# The Good Skiing & Snowboarding Guide **2005**

CW00351194

# The Good Skiing & Snowboarding Guide **2005**

Peter and Felice Hardy

WHICH?
BOOKS

CONSUMERS' ASSOCIATION

Which? Books are commissioned by Consumers' Association and published
by Which? Ltd, 2 Marylebone Road, London NW1 4DF
Email: books@which.net
Resort reports to: goodskiandsnowguide@which.net

Distributed by The Penguin Group
Penguin Books Ltd, 80 Strand, London WC2R 0RL

First edition of *The Good Skiing Guide*: 1985
This edition September 2004


Editors        Peter and Felice Hardy
Researchers    Jo Crossley, Kate Parker
Contributors   Minty Clinch, Neil English, Arnie Wilson
Cover photo    Graham Plant / Skishoot
Maps           Holmes Linnette

British Library Cataloguing-in-Publication Data:
A catalogue record for *The Good Skiing & Snowboarding Guide* is available from the British Library

**ISBN 0 85202 996 9**

For a full list of Which? Books, please call 0800 252100, access our website at www.which.net,
or write to Which? Books, P.O. Box 44, Hertford SG14 1SH


Editorial      Joanna Chisholm, Alethea Doran, Ian Robinson
Production     Joanna Bregosz
Typeset by     Saxon Graphics Ltd, Derby
**Printed and bound in Spain by** Bookprint, S.L. Barcelona



**Photographic acknowledgements**

pp.161, 166, 167, 196, 197 Graham Plant / Skishoot; p.176 Office du Tourisme Val d'Isère; p.177 Skishoot

# Contents

# Using the Guide

*The Good Skiing & Snowboarding Guide* features what we consider to be the Top 100 ski resorts in the world. These are listed by country in alphabetical order. Longer chapters include full resort statistics in the *At a glance* box. Shorter chapters have a truncated version of this box, with resort contact and lift details.

At the beginning of each chapter we highlight the key strengths of that resort and the types of people who would be most likely to enjoy it – as well as those for whom it might be unsuitable.

Over 150 additional resorts that are particularly worthy of note are covered in the *World resort index*. This index also lists the tour operators that go to every resort included in the Guide. Details of the tour operators are given at the back of the book.

Throughout the Guide, the name of a resort in bold indicates a cross-reference to its own entry, or shows the first instance of where it is described.

## Runs and maps

In most cases we have described runs by their colour grading, rather than more generally as, for example, 'easy' or 'intermediate', since grading can vary from resort to resort. An explanation of the colour grading for runs in both Europe and North America is given in the map key on page 161.

## Lift symbols

In the *At a glance* boxes, symbols denote the types of lift in each resort. The map key explains these symbols. Mountain railways and funiculars have been grouped together, as have all types of drag-lift. The difference between gondolas and cable-cars is becoming increasingly difficult to define, so both types of cableway are similarly combined. We have chosen not to include nursery-slope magic carpet lifts, nor lifts specifically used for tobogganing and tubing runs, because these tend to distort a resort's statistics when trying to judge the overall extent of its ski area.

## Lift passes

Lift passes are free for small children and for pensioners in all age ranges not stated in the *At a glance* boxes.

## Lift opening dates

Where possible we have supplied the exact dates when resorts plan to open and then close at the end of the season. Dates are given in more general terms (such as 'mid-December to mid-April') for those resorts that had not finalised their plans at the time of going to press. Obviously actual dates are liable to change, depending on snowfall. We therefore advise you not to make any firm early- or late-season plans without contacting your chosen resort to confirm that a sufficient number of lifts are operating.

## Dialling codes

Telephone numbers for accommodation are given throughout. However, for reasons of space we have omitted country codes in the resort chapters (although these can be found in the *At a glance* boxes). We have also omitted the '0' that precedes most numbers when dialled locally, but which is not part of the international dialling code. Please note that the initial '0' in Italian numbers is not omitted when dialling from outside the country.

# Introduction

The volatile pricing of package European ski holidays now bears a worrying resemblance to the UK housing market, and may be equally unsustainable in the long term. Unless they come – or are brought – swiftly to their senses, a number of tour operators risk joining the ranks of the unemployed during the course of this winter.

By inflating prices at February half-term and New Year, and charging unfeasibly high sums for other dates – only to reduce them as 'last-minute offers' in the weeks prior to departure – ski travel firms are leaving British skiers and snowboarders confused as to what they should realistically pay for their holiday. Last season, for example, we noted a chalet in Val d'Isère that was reduced from £1,675 to £795 in March. One in St Anton was discounted from £570 to £285, and another in Chamonix from £1,280 to £795.

This is not a sensible way to run any business. A customer who has paid the full brochure price is hardly likely to enjoy his or her week in a chalet shared with another who has paid the reduced price. And the second customer will surely never consider paying the full price with that firm in the future.

The reasoning behind these questionable pricing practices is the ever-increasing polarisation of those dates termed as high and low season. For British tour operators, these are largely dictated by school holidays (high season), which are easy to sell, and by term-time weeks in January and March (low season), which are becoming increasingly difficult to shift. As we have said before in this Guide, this problem would largely be rectified if the UK government staggered half-term holidays by region, as France has done for many years.

However, holidaymakers' options have evolved considerably in recent years. The advent of the Internet has meant that the consumer now has far greater choice when making travel plans: he or she can book accommodation and low-cost flights directly and is no longer tied to the traditional package holiday.

Indeed, before booking a hotel through a tour operator, it could be well worth contacting the chosen hotel, getting an individual quote, and weighing up the advantages and disadvantages of cutting the operator out of the equation. Obvious advantages are that organising your own flights, transport and accommodation can result in a considerable saving. On the down-side, however, your payment will not necessarily be secure in the event of an unforeseen problem such as overbooking, nor will you have the services of a travel firm representative in the resort.

Skiers and snowboarders are now likely to vote with their feet. If the tour operators want to safeguard their business and, in an age of transparency and increasingly informed consumers, ensure continuing public faith in package holidays, they need to put their house in order.

## Whiter than white

The start of each ski season is a bit like dropping off a high cornice into a bowl of deep snow. You hope for the best, but you never quite know what to expect until you are up to your knees in it. The 2003–4 season began badly, quickly improved, and ended with so much snow across Europe that some high Alpine pastures were still winter-white in June.

Austria got off to a poor start, with St Anton and others having to postpone their opening dates. But when the snow finally arrived, it just kept on coming. Elsewhere, timely top-ups were delivered for Christmas and February half-term. Andorra and other resorts in the Pyrenees were blessed with excellent skiing throughout. Even oft-blighted Bulgaria was able to offer pristine powder skiing in March.

Across the Atlantic, Snowbird and other destinations in Utah broke every snowfall record, and nowhere else had cause for complaint. All in all, it was a vintage winter that will be savoured for many years to come.

Such admirable snow cover lends apparent weight to the argument of those sceptics who do not believe that our climate is becoming warmer. But even huge falls like these could do little to repair the damage to the Alps created by the heatwave of August 2003. A layer of permafrost built up over a million years melted in a single weekend, changing forever the face of major peaks such as the Aiguille du Midi above Chamonix. Ancient ice bridges collapsed, new crevasses yawned, and the famous Vallée Blanche remained closed for the first part of last season. One good winter does not necessarily end the climatic uncertainty that dogs the ski industry worldwide.

Those who dismiss global warming as scaremongering should be aware that exceptionally high winds and occasional periods of rain at high altitude, such as occurred throughout the season in both Europe and North America, are classic indicators of climate change. It is also worth noting that heli-skiing operations in remote northern British Columbia recorded a third less snow than usual last winter, along with the highest March temperatures since records began.

## Difficult dates

Choose your ski-break dates with care this year. An early Easter (Sunday 27 March) makes the 2004–5 season shorter than usual. Regardless of snow conditions, most tour operators start to wind up their programme immediately after this holiday. The majority of UK state schools start their break on Good Friday, and it is worth remembering that the second of the two school-break weeks is proving by far the most popular for skiing.

The February 2005 half-term falls early, with most schools in England and Wales opting once again for the same week: this year, the one commencing Saturday 12 February. For once, the timing does not clash with either the Paris school break (19 February to 7 March) or President's Day Weekend, America's biggest winter bank holiday (19 to 21 February). This means that the slopes shouldn't be too crowded in the main resorts of the French Alps and throughout North America. However, the half-term dates do clash with the spring break for Lyon and Grenoble, which could result in long-than-usual lift queues in popular resorts in the French Alps. At the same time, in Andorra and elsewhere in the Pyrenees, an influx of families from Toulouse will augment the number of snow-users.

Avid American skiers tend to spend the rest of their bank holiday week on the slopes, making it the busiest week of the season in the States, which also has a knock-on effect on Canadian resorts.

To compound the difficulty of organising your ski holiday, Christmas Day and New Year's Day both fall on Saturday, the traditional change-over day, forcing some operators to offer either weekday travel or ten-day breaks over the period.

## Swiss departure

A worrying development for skiers and snowboarders this season is the takeover by British Airways of Swiss International's daily flights between Heathrow and Geneva. Low prices and skier-friendly schedules have long made Swiss, and its predecessor Swissair, the favourite airline for those who commute frequently during the winter to resorts in France and Switzerland from Heathrow and London City.

There are fears that BA will introduce smaller aircraft on the route. No doubt this will improve profitability during the week, but add to the already considerable difficulty of finding seats at weekends. Passengers on Swiss who are used to travelling with their skis may also be in for a financial shock. For while Swiss, like easyJet, carries skis free of charge, British Airways includes ski and snowboard carriage in its standard

23kg baggage allowance – so many skiers may have to pay extra if they exceed the weight limit.

Other Swiss flights to destinations in Switzerland from Heathrow and London City are not affected. But it should come as no surprise to the bosses of BA if loyal Geneva-bound passengers abandon BA/Swiss and join the growing ranks of customers choosing easyJet and other budget airlines for their lower prices and more skier-friendly service.

## Helmets and body armour

Six years have now passed since the much-publicised deaths in the United States of Sonny Bono and Michael Kennedy, both of whom died from head injuries in unrelated ski accidents. The tragedies sparked a furore of debate on ski safety, and led a significant number of recreational skiers to wear helmets for the first time. The sale of safety helmets for adults continues to increase in America, and hard hats are now commonplace across Europe, particularly in France. Young skiers and snowboarders who spend their time in terrain parks are now also wearing spinal supports similar to those worn by horse riders – either separately or as an integral part of their clothing.

Contrary to popular belief, the risk of any form of injury on a ski holiday remains extremely low – only five per thousand visitors to a ski area sustain an injury, and only ten per cent of those cases are likely to involve head injuries. However, with intermediate skiers regularly exceeding speeds of 30mph on piste, a full-on collision with a tree or lift pylon is an accident to avoid whether you wear a helmet or not.

No satisfactory statistical evidence has yet been published to show that wearing a helmet significantly lowers the risk of head injury. Similarly, no published research to date has analysed the effectiveness of spinal supports in protecting against injuries. It is still not mandatory to wear a helmet on the mountain, and it is unlikely that it ever will be. But surely any measure that prevents or reduces the risk of serious damage in a high-speed fall on a hard piste must make sense. As committed helmet-wearers ourselves, we applaud this trend. Fortunately, both helmets and spinal protectors are now seen as cool by teen and twenty-something freeride skiers and snowboarders.

## Ski running

The biggest threat to skiers' health last season went largely unreported – and it had nothing to do with collisions, maladjusted bindings or poor piste markings. Throughout much of the season, doctors' waiting rooms in major French resorts were inundated with holidaymakers suffering not from broken bones but from severe gastroenteritis.

'"Epidemic" is a strong word to use', said Dr Alan Griffiths, the British doctor in Val d'Isère, 'but a ski resort is just like a cruise ship. Once a resistant bug like this one takes hold, it just goes round and round. The only way to stop it spreading is by extra hygiene precautions – in particular hand-washing, and disinfecting surfaces and doorknobs'. Tour operators and chalet staff please take note.

## Help with the Guide

We need your help to update *The Guide* accurately each year. Our team of researchers tries to visit as many destinations as possible, but it is not feasible to visit every resort in the Guide in a 20-week season. Lifts are constantly being upgraded, the standards of hotels and restaurants rise and fall, and the tuition given at ski and snowboard schools can vary from season to season. Please tell us about your ski holiday experiences – both the good and the bad – in as much detail as possible. Guidelines on reporting on resorts are given at the back of this book.

# Simply the best

The resorts listed below are those considered by the editors and contributors to the Guide to be the best in a variety of categories. The ten entries in each category are listed in alphabetical order, rather than by ranking.

## Beginners

| | |
|---|---|
| Beaver Creek | Poiana-Brasov |
| Big White | Saas-Fee |
| Cervinia | Soldeu–El |
| Flaine | Tarter–Canillo |
| Livigno | Wengen |
| Mayrhofen | |

## Intermediates

| | |
|---|---|
| Gasteinertal | Park City Resorts |
| Banff–Lake Louise | Serre Chevalier |
| Courchevel | Sestriere |
| Engelberg | Vail |
| La Plagne | Wengen |

## Advanced

| | |
|---|---|
| Alpe d'Huez | Snowbird and Alta |
| Chamonix | St Anton |
| Crested Butte | Val d'Isère |
| Fernie | Verbier |
| Jackson Hole | Zermatt |

## Skiing for all standards

| | |
|---|---|
| Aspen | Méribel |
| Banff–Lake Louise | Selva Gardena |
| Courchevel | Tignes |
| Flaine | Vail |
| Les Arcs | Whistler |

## Snowboarding

| | |
|---|---|
| Avoriaz | Serre Chevalier |
| Axamer Lizum | Squaw Valley |
| Chamonix | St Anton |
| Davos | Vail |
| Red Mountain | Whistler |

## Off-piste

| | |
|---|---|
| Alagna | La Grave |
| Banff–Lake Louise | Snowbird and Alta |
| Chamonix | Val d'Isère |
| Jackson Hole | Verbier |
| Kicking Horse | Zermatt |

## Moguls

| | |
|---|---|
| Avoriaz | Red Mountain |
| Breckenridge | St Anton |
| Killington | Taos |
| Klosters | Telluride |
| Mürren | Verbier |

## Mountain restaurants

| | |
|---|---|
| Alpe d'Huez | Kicking Horse |
| Cervinia | Klosters |
| Cortina d'Ampezzo | Megève |
| Courchevel | St Moritz |
| Courmayeur | Zermatt |

## Luxury accommodation

| | |
|---|---|
| Aspen | Klosters |
| Beaver Creek | Lech and Zürs |
| Courchevel 1850 | Méribel |
| Deer Valley | St Moritz |
| Jackson Hole | Zermatt |

## Eating out

| | |
|---|---|
| Aspen | Megève |
| Cortina d'Ampezzo | Park City Resorts |
| Courchevel | St Anton |
| Courmayeur | Whistler |
| Kitzbühel | Zermatt |

## Après-ski

| | |
|---|---|
| Banff | Pas de la Casa |
| Baqueira–Beret | Sauze d'Oulx |
| Chamonix | St Anton |
| Ischgl | Thredbo |
| Kitzbühel | Zermatt |

## Families

| | |
|---|---|
| Big White | Lech |
| Deer Valley | Megève |
| Fernie | Schladming |
| Hemsedal | Smugglers' Notch |
| Lake Louise | Villars |

## Non-skiers

| | |
|---|---|
| Åre | Kitzbühel |
| Aspen | Megève |
| Banff | Seefeld |
| Cortina d'Ampezzo | St Moritz |
| Heavenly | Zermatt |

## Value for money

| | |
|---|---|
| Barèges | Schladming |
| Fernie | Serre Chevalier |
| Levi | Soldeu–El |
| Livigno | Tarter–Canillo |
| Poiana Brasov | Söll |
| Red Mountain | |

## Ski-and-shop

| | |
|---|---|
| Aspen | Megève |
| Breckenridge | Park City Mountain |
| Cortina d'Ampezzo | Resort |
| Jackson Hole | Whistler |
| Livigno | Zermatt |
| Mammoth | |

## Ski and spa

| | |
|---|---|
| Aspen | Megève |
| Banff | St Moritz |
| Beaver Creek | Snowbird |
| Crans-Montana | Telluride |
| Kitzbühel | Whistler |

## Snow-sure resorts

| | |
|---|---|
| Cervinia | Saas-Fee |
| Kaprun | Solden |
| Levi | Tignes |
| Obergurgl– | Val Thorens |
| Hochgurgl | Zermatt |
| Obertauern | |

## Purpose-built convenience

| | |
|---|---|
| Alpe d'Huez | La Plagne |
| Les Arcs | Snowbird |
| Courchevel 1850 | Tignes |
| Flaine | Valle Nevado |
| Kicking Horse | Valmorel |

## Romantic/charming resorts

| | |
|---|---|
| Alpbach | Mürren |
| Courmayeur | Stowe |
| Jackson Hole | Telluride |
| Kitzbühel | Zell am See |
| Megève | Zermatt |

## Resorts in exotic locations

| | |
|---|---|
| Chamonix | Mammoth |
| Cortina d'Ampezzo | Mt Ruapehu |
| Grindelwald | Portillo |
| Heavenly | Thredbo |
| La Leñas | Zermatt |

## Small, attractive villages in big ski areas

| | |
|---|---|
| Arabba (Sella Ronda) | Montchavin (La Plagne/Paradiski) |
| Champagny (La Plagne/ Paradiski) | St Christoph (St Anton) |
| Champéry (Portes du Soleil) | St-Martin-de Belleville (The Trois Vallées) |
| Dorf Gastein (Gasteinertal) | Samoëns (Flaine) |
| Flachau/Wagrain (Salzburger Sportwelt Amadé) | Vaujany (Alpe d'Huez) |

## Close to an interesting city / airport convenience

| | |
|---|---|
| Gasteinertal (Salzburg) | Sauze d'Oulx (Turin) |
| Chamonix (Geneva) | Seefeld (Innsbruck) |
| Cortina d'Ampezzo (Venice) | Valle Nevado (Santiago) |
| Mont-Sainte-Anne (Québec City) | Whistler (Vancouver) |
| Park City Resorts (Salt Lake City) | Winter Park (Denver) |

# The Golden Ski Awards 2005

The Golden Ski Awards are judged annually by the editors and contributors of *The Good Skiing & Snowboarding Guide*. These prestigious 'White Oscars' go to those resorts and establishments that we consider have provided an outstanding level of service to skiers and snowboarders during the 2003–4 season. Two winners have been selected for each category: one in Europe and one in North America (chalets are an exception).

## Resort of the Year

Val d'Isère (France)

Jackson Hole (Wyoming)

## Most Improved Resort of the Year

Engelberg (Switzerland)

Heavenly (California)

## Small Resort of the Year

Alpbach (Austria)

Kicking Horse (BC)

## Family Resort of the Year

Megève (France)

Banff–Lake Louise (Alberta)

## Hotel of the Year

Barmes de l'Ours (Val d'Isère)

Ritz-Carlton Bachelor Gulch (Beaver Creek)

## Budget Accommodation of the Year

The Ram's Head Inn (Red Mountain, BC)

## Luxury Chalet of the Year

Chalet Aurea, Courchevel 1850 (Scott Dunn Ski)

## Tour Operator Chalet of the Year

Chalet Montana, Morzine (Snowline)

## Resort Restaurant of the Year

The Rosengarten (Kirchberg)

Kicking Horse Grill (Kicking Horse)

## Après-ski Venue of the Year

Hotel Farinet (Verbier)

The Tap Room & Sanctuary (Vail)

## Mountain Restaurant of the Year

Au Vieux Verbier (Verbier)

Eagle's Eye (Kicking Horse)

## Ski School of the Year

New Generation (Courchevel)

Jackson Hole Mountain Sports School (Jackson Hole)

## Children's Ski School of the Year

Oxygène (Val d'Isère)

Jackson Hole Mountain Sports School (Jackson Hole)

## Ski Shop of the Year

Precision Ski (Val d'Isère)

Base Mountain Sports, Vail

Readers are invited to submit their nominations for The Golden Ski Awards 2006, together with a short explanation. Please send them to: Dept CD, Consumers' Association, FREEPOST, 2 Marylebone Road, London NW1 4DF. No stamp is needed. Alternatively, you can email them to us at *goodskiandsnowguide@which.net*.

# ANDORRA

# Pas de la Casa

ALTITUDE 2,095m (6,872ft)

❋ **Andorra's largest and highest ski area** ❋ **duty-free shopping**
❋ **wild nightlife** ❋ **cheap-and-cheerful accommodation**

> **Best for:** intermediate cruisers, young skiers and riders on a budget, night-owls
> **Not recommended for:** families, older skiers, advanced and off-piste skiers

Pas de la Casa is a border town that divides countries and cultures. Every weekend, the youth of Toulouse cross the frontier in search of day-time snow, duty-frees and night-time action. They are joined by hordes of Brits seeking snow, sex and sangria.

The fundamental impression is of giant advertising hoardings and scores of tacky bars. Duty-free perfume shops, and supermarkets selling booze, cigarettes, clothing and equipment at knock-down prices are ubiquitous, despite the €100 million invested in the ski areas in recent years in an attempt to remodel this image.

## On the snow

top 2,580m (8,465ft) bottom 2,095m (6,872ft)

Pas de la Casa has finally buried the hatchet with neighbouring **Soldeu**, ending an argument that originated in the eighteenth century over disputed communal grazing rights. They have now officially joined forces to form a joint ski area covered by one pass and known as **Grand Valira**. The 60 lifts serve some 200km of mainly beginner and intermediate terrain that encompasses five villages – Pas, Grau Roig, Soldeu, El Tarter and Canillo – as well as the town of Encamp, linked by the long Funicamp gondola. The Pas and Grau Roig end of the circuit has the pick of the runs and Grau Roig has a new beginner area.

The standard of English spoken by instructors is high, but at peak times classes can be 'ridiculously overcrowded'. Another complaint is that beginners are forced to buy a full area lift pass just to use the two short drag-lifts on the nursery slopes.

Snowboarders – and skiers – congregate at the snowpark with its rails, half-pipe, skiercross and boardercross courses on the Tubs piste in Pas de la Casa.

The gastronomic Solanelles restaurant at the top of the Funicamp is supplemented by six mountain eating-places that are little more than snack bars. The Bar El Piolet is recommended, and Refugi dels Llacs Pessons has 'a log fire and pleasant food and service'.

## In the resort

Four-star hotels include the Sporting (☎ 85 54 51), the Grau Roig (☎ 85 55 56) and the Himalaia (☎ 85 62 19). The budget Hotel Central (☎ 85 53 75) is praised.

Restaurants are cheap and cheerful, serving mainly fresh seafood and paella. Nightlife is frenetic: 'We were kept awake until 3am every night,' complained one reporter. The Marseillais 'is the place for a quiet drink and has great lasagne', and the West End is popular. Other favourite nightspots include Milwaukee's, Billbord, KYU and Le Pub.

Both Pas de la Casa and Grau Roig have ski kindergartens for children aged three to six. Grau Roig also has a nursery.

> ## Pas de la Casa: At a glance
>
> **Tel** Pas de la Casa 376 80 10 60 / Grand Valira 376 80 89 00
> **Email** info@pasgrau.com / info@grandvalira.com
> **Websites** www.pasgrau.com / www.grandvalira.com
> **Lifts in area** 60: 5🚡 27🚟 28🎿
> **Lift opening dates** beginning of December 2004 to 20 April 2005

# Soldeu–El Tarter–Canillo

ALTITUDE 1,710m (5,610ft)

## ❄ Andorra's largest ski area ❄ excellent skiing tuition ❄ modern lift system ❄ value for money

**Best for:** beginners to low intermediates, families, snowboarders

**Not recommended for:** advanced and off-piste skiers, those in search of high-mileage skiing, ski-to-lunchers

Soldeu, together with the adjoining villages of El Tarter and Canillo, now forms part of the new **Grand Valira** ski area that incorporates **Pas de la Casa**, Grau Roig and Encamp. This corner of the 60-lift area provides the best combination of skiing, accommodation, architecture, scenery and ambience of any resort in Andorra. While Pas de la Casa has marginally the more challenging terrain, Soldeu is a much more attractive and comfortable destination. Like Pas, the resort offers a wild nightlife throughout the season, but revellers here are not confined to the 16-to-25 age bracket of its brasher rival.

### WHAT'S NEW

8-person gondola from El Tarter base to Riba Escorxada for 2004–5
4-seater chair replaces 2-seater at El Tarter base for 2004–5
New chair replaces TK Enllac between El Tarter and Canillo for 2004–5

Both Soldeu and El Tarter consist of little more than a ribbon of stone-and-wood buildings alongside the main road. Canillo is an ancient Andorran community that is now rapidly expanding and provides an alternative mountain-linked bed base.

The majority of reporters are extremely enthusiastic about the resort: 'I would recommend Soldeu to anyone. It is especially great for beginners, and the ski school is excellent for all levels'. But one warned: 'Prices have now caught up with the rest of Europe. Andorra is no longer the cheap option'.

## On-piste
top 2,560m (8,399ft) bottom 1,710m (5,610ft)

The local skiing spans the mountainside above the three villages, all situated within a 5-km stretch of the valley road. In recent years this part of the ski area has been transformed by the building of a host of new lifts, including two gondolas that provide mountain access from the centre of Soldeu and from Canillo. A chair-lift links the mid-mountain area of Pla Riba Escorxada above El Tarter with the 2,560-m summit of Tossal de la Llosada. New for the 2004–5 season are an eight-person gondola from El Tarter's base to Riba Escorxada, a four-seater chair replacing the two-seater at El Tarter's base, and a chair replacing TK Enllac between El Tarter and Canillo.

Like other Andorran resorts, Soldeu is particularly busy at British half-term, which coincides with both French and Spanish school holidays. However, improvements to the lift system and the creation of Grand Valira have done much to disperse skiers on the mountain.

Nearly all the terrain is best suited to beginners and intermediates, but there is little here to attract advanced skiers. We have good reports of the nursery slopes, which are 'well prepared and fenced off from the rest of the pistes'. Soldeu has an ungroomed snowboard zone (also for skiers) called ACG Free Set Area.

## Off-piste
The intermediate profile of the average Andorran skier means that whole tracts of powder remain untouched, often for days after a snowfall. With the help of a local guide there is plenty of terrain to explore within easy reach of the lift system ('superb back-country skiing'). Good value heli-skiing is also available.

## Tuition and guiding
Soldeu ski school has an enduring reputation as one of the best in Europe and is a contributory reason for Andorra's

success ('fabulous, with friendly English-speaking instructors who really know their job'). El Tarter and Canillo have their own ski and snowboard schools.

## Mountain restaurants

Eating on-piste is Soldeu's weakest point. The handful of restaurants are described as 'refuelling stops serving cheap, fast food'. The exception is the gastronomic Roc de les Bruixes at Canillo, which is open in the evening and reached by gondola. Another reporter commented: 'there are too few restaurants actually on the piste, but they are functional and the service is quick'. Espiolet above Soldeu and Riba Escorxada are both recommended.

## Accommodation

All accommodation can be booked through a central reservations office (☎ 89 05 01). In Soldeu, The four-star Hotel Sport Village is unanimously picked by reporters as the best. Four-star Piolets is also praised. The refurbished four-star Hotel Himalaia Soldeu is said to be 'quite luxurious with a great restaurant'.

In El Tarter, the three-star Hotel del Tarter has 'brilliant accommodation, food and service'. Three-star Hotel del Clos has 'nice rooms, good food, and is altogether great for a family party'. At the foot of the slopes is the conveniently placed Hotel Llop

Gris, with a swimming-pool and squash courts. Parador Canaro offers 'the highest standard of comfort'.

In Canillo, the five-star Hotel Ski Plaza is warmly praised, along with the three-star Hotel Bonavida.

## Eating in and out

Cort de Popaire in Soldeu is famous for its grilled lamb and beef. La Fontanella in the Hotel Piolets 'is the best or possibly the only Italian restaurant in town'. Borda de l'Horto outside Canillo serves 'rustic fare in atmospheric surroundings'. Cantina dels Racons in Canillo is recommended for its chargrilled steaks.

## Après-ski

Nightlife thrives in Soldeu but does not try to compete with the fleshpots of Pas de la Casa. The Avalanche, Slim Jim's and Fat Alberts are three popular British-owned pubs. The Piccadilly and Aspen attract big crowds, along with Pussycat and Capital. In Canillo, Pub la Roda and Pub Camping keep similarly late hours.

## Childcare

The Mickey Snow Club kindergarten cares for children aged three to ten, with ski lessons for older children. The nursery takes non-skiing children from two years old. The resorts have five magic carpet lifts and nine rope-tows.

# Soldeu–El Tarter–Canillo: At a glance

**Tel** Soldeu 376 89 05 00/ Grand Valira 376 80 89 00
**Email** soldeu@soldeu.ad / info@grandvalira.com
**Websites** www.soldeu.ad / www.grandvalira.com

### GETTING THERE
**Airports** Toulouse 3hrs, Barcelona 3hrs
**Rail** Barcelona, daily coach connection
**Road** N20 from Toulouse to Foix and Ax-Les-Thermes, through Pas de la Casa to Soldeu

### THE SKIING
**Linked/nearby resorts** Arinsal, Pas de la Casa
**Total of trails/pistes** 192km (49% easy, 45% intermediate, 6% difficult)
**Lifts in area** 60: 5⬡ 27⬡ 28⬡
**Lift opening dates** beginning of December 2004 to 20 April 2005

### LIFT PASSES
**Area pass** €163–168 for 6 days

**Pensioners** 65yrs and over €123–129 for 6 days, free for 70yrs and over

### TUITION
**Ski & board** Canillo Ski School (☎ 89 06 91), Cortals Ski/Snowboard School (☎ 83 47 21), El Tarter Ski School (☎ 89 06 41), El Tarter Snowboard School (☎ 89 06 44), Soldeu Ski School (☎ 89 05 91), Soldeu Snowboard School (☎ 89 06 15)
**Guiding** through ski schools

### CHILDREN
**Lift pass** €123–129 for 6 days
**Ski & board school** as adults
**Kindergarten** Mickey Snow Club and nursery

### FOOD AND DRINK
Coffee €1.20, bottle of house wine €8–10, small beer €2, soft drink €2, dish of the day €6–7

# ARGENTINA

# Las Leñas

ALTITUDE 2,240m (7,349ft)

## ❊ superb off-piste ❊ value-for-money hotels ❊ exotic location

> **Best for:** hard-core skiers and boarders, night-owls
> **Not recommended for:** beginners, those wanting skiing convenience

The resort of Las Leñas is said by *aficionados* to be one of the most challenging ski resorts in South America. Purpose-built 20 years ago with the help of French advisers, it is located in a remote part of the Andes, close to the Chilean border. The easiest way to reach the resort is by a 90-minute flight from Buenos Aires to Malargue Airport, followed by a one-hour bus journey. You can also fly to San Rafael, 125 miles away. The alternatives are to drive the 740 miles from Buenos Aires, which takes at least 15 hours, or to travel by overnight coach from the capital.

In spite of its fairly modest 70km of groomed runs, the area's off-piste potential is limitless. Las Leñas is laid out like a lunar village in a treeless wilderness, yet the valley is named, rather tamely, after a yellow shrub.

## On the snow
### top 3,431m (11,257ft) bottom 2,240m (7,349ft)

Las Leñas has a Jekyll-and-Hyde identity – and which personality visitors encounter depends entirely on the weather, which dictates whether or not the Marte lift is operational. This exposed chair – prone to high winds and avalanche danger – provides the sole link to the extensive off-piste, regarded by some as the best in the southern hemisphere, and the reason why more than two-thirds of the skiing is designated advanced. Hardened skiers and boarders routinely climb as high as 3,740m (12,272ft) to reach the most challenging terrain. But great care must be taken: many of the couloirs cannot be completely descended because of cliffs, and a guide is essential.

However, when the Marte lift is closed, the resort reverts to its other, less interesting, persona as just another family ski area in the Andes. 'The Marte lift', said one reporter, 'is essential to access the mind-blowing open bowls and intense couloirs – things can get a little tedious when the upper part of the mountain is closed'.

## In the resort

All accommodation is in piste-side hotels and lodges within a short walk or ski of a lift. The five-star Hotel Piscis (☎ 262 747 1100) is the most luxurious, featuring what claims to be the highest ski-resort casino in the world. The Aries (☎ 262 742 7120) is more modestly priced and has its own cinema.

The Innsbruck, at the mountain base, and La Cima, on the Eros ski trail, serve food all day. The Santa Fe bar-restaurant and the Elurra both serve lunch and dinner. El Brasero is warmly recommended. The Restaurant Club de la Nieve specialises in steak, fish and fondues, and the Edelweiss bar serves meals prepared by university culinary students. The Las Cuatro Estaciones restaurant and the Bar Estar are good for late-night food.

There are numerous bars, discos and nightclubs, and the après-ski is frenzied. The Ku nightclub, in the Pyramid shopping centre, says open until 5am. The UFO Point nightclub, next to the Brasero, shuts at 3am.

> ## Las Leñas: At a glance
>
> **Tel** 54 262 747 1100 (1 313-1300 in Buenos Aires)
> **Email** ventas@laslenas.com
> **Website** www.laslenas.com
> **Lifts in resort** 11: 7🚡 4 🚠
> **Lift opening dates** mid-June to mid-November

# AUSTRALIA

## Thredbo

ALTITUDE 1,370m (4,495ft)

❉ **Australia's answer to the Alps** ❉ **extensive snowmaking**
❉ **some of the longest runs on the continent**

> **Best for:** intermediates, party animals
> **Not recommended for:** resort-to-resort skiers, powderhounds

Thredbo, in the Kosciuszko National Park of New South Wales, is Australia's premier resort. It was founded in the early 1950s by Austrian and Czech immigrants who helped build the Snowy Mountain hydroelectric scheme.

The resort is named after the country's highest mountain, which is visible some 6km from the top of the ski area. The lifts serve some of the best intermediate terrain in Australia. This is the country's nearest equivalent to a European ski resort but, although the glades through the gum trees have considerable charm, the gradient is modest and the comparison carries little weight.

However, this does not deter Aussies from making either the six-hour drive from Sydney or the two-and-a-half hour journey by road from Canberra (you can also fly to Cooma, 80km away).

### On the snow
top 2,037m (6,683ft) bottom 1,365m (4,478ft)

Four quads among the dozen lifts speed skiers and snowboarders above the tree-line on Mount Crackenback. From here they can move nearer the summit on T-bars, which are better suited to the windier conditions at this altitude. For the 2004–5 season, a gondola replaces one of the chair-lifts at night, to take diners to the Eagle's Nest – the highest mountain restaurant in Australia, which sometimes opens for sunset dinners. The longest run is almost 6km. Because the snow record in the Australian Alps is unpredictable, the resort has invested heavily in snowmaking, and claims the largest system in the southern hemisphere.

Thredbo Snowsports School offers lessons for skiers and riders. The Avalanche Café, at the base of the lift, is recommended. Black Sallees, at the top of the Snow Gums chair-lift, is popular for barbecues. At Friday Flat, the River Rock Café & Bistro has live entertainment on the deck.

### In the resort

Hotels include the Thredbo Alpine Hotel (☎ 2 6459 4100), High Country Mountain Resort (☎ 2 6456 2511), the Alpenhorn (☎ 2 6457 6223), the Tyrolean-style Black Bear Inn (☎ 2 6457 6216) and the Candlelight Lodge (☎ 2 6457 6049). The nearby Crackenback Farm (☎ 2 6456 2198) is a four-star country guesthouse.

Recommended restaurants include Segreto in the Thredbo Alpine Hotel, Alfresco Pizzeria and Kebabz. The T-Bar serves seafood, steaks and the occasional kangaroo. Altitude 1380 is a café by day and a BYO restaurant by night. Both the Candlelight Lodge and Drakes pride themselves on their international cuisine. Credo is celebrated for its roast duck and stuffed Snowy River trout.

Thredbo Snowsports School offers tuition for children from four years. Thredbo Childcare Centre is for babies from six months, and Thredboland is for three- to six-year-olds. There is a magic carpet lift in the resort.

> ## Thredbo: At a glance
>
> **Tel** 61 2 6459 4100
> **Email** info@thredbo.com.au
> **Website** www.thredbo.com.au
> **Lifts in resort** 12: 7Ⓢ 5Ⓣ
> **Lift opening dates** 12 June 2005 to 4 October 2005

# AUSTRIA

# Alpbach

**ALTITUDE 1,000m (3,280ft)**

## ❄ attractive village ❄ Alpine charm ❄ family skiing ❄ extensive off-piste opportunities

> **Best for:** anyone who enjoys the ambience of a traditional Austrian village, intermediate skiers, families
>
> **Not recommended for:** night-owls (except high-season weeks), those looking for skiing convenience

Alpbach is a small, sunny village on a steep hillside in the heart of the Tyrol. It has nurtured an intimate relationship with British skiers over the past 45 years. A pretty green-and-white church, surrounded by old wooden chalets and the buttressed walls of the two medieval inns, dominates the compact centre. New buildings have been kept to such an absolute minimum that only Alta in Utah can match Alpbach for retro-chic.

Apart from the nursery slopes, nearly all the skiing is a five-minute bus ride from the village on the Wiedersbergerhorn. This is a drawback, but the free bus service is efficient.

The next-door village of Reith shares a lift pass and has three lifts as well as an eight-person gondola. Plans are in place to create a link to the neighbouring **Wildschönau** area.

## On the snow
**top 2,100m (6,890ft) bottom 1,000m (3,280ft)**

The ski area offers a surprising variety of terrain, best suited to intermediates. Alpbach's main mountain access to the Wiedersbergerhorn is by a two-stage gondola, which takes you up to Hornboden at 1,850m and the start of a complex of 15 chair- and drag-lifts.

Compact it may be, in comparison to Kitzbühel or its other grand cousins in this corner of the Tyrol, but Alpbach's local lift map completely fails to do justice to a surprisingly diverse and challenging area of easily accessible off-piste, above and below the tree-line. The old downhill course that follows

the fall-line from the gondola is a popular run. With modern safety controls, it is too narrow to be officially raced these days, but at recreational speeds it provides an exhilarating drop to the valley floor. The undulating topography is a dream for riders, and the area boasts two terrain parks and a half-pipe.

Alpbach-Inneralpbach Ski School is still run by legendary teacher and ex-racer Sepp Margreiter. Alpbach Aktiv Ski School is the equally friendly alternative.

The Hornboden is 'much the best mountain restaurant', but one reporter commented that 'you are spoilt for choice'.

## In the resort
The four-star hotels are the Romantikhotel Böglerhof (☎ 5336 52270), Alpbacherhof (☎ 5336 5237) and the Alphof (☎ 5336 5371). Three-star Hotel Post (☎ 5336 5203) is 'absolutely wonderful, with a popular bar and great restaurant'. Other eateries of note include Gasthof Wiedersbergerhorn, Gasthaus Rossmoos, Gasthof Jakober and the intimate Fuggerstube in the Romantikhotel Böglerhof. The Messnerwirt, Postalm and the Waschkuchl are the liveliest bars, along with the Jakober, which suits all ages. Both ski schools operate all-day ski kindergartens for children from four years. Alpbach Kindergarten accepts children from three years.

> ## Alpbach: At a glance
>
> **Tel** 43 5336 5233
> **Email** info@alpbach.at / info@alpbacher-bergbahnen.at
> **Websites** www.alpbach at / www.alpbacher-bergbahnen.at
> **Lifts in area** 20: 2⛷ 7⛷ 11⛷
> **Lift opening dates** late November 2004 to mid-April 2005

# The Gasteinertal

ALTITUDE 1,100m (3,608ft)

map: see page 162

❋ **large intermediate ski area** ❋ **easy rail access**
❋ **reasonable prices** ❋ **spa resorts**

> **Best for:** all standards of skier, high-mileage skiers, non-skiers, ski-to-lunchers
>
> **Not recommended for:** beginners, families with small children (Bad Gastein), people wanting skiing convenience, night-owls

The Gasteinertal offers a better class of skiing than the lowland pastures of the Tyrol and an altogether more cosmopolitan atmosphere. **Bad Gastein**, the main resort in the valley, is a collection of once-grand hotels painted mostly in the imperial yellow of Vienna's Schönbrunn Palace and stacked dramatically up a steep hillside around a waterfall that plunges into the River Ache. The resort's elegant casino harks back to the days when this was one of the greatest spas of Europe. Franz Schubert and Johann Strauss composed here, and the guest list never failed to include at least a couple of crowned heads. These days – with 'wellness' being seen by the predominantly German, northern and eastern European clientèle as an essential feature of any holiday – the people of Gasteinertal have switched their focus from curing bad health to promoting good health.

Some 23 million litres of hot water per day bubble up from 17 natural springs and are piped into all the main hotels. About 4.5 million litres of this are also piped down the road to Bad Gastein's sister spa of **Bad Hofgastein**, a spacious and comfortable resort that is popular with families and a good base for walking and cross-country skiing. Here busy ice-rinks complete the winter scene, and there are indoor and outdoor thermal pools as well as a modern sports centre.

Dorfgastein is the first of the settlements you reach on entering the Gasteinertal. The sleepy and unspoilt village is lined with arcades, while horses and carts clatter along the narrow streets past the old church. The village has its own attractive ski area that extends over the 2,027-m Kreuzkogel to the resort of Grossarl in a neighbouring valley. Sportgastein, at the head of the valley, is a separate ski area based around an abandoned gold-mining village. In the Middle Ages the area was responsible for ten per cent of the world's gold and silver output.

The Gastein resorts are included in the regional Skiverbund Amadé lift pass, which covers resorts in this corner of Austria. It gives access to 270 lifts serving 860km of piste. In practice, this means that the visitor with a car can also ski in **Schladming** or, for a day, join the giant **Salzburger Sportwelt Amadé** circuit, which includes Flachau and Wagrain.

## On-piste

top 2,686m (8,810ft) bottom 850m (2,788ft)

The lift system has undergone a £20-million upgrade in recent years, but first you have to get to a lift. If you are accustomed to clicking into your bindings outside your hotel door and skiing home at the end of the day, then the Gasteinertal is not for you. Bad Gastein was built as a medical spa, not a ski resort, and a considerable amount of walking is unavoidable. The main Stubnerkogel ski area is situated on the western side of the valley and is reached by a modern, two-stage gondola from the top of the town near the railway station.

At the top of the Stubnerkogel a choice of manicured pistes takes you 1,100m vertical down to the floor of the Anger valley. You can return by a four-seater chair or ride a gondola up the Schlossalm above Bad Hofgastein. The Kitzstein funicular followed by the choice of cable-car or chair-lift provides alternative access to Schlossalm from Bad Hofgastein.

The best piste skiing lies a few minutes by car further down the valley above Dorfgastein. From here, a two-stage gondola brings you to the summit of the Fulseck. A series of demanding red and token black runs takes you back down to Dorfgastein or over the top to Grossarl.

Sportgastein is a small ski area with no village. It has the advantage of a 1,590-m base and a gondola that takes you up to 2,686m. The higher altitude often attracts better snow cover than anywhere else in the region.

The small Graukogel area above Bad Gastein on the far side of the valley completes the skiing possibilities with descents that include a World Cup course.

The area has five nursery slopes served by drag-lifts, but overall it cannot be recommended for beginners. From Bad Gastein, the main novice slopes are a bus ride away at Angertal. The entire valley is best suited to those looking for a combination of mileage and challenge. A ski bus service links the separate ski areas. Taxis are plentiful but in order to explore the area fully a car is a necessity.

Bad Gastein, Bad Hofgastein and Sportgastein all have commendable half-pipes, but most freestyle riders congregate in the terrain park at Dorfgastein.

## Off-piste
Untracked opportunities abound above the Schlossalm next to Hohe Scharte. Both the north and south faces of Sportgastein can provide excellent powder runs after a new snowfall. Graukogel has superb tree-level skiing and is the place where the locals go on a snowy day.

## Tuition and guiding
The Gastein Valley has five ski and board schools with the principal Bad Gastein and Bad Hofgastein ones run under the joint umbrella of the Schneesportschule Gastein. We have positive reports of these as well as Dorf Aktiv in Dorfgastein: 'friendly teacher with a gift for instruction'.

## Mountain restaurants
The area is plentifully served with pleasant huts on the slopes and self-service cafeterias at the lift stations. Prices are no higher than in the valley, where they are low by Austrian standards. Aeroplanstadl, on the home run to Bad Hofgastein, houses some of the finest WCs in the Alps: 'Both the Damen and the Herren bear witness to the fact that this whole valley is obsessed with waterworks. Together they form an underground ablutionary palace decorated with granite cattle troughs, giant boulders and ancient cast-iron village pumps'.

The Jungerstube and the Wengeralm are highly rated. The Waldgasthof in the Angertal earned praise for its 'roaring log fire, cosy dining booths and the best *Gulaschsuppe* we have ever tasted'.

## Accommodation
'Stay near the station,' recommended one reporter. Where you stay in Bad Gastein is crucial because of the steep layout of the resort, which also has an annoyingly complicated one-way system and heavy traffic. However, many of the hotels have their own car parks and a ski bus operates between 8am and 6pm daily. The old hotels are flanked by smart boutiques and expensive jewellers, who set their sights on Bad Gastein's wealthy Austrian and German visitors, here for the health treatments, rather than on the skiers and boarders.

The modern Arcotel-Elizabethpark (☎ 6434 2551) is said to be comfortable, with an indoor pool, but is a ten-minute walk from the snow. Hotel Wildbad (☎ 6434 3761), conveniently situated near the top of the town, is warmly recommended. Hotel Mozart (☎ 6434 2686) is spacious and well positioned. Hotel Grüner Baum (☎ 6434 2516), built in 1831 by Archduke Johann as a hunting lodge, is in a rural setting and has a justified reputation as one of the great hotels of Austria.

Although smaller than Bad Gastein, Bad Hofgastein is still sizeable, with 50 hotels and guesthouses built around a pedestrianised centre. The four-star Osterreichischer Hof (☎ 6432 62160) is described as 'delightful', and the palatial Grand Park Hotel (☎ 6432 6356) boasts its own spa.

There are several friendly hotels in the centre of Dorfgastein: Hotel Römerhof (☎ 6433 7777) has a swimming-pool and spa, while Gasthof Steindlwirt (☎ 6433 7219) and Hotel Kirchenwirt (☎ 6433 7251) are recommended by reporters. Gasthof Mühlbachstüberl (☎ 6433 7367) is 'very friendly with good food'.

## Eating in and out
The choice of eateries is limited mainly to the hotels, but the Fischer Stüberl, the Orania Stüberl and the Bahnhofrestaurant are recommended as good value for money. The Bellevue Alm and the Hofkeller both specialise in fondue. The Sponfeldner Restaurant am Wasserfall is 'inexpensive and cheerful', as is the Mozartstuben in

Hotel Mozart. The China-restaurant, according to one reporter, 'makes a pleasant change from *Wienerschnitzel*'. Hotel Rader and Gasthof Radhausberg in Böckstein are commended, while Villa Solitude's Thom and the restaurant in Hotel Grüner Baum provide the best gourmet fare in town.

## Après-ski

'The pampered alternative après-ski experience' is how one reporter put it. The new Felsentherme, opposite the Bahnhof restaurant, boasts thermal indoor and outdoor pools as well as a bar, and attracts the crowds as they come off the slopes. No visitor should miss the chance to improve his or her health by taking a train ride to the Healing Galleries, 2km inside the mountain near Böckstein.

The Gatz Music Club and Hägblom's are the hot-spots at teatime and again much later in the evening. Their late-night rival is the Central Park Entertainment. Eden's Pub is said to be crowded, 'not least because a giant moose head takes up most of the room'. Ritz in the Salzburgerhof Hotel has live music and is more sophisticated. The casino is worth a visit, and the Manfreda and Kir Royal bars are popular. Other late bars to check out include Oslag, which usually has a live band, Silver Bullet, Hexn-Häusl, Weinfassl, Highlife, Pub am Wasserfall and the Zirbenstube. The bar at the British-owned Hotel Tannenburg offers the cheapest drinks in town.

The nightlife at Bad Gastein is considered too staid by riders ('too little après-ski', complained one), with Bad Hofgastein a preferable lodging base boasting five discos and more than a dozen bars.

## Childcare

As with all resorts with a disparate ski area, it is difficult to recommend Bad Gastein for children. However, the valley operates non-ski kindergartens in the three principal resorts for children from three years of age, and Hotel Grüner Baum also runs a crèche for its small residents. All the ski schools offer lessons from four years of age: Schneesportschule Bad Gastein boasts the Kids Park in the Angertal Ski Centre, and Schneesportschule Dorfgastein has a children's ski playground.

# The Gasteinertal: At a glance

**Tel** Bad Gastein 43 6434 2531 560 / Bad Hofgastein 43 6432 7110 / Dorfgastein 43 6433 7277
**Email** info@badgastein.at / info@badhofgastein.com / info@dorfgastein.com
**Websites** www.badgastein.at / www.badhofgastein.com / www.dorfgastein.com

**GETTING THERE**
**Airport** Salzburg 1½hrs
**Rail** station in Bad Gastein
**Road** leave Salzburg–Klagenfurt Autobahn at Bischofshofen

**THE SKIING**
**Linked/nearby resort** Grossarl, Saalbach–Hinterglemm
**Total of trails/pistes** 201km (30% easy, 58% intermediate, 12% difficult), 860km in Skiverbund Amadé area
**Lifts in area** 48: 1 10 19 18. 270 in Skiverbund Amadé area
**Lift opening dates** 3 December 2004 to 1 May 2005

**LIFT PASSES**
**Area pass** Skiverbund Amadé (covers 25 resorts) €149.50–161 for 6 days

**Pensioners** no reductions

**TUITION**
**Ski & board** Bad Gastein: Schneesportschule Bad Gastein (☎ 6434 2260), Skischule Schlossalm (☎ 6432 3298). Bad Hofgastein: Schneesportschule Bad Hofgastein (☎ 6432 6339). Dorfgastein: Dorf Aktiv (☎ 6433 20048), Schneesportschule Dorfgastein (☎ 6433 7538)
**Guiding** L. Kravanja (☎ 6434 2941), F. Sendlhofer (☎ 6434 2879), Hans Zlöbl (☎ 6434 5355) and through ski schools

**CHILDREN**
**Lift pass** Skiverbund Amadé 6–15yrs €75–80.50 for 6 days
**Ski & board school** as adults
**Kindergarten** (ski) through ski schools, (non-ski) Gastein Kindergartens in Bad Gastein, Bad Hofgastein and Dorfgastein (☎ 6432 3393 560 for all)

**FOOD AND DRINK**
Coffee €2.20–3, bottle of house wine €14, small beer €2.50–3, soft drink €2.20, dish of the day €10–14

# Ischgl

ALTITUDE 1,400m (4,592ft)                                  map: see page 163

## ❋ large ski area ❋ beautiful scenery ❋ huge terrain park ❋ reliable snow ❋ lively après-ski

> **Best for:** intermediate skiers, powderhounds and ski-tourers, snowboarders, night-owls
>
> **Not recommended for:** beginners, ski-to-lunchers, people on a budget

Ischgl has some of the best intermediate skiing in Austria and is the après-ski capital of the Alps, yet this established resort on the Austrian–Swiss border remains almost unknown to the British. This is largely due to the fact that tour operators find it difficult to secure favourable hotel rates against heavy German competition.

Over the years this farming village has transformed itself into a bustling, attractive hill-side community. A tunnel with airport-style moving walkways has been driven through the hill to provide a curious and convenient pedestrian link between the two halves of the otherwise spread-out resort.

'Pretty much everything is expensive', said one reporter, 'especially as many bar staff seem to have big problems giving you the correct change'.

Ischgl is linked by lift to duty-free **Samnaun** in Switzerland, and on sunny days skiers flock across the frontier, attracted by the promise of a Swiss lunch and bargain-priced perfume, electrical goods and alcohol.

## On-piste
### top 2,864m (9,394ft) bottom 1,377m (4,517ft)

The resort's 205km of groomed pistes are served by a network of 42 lifts that are being systematically upgraded. The long, cold T-bars, which used to be a central feature of the lift system, are now outnumbered by modern chair-lifts. However, 16 drag-lifts still remain.

Three gondolas provide comfortable and rapid access from town to the mid-mountain plateau of Idalp. From this focal point the pistes fan out over the upper slopes, with extensive and well-linked opportunities for fast cruising. Further chair-lifts take you up to the ridge that marks the Swiss border for the long run down to Samnaun. After eating and shopping there, snow-users take a short road-side descent below the village to Ravaisch for the return journey, which involves a ride on the Pendelbahn, which was the world's first double-decker cable-car.

With the two home runs both coloured red, Ischgl is not user-friendly for first-timers or wobbly second-weekers, who have no sensible choice but to return to the village by gondola. Idalp's sunny nursery slopes are inviting, although frequently crowded with ski-school classes. Blue runs are also interrupted on occasion by short, sharp, red stretches.

The Silvretta area has established itself as a major snowboard centre, with the Boarders Paradise Funpark at Idjoch, which lays claim to being the largest in Europe. It contains a good half-pipe and 30 obstacles.

## Off-piste
Although the Paznaun Valley is famous for its spring ski-touring, Ischgl itself is not widely known as a resort for advanced skiers. In consequence, the powder is not skied out the moment the lifts open. Some of the most favourable terrain is off the Gampenalp chair.

## Tuition and guiding
The Ischgl Ski and Snowboard School (SSS) offers tuition in English for groups of 10 to 12 people. One reporter said: 'teaching is cheerful, but very much in the old style'.

## Mountain restaurants
There is not a huge choice on the Austrian side, but the best options include the restaurant in the hotel at Bodenalp, Restaurant Idalp and the small Ski Haus Alp Trida ('excellent service and atmosphere'). You can eat typical Swiss fare in Samnaun, with choices that include the Schmugglers Alms ('try the vodka and homemade strawberry ice-cream'), the

Chasa Montana ('the best pizzas') and the Samnaunerhof.

## Accommodation

The five-star Trofana Royal is an extremely comfortable hotel that heads a list of luxurious establishments, but almost any hotel makes a convenient base for at least one of the three lifts up to the mid-station. The exception is the Hotel Antony (☎ 5444 5427), which is isolated on the hill-side opposite the village but is highly recommended in other respects. Hotel Elisabeth (☎ 5444 5411) is a resort meeting-place and a firm favourite with reporters. Hotel Madlein (☎ 5444 5226) is a minimalist hotel with a Zen theme and a spa that overlooks a Japanese garden. Hotel Post (☎ 5444 5232) is warmly praised as 'a quality four-star with a family atmosphere and a fantastic swimming-pool'.

## Eating in and out

Celebrity chef Martin Sieberer presides over the elegant Paznauner Stube in the Trofana Royal, which is considered one of the best restaurants in Austria. Cuisine in both the Hotel Post and the Hotel Elisabeth is warmly praised; the former has 'a gourmet seven-course dinner every night'. The Goldener Adler is recommended for its ambience and its fresh trout. The

Heidelberger Hütte specialises in fondue evenings, with transport by snowcat.

## Après-ski

Ischgl is a resort 'where tippling and tobogganing become the two frenetic focal points when the lifts close for the day'. By mid-afternoon the entire village throbs to a heady mix of Europop and post-modern oompah. Fun-seeking Austrians and Germans crowd to watch go-go dancers at the Hotel Elisabeth before moving to Niki's Stadl, the Kitzlock, Trofana Alm and the Kuhstall for hard drinking and tabletop dancing. Later on the clubbing scene focuses on the Pacha in the Hotel Madlein, and Feuer & Eis. Lap-dancing at the Coyote Ugly carries on until 6am and can exceed the bounds of good taste for some visitors.

The 7-km toboggan run from Idalp on Thursday and Saturday evenings is not for the faint-hearted.

## Childcare

Three-year-olds can learn the basics in the ski kindergarten then graduate to the children's ski school from four years of age, according to ability. The meeting-point is beside the adventure garden, and lunch is served in the youth centre. There is also a kindergarten in the Silvretta cableway building on Idalp.

# Ischgl: At a glance

**Tel** 43 5444 5266
**Email** info@ischgl.com
**Website** www.ischgl.com

### GETTING THERE
**Airports** Innsbruck 1½hrs, Zurich 2½hrs
**Rail** Landeck 30km, frequent buses from station
**Road** through Arlberg tunnel, then before Landeck take highway 188 up the Paznaunertal

### THE SKIING
**Linked/nearby resorts** Galtür, Kappl, Samnaun, See
**Total of trails/pistes** 205km in area (27% easy, 63% intermediate, 10% difficult)
**Lifts in area** 42 in Ischgl–Samnaun linked area:
2 🚡 3 🚠 21 🚡 16 🚡
**Lift opening dates** 26 November 2004 to 1 May 2005

### LIFT PASSES
**Area pass** Silvretta Regional (covers Galtür, Ischgl,

Kappl, Samnaun, See) €197, VIP (covers Ischgl, Samnaun) €173.50, both for 6 days
**Pensioners** Silvretta Regional 60yrs and over €167.50, VIP 60yrs and over €142.50, both for 6 days

### TUITION
**Ski & board** Ischgl Ski and Snowboard School
(☎ 5444 5257)
**Guiding** through ski school

### CHILDREN
**Lift pass** Silvretta Regional 7–15yrs €112, VIP 7–15yrs €101, both for 6 days. Family discounts available
**Ski & board school** as adults
**Kindergarten** as ski school

### FOOD AND DRINK
Coffee €2.60, bottle of house wine €16, small beer €3.20, soft drink €2.50, dish of the day €20

# Kitzbühel

ALTITUDE 760m (2,493ft)                                    map: see page 164

## ❄ beautiful architecture ❄ Alpine charm ❄ lively après-ski
## ❄ intermediate slopes

> **Best for:** beginners, intermediates, party-goers, non-skiers
>
> **Not recommended for:** skiers in search of radical terrain, early-nighters, doorstep skiers

Kitzbühel's world renown is based largely on the Streif, the annual televised downhill race on the Hahnenkamm. But in reality its extensive ski area is largely intermediate, with few pisted challenges for experts.

The charming town is a walled, medieval settlement painted with delicate frescoes. The centre is mercifully traffic-free, and a bus service ferries skiers to and from the Hahnenkamm and the Kitzbüheler Horn mountains.

Changes come slowly here. But for the 2004–5 season, after a 15-year debate, a new gondola spans the valley between the top of the Jochberg ski area and the top of Pengelstein. This means that the Ski Safari route from the Hahnenkamm to Jochberg and Pass Thurn can now be made in both directions without an annoying walk or a return bus journey.

Kitzbühel's insuperable problem is its lack of altitude. In recent seasons it has been blessed with good cover, but conditions in early- and late-season weeks remain a gamble.

## WHAT'S NEW
Gondola linking Kitzbühel and Jochberg ski areas

## On-piste
top 2,000m (6,562ft) bottom 760m (2,493ft)

The main skiing is divided between the Kitzbüheler Horn and the more challenging Hahnenkamm, which is easily accessed from near the centre of town by a six-person gondola, from neighbouring **Kirchberg** by the Fleckalmbahn or from a giant car park between Kirchberg and Aschau by another gondola.

The Kitzbüheler Horn lies to the east of town and towers above the resort. A cable-car takes you up to 2,000m, where the views are spectacular. The skiing is pleasant and gentle, but experienced skiers will quickly find the Horn a disappointment.

Aurach, a ten-minute ski bus ride away from Kitzbühel, is a third separate area with three gentle blue runs and a marginally steeper reddish alternative.

Kitzbühel has four good nursery slopes near the town and plenty of easy cruising on both mountains for second-weekers.

The celebrated Ski Safari, marked by elephant signposts, is an enjoyable pisted itinerary that takes you from the Hahnenkamm up the Kitzbühel Valley to Jochberg and Pass Thurn. Anyone with a couple of weeks' ski experience can manage the outing, which consists of a series of blue and gentle red runs linked by lifts along the east-facing slopes of the valley. The new gondola allows you to ski back to Kitzbühel.

Riders tend to congregate on the Horn, which has a well-equipped terrain park with a half-pipe and boardercross course.

## Off-piste
After a fresh snowfall, there is plenty of easy powder skiing close to the pistes in the Hahnenkamm area. Bichlalm is another enjoyable spot, and Pass Thurn is particularly recommended. Alpinschule Kitzbühel is the specialist off-piste ski school.

## Tuition and guiding
Competition is keen among the ski schools, and all work hard to provide a good service to customers. The famous Rote Teufel received a couple of extremely positive reports in 2003–4: 'friendly teacher who not only knew his stuff but also how to impart it'.

## Mountain restaurants
The Hoch Kitzbühel restaurant at the top of the Hahnenkamm gondola ('superb *Gulaschsuppe* and enormous veal cutlets') has a sun terrace. Don't miss the adjoining

Hahnenkamm museum. Trattenbergalm between Jochberg and Pass Thurn has some of the best simple food in the region. Panorama-Alm above Pass Thurn has an outside bar with glass walls. The Pengelstein restaurant offers 'exceptionally good service and food'. The Staudachstub'n on the main run down to the Fleckalm gondola is 'a real delight', and the Streifalm has 'wonderful fresh ravioli'.

## Accommodation

Hotel Tennerhof (☎ 5356 6318 170) and Weisses Rössl (☎ 5356 63472) head a long list of luxury establishments. Goldener Greif (☎ 5356 64311), Jägerwirt (☎ 5356 64067) and Maria Theresia (☎ 5356 64711) are popular four-stars, and Sporthotel Astron (☎ 5356 63211) is also warmly recommended, as is Golfhotel Rasmushof (☎ 5356 652520). The converted hunting lodge of Schloss Lebensberg (☎ 5356 6901), on the outskirts, has a medieval-style interior complete with four-poster beds, and a health centre. Zur Tenne (☎ 5356 64444), in the town centre, is a comfortable designer hotel. Of the three-stars, Haselsberger (☎ 5356 62866) is 'small, pleasant, with good food' and Golfhotel Bruggerhof (☎ 5356 62806), outside town, has 'fabulous food and wonderful hosts'.

## Eating in and out

Goldener Greif is renowned for its *Salzburger Nockerl*, a kind of hot meringue soufflé, and Weisses Rössl has a private Weinstube for small parties. Geniesserrestaurant Rosengarten in Hotel Taxacherhof at Kirchberg is one of the finest restaurants in the Tyrol. Acclaimed chef Simon Taxacher has created his own outstanding style of Austrian nouvelle cuisine: 'not to be missed'.

## Après-ski

Après-ski begins in The Londoner, a British pub with Austrian overtones, and for many it ends there in the early hours. Bergsinn is the cooler hang-out. Other bars include S'Lichtl, Jimmy's, La Fonda and Barrique, while discerning drinkers opt for the tiny Waschkuchl, Fünferl and the Schirmbar in the Sporthotel Reisch. Late-night clubbers head for Club Take Five, Olympia and Royal. The Casino is 'large, comfortable and sophisticated with security checks at the door and a dress code'.

## Childcare

Beginner children are well catered for, with five lifts that make up the extensive nursery area at the foot of the Hahnenkamm. All the ski schools accept children. Anita Halder Nursery cares for non-skiers from newborn.

# Kitzbühel: At a glance

**Tel** 43 5356 777
**Email** info@kitzbuehel.com
**Website** www.kitzbuehel.com

## GETTING THERE
**Airports** Salzburg 1½hrs, Innsbruck 2hrs, Munich 2½hrs
**Rail** station in resort
**Road** 30-minute drive up winding road from the A12 Munich–Innsbruck Autobahn

## THE SKIING
**Linked/nearby resorts** Aurach, Jochberg, Kirchberg, Pass Thurn, Reith, Söll, St Johann in Tyrol
**Total of trails/pistes** 150km in linked area (39% easy, 46% intermediate, 15% difficult)
**Lifts in linked resorts** 57: 6🚠 29🚡 22🎢
**Lift opening dates** early December 2004 to late April 2005

## LIFT PASSES
**Area pass** (covers Jochberg, Kitzbühel, Kirchberg, Pass Thurn; includes ski bus, swimming-pool and reduction for sauna) €139–160 for 6 days
**Pensioners** 60yrs and over €126, 79yrs and over €77, both for 6 days

## TUITION
**Ski & board** Hahnenkamm Egger (☎ 5356 63177), Kitzbüheler Horn (☎ 5356 64454), Rote Teufel/Red Devils (☎ 5356 62500), Total (☎ 5356 72011)
**Guiding** Alpinschule Kitzbühel (☎ 5356 73323)

## CHILDREN
**Lift pass** 6–15yrs €86 for 6 days
**Ski & board school** as adults
**Kindergarten** (ski) through ski schools, (non-ski) Anita Halder Nursery (☎ 5356 75063)

## FOOD AND DRINK
Coffee €2.50, bottle of house wine €16, small beer €3, soft drink €2.25, dish of the day €8–15

# Lech and Zürs

ALTITUDE Lech 1,450m (4,756ft), Zürs 1,720m (5,642ft)                map: see page 165

## ❄ long cruising runs ❄ luxury accommodation ❄ compact village centre

> **Best for:** intermediates, families, comfort-seekers
>
> **Not recommended for:** people on a budget, advanced skiers and riders, serious mountain-lunchers

'Save your pennies and come here at least once. It really is worth it,' enthused a reporter. Lech and neighbouring Zürs are the most exclusive resorts in Austria, attracting the rich and famous to their portfolio of six five-star hotels. But by day their number is augmented by a considerably wider cross-section of skiers and riders who make the bus journey from **St Anton**, with which the resorts share a hands-free lift pass. The reason for this is that the terrain at this end of the combined area is considerably more benign than the notoriously tough slopes above St Anton: 'we had booked to stay in St Anton, but both of us found the skiing at Galzig too difficult to be enjoyable. We caught a bus to Lech each day – and that is where we will be booking our next holiday'.

Despite the luxury hotels, Lech clings charmingly to its farming origins and remains a traditional village. Over the years, the biggest expansion has been in Oberlech, a satellite 200m up the mountain, which was once the summer home of herdsmen and shepherds. Today it provides a safe and car-free centre for families with small children, and the hotels are ideally placed for the skiing. Access is by cable-car from Lech and your luggage is transported to and from your hotel through an ingenious set of underground service tunnels, thus avoiding a difficult walk with suitcases across the piste.

Zürs is little more than a collection of four- and five-star hotels in an isolated position astride the Flexen Pass and connected with Lech by free ski bus. The village lacks much of Lech's charm, although resort-level snow is guaranteed into spring. Zug, 3km by road through the

woods from Lech and fully integrated into the lift system, offers rural tranquility.

The resorts share a varied and extensive ski area, although advanced skiers will be more interested in the abundant off-piste and ski-touring opportunities of St Anton. The car park at Alpe Rauz is 20 minutes' drive from Lech and provides a back-door entrance into St Anton's ski area, which can also be reached by the regular and comfortable postbus.

Access across the Flexen Pass to Lech and Zürs can be restricted by avalanche danger in mid-winter. Plans to build a road tunnel from **Stuben** to Zug remain on the drawing board. Technically, this is not as difficult as it sounds and a feasibility study has been completed. However, improvements to the protective avalanche galleries on the pass road have removed the immediate need for a tunnel.

## On-piste
### top 2,450m (8,036ft) bottom 1,450m (4,757ft)

The Lech/Zürs circuit is spread over three mountains and provides mainly intermediate skiing of the highest quality. The lift system is being steadily upgraded and most of the annoying bottlenecks have been eliminated. However, the fact that the full circuit can be skied only in a clockwise direction inevitably leads to some delays during high-season weeks.

Mountain access to the circuit is via the twin Rüfikopf cable-cars, which scale an impressive wall from the centre of Lech. But many of Lech's well-heeled skiers prefer to spend their day in and around Oberlech on the sunny side of the valley. Above Oberlech, lifts and pistes spread throughout a wide, fragmented basin below the peaks of the Kriegerhorn and the Mohnenfluh. The two are linked by a cable-car with spectacular views.

Lech has excellent nursery slopes behind the church as well as at Oberlech. Second-weekers should be able to negotiate the blue run from the Rüfikopf all the way to Zürs.

Follow the local lift map with care: appropriately coloured circles indicate pisted runs, while ski routes are marked by diamonds. It is easy to think that a red diamond with a thin black border is a hard intermediate run. In fact it is an extreme itinerary that is neither patrolled nor pisted, although some are so well skied that they become pistes.

Zürs has the steeper skiing of the two main resorts, including a couple of short, sharp black pistes, notably the Hexenboden Direkte.

Lech's Boarderland terrain park on the Schlegelkopf is 300m long, with a half-pipe, a quarter-pipe and a series of obstacles. Zug has myriad gullies and drops, as well as a natural half-pipe when snow conditions allow.

## Off-piste

After fresh snowfalls both Lech and Zürs are a delight. Advanced skiers can try the various descents of the 2,173-m Kriegerhorn and the Zuger Hochlicht beyond it. The long run down from the top to Zug via the narrow Zuger Tobel can be spectacular in powder conditions. Langerzug and Tanngg, around the shoulder of the Rüfikopf, are dramatic in the extreme. For environmental reasons, it is forbidden to ski off-piste through the trees – anyone caught risks having his or her lift pass confiscated. Ski-touring is popular and limited heli-skiing is available.

## Tuition and guiding

Ski Schools Lech, Oberlech and Zürs received mixed reports. We have no reports of the Alpine Centre Lech. Eighty per cent of ski teachers in Zürs and more than 50 per cent in Lech are booked for private rather than group lessons each day. Reporters advised that it is essential to book both private and group lessons well in advance.

## Mountain restaurants

Indulgent lunch opportunities are surprisingly limited. 'The food is unremarkable and the choice is confined to which has the sunniest terrace,' commented one reporter. These belong mainly to hotels in Oberlech. The atmospheric Alte Goldener Berg above Oberlech is recommended, as is the Gasthof Auerhahn in Zug, which is 'wood-panelled, chintzy and quite exquisite – an exception in the gastronomic wilderness'. The Rote Wand, also in Zug, is 'superb, but moderately expensive'. The Seekopf at Zürs is also rated.

## Accommodation

Lech is fairly compact, and location is not particularly important. The smartest hotel – indeed one of the most celebrated five-stars in Austria – is the sumptuous Gasthof Post (☎ 5583 22060). It has only 38 rooms, including ten suites with private steam baths, and you need to book a year in advance. Hotel Kristiania (☎ 5583 2561) is set in a quiet position 500m from the centre.

The Arlberg (☎ 5583 2134), Gotthard (☎ 5583 3560) and the Schneider-Almhof (☎ 5583 3500) ('the height of luxury') are all warmly recommended by regulars.

The Romantik-Hotel Krone (☎ 5583 2551) boasts the Moroccan-influenced Wasserschlössl spa. The Tannbergerhof (☎ 5583 3313) is popular with the British and is the hub of Lech's social life. Hotel Elizabeth (☎ 5583 2330) is said to be 'very comfortable', as is the Monzabon (☎ 5583 2104). It is worth noting that even the best hotels do not generally accept credit cards. One reporter strongly recommended Haus Lechblick apartments (☎ 5583 3839).

In Oberlech, the four-star Sonnenburg (☎ 5583 2147) is 'delightfully convenient and much the best hotel in the hamlet'. Bergkristall (☎ 5583 2678) has 'excellent food and service with easy access to the slopes'. In Zug, the four-star Rote Wand (☎ 5583 3435) is 'wonderfully peaceful'. It also has an annexe of apartments: 'modern design and perfect for families'.

Zürs has three five-star hotels including Thurnhers Alpenhof (☎ 5583 21910). The four-star Arlberghaus (☎ 5583 2258) receives glowing reports and has a roof-top curling-rink.

## Eating in and out

Good restaurants abound, but most are in the hotels and none is cheap. Hus No. 8 in Lech, opposite the Post Hotel, is intimate, with good food and a superb wine list. Booking is essential. Fux is a surprisingly modern restaurant in such a traditional resort ('sushi and other oriental delights served from an open-plan kitchen'). The Brunnenhof is highly acclaimed, together with Bistro s'Casserole, Rudi's Stamperl and the Dorf Stüberl. Don Enzo serves pizzas and pasta. In Zürs, the Chesa Rose is an award-winning restaurant, while in Zug the Rote Wand is highly praised.

## Après-ski

The average age of the clientèle in Lech and Zürs is higher than that in other Alpine resorts; bronzed and fit 60-year-olds wearing the latest designer ski suits abound. Consequently, après-skiers at these resorts prefer to put their hair up, rather than let it down.

The floodlit toboggan run is the quickest way to travel down from Oberlech to Lech at the start of the evening's entertainment. The ice-bar outside the Tannbergerhof in Lech is where the evening begins, with tea-dancing, as the slopes close. The hotel also hosts a disco, often with live music later on in the evening. The Sidestep Bar in the Romantik-Hotel Krone attracts the over-25s for dancing, and the Klausur Bar in the Schneider-Almhof is popular. The s'Pfefferkörndl bar has youth appeal. Hotel Petersboden at Oberlech has an Internet café. Fux has armchairs in the bar and an open log fire.

Schneggare, at the bottom of the Schlegelkopf run, has a cosy wooden interior with two log fires, a bar serving snacks and a pizzeria.

Die Vernissage in Zürs is recommended, and the Zürserl in the Hotel Edelweiss is the biggest disco in town, while the Rote Wand and the Sennkessel in Zug are both lively.

Public transport comes to a halt in the early evening. Taxis are expensive, but a bus collection service called 'James', which runs until 4am, will return you to wherever you are staying in Lech, Zürs or Zug for a reasonable flat fee.

## Childcare

The area lends itself to family skiing, particularly at Oberlech, the site of the main nursery slopes. Children six years and under ski for €10 for the whole season. A number of hotels run their own crèches. We have positive reports of Kinderland Oberlech. The ski school takes small skiers all day and supervises lunch. Little Zürs kindergarten takes children from three years old and provides ski instruction for little ones from four years. Miniclub Lech is for children from three to five years of age, 9am–4pm except Saturday.

# Lech and Zürs: At a glance

**Tel** 43 5583 2161 229
**Email** info@lech-zuers.at
**Website** www.lech-zuers.at

**GETTING THERE**
**Airports** Innsbruck 2hrs, Zurich 2½hrs
**Rail** Zurich–Langen (17km by postbus)
**Road** motorway from Zurich to Arlberg, and Flexenpass to Zürs and Lech

**THE SKIING**
**Linked/nearby resorts** Klösterle, Pettneu, St Anton, St Christoph, Stuben, Zug
**Total of trails/pistes** 110km in Lech/Zürs (36% easy, 42% intermediate, 22% difficult). 280km in Arlberg Ski Pass area
**Lifts in linked resorts** 33: 4⬚ 18⬚ 11⬚. Alberg Ski Pass area: 82: 10⬚ 38⬚ 34⬚
**Lift opening dates** 3 December 2004 to 24 April 2005

**LIFT PASSES**
**Area pass** Arlberg Ski Pass (covers Klösterle, Lech and Zürs, Pettneu, St Anton, St Christoph, Stuben, Zug) €169–184 for 6 days

**Pensioners** Arlberg Ski Pass women 60yrs and over, and men 65yrs and over, €147–160, both for 6 days. 75yrs and over €10 for whole season

**TUITION**
**Ski & board** Alpine Centre Lech (☎ 5583 39880), Ski School Lech (☎ 5583 2355), Ski School Oberlech (☎ 5583 200), Ski School Zürs (☎ 5583 2611)
**Guiding** Wucher Heli-skiing (☎ 5583 2950) and through ski schools

**CHILDREN**
**Lift pass** Arlberg Ski Pass 7–15yrs €101–111 for 6 days. 6yrs and under €10 for whole season
**Ski & board school** as adults
**Kindergarten** (ski/non-ski) Kinderland Oberlech (☎ 5583 2007), Little Zürs (☎ 5583 2245 252), (non-ski) Miniclub Lech (☎ 5583 3530)

**FOOD AND DRINK**
Coffee €2.60, bottle of house wine €17, small beer €3.20, soft drink €2.80, dish of the day €10–18

# Mayrhofen

ALTITUDE 630m (2,066ft)  map: see page 168

## ❄ big intermediate ski area ❄ well-regarded ski schools
## ❄ exemplary childcare ❄ glacier skiing

**Best for:** families with small children, intermediate cruisers, snowboarders, night-owls

**Not recommended for:** advanced skiers and riders, people who want skiing convenience, those expecting quiet slopes

Mayrhofen somehow manages to combine the opposing images of family resort in the gentle Tyrolean pastureland and wild party resort in a modern, vibrant village.

Outlying hamlets have now been linked into the lift system to create Zillertal 3000, which is one of the largest networks in the Ziller valley. Skiing is possible for the entire year on the Hintertux Glacier, 19km away at the head of the valley. This means that Christmas visitors have guaranteed skiing during their holiday, even if cover in much lower Mayrhofen is inadequate. However, when such conditions prevail, the glacier becomes extremely crowded.

The Zillertal Superskipass covers 11 different local areas, stretching down to the River Inn and the Germany–Innsbruck Autobahn, and up the valley sides east as far as Königsleiten and Gerlos and west as far as **Hintertux**. Individually, no one area offers much more than a single day's interesting skiing, but bus transport is free and generally efficient, and a free train goes from Mayrhofen down the valley to **Zell am Ziller**, and on to Fügen and the mainline junction at Jenbach.

### WHAT'S NEW
Knorren chair-lift upgraded to covered 6-seater

## On-piste
top 2,300m (7,546ft) bottom 630m (2,066ft)

Mayrhofen's main mountain is the Penken, to which a gondola rises from the town centre as well as from the outlying hamlets of Finkenberg and Schwendau. There is no route whatsoever back down to Mayrhofen, and at the end of the day you must download on the Penkenbahn or ski down to the satellite villages and complete your journey by ski bus.

The Ahorn, on the other side of the valley, is reached by cable-car and is best suited to beginners, although the 5.5-km black Ebenwald piste from the top attracts more accomplished skiers and riders. Plans are in place for a complete restructuring of the lifts here.

Mayrhofen has a funpark with a 150-m half-pipe and an assortment of advanced and medium jumps and rollers, which is served by the Hintertrett lift. The highlight is a mega-spine leading to a triple-kicker table-top with a 30-m landing.

## Off-piste
The ingenious will find short, steep descents through rocks and woods on Penken and Gerent. Peter Habeler, who climbed Everest without oxygen in 1978, offers off-piste tours with overnight stops in a mountain hut, through his company Mount Everest.

## Tuition and guiding
Mayrhofen has more than 100 instructors from five competing schools: Die Roten Profis, Mount Everest, Mayrhofen Total, Mayrhofen 3000 and Mike Thanner. Despite typical high-season class sizes of 12, most students give the teaching high marks. All five schools offer snowboarding.

## Mountain restaurants
Numerous 'umbrella bars', some open-air and others covered, serve quick snacks, Schnapps and beer – generally to the accompaniment of raucous accordion music. Josef's Biohütte is arguably the world's first organic mountain restaurant. The Schneekarhütte serves 'wonderful prawns and salmon steaks'. The Grillholfalm by the terrain park is popular for pizzas. Vroni's Skialm, the Penkentenne and Hilde's Skitenne are also recommended.

## Accommodation

The general standard is superlative, with many hotels featuring swimming-pools, saunas or Turkish baths. The five-star Elisabethhotel (☎ 5285 6767) sets the pace in luxury. Four-star Hotel Strass (☎ 5285 6705) is next door to the Penken lift and home to both the Ice Bar and Sports Arena disco. Just up the road is the four-star Waldheim (☎ 5285 62211), which has comfortable rooms with views. The impeccable Hotel Berghof (☎ 5285 62254) has its own indoor tennis courts. The three-star Hotel Siegelerhof (☎ 5285 62493) is 'a real traditional Tyrolean experience'. Alpenhotel Kramerwirt (☎ 5285 6700) is also recommended, along with Hotel-Gasthof Perauer (☎ 5285 62566).

## Eating in and out

Mayrhofen has fewer independent dining venues than one might expect. The Wirthaus zum Griena, which is a listed 400-year-old building, provides what one reporter described as a menu of 'local mountain food'. Singapore is an average Chinese restaurant, Mo's serves Cajun burgers, and Mamma Mia is a bright Italian. Grill Kuchl has a good, inexpensive menu. Café Dengg has the best pizzas. The Sports Bar Grill in Hotel Strass serves Mexican food.

## Après-ski

The Ice Bar at the foot of Penken gondola becomes a seething mass of humanity at the end of the day and claims to be Europe's biggest sales point for Grolsch beer. Uli Spiess' Happy End is a quieter alternative. The Lobby and the Speakeasy are both popular bars. The Sports Arena is one of the more hi-tech discos in the Alps. The Scotland Yard Pub is a popular hang-out for riders and has British beer. The Garage attracts the younger set, but Schlusselalm is the busiest.

Erlebnis Mayrhofen, a swimming-pool complex with a 101-m chute, ranks as one of the top five waterparks in the Tyrol.

## Childcare

The concept of the ski kindergarten was born in Mayrhofen a generation ago and the standard of childcare here remains among the best in Austria. Wuppy's Kinderland minds little ones from three months, Die Roten Profis caters for children from twelve months, and Max Rahm's Mayrhofen Total accepts children from two years old.

# Mayrhofen: At a glance

**Tel** 43 5285 6760
**Email** info@mayrhofen.at
**Website** www.mayrhofen.at

**LIFT PASSES**
**Area pass** Zillertal Superskipass €165 for 6 days
**Pensioners** no reductions

**GETTING THERE**
**Airports** Innsbruck 1hr, Munich and Salzburg 2½hrs
**Rail** station in resort, mainline connection at Jenbach
**Road** easy access up Zillertal from Kufstein–Innsbruck A12 Autobahn

**THE SKIING**
**Linked/nearby resorts** Finkenberg, Fügen, Fügenberg, Gerlos, Hintertux, Hippach, Juns, Kaltenbach, Kramsach, Lanersbach, Madseit, Ramsau-im-Ziller, Schwendau, Vorderlanersbach, Zell am Ziller
**Total of trails/pistes** 146km in the Zillertal 3000 (27% easy, 59% intermediate, 14% difficult), 590km in whole of Zillertal
**Lifts in area** 46 in the Zillertal 3000: 8🚠 18🚡 20🚦. 173 in whole of Zillertal.
**Lift opening dates** mid-December 2004 to mid-April 2005. 21 lifts for summer skiing on Hintertux Glacier open throughout the year

**TUITION**
**Ski & board** Die Roten Profis (☎ 5285 63800), Mount Everest (☎ 5285 62829), Mayrhofen Total (☎ 5285 63939), Mayrhofen 3000 (☎ 5285 64015), Mike Thanner (☎ 5285 64015)
**Guiding** Mount Everest

**CHILDREN**
**Lift pass** Zillertal Superskipass €98 for 6 days. 6yrs and under free
**Ski & board school** as adults
**Kindergarten** (ski) Mount Everest, (ski/non-ski) Die Roten Profis, Mayrhofen Total, (non-ski) Wuppy's Kinderland (☎ 5285 63612)

**FOOD AND DRINK**
Coffee €2.20, bottle of house wine €18, small beer €2.40, soft drink €2.30, dish of the day €9–14

# Obergurgl–Hochgurgl

**ALTITUDE 1,930m (6,330ft)**                                      **map: see pages 166–167**

❄ **resort charm** ❄ **long skiing season** ❄ **magnificent scenery**
❄ **atmospheric lunch spots**

---

**Best for:** families, first-timers, ski-tourers, older intermediates, Easter skiers

**Not recommended for:** upper intermediates and experts looking for challenge, non-skiers, budget skiers, party-goers

---

Obergurgl–Hochgurgl provides snowsure, high-altitude skiing from November until the end of April. Situated at the head of the Ötz Valley, a 90-minute drive from **Innsbruck**, Obergurgl remains a small and charming village, set around the church, a handful of shops and an open-air ice-rink. Cars are banned after 11pm and 6am, and parking is not easy.

Hochgurgl is a collection of modern hotels perched by the side of the road. The resort is linked to Obergurgl by gondola.

## On-piste

**top 3,080m (10,104ft) bottom 1,793m (5,881ft)**

The slopes of Obergurgl and Hochgurgl occupy a north-west-facing area, linked via a 3.6-km gondola. Skiing takes place in three areas, naturally divided by the contours of the terrain. The Festkogel sector is the most extensive, and access is provided via a four-seater enclosed chair. Alternatively, you can take the Festkogelbahn gondola.

The smaller Gaisberg area, to the south of the village, offers some varied runs above and between the trees. The first part of the only official run down is a ski route, which in turn becomes a black piste, but the 1.8-km descent is not difficult when snow cover is deep.

The third ski area is at Hochgurgl. High glacial terrain here offers a far more comprehensive selection of broad blue pistes as well as a greater vertical drop. The Schermer-Spitz chair gives access to a wide and easy red piste, which is the start of nearly 1,500m vertical all the way down to

Pill. 'The pistes never feel overcrowded', commented one reporter.

This is also a pleasant region for snowboarders of all levels: Wurmkogl has a 120-m half-pipe and a terrain park, and in the Festkogl ski area is a quarter-pipe.

## Off-piste

Obergurgl, with its 23 glaciers, is one of the great ski-touring centres of Europe. An off-piste run in good powder conditions off the back of the Hohe Mut takes you on a glorious descent that ends up near the Schönwieshütte.

## Tuition and guiding

We have received favourable reports of both the Obergurgl and Hochgurgl schools, which have been the subject of criticism in the past: 'I commend the Obergurgl school, particularly for its handling of young children'.

## Mountain restaurants

The Hohe Mut Hütte, at Gaisberg, provides magnificent views of the Ötztal and the Dolomites. The Schönwieshütte is a touring refuge that serves simple meals ('best *Gulaschsuppe* and *Kaiserschmarren* ever').

David's Schihütte at the bottom of the Steinmannlift received mixed reports of good food but slow service. The Festkogl mountain restaurant has 'an excellent range of salads, soups and traditional main dishes'. The Nederhütte is commended.

In Hochgurgl, the Wurmkoglhütte offers 'a good range of mountain food'. Toni's Almhütte is highly praised. The sun terrace of the Hotel Riml has great views.

## Accommodation

Most of this is in smart hotels and, to a lesser extent, in guesthouses and pensions. In Obergurgl, Hotel Crystal (☎ 5256 6454) is a monster of a building but extremely comfortable inside. The Deutschmann (☎ 5256 6594) takes its name from the Obergurgl family owners. The Bergwelt

(☎ 5256 6274) ('a great pool'), the Austria (☎ 5256 6282) and Hotel Gotthard-Zeit (☎ 5256 6292) are all highly recommended.

In the centre, the Hotel Edelweiss & Gurgl (☎ 5256 6223) is still popular, although its bedrooms are smaller and less well equipped than those in the newer four-stars. The Jenewein (☎ 5256 6203) is praised for its friendly service and 'quite exceptional demi-pension food'. Hotel de Luxe Alpina (☎ 5256 600) is described as having 'fine service and hospitality'. Haus Schönblick (☎ 5256 6251) has 'helpful owners, large rooms and excellent buffet breakfasts'.

In Hochgurgl, the five-star Top Hotel Hochgurgl (☎ 5256 6265) leads the field and has a crèche and a health club. We have good reports of the Hotel Riml (☎ 5256 6261) and the Sporthotel Ideal (☎ 5256 6290). The three-star Alpenhotel Laurin (☎ 5256 6227) is applauded for its 'first-rate food'.

## Eating in and out

Dining is largely confined to the main hotels, most of which have separate à la carte restaurants. In Obergurgl, Pizzeria Romantika in the Hotel Madeleine and Pizzeria Belmonte in Haus Gurgl ('the best pizzas in town') provide some respite from the ubiquitous rounds of *Wienerschnitzel*. The Edelweiss & Gurgl has a comfortable candlelit *Stübli* with an atmosphere of 'relaxed elegance'. The Bergwelt's restaurant is recommended for its nouvelle cuisine. Restaurant Pic-Nic is also praised. Restaurants in Hochgurgl are nearly all attached to the smart hotels.

## Après-ski

Obergurgl is geared towards family groups and older intermediates and consequently non-skiing activities are limited. As one reporter put it: 'sleep is not disturbed by drunks, traffic or loud music'. The Nederhütte ('by far the best') at the top of the Gaisberg lift becomes crowded as the lifts close. The Joslkeller has a cosy atmosphere and good music. The Krump'n'Stadl is lively. Hexenkuch'l has live music, as does Toni's Almhütte in Hochgurgl. The Austriakeller and the Edelweissbar in Obergurgl, and the African Bar in Hochgurgl, are the late-night spots.

## Childcare

The resort allows children aged eight years and under to ski for free – a higher age limit than in many other resorts in the Alps. Bobo's Kinderclub takes non-skiing children from three years old. A number of hotels operate their own crèches, usually free of charge. These include the Alpina, Austria, Bellevue, Bergwelt, Crystal, Hochfirst, Top Hotel Hochgurgl and Olymp. Both Obergurgl and Hochgurgl ski schools accept children as young as three years for lessons.

# Obergurgl–Hochgurgl: At a glance

**Tel** 43 5256 6466
**Email** info@obergurgl.com
**Website** www.obergurgl.com

### GETTING THERE
**Airport** Innsbruck 1½hrs
**Rail** Ötztal 54km, regular buses from station
**Road** easy access up the dead-end Ötz valley from Arlberg–Salzburg Autobahn

### THE SKIING
**Linked/nearby resorts** Sölden, Vent
**Total of trails/pistes** 110km (32% easy, 50% intermediate, 18% difficult)
**Lifts in linked resorts** 23: 4🚠 11🚡 8🚟
**Lift opening dates** 12 November 2004 to 1 May 2005

### LIFT PASSES
**Area pass** Gurgl (covers Obergurgl/Hochgurgl) €167–187 for 6 days
**Pensioners** 60yrs and over €150 for 6 days

### TUITION
**Ski & board** Hochgurgl (☎ 5256 6265), Obergurgl (☎ 5256 6305)
**Guiding** through Obergurgl ski school

### CHILDREN
**Lift pass** 9–16yrs €110 for 6 days
**Ski & board school** as adults
**Kindergarten** Bobo's Kinderclub (☎ 5256 6305)

### FOOD AND DRINK
Coffee €2.50, bottle of house wine €15, small beer €2.50–3.50, soft drink €2–2.60, dish of the day €10–12

# Obertauern

ALTITUDE 1,740m (5,708ft)

✳ **excellent snow record** ✳ **purpose-built convenience**
✳ **well-linked ski circuit**

> **Best for:** all levels of skier and boarder,
> off-piste skiers, early- and late-season
> skiers
> **Not recommended for:** non-skiers,
> night-owls

Obertauern is Austria's best shot at a
purpose-built resort, with a reputation based
largely on its exceptionally good snow cover.
Indeed, if there is decent snow anywhere in
Austria, you will find it here. The resort
consists of a long straggle of road-side hotels
and bars and looks more like a Wild West
town than a traditional ski village, but it is
by no means devoid of charm. It lies on a
high pass in the Niedere Tauern mountains,
90km south of Salzburg. The main cluster of
buildings, which constitutes the centre, is
around the village nursery slope and the
tourist information office.

## On the snow
top 2,313m (7,587ft) bottom 1,640m (5,379ft)

The impressive peaks of the Niedere Tauern
mountains surround the road around the
resort, allowing the construction of lifts
from a central point to fan out into a
natural ski circus covering 95km of piste.
The ski area provides an interesting variety
of gradient and terrain.

In powder conditions the off-piste is
spectacular, with long runs above and
below the tree-line. To find the best and
safest runs you need the services of a local
guide – Vertical is the off-piste mountain
guiding company. Obertauern has six ski
and snowboard schools, including Ski &
Snowboardschule Krallinger, which is much
favoured by tour operators. The others are
CSA (known as Ski & Snowboardschule
Willi Grillitsch), Ski & Snowboardschule
Top, Ski & Snowboardschule Frau Holle,
Blue Tomato Snowboardschule and
Skischule Koch. Two more unusual schools
are Snowbikeschule Koch and Snow-Kite-
Schule Tony Ully.

## In the resort
Hotel location is not particularly critical
unless you have small children (pick a hotel
within easy walking distance of your chosen
kindergarten). Sporthotel Edelweiss
(☎ 6456 7245), Hotel Römerhof (☎ 6456
72380) and Alpenhotel Perner (☎ 6456
7236) are all recommended four-stars, as is
Sporthotel Cinderella (☎ 6456 7589) and
Hotel-Restaurant Montana (☎ 6456 7313).
Haus Kärntnerland (☎ 6456 7250) is said
to be 'clean, comfortable and friendly, with
exceptional food'. The Alpenrose
apartments in the village centre are
described as 'cosy and well-appointed'.
Hotel Petersbühel (☎ 6456 72350) is in a
quiet location with rooms 'cheerfully and
comfortably decorated'. The lavish
Sportinghotel Marietta (☎ 6456 7262)
remains a favourite with reporters.

The Stüberl restaurant in Hotel Regina is
said to be extremely good value ('quiet,
candlelit and serves enormous portions'),
while the Lurzeralm requires reservations
and serves 'well-presented, good food'. The
Stüberl at Hotel Latschenhof boasts friendly
service and well-prepared food.

Après-ski begins at the Edelweisshütte
before the lifts close, along with the
Achenrainhütte. Later on the action moves
to Römerbar and Der Turn. The Gasthof
Taverne reportedly has the liveliest disco.

Non-skiing children from three years old
are cared for in the Petzi-Bär crèche or in
the Haus des Gastes. All the ski schools run
ski kindergartens, with optional lunch
provided. The resort boasts four magic
carpet lifts.

> ## Obertauern: At a glance
> **Tel** 43 6456 7252
> **Email** info@obertauern.com
> **Website** www.obertauern.com
> **Lifts in resort** 26: 1🚡 18🚠 7🎿
> **Lift opening dates** 27 November 2004 to 1 May
> 2005

# Saalbach–Hinterglemm

ALTITUDE 1,000m (3,280ft)                                   map: see page 169

❄ extensive ski area ❄ confidence-building slopes
❄ modern lift system ❄ reliable snow cover

> **Best for:** intermediate to advanced skiers and riders, ski-to-lunchers, night-owls, cross-country skiers, snowboarders
> **Not recommended for:** those wanting a compact and peaceful village

Saalbach–Hinterglemm is the collective marketing name of two once-separate villages in the pretty Glemmtal near **Zell am See**. The narrow valley, with uniform 2,000-m peaks on either side, lends itself to a natural ski circus ('superb . . . almost as good as the French Alps'), which can be skied as happily in one direction as in the other. It provides some of the best intermediate and advanced skiing in Austria, second only to that in the Arlberg region. 'It is a lively and friendly resort with an extensive and varied range of skiing', said one reporter.

The two villages are a 5-minute drive or 40-minute walk apart along the bank of the river Glemm. The steep pedestrianised main street of Saalbach, with its smart hotels and fashion boutiques, contrasts with Hinterglemm, which is much quieter and more family-oriented, thanks largely to a road tunnel that keeps traffic away from the village centre.

## WHAT'S NEW
Both Westgilpfel double chair-lifts replaced by an 8-person gondola

## On-piste
top 2,096m (6,877ft) bottom 1,000m (3,280ft)

'I would recommend Saalbach to anyone', said one reporter, 'the skiing is always fantastic and just keeps getting better with the improved lift system'. Another was also 'very impressed with the lift system'. Both sides of the valley are lined with a network of mainly modern lifts that provide an easy traffic flow around the 200-km circuit of prepared pistes.

From Saalbach, the Schattberg Ost gondola gives direct access to the southern half of the circuit; a triple-chair at the top end of the village is the starting point for the northern part of the area, including Hochalm where three modern detachable chair-lifts serve an extensive intermediate area beyond the Reiterkogel. From Vorderglemm, the Schönleitenbahn gondola takes you up to Wildenkarkogel and the more remote and demanding Leogang ski area. The Glemmtal offers considerable Langlauf opportunities.

The north side of the valley is dotted with T-bars serving an unusual variety of beginner terrain. Schattberg Ost, Schattberg West and Zwölferkogel make up the more challenging north-facing slopes. The north face of the Zwölfer is a classic harsh black run, which can be heavily mogulled.

Saalbach–Hinterglemm is recognised as a major resort for snowboarders. The snowboard-only terrain park at Hinterglemm is vast, while Saalbach and neighbouring **Leogang** also have half-pipes.

## Off-piste
The north side of the valley offers some outstanding powder runs. Sepp Mitterer, as well as all the regular ski and board schools, can arrange off-piste guiding.

## Tuition and guiding
Since deregulation permitted the establishment of alternative ski and snowboard schools in Austria, no fewer than eight compete for the resort's big business. Activ in Hinterglemm has a sound reputation.

## Mountain restaurants
As one reporter put it: 'there are almost as many delightful restaurants as there are runs. The Pfefferalm above Hinterglemm is the most picturesque old farmhouse we have ever encountered'. Another remarked on the 'reasonable mountain restaurant prices'. The rustic GoassStall is recommended for its

Glühwein. The good-value Rosswaldhütte, beside the Rosswald lift, is an attractive chalet where the friendly staff wear traditional costume. The Wildenkarkogel Hütte at the top of the Vorderglemm gondola is accessible for non-skiers. Also recommended are the Gerstreitalm in Hinterglemm, the Maisalm above Saalbach, and the Grabenhütte below Schattberg West.

## Accommodation

The area has a total of 31 four-star hotels. In Saalbach these include the Alpenhotel (☎ 6541 6666) ('wonderful food cooked superbly, and staff treated guests as royalty'), the Ingonda (☎ 6541 6262), the Kristiana (☎ 6541 6253) and the Saalbacherhof (☎ 6541 7111).

In Hinterglemm, Hotel Dorfschmiede (☎ 6541 7408) has 'delicious food and helpful staff', Hotel Glemmtalerhof (☎ 6541 7135) is 'ideally situated and comfortable' and the Blumenhotel Tirolerhof (☎ 6541 6497) is also rated. Hotel Hasenauer (☎ 6541 6332) is convenient for the lifts, and three-star Hotel Sonnblick (☎ 6541 6408) is said to have 'Austrian charm and excellent food'.

## Eating in and out

Bäckstättstall is the most exclusive restaurant in Saalbach. Hotel Bauer is said to be 'good value, with a much more varied menu than you would expect in Austria'. In Hinterglemm, the Gute Stube in the Hotel Dorfschmiede has 'the best gourmet food in the region', Hotel Hasenauer is 'cheaper than anywhere else', while the Bärenbachhof is 'better than most'. Two reporters spoke warmly of Hotel Gollingerhof's restaurant.

## Après-ski

Après-ski starts with a drink at the Hinterhagalm above Saalbach or the GoassStall above Hinterglemm. Both are situated on the home runs and are 'packed from 4pm until 6pm with live music, singing and dancing'. Bauer's Schialm by the church in Saalbach has Glühwein on draught. In Hinterglemm, the snow-bar outside the Hotel Dorfschmiede is always crowded. The Hexenhäusl attracts crowds as they leave the slopes, and Bla Bla has a good atmosphere. The Road King is a popular late-night bar. Other late-night venues include Classics Dancing in Saalbach and Tanzhimmel in Hinterglemm. A regular bus service runs until 3am.

## Childcare

Schischule Fürstauer and Snow & Fun both operate their own ski kindergartens.

# Saalbach-Hinterglemm: At a glance

**Tel** 43 6541 680068
**Email** contact@saalbach.com
**Website** www.saalbach.com

## GETTING THERE
**Airport** Salzburg 1½hrs
**Rail** Zell am See 19km
**Road** Siegsdorf exit off Munich–Salzburg Autobahn

## THE SKIING
**Linked/nearby resorts** Bad Gastein, Bad Hofgastein, Grossarl, Kaprun, Leogang, Zell am See
**Total of trails/pistes** 200km (45% easy, 47% intermediate, 8% difficult)
**Lifts in linked resorts** 55: 11🚠 21🚡 23🎿
**Lift opening dates** 3 December 2004 to 10 April 2005

## LIFT PASSES
**Area pass** (covers Saalbach–Hinterglemm and Leogang) €126–168 for 6 days, Europa Sport Region (see Zell am See and Kaprun) €154–168 for 6 days

**Pensioners** no reduction

## TUITION
**Ski & board** Hinterglemm: Activ (☎ 6765 171325), Snow & Fun (☎ 6541 7511). Saalbach: Snow Academy/Aamadall (☎ 6541 668256), Fürstauer (☎ 6541 8444), Heugenhauser (☎ 6541 8300), Hinterholzer (☎ 6541 7607), Snowboardschule Saalbach (☎ 6541 3453838, Zink (☎ 6541 8420)
**Guiding** Sepp Mitterer (☎ 6541 7008) and through ski schools

## CHILDREN
**Lift pass** 7–15yrs €60–84, 16–18yrs €96–134.50, both for 6 days. Europa Sport Region 6–15 yrs €77–84, 16–18 yrs €138–151, both for 6 days
**Ski & board school** as adults
**Kindergarten** (ski/non ski) Fürstauer, Snow & Fun

## FOOD AND DRINK
Coffee €2.50, bottle of house wine €15, small beer €2–3.50, soft drink €2–2.50, dish of the day €10–14

# Schladming

ALTITUDE 745m (2,224ft)                                              map: see page 170

✳ **large intermediate ski area** ✳ **easy airport access**
✳ **excellent childcare** ✳ **glacier skiing**

> **Best for:** families, ski-to-lunchers, cross-country skiers
>
> **Not recommended for:** beginners, people seeking a skiing challenge, off-piste skiers

Schladming is a charming and unspoilt provincial town with an onion-domed church and magnificent eighteenth-century town square. It has its own regional lift pass, and the ski area is also included in the 25-resort Skiverbund Amadé lift pass, which covers 270 lifts serving 860km of piste.

The resort is therefore a very attractive base from which to explore huge tracts of mostly linked intermediate skiing and snowboarding that are entirely unknown to the majority of British snow-users. Anyone looking for *Lederhosen-und-oompah Gemütlichkeit* will discover that it still thrives here. Schladming is extremely popular with Austrian families, and the slopes are subject to overcrowding during the local school break in early February.

## On-piste
top 2,015m (6,609ft) bottom 745m (2,224ft)

Schladming lies in the centre of a long and beautiful valley. The main slopes are spread disparately across the southern side, which makes it unsuitable for beginners. Planai, at 1,894m, Hochwurzen, at 1,850m, and Reiteralm, at 1,860m, are the three adjoining mountains that form the linked ski area to the west of the town. Easiest access is by gondola from the edge of the resort. The Kessleralm mid-station of the gondola can also be reached by car.

Above Schladming, on the eastern side of Planai, two chair-lifts provide a gateway to Hauser Kaibling, a 2,015-m peak that towers over the pretty village of **Haus-im-Ennstal**. Still farther to the east along the valley, the Galsterbergalm, at 1,976m, offers a few (mainly gentle) slopes reached by cable-car from the village of Pruggern.

A scattering of other lifts along the valley is included in the lift pass and limited high-altitude skiing is available throughout most of the year on the nearby Dachstein Glacier.

The gentle Rohrmoos meadows on the lower slopes of Hochwurzen provide the best arena for first turns when snow cover permits, with plenty of easy alternatives on the higher slopes of the main mountains.

Despite the lack of variety, the red and blue cruising terrain is plentiful enough to keep any skier busy for a week. The World Cup racecourses on both Planai and Hauser Kaibling should please fast intermediates, and the long downhill course on Hochwurzen is thigh-burning.

Planai and the Dachstein Glacier both have good half-pipes. The Schladming area provides some of the best cross-country skiing in Austria, with 250km of trails against a dramatically scenic backdrop and plenty of small huts to call in at for refreshments.

## Off-piste
Skiing outside the marked pistes is discouraged on the main mountains, except on marked ski routes. In good snow conditions the north face of Hauser Kaibling offers great scope, and the runs through the trees from Bergstallalm on Planai are recommended.

## Tuition and guiding
Three schools – Hopl, Tritscher and Blue Tomato – now provide the full range of ski and snowboard lessons. We have positive reports of all three, and in particular Hopl: 'our instructor was good fun, and his sense of humour was a major enjoyment factor of the whole week'.

## Mountain restaurants
'The mountain restaurants are tremendous', said one reporter, 'service was invariably friendly and efficient, with large helpings'. The Seiterhutte below the summit of Hochwurzen is singled out for particular

praise and the Krömmelholze at Haus is also rated. Panorama Alm on Reiteralm and Kessleralm on Planai are 'pleasant self-services with reasonable prices'. Onkel Willy's Hütte ('buzzing with atmosphere') has live music and a sunny terrace. The Eiskarhütte on Reiteralm is also popular.

## Accommodation

Sporthotel Royer (☎ 3687 200) is acclaimed as by far the best hotel in town. The once popular Alte Post (☎ 3687 22571) has received mixed reports. Hotel Zum Stadttor (☎ 3687 24525) is 'spotlessly clean with acceptable food and an unfailingly pleasant and helpful owner'. Haus Stangl (☎ 3687 22150), a simple B&B, is also praised.

## Eating in and out

We have positive reports of the Rôtisserie Royer Grill in Sporthotel Royer, while the Alte Post is recommended for 'excellent trout and other dishes in a pretentious but friendly atmosphere'. The Neue Post has two recommended à la carte restaurants: the Jägerstüberl and the Poststüberl. Le Jardin is a warmly commended French restaurant, and Gasthof Kirchenwirt is 'unmatched for quality of food, price, atmosphere and service'. Charly Kahr's Restaurant is also noted for its 'outstanding Salzburg cuisine'.

## Après-ski

The fun starts early at Onkel Willy's Hütte on Planai. Later on the action moves to The Pub, La Porta, the Hanglbar and – still later – to the Sonderbar disco. The Planaistub'n, also known as Charly's Treff, is a popular meeting-place, as is Ferry's Pub. The Beisl is 'intimate and lively with good music', and La Porta is 'small, crowded, with a great atmosphere'.

The Schwalbenbrau brewery is worth a visit, although the intentionally cloudy beer it produces is not to everyone's taste.

The 8-km toboggan run from the top of Hochwurzen is open in the evenings. Schladming also has a large swimming-pool and leisure complex.

## Childcare

Few resorts receive such resounding reviews for their kindergartens. 'Outstanding facilities for very young children,' commented one reporter. 'Facilities were brilliant; this is definitely the area to bring small children to be well looked after and to learn to ski,' said another. The ski kindergartens are operated by the three schools. Frau Ladreiter and Meine Kleine Schule are the resort's two non-ski kindergartens.

# Schladming: At a glance

**Tel** 43 3687 22777
**Email** info@schladming-rohrmoos.com
**Website** www.schladming-rohrmoos.com

### GETTING THERE
**Airports** Salzburg 1hr, Munich 2½hrs
**Rail** station in resort
**Road** easy access, 40 mins from Salzburg

### THE SKIING
**Linked/nearby resorts** Haus-im-Ennstal, Obertauern, Pruggern, Ramsau/Dachstein, Rohrmoos, St Johann im Pongau
**Total of trails/pistes** 115km in linked area (29% easy, 59% intermediate, 9% difficult, 3% very difficult), 860km in Skiverbund Amadé area
**Lifts in area** 64: 7⃞ 19⃞ 38⃞
**Lift opening dates** Late November 2004 to mid-April 2005. Summer skiing on Dachstein Glacier from mid-June

### LIFT PASSES
**Area pass** Skiverbund Amadé (covers 25 resorts) €149.50–161 for 6 days
**Pensioners** no reductions

### TUITION
**Ski & board** Blue Tomato (☎ 3687 24223), Skischule Hopl (☎ 3687 61268), Skischule Tritscher (☎ 3687 61142)
**Guiding** through ski schools, Helli Team Bedarfsflug (☎ 3687 81323)

### CHILDREN
**Lift pass** Skiverbund Amadé 6–15yrs €75–80.50 for 6 days
**Ski & board school** as adults
**Kindergarten** (ski) through ski schools, (non-ski) Frau Ladreiter (☎ 3687 61313), Meine Kleine Schule (☎ 3687 24407)

### FOOD AND DRINK
Coffee €2.30, bottle of house wine €15, small beer €2.40, soft drink €2.20, dish of the day €7.50–14

# Sölden

ALTITUDE 1,377m (4,517ft)

## ❋ snow-sure resort ❋ lively village atmosphere ❋ glacier skiing

> **Best for:** intermediates, ski-to-lunchers, night-owls
>
> **Not recommended for:** people looking for a quiet village, families with non-skiing children

Sölden is a high-altitude resort spread out for over 2km along the main road of the isolated Ötz Valley. Although it consists of an untidy sprawl of hotels, restaurants and bars, the village has considerable atmosphere and lively après-ski fuelled by the high number of young German and Dutch visitors.

Hochsölden is little more than a ski-in, ski-out collection of hotels set 700m up the mountainside with dramatic views.

> ## WHAT'S NEW
>
> Seiterkar chair-lift upgraded to 6-seater

## On the snow
### top 3,250m (10,663ft) bottom 1,377m (4,517ft)

Sölden's 1,873-m vertical drop is substantial by Austrian standards, and its skiing is suited mainly to intermediates. The ski area is in two sections, connected by chairs up both walls of the narrow Rettenbachtal, which provides the toll road up to the Rettenbach and Tiefenbach glaciers. Both sectors are also reached by gondolas from the village. Complete snow security is ensured by the glaciers, which are linked into the main ski system. The Glacier Express gondola connects the winter and year-round glacial areas.

Sölden's four ski schools – Sölden-Hochsölden, Yellow Power, Vacancia and Aktiv – all have solid reputations.

The terrain park at Giggijoch contains a half-pipe, boardercross course and a range of obstacles and jumps. A second terrain park, on the Rettenbach Glacier, is open in the autumn.

The choice of mountain restaurants is large. Gampe Thaya is an authentic mountain hut with a cosy atmosphere, and Heidealm has 'a really varied menu and a beautiful setting'. Sonneck at Gaislach is said to be good value.

## In the resort
The position of accommodation is important, and a hotel near one of the two main lift stations is a must. Hotel Regina (☎ 5254 2301), right by the Gaislachkoglbahn, is strongly recommended. Nearby Gasthof Sonnenheim (☎ 5254 2276) is praised for being 'extremely cheap'. Hotel Stefan (☎ 5254 2237) by the Giggijoch gondola station has a good restaurant, and Haus Karl Grüner (☎ 5254 2277), above town on piste 8, is ski-in, ski-out.

Restaurants include s'Pfandl, ('interesting cuisine'), Alpengasthof Grüner ('lovely views') and the Waldcafé. Dominic is said to be the best eatery in the village. The Alpina, Stefan and Hubertus à la carte restaurants are recommended, while Hotel Liebe Sonne boasts a cosy *Stübli*. At Innerwald, Pension Café Elisabeth serves 'simple good food' and Rauthalm is praised.

Sölden's buzzing nightlife begins at Café Philipp at Innerwald and Tino's Eisbar near the Gaislachkoglbahn. Sonnenschirm and Bla Bla are both extremely popular, as are Hinterher and Café Heiner. Later in the evening, Jakob's Weinfassl attracts the 30-somethings. Discos include the sophisticated Alibi Bar in Hotel Central.

The ski schools all accept children from three years old. The Sölden-Hochsölden school provides a crèche for children from six months.

> ## Sölden: At a glance
>
> **Tel** 43 5254 5100
> **Email** info@soelden.com
> **Website** www.soelden.com
> **Lifts in resort** 35: 7⊝ 19⊝ 9⊠
> **Lift opening dates** late November 2004 to late April 2005. Summer skiing on glaciers: 26 June 2004 to mid-May 2005

# Söll and the SkiWelt

ALTITUDE 703m (2,306ft)                                     map: see page 171

✳ **large linked ski area** ✳ **low-key atmosphere** ✳ **short airport transfer**
✳ **value for money**

> **Best for:** beginners, families, skiers on a budget
>
> **Not recommended for:** non-skiers, expert skiers and riders, late-season skiers, people wanting skiing convenience, gourmets

Söll is the central hub of the SkiWelt, one of Austria's largest networks of interconnected pistes and particularly popular with Dutch and British beginners and lower intermediates, along with anyone else who enjoys easy cruising on the rolling pastures of the Tyrol. It is also suitable for skiers and riders who do not mind short runs and uphill traverses. The SkiWelt is only 70km from Innsbruck and within easy reach of the German border.

The region counts 93 lifts and 250km of pistes spread around an oval of nine resorts linked on snow. Two further resorts, Kelchsau and **Westendorf**, are also included on the lift pass but are connected by bus. They are all sandwiched between the Kitzbüheler Alps to the south and the craggy Wilder Kaiser peaks to the north. All the skiing in the region is well below 2,000m, but an extensive range of 250 snow-cannon covers most of the lower slopes, allowing skiing to continue into April when temperatures permit. High grooming standards are ensured by 45 snowcats.

One reporter complained that 'all the runs seem the same, with little variation in terrain from valley to valley – however, the beautiful scenery makes up for this'.

## On-piste
top 1,829m (6,001ft) bottom 622m (2,040 ft)

Söll's skiing starts with a free bus ride (the bus runs every 30 minutes) to a modern eight-person gondola. A second gondola takes you swiftly up to Hohe Salve, which, at 1,829m, is the highest point in the linked SkiWelt circuit. From Hohe Salve it is

possible to ski to seven of the SkiWelt resorts; Westendorf requires a short bus transfer from Brixen-im-Thale, and Kelchsau a less frequent and longer bus trip from the village of **Hopfgarten**. There is no ski bus itinerary connecting the resorts, so care must be taken when skiing far afield.

The region has more than 100km of blue runs. Most beginner areas are at the base of the ski area, where the snow often melts away. **Scheffau** is the only resort with a top-to-bottom blue piste. Söll has a simple, wooded run from mid-mountain. Zinsberg and Brandstadl runs offer ample easy terrain.

More than half the pistes in the SkiWelt are graded intermediate, but most are short runs down to lifts, rather than from village to village. The red trail down to Hopfgarten, and the run to Söll from Hohe Salve, are good cruisers, as is the 7.5-km Kraftalm run to Itter.

Advanced terrain is often limited by a lack of snow. From Hohe Salve the Lärchenhang is one of the unmarked local runs on the north side, where a bowl region called Mulde presents some challenge and a reasonable pitch.

Söll has a well-maintained terrain park above Salvenmoos, with a half-pipe and some jumps.

## Off-piste
Short, steep sections that require ducking under warning ropes do appear in Westendorf and are regularly skied by locals. The SkiWelt offers a wealth of guided ski-tours, for example to Brechhorn, which demands little uphill effort.

## Tuition and guiding
Söll now has two schools. The main Söll–Hochsöll has enormous experience in teaching British novices: 'a great place to take first steps on skis with a really friendly instructor', and 'very good for learning – the ski school is second to none'. Ted Kaufmann's Pro-Söll limits groups to five people and promises rapid progress.

## Mountain restaurants

The SkiWelt lists a total of 63 mountain eateries, six of which are above Söll, and most suffer from peak-season lunchtime crowds. Self-service and simple meals abound. Schernthannstuberl is praised for its 'fairly large choice, big portions and hot food'. Stöcklalm, Kraftalm and Gründalm are typical, unexceptional inns, all with terraces. Hochschwendt is said to be the cheapest. The glass-walled Siglu Bar at Hochsöll is popular with children.

## Accommodation

Nine of Söll's 70 hotels are rated four-star and the remainder are reasonably priced inns and guesthouses. The main hotel is the Gasthof Postwirt (☎ 5333 5081) with an outdoor heated swimming-pool. The Alpenschlössl (☎ 5333 6400) is even more luxurious, but a 30-minute walk from the centre. Other hotels include the lively Christophorus (☎ 5333 5264) as well as the out-of-town Agerhof (☎ 5333 5340). Hotel Greil (☎ 5333 5289) and Ferienhotel Tyrol Söll (☎ 5333 5273) are both ski-in, ski-out.

## Eating in and out

Most visitors are on hotel half-board packages. For Austrian coffee-and-cakes it is worth making the hike to Panorama, and the modest Söller Stube on the main street also merits a visit. Schindlhaus is advertised as a gourmet restaurant. Venezia and Don Giovanni serve cheap Italian fare, while the Hexenkessel pizzeria is in the Schirast guesthouse.

## Après-ski

At the Whisky Mühle, scantily clad go-go girls (and boys) kick away each Friday night until 3am. The Salvenstadl ('still the place to be') plays live music, and the quality of 'food, beer and atmosphere' of Pub Austria was recommended. Buffalo's has a Wild West theme. Rossini is 'the wildest of all daily après-ski venues'. The Sports has karaoke, and live music three times a week. The Dorfstadl in Hotel Tyrol has a disco, and Pub 15 and the Salvenstadl are both local bars. The Hexenalm at the Söll gondola station was also praised.

## Childcare

The Söll–Hochsöll ski school has the most extensive programmes for children of all ages. Bobo's Children's Club is part of this school and accepts children from five to fourteen years of age. Bobo the Penguin is the symbol of an Austrian association that guarantees English-speaking, certified teachers. The Mini-Club takes children from three to five years.

# Söll and the SkiWelt: At a glance

**Tel** 43 5333 5216
**Email** info@soell.com
**Website** www.soell.com

**GETTING THERE**
**Airports** Innsbruck 45mins, Salzburg 1hr, Munich 2hrs
**Rail** Kufstein 15km, Wörgl 15km, St Johann 25km
**Road** situated 15km up a winding road off the A12 Munich–Innsbruck Autobahn

**THE SKIING**
**Linked/nearby resorts** Brixen-im-Thale, Ellmau, Going, Hopfgarten, Itter, Kelchsau, Kirchberg, Kitzbühel, Scheffau, Westendorf
**Total of trails/pistes** 34km in Söll, 250km in SkiWelt (43% easy, 51% intermediate, 6% difficult)
**Lifts in area** 93 in SkiWelt: 11🚡 34🚠 48🎿
**Lift opening dates** mid-December 2004 to mid-April 2005

**LIFT PASSES**
**Area pass** SkiWelt €131.50–153 for 6 days
**Pensioners** no reductions

**TUITION**
**Ski & board** Ski & Snowboard School Pro-Söll (☎ 6642 560184), Söll–Hochsöll (☎ 5333 5454)
**Guiding** through ski schools

**CHILDREN**
**Lift pass** SkiWelt 6–16yrs €79–92 for 6 days
**Ski & board school** as adults
**Kindergarten** (ski) Bobo's Children's Club (☎ 5333 5454), (non-ski) Mini-Club (☎ 5333 5454)

**FOOD AND DRINK**
Coffee €2.20, bottle of house wine €14.70, small beer €2.30–2.50, soft drink €1.80–2.40, dish of the day €6.50–14

# St Anton

ALTITUDE 1,304m (4,278ft)                                          map: see page 165

## ✳ challenging terrain ✳ excellent restaurants ✳ village atmosphere ✳ lively après-ski

**Best for:** high intermediate/advanced skiers and riders, party-goers, gourmet skiers, off-piste enthusiasts
**Not recommended for:** second/third weekers, early-nighters, budget skiers

St Anton is a member of that exclusive club of world-class ski resorts where the terrain is tough enough to raise the adrenaline level of even the most jaded powderhound. Those who otherwise pound the slopes of Chamonix, Verbier, and Jackson Hole in Wyoming try to make time each winter for at least a few linked turns in the resort that is to skiing what St Andrews is to golf. The Arlberg region, of which St Anton is the capital, is the birthplace of modern technique and in part responsible for the way in which we ski today. Over the years the resort has embraced snowboarding with the enthusiasm it once reserved for two planks, but this is not the place for beginners or even near-beginners of either discipline. Riders on the mountain may be fewer in number than in many resorts, but they know their business.

The awesome quality of these mountains remains, of course, unchanged. Happily the same cannot be said for the lift system, which was substantially improved for the 2001 World Ski Championships.

Visitors returning after an absence of several years will find the village transformed by the removal of the mainline railway track that used to bisect it. The track has been discreetly relocated to the south and much of the vacated space is filled by a giant complex, originally built for the Championships and now turned into a sports hall with ice-rink, swimming-pool, health club and gourmet restaurant.

The village architecture is a blend of old and new and is surprisingly successful, with a pedestrian zone lined with shops, cafés and handsome traditional hotels. The rest of the village straggles along the road in both directions, towards Mooserkreuz to the west, and towards the satellite villages of Nasserein and St Jakob to the east. A regular shuttle bus runs until 2am connecting the resort with its satellites.

## On-piste
top 2,811m (9,222ft) bottom 1,304m (4,278ft)

St Anton's skiing takes place on both sides of the valley, but the most challenging area is on the northern slopes dominated by the 2,811-m Valluga. A high-speed quad-chair to Gampen takes the morning strain off the Galzig cable-car, and the Nasserein gondola ('a big improvement') provides a third, swift means of access. The volume of high-season skiers can create a busy morning rush-hour, while Happy Valley, the end-of-the-day home run, can be intimidating to the unaccomplished or uncommitted, with skiers and boarders jostling for position like Parisian taxi drivers.

On this side at mid-mountain level, the ski area splits into two, separated by a steep gully. Gampen, at 1,850m, is a sunny plateau with a six-person chair-lift rising to the higher slopes of Kapall at 2,330m. But Galzig is the focal point of the serious skiing, and from here you can ski down to **St Christoph**. Above Galzig lie the more sublime challenges of the Valluga and the Schindlergrat at 2,650m. The Valluga is reached by a second and oversubscribed cable-car from Galzig; alternatively you can ski down into the valley behind Galzig and take the chair-lift up to the Schindlergrat. The skiing from here is some of the best in St Anton.

The Rendl is a separate ski area on the other side of the St Anton valley and is reached by the Rendlbahn gondola, a short bus ride from town. It offers interesting and often uncrowded skiing.

Almost all of St Anton's skiing can be considered advanced. Within hours of a new snowfall the major runs, such as the notorious Schindlerkar, quickly become bumped up to create a mogul marathon.

The few blue slopes would nearly all be classified as intermediate elsewhere. Those with a little experience may find some of the runs on the Rendl negotiable, and Nasserein has some easier slopes.

St Anton has some of the best freeride snowboarding terrain in Austria, with a seemingly endless choice of natural obstacles and gullies, as well as sensational freeriding in the steep powder fields and drop-offs. Gampen, Kapall and Rendl are particularly good areas to ride, and Rendl has a terrain park.

## Off-piste

The possibilities are limitless, and an experienced skier or rider wanting to enjoy St Anton to the full should view the services of a local guide as part of the basic holiday cost. However, the mainly south-facing slopes harbour an extremely high avalanche risk.

From the top of the Valluga, which is accessible to skiers and riders accompanied by a qualified guide, it is possible to ski down the Pazieltal into **Lech and Zürs**. The Malfon Valley over the back of the Rendl is a wide, enjoyable off-piste run which, when there is sufficient snow, ends on a road near the base of the lift. Above Stuben, a 20-minute walk up the Maroi Köpfe gives entry to the Maroi Valley. Reporters recommend hiking up to a col from the top of Hinterrendl and descending the valley to Pettneu ('excellent and beautiful, although there is a long run out').

## Tuition and guiding

The two once-rival ski schools now operate under one financial umbrella, but retain their separate names. In effect, the Arlberg Ski School, with its 250 instructors, has swallowed up the much smaller St Anton Ski School. Both have solid reputations ('expert and friendly instruction from a 30-something Arlberg instructor, although I didn't feel he straddled the cutting edge of modern technique'). We continue to receive enthusiastic reports of Piste to Powder Mountain Guided Adventures, a British-run teaching and guiding organisation ('outstanding instruction and safe guiding with a smile from true experts').

## Mountain restaurants

The waiter-service Verwall Stube, at the top of Galzig cable-car, heads a strong list of mountain eateries ('outstanding modern Austrian cuisine with an emphasis on fresh fish and seafood'). The adjoining self-service gets overcrowded but has panoramic views over the slopes. The Albonagrat is highly rated for its atmosphere and reasonably priced food. The Ulmerhütte, on the descent from the Schindler Spitze, is praised, as are the Sennhütte, Kaminstube and Rodelhütte.

The sunny terrace of the Arlberg-Hospiz-Alm in St Christoph, with lunch served by waiters in traditional dress, is a favourite with reporters. The Maiensee Stube in St Christoph and the Hotel Post in Stuben both have a warm atmosphere and good food.

## Accommodation

The area has two five-star hotels: the historic and expensive Arlberg-Hospiz (☎ 5446 2611) at St Christoph and the modern St Antoner Hof (☎ 5446 2910) near the bypass. The four-star options include the Neue Post (☎ 5446 2213) ('excellent') and the Hotel Alte Post (☎ 5446 2553), both much richer in tradition and closer to the lifts. The latter has a good spa.

Hotel Karl Schranz (☎ 5446 25550), owned by the former world champion, is said to be 'a very comfortable four-star with good food but quite far from the centre'. Hotel Arlberg (☎ 5446 22100) has 'excellent food and rooms, and friendly, helpful, English-speaking staff'. Hotel Tyrol (☎ 5446 2340), near the church, is 'a friendly and comfortable base in traditional Austrian style'.

St Anton has a large number of tour operator chalets and B&B pensions as well as a wide choice of reasonably priced apartments. Those who find themselves uncomfortably far away from the slopes can leave their skis and boots overnight in storage at the bottom of the Galzig cable-car. Hotels in the centre can suffer from late-night street noise.

## Eating in and out

The standard of restaurants has improved so much in recent years that the resort has become one of the major gastronomic centres of the Alps, thanks largely to the input of the Werner family. Their Arlberg-Hospiz-Alm in St Christoph is transformed by night from mountain pit-stop to gourmet restaurant with a renowned wine cellar. Its parent restaurant in the Arlberg Hospiz hotel is even more impressive, but more formal.

Benvenuto serves a wonderful array of mainly oriental dishes in a minimalist warehouse-style dining-room reminiscent of one of the London Conran creations. Floriani is warmly recommended, as is the fashionable Hazienda. The Museum, which houses a permanent exhibition of ski memorabilia and folklore, 'is like eating inside a large private house that boasts a fine chef'. The Funky Chicken, Sportcafé Schneider and the 1960s-style Café Aquila are all praised. The Brunnenhof in St Jakob has 'some of the best food in the region'. San Antonio is a popular pizzeria in Nasserein.

## Après-ski

St Anton's vibrant après scene starts to warm up from lunch-time in the Sennhütte before snow-users make their way down to the noisy Mooserwirt just above the final descent to the resort. The Australian-inspired and Swedish-owned Krazy Kanguruh just above it is equally popular; long before the lifts close for the day the bar is packed tighter than Bondi Beach. Most guests, after dancing in their ski boots and consuming copious amounts of alcohol, still manage to negotiate on skis the final 800m home in the dark.

Down in the resort the action continues until sundown on the terrace of the Hotel Alte Post before switching to the Underground ('the entertainment here is unbelievable'), Postkeller or the Platz'l, which have live music. The St Antoner Hof bar is recommended as more 'quiet and sophisticated'. Scottie's Bar in the Hotel Rosanna is a rendezvous for Brits, and Vino is a pleasant place for a drink. After midnight the youth scene switches to the Piccadilly, Bar Cuba and the Kandahar. The Funky Chicken is popular with snowboarders. The Fang Bar beside the Nasserein gondola has 'a great atmosphere', and Tom Dooley's, also in Nasserein, is 'a convenient spot for a quiet drink'.

## Childcare

The Arlberg Ski School runs Kinderwelt, a kindergarten with four bases: at the ski school meeting-place, on the Gampen, in Nasserein and at St Christoph. Small skiers are accepted once they are out of nappies. Kiki Club, organised by the St Anton Ski School, runs ski classes for children.

# St Anton: At a glance

**Tel** 43 5446 22690
**Email** info@st.antonamarlberg.com
**Website** www.stantonamarlberg.com

## GETTING THERE
**Airports** Innsbruck 1hr, Friedrichshafen 1½hrs, Zurich 2–3hrs, Munich 3–4hrs
**Rail** station in resort
**Road** Arlberg tunnel from Switzerland

## THE SKIING
**Linked/nearby resorts** Klösterle, Lech and Zürs, Pettneu, St Christoph, Stuben, Zug
**Total of trails/pistes** 260km (30% easy, 40% intermediate, 20% difficult, 10% very difficult)
**Lifts in area** 82 on Arlberg Ski Pass: 10🚡 38🚠 34🎿
**Lift opening dates** 3 December 2004 to 1 May 2005

## LIFT PASSES
**Area pass** Arlberg Ski Pass (covers Klösterle, Lech and Zürs, Pettneu, St Anton, St Christoph, Stuben, Zug) €169–184 for 6 days
**Pensioners** Arlberg Ski Pass women 60yrs and over, and men 65yrs and over, €147–160, both for 6 days. 75yrs and over €10 for whole season

## TUITION
**Ski & board** Arlberg Ski School (☎ 5446 3411), St Anton Ski School (☎ 5446 3563)
**Guiding** Piste to Powder Mountain Guided Adventures (☎ 6641 7462 820, 01661 824318 in UK)

## CHILDREN
**Lift pass** Arlberg Ski Pass 7–15yrs €101–111 for 6 days, 6yrs and under €10 for season
**Ski & board school** as adults
**Kindergarten** (ski/non-ski) Kinderwelt (☎ 5446 2526), Kiki Club (☎ 5446 3563)

## FOOD AND DRINK
Coffee €2.60, small beer €3.20, bottle of house wine €17, soft drink €2.50, dish of the day €10–18

# Wildschönau

ALTITUDE 830m (2,722ft)

❋ traditional Tyrolean villages ❋ easy skiing ❋ reasonable prices
❋ short airport transfer

> **Best for:** beginners and unadventurous intermediates, budget skiers, party-goers
> **Not recommended for:** expert skiers, snowboarders, late-season skiers

The Wildschönau is a quiet corner of the Tyrol, 70km from Innsbruck, with four resorts (**Niederau, Oberau, Auffach** and the old silver-mining village of Thierbach) offering a traditional Austrian welcome and easy skiing. Niederau is the best known to British skiers, although Auffach has the best terrain. Oberau, 3km from Niederau, is the regional centre. Free ski buses link Niederau, Auffach and Oberau, and plans are at an advanced stage to connect the Wildschönau with the neighbouring **Alpbach** valley.

The appeal of Wildschönau, with its 63km of low-altitude pistes, seems to be its very benign slopes: 33 per cent of them being classified as easy.

## On the snow
top 1,903m (6,243ft) bottom 830m (2,722ft)

A modern eight-person gondola provides access from Niederau to the top of the 1,500-m Markbachjoch. From there, three pisted and one unpisted run lead back to the bottom. Niederau has ten lifts, eight of which are drags, and Oberau has a further seven short drags that are suited to beginners. The slopes in Auffach rise to to 1,903m and provide much the best skiing in the area, despite not being featured in any British tour operators' brochures. A four-person gondola rises in two stages through woods to give access to five drag-lifts and a new six-person chair. Thierbach has only two drag-lifts.

Auffach has a terrain park with a half-pipe, while Niederau boasts a boardercross course in its Race 'n' Board Arena.

For ski-tourers, a black itinerary run from the summit of the Schatzberg down to the valley floor beyond Auffach is fun in powder conditions.

Niederau has two ski and board schools: Aktiv and Wildschönau. Both have ample experience with beginners, and English is widely spoken. Along with schools at Oberau and Auffach, they offer lessons to children from four years of age.

Mountain restaurants are limited in number but are of a generally high quality. At the top of Niederau, Rudi's is renowned for its plum pancakes, and the Anton Graf Hütte is an authentic touring hut. Auffach's Schatbergalm and Koglmoos are large self-service eateries.

## In the resort

In Niederau, Hotel Sonnschein (☎ 5339 8353) has an indoor swimming-pool and 'sumptuous rooms'. The older Hotel Austria (☎ 5339 8188) also offers an indoor pool. In Oberau, the four-star Hotel Silberberger (☎ 5339 8407) is warmly praised, as are the Tirolerhof (☎ 5339 83160) and Gasthof Kellerwirt (☎ 5339 8116). In Auffach, Gasthof Weissbacher (☎ 5339 8934) and the three-star Gasthof Platzl (☎ 5339 8928) are both recommended.

Most dining is in hotels and guesthouses. Nightlife in Niederau can be raucous, with Hotel Vicky providing live music and British beer. Serious drinking takes place at the Cave Bar, while the Dorfstub'n is more salubrious. Almbar provides a late-night disco, while Charlie's Pub and the Grutt'n Bar are other après-ski venues. Entertainment in Oberau is largely confined to the SnoBlau Pub.

The Wildschönau's crèche, based in Niederau, accepts children from two years of age, and Bobo's Kinderclub provides daycare for two- to six-year-olds. Children under six ski for free.

> ## Wildschönau: At a glance
>
> **Tel** 43 5339 8255
> **Email** info@wildschoenau.tirol.at
> **Website** www.wildschoenau.com
> **Lifts in resort** 26: 2🚠 2🚡 22🎿
> **Lift opening dates** mid-December 2004 to 3 April 2005

# Zell am See and Kaprun

ALTITUDE 758m (2,487ft)      map: see page 172

## ❋ glacier skiing ❋ easy airport access ❋ attractive resorts

> **Best for:** intermediates, non-skiers, night-owls, novice snowboarders, cross-country skiers, ski-to-lunchers (Zell)
>
> **Not recommended for:** those who want skiing convenience, off-piste skiers

The medieval lake-side town of Zell am See is one of Austria's most appealing winter and summer resorts. Its huge international popularity rests on its hard-to-beat setting on the shore of a beautiful lake at the foot of the 2,000-m Schmittenhöhe.

The mountain provides ample easy intermediate skiing, and the towering presence of the Kitzsteinhorn Glacier above the delightful neighbouring village of Kaprun (a ten-minute journey by free ski bus) means that snow is guaranteed in winter. The glacier used to offer year-round skiing on the upper slopes, but now closes for ten days each June and for a further ten days in September.

## On-piste
### top 3,029m (9,938ft) bottom 750m (2,460ft)

Mountain access is by the newly named City Express gondola from the town, by cable-car from Schmittental (2km from the centre of Zell) or by the modern Areitbahn gondola from the village of Schüttdorf. This satellite acts as a much less attractive, but convenient, alternative bed base, to which the free bus runs every 20 minutes.

The Schmittenhöhe's moderate slopes provide long, gentle red and blue runs back down towards Zell and along the southern flank to Schüttdorf. Steeper slopes drop from a bowl and provide the resort's most challenging skiing.

Kaprun also has its own gentle ski area above the village. However, the best of its skiing is on the glacier, reached by two gondolas at the head of the valley. A network of lifts going up to 3,029m serves good, but exposed, blue and red runs.

The main novice slopes at Zell are on the top of the Schmittenhöhe. There are also nursery slopes at the bottom of the cable-car and at Schüttdorf. Kaprun has its own winter beginner slope at the edge of the village.

Zell am See is ideal for novice riders and has a permanent half-pipe. Kaprun also offers a terrain park with a half-pipe on the glacier.

## Off-piste
Zell's environmental policy means that off-piste skiing is restricted to the point of being almost forbidden. After a fresh fall, a number of tree-line trails look particularly enticing, but the protection of saplings is a priority and you risk confiscation of your lift pass if you ski here.

## Tuition and guiding
Ski and snowboard schools in the valley seem to vary in quality, and we have mixed reports of the schools in the region. Of the four ski schools in Zell am See, the Schmittenhöhe receives the most praise. The Ski und Rennschule Kitzsteinhorn in Kaprun has a high standard of instruction, which includes race training.

## Mountain restaurants
Zell am See has a good choice of mountain eating-places, and prices are reasonable. The black run down from Sonnalm has a pleasant hut for those who can get to it. Schmiedhofalm has amazing views from its sunny terrace. Glocknerhaus, on the way down to Schüttdorf, is also popular. Hans' Schnapps Bar on the summit boasts a live rock band two days a week.

## Accommodation
In Zell, the luxurious, five-star Grand Hotel (☎ 6542 788) and Salzburgerhof (☎ 6542 765) are the most comfortable hotels in town; the latter has an exquisite spa. The four-stars are the Alpin (☎ 6542 769), Sporthotel Alpenblick (☎ 6542 5433) and the Romantikhotel Zum Metzgerwirt (☎ 6542 72520), which a honeymooning reporter recommended for its 'very high

standard of accommodation'. One of this hotel's suites has a waterbed. Hotel Bellevue (☎ 6542 73104) is a recommended three-star, and Hotel St Georg (☎ 6542 768) has smart, pine-panelled rooms and views of the lake. Hotel Berner (☎ 6542 779), set above the town, has a heated outdoor swimming-pool. Two of the best hotels for families are at Schüttdorf: Hotel Porscherhof (☎ 6542 55355) and Baby und Kinderhotel Hagleitner (☎ 6542 571870).

In Kaprun, the four-star Orgler Hotel (☎ 6547 8205) is recommended, as are the Salzburgerhof B&B (☎ 6547 8601) and Pension Heidi (☎ 6547 8223). The Sonnblick (☎ 6547 8301) and the Kaprunerhof (☎ 6547 7234) cater for families.

## Eating in and out

The Steinerwirt is considered the best value for money, along with the Kupferkessel and the Saustall. Hotel St Georg, Zur Einkehr, Landhotel Erlhof and the Salzburgerhof are praised for their high standard of cuisine. The Baum-Bar in Kaprun has a large conservatory restaurant.

## Après-ski

Zell am See is lively by any standards, and the Crazy Daisy and the Diele attract a young international crowd. Classic is for the over-25s. Late-night action switches to the Viva nightclub, the Insider pub and the B17 bar.

In Kaprun, Kitsch and Bitter has a live band mid-week. The Baum-Bar offers a late-night disco, and the Austrian Pub attracts snowboarders. The Optimum sports centre contains an indoor pool, sauna and fitness centre, as well as a giant outdoor water-slide.

## Childcare

The Play and Fun kindergarten takes small non-skiers from twelve months and skiers from two years. Ski lessons are given at all the ski schools for children from the age of four. Hotel Porscherhof and Baby und Kinderhotel Hagleitner at Schüttdorf both have crèches.

# Zell am See and Kaprun: At a glance

**Tel** 43 6542 770
**Email** welcome@europasportregion.info
**Website** www.europa-sport-region.info

### GETTING THERE
**Airport** Salzburg 1hr
**Rail** station in resort
**Road** Siegsdorf exit from Munich–Salzburg Autobahn or Bischofshofen exit from Salzburg–Villach Autobahn

### THE SKIING
**Linked/nearby resorts** Leogang, Maria Alm, Saalbach–Hinterglemm
**Total of trails/pistes** 75km in Zell am See (38% easy, 50% intermediate, 12% difficult), 55km in Kaprun
**Lifts in linked resorts** 57 in Zell am See/Kaprun: 12🚡 15🚠 30🎿
**Lift opening dates** 27 November 2004 to 17 April 2005. 15 lifts for summer skiing on Kitzsteinhorn Glacier (Kaprun), open all year except 14–25 June 2005

### LIFT PASSES
**Area pass** Europa Sport Region (covers Abtenau, Kaprun, Leogang, Saalbach–Hinterglemm, Zell am See) €154–168 for 6 days

**Pensioners** no reductions

### TUITION
**Ski & board** Zell am See: Schmittenhöhe (☎ 6542 732070), Ski und Snowboardschule Zell am See (☎ 6542 56020), Snowboard Academy (☎ 6642 530381), Sport-Alpin (☎ 6644 531417). Kaprun: Hartweger (☎ 6547 77668), Oberschneider (☎ 6547 8232), Ski & Snowboarding Kaprun (☎ 6547 8070), Skischule Kaprun M. Handl (☎ 6547 7562), Skischule Kaprun Schernthaner (☎ 6547 20091), Ski und Rennschule Kitzsteinhorn (☎ 6547 8621363)
**Guiding** Safari in Austria (☎ 6643 361487)

### CHILDREN
**Lift pass** Europa Sport Region 6–15yrs €77–84, 16–18yrs €138–151, both for 6 days. Free for 6yrs and under if accompanied by parent
**Ski & board school** as adults
**Kindergarten** (ski/non-ski) Play & Fun (☎ 6542 56020)

### FOOD AND DRINK
Coffee €2.60–3, bottle of house wine €15–18, small beer €3–4, soft drink €2.50–3, dish of the day €12–18

# CANADA
# Banff–Lake Louise

ALTITUDE 5,350ft (1,631m)                                    map: see page 173

✻ **stunning scenery** ✻ **skiing variety** ✻ **lively town (Banff)** ✻ **few queues**
✻ **snow-sure slopes** ✻ **wide choice of children's facilities**

**Best for:** all standards of skier and rider, night-owls (Banff), off-piste enthusiasts, budget skiers, ski-age children

**Not recommended for:** people who dislike low temperatures, those who want skiing convenience

Banff–Lake Louise has long been known as a cheap-and-cheerful destination for lower intermediate skiers in search of wild nightlife. It is true that prices are extremely reasonable, the nightlife in Banff itself is lively, and there is plenty of skiing for the less adventurous. But what is not widely appreciated is that there is some truly excellent skiing and riding for good intermediates and experts, and – on new snow days – some exquisite off-piste that remains untracked for hours.

The bustling tourist town of Banff is the gateway to Banff National Park and three very different ski resorts, collectively marketed as Banff–Lake Louise. The biggest and best-known but farthest from Banff is Lake Louise – 35 miles away along the Trans-Canadian Highway. The view from Lake Louise across the Bow Valley, lined with one huge chiselled peak after another, is outstanding. Sightings of elk, mule deer and bighorn sheep are not uncommon.

## WHAT'S NEW
High-speed quad replaces double-chair on Mount Standish at Sunshine Village

Although Lake Louise boasts a famous and picturesque hotel, the neo-Gothic Fairmont Chateau Lake Louise, it is fundamentally a large ski area with a very small village, while Banff is quite a large town with a small family ski hill – four

miles away at Mount Norquay (officially known as Ski Banff@Norquay). The way to get the best of the skiing and the nightlife is to stay in the vibrant town of Banff and visit a different ski area each day. All three are covered on one lift ticket.

**Sunshine Village**, ten miles from Banff, is also a ski area rather than a village. It has some of the highest, most snow-sure slopes in Canada, and a correspondingly long season.

## On-piste
top 8,650ft (2,637m) bottom 5,400ft (1,662m)

Lake Louise's two mountains, Whitehorn and Lipalian, provide three distinct skiing areas: the Front Side/South Face, the Back Bowls and Ptarmigan/Paradise, and the Larch area. Between them they offer a large network of trails, including an easy run from the top of every major lift. All three areas have terrain parks.

The Front Side alone is big enough to keep less ambitious skiers and boarders happy for two or three days, but sooner or later they will be tempted up and over Mount Whitehorn to explore the rest of the area. Most of the trails are ideal for intermediates. Lake Louise's terrain park, at the foot of the slopes, is arguably one of the most impressive and extensive anywhere in the world.

Sunshine Village, with a splendid view of Mount Assiniboine – Canada's 'Matterhorn' – comprises three mountains. Goat's Eye has a mix of challenging black-diamond runs and a few easier blues that start above the tree-line and end in gladed trails. The more-exposed traditional peak, Lookout Mountain, is a big blustery place mainly suitable for intermediates and above. Mount Standish is a more leisurely location with skiing and riding to suit all comers. A new high-speed quad replaces the old double-chair.

Ski Banff@Norquay may not be as extensive as its rivals, but in spite of its size its slopes have enough variety to lure locals up for a quick workout during their lunch hour. It has the entire range of possibilities: very easy skiing in the Cascade area, a wealth of cruising off the Spirit and Pathfinder lifts, and some demanding runs served by the North American chair.

## Off-piste

At Lake Louise, there are plenty of challenging opportunities for off-piste excursions on the Front Side/South Face as well as the celebrated Back Bowls, reached principally by the Summit Platter lift and the Top of the World six-person chair. A huge variety of chutes – some with unnervingly high cornices – lead down from the ridge into glorious bowls. On a fresh powder day you will not want to ski anywhere else.

The Ptarmigan area has a widely scattered selection of gladed runs, many of them double-black. The Paradise area is also dotted with single- and double-black-diamond runs above the tree-line. Firm favourites with tree skiers are the lookout Chutes and Tower 12, off the Larch chair-lift.

At Sunshine, Delirium Dive on Goat's Eye Mountain is fast acquiring notoriety as one of the world's classic steeps. Before attempting it, the ski patrol insists on checking that you are carrying a transceiver and shovel. However, this measure is aimed principally at deterring anyone who is not already a committed off-piste skier. The entrance is stomach-churningly steep, but involves a sideslip more than a jump. The terrain quickly opens up into some wonderful bowl skiing with a choice of two exit routes: the more direct involves a walk-out, while a lengthy traverse to the skier's right offers more powder and a speedier return to a lift.

## Tuition and guiding

The Lake Louise, Ski Banff@Norquay and Sunshine Village Ski and Snowboard Schools all offer group and private lessons. Club Ski/Snowboard runs three-day courses that include instruction and video analysis.

## Mountain restaurants

At Lake Louise, Sawyers Nook upstairs at the Temple Lodge provides waiter-service as well as 'good food and great atmosphere'. The World Cup Restaurant at

Whiskeyjack Lodge has replaced the Northface. Whitehorn Lodge is a mid-mountain cafeteria on the Front Face, while Kokanee Kabin at the base has barbecues and beer. Lodge of the Ten Peaks houses a cafeteria and the Powderkeg Lounge.

At Sunshine, all the restaurants are at the mid-mountain base area. Choose from the Deli, Alpine Grill and Lookout Pasta Company at the Day Lodge, the Chimney Corner and Eagle's Nest at the Sunshine Inn, soups and sandwiches at Mountainhilm, and Goat's Eye Gardens at the base of Goat's Eye Mountain. The Mad Trapper's Saloon, at Old Sunshine Lodge, offers a wide selection of fast food. Norquay's Cascade Lodge houses Kika's Café, the Lone Pine Pub, and a delicatessen.

## Accommodation

The big decision is whether to stay in bustling Banff or more serene Lake Louise, where the century-old Fairmont Chateau Lake Louise (☎ 403 522 3511), with its stunning bedroom views across the frozen lake, is one of the wonders of the Canadian Rockies. The Post Hotel (☎ 403 522 3989) has recreated the style of the 1900s down to the smallest detail, and nearby Deer Lodge (☎ 403 522 3747) is warmly recommended.

Alternatively you could base yourself 'in the middle', at the ski-in, ski-out Sunshine Inn (☎ 403 762 6564) at Sunshine Village, where many of the rooms were renovated in summer 2003. Be warned that the mid-mountain base area has precious little else to offer the overnight visitor, but the bonus is being able to create the first tracks each morning.

In Banff, the Chateau's 'sister' hotel, the Fairmont Banff Springs (☎ 403 762 2211), is designed in the style of a Scottish baronial castle and boasts one of the best spas in North America, the Willowstream, with heated indoor and outdoor swimming-pools. Buffalo Mountain Lodge (☎ 403 410 7417) has a style that could best be described as rugged luxury, with log fireplaces and lots of beams. Its restaurant serves local cuisine, with game a speciality.

The 'elegant, bright and modern' Rimrock Resort Hotel (☎ 403 762 3356) has luxury accommodation, the Mount Royal (☎ 403 762 3331) – close to the Banff Avenue après-ski action – and Banff Caribou Lodge (☎ 403 762 5887) are popular, and the Banff King Edward (☎ 403 762 2202), the town's second oldest hotel, is a favourite with reporters. Siding 29 Lodge (☎ 403 762 5575) is described as 'a no-frills hotel with large comfortable rooms'. Similarly, the Red Carpet Inn (☎ 403 762 4184) is rated as 'extremely accommodating and friendly' and the Rundle Manor apartments (☎ 403 762 5544) are 'spacious, comfortable and cheap'. Ski Banff@Norquay offers 'homey chalets and suites' at the Timberline Inn (☎ 403 762 2281).

## Eating in and out

Banff is the location for an eclectic choice of restaurants, with cuisine from at least a dozen countries: Maple Leaf Grille or Melissa's (Canadian), Le Beaujolais (French), Giorgio's Trattoria or Guido's (Italian), El Toro (Greek), Typhoon (Far Eastern), the Silver Dragon (Chinese) and Miki (Japanese). The Fairmont Banff Springs hotel offers a number of different restaurants, including Japanese and Italian, and a German/Swiss/Austrian selection at the Waldhaus.

In Lake Louise Village, the Post Hotel and Deer Lodge are the pick of a limited choice. The Fairmont Chateau Lake Louise has four restaurants, ranging from the elegant Edelweiss to the Glacier Saloon. The old Canadian Pacific railway station, built in grand style more than a century ago, has been converted into a restaurant complex, including a selection of dining cars.

## Après-ski

There are more than sufficient bars and pubs in Banff, particularly in Banff Avenue, to provide a week's worth of lively après-ski. Apart from Tommy's Neighbourhood Pub, there are two Irish bars: the Rose & Crown and St James's Gate, which was built in Dublin and reassembled in Banff. Wild Bill's, a Western Saloon, has Country and Western bands, and the Barbary Coast has rock/blues bands. Hoodoo and Aurora are both popular clubs with late-night dancing. The nightlife at Lake Louise is considerably quieter, and pretty much restricted to the Glacier Saloon at the Fairmont Chateau Lake Louise.

## Childcare

Each of the three areas has good children's programmes. At Lake Louise, Telns Play Station takes babies from 19 months. Club Ski Junior offers guided tours for 6- to 12-year-olds to all three areas. Tiny Tigers Daycare at Sunshine Village and The Kids' Place at Ski Banff@Norquay look after toddlers over 19 months. The ski schools all provide children's programmes, nursery and daycare. The area boasts five magic carpets.

# Banff–Lake Louise: At a glance

**Tel** 1 403 762 4561
**Email** info@skibig3.com
**Website** www.skibig3.com

### GETTING THERE
**Airport** Calgary 1½–2hrs
**Road** 1–2hr scenic drive from Calgary

### THE SKIING
**Linked/nearby resorts** Fortress Mountain, Kicking Horse, Nakiska
**Total of trails/pistes** 7,558 acres in area: 4,200 acres at Lake Louise, 3,168 acres at Sunshine Village, 190 acres at Ski Banff@Norquay (25% easy, 45% intermediate, 30% difficult)
**Lifts in area** 24: 1⑤ 21⑤ 2⑨
**Lift opening dates** 9 November 2004 to 24 May 2005

### LIFT PASSES
**Area pass** CDN$396 for 6 days
**Pensioners** 65yrs and over CDN$354 for 6 days

### TUITION
**Ski & board** Club Ski/Snowboard (all areas) (☎ 403 760 7731), Lake Louise Ski and Snowboard School (☎ 403 522 1333), Ski Banff@Norquay Ski and Snowboard School (☎ 403 760 7717), Sunshine Village Ski and Snowboard School (☎ 403 762 6560)
**Guiding** RK Heli-ski Panorama (☎ 250 342 3889)

### CHILDREN
**Lift pass** 6–12yrs CDN$162 for 6 days
**Ski & board schools** as adults, Club Ski Junior programme (☎ 403 760 7731)
**Kindergarten** (ski/non-ski) Lake Louise: Telus Play Station (☎ 403 522 1333). Ski Banff@Norquay: The Kids' Place (☎ 403 760 7717). Sunshine Village: Tiny Tigers Daycare (☎ 403 762 6560)

### FOOD AND DRINK
Coffee CDN$1.75–2, bottle of house wine CDN$20–21, small beer CDN$3–5, soft drink CDN$2.50–3, dish of the day CDN$10–14

# Big White

ALTITUDE 5,706ft (1,755m)

## ❄ attractive ski village ❄ modern lift system ❄ skiing convenience ❄ varied terrain

> **Best for:** strong intermediates, families, powder-skiers, snowboarders
>
> **Not recommended for:** mountain-lunchers, night-owls

Big White is one of a charming trio of resorts tucked away in the beautiful Okanagan Valley of British Columbia. It is within easy driving distance of **Silver Star** and **Sun Peaks**, and the scenery is magnificent. Local lore has it that Big White is named after the cloud that often conceals it. The resulting humidity creates a phantom forest of 'snow-ghosts': trees frozen into eerie, monster-like formations. On clear days, the view of the Monashees mountain range is spectacular.

The resort is Australian-owned and, together with Silver Star, the recipient of lavish and enviable funding. But the welcome here is raw Canadian rather than overtly commercial.

### WHAT'S NEW

Chair-lift in the Cliff area
Ski terrain expanded into East Peak
State-of-the-art terrain park

## On the snow
### top 7,606 ft (2,319m) bottom 4,950ft (1,508m)

The extensive but predominantly intermediate ski area is better suited to families than radical adventurers but, given sunshine and powder, Big White is a magical place.

The modern lift system, which includes a gondola, seven chair-lifts and a T-bar, serves 118 trails with a vertical drop of 2,656ft and 7,355 acres of terrain. The Plaza quad-chair serves a first-timer's area and children's park with magic carpet below the main village. In summer 2004 a new double chair-lift is being installed in the Cliff area, giving access to East Peak.

More adept skiers will find a wealth of intermediate trails, accessed initially by the Ridge Rocket Express quad. The Gem Lake Express quad, on the edge of the 10km-wide ski area, opens up Sun Ripe Bowl for sensational powder skiing between snow ghosts, as well as long, challenging groomed runs with lots of rollers. Heli-skiing in the Monashees is available directly from the resort.

The snowboarding at Big White is superlative. New for the 2004–5 season is a floodlit terrain park accessed by the new Cliff double-chair, offering a rail garden, half-pipes, a 450-ft super-pipe with 17-ft walls, boarder- and skiercross, and a family fun racing area.

Most people return to the resort for lunch. The restaurant at the bottom of the Gem Express is said to be 'a good place, friendly, spacious, good food – but no alcohol'.

Big White's Ski and Snowboard School has a solid reputation. The Kids' Centre is one of the best in North America, with a full range of all-day programmes for children aged 18 months to 12 years.

## In the resort
All the accommodation is ski-in, ski-out, with a choice of four hotels and a wide range of condos. All can be booked on ☎ 250 765 8888. Chateau Big White has the smartest piste-side accommodation, and the White Crystal Inn has large rooms and a good restaurant. The best gourmet food in town is found at the Kettle Valley restaurant. The Swiss Bear offers reasonably priced fare. Snowshoe Sam's is rough-hewn and friendly, with pool tables, a dance area and a restaurant.

## Big White: At a glance

**Tel** 1 250 765 3101
**Email** bigwhite@bigwhite.com
**Website** www.bigwhite.com
**Lifts in resort** 10: 1⬆ 7⬆ 2⬆
**Lift opening dates** mid-November 2004 to mid-April 2005

# Fernie

ALTITUDE 3,500ft (1,068m)                    map: see page 174

❊ uncrowded slopes ❊ skiing convenience ❊ good snow record
❊ value for money ❊ extensive piste grooming

> **Best for:** skiers and snowboarders of all
> standards, families, off-piste skiers
> **Not recommended for:** night-owls, ski-
> to-lunchers

Within less than a decade, Fernie has grown
from a little-known and unfashionable ski
centre into an international destination
favoured by powderhounds in their eternal
quest for fresh and ever-more-challenging
pastures. Few destinations offer such a
demanding menu of steep piste and powder
in such a friendly and relaxed environment.

Ski tycoon Charlie Locke set the ball of
progress rolling when he bought the resort
above the Victorian railway town of the
same name in 1998. Most of his initial
CDN$100 million investment was directed
at building on-mountain accommodation,
which greatly enhanced the appeal of the
resort, but the promised new lifts failed to
materialise. Fernie has since changed hands
again and is now part of an impressive
portfolio of seven Canadian resorts that
includes Banff–Lake Louise, Kimberley,
Stoneham and Mont-Sainte-Anne. Resorts
of the Canadian Rockies, Fernie's new
owners, have invested a much-needed
CDN$3.5 million in the resort, most of it in
improved facilities at the mountain base.

Fernie's problem is its remote position.
A tricky three-and-a-half-hour drive from
Calgary deters day and weekend visitors,
who prefer the easier journey to **Banff–Lake
Louise**. A high standard of new
accommodation is now attracting visitors to
Fernie in increasing numbers, but the new
owners have yet to take the plunge and
decide that these are of sufficient volume to
warrant the full makeover of the lift system
that is required.

The up-side of this is that Fernie, for the
present, remains delightfully unspoilt. Four
of the six chair-lifts are quads, while an
infamous drag looks as though it escaped
from a New Zealand ski-club field. But the
fact that the skiing remains raw has
detracted not at all from Fernie's growing
popularity as a cult resort for serious snow-
seekers from all over the world ('North
America's best-kept secret'). Many of its
band of supporters believe it to be the finest
resort north of the 49th parallel and a hot
contender for Whistler's successor as
Canada's – if not North America's – premier
destination. In the economic life cycle of ski
resorts, the 'window' between commercial
success and mass-market saturation is an
increasingly narrow band of seasons, and
for many the overdevelopment of Whistler
means that its window has already closed.
Fernie is seen as the natural successor,
although Kicking Horse is a strong
contender.

> ## WHAT'S NEW
> Mojo Risin' restaurant at the Royal Hotel and
> Yamagoya Japanese restaurant in town

The old town of Fernie, three miles
below the resort, provides an alternative
bed base and a modicum of off-slope
entertainment. Despite its colourful mining
heritage, this is no Telluride or Crested
Butte. Fernie likes to call itself
unpretentious – and it is. The centre has
considerable Victorian charm that remained
intact throughout the twentieth century and
has as yet barely been touched by the
twenty-first. However, the gentrification
process of some of the old buildings has
begun, and each year more sports shops,
restaurants and bars are opened. A regular
ski bus service operates between town and
mountain village.

Day-trips or overnight excursions to
other resorts are possible. **Panorama
Mountain Village**, and Big Mountain across
the US border in Montana are both –
frontier controls permitting – a two-hour
drive away. **Kimberley** is a 90-minute drive
and **Kicking Horse** is three hours away,
while Schweitzer in Idaho, Banff–Lake

Louise and **Red Mountain** are all four hours away.

## On-piste
**top 6,316ft (1,925m) bottom 3,500ft (1,068m)**

Fernie's antique lift system serves 2,504 acres of skiing in what lays claim to be the fourth-largest ski area in Canada. None of the lifts has protective coverings, and temperatures in mid-winter can be extremely cold.

One reporter described the terrain, with its impressive vertical drop of 2,816ft, as 'like Argentière minus the glacier and minus the crowds'. Certainly the five alpine bowls offer a variety of challenging skiing that, with exceptions such as Jackson Hole, is more reminiscent of the Alps than North America. Another reporter described Fernie as 'a paradise for strong skiers, with good glades and off-piste'. A third praised the runs as 'long, superb and empty'. Mountain access is by two quad-chairs from either end of the base-area village.

There is a decent nursery slope next to the ski-school meeting-place at the base of the lifts, and three beginner lifts serve more than 20 green trails ('well-groomed runs, and plenty for beginners too'). However, a few of them are quite steep for novices. The Mini Moose and Mighty Moose lifts are where first-timers start, while the Deer and Elk chair-lifts access some wide and gentle slopes. The shape of the mountain-side lends itself to plenty of long, rolling runs – a playground for cruisers – but the terrain rarely allows you to relax your concentration. Reporters rated the trails off Timber Bowl high-speed quad as 'superb'. Those off the Elk chair-lifts are good warm-up runs, followed by taking the Boomerang chair to Cedar Bowl. Most of the runs in Cedar and Lizard bowls are intermediate.

Fernie boasts 12 double-black-diamond trails, including Siberia Ridge, and a cluster of four adjacent gullies off the spine between Lizard and Currie bowls. Boomerang and Boomerang Ridge, reached by the triple-chair of the same name, also provide plenty of challenge, as does Bootleg Glades. Beware of the notorious Face Lift handle-tow, or 'meat-hook', at the top of the Great Bear Express quad. It serves some worthwhile skiing in Lizard Bowl but reporters warned: 'if you don't get on properly, let go and don't let it drag you up by your arms – it could put your back out'.

Fernie is a good resort for learning to snowboard, with plenty of suitable trails. The terrain park is on Upper Falling Star, accessed by the Timber chair-lift, and the half-pipe is on Bambi trail close to the base area.

## Off-piste
Fernie is famous for its massive snowfalls, deep powder and tree skiing. The five bowls of Cedar, Lizard, Currie, Timber and Siberia spread along the south-facing slopes of the Lizard mountain range, and snowcat-skiers and -boarders will be in their element. Several companies can arrange trips, including Island Lake Lodge, Fernie Wilderness Adventures, and Powder Cowboy, which has 7,000 acres of terrain six miles farther along the valley.

## Tuition and guiding
Fernie Alpine Resort Winter Sports School gives lessons in skiing and snowboarding and offers a variety of other courses including telemarking, women's ski clinics, Powder & Crud, Turn & Burn, teen skiing and race camps.

## Mountain restaurants
Gourmet lunching on snow has yet to reach Fernie, although The Wood on the Hill heads the growing list of eateries catering for the more sophisticated palates of out-of-town visitors and is open for lunch. Bear's Den at mid-mountain is an open-air snack bar. The alternative, preferable on the average chilly day, is to return to the village. Kelsey's in the Cornerstone Lodge in the village centre is warmly recommended ('wonderful English-style fish and chips and Mexican dishes'). Lizard Creek is another good option, with a reasonably priced bar menu, and the Mean Bean Coffee & Deli serves gourmet soups and sandwiches.

## Accommodation
The base area includes condominiums and an assortment of chalets and town houses, available through the Canadian Rockies Lodging Company (☎ 403 256 8473). Lizard Creek Lodge is the prime place to stay ('superb accommodation with excellent service'). It has a gym, an outdoor hot-tub, a swimming-pool, a comfortable lounge with a roaring log fire and a gourmet restaurant. Its large and comfortable condos contain well-fitted

kitchens and are ideal for families. In the evening, the bar menu is an attractive option for families, who can sit and eat on the comfortable sofas around the fireplace. Snow Creek Lodge has smaller condos than Lizard Creek, serves light breakfasts and lunches, and is in a good location with an outdoor heated pool. Cornerstone Lodge lies at the base of Deer chair and above Kelsey's Restaurant. Five minutes' drive away in town, Park Place Lodge is 'spacious and modern' but with 'disappointingly impersonal service', while the Old Nurses Residence is a B&B with large Victorian rooms. The Victorian-built Royal Hotel has considerable atmosphere.

## Eating in and out

Lizard Creek is recommended both for its bar menu and fine dining ('the finest food and service in the ski village'), while River Rock Bistro in Park Place Lodge is praised for its 'sumptuous steaks and bacon-wrapped rainbow trout'. Gabriella's is Italian and serves good-value pasta dishes. The Alpine Lodge above the base area now specialises in fondue. In old Fernie, Yamagoya serves sushi, and the Old Elevator has an open fire and a good wine list. Rip 'n' Richard's and the Curry Bowl

are both popular, while the Old Elevator and El Guapo ('Mexican diner with a funky, relaxed atmosphere') are also recommended. Mojo Risin' is a new restaurant in the historic Royal Hotel, featuring French quarter New Orleans cuisine.

## Après-ski

This is a resort suited to families and individuals whose priority is skiing rather than a lively nightlife. On the mountain you can enjoy a barbecue around the fire at Bear's Den before finishing with torchlight skiing down the Elk run. Alternatives include dog-sledding and ski-jöring. In the old town you can go ice-skating and curling, or try the indoor climbing wall. Here too the Eldorado Lounge has live music, as does the Grand Central Hotel & Bar and the Royal Hotel. The on-mountain Grizzly Bar offers live music at weekends.

## Childcare

Daycare is available for newborn to six-year-olds from 8.30am to 4.30pm, and the children's ski programme is extensive. There is a Freeriders Programme for experienced skiers up to the age of 17. The nursery area has a magic carpet lift.

# Fernie: At a glance

**Tel** 1 250 423 4655
**Email** info@skifernie.com
**Website** www.skifernie.com

### GETTING THERE
**Airport** Calgary 3½hrs
**Road** scenic drive on Highway 22 from Calgary via Crowsnest Pass

### THE SKIING
**Linked/nearby resorts** Big Mountain, Kimberley, Panorama
**Total of trails/pistes** 2,504 acres (30% easy, 40% intermediate, 30% difficult)
**Lifts in area** 9: 6🪑 3🚡
**Lift opening dates** 6 December 2004 to 18 April 2005

### LIFT PASSES
**Area pass** CDN$336 for 6 days
**Pensioners** 65yrs and over CDN$258 for 6 days

### TUITION
**Ski & board** Fernie Alpine Resort Winter Sports School (☎ 250 423 4655)
**Guiding** Fernie Wilderness Adventures snowcat skiing (☎ 250 423 6704), Island Lake Lodge and Powder Cowboy Cat Skiing (☎ 250 423 3700), RK Heli-ski in Panorama (☎ 250 342 3889)

### CHILDREN
**Lift pass** 6–12yrs CDN$114, 13–17yrs CDN$258, both for 6 days
**Ski & board school** as adults
**Kindergartens** (ski) through ski & board school, (non-ski) Telus Resort Kids Daycare (☎ 250 423 4655)

### FOOD AND DRINK
Coffee CDN$1.25, bottle of house wine CDN$20, small beer CDN$4–5.25, soft drink CDN$2, dish of the day CDN$6–9

# Kicking Horse

ALTITUDE 3,902ft (1,190m)

## ❄ tough terrain ❄ top-rate mountain restaurant
## ❄ excellent on-mountain accommodation

> **Best for:** steep-and-deep enthusiasts, adventurous skiers and riders
> **Not recommended for:** beginners, après-skiers, those wanting a lively resort, non-skiing children

Since its development four years ago, the rugged ski area of Kicking Horse has attracted a passionate following among snow *aficionados*. The small community-owned hill of White Tooth, situated a three-hour drive from Calgary, is being transformed, at a projected cost of CDN$300 million, into what is destined to be a world-class resort with tough terrain comparable to Whistler, Red Mountain and the best of Banff–Lake Louise. Progress has been slow and has not been helped by a couple of winters of bad snow that did nothing to attract investment. However, cover was good in 2003–4, and an embryo village with ski-in, ski-out accommodation is now taking shape. This is just as well, because the valley town of Golden is no quaint Victorian mining town awaiting a little gentrification, but a busy railway junction awkwardly sprawled across both sides of the tracks and without a modicum of charm. You need to be a truly dedicated skier to spend a whole week in a motel in Golden. Fortunately, the development of the base area is beginning to alleviate accommodation problems.

## On-piste
### top 8,037ft (2,450m) bottom 3,902ft (1,190m)

The hi-tech Golden Eagle Express gondola provides the only full mountain access and is the resort's showpiece. The number of cabins has been doubled since it was first built, but its monopoly inevitably results in queues on big powder days, when the shutters come down on the shops in Golden and commercial life in the valley comes almost to a halt as the locals head for the hills.

The concept and construction of the gondola, which takes you up 4,135ft, is

faultless, but it is a shame that the Dutch consortium that developed the resort could not have found the extra finance to build a mid-station. However, queues are fast-moving, and once you are up the mountain the Stairway to Heaven quad-chair gives access to plenty of terrain without immediately having to return to base.

Essentially, this is a resort for accomplished skiers and riders looking for challenge. Anyone who has skied in Jackson Hole or Snowbird will feel at home here. But, unlike Jackson, there is always one easy way down, making it a good choice of destination for a party of mixed abilities. The lower third of the mountain, served by two chair-lifts, also provides easy beginner and intermediate terrain.

### WHAT'S NEW
Lodge and luxury condominium accommodation at base area

## Off-piste
The main course starts outside the door of the Eagle's Eye restaurant at the top of the gondola, where black-diamonds fall away from both sides of the ridge to produce some sensational tree and bowl skiing. Some of this is steep by any standards, and for anyone lacking in confidence it pays to study the topography before committing yourself to runs that may test your ability to its limits.

Redemption Ridge, reached from the Stairway to Heaven lift, also offers outstanding steep skiing in the huge alpine expanse of Feuz Bowl. Kicking Horse's 2,750-acre ski area is now larger than Breckenridge and is set to expand further, to 4,000 acres, over the next few years. One of Canada's oldest heli-skiing companies, Purcell Heli Skiing, operates in the region.

## Tuition and guiding
Kicking Horse Snow School offers tuition for all levels, from beginners to powder and

mogul skiing. Girl Powder classes are for women, with top female coaches.

## Mountain restaurants

The base-lodge is attractive and contains a self-service restaurant, and a mid-mountain yurt – called Heaven's Door – serves sushi. But the most staggering gastronomic find is the Eagle's Eye restaurant at the top of the gondola. Here the best of Alpine dining is mixed with Canadian service and style in a surrounding of wooden beams, floor-to-ceiling windows and a roaring log fire. The result is a memorable experience not normally associated with North American skiing.

## Accommodation

The charming and well-equipped chalet homes, near the mountain base area, are ski-in, ski-out and boast state-of-the-art kitchens, large living-rooms, bedrooms with en-suite bathrooms, outdoor hot-tubs and garages. The 2004–5 season sees the opening of Highland Lodge, an additional building on the edge of the piste comprising 12 rooms. Other hotel condominium units are being built.

Golden, a ten-minute drive away down a paved all-weather road, has a youth hostel, half-a-dozen B&Bs, and ten motels and lodges including the Ramada Inn (☎ 250 439 1888) and the Prestige Inn (☎ 250 344 7990). About 30 miles on the other side of the scenic Kicking Horse Pass, the isolated lake-side cabins of Emerald Lake Lodge (☎ 250 439 5400) are uniquely Canadian.

## Eating in and out

The Eagle's Eye restaurant is open in the evenings at weekends, when you can also stay the night up here in two luxury suites and make 'first tracks' down in the morning. Golden boasts a number of coffee shops, bars and cafés, such as the smoky Mad Trapper Pub and the Dogtooth Café. Cedar House, on the edge of town, is a gourmet option. The Kicking Horse Grill, which has a Dutch chef/owner, is highly recommended for its atmospheric log cabin setting and adventurous cuisine, while the quirky Sisters & Beans and the Country Garden are also praised.

## Après-ski

The Mad Trapper Pub in Golden has been the only establishment to rise to the evening needs of skiers and snowboarders. However, a slope-side pub is promised as part of the first lodge development at the base. For the present, Kicking Horse has no after-hours entertainment.

## Childcare

The ski school teaches children aged three to twelve years. Apart from a magic carpet lift, there are no other child facilities at present.

# Kicking Horse: At a glance

**Tel** 1 250 439 5400
**Email** guestservices@kickinghorseresort.com
**Website** www.kickinghorseresort.com

### GETTING THERE
**Airport** Calgary 3hrs
**Road** 2½ hr drive from Calgary

### THE SKIING
**Linked/nearby resorts** Banff, Lake Louise, Panorama
**Total of trails/pistes** 2,750 acres (20% easy, 20% intermediate, 60% difficult)
**Lifts in area** 4: 1🚡 3🚠
**Lift opening dates** mid-December 2004 to mid-April 2005

### LIFT PASSES
**Area pass** CDN$305 for 6 days

**Pensioners** 65 yrs and over CDN$242 for 6 days

### TUITION
**Ski & board school** Kicking Horse Snow School (☎ 250 439 5424)
**Guiding** Purcell Heli Skiing (☎ 250 344 5410)

### CHILDREN
**Lift pass** 7–12 yrs CDN$132, 13–18 yrs CDN$242, both for 6 days
**Ski & board school** Kicking Horse Snow School
**Kindergarten** none

### FOOD AND DRINK
Coffee CDN$1.50, bottle of house wine CDN$20, small beer CDN$5, soft drink CDN$1.50, dish of the day CDN$7

# Red Mountain

**ALTITUDE 3,888ft (1,1296m)**

❄ **cult resort with tough skiing** ❄ **excellent value for money**
❄ **exhilarating on- and off-piste skiing**

> **Best for:** people on a budget, advanced skiers and snowboarders
>
> **Not recommended for:** beginners, those wanting a modern lift system, ski-to-lunchers

Red Mountain has managed to achieve and maintain a rugged reputation as the spiritual home of the hard men – and women – of skiing in North America. Frontier machismo is still much in evidence, but whether this retro-charm survives a change of ownership remains to be seen. In summer 2004 the resort was in the process of being acquired by a San Diego businessman with close ties to the area. He has dynamic plans to improve mountain facilities.

Red Mountain is served by Rossland, a small mining town that had its heyday in the 1890s, when the discovery of gold and copper attracted fortune hunters. The town is a two- to three-hour drive away from Spokane in Washington State, although it is also possible to fly into Castlegar via Calgary or Vancouver.

## On the snow
**top 6,800ft (2,266m) bottom 3,888ft (1,1296m)**

By refusing to invest in state-of-the-art lifts, the resort has kept the pioneering spirit intact, and the terrain has done the rest. Red Mountain and Granite Mountain, where the main ski area is to be found, share 83 trails, of which 45 per cent is graded at least black-diamond. The longest run is an exhilarating roller-coaster, Long Squaw, which continues for 7km.

Red's hard core is made up of ski bums, while most of the passing visitors see their visit as a rite-of-passage pilgrimage to a resort with a reputation for testing the best. Snowboarders view the resort as one of the top two in Canada (the other being Whistler).

Paradise Lodge provides simple but good on-mountain dining, while Rafters at the base-lodge has a substantial lunch menu and a well-stocked bar. Sourdough Alley, also in the base-lodge, offers a wide choice of food.

Whitewater, near the town of Nelson, is well worth a day-trip for some alternative steep-and-deep skiing and riding.

## In the resort
The main hotel in Rossland is the Uplander (☎ 250 362 7375), which has simple rooms but serves unexpectedly good meals in the Louis Blue Dining Room. The hotel also features a fitness centre and the Powder Keg Pub, the town's hot-spot. Angela's B&B (☎ 250 362 7790) is decorated with local antiques and has an outdoor hot-tub. The Ram's Head Inn (☎ 250 362 9577), a comfortable and good-value B&B, is close enough to the slopes to ski back to, and is run chalet-style with communal breakfast-time dining. Another convenient place to stay is the Red Shutter Inn (☎ 250 362 5131). Red Mountain Rentals has Carolyn's Corner luxury condos (☎ 250 362 5553), with hot-tubs and fireplaces, at the mountain base. Mountain Rose café and Idgies are both recommended restaurants for dinner.

Despite Red's steep-and-deep reputation, children love the hidden trails through the woods between the pistes. Red Mountain Kindercare caters for little ones from eighteen months, and Kinderski combines skiing and childcare for three- to six-year-olds.

> ## Red Mountain: At a glance
>
> **Tel** 1 250 362 7384
> **Email** info@ski-red.com
> **Website** www.ski-red.com
> **Lifts in resort** 5: 4🚠 1🚡
> **Lift opening dates** mid-December 2004 to beginning of April 2005

# Silver Star

ALTITUDE 3,780ft (1,152m)

❆ **colourful Victorian-style village** ❆ **renowned ski school**
❆ **skiing convenience** ❆ **demanding terrain**

**Best for:** families, intermediate and advanced skiers seeking fresh challenges
**Not recommended for:** those looking for a lively nightlife, non-skiers

Silver Star, situated in the beautiful Okanagan Valley near the town of Vernon, looks remarkably like what it is not – a carefully restored British Columbian mining town of the 1890s. The brightly-painted town houses, sodium street lamps, shops and restaurants are entirely without provenance, but very skilfully executed. For a purpose-built village it has an unusual amount of ambience. The nearest airport is Kelowna, 55 minutes' drive away.

The resort is owned by the Australian proprietors of nearby **Big White** and is now the subject of a substantial further expansion. **Sun Peaks** is its other worthy neighbour in the valley. Snow cover is exceptionally good, with an annual average of 23ft (700cm).

## On the snow
top 6,280ft (1,915m) bottom 3,780ft (1,152m)

Silver Star manages to provide the full menu of skiing, from easy nursery slopes to some technically demanding 'steeps' that allow little room for error. The village is situated mid-mountain. The south-facing Vance Creek area, overlooking the village, possesses long cruises suitable for intermediates. Accomplished skiers will quickly head for the north face to explore what is the highest number of double-black-diamond trails in British Columbia. Runs such as Free Fall are not for the faint-hearted, while reverse-cambered Gowabunga consistently tries to pitch you into impenetrable pine forest. The skiable terrain covers 2,725 acres and another 340 acres of unpatrolled off-piste. The number of flats on the north side of the mountain makes it hostile for snowboarders.

The terrain park features some challenging and varied terrain, with a boardercross course, a half-pipe, and a Freestyle Aerial Site.

Silver Star Ski and Board School is one of the best in the country, and regularly wins awards.

Paradise Camp, on the north side, offers the only on-mountain lunch. It has music and a varied menu that includes buffalo burgers. Longjohn's Pub is a popular lunch spot located in the village.

Non-skiing activities include snowmobiling, snowshoeing, dog-sledding, tubing, ice-skating, and 55km of cross-country trails.

## In the resort
The Silver Star Club Resort has extremely comfortable suites. Creekside condos are said to be 'ideal for families'. Victorian Vacation Homes range from simple studios to five-bedroomed townhouses with private hot-tubs. All can be booked through the resort (☎ 250 542 0224).

Recommended restaurants include the Craigellachie Room at Putnam Station Inn, complete with its own model train that circuits the room, The Italian Garden Restaurant and Clementine's Dining Room, as well as the Silver Lode Restaurant. Nightlife centres around the pool table in the Saloon. The best place for early evening après-ski is the atmospheric Wine Cellar downstairs from Putnam Station, which serves tapas with Okanagan wines.

The Children's Center at the ski school accepts newborn to six-year-olds, while Star Kids Skiing & Snowboarding Program takes youngsters aged three to ten.

### Silver Star: At a glance

**Tel** 1 250 542 0224
**Email** star@skisilverstar.com
**Website** www.skisilverstar.com
**Lifts in resort** 8: 5 3
**Lift opening dates** mid-November 2004 to mid-April 2005

# Sun Peaks

**ALTITUDE 4,117ft (1,255m)**

❄ **sophisticated resort** ❄ **skiing for all standards** ❄ **good restaurants**
❄ **busy nightlife** ❄ **skiing convenience**

> **Best for:** anyone who enjoys Whistler but seeks new and less overtly commercial horizons
>
> **Not recommended for:** non-skiers, mountain-lunchers

This ski-in, ski-out resort is one of a trio in the delightful Okanagan Valley of British Columbia, which deserves international recognition. Together with **Silver Star** and **Big White**, the area is worthy of a ten-day holiday. All the resorts have entirely different characters, are within easy driving distance of each other and are accessible from Kamloops or Kelowna airport.

Sun Peaks used to be called Tod Mountain, the local hill for the logging town of Kamloops, until it received an injection of CDN$75 million of Japanese money. Hotel developers have since invested three times this amount.

Nancy Greene, who became the *grande dame* of Canadian ski-racing after winning the Olympic gold at Grenoble in 1968, and her husband Al Raine played the pivotal roles in organising the transition. Although still small, Sun Peaks is now one of the most attractive and sophisticated ski villages in Canada. It has picked up a number of national accolades.

## On the snow
**top 6,824ft (2,080m) bottom 3,933ft (1,199m)**

The skiing takes place on three mountains linked at the base, of which much the most important is Mount Tod. Two quads and a triple-chair take you up to the Top of the World, the highest point in the patrolled ski area. From here there are black-diamond descents in chutes and bowls, as well as easier intermediate runs and one beginner route back down. Challenger is one of the steepest marked trails in Canada. A cat-ski operation enables advanced skiers and boarders to explore the higher slopes of Mount Tod outside the ski area boundary –

'A truly outstanding raw mountain experience for anyone who can ski parallel', according to one reporter.

Sundance, the second mountain, is accessed by a quad-chair. Its mainly blue runs are ideal intermediate terrain and it also has a large terrain park with a half-pipe. Mount Morrisey, the third ski area, has a quad-chair that opens up an enormous gladed area of undemanding, confidence-building runs.

Sun Peaks Snowsports School offers tuition for adults and children. Mountain restaurants are limited to one grim self-service at the top of the Sunburst Express lift.

## In the resort
Delta Sun Peaks Resort (☎ 250 578 6000) has established itself as one of the finest mountain hotels in Canada. Other slope-side hotels include the three-stars Fireside Lodge (☎ 270 578 7842) and Hearthstone Lodge (☎ 250 578 8588). Nancy Greene's Cahilty Lodge (☎ 250 578 7454), although rated three-star, offers four-star comfort.

Sun Peaks Village boasts the Kids' Adventure Park (featuring snowmobiling and tobogganing), a pedestrian mall and eateries ranging from steakhouses to a Japanese restaurant. Val Senales and Macker's Bistro are both recommended. Macdaddies is the wildest nightspot.

Other activities include snow tubing in the resort's new tube park, which has a choice of three runs down.

Sun Peaks Childminding cares for babies from 18 months, and small beginners now have two magic carpet lifts.

### Sun Peaks: At a glance
**Tel** 1 250 578 7842
**Email** info@sunpeaksresort.com
**Website** www.sunpeaksresort.com
**Lifts in resort** 8: 5🚠 3🎏
**Lift opening dates** 20 November 2004 to 10 April 2005

# Tremblant

ALTITUDE 870ft (265m)

❄ state-of-the-art lift system ❄ well-groomed slopes
❄ attractive village ❄ widespread snowmaking

**Best for:** families, lower intermediates, snowboarders, gourmet skiers

**Not recommended for:** advanced skiers, people who hate the cold

Located in the Laurentian Mountains, 75 miles north-west of Montréal, Tremblant offers skiing in a cold climate combined with a chance to appreciate Québeçois culture and cuisine in a contrived but charming ambience. A massive investment by the owner, Intrawest, has transformed the traditional ski village into a modern ski resort.

Intensive piste-grooming and snowmaking do much to combat the prevailing icy conditions, but the climate can be hostile in January and February, and parents with young children may consider it too cold for comfort here at February half-term. Vieux Tremblant, the old village, has been meticulously restored, and the newer pedestrian-only Tremblant Village includes steeply terraced main streets with painted wooden buildings that are modelled on the old quarter of Montréal. The numerous boutiques in the Place St-Bernard in Tremblant Village are enticing. A short shuttle-bus ride links Vieux Tremblant with the modern ski base area.

## On-piste

top 3,001ft (915m) bottom 870ft (265m)

Tremblant features varied pistes and trails spread around four sectors of the mountain. A heated, high-speed gondola provides the nine-minute ride up from the village at the foot of South Side to the summit, where the longer lifts meet at Le Grand Manitou Lodge. From here, pistes lead down the three main faces of the mountain. The fourth face, the Edge, is set on a neighbouring flank. The resort possesses Canada's largest snowmaking system.

Seventeen per cent of the runs are for beginners, so second-weekers and early intermediates are able to ski both sides of the mountain. However, the freezing temperatures mean conditions are not ideal for first-timers. Most of the intermediate trails are on the generally easier South Face with its main Équilibre beginner area just above the village.

Over the top, those in search of greater challenge will find runs such as Dynamite, a double-black-diamond trail located on the North Side of the mountain; it has a 42-degree pitch, making it one of the steepest trails in eastern Canada.

The Edge is set aside for better skiers and riders, and is served by its own quad-chair. It contains three demanding trails, the difficulty of which are accentuated by the icy, hard-packed snow conditions.

The main terrain park, Parc Gravité, on the North Side, has a super-pipe, quarter-pipe and variety of obstacles.

## Off-piste

Some 77 acres are given over to wooded glades. At the Edge, the intermediate runs of Réaction and Sensation through the frozen spruces provide a dramatic introduction to tree-skiing, as does Windigo on the North Face.

## Tuition and guiding

The Tremblant Snow School offers a great variety of courses, including 'Super Group 4' classes in groups of four, tuition for disabled skiers and riders, race training, cross-country, telemark, seniors, teen skiing and boarding, and women's clinics.

## Mountain restaurants

On-mountain eating opportunities are disappointing – Le Grand Manitou Lodge at the summit is the only restaurant, and offers cafeteria-style self-service. Le Refuge du Trappeur on the Versant Soleil is an attractive, simple log cabin that serves soups and drinks.

## Accommodation

Of the ten hotels and lodges that have been built at the foot of the slopes, Le Westin

Resort & Spa (☎ 819 681 8000) is one of the smartest places to stay, with a choice of restaurants and a lavish spa. L'Ermitage du Lac is a new five-star, while stylish five-star Fairmont Chateau Tremblant (☎ 819 681 7000) has two restaurants and a large spa. Other hotels include the rustic-style Lodge de la Montagne, La Tour des Voyageurs in Tremblant Village and the Le Sommet des Neiges, 100ft from the main Express gondola. Most other properties are condominium developments. All of the above, apart from the Fairmont Chateau Tremblant and Le Westin Resort & Spa, are booked through central reservations (☎ 819 681 2000).

There are several options, too, outside Tremblant Village. Both within a ten-minute shuttle journey are Club Tremblant (☎ 819 425 8781) on the shore of Lake Tremblant, with its fine views over the lake and to the ski slopes, and Le Grand Lodge (☎ 819 425 2734), a four-star, log-cabin-style hotel close to the Gray Rocks ski area.

## Eating in and out

In contrast to the better-known Canadian resorts, restaurant prices in Tremblant are high. However, the choice of eating-places is wide, ranging from pizzerias to atmospheric establishments offering cuisine Québeçois. La Grappe à Vin is an intimate wooden house with an extensive wine list, and serves local game and regional dishes. Aux Truffes offers progressive French *haute cuisine*, and La Forge has steaks and grills. Coco-Pazzo boasts fine Italian food, and Crêperie Catherine serves Breton crêpes. Mexicali Rosa's specialises in Californian-Mexican, and Java-U Sushi provides Japanese cuisine.

## Après-ski

The nightlife is concentrated at Vieux Tremblant, which has several lively bars and clubs including the popular Café de l'Époque, Le P'tit Caribou and Octobar Rock. Microbrasserie La Diable brews its own beer, and is a popular early-evening watering-hole. The pool at La Source Aquaclub makes good family entertainment. A more soothing spot for adults is Spa Le Scandinave, about four miles away on the wooded bank of a creek. Other activities nearby include deer observation outings and snowshoe hikes by moonlight.

## Childcare

Low temperatures aside, this is an ideal resort for families. At the base of the slopes is the Kidz Club with its own magic carpet. The club organises daycare for non-skiing children over twelve months old, and runs ski programmes for three- to twelve-year-olds. There are three magic carpets.

# Tremblant: At a glance

**Tel** Mont Tremblant 1 819 425 2434 / Tremblant/Intrawest 1 819 681 2000
**Email** info_tremblant@intrawest.com
**Website** www.tremblant.ca

### GETTING THERE
**Airport** Montréal 90 mins
**Road** autoroute 15 North 73 miles from Montréal to St-Jovite exit and continue for 6 miles to resort

### THE SKIING
**Linked/nearby resorts** Gray Rocks at St-Jovite
**Total of trails/pistes** 627 acres (17% easy, 33% intermediate, 39% difficult, 11% very difficult)
**Lifts in area** 9: 1🚠 8🚡
**Lift opening dates** 20 November 2004 to 17 April 2005

### LIFT PASSES
**Area pass** CDN$267–298 for 6 days

**Pensioners** 65yrs and over CDN$197–219 for 6 days

### TUITION
**Ski & board** Tremblant Snow School (☎ 819 681 5666)
**Guiding** through ski school

### CHILDREN
**Lift pass** 6–12yrs CDN$145–163, 13–17yrs CDN$197–219, both for 6 days
**Ski & board school** as adults
**Kindergarten** (ski/non-ski) Kidz Club (☎ 819 681 5666)

### FOOD AND DRINK
Coffee CDN$2–2.50, bottle of house wine CDN$22, small beer CDN$5.50–6, soft drink CDN$2.50–3, dish of the day CDN$9–22

# Whistler

ALTITUDE 2,214ft (675m)                    map: see page 175

✳ **long vertical drop** ✳ **extensive off-piste** ✳ **cosmopolitan atmosphere**
✳ **modern lift system** ✳ **buzzing nightlife**

**Best for:** all standards of skier and
snowboarder, gourmet diners, night-owls,
non-skiers

**Not recommended for:** sun worshippers,
those in search of peace and quiet

Whistler remains by far the most popular
destination in Canada. Its twin peaks offer
the longest continuous vertical drops in
North America, and the skiing and riding
for all standards falls nothing short of
superb. Few resorts provide such an
inspiring combination of awesome terrain,
comfortable accommodation and
cosmopolitan atmosphere, and it has justly
won the honour of staging the 2010 Winter
Olympics. However, an increasing number
of visitors feel that the resort has become a
victim of its own success through
overbuilding by owners Intrawest. As one
reader put it: 'after an absence of some
years, I was truly shocked that what was
once a tiny village with great skiing could
have sold its soul to become a metropolis of
Mammon on such a scale'.

But the enormous construction
programme is now complete, and the once-
unconnected villages of Whistler and
Blackcomb have merged into a not-
unpleasing conurbation that now extends to
a whole new village at Whistler Creek. Even
so, reporters moan about 'ridiculously high
prices for Canada' and 'lengthy lift queues
at weekends', but most confess that such
drawbacks do not detract from their
enjoyment, and that they will return. The
resort plans to invest a further $14.2
million in on-mountain improvements.

Whistler's only real failing is its
maritime position, which means that much
of the heavy winter precipitation falls as
rain in the village and as snow only higher
up. The number of blue-sky days in winter
is markedly lower than in rival resorts in
Colorado and Utah. Changes in temperature
between village and summit can be
frostbitingly dramatic, although not as
extreme as in Banff–Lake Louise.

## On-piste
top 7,494ft (2,284m) bottom 2,140ft (652m)

Part of Whistler's charm is the contrast
between Whistler and Blackcomb mountains.
Both offer exhilarating top-to-bottom skiing,
much of it below the tree-line. Each claims
more than 100 runs and each has long
cruising trails. But whereas Whistler is
known for its bowls, Blackcomb prides itself
on its two glaciers and some dramatic
couloirs. The two mountains share a lift pass,
but they are divided by Fitzsimmons Creek
and are at present linked only at the foot.

From the resort, Whistler Village Gondola
climbs to Roundhouse Lodge at 6,069ft on
Whistler Mountain. Queues can develop here
during the morning rush-hour in high season,
and those in the know take the Fitzsimmons
Express quad-chair and work their way up
the lift system. From the same corner of the
village, Excalibur Gondola takes skiers up
Blackcomb. The Wizard Express quad at
Blackcomb base provides alternative access to
Blackcomb, while skiers staying in Whistler
Creek can take Creekside Gondola up
Whistler Mountain.

Both mountains have dedicated learning
areas near the bottom as well as easy trails
higher up on the mountain, so novices can
enjoy the wide-open spaces and a vertical
drop usually associated with intermediate
ambitions. On Blackcomb Mountain, catch
the Wizard Express quad-chair and switch
to the Solar Coaster Express. From here you
can take the easy Expressway link to the
Seventh Heaven Express quad, or explore
the gentler runs served by the Jersey Cream
and Glacier Express quads. At Whistler, ski
trails such as Upper Whiskey Jack and Pony
Trail can be accessed via the gondola.
Papoose, Bear Cub and Expressway are
other options lower down.

On Blackcomb, intermediates should
head for the Seventh Heaven Zone, where a
quad-chair serves runs such as Cloud Nine

Panorama and Southern Comfort. Crystal Chair also leads to a wide sector of blue trails cut between the trees. On Whistler Mountain, a choice of blue runs leads from Big Red Express or Franz's Chair into Franz's run, an invigorating high-velocity cruiser that drops all the way to Whistler Creek. The Harmony Express quad also gives access to some classic intermediate trails including Crescendo down Symphony Bowl.

Advanced skiers and riders have plenty of challenges on both mountains, including the infamous Couloir Extreme on Blackcomb, which lives up to its name ('nerves of steel are a distinct advantage') and the double-diamond Couloir and Cirque on Whistler Mountain.

Whistler is one of the best snowboarding resorts in North America. Blackcomb offers a sequence of adjoining parks on 40 acres of mountain-side for different ability levels. These include a world-class half-pipe and boardercross course. Entry to the Highest Level, set aside for true experts, is by special pass obtained from Guest Relations at the base area. Whistler Mountain also has a terrain park featuring rails and a half-pipe.

## Off-piste

A short hike from the top of the Showcase T-bar on Blackcomb gives access to a delightful intermediate off-piste run down the Blackcomb Glacier. After a fresh dump Whistler's bowls become a giant playground for all levels of powder enthusiasts. For those prepared to hike, off-piste opportunities extend into a further sequence of bowls from the top of Whistler Mountain. Five heli-ski companies operate in and around Whistler, including Whistler Heli-skiing, which runs daily excursions, and Coast Range Heliskiing, which operates out of Pemberton, 25 miles away.

## Tuition and guiding

Whistler Blackcomb Ski and Snowboard School (SSS) has an excellent reputation: 'the tuition was so illuminating, with smooth and rapid progress, that I wondered how we had ever skied without it'. The resort's regular free tours of the pistes with some of Canada's greatest skiers are strongly recommended: 'it was an extraordinary experience to ski with someone of world class, and one that I will never forget'. Extremely Canadian provides lessons in extreme skiing and snowboarding.

## Mountain restaurants

On Whistler Mountain, Roundhouse Lodge promises 'everything from burgers and fries to fresh pasta and Asian cuisine'. The Raven's Nest at the top of Creekside Gondola specialises in pasta and homemade soup.

On Blackcomb, Christine's Restaurant in Rendezvous Lodge received mixed reports. The Rendezvous offers more casual but faster service. Crystal Hut at the top of Crystal Chair is 'just like an atmospheric Swiss or Italian Alpine hut, with the same primitive toilets'. The River Rock Grill, upstairs at the Glacier Creek, is praised for both cuisine and view.

Monk's Grill in the Upper Village is highly recommended, as is Dusty's at Creekside base. Early birds can start the day at Roundhouse Lodge with the Fresh Tracks programme. You board the Whistler gondola at 7.15am for an all-you-can-eat breakfast before setting off down the mountain as soon as the ski patrol declares it open. 18 Below in the Excalibur Base II Day Lodge serves all-day breakfast.

## Accommodation

The 13-storey Fairmont Chateau Whistler (☎ 604 938 8000) remains one of the truly great ski hotels of the world, with the addition of a first-rate spa. The Four Seasons Resort (☎ 604 935 3400), near Blackcomb Base, opened in summer 2004 and is liable to prove a worthy rival. Westin Resort & Spa (☎ 604 905 5000) at the base of Whistler Mountain contains a shopping mall and a sushi restaurant and is 'almost a village in itself'. We also received good reports of Delta Whistler Resort (☎ 604 932 1982) and Pan Pacific Lodge (☎ 604 905 2999). Timberline Lodge (☎ 604 932 5211) is 'comfortable, well situated and friendly', while Crystal Lodge (☎ 604 932 2221) is 'comfortable, conveniently located and the staff were helpful' and Listel Whistler Hotel (☎ 604 932 1133) are both popular. Summit Lodge (☎ 888 913 8811), in the heart of Whistler Village North, has an outdoor swimming-pool and hot-tub, a spa and a free in-room yoga programme.

Whistler Chalets (☎ 604 905 5287) boasts a portfolio of luxury self-catering homes for rental. Alpine Springs B&B (☎ 604 905 2747) and Blue Spruce Lodge (☎ 604 932 3508) charge moderate prices. Shoestring Lodge (☎ 604 932 3338) is one of the most affordable places to stay, with a choice of private or dormitory rooms all with television and private bath.

## Eating in and out

The Rimrock Cafe is the crowning glory of Whistler's eateries; it specialises in seafood. Another excellent restaurant is Bearfoot Bistro ('a luxurious candlelit place with exquisite food'). Trattoria di Umberto ('very fine') and Il Caminetto di Umberto are also praised, along with Zueski's Taverna ('soundly priced and tasty meals') and La Rua. Sushi Village is a perennial favourite. Ingrid's Café is 'cheap, cheerful and wholesome'. Ristorante Araxi specialises in Mediterranean cuisine and is 'absolutely delightful', and Citta's is a friendly little bistro. Splitz Burger in the Upper Village is warmly praised. You can also cook your own dinner at Whistler Cooking School – students participate in the cooking with the help of a chef, and eat the results. The IGA supermarket has 'an amazing range of food'.

## Après-ski

Whistler's nightlife is highly praised by reporters: 'the bars and nightlife were wonderful – no drunks and hooligans, just loads of friendly, happy people'. Dubh Linn Gate is an Irish pub described by one reporter as 'a great place to step out of your wet clothes and into a dry Martini'. The Longhorn Saloon at the foot of the slopes catches skiers and snowboarders as they come off the mountain ('beers gush from the tap like oil from a pipeline, a great place for anyone slightly deaf and with a cast-iron liver'). Merlin's Bar at Blackcomb base is lively, and Tapley's Pub is 'friendly, cheap and used by the locals'. Garfinkel's, Tommy Africa's and the Savage Beagle Bar are all extremely popular nightclubs, while Blacks Pub employs 'friendly staff and was not too noisy'. One of the 'in' places for riders is the Maxx Fish disco.

The shopping – which continues until 10pm – is a core part of the evening entertainment.

## Childcare

Whistler Kids caters for children aged three months to twelve years on both mountains with all-day care and lessons for appropriate ages: 'my four-year-old daughter learned more in a week than she had done in two previous weeks in France'. It also runs special classes for teenagers. The Nanny Network provides babysitters who will come to your lodging during the day or evening.

# Whistler: At a glance

**Tel** 1 604 664 5625
**Email** wbgr@intrawest.com
**Website** www.whistlerblackcomb.com

### GETTING THERE
**Airport** Vancouver 2hrs
**Road** scenic 2-hr drive up Sea-to-Sky highway from Vancouver

### THE SKIING
**Linked/nearby resorts** Grouse Mountain
**Total of trails/pistes** 7,071 acres (20% easy, 55% intermediate, 25% difficult)
**Lifts in area** 33: 3⬡ 18⬠ 12⬡
**Lift opening dates** 21 November 2004 to 5 June 2005. Summer skiing mid-June to mid-August on Horstman Glacier

### LIFT PASSES
**Area pass** CDN$390 for 6 days
**Pensioners** 65yrs and over CDN$333 for 6 days

### TUITION
**Ski & board** Extremely Canadian (☎ 604 932

4105), Lauralee Bowie Ski Adventures (☎ 604 689 7444), Whistler Blackcomb SSS (☎ 604 932 3434)
**Guiding** Blackcomb Helicopters (☎ 604 938 1700), Coast Range Heliskiing (☎ 604 894 1144), Helico Presto (☎ 604 938 2927), Spearhead Mountain Guides (☎ 604 932 8802), TLH Heliskiing (☎ 250 558 5379), Whistler Alpine Guides Bureau (☎ 604 932 4040), Whistler Heli-skiing (☎ 604 932 4105)

### CHILDREN
**Lift pass** 7–12yrs CDN$201, 13–18yrs CDN$305, both for 6 days
**Ski & board school** Whistler Kids (☎ 604 932 3434)
**Kindergarten** (ski/non-ski) Whistler Kids, (non-ski) The Nanny Network (☎ 604 938 2823)

### FOOD AND DRINK
Coffee CDN$1.80, bottle of house wine CDN$22–25, small beer CDN$5.20–6, soft drink CDN$2.50, dish of the day CDN$9.50–22

# CHILE

# Portillo

ALTITUDE 2,512m (8,241ft)

## ❄ exotic, idiosyncratic resort ❄ lack of crowded pistes and lift queues

**Best for:** adventurous skiers, off-piste enthusiasts

**Not recommended for:** beginners, people who hate T-bars, night-owls, those looking for a large and lively resort

Chile's oldest ski area, in a steep-sided valley next to the breathtakingly beautiful Laguna del Inca, is picturesque and slightly quirky. Portillo is situated 160km north of Santiago, on the awe-inspiring Uspallata Pass that marks the frontier with Argentina. Aconcagua, at 6,960m the highest mountain in the southern hemisphere, is nearby.

The area was first skied by Norwegian and British engineers, who were building the now largely abandoned trans-Andes railway. The resort is owned and run by a veteran American, Henry Purcell.

### WHAT'S NEW

Additional quad-chair on plateau side of the resort for 2004–5

## On the snow
### top 3,348m (10,984ft) bottom 2,512m (8,241ft)

The grooming and signposting on the 23 trails, served by 12 lifts, are as efficient as you would expect to find in any North American resort. There are seven US and five European ski instructors, in addition to the 13 Chilean. Unlike its North American counterparts, however, Portillo is not striving for expansion. Its ecologically minded owner limits the number of guests to just 450 and reinvests revenue in hotel facilities. Reporters say there are no lift queues, and powder does not get tracked out for days. 'I've been to more than 200 resorts and I've never seen anything as fun and as intimate as Portillo, nor have I skied such

empty runs,' said one. Skiers can access an enormous amount of off-piste terrain and finish by skating back across the frozen lake.

There are two bizarre but exhilarating *va* *et vient* lifts, including the celebrated Flying Kilometre run, which are unique to Portillo and designed for accessing the steep chutes in avalanche-prone areas on both sides of the valley. The larger lift, Roca Jack, hauls five skiers at a time on linked platters at 27kph to the top of the chute before suddenly coming to a halt; skiers disengage backwards. The resort has a new quad-chair for the 2004–5 season.

## In the resort
Most visitors stay at the bright yellow Hotel Portillo, which dominates the resort. A touch of a bygone era still pervades in the lakeside dining-room, with its antique leather walls and waiters in bow-ties and red jackets. The rooms, however, are rather small. Low-budget travellers using the bunk beds at the Octagon Lodge still eat at the hotel, while backpackers at the Inca Lodge have access to all hotel facilities. There is a new sushi bar in the resort.

Children are welcomed in Portillo, with 'Kids Ski Free' weeks, when each parent can bring one child aged 12 years or younger for free lodging, meals and skiing. There is a free daycare centre for children up to six years old. A daily entertainment programme is offered to kids every afternoon.

## Portillo: At a glance

**Tel** 56 2 263 0606
**Email** info@skiportillo.com
**Website** www.skiportillo.com
**Lifts in resort** 12: 5⬆ 7⬆
**Lift opening dates** 12 June 2005 to 9 October 2005

# Valle Nevado

**ALTITUDE 3,200m (10,498ft)**

❋ **exotic destination** ❋ **largest ski area in South America**
❋ **proximity to a capital city** ❋ **good-value heli-skiing**

> **Best for:** adventurous skiers, all standards of skier and snowboarder, those who want a combined ski-and-city holiday
> **Not recommended for:** people who suffer altitude sickness

Constructed by the French in the 1980s, Valle Nevado is situated only 64km from Santiago, although the steep approach road lined with cacti and spicy-scented scrub takes a couple of hours. Higher up, foxes pad the snow in search of food, while giant condors soar in the thermals around the 5,428-m summit of El Plomo.

The resort is linked by lift to the adjoining ski villages of **La Parva** and **El Colorado** to form the nearest equivalent to a European ski circuit such as the Trois Vallées or Espace Killy in France. These are the closest major slopes in the world to a capital city. Add to the high-quality skiing a day or two in Santiago and wine-tasting at one of the vineyards an hour from the city centre, and Valle Nevado beats the Alps in culture if not in lift capacity. Skiers flock to the region from Santiago at weekends, but the slopes are relatively quiet during the week.

The resort has a village altitude of a heady 3,200m, with pistes going up to 3,670m. Visitors arriving directly from sea level may experience some discomfort for the first couple of days and are advised to consume copious amounts of water and refrain from drinking alcohol.

## On the snow
**top 3,670m (12,040ft) bottom 2,430m (7,972ft)**

Well-prepared slopes cover some 100km of mainly intermediate skiing. Experienced skiers and riders can also take advantage of some of the world's best-value heli-skiing: just £60 for a well-organised morning of 4,000 vertical metres is a bargain by Canadian or European standards, and the price includes equipment and the services of an expert guide. The heli-skiing goes up to a breathtaking 5,000m.

Snow School Valle Nevado provides the ski and snowboard tuition, while Mini School is for four- to seven-year-olds.

## In the resort
A landmark on the slopes, and the most comfortable place to stay, is the Hotel Valle Nevado. The slightly cheaper options are La Puerta del Sol and Tres Puntas. There are two condominium complexes, one of which is new for 2005. Of six good restaurants, La Fourchette d'Or serves fine French cuisine and the Café de la Plaza offers traditional Chilean dishes. The resort has a handful of shops, mainly selling ski clothing and accessories, and a fitness centre.

> **WHAT'S NEW**
> Valle de La Luna condominiums open for winter 2005
> Heli-ski packages offered by the 3 hotels of Valle Nevado

La Parva is a smart enclave of holiday homes for wealthy city dwellers, while El Colorado is little more than a purpose-built base area for the adjoining old village of Farellones.

The Day Care Center in Hotel Valle Nevado offers indoor and outdoor activities for children.

## Valle Nevado: At a glance

**Tel** 56 2 206 0027
**Email** info@vallenevado.com
**Website** www.vallenevado.com
**Lifts in area** 11: 4🚠 7🚡
**Lift opening dates** June 2005 to October 2005

# FINLAND

## Levi

ALTITUDE 400m (1,312ft)

❄ **attractive resort in the Arctic Circle** ❄ **guaranteed snow cover**
❄ **long ski season** ❄ **value for money**

> **Best for:** beginners and intermediates, families, snowboarders, reindeer enthusiasts, dog-sledders
>
> **Not recommended for:** advanced skiers and powderhounds, vegetarians, teetotallers, those looking for sophisticated nightlife

This small and unusual resort lies 161km by road north of Rovaniemi, the capital of Finnish Lapland, but only 15km from Kittilä airport. It receives mixed reviews: 'a gigantic car park with a few hotels and chalets built as an afterthought. It seems a soulless place', commented one reporter. 'Magical and surreal surroundings – the place to come for a winter holiday as opposed to just a ski holiday,' said another.

> **WHAT'S NEW**
>
> Additional drag-lift
> 5 new beginner slopes
> New snow park

The resort possesses 22 lifts and is at the centre of 230km of cross-country trails. Snow is guaranteed from mid-October/early November until mid-May. From November to January the sun hardly rises and the day passes in a gentle twilight, but 13 runs covering 28km are floodlit and the ski area remains open from 10am to 7.45pm. By night, if you are lucky, the Northern Lights provide nature's supreme fireworks display. The hours of daylight increase each month until the late spring, when the ski area is open from 10am to 8pm.

It is worth visiting a traditional Lapp farm for a reindeer sleigh ride, and families with young children should not miss Santapark at Rovaniemi.

## On the snow
top 531m (1,742ft) bottom 200m (656ft)

A gondola provides uphill transport in a lift system serving 50 runs. However, it should be noted that all but one of the lifts are slow drag-lifts, although 'lift queues were non-existent'. New for the 2004–5 season are five additional beginner slopes.

Snowboarding is popular in Finland, and Levi boasts a new snow park containing a boardercross trail. There are 230km of flat cross-country runs across the frozen lakes, together with some more challenging routes and 9km of floodlit trails.

## In the resort

Recommended hotels include Hullu Poro, with 'enormous, comfortable apartment rooms with private saunas'. Hotel Levitunturi received mixed reports: 'my room was spotless', but 'I had expected better facilities'. Hotel K5 Levi is a luxury hotel with private saunas or hot-tubs in each room. The Matkalumaija Chalets are said to be 'beautiful'. Accommodation can be booked through a central office (☎ 166 393300).

Levi has good facilities for small children and offers a ski- and non-ski kindergarten. Children under seven years, accompanied by parents and wearing helmets, can ski free.

Most restaurants are in hotels, with reindeer on every menu. A new Italian and a Chinese restaurant will open for the 2005 season. The nightlife is limited.

> ## Levi: At a glance
>
> **Tel** 358 166 41246
> **Email** leviskiresort@levi.fi
> **Website** www.levi.fi
> **Lifts in resort** 22: 1🚠 21🎿
> **Lift opening dates** early November 2004 to mid-May 2005

# FRANCE

# Alpe d'Huez

ALTITUDE 1,860m (6,100ft)  map: see page 178

❋ **extensive ski area** ❋ **late-season skiing** ❋ **lively après-ski**
❋ **excellent off-piste skiing** ❋ **variety of mountain restaurants**

> **Best for:** families and other groups of
> mixed ability, off-piste skiers,
> snowboarders, gourmets, party-goers
> **Not recommended for:** people wanting
> Alpine charm, skiers preferring empty
> slopes

Alpe d'Huez is the capital of the fifth largest
ski area in France and the hub of 238km of
linked skiing. Though not a purpose-built
resort, so great are the additions to the
original village that it has all the
convenience of one. Reporters' main
criticism is its lack of atmosphere, although
one did admit that 'the town was more
charming than I had been led to believe and
has excellent non-skiing facilities'. Alpe
d'Huez's high altitude ensures that the
mountain remains snow-sure even for the
latest Easter holiday.

## On-piste
**top 3,330m (10,922ft) bottom 1,120m (3,674ft)**
'Without a doubt the best ski resort I have
ever been to,' enthused one reporter. Alpe
d'Huez is a genuine all-rounder, with
excellent nursery slopes, good red runs, long
black trails and extremely serious off-piste
opportunities. Mountain access is multiple:
two modern gondolas feed traffic out of the
village into the Pic Blanc sector and to the
neighbouring resorts of Oz-en-Oisans and
**Vaujany**, while chair- and drag-lifts give
access to the lower satellites of **Villard-
Reculas**, Huez and **Auris-en-Oisans**.
 Pic Blanc, at 3,330m, is reached by a
cable-car, and two quad chair-lifts on the
glacier give access to some excellent high-
altitude skiing. The area boasts the 16-km
Sarenne, which is Europe's longest black
run, but is considered by reporters to be
'more like a red'.

The terrain park on the Signal piste has
a half-pipe and a boardercross course. The
Signal blue run is now floodlit twice a week
throughout the winter for night-
skiing/boarding. The area has numerous
natural drop-offs and is well suited to
freeriding.

## Off-piste
Opportunities for *ski sauvage* from the top
of Pic Blanc are superb. Variations include
the Grand Sablat, the Combe du Loup and
a long, tricky descent via the Couloir de
Fare. A 20-minute climb from the cable-car
station takes you to the top of La Pyramide,
the off-piste starting point for more than
2,000m of vertical drop, bringing you down
to Vaujany.

## Tuition and guiding
The French Ski School (ESF) claims that two-
thirds of its instructors are English-speaking:
'we were very impressed,' remarked a couple
of reporters. The International Ski School
(ESI) offers ski and snowboarding classes
restricted to ten, with tuition in English, while
British Masterclass courses 'were superb',
said one reporter. 'I can't recommend the
Masterclass people highly enough.'

## Mountain restaurants
At La Cabane du Poutat, above Alpe
d'Huez, 'staff may be a little distant, but the
menu is extensive'. La Bergerie, on the red
run down to Villard-Reculas, is an Alpine
museum that doubles as a restaurant. The
Chalet du Lac Besson, on the cross-country
trail between the DMC gondola and
Alpette, offers some of the best mountain
cuisine in the region. Equally good is the
Chalet Alti-Bar next to the altiport. The
Signal restaurant has panoramic views.
 Le Tetras in Auris serves fine pizzas and
has a varied wine list, while Combe Haute in
the Sarenne Gorge is renowned for its salads.

## Accommodation

The Royal Ours Blanc (☎ 476 80 35 50) and Chamois d'Or (☎ 476 80 31 32) form the hard core of four-stars. The Pic Blanc (☎ 476 11 42 42) and the charming Printemps de Juliette (☎ 476 11 44 38) are welcoming three-stars, and the Christina (☎ 476 80 33 32) is friendly and charming, and one of the few attractive chalet-style buildings at the top of the resort. The best apartments include those in the Pierre et Vacances building (☎ 476 80 85 00), which has its own outdoor heated swimming-pool and optional self-catering.

## Eating in and out

Dining is an important business in Alpe d'Huez. Au P'tit Creux ('intimate atmosphere and wonderful, but avoid it at weekends') is one of the best restaurants here, while Passe Montagne is 'good value with friendly staff and an open fireplace'. Les Caves has 'exceptionally good food and wine'.

## Après-ski

'At night Alpe d'Huez comes alive,' enthused a reporter, and 'there's a huge variety of bars to suit absolutely everyone', added another. However, the prices were rated 'very expensive'. The Underground has live music, as does Le Sporting ('come here to mix with French locals'). Try Sphere Bar if you want to meet Brits. Les Caves is a firm favourite among older reporters, and Zoo Music Bar, Freeride Café and L'Etalon attract a younger crowd. Magoos is lively, but for 'a completely different night that's a lot more chilled head for DT's Tapas Bar or Cactus Winebar', advised one reporter.

The Circuits de l'Oisans ice-driving school is a racing drivers' training ground and also provides lessons for the public, and the Sports Centre has a choice of 26 indoor activities including ice-skating, indoor climbing and a swimming-pool.

## Childcare

The ESF ski school guarantees class sizes of no more than ten and gives lessons to children from four years old. The ESI teaches children from three-and-a-half, and Les Eterlous takes skiing and non-skiing children from three. Les Crapouilloux is a crèche for children from two years old. Its staff will meet older children from ski school and provide lunch and afternoon supervision. Les Intrépides is the alternative non-ski kindergarten.

# Alpe d'Huez: At a glance

**Tel** 33 476 11 44 44
**Email** info@alpedhuez.com
**Website** www.alpedhuez.com

### GETTING THERE
**Airports** Grenoble 1½hrs, Lyon 2hrs
**Rail** Grenoble 63km
**Road** access via steep D211 mountain road from N91 Grenoble–Briançon

### THE SKIING
**Linked/nearby resorts** Auris-en-Oisans, Les Deux Alpes, Huez, Serre Chevalier, Oz Station, Vaujany, Villard-Reculas
**Total of trails/pistes** 238km (36% beginner, 28% easy, 24% intermediate, 12% difficult)
**Lifts in area** 85: 16⛆ 24⛆ 45⛆
**Lift opening dates** 4 December 2004 to 30 April 2005. Summer skiing on Sarenne Glacier in July

### LIFT PASSES
**Area pass** (covers linked resorts and 1 day in Les Deux Alpes, La Grave, The Milky Way, Puy-St-

Vincent, Serre Chevalier) €182 for 6 days
**Pensioners** 60–70yrs €129 for 6 days. Free for over 70yrs

### TUITION
**Ski & board** British Masterclass (☎ 01237 451099 in UK), ESF (☎ 476 80 31 69), ESI (☎ 476 80 42 77)
**Guiding** Bureau des Guides (☎ 476 80 42 55), SAF Isère Heliskiing (☎ 476 80 65 49)

### CHILDREN
**Lift pass** 5–15yrs €129 for 6 days
**Ski & board school** as adults
**Kindergarten** (ski) La Garderie des Neiges (ESF) (☎ 476 80 31 69), (ski/non-ski) Les Eterlous (☎ 476 80 67 85), ESI Baby Club 476 80 42 77, (non-ski) Les Crapouilloux (☎ 476 11 39 23), Les Intrépides (☎ 476 11 21 61)

### FOOD AND DRINK
Coffee €2–2.50, bottle of house wine €15, small beer €3–3.50, soft drink €3, dish of the day €15

# Les Arcs

ALTITUDE 1,600–2,000m (5,249–6,560ft)                    map: see pages 176–177

## ❋ giant ski area ❋ extensive and varied pistes ❋ skiing convenience ❋ excellent off-piste opportunities

**Best for:** intermediates, snowboarders, families, high-mileage skiers
**Not recommended for:** those looking for traditional Alpine charm

**Paradiski** is the name given to the newly married resorts of Les Arcs and **La Plagne**. The opening of the 200-passenger double-decker Vanoise Express cable-car across the Ponturin gorge has created a joint ski area so vast that even an accomplished skier is hard put to travel from one end to the other and back in a single day. The construction of the £11-million link has inevitably resulted in a serious increase in the price of the lift pass. Both resorts have also surreptitiously changed the rules for children's lift passes by lowering the age threshold for free tickets.

Critics of the marriage question whether the expense of construction is justified. The number of skiers using the Vanoise Express has not exceeded the expected 30 per cent in either resort, but whether in the long term Paradiski will be paradise found or paradise lost remains to be seen.

Equally exciting for Les Arcs last season was the opening of the Intrawest-designed village of Arc 1950. Despite the unsightly presence of a crane throughout the season, the village developed instant atmosphere, and reporters who stayed there were enthusiastic: 'if I could afford to buy here, I certainly would. Guaranteed snow, sympathetic architecture, and a level of comfort you don't expect to find in a French apartment'. The village will continue to expand until its projected completion in 2008.

The original village of Les Arcs is on a plateau above Bourg-St-Maurice and is known as Arc 1600. When it opened in 1968 it embodied a novel concept – accommodation purposely built for convenience skiing, with doorstep access to the slopes. Further new ground was broken over the coming decade, with the idea of building more resort villages to share the same ski area. Accordingly, Arc 1800 was inaugurated in 1975, followed by Arc 2000.

Arc 1600 is still the most compact village and, for many die-hards, it is regarded as the friendliest place to stay. Arc 1800 is the largest, liveliest and most cosmopolitan and is divided into four sub-villages of Le Charvet, Le Chantel, Les Villards and Charmettoger. Arc 2000 sits in its own secluded bowl at the foot of the Aiguille Rouge (3,226m), close to much of the best skiing. Just below Arc 2000 is the new Arc 1950, to which it is linked by lift for skiers and foot passengers.

## On-piste
### top 3,226m (10,581ft), bottom 1,200m (3,936ft)

The 200km of pistes open to skiers in the Les Arcs area alone offer a tremendous variety of skiing. The resort has a wealth of long, smooth runs that start way above the tree-line and progress down through the woods to outlying villages linked by lift, such as Le Pré and Villaroger. A classic of this genre is the 7-km Aiguille Rouge black run from the resort's highest point down to Villaroger, a vertical drop of more than 2,000m.

### WHAT'S NEW
A 6-seater chair-lift at Vallandry
Hands-free ski pass

The greatest concentration of lifts, slopes and skiers is above Arc 1800, where wide, smooth cruising runs attract intermediates and families. There are more reds and blues on the way down to the outpost villages of Plan-Peisey and Vallandry, near the new Vanoise Express link to La Plagne.

For beginners, there are nursery slopes above all the villages, with the most extensive at 1800.

Les Arcs pioneered *ski évolutif*, an easy means of learning, in which you start on short skis and progress to longer ones as your technique and confidence improve. The resort has also long led the way in *les nouvelles glisses* – alternative ways of sliding down mountains – and is an important centre for snowboarding. There is an excellent terrain park between Arc 1800 and Arc 1600, incorporating seven jumps, a half-pipe and a boardercross course. Another claim to fame for this resort is its Olympic speed-skiing track on the face of the Aiguille Rouge. The track can be tested by members of the public, starting at various heights according to experience and sheer pluck.

## Off-piste
In fresh snow conditions, Les Arcs' most exhilarating and steepest powder skiing is below the Aiguille Rouge. There is also decent off-piste in the bowl beneath the Crête de l'Homme, behind the Aiguille Grive and Aiguille Rouge on the south-western edge of the Arc 1800 ski area. However, the accessibility of La Plagne via the Vanoise Express opens up some truly outstanding powder skiing. In terms of safety and finding the best terrain, it really does pay to hire a guide for all off-piste ventures.

## Tuition and guiding
The French Ski School (ESF) operates in the main resort villages in Les Arcs. Ski and snowboard classes are offered at all levels. The smaller school, Arc Aventures, is the main competition in Arc 1800. Spirit 1950 is a new school in the new village ('very capable instruction from a friendly, helpful teacher'). Optimum is a British-run ski school based in Villaroger. Initial Snow is based in Bourg St Maurice, with offices in Arc 1600, 1800 and 2000, taking skiers and riders to the other Haute Tarentaise resorts also. Also in Bourg St Maurice is Darentasia, which specialises in small groups for freeride, off-piste, and parapente.

## Mountain restaurants
Lunching at high altitude is improving in Les Arcs, with plenty of places to eat, but these receive mixed reports: 'wine lists were fabulous and good value for money, but ordinary food a bit expensive', said one reporter, and 'poor-quality food at rip-off prices', complained another. However, the

Aiguille Grive offers 'great food, great value, in a lovely setting', and Blanche Murée is recommended. The outpost villages have some excellent rustic-style restaurants, including Bélliou La Fumée, a 500-year-old hunting lodge in Pré-St-Esprit below Arc 2000. Les Chalets de l'Arc 2000 is decorated Savoyard style and serves traditional local dishes.

## Accommodation
About two-thirds of the skiers and snowboarders visiting Les Arcs stay in self-catering apartments including those in the new village of Arc 1950 (☎ 479 07 68 00 or 020-7584 2841 in UK), while a smattering of hotels and two large Club Meds at Arc 1800 and Arc 2000 (☎ 0845 367 6767 in UK) account for almost all the remainder. There are virtually no catered chalets. The new Arc 1950 apartments include features that will be familiar to people who have skied in North America, such as spacious, condominium-style living areas and outdoor hot-tubs. Le Prince des Cimes and Les Jardins are two new apartment buildings in Arc 1950. Also luxurious, although more compact, are Les Chalets des Neiges and Chalet Altitude apartments in Arc 2000, and the piste-side Les Alpages du Chantel apartments ('fantastic swimming-pool') above Arc 1800.

The top hotels in 1800 are the three-star Maeva Hotel du Golf (☎ 479 41 43 43) at the edge of Le Charvet, and Grand Hotel Mercure Coralia (☎ 479 07 65 00) in Charmettoger. In Arc 1600 are three-star La Cachette (☎ 479 07 70 50), which has won a reputation as one of the best family hotels in the Alps, as well as the smaller, simpler Hotel Béguin (☎ 479 07 72 61) and Hotel Explorers (☎ 479 04 16 00). Arc 2000's hotels are Les Mélèzes (☎ 479 07 50 50) and the Aiguille Rouge (☎ 479 07 57 07), which was strongly criticised by one reporter as 'a scruffy, decrepit, uncaring and uncomfortable joint'. The other option is to stay down in the valley town of Bourg-St-Maurice, which links directly into the lift system via a funicular to Arc 1600, and is convenient for visiting other resorts such as **Val d'Isère**. The 24-room Hostellerie du Petit-St-Bernard (☎ 479 07 04 32) has a renowned restaurant. La Petite Auberge (☎ 479 07 05 86), on the edge of town (less convenient for the funicular) is smaller still and run by an English couple.

# Eating in and out

The best choice of restaurants is at Arc 1800. The pricy, designer-rustic Casa Mia enjoys an excellent reputation, along with Onglet and Marmite in Le Charvet and Le Coq Hardy in Villard. The large L'Equipe remains popular, and Le Chalet de Bouvier is new. La Casa is an Italian restaurant at Arc 1950. In Arc 2000, Latino Lococafé and Pierre Chaud have both won praise. L'Arc à L'Os below 1600 serves spectacular Savoyarde dishes with novel flourishes. L'Ancolie at Nancroix, five minutes by bus or taxi from the Vanoise Express terminus, attracts gourmets from a wide radius. If you are self-catering, prices are lower and the variety much wider at the two hypermarkets on the outskirts of Bourg. Arc 1800 has the best selection of food shops.

# Après-ski

For all-night revellers and seekers of chic après-ski venues, Les Arcs has little to compete with the likes of Val d'Isère or Courchevel 1850. 'Après-ski in Arc 1800 is truly dreadful,' complained one reporter, even though it does have several lively bars and nightspots, such as the Fairway and Apocalypse nightclubs, the J.O. bar and Le Benji Bar. In Arc 2000, Red Rock bar draws a crowd from when the lifts close until the wee hours – the alternatives being the new Crazy Fox and The Whistler pubs. Arc 1600 is more muted, with activity centred on the Arcelle disco. Arc 1950 is quieter still, although Les Belles Pintes pub is a welcome addition.

# Childcare

Nearly all the adult ski and snowboard schools offer tuition for children. Hotel La Cachette in Arc 1600 has a crèche for infants from four months to two years, and a mini-club for under-twelves. Les Pommes des Pins in 1800 caters for kids aged one to six. The Pom d'Api nursery in Bourg is said to be 'excellent and accommodating'.

# Les Arcs: At a glance

**Tel** 33 479 07 12 57
**Email** lesarcs@lesarcs.com
**Website** www.lesarcs.com

## GETTING THERE
**Airports** Chambéry 2hrs, Geneva 2½hrs, Lyon 2½hrs
**Rail** Eurostar from Waterloo and Ashford to Bourg-St-Maurice 15km, buses and funicular to Arc 1600
**Road** autoroute to Albertville, steep climb from Bourg-St-Maurice

## THE SKIING
**Linked/nearby resorts** Bourg-St-Maurice, Peisey–Nancroix, La Plagne, Le Pré, Vallandry, Villaroger
**Total of trails/pistes** 200km in Les Arcs–Peisey Vallandry (5% beginner, 56% easy, 27% intermediate, 12% difficult), 425km in Paradiski area
**Lifts in area** 141 in Paradiski: 1🚡 16🚟 66🚠 58🎋
**Lift opening dates** 4 December 2004 to 30 April 2005

## LIFT PASSES
**Area pass** Les Arcs only €181, Paradiski (covers linked Les Arcs/La Plagne area and one day in each of Val d'Isère/Tignes, Pralognan–La-Vanoise, Les Saisies) €225, both for 6 days

**Pensioners** Les Arcs only 60–71yrs €150, Paradiski 60–71yrs €191, both for 6 days

## TUITION
**Ski & board** 1600: ESF (☎ 479 07 43 09), Initial Snow (☎ 612 45 72 91). 1800: Arc Aventures (☎ 479 07 41 28), ESF (☎ 479 07 40 31), Initial Snow, Ski Virages (☎ 479 07 78 82). 1950: Spirit 1950 (☎ 479 04 25 72). 2000: ESF (☎ 479 07 47 52), Initial Snow. Bourg St Maurice: Darentasia (☎ 479 04 16 81), Initial Snow. Villaroger: Optimum (☎ 01992 561085 in UK)
**Guiding** Bureau des Guides (☎ 479 07 71 19)

## CHILDREN
**Lift pass** Les Arcs only 6–13yrs €136, Paradiski 6–13yrs €169, both for 6 days
**Ski & board school** Arc Aventures, ESF, Initial Snow, Ski Virages
**Kindergarten** 1600: (ski/non-ski) La Cachette (☎ 479 07 70 50). 1800: (ski/non-ski) Pommes des Pins (☎ 479 04 24 31). 2000: (ski/non-ski) Les Marmottons (☎ 479 07 64 25). Bourg-St-Maurice: (non-ski) Pom d'Api (☎ 479 07 59 31)

## FOOD AND DRINK
Coffee €2–3, bottle of house wine €12, small beer €2.50–3.50, soft drink €3.20, dish of the day €12–14

# Avoriaz

**ALTITUDE 1,800m (5,904ft)**                                      map: see page 179

## ❄ vast ski area ❄ skiing and snowboarding for all standards
## ❄ dramatic setting ❄ car-free resort

> **Best for:** high-mileage cruisers, snowboarders, cross-country skiers, families
>
> **Not recommended for:** non-skiers, early-season skiers

Avoriaz is the highest resort in the **Portes du Soleil**, a long-established circuit of a dozen villages that straddles the Swiss border. The published statistics refer to 650km of piste (although how this figure is arrived at is best not examined) served by 207 lifts that are regularly upgraded, to create a well-linked circus covering vast tracts of land bordered by Lac Léman. In reality, the Portes du Soleil consists of a series of naturally separate ski areas. Most are joined by awkward and often confusing mountain links, while a few, such as St-Jean d'Aulps, Val d'Illiez and Abondance, are entirely independent.

> **WHAT'S NEW**
>
> Le Fornet chair upgraded to a 6-person detachable chair-lift
> Zore lift replaced by a quad-chair
> Widening of Zore and Tetras pistes

The region might well be considered to be one of Europe's greatest overall ski areas were it not for one major fault: it is too low. With a top height of only 2,466m and the villages mostly below 1,200m, snow cover is by no means guaranteed in the Portes du Soleil and the links are liable to rupture at any time, especially if there is a strong wind. Avoriaz, at 1,800m, is the 'safest' destination for snow in early April. When cover is poor or non-existent elsewhere, the overcrowding here can become unacceptable, but keen skiers and snowboarders should still base themselves at this end of the circuit, where the slopes are the most challenging.

While it is possible to complete a tour of the main Portes du Soleil resorts in one day, this actually involves limited enjoyable skiing and a considerable amount of time spent on lifts.

The overall Portes du Soleil piste map is confusing, but fortunately individual maps covering the different areas are available from tourist offices. Snow-users are advised to carry passports as well as two sets of currency. Although Switzerland willingly accepts euros in border areas, the rate is not always advantageous to visitors.

Avoriaz is mainly a collection of wood-clad apartment buildings dramatically perched on the edge of a cliff far above **Morzine** and built in what was for the 1960s a truly futuristic style. The French government recently declared it a Landmark of the Twentieth Century. Much has been done to revamp the original façades, and the 'rabbit-hutch' Elinka and Saskia buildings have been gutted to provide a smaller number of better-sized apartments. The newer constructions in the Falaise and Festival *quartiers* are altogether more attractive.

The resort is reached either by a narrow, winding road or by cable-car from the hamlet of Les Prodains near Morzine. A vehicle has no useful purpose in car-free Avoriaz, and the car park is expensive (€40–70 per week). Transport to your apartment or hotel is via horse-drawn sleigh, snow tractor or on foot. When not on skis, moving around is made easier by public lifts within the *résidences* to different levels of this steep resort. The busiest area is around the foot of the nursery slopes by the supermarkets, bars, nightclubs and restaurants.

## On-piste
### top 2,466m (8,090ft) bottom 1,000m (3,280ft)

The skiing is suited to all standards. Above the village is an extension of the main nursery slopes, with a variety of lifts serving a series of confidence-building green runs

linked with the lifts coming up from
Morzine.

The best skiing is on both sides of the
Swiss border, reached by two high-speed
chairs from Avoriaz. This is the top of La
Chavanette – more commonly known as
The Wall – which is one of Europe's most
notorious black pistes and which takes you
down towards **Les Crosets**, **Champéry** and
the rest of the Portes du Soleil. A sign at the
top warns that it is to be attempted only by
experts, and the initial angle of descent is
such that you cannot see what lies ahead.
Beginners and less accomplished skiers can
ride the chair-lift down.

On the Swiss side, Les Crosets sits above
the tree-line, surrounded by abundant wide
pistes, some of them north-facing but most
of them sunny. From here there are
connections with **Champoussin** and
**Morgins**. Morgins has little skiing on the
approach side from Champoussin, but it
includes an excellent north-facing red run
cut through the woods above the village.
Those who wish to continue skiing the
Portes du Soleil circuit must walk across the
village or take a short bus ride to the
nursery slopes and the lifts for Super-Châtel
and France. In strong contrast to the
sometimes bleak ski-fields of Avoriaz, the
pistes here wind through the trees and are
connected by a series of short drag-lifts.

The Morclan chair from Super-Châtel up
to 1,970m serves a challenging mogul field.
The top of this chair is the departure point
for Torgon, one of the farther extremities of
the Portes du Soleil, back across the border
in Switzerland.

The circuit breaks down at the village of
**Châtel** and, whichever way you are
travelling, the link cannot be made on skis.
You have to take a bus across the village to
the gondola up to Linga; this is the first of a
long chain of lifts and pistes towards
Avoriaz and provides one of the best
intermediate playgrounds in the region,
with a seemingly endless variation of terrain
and gradients.

More good skiing for experts is to be
found in Les Hauts Forts sector, reached by
a chair-lift just above the resort. There,
skiers can explore demanding ungroomed
slopes in and above the tree-line. Le Plan
Brazy is the starting point for a challenging
FIS downhill course that takes you all the
way down to Les Prodains and the bottom
of the cable-car.

Avoriaz was the first resort in Europe to
appreciate the importance of snowboarding
when the sport was in the early stages of
development. It was also the first (in 1993)
to build a half-pipe and is recognised as
one of the world's major snowboarding
centres. The resort now has three terrain
parks, including the La Chapelle park,
specifically designed for youngsters and
beginners. The Tête aux Boeufs, which is
120m long and 4.5m high, plays host to a
number of international snowboard
competitions.

## Off-piste
Although Les Hauts Forts sector above the
resort provides considerable challenge, the
best powder runs are found on both sides of
the Swiss border. After a fresh snowfall
various itineraries parallel to The Wall can
be exhilarating. The area is prone to
considerable avalanche danger, and the
services of a qualified guide are essential.
Other off-piste opportunities include the
Crêtes, Le Fornet and La Suisse.

## Tuition and guiding
Avoriaz has the ESI Ecole de Glisse and the
French Ski School (ESF). Both schools also
teach snowboarding, in healthy competition
with Emery Snowboard School and Free
Ride. The British Alpine Ski and
Snowboarding School received a number of
positive reports last winter. As one reader
commented: 'the advantage of being taught
by a native English-speaker is
overwhelming'.

## Mountain restaurants
The Portes du Soleil offers a mixed bag of
eateries, ranging from overcrowded self-
services to wonderful old huts off the
beaten track. Prices are generally high on
both sides of the border, and there are
simply not enough restaurants. Coquoz at
Planachaux has a circular open fire and
offers wonderful local Swiss specialities.
Les Lindarets, the hamlet just north of
Avoriaz, has the best concentration of
eating-places with competitive prices, and
La Chanterelle at the foot of the Chéry
Nord chair is warmly recommended too.
La Cabushe near Le Ranfoilly is 'simple,
but brilliant value', while Plaine Dranse is
'where the locals eat, so prices must be
fair'.

## Accommodation

Most visitors to Avoriaz stay in apartments. Bookings can be made through Pierre & Vacances (☎ 825 82 08 20), Agence Immobilière des Dromonts (☎ 450 74 00 03), Agence Immobilière des Hauts Forts (☎ 450 74 16 08) and Selectis (☎ 450 74 13 33).

The two three-star hotels are the recently renovated Dromonts (☎ 450 74 08 11), and La Neige et Roc (☎ 450 79 03 21) down at Les Prodains. Location within the resort is of no significance for skiing purposes as all skiing is door-to-door, with some of the village streets doubling as pistes.

## Eating in and out

Avoriaz boasts a choice of 32 restaurants, most of which are rather overpriced. Two gastronomic eateries, La Table du Marché and Restaurant Gastronomique, are in Les Dromonts hotel. Others include La Réserve and Le Petit Vatel. Le Bistro opposite Le Village des Enfants is said to be 'good, but expensive'. Les Trappeurs is above Résidence Le Sepia and specialises in Savoyard fare, with five types of *croûtes aux fromages*.

## Après-ski

The Place, Shooter's and the Globe are pubs with live, non-French music. Le Choucas and Le Fest are hang-outs for riders; the latter offers live music and is usually not too crowded. Pub Le Tavaillon was described by one reporter as 'the British nerve centre of Avoriaz'. The nightclubs are said to be generally overpriced and empty, except on striptease nights, when audience participation is invited. Le Festival disco charges an entrance fee 'but is well worth the money'. Globe Trotters Café and Le Yéti are two local bars.

## Childcare

Le Village des Enfants/Le Village Snowboard in Avoriaz has a justified reputation as one of the better childcare establishments in France. Children from three years old are taught in the centre of the resort, using methods developed by the celebrated French ski champion Annie Famose. Younger non-skiing children are looked after by Les P'tits Loups day nursery, of which we have good reports.

## Avoriaz: At a glance

**Tel** 33 450 74 02 11
**Email** info@avoriaz.com
**Website** www.avoriaz.com

### GETTING THERE
**Airport** Geneva 2hrs
**Rail** Thonon les Bains 43km, Cluses 40km
**Road** take the Cluses exit 18 off the Autoroute Blanche towards Taninges and Morzine

### THE SKIING
**Linked/nearby resorts** Abondance, Champéry, Champoussin, La Chapelle d'Abondance, Châtel, Les Crosets, Les Gets, Montriond, Morgins, Morzine, St-Jean d'Aulps, Torgon, Val d'Illiez
**Total of trails/pistes** 150km in Avoriaz (8% beginner, 55% easy, 27% intermediate, 10% difficult), 650km in Portes du Soleil
**Lifts in area** 207 in Portes du Soleil: 14🚠 82🚡 111🎿
**Lift opening dates** mid-December 2004 to end of April 2005

### LIFT PASSES
**Area pass** Portes du Soleil (covers 14 resorts) €176 for 6 days
**Pensioners** Portes du Soleil 60yrs and over €141 for 6 days

### TUITION
**Ski & board** British Alpine Ski and Snowboarding School (☎ 01237 451099 in UK), Emery Snowboard School (☎ 450 74 12 64), ESF (☎ 450 74 05 65), ESI Ecole de Glisse (☎ 450 74 02 18), Free Ride (☎ 450 74 00 36)
**Guiding** Mont Blanc Helicopters (☎ 450 74 22 44)

### CHILDREN
**Lift pass** Portes du Soleil 5–16yrs €118 for 6 days
**Ski & board school** as adults
**Kindergarten** (ski) Le Village des Enfants/Le Village Snowboard (☎ 450 74 04 46), (non-ski) Les P'tits Loups (☎ 450 74 00 38)

### FOOD AND DRINK
Coffee €2–3, bottle of house wine €12, small beer €3–3.50, soft drink €3, dish of the day €12–15

# Chamonix and Argentière

ALTITUDE 1,035m (3,396ft)                                      map: see page 180

❋ rugged off-piste skiing ❋ beautiful scenery ❋ cosmopolitan atmosphere
❋ short airport transfer ❋ outstanding mountain guides

**Best for:** expert skiers and
snowboarders, non-skiers, night-owls

**Not recommended for:** beginners to
lower intermediates, families, fair-
weather skiers, nervous skiers, those
wanting skiing convenience

Chamonix is truly different from any other
ski resort in the world. Anyone who has
learned the basics on the rolling pastures of
the Austrian Tyrol or in the purpose-built
'ski factories' of the French Tarentaise is in
for a stupendous shock. Acknowledged as
the climbing and extreme skiing capital of
the world, this is high Alpine territory,
where misjudging the severity of a run or
the sudden changes of weather above
3,000m can cost a life.

Not so much a single resort as a chain of
unconnected ski areas set along both sides
of the valley dominated by Mont Blanc,
Chamonix is glitteringly beautiful and
deceptively tranquil on a sunny day. On
stormy days, of which there are many, it is a
brooding place, menaced by razor-sharp
peaks and tumbling walls of ice.

Chamonix town itself is based around a
core of hotels and villas built at the end of
the nineteenth century. The original village
square is fully pedestrianised, and the main
street is closed to traffic during daylight
hours. The bus service links the base-
stations with moderate efficiency, but
having a car is a distinct advantage.

Along with a string of lesser hamlets
scattered along the road, the attractive little
village of Argentière, situated 8km away up
the road towards the Swiss border, acts as
an alternative bed base for the skiing.

## On-piste
top 3,842m (12,605ft) bottom 1,035m (3,396ft)

Four main base-stations give access to most
of the skiing. The only one within easy
walking distance of the town is the
celebrated cable-car that climbs the Aiguille
du Midi, a 3,842-m granite needle that is
the starting point for some of the most
beautiful off-piste skiing in the Alps.

A short bus ride away, the linked area of
Le Brévent and La Flégère is an often
underrated circuit with excellent terrain for
all levels of intermediate and advanced skier
and snowboarder. However, the toughest
skiing lies at Argentière, access point for the
Grands Montets. This is a truly magnificent
mountain for expert skiers and riders –
steep, complex and dramatic with seemingly
unlimited possibilities. It is reached by the
80-person cable-car to Lognan or the high-
speed quad-chair to Plan Joran from just
outside the village.

The Grands Montets cable-car at Lognan
is extremely popular despite the €5
supplement payable on top of the Mont
Blanc lift pass (the first two rides are
included) and the 200 slippery metal steps
leading from the top-station to the start of
the step descents.

Still further up the valley, Le Tour has
beginner slopes and some enjoyable
intermediate terrain. The Tête de Balme
gives access to delightful skiing down
towards Vallorcine in Switzerland.

Other easier slopes are scattered along
the valley, but this is not a resort that
recommends itself to novices or even
second-weekers. The terrain is steep and the
chances of linking up before nightfall with
more experienced family or friends are slim.

The Grands Montets and Le Tour both
have terrain parks but the majority of
snowboarders here are found shredding the
powder. Day trips are possible to
neighbouring **Les Houches**, but this is no
longer covered by the lift pass.

## Off-piste
On powder mornings the rush for the
Grands Montets is fierce, but the area is so
enormous that skiing it out quickly is even
beyond the powers of Europe's most
dedicated first-track pack. The glacier is
wild and dangerous terrain, a web of

shifting crevasses and seracs, and the services of an expert and qualified local guide are essential. The most challenging descent is the Pas de Chèvre, a run from the top of Bochard via one of several extreme couloirs down to the Mer de Glace.

No visit to Chamonix is complete without a ride up the two-stage Aiguille du Midi cable-car, the highest in Europe. The first stage gives access to the Pré des Rochers, a delightful steep powder run back into Chamonix. The top of the second stage is the departure point for the 22-km glacier run down the Vallée Blanche, which, depending on the route your guide takes, is either a gentle cruise through some of the most awesome mountain scenery in the world or a character-building encounter with ice-screws, karabiners and the other ironmongery of ski mountaineering.

## WHAT'S NEW
High-speed 6-seater chair replaces Herse 2-seater

The easiest route can be attempted (and, once you start, there is no alternative but to finish it) by any intermediate who can ski parallel. The trickiest part comes early on, in the shape of the infamous steps cut into the spine of the ridge from the cable-car station. To avoid hidden and yawning crevasses you must follow your guide's tracks, but the gradient is gentle enough. The return to Chamonix is by rack-and-pinion railway from Montenvers or via a short climb and a long descent down a narrow path and short piste into the centre of Chamonix.

## Tuition and guiding
The Chamonix branch of the French Ski School (ESF) offers traditional teaching methods. Sensation Ski Ecole Internationale takes a wilder approach to the learning curve. We have particularly positive reports of Evolution 2: 'expert, friendly guiding with plenty of tips for off-piste and a well-organised day of heli-skiing through the tunnel in Courmayeur', and 'if you want to learn how to ski steeps, then these are the people to teach you'. We have no reports of the other ski schools. The ESF also has an office in Argentière, and Summit Ski Montagne is the specialist board school in Argentière.

## Mountain restaurants
The Bergerie above the top of the Brévent cable-car has 'excellent food in a warm

atmosphere'. Plan Joran at Lognan is probably the best mountain restaurant in the valley. La Crèmerie du Glacier in the woods at the bottom of the Grands Montets is warmly praised for its special of *croûte fromage* ('one of the best dishes I have ever eaten'). Robinson, tucked away on the cross-country track on the outskirts of Chamonix, is 'a wonderful atmospheric lunch spot known only to the locals'.

## Accommodation
Chamonix offers the full spectrum, from youth hostels to four-star hotels, plus a wide choice of chalets and apartments. All bookings should be made through the Chamonix Reservations Centre (☎ 450 53 23 33). The most luxurious hotels are Le Hameau Albert 1er and L'Auberge du Bois Prin, both owned by the Carrier brothers. Hotel Mont-Blanc is the third four-star, and a fourth, Grand Hotel Des Alpes (☎ 450 55 37 80), is opening for the 2004–5 season. In the three-star category, the Sapinière is said to be 'very comfortable and hospitable', Hotel Richemond is popular, while hotels Alpina and Gustavia are centrally located.

Hotel Le Dahu (☎ 450 54 01 55) in Argentière is recommended for comfort and food. In the same village, La Chapelle d'Elise (☎ 450 54 56 35) is a converted chapel that sleeps just two people in bijou comfort. Les Chalets de Philippe (☎ 450 54 56 35), in the nearby hamlet of Lavancher, offer accommodation of a similar luxurious style in tiny converted wood-and-stone *mazots* (ancient barns).

## Eating in and out
No one denies that the Michelin-rated Le Hameau Albert 1er has the best food in Chamonix, but prices have risen to such a level that even the seriously wealthy hesitate to visit the restaurant except on special occasions. The hotel's second restaurant, Les Fermes, is much more relaxed. L'Auberge du Bois Prin follows Le Hameau Albert 1er closely in quality and price, and the food at the Hotel Eden in Les Praz is also recommended. Reporters praised the Rusticana ('exceptionally good meal') in Argentière.

## Après-ski
'The après-ski is wild,' remarked one reporter. The ski- and board-mad early-evening trade starts at 5pm at bars such as

the Chambre Neuf. The video bars of Le Choucas and Expedition are fashionable, and there is no shortage of lively watering-holes along the rue du Docteur Paccard. The bars empty at about 7.30pm, when snow-users return to their chalets or apartments for dinner. From about 10.30pm the partying starts up again at Arbat, which has the best live music in town. Wild Wallabies is a top choice for riders, as is Jekyll and Hyde, while real late-nighters end up at the BPM or the Arbate. The Bumble Bee, Bar du Moulin, La Cantina and the Bar d'Up in Chamonix are all popular. Le Pub and the Garage in Chamonix Sud are also well frequented; the latter is a large basement bar incorporating half a truck and various motorbikes and is packed until the early hours. Dick's Tea-Bar has a branch here.

In Argentière, the Office Bar has been redecorated and is the favoured British watering-hole. The Stone Bar is also popular.

## Childcare

The ESF schools in Chamonix and Argentière have classes for children from the age of four; they also have a crèche with full daycare. The Panda Club in Argentière provides care for children from six months, and Panda-Ski offers small skiers daily sessions in the Jardin des Neiges near the Lognan lift station. A municipal crèche, Halte Garderie, in Chamonix provides entertainment for children aged between eighteen months and six years, but this is available only through tour operators. There is a magic carpet lift.

# Chamonix and Argentière: At a glance

**Tel** 33 450 53 00 24
**Email** info@chamonix.com
**Website** www.chamonix.com

## GETTING THERE
**Airport** Geneva 1hr
**Rail** station in Chamonix
**Road** Autoroute Blanche from Geneva

## THE SKIING
**Linked/nearby resorts** Courmayeur, Les Houches, Megève, St-Gervais
**Total of trails/pistes** 150km (52% easy, 36% intermediate, 12% difficult)
**Lifts in area** 46: 1🚠 12🚡 17🚡 16🎿
**Lift opening dates** early December 2004 to 8 May 2005

## LIFT PASSES
**Area pass** Cham'Ski (covers Chamonix valley except Les Houches) €181, Ski Pass Mont Blanc (covers all local resorts including Courmayeur, Les Houches, Megève) €205, both for 6 days
**Pensioners** Cham'Ski 60yrs and over €154 for 6 days, Ski Pass Mont Blanc €174, both for 6 days

## TUITION
**Ski & board** Argentière: ESF (☎ 450 54 00 12), Summit Ski Montagne (☎ 450 54 05 11).

Chamonix: ESF (☎ 450 53 22 57), Evolution 2 (☎ 450 55 90 22), Kailish Adventure (☎ 450 53 18 99), Sensation Ski Ecole Internationale (☎ 450 53 56 46), Stages Bernard Muller (☎ 450 53 18 99), Summit Ski Montagne (☎ 450 54 05 11).
**Guiding** Association Internationale des Guides du Mont-Blanc (☎ 450 53 27 05), Compagnie des Guides de Chamonix (☎ 450 53 00 88), Mont Blanc Ski Tours (☎ 450 53 82 16), Roland Stieger (☎ 450 54 43 53), Sensation Ski Ecole Internationale (☎ 450 55 94 26), Stages Vallençant (☎ 450 54 05 11), Yak & Yeti (☎ 450 53 53 67)

## CHILDREN
**Lift pass** Cham'Ski 4–11yrs €127, 12–15yrs €154. Ski Pass Mont Blanc 4–11yrs €164. All for 6 days
**Ski & board school** as adults
**Kindergarten** Argentière: (ski/non-ski) ESF, Panda Club (☎ 450 54 08 88), Chamonix: (ski/non-ski) ESF, (non-ski) Halte Garderie (☎ 450 53 36 68)

## FOOD AND DRINK
Coffee €2–2.50, bottle of house wine €10–15, small beer €3.50–4, soft drink €3.50, dish of the day €15–16

# Courchevel

ALTITUDE 1,300–1,850m (4,265–6,068ft)                        map: see page 181

## ✳ giant ski area ✳ big vertical drop ✳ high standard of accommodation ✳ skiing convenience

> **Best for:** skiers and snowboarders of all standards, gourmet skiers, hedonists, off-piste skiers, families
>
> **Not recommended for:** those on a budget (1850), people wanting an intimate ski area, non-skiers

Courchevel is the unquestioned queen of **The Trois Vallées**, a resort for everyone, regardless of the depth of his or her pocket. At the top end of the scale, its clutch of four-star de luxe hotels (France does not have five-stars) and gilded chalets has few mountain rivals for comfort, and none for cost. It caters for a cosseted international clientèle for whom prices are irrelevant details on credit-card statements. At the lower end of the scale, self-catering couples and families stay in modest apartments and make their own packed lunches and sneak at midday onto the 'picnic forbidden' sun terrace of mountain restaurants to eat their sandwiches.

Both groups have one common desire: to explore as much as they can, in a week or a fortnight, of what is justly billed as the world's largest truly linked ski area. Indeed, the Trois Vallées is now so vast – it continues to extend into a fourth valley, the Maurienne – that none of the principal players can agree on the correct total of lifts. The most reliable statistics claim 189 lifts serving 600km of piste.

What puts the Trois Vallées ski-lengths ahead of its rivals in the super-circus league is the range and sophistication of the resorts it contains, coupled with the variety of mainly intermediate skiing. However, the Trois Vallées still provides more than adequate scope for those of greater or lesser ability.

Courchevel is not one but four quite separate resorts at different altitudes above the Bozel Valley, linked on piste but with little else in common. A free bus service connects the different villages.

Courchevel 1850 is the international resort with the jet-set image. Like its stylistic rival, Megève, a high proportion of its designer-clad visitors come here to see and to be seen. A covered mall houses expensive boutiques, and a couple of supermarkets cater for the more mundane needs of self-caterers. The secluded Jardin Alpin sector is a Millionaire's Row of sumptuous chalets and shockingly expensive hotels tucked away in trees that provide at least an illusion of privacy.

Courchevel 1650 is 200m vertical lower down both the mountain and the price scale. Many would argue that this is *le vrai* Courchevel, with its year-round population and atmosphere of the farming community it once was.

Courchevel 1550 is away from the heart of the skiing. It is little more than an attractive cluster of apartment buildings, chalets and a few hotels, but looks set to expand as it becomes better integrated into the Trois Vallées. A new six-person lift up to 1850 is being installed for this season, and the main piste has been widened.

Le Praz (Courchevel 1300) is a farming village at the foot of the lift system and a cheap base for Courchevel's skiing. Two gondolas ('always free of queues') swiftly take you up towards the Col de la Loze, which connects with **La Tania**, or to Courchevel 1850.

> ## WHAT'S NEW
> Dou du Midi fixed chair and Les Tovets drag-lift replaced by 6-person detachable chair
> Widening of the Plantrey piste

## On-piste
### top 2,738m (8,983ft) bottom 1,300m (4,265ft)

From La Croisette – the giant central lift station at Courchevel 1850 – a gondola rises to La Vizelle at 2,659m, and at the half-way station you can swap to a giant cable-car that makes a rapid ascent to La Saulire, the high point of the ski area and the link with **Méribel** and the rest of the Trois Vallées.

Courchevel 1550 is below La Croisette and can be reached directly by the newly widened piste. To ski down to Le Praz you must first take one of a choice of lifts up to the Col de la Loze, starting point for Jockeys and Jean Blanc, two demanding black pistes which bring you down to the farming village.

Courchevel 1650 has its own large ski area for all standards, which offers some of the best piste skiing in the region. Because it is off the beaten track, the runs here remain wonderfully uncrowded at times when the main home-run motorway from Saulire to La Croisette resembles an ant-hill.

The trails surrounding the altiport at Courchevel are ideal for beginners, with enough length to help build confidence. Once the basics have been conquered, the area lends itself to easy exploration.

On the Verdons piste, impossibly high moguls are interspersed with steep canyons for the use of skiers as well as snowboarders. Plantrey boasts a terrain park with an obstacle course, dedicated trick space and a giant half-pipe. A third terrain park has been created at Biolley.

## Off-piste

Roc Merlet above Courchevel 1650 is the jump-off point for a glorious descent around the shoulder into the Avals Valley, which brings you back, after a short walk, to 1650.

The infamous Courchevel Couloirs, reached from the top of the Saulire cable-car, were once marked as pistes but have been re-graded as off-piste itineraries. In good conditions they are by no means as difficult as they appear from below. However, care should be taken on the entry route, which is prone to ice. When snow cover is sufficient it is also possible to ski from Saulire all the way down to Bozel, a descent of 2,000m.

## Tuition and guiding

The French Ski School (ESF) has more than 600 instructors here. Magic in Motion has a sound reputation, although reporters commented that not all instructors speak fluent English. Supreme in Courchevel 1850 is an all-British school of which we received mixed reports. One reporter said: 'a great lesson from an expert and really friendly

instructor', while another complained: 'what was a small specialist school is in danger of becoming part of the establishment – with customary loss of service'. We continue to receive favourable reports of New Generation (also known as Le Ski School).

## Mountain restaurants

Reporters praise Bel-Air, at the top of the Courchevel 1650 gondola, as 'the best-value waiter-service restaurant in the region'. Higher up the mountain and the price scale, Le Cap Horn offers gourmet dishes served by liveried waiters ('standards are rigidly maintained, with some of the best food in the resort'). Rival Chalet de Pierres is a resort institution 'but you pay handsomely for the privilege of lunching in style beside the piste'. Le Petit Savoyard and L'Eterlou at 1650 are warmly recommended.

## Accommodation

The Byblos de Neige (☎ 479 00 98 00) is the glitzy centrepiece, while Les Airelles (☎ 479 09 38 38) is more discreet. Hotel des Neiges (☎ 479 03 03 77) is an established favourite and the Trois Vallées (☎ 479 08 00 12) is 'intimate and charming'. The family-run, three-star La Sivolière (☎ 479 08 08 33) provides four-star comfort and has a health centre. Le Mélézin (☎ 479 08 01 33) is the luxurious Alpine headquarters of Amanresorts. Le Saint Joseph (☎ 479 08 16 16) is designed to look like a traditional Savoyard hotel, with antiques, retro décor and the service of a bygone age. Ducs de Savoie (☎ 479 08 03 00), Le Lana (☎ 479 08 01 10), Kilamanjaro (☎ 479 01 46 46) and La Loze (☎ 479 08 28 25) are also singled out for praise.

Courchevel 1650 consists mainly of chalets. However, the ski-in ski-out Hotel du Golf (☎ 479 00 92 92) 'cannot be beaten for convenience'. Le Praz contains the comfortable Hotel Les Peupliers (☎ 479 08 41 47) ('a delightful base from which to ski Courchevel without paying through the nose').

## Eating in and out

Courchevel 1850 abounds in fine restaurants, some of them at truly stratospheric prices. The Chabichou Hotel has two coveted Michelin stars, as does Le Bateau Ivre ('much better value than

London and a real gastronomic treat'). La Saulire (known as Jacques' Bar) in the square at 1850 offers *haute cuisine* at far more wallet-friendly prices and is 'a resort institution with a passionate following'.

Restaurants at Courchevel 1650 are less Parisian in style and cost. L'Eterlou is 'family-run, welcoming and reasonably priced' and La Montagne is 'extremely popular on chalet-staff night off'. In Courchevel 1550 the Oeil de Boeuf is 'good, but rather smart'.

In Le Praz, the famous Bistro du Praz 'is still as good and as expensive as ever'. Hotel Les Peupliers, the original village inn, 'has much the best *haute cuisine* in the region. Why it does not have two Michelin stars is a mystery to me and other French devotees'.

## Après-ski

At Prends Ta Luge et Tire-toi in the Forum complex at Courchevel 1850 you can surf the Net, have a drink or buy a snowboard. Le Grenier is usually the most crowded piano bar, while Le Pyggys Pub has a dedicated following. La Grange and Les Caves are the main, but prohibitively expensive, late-night venues.

At Courchevel 1650, Le Bubble is the 'in' place 'for a drink, catch up on your email – or both', while Le Plouc is a small, smoky and busy bar. At Courchevel 1550, après-ski revolves around La Taverne ('very French, very friendly') and the Glacier Bar ('full of British resort staff'). Chanrossa provides some of the best late-night action.

Le Praz is not the place for raucous nightlife. Its crêperie makes 'the best *vin chaud* in the business', and the Bar Brasserie is 'the only place with any life'.

## Childcare

All the villages are well served with ESF ski kindergartens, although we have received critical reports of the ESF in Courchevel 1850, which is said to be over-serious and 'chaotic during high-season weeks'. Many parents staying here feel that Le Praz has a better ski school. The instructors will come up to 1850 to collect children.

Magic in Motion in Courchevel 1850 runs lessons in English for four- to six-year-olds, and Supreme offers group lessons for children from age six during school holidays.

# Courchevel: At a glance

**Tel** 33 479 08 00 29
**Email** pro@courchevel.com
**Website** www.courchevel.com

## GETTING THERE
**Airports** Chambéry 2hrs, Lyon 2½hrs, Geneva 3hrs
**Rail** Eurostar from Waterloo and Ashford to Moûtiers, 25km away
**Road** autoroute to Albertville, steep climb from Moûtiers

## THE SKIING
**Linked/nearby resorts** Les Menuires, Méribel, St-Martin-de-Belleville, La Tania, Val Thorens
**Total of trails/pistes** 180km in Courchevel area (26% beginner, 27% easy, 36% intermediate, 11% difficult), 600km in Trois Vallées
**Lifts in area** 189 in Trois Vallées: 40🚠 68🚡 81🎿
**Lift opening dates** 11 December 2004 to 24 April 2005

## LIFT PASSES
**Area pass** Trois Vallées €204 for 6 days
**Pensioners** Trois Vallées 60–72yrs €164 for 6 days

## TUITION
**Ski & board** 1300: ESF (☎ 479 08 07 72). 1550: ESF (☎ 479 08 21 07). 1650: ESF (☎ 479 08 26 08). 1850: ESF (☎ 479 08 07 72), Magic in Motion (☎ 479 01 01 81), New Generation/Le Ski School (☎ 479 01 03 18), Ski Académie (☎ 479 08 11 99), Supreme (☎ 479 08 27 87)
**Guiding** Bureau des Guides (☎ 479 01 03 66)

## CHILDREN
**Lift pass** Trois Vallées 5–13yrs €153.50 for 6 days
**Ski & board school** as adults
**Kindergarten** 1300: (ski) ESF. 1550: (ski) ESF. 1650: (ski) ESF, Magic in Motion, Supreme (non-ski) Les Pitchounets 1650 (☎ 479 08 33 69). 1850: (ski) ESF, (non-ski) ESF Village des Enfants 1850 (☎ 479 08 08 47)

## FOOD AND DRINK
Coffee €3.60, bottle of house wine €14–20, small beer €3.50–5, soft drink €3.50–4, dish of the day €12–20

# Les Deux Alpes

ALTITUDE 1,650m (5,412ft)                                   map: see page 182

## ❄ large ski area ❄ snow-sure slopes ❄ modern lift system
## ❄ excellent children's facilities ❄ glacier skiing

**Best for:** snowboarders, intermediate cruisers, off-piste novices, families, night-owls

**Not recommended for:** beginners, those seeking a traditional Alpine village, people preferring quiet slopes, those wanting to ski back to the resort

This efficient and only partly purpose-built resort lies between Grenoble and Briançon, within easy reach of **Alpe d'Huez** in one direction and **Serre Chevalier** and **Montgenèvre** in the other. Its primary asset is the height of the skiing, which means that snow is assured at any stage of the season. The glacier is also open for summer skiing mid-June to September, and the resort is linked – by a 20-minute hike – to the top of neighbouring **La Grave**, which is one of the most dramatic off-piste ski areas in Europe.

Although Les Deux Alpes town itself is visually unappealing, it is by no means the worst example of modern French architecture. Both village and ski area are long and narrow, and there is less skiing terrain than one would imagine for such a long vertical drop.

A quieter, alternative base is the quaint old hamlet of Venosc in the Vénéon Valley below Les Deux Alpes. Its ancient cobbled streets are lined with craft shops and studios, and it has three extremely pleasant and inexpensive restaurants. The village is linked by an efficient modern gondola that you have to take down again at the end of the day, as you cannot ski back from the resort.

## On-piste
top 3,600m (11,808ft) bottom 1,600m (5,249ft)

At Les Deux Alpes it is easy to be confused by the multitude of lifts on the 220km of piste within a relatively confined area. Apart from a smaller, uncrowded sector to

the west of the village, between Pied Moutet at 2,339m and the Alpe du Mont de Lans, the bulk of the skiing is between the village and La Toura (2,600m) to the east. The principal lift is the Jandri Express jumbo gondola, which deposits skiers on the glacier in 45 minutes. It is prone to rush-hour queues, as are the alternative gondolas and chairs out of the resort.

Above the 2,600-m mid-station the terrain narrows down to a bottleneck, and Le Jandri pistes have 'too many skiers of too many ability levels thrown together'. The broad plateau on the Glacier du Mont de Lans provides extensive nursery slopes and even a sub-glacial funicular for novice skiers, for whom the very exposed drag-lifts are extremely daunting. However, 'the green runs up the mountain are incredibly busy every day and the queues are long', according to one reporter. A compensation is the excitement of being able to experience your first slither on skis high up the mountain with magnificent views. The slopes immediately above the village are steep, and learners can either download by gondola or take a green path, Chemin Demoiselles, from 2,200m to return to the village. However, this is 'only a narrow track, very crowded, icy in places, tiring and not at all enjoyable'.

Competent cruisers can enjoy themselves on most of the upper slopes at Les Deux Alpes, although less experienced skiers may find themselves overwhelmed by the steep homeward-bound runs, which can become crowded at the end of the day. One method of escaping from the mainstream skiing is to try one of the rare runs through the trees. There is an enjoyable piste down to the village of Bons at 1,300m, while Mont de Lans can be reached from both ski areas.

Experienced skiers and riders gravitate towards the Tête Moute area, which provides some of the steepest terrain on the mountain. They will be tempted to go straight from the Venosc end of the village by gondola to Le Diable. From here, the

Grand Diable chair reaches the Tête Moute itself, where steep, north-facing runs lead to Lac du Plan and onwards towards the Thuit chair. Le Diable offers a challenging and often mogulled 1,200-m descent to the village. One reporter noted that 'the last section just drops away into icy, inky blackness'. There are seven other black runs.

Riders rate the resort, and the layout of the pistes is such that they need never take a drag-lift. The terrain park is set up on La Toura piste in winter and moves to the glacier in the summer. Facilities include a boardercross course and a half-pipe, plus a barbecue and sound system. Each October the resort hosts the World Snowboard Meeting (along with the World Ski Meeting), which claims to be 'the highest and biggest exhibition of snowboarding on the planet'.

## Off-piste

Les Deux Alpes has enclosed bowl-skiing, which is ideal for those wanting to try off-piste for the first time. For seasoned deep-snow skiers there are a number of easily accessible (but not so easily skiable) couloirs. La Grave, one of the most exciting and scenic off-piste ski areas in the Alps, can be accessed from the top of the ski area via the Glacier du Mont de Lans.

## Tuition and guiding

The main ski schools are the French Ski School (ESF) ('very good') and the rival International Ski School (ESI). The British-run European Ski and Snowboard School offers tuition (in English) to classes of up to four pupils: 'I cannot speak highly enough of the teachers, who explained everything fully and taught with a high degree of understanding and patience,' said one reporter. Courses include video analysis and computerised ski simulators, and there is an extensive summer skiing programme in July. We have no reports on Ski Privilège. Primitive Snowboard School is the specialist for wannabe riders.

## Mountain restaurants

Les Deux Alpes receives few bouquets for its eight mountain restaurants, and, if it were not so inconvenient, more skiers might consider lunching in town or downloading by gondola to Venosc. The Panoramic ('friendly and efficient') is a convenient

meeting-point. The highest restaurant is Les Glaciers. Chalet de La Toura, over the back of the mountain, is 'in an excellent location with very good food', and La Fée Refuge is 'attractive and friendly but the menu choices are pedestrian'. La Meije offers a 'friendly, efficient service of local specialities at very reasonable prices', and La Patache and La Petite Marmite are also recommended.

## Accommodation

Most of the accommodation is in apartments, with the remainder in the resort's 40 hotels and pensions. The top end of the market boasts two four-star hotels, the Bérangère (☎ 476 79 24 11) and La Farendole (☎ 476 80 50 45), which both have indoor swimming-pools. There are ten three-star hotels and 16 two-stars. The Hotel-Club Edelweiss (☎ 476 79 21 22) is warmly recommended for its 'wonderful gourmet dinners, with local produce properly cooked and well presented; the staff were patient and helpful and the bedrooms large, if a little spartan'. It has a crèche for its small guests, as well as an evening entertainment programme. Hotel Les Marmottes (☎ 476 79 21 91) is 'superb, with a five-course dinner and large bedrooms'. Le Souleil d'Or (☎ 476 79 24 69) has 'friendly owners and decent accommodation', and Hotel Chalet Mounier (☎ 476 80 56 90) is praised for its 'wonderful feminine touch'. La Brunerie (☎ 476 79 22 23) is said to be 'a very good hotel for families, in a reasonable location for the skiing and the shopping. Hotel Côte Brune (☎ 476 80 54 89) is a family-run two-star hotel with an Austrian-style restaurant.

## Eating in and out

L'Abri and La Spaghetteria are both recommended for pizza and pasta. Blue Salmon Farm specialises in fish dishes and Il Caminetto is a much-praised Italian restaurant. Le P'tit Polyte is praised for its 'fabulous wine list'. Le Four à Bois is renowned for its regional specialities, while Le Saxo serves Tex-Mex cuisine, and La Patate is reputed to have 'a good atmosphere'. Hotel Chalet Mounier restaurant serves 'high-quality French cuisine at reasonable prices, with attentive service, sumptuous and romantic surroundings'. Reporters also praised

Smokey Joe's: 'good-value Mexican food with superb background music'.

## Après-ski

Les Deux Alpes scores highly for après-ski among those who like lively, noisy bars and discos and do not mind bumping into lots of other British people (more than 25 per cent of non-French visitors are British). GoGo Café Bar is a 'cosy wooden chalet-type coffee bar with a log fire, English newspapers and entertaining French cartoon books for children', and Pub Windsor is an enduringly popular haunt. The Irish Bar, Windsor Pub and Smokey Joe's are recommended. Rodéo Saloon, at the Venosc end of town, displays a mechanical bull, which inevitably attracts the wilder element of après-skiers. The Asterix Bar, in the hotel of the same name, is 'not very pretty, but offers friendly service'. Le Pressoir and Le Tonic are described as 'useful watering-holes'. The Secret Bar is attached to the European Ski and Snowboard School office, and serves snacks to a background of live music. The three discos are Waaza, L'Avalanche and L'Opéra Music Temple.

## Childcare

Among the bridges, tunnels and animal characters at the Espace Loisirs playground are a trampoline, a small slalom course, toboggan run, ski-biking, tubing and an inflatable bob-run. Qualified staff welcome children from six months to two years old at the slope-side La Crèche du Clos des Fonds, and Le Bonhomme de Neige caters for two- to six-year-olds.

The ESF operates a kindergarten slope in the centre of town close to the Jandri Express, and the ESI has its own kindergarten. Both ski schools offer half- or full-day courses for children over four who wish to ski or snowboard. We have positive reports of the ESF children's ski school: 'the French instructors spoke adequate English and even in the worst of the weather they took the wee souls out for at least part of the three-hour lesson. When they got cold, wet and fed up they returned to the ESF chalet to dry out and watch videos'. The European Ski School received mixed reports: 'our kids enjoyed ski school with friendly English-speaking instructors', and 'lack of technical tuition'.

# Les Deux Alpes: At a glance

**Tel** 33 476 79 22 00
**Email** les2alp@les2alpes.com
**Website** www.les2alpes.com

### GETTING THERE
**Airports** Grenoble 1½hrs, Lyon 2hrs
**Rail** Grenoble 70km
**Road** a short, steep climb from the main Grenoble–Briançon road

### THE SKIING
**Linked/nearby resorts** Alpe d'Huez, La Grave, Montgenèvre, Puy-St-Vincent, Serre Chevalier, St-Christophe-en-Oisans, Venosc
**Total of trails/pistes** 220km with La Grave (24% easy, 44% intermediate, 16% difficult, 16% very difficult)
**Lifts in area** 55 including La Grave: 1🠖 7🠗 25🠗 22🠗
**Lift opening dates** 27 November 2004 to 30 April 2005. 16 lifts open for summer skiing mid-June–Sept

### LIFT PASSES
**Area pass** (includes 1 free day in Alpe d'Huez, La Grave, The Milky Way, Puy-St-Vincent, Serre

**Chevalier**) €158 for 6 days
**Pensioners** 60–74yrs €118.50 for 6 days, free for over 74yrs

### TUITION
**Ski & board** ESF (☎ 476 79 21 21), ESI (☎ 476 79 04 21), European Ski and Snowboard School (☎ 476 79 74 55), Primitive Snowboard School (☎ 476 79 09 32), Ski Privilège (☎ 476 79 23 44)
**Guiding** Bureau des Guides ESF (☎ 476 79 50 12)

### CHILDREN
**Lift pass** 6–13yrs €118.50 for 6 days
**Ski & board school** ESF, ESI, European Ski School
**Kindergarten** (ski) ESF, ESI, (non-ski) Le Bonhomme de Neige (☎ 476 79 06 77), La Crèche du Clos des Fonds (☎ 476 79 02 62)

### FOOD AND DRINK
Coffee €2, bottle of house wine €12–15, small beer €3–3.50, soft drink €3, dish of the day €12–15

# Flaine

**ALTITUDE 1,600m (5,248ft)** | **map: see page 183**

## ❋ large ski area ❋ short airport transfer ❋ lack of lift queues ❋ good snow record ❋ skiing convenience

**Best for:** intermediates, off-piste skiers, families who want a no-frills holiday, budget skiers, snowboarders

**Not recommended for:** night-owls, those wanting an atmospheric resort, gourmet skiers

Despite its modest altitude, Flaine has a better snow record than any comparable resort in Europe. The locals put this down to a micro-climate created by its proximity to Mont Blanc. Whatever the reason, this purpose-built ski village has virtually guaranteed snow cover from mid-December until after Easter.

Flaine is the focal point of the Grand Massif, France's fourth biggest ski area with 72 lifts spread between its own contained bowls and the three lower and more traditional villages of **Samoëns**, **Morillon** and **Les Carroz**. A long piste also takes you down to the charming village of Sixt.

### WHAT'S NEW

Hands-free lift passes

Reporters described Flaine as 'a good ski resort that doesn't pretend to be anything else. The drawbacks are limited nightlife and a general lack of charm and ambience'. The first view down into the village from the approach road is an unexpected one: Flaine sits ostentatiously in an isolated little valley where you would not expect to find any habitation. The grey concrete of the resort matches the grey rock formation. Two enclosed people-mover lifts operate day and night between Flaine Forêt and Flaine Forum – the higher and lower villages. The separate Hameau de Flaine, an attractive development of Scandinavian-style chalets, is served by a free bus, which runs every 15 to 30 minutes until midnight to Flaine Forum, where most of the shops

and restaurants and the ski school meeting-place are located.

Flaine has had a chequered financial history since it opened in 1968, but the resort now belongs to the giant Compagnie des Alpes and a £20-million investment plan is in progress. Its future once again looks rosy.

## On-piste
### top 2,480m (8,134ft) bottom 700m (2,296ft)

The area divides naturally into separate segments. Flaine's own skiing is ranged around the north-facing part of its home bowl, with lifts soaring to nearly 2,500m around the rim. Most of the skiing is open and unsheltered. The main mountain access from the village centre is by gondola up to Grandes Platières, a high, wide plateau with panoramic views. A large number of runs go from here down to the resort; most are graded red or blue. In general, the skiing in the enclosed Flaine bowl is somewhat limited, and its real attraction lies in its link with the remainder of the Grand Massif area.

An eight-person chair ('extremely comfortable and fast with no queues') acts as the main, swift link out of Flaine to the rest of the Grand Massif. The Tête du Prè des Saix is the central point of the entire Grand Massif system. From here, north-facing runs drop down steep mogul slopes towards Samoëns ('most enjoyable, challenging blacks up top, opening up to fast cruising lower down'). On the other side of the valley, the parallel easier pistes towards Morillon comprise long and gentle trails in the tree-line.

The runs to Les Carroz are short but offer a wide variety of trails, including more difficult sections at the top of the red runs and some good off-piste. Sixt has its own small ski area and is directly linked into the Grand Massif via a piste, but ski buses provide the only return.

Flaine has extensive novice slopes in the middle of the village, and improvers can try wide, snaking blue runs on the bowl's west-facing slopes. Crystal and Serpentine are long runs around the shoulder of the mountain that beginners can tackle by the end of their first week.

However, the whole area is designed for intermediates. Day-long forays into the far corners of the Grand Massif are well within the capabilities of most snow-users with a few weeks' experience. It is important to allow plenty of time for the return journey.

The more difficult skiing sections of the Flaine bowl are in the middle, graded black under the gondola and red to each side. The black Diamant Noir is an enjoyable mogul slope ('the highlight of a week's skiing') with 'a narrow gully to negotiate under the scrutiny of those going up the chair'. The Agate piste from the Tête des Lindars is 'an interesting black with a couple of awkward bits that get the adrenaline going a little'.

Flaine is recommended for first-time snowboarders and also has one of the biggest terrain parks in Europe. The 1,500-m-long Jam-Park has a boardercross course and half-pipe as well as enough hips, table-tops and quarter-pipes to keep even the most hard-core rider happy. Fantasurf has a designated kids' half-pipe.

## Off-piste

Flaine and the Grand Massif area offer outstanding off-piste possibilities. The rocky terrain means that powder hunts can all too easily end on a cliff, and the services of a local guide who really knows the region are essential. As one off-piste guide explained: 'Flaine – c'est un Gruyère,' because of the many holes that suddenly open up off-piste. Mont Blanc Helicopters will pick you up after an off-piste trip and return you to the resort.

## Tuition and guiding

Flaine has two main ski schools, the French Ski School (ESF), of which we have received mixed reports, and the International Ski School (ESI) ('small classes and everybody improved hugely'), as well as three small independent ones. Flaine Super Ski offers half-day improvement courses. Ski Action was set up by two former members of the French ski team and has a growing reputation. Other qualified independent instructors can be booked through the Association of Independent Ski Instructors (Moniteurs Indépendants).

## Mountain restaurants

Those in the immediate Flaine vicinity are limited, especially in the Aujon area, but there is a wide choice further afield. Close to the resort, the Blanchot received mixed reports: 'excellent French onion soup and exceptionally tasty *vin chaud*', but other reporters complained: 'we had to pay 50 cents for the toilet even when we'd eaten there. Not impressed with the food either'. Le Bissac had 'terribly long queues for self-service, with everyone in a bad mood', while Epicéa, on a green run between Flaine Forêt and Forum, had 'waiter service but was quick. Good pasta but a bit heavy on the garlic'. L'Eloge, by the Flaine gondola, provides a simple choice of food and friendly service, and La Combe, in the Morillon area, has 'terrific ambience'. The Oréade, at the top of the Kédeuse gondola, is praised for its food and large, sunny terrace. The restaurant on the Chariande piste at Samoëns has reasonable prices and a stunning view from the terrace.

## Accommodation

The original independent hotels are now all run by tour operators, and all other accommodation is in self-catered apartments and chalets. Les Lindars and the Totem are run by Club Med (☎ 020-7348 3333 in UK) and Crystal (☎ 0870 160 6040 in UK) respectively, while the alternatives are Le Flaine (☎ 450 90 47 36) ('spacious rooms and the food was good') and the two-star Aujon (☎ 450 90 80 10) ('comfortable, clean rooms. Food is OK but not very child-orientated, with unlimited wine at dinner but no soft drinks for kids').

The apartments are small, even by French standards, but cheap compared with more fashionable resorts. Résidence de la Forêt (☎ 450 90 86 99), situated at the top of the resort, has old-type Pierre & Vacances apartments ('clean but cramped'). The Andromedes block (☎ 450 90 80 01) is said to be 'surprisingly spacious and clean, but decidedly tired'. The Doris block is 'as far from the slopes as you can get'. Le Hameau de Flaine (☎ 450 90 40 40), on the mountain at 1,800m, is a later development of attractive Scandinavian-style chalets inconveniently situated for the ski area. All accommodation can also be booked through a central reservations office (☎ 450 90 89 09).

## Eating in and out

Chez La Jeanne is 'small and friendly with excellent pizzas and good house wine'. Also in Flaine Forum, the White Grouse Pub provides snacks, pizzas and fondues, and the Brasserie has 'excellent pizzas, salads and vin chaud'. L'Auroch in the Forum shopping centre serves traditional French cuisine. Chez Daniel has 'good *tartiflette* and fondues in an Alpine atmosphere', La Pizzeria Chez Pierrot is said to be 'very good', and Le Grain de Sel offers traditional French food. La Perdrix Noire in Flaine Forêt serves regional specialities and is voted best restaurant by a number of reporters. Les Chalets du Michet is commended for 'excellent atmosphere, good food and plenty of it'. There are well-stocked supermarkets on both Forum and Forêt levels. La Ruche is the only restaurant in Le Hameau sector.

## Après-ski

'Quite quiet,' said one reporter of the nightlife, and 'not much to do after skiing', commented another. People do not come to Flaine for the nightlife and many, especially those with small children, tend to opt for quiet evenings in. If you do want to go out, the Flying Dutchman in Flaine Forêt has karaoke, and the White Grouse Pub is a Flaine institution. Le Diamant Noir is 'noisy, sometimes until 3am, with drunks in the street'. Fun disco provides late-night entertainment.

The ice-driving school is one of the most famous in France ('fantastic fun as long as you miss the trees'). Ice-quad biking takes place on a prepared circuit for adults and children of seven and over.

## Childcare

All five ski schools offer lessons, with La Souris Verte at the ESI taking children all day ('a great hit and the groups were small'), as does the more French-oriented ESF Rabbit Club. Both collect children from their accommodation each morning and return them at the end of the day. Hotel-Club Le Flaine and Club Med have kindergartens for their residents. Les P'tits Loups cares for children from six months to four years. The ski area has three rope-tow lifts. The resort organises puppet shows and tobogganing competitions throughout the season.

# Flaine: At a glance

**Tel** 33 450 90 80 01
**Email** welcome@flaine.com
**Website** www.flaine.com

## GETTING THERE
**Airport** Geneva 1½hrs
**Rail** Cluses 25km, frequent bus service to resort
**Road** steep climb from Autoroute Blanche

## THE SKIING
**Linked/nearby resorts** Les Carroz, Morillon, Samoëns, Sixt
**Total of trails/pistes** 265km in Le Grand Massif (12% easy, 42% intermediate, 37% difficult, 9% very difficult)
**Lifts in area** 72: 6⊙ 28⊙ 38⊙
**Lift opening dates** 11 December 2004 to 1 May 2005

## LIFT PASSES
**Area pass** Grand Massif (covers Les Carroz, Flaine, Morillon, Samoëns, Sixt) €160 for 6 days

**Pensioners** Grand Massif 60–74yrs €136 for 6 days

## TUITION
**Ski & board Association of Independent Ski Instructors** (☎ 450 47 84 54), ESF (☎ 450 90 81 00), ESI (☎ 450 90 84 41), Flaine Super Ski (☎ 450 90 82 88), Ski Action (☎ 450 90 80 97)
**Guiding** Mont Blanc Helicopters (☎ 450 92 78 21) and through ski schools

## CHILDREN
**Lift pass** Grand Massif 5–11yrs €117, 12–15yrs €128, both for 6 days
**Ski & board school** as adults
**Kindergarten** (ski) Rabbit Club (ESF), La Souris Verte (ESI), (non-ski) Les P'tits Loups (☎ 450 90 87 82)

## FOOD AND DRINK
Coffee €2–3, bottle of house wine €10–12, small beer €2.30–3.50, soft drink €3–4, dish of the day €10–14

# La Grave

ALTITUDE 1,450m (4,757ft)

## ❋ rugged off-piste skiing ❋ unspoilt 200-year-old village ❋ dramatic scenery

**Best for:** highly experienced skiers and riders, ski-mountaineers

**Not recommended for:** anyone below expert level, people skiing or riding without a qualified mountain guide, children, après-skiers

The towering presence of mighty La Meije, at 3,982m, dominates this ancient, rugged village that straddles the road up to the Col du Lauteret, a two-hour drive from Grenoble in one of the least populated and most wildly beautiful parts of France.

Although La Grave is an important summer climbing centre, it also provides some of the most challenging advanced skiing and snowboarding in Europe. Its steep, unpisted routes down to the resort entail a mighty 655-m descent through glaciers. As the glacial area is heavily crevassed and the couloirs are steep, skiers and riders are strongly advised to use the services of a local guide at all times. The top of the ski area can be reached by gondola and drag-lift or by a 20-minute hike over the back of **Les Deux Alpes**.

## On the snow

top 3,550m (11,647ft) bottom 1,450m (4,757ft)

The high-altitude glacial landscape is dotted with giant séracs and yawning crevasses. Only Chamonix has such comparably beautiful scenery. Two runs are ungroomed but skied until they are almost pisted, and thus provide safe descents that can be tackled by any strong intermediate.

However, once you stray from the well-beaten track you encounter viciously steep couloirs between the cliffs. This is not a place for the faint-hearted, even when accompanied by a local guide. Runs such as the Pan de Rideau, which begins with a truly terrifying traverse along the edge of cliffs, require both skill and nerve. The severity and safety of the couloirs depends on the weather and snow conditions. Those

such as the Couloir des Tryfides can usually be negotiated relatively easily in mid-winter but require the use of ropes and ironmongery when glazed with ice in April. Any mistake here can be fatal.

The gondola takes 30 minutes to reach the top station at 3,200m, where two drag-lifts climb a further 300m to the top of the ski area. From there it is possible to ski to the remote climbing village of St-Christophe-en-Oisans, from where you take a taxi back to Venosc for the climb back up through the lift system of Les Deux Alpes. The run is demanding more because of its length – particularly in tricky snow conditions – rather than its gradient.

## In the resort

La Grave and the nearby resort of Villar d'Arène, 3km away, have one three-star hotel, seven two-stars and a dozen simple guesthouses and gîtes between them. In La Grave there is Le Castillan (☎ 476 79 92 80), L'Edelweiss (☎ 476 79 90 93) and Le Serac (☎ 476 79 91 53), all of which have restaurants. La Grave itself has little to offer anyone who does not climb or ski off-piste, although Kite Surf-Air organises wind-powered kite-surfing and kite-skiing on the nearby Lauteret Pass, for those searching for new experiences. The Bureau des Guides provides local guides, which are essential in this extreme area, but the ESF is 5km away at Le Chazelet. The other beginner ski areas are at Villar d'Arène and the Col du Lauteret. There is no crèche, although children are taught by Juge Raymond, who can be contacted through the tourist office.

## La Grave: At a glance

**Tel** 33 476 79 90 05
**Email** ot@lagrave-lameije.com
**Website** www.lagrave-lameije.com
**Lifts in resort** 4: 2⬡ 2⬡
**Lift opening dates** 18 December 2004 to 1 May 2005

# Megève

ALTITUDE 1,113m (3,651ft)                          map: see page 184

❋ **large linked ski area** ❋ **resort atmosphere** ❋ **smart restaurants**
❋ **designer hotels** ❋ **sophisticated nightlife**

---

**Best for:** beginners, families, intermediate cruisers, gourmets, non-skiers, cross-country skiers, night-owls
**Not recommended for:** expert skiers, people on a budget, early- or late-season skiers

---

A combination of extensive gentle skiing, excellent children's facilities, lavish hotels and superlative restaurants makes Megève a serious contender for the most stylish resort in the Alps. The village is built around a fine medieval church set in a traffic-free main square, where you can hire brightly painted sleigh-taxis. Free buses link the mid-town with the lifts, and coaches run to other nearby resorts covered on the Evasion Mont Blanc lift pass.

Provided you have a car, Megève is the most pleasant base in the Mont Blanc area from which to enjoy the 16 resorts (including **Chamonix**, **Courmayeur** and **Argentière**) covered by the Ski Pass Mont Blanc. Day-trips are also possible to **Les Contamines–Montjoie**, with 120km of slopes, and to attractive Val d'Arly with its linked resorts of Nôtre-Dame-de-Bellecombe, Flumet and Praz-sur-Arly.

## On-piste
### top 2,350m (7,708ft) bottom 850m (2,788ft)

The ski area is large, with smooth and well-groomed pistes, but the low altitude normally makes the season a short one. Anyone planning to spend Christmas or New Year here must be aware that resort-level snow is by no means assured. Two of the three areas, Mont d'Arbois and Rochebrune, are connected at their bases by cable-car.

The Princesse eight-person gondola provides access to Mont d'Arbois by routing day visitors away from the town centre. The lift, with a large car park, is only 10km from the Autoroute Blanche.

The nursery slopes at Mont d'Arbois are easily accessible by cable-car or ski bus. The resort abounds in green slopes and gentle blue runs. From Mont Joux, long blues descend to Les Communailles near Le Bettex, with drag-lifts back up to the ridge. The runs into Megève itself are mostly wide and easy and include a long green piste. There is a drag-lift in the trees at the top-station of Le Jaillet for novices.

The slopes are superb for intermediates who enjoy easy cruising amid beautiful scenery and don't want to push themselves. The skiing at Mont d'Arbois rises to its highest point of the area at Mont Joly, at 2,350m. A choice of long and fairly gentle red runs takes you into the attractive village of St-Nicolas-de-Véroce as well as to **St-Gervais**.

Access to the Rochebrune area is by a swift gondola from the town centre. The area offers arguably the most attractive runs in the resort and is usually less crowded than Mont d'Arbois. From the top of the gondola, further lifts take you up to L'Alpette. The highest point and the start of Megève's downhill course is Côte 2000, which provides some of the toughest skiing in the area and the best snow.

---

### WHAT'S NEW
2 drag-lifts linking Le Jaillet with La Giettaz

---

Megève's third skiing area is Le Jaillet – self-contained and reached by gondola only after a lengthy walk or bus ride from the middle of town. This season sees an expansion across the back of the area in the form of two drag-lifts to the neighbouring small resort of La Giettaz. The hamlet has three main lifts that serve some surprisingly steep pistes.

Langlaufers have a choice of four circuits totalling 70km, including a long, scenic track from the Mont d'Arbois cable-car to Le Bettex and St-Nicolas-de-Véroce. Another loipe links with the resort of Praz-sur-Arly. The resort's only terrain park is at Mont Joux, and there is a boardercross course at Rochebrune.

# Off-piste
The area through the trees towards La Princesse provides superlative powder-skiing after a fresh snowfall, as does Côte 2000. Megève is not a resort that normally attracts hard-core powderhounds (although the cognoscenti from Chamonix come here when conditions at home are too stormy). As a result, the off-piste is far less skied than in most of the other Mont Blanc resorts. The new link to La Giettaz provides some outstanding off-piste opportunities on the forested slopes beneath the Tête de Bonjournal, as well as runs from La Torraz, at 1,930m, to the meadows above the pretty resort of Praz-sur-Arly at 1,250m. A 90-minute walk up Mont Joly takes you to a point where you can ski down to Les Contamines.

## Tuition and guiding
Megève's four ski schools have fine reputations, particularly for beginners, who progress speedily from the nursery areas to the long and flattering easy and intermediate slopes. 'I can't praise the ESI enough,' commented one reporter. Another lauded the ESF for its 'professional and wonderful teachers'. We have enthusiastic reports of the British-run White Sensations ski school: 'truly excellent tuition from a BASI-qualified instructor who really knew his onions'. Ecole Freeride runs ski and snowboard classes. The long-established Bureau des Guides de Megève is also warmly recommended.

## Mountain restaurants
Megève has elevated the Alpine lunch to an art form, albeit an expensive one. L'Alpette at Rochebrune has been a celebrated beacon of mountain eating since 1935 ('try the poached *foie gras* and lamb shanks in a rich wine sauce'). Others warmly recommended are Chalet du Radaz at Côte 2000, Auberge Côte 2000, Les Mandarines at Mont d'Arbois and Auberge du Christomet at Le Jaillet. L'Igloo has a sunny terrace with magnificent views of Mont Blanc; reporters, however, considered it 'owes more to school dinners than *cordon bleu*'.

## Accommodation
The standard of Megève's eight four-stars is outstanding. Chalet Relais et Châteaux du Mont d'Arbois (☎ 450 21 25 03) used to be the Rothschild family home and is located some distance from the town near the Mont

d'Arbois cable-car. Le Fer à Cheval (☎ 450 21 30 39) is rated for its English breakfast, and chalet-style Le Manège (☎ 450 21 41 09) is one of the resort's newest places to stay. Hotel Chalet Saint Georges (☎ 450 93 07 15) is 'excellent in every way'. The Mont Blanc (☎ 450 21 20 02), in the centre of the pedestrian zone, is one of the finest hotels in the Alps. Lodge Park (☎ 450 93 05 03), decorated in eclectic style, has the atmosphere of a private club. Ten minutes' walk from the centre is Les Fermes de Marie (☎ 450 93 03 10), based around a sixteenth-century cowshed with a vaulted frescoed ceiling. The hotel's spa ranks among the finest in Europe. Le Chalet Saint Philippe et Son Hameau (☎ 450 91 19 30) is the eighth four-star.

The best three-stars include Au Vieux Moulin (☎ 450 21 22 29), which is said to be 'warm, spacious and tastefully decorated. Only a short stroll from the hustle and bustle, and the food was excellent'. We also have good reports of the delightful Hotel Coin du Feu (☎ 450 21 04 94) and Hotel Grange d'Arly (☎ 450 58 77 88) ('small and comfortable'). La Chauminé (☎ 450 21 37 05) is a recommended two-star, while the Gollet (☎ 450 47 34 34) and the Richmond (☎ 450 21 43 25) are self-catering apartments.

## Eating in and out
Le Cintra is famed for its seafood. Chef Emmanuel Renaut has been awarded a Michelin star at Flocons de Sel for his imaginative modern French cuisine. L'Alpage has a cosy atmosphere and Savoyard specialities such as fondue and raclette, and Chalet St Georges has separate fish and meat restaurants. Jacques Megean in the restaurant of the same name has built a reputation throughout France for his gourmet dishes created with fresh truffles. La Ferme de Mon Père, built as an old-style farmhouse complete with sheep, cows and goats outside the window, has three Michelin stars and is one of the best restaurants in France ('a spiritual experience for anyone who appreciates fine cuisine'). Le Prieuré is recommended for tea and cakes as well as its 'high-quality' cuisine, and the Mirtillo is said to be 'a first-class Italian experience'. Le Bar du Chamois is a lively and less expensive bistro serving fondue and local white wines.

## Après-ski

This is taken almost more seriously than the skiing, and the choice of venues is enormous, with the après-ski revolving largely around Megève's piano bars and eight nightclubs. Club de Jazz Les Cinq Rues, set in cosy surroundings complete with open fire during the ski season, attracts some of the big international names in jazz and has live music from early evening until late. The Palo Alto complex houses two popular discos, and for insomniacs the bar of the Cocoon Club stays open until 5am. The casino, originally a 1930s' bus station, also houses a restaurant. Rosie Crève Coeur is an unusual bar that looks as if it has stepped out of a 1940s' US airforce base. Le Palace Café is popular with a young crowd, Bar St-Paul is frequented by locals, while Les Caves de Megève attracts the 40-somethings.

The Palais des Sports contains an outdoor Olympic-size skating-rink and a vast swimming-pool. Electric-powered ice bumper-cars are an unusual sport on the skating-rink. Shopping is a major pastime here ('a window-shopper's paradise'), headed by the original Aalard department store, antiques and jewellery shops, designer clothing boutiques and some delightful interior decoration outlets.

## Childcare

Megève boasts some of the most extensive nursery slopes and comprehensive childcare facilities of any resort in France. The non-ski kindergarten, Meg'loisirs, is housed in a well-equipped building next to the Palais des Sports and accepts children from 12 months to 14 years. Club Piou-Piou La Caboche accepts small skiers from three to five years, while La Princesse has a snow kindergarten with magic carpet and takes two-and-a-half-year-olds and above. Ecole Freeride offers children's ski and snowboard lessons with a maximum class size of six.

# Megève: At a glance

**Tel** 33 450 21 27 28
**Email** megeve@megeve.com
**Website** www.megeve.com

### GETTING THERE
**Airport** Geneva 1hr
**Rail** Sallanches 10km, regular bus service to resort
**Road** Autoroute Blanche from Geneva and short climb

### THE SKIING
**Linked/nearby resorts** Argentière, Le Bettex, Chamonix, Combloux, Les Contamines–Montjoie, Courmayeur, Flumet, La Giettaz, Les Houches, Nôtre-Dame-de-Bellecombe, La Prairon, Praz-sur-Arly, Les Saisies, St-Gervais, St-Nicolas-de-Véroce
**Total of trails/pistes** 300km in resort, 450km in linked area (30% easy, 45% intermediate, 25% difficult), 729km in Mont Blanc ski area
**Lifts in area** 107 with Les Contamines–Montjoie: 12⊙ 36⑤ 59⊗
**Lift opening dates** mid-December 2004 to late April 2005

### LIFT PASSES
**Area pass** Evasion Mont Blanc (covers Les Contamines–Montjoie, Mègeve, La Prairon) €151, Ski Pass Mont Blanc (covers whole region including Argentière, Chamonix and Courmayeur) €205, both for 6 days
**Pensioners** Evasion Mont Blanc 60yrs and over €121, Ski Pass Mont Blanc 60yrs and over €174, both for 6 days

### TUITION
**Ski & board** Ecole Freeride (☎ 450 93 03 52), ESF (5 centres) (☎ 450 21 00 97), ESI (☎ 450 58 78 88), White Sensations (☎ 450 91 14 25 or 0870 241 5801 in UK)
**Guiding** Bureau des Guides (☎ 450 21 55 11), Hélico de France (☎ 450 58 94 50), Mont Blanc Helicopters (☎ 450 92 78 21) and through ski schools

### CHILDREN
**Lift pass** Evasion Mont Blanc 5–14yrs €116, Ski Pass Mont Blanc 5–14yrs €164, both for 6 days
**Ski & board school** as adults
**Kindergarten** (ski/non-ski) Club Piou-Piou La Caboche (☎ 450 58 97 65) (non-ski), Meg'loisirs (☎ 450 58 77 84), Princesse (☎ 450 93 00 86)

### FOOD AND DRINK
Coffee €2.50–3.50, bottle of house wine €14–20, small beer €3.50–5, soft drink €2.50–3.50, dish of the day €12–18

# Méribel

ALTITUDE 1,450–1,800m (4,756–5,905ft)          map: see page 181

✳ **giant resort in The Trois Vallées** ✳ **extensive pistes for all standards**
✳ **most popular resort for British skiers**

> **Best for:** high-mileage cruisers, luxury chalet dwellers, powderhounds
> **Not recommended for:** Francophiles, budget skiers, those seeking ski-in ski-out accommodation or who dislike crowded pistes, older night-owls, non-skiers

Méribel markets itself as 'the heart of The Trois Vallées' and it is certainly the most convenient base from which to explore the 189 lifts and 600km of piste that make up what is the largest truly linked ski area in the world. Others claim more terrain and a greater number of lifts, but the ideal topography of the Trois Vallées means that even the links are serious runs in their own right.

The resort, which was founded by Englishman Colonel Peter Lindsay just before World War II, consists of an ever-expanding series of purpose-built hamlets of mainly luxury chalets. These sprawl up 250m of hillside on a winding road 18km above the valley town of Moûtiers. It is also connected by gondola to the much lower spa resort of Brides-les-Bains, which acts as an alternative budget bed-base.

Méribel has more top-of-the-range chalet accommodation – six bedrooms and six bathrooms is the norm rather than the exception – than any other resort in the world, and no one can deny the extent and quality of its own ski area or the easy lift links to **Courchevel**, **La Tania**, **Les Menuires** and **Val Thorens** in the neighbouring valleys. Planning regulations insist that all buildings are made of stone, timber and slate – sticking rigidly to the rules laid down by its founder.

But despite all this – or perhaps because of its British ex-pat heritage – Méribel lacks soul. Teenagers hoping to put in a little final evening practice for GCSE French oral will find themselves in the wrong place. So many British people holiday or work in Méribel during the winter that any attempt to order a drink or a meal in French can be met with a look of blank incomprehension ('I did actually forget I was in France, until I heard a radio one day').

Heart of the Trois Vallées it may be, but the diffuse layout means that the resort itself is devoid of a single heart, and its atmosphere is accordingly muted. The convenience of the various hamlets for skiing, shopping and nightlife varies considerably.

Méribel Centre (1,450m) is the commercial core – a one-street village with the tourist office as its focal point. It has a number of boutiques and souvenir shops beyond the usual sports shops, and one main supermarket. The bi-weekly street market provides colour and bargains. Méribel Mottaret (1,700–1,800m) is a ski-in, ski-out satellite situated further up the valley and is also divided into individual hamlets. The village is praised by reporters: 'not only does it offer the ski-in, ski-out advantage over its larger cousin, but it also provides much more entertainment and restaurants than its satellite status suggests'.

Others commented that the free bus service, which in theory runs every 20 minutes during the day and hourly in the early evening, is irregular and overcrowded ('an absolutely awful way to end a wonderful day's skiing').

## On-piste
top 2,952m (9,685ft) bottom 1,400m (4,593ft)

Both sides of the open valley are extensively networked with modern lifts, which improve each year. A hands-free lift pass is desperately needed, but is unlikely to materialise for the present. The lift capacity is so high that queues are a rarity but, as a result, the main runs inevitably become overcrowded.

The western side of Méribel culminates in a long skiable ridge, which separates it from the beautiful Belleville Valley and the resorts of Val Thorens, Les Menuires and **St-Martin-de-Belleville**. The eastern side rises to the rocky 2,738-m summit of Saulire and the Col de la Loze at 2,274m. Beyond lie La Tania, the Bozel Valley and Courchevel. At the head of Les Allues Valley rises Mont du Vallon (2,952m) – the most easterly of the horseshoe of 3,300-m peaks accessed from Méribel and Val Thorens.

The runs surrounding Méribel's altiport are ideal beginner areas with enough length to help build confidence. Higher nursery slopes at Mottaret are subject to the heavy traffic of more experienced skiers and snowboarders passing through at speed. Second-week skiers will quickly find that they can cover considerable distances on green and blue runs, an experience that greatly adds to the feeling of achievement.

The Trois Vallées constitutes what many skiers rightly regard as the greatest intermediate playground in the world: a seemingly endless network of moderately graded runs that provide a challenge to all levels of skier. As one reader put it: 'we have been spoilt by the Trois Vallées and now look upon most other resorts with disdain'. The Combe de Vallon is a magnificent cruise of 1,100m vertical from the top of Mont du Vallon all the way down to Méribel Mottaret.

There is a terrain park above Arpasson on the Tougnète side of Mottaret and a designated snowboard area below the second Plattières station above Mottaret.

## Off-piste

Mont du Vallon and the Col du Fruit offer outstanding off-piste opportunities, but the services of a local guide are essential. A number of narrow chutes including the frighteningly named Death Couloir, reached by a metal staircase from the top of Saulire, satisfy those who need fear in order to work up an appetite for lunch. Méribel's central position makes off-piste easy to access in both the Bozel and Belleville valleys.

## Tuition and guiding

The French Ski School (ESF), which has been the subject of severe criticism in the past, received more favourable comments this year: 'the tuition seemed to have improved. I think the ESF has finally realised that it needs to compete'. But the sheer volume of business during the main weeks of the season inevitably turns the larger ski and snowboarding schools into

'sausage factories'. Unless you feel you benefit from the 'follow-me' type of instruction, or decide that the lift priority given to a class warrants the cost, you might do better to save your money.

Reporters continued to praise Magic in Motion ('excellent' – no more than seven in a class'), although not all instructors speak fluent English. We have received a favourable reports of British-run New Generation.

Ian and Susan Saunders (BASI instructors who work for the ESF in Méribel) have their own company, Ski Principles, which provides 'great instruction by sympathetic teachers'. The new British ski school, Parallel Lines, has BASI instructors and received much praise: 'the standard of tuition was excellent, sympathetic and attentive, and completely tailored around what I wanted to get out of the lesson', said one reporter, and 'the class size was small and it was good value for money', commented another.

## Mountain restaurants

The price of food on the mountains is a constant complaint. 'Prices remain as scandalous as ever. Lunch is nothing short of daylight robbery, with every waiter acting as an Alpine Dick Turpin'. However, some reporters said that shopping around paid dividends.

Les Castors, at the foot of the Truite run in Méribel, receives mixed comments: 'crowded but still excellent', and 'well situated and popular but extremely pricy compared to restaurants only a short distance away'. Roc des Trois Marches offers consistently good value and Le Grain de Sel has a sunny terrace. Les Rhododendrons waiter-service restaurant has 'seriously improved', while the self-service below was 'overcrowded with poor service and poor food'. Le Rond Point provides 'some of the best lunchtime fare in the region', while Le Bibi Phoque at Chaudanne makes 'excellent crêpes and galettes'. Chalet Tougniat at the top of the Combes chair out of Mottaret received praise: 'it gets less crowded than most, as it is slightly off the beaten track'.

## Accommodation

Those who don't like walking in their ski boots are strongly advised to check out the location of their chalet before booking. Of the hotels, the four-star Grand Coeur

(☎ 479 08 60 03) was one of the resort's first and remains its finest: 'the food and service are excellent; its understated luxury appeals equally to the Brits and the French'. The Marie Blanche (☎ 479 08 65 55) and Le Yeti (☎ 479 00 51 15) are also recommended. In Mottaret, the four-star Mont Vallon (☎ 479 00 44 00) is praised.

## Eating in and out

Méribel has a surprisingly limited choice of recommended restaurants for a resort of its size, mainly because such a large proportion of its clientèle eat in their catered chalets. Les Enfants Terribles has 'typical French fare of a high quality'. La Cava is recommended for fondue, while La Taverne offers pizzas and Savoyard dishes and has established itself as one of the resort's main rendezvous. Chez Kiki specialises in charcoal grills, and the surroundings are appealing. La Chaumière is 'old-style traditional French' and Le Boa à Mil is 'an excellent cellar dive'. In Mottaret, Ty Sable is strongly recommended, and Hotel Tarentaise, on the edge of the piste, is British-managed and popular with the French for its food. The central Côte Brune is still a culinary mainstay. Au Temps Perdu ('extensive range of crêpes') and Pizzeria du Mottaret ('the restaurant with the best ambience and prices') are both praised, while Le Croix Jean-Claude is also warmly recommended.

## Après-ski

Méribel Jack's Bar close to the piste puts on a popular après-ski happy hour: 'lively, happy atmosphere, value for money', said one reporter, but 'full of sad, middle-aged English drinking lager and playing bar billiards to the strains of old Beach Boys tapes', commented another. Le Rond Point is equally busy as the lifts close. Le Loft, located above the ice-rink, has live music, a fun atmosphere and stays open late. Le Bowling has a six-lane alley and a bar with pool table. Dick's Tea-Bar, a branch of the Val d'Isère original, is also extremely popular.

## Childcare

The Méribel ESF ski school continued to receive mixed reviews for its children's classes: 'although the classes were large, the teachers made the lessons fun', and 'the teacher just didn't bother to speak to our son at all because all the other children spoke French'. Both the ski and non-ski kindergarten were said to be 'well organised, but staff were not as friendly as we would have liked'.

# Méribel: At a glance

**Tel** 33 479 08 60 01
**Email** info@meribel.net
**Website** www.meribel.net

### GETTING THERE
**Airports** Chambéry 2hrs, Lyon 2½hrs, Geneva 3hrs
**Rail** Eurostar from Waterloo and Ashford to Moûtiers, 18km away
**Road** autoroute to Albertville and steep climb from Moûtiers

### THE SKIING
**Linked/nearby resorts** Courchevel, Les Menuires, St-Martin-de-Belleville, La Tania, Val Thorens
**Total of trails/pistes** 150km in Méribel area (15% easy, 71% intermediate, 14% difficult), 600km in Trois Vallées
**Lifts in area** 189 in Trois Vallées: 40🚠 68🚡 81🎿
**Lift opening dates** 11 December 2004 to 24 April 2005

### LIFT PASSES
**Area pass** Trois Vallées €204 for 6 days
**Pensioners** Trois Vallées 60–72yrs €164 for 6 days

### TUITION
**Ski & board** ESF (☎ 479 08 60 31), Magic in Motion (☎ 479 08 53 36), New Generation/Le Ski School (☎ 479 01 03 18), Parallel Lines (☎ 01702 589580 in UK), Ski Principles (☎ 479 00 52 71)
**Guiding** Bureau des Guides (☎ 479 00 30 38)

### CHILDREN
**Lift pass** Trois Vallées 5–13yrs €153.50 for 6 days
**Ski & board school** as adults
**Kindergarten** (ski) Les P'tits Loups (☎ 479 08 60 31), (non-ski) Les Saturnins (☎ 479 08 66 90)

### FOOD AND DRINK
Coffee €3–3.50, bottle of house wine €14–20, small beer €3.50–5, soft drink €3.50–4, dish of the day €12–20

# Morzine and Les Gets

**ALTITUDE 1,000m (3,280ft)** map: see page 179

## ❋ skiing for all standards ❋ vast ski area ❋ short airport transfer

> **Best for:** intermediate cruisers, families, night-owls, town dwellers, cross-country skiers
> **Not recommended for:** early- or late-season skiers, those looking for quiet village atmosphere

Morzine is an attractive market town, situated a 90-minute drive from Geneva, and it forms one of the principal resorts of the giant **Portes du Soleil** ski area. This uneasy marketing consortium of a dozen ski villages, ranging from large, internationally recognised resorts to the tiniest of unspoilt hamlets, straddles the Swiss border and comprises some 207 lifts on a single lift pass, serving 650km of piste. Les Gets is situated on a mountain pass 6km from Morzine.

Les Portes du Soleil takes its name from a mountain pass just above the Swiss hamlet of Les Crosets. The trans-frontier ski area dates back 40 years. Jean Vuarnet from Morzine, gold medallist at the 1960 Winter Olympics in Squaw Valley, was given the job of creating the futuristic resort of **Avoriaz** on the cliffs above the town. Vuarnet, better remembered for his sunglasses than his skiing prowess, saw the potential for expanding his ski area across the Swiss frontier down to Les Crosets, and the first link was installed in 1968 and a regional lift pass introduced in 1974.

This enormous area is now an enjoyable intermediate playground where skiers and riders can clock up impressive daily mileage in two countries. The lift system is steadily being upgraded. However, most of the resorts are joined by awkward and often confusing mountain links, while a few, such as St-Jean d'Aulps and Abondance, are entirely independent. It is possible to complete a tour of the main resorts in one day, but this involves limited enjoyable skiing and a considerable amount of time spent on lifts. It is far better to confine yourself to a couple of areas to explore in detail before making the obligatory Portes du Soleil tour.

Snow cover is not always reliable and Morzine's low altitude of 1,000m means that poor conditions on the lower slopes are not unusual. However, lift links to the higher resort of Avoriaz at 1,800m, with its top lifts at 2,350m, ensure that skiing continues throughout the season.

Morzine is also linked on the other side of town to Les Gets, which has a further extensive ski area with upgraded lifts. This attractive old farming community has expanded almost out of recognition, boasting a large and under-used floodlit piste. Parts of the ski area and many of the mountain restaurants are accessible on foot. By road, the two resorts are only 6km apart.

Unlike purpose-built Avoriaz, Morzine has all the appeal of an old-style chalet resort set in charming, wooded surroundings. The town covers a large area on both sides of a river gorge and is on several levels. It has seen considerable growth in recent years, and the resort is becoming increasingly popular with British skiers, who enjoy the fact that Morzine is a real market town with a life that goes beyond tourism ('the standard and range of shops was far higher than I have ever before encountered in a ski resort').

### WHAT'S NEW

Zore lift upgraded to a quad-chair
Widening of Zore and Tetras pistes
Charniaz chair replaced by a 6-person chair-lift

The town has a serious traffic problem, but a high footbridge over the river makes movement less tortuous for pedestrians than for motorists. The main congested shopping street climbs from the old village centre beside the river to more open ground at the foot of Le Pleney, where the resort has developed, with hotels and shops around the tourist office.

Such is the diffuse nature of the resort that the free buses and a miniature road rain are essential forms of transport. Horse-drawn taxis are an alternative means of getting around.

## On-piste
top 2,350m (7,708ft) bottom 1,000m (3,280ft)

Morzine's own ski area is accessed by a choice of cable-car or gondola leading up to Le Pleney at 1,554m. From here you can return to the valley or ski on into the system towards Les Gets. A refurbished gondola on the other side of Morzine takes you up into the town's second ski area of Super-Morzine, from where a network of lifts links with Avoriaz, as does a cable-car from the hamlet of Les Prodains, reached by free ski bus from Morzine.

Morzine and Les Gets both have terrain parks, and riders are generally well catered for in the area.

## Off-piste
The best powder runs are above Avoriaz on both sides of the Swiss border, but Les Gets also offers plenty of opportunities after a fresh dump. The area is prone to considerable avalanche danger, and the services of a qualified guide are essential.

## Tuition and guiding
In Morzine, the French Ski School (ESF) is recommended for its innovative programmes and 'friendly instructors'. There is also a branch of the much-praised British Alpine Ski and Snowboarding school, which was described by one reporter as 'everything the ESF is not – small classes and good technical advice in one's mother tongue'. A reporter who attended classes with the ESI found the classes 'disappointing'. Ski Snowboard et Adventures is Morzine's specialist board school, while Bureau de la Montagne and Maison de la Montagne are the mountain guiding companies.

In Les Gets, the British Alpine Ski and Snowboarding School has a branch too ('we were all extremely happy with the instruction provided'), while 360 International is a ski and snowboard school that quickly established a good reputation during its first season.

## Mountain restaurants
The Portes du Soleil offers a mixed bag of eateries, ranging from overcrowded self-services to wonderful old huts off the beaten track. Les Prodains, at the bottom of the Vuarnet run from Avoriaz, is much praised, not least for its reasonable prices. The two restaurants at the top of Le Pleney are said to be 'always busy, but the wait is worth it', and the Perdrix Blanche at Pré-la-Joux is good value and recommended for its warm atmosphere. One reporter rated Restaurant Lhotty, on the piste from the Chamosière to Morzine, as 'one of the best restaurants I've ever been to for quality and value'. The restaurant at the Pointe de Chéry mid-station is said to have 'reasonably priced and extremely well-prepared meals'.

## Accommodation
Morzine has a plentiful supply of hotels in each price bracket; most are chalet-style and none is luxurious. In the central area, the three-star Les Airelles (☎ 450 74 71 21) is one of the more comfortable. Other three-stars include Hotel Le Tremplin (☎ 450 79 12 31) on the edge of the piste with a grandstand view of the night-skiing and -snowboarding arena, and Hotel Le Dahu (☎ 450 75 92 92), which is a long-established favourite with reporters and continues to receive favourable comments: 'the half-board food is some of the best I have ever found in a ski resort'. Hotel Fleur des Neiges (☎ 450 79 01 23) is a reasonable two-star built in chalet style. La Neige et Roc (☎ 450 79 03 21) at Les Prodains is recommended: 'cosy, comfortable and convenient for the cable-car up to Avoriaz'.

In Les Gets, much of the accommodation is in chalets. Some of the apartments are said to be 'very dated'. The Australian-owned three-star Boomerang (☎ 450 79 80 65) is warmly praised: 'a welcome bit of Oz in the French outback' and 'I can recommend it to anyone – the food is wonderful and the atmosphere fantastic'. Hotel Labradar (☎ 450 75 80 00) has a restaurant and swimming-pool. Other recommended three-stars are Hotels Alpages (☎ 450 75 80 88), Marmotte (☎ 450 75 80 33), Nagano (☎ 450 79 71 46) and Mont-Chéry (☎ 450 75 80 75). Hotel Marmotte has an indoor swimming-pool and spa.

## Eating in and out
Le Tremplin in Morzine is praised by reporters. L'Etale serves regional specialities in a 'wonderful, authentic mountain atmosphere', and La Chamade and La Grange are both highly acclaimed

for a special night out. The Neige Roc at Les Prodains is 'well worth the journey from Morzine'. In Les Gets, Le Flambeau and le Tourbillon are both recommended, along with Le Vieux Chêne.

## Après-ski
Morzine's après-ski receives mixed comments: 'average', said one mature reporter, and 'it rocks', enthused a 21-year-old. The town abounds with civilised tea-rooms and bars. Inside the Wallington complex are a bowling alley, pool hall, bar and disco. L'Opéra and Le Paradis de Laury's are the nightclubs. 'The bars and nightclubs are a lot of fun – especially the Cavern,' was one reporter's verdict.

In Les Gets, Bar Bush was rated 'better than ever'. Bar Canadie provides 'good bar snacks of local charcuterie and cheese', while the Boomerang bar is 'lively'. For

dancing, the Iglu nightclub was considered 'small, but very accommodating and good fun'. The leisure centre has a swimming-pool and a range of other facilities ('really clean with friendly staff').

## Childcare
Morzine's L'Outa crèche takes youngsters from two months to six years, while Le Club des Piou-Piou provides daycare with ski lessons for children from three to twelve years.

In Les Gets, the ESF is 'brilliant for kids of all ages'. Both the ESF Fantaski Club and Ile des Enfants take beginners from three years 'quite Gallic but lots of fun'. Ski Plus is praised: 'my kids really enjoyed the classes'. Les Fripouilles welcomes children from three months to four years, and Les P'tits Montagnys takes non-skiing children from four to twelve years.

# Morzine and Les Gets: At a glance

**Tel** Les Gets 33 450 75 80 80 / Morzine 33 450 74 72 72
**Email** lesgets@lesgets.com / info@morzine-avoriaz.com
**Websites** www.lesgets.com / www.morzine-avoriaz.com

**GETTING THERE**
**Airport** Geneva 1½hrs
**Rail** Thonon les Bains 31km, Cluses 25km
**Road** take the Cluses exit 18 off the Autoroute Blanche towards Taninges

**THE SKIING**
**Linked/nearby resorts** Abondance, Avoriaz, Champéry, Champoussin, La Chapelle d'Abondance, Châtel, Les Crosets, Montriond, Morgins, St-Jean d'Aulps, Torgon, Val d'Illiez
**Total of trails/pistes** 260km in Morzine and Les Gets (10% beginner, 44% easy, 36% intermediate, 10% difficult), 650km in Portes du Soleil
**Lifts in area** 207 in Portes du Soleil: 14⑤ 82⑤ 111⑨
**Lift opening dates** mid-December 2004 to end of April 2005

**LIFT PASSES**
**Area pass** Portes du Soleil (covers 14 resorts) €176 for 6 days

**Pensioners** Portes du Soleil 60yrs and over €141 for 6 days

**TUITION**
**Ski & board** Les Gets: 360 International (☎ 450 79 80 31), British Alpine SSS (☎ 450 79 85 42 during season, ☎ 01485 572596 in UK all year), ESF (☎ 450 75 80 03) Morzine: British Alpine SSS (☎ 450 74 78 59 during season, ☎ 02392 528497 in UK all year), ESF (☎ 450 79 13 13), ESI (☎ 450 79 05 16), Ski Snowboard et Aventures (☎ 450 79 05 16)
**Guiding** Bureau de la Montagne (☎ 450 79 03 55), Maison de la Montagne (☎ 450 75 96 65)

**CHILDREN**
**Lift pass** Portes du Soleil 5–16yrs €118 for 6 days
**Ski & board school** as adults
**Kindergarten** Les Gets: (ski) Ile des Enfants (☎ 450 75 84 47), Ski Plus (☎ 450 75 86 01), (ski/non-ski) ESF Fantaski Club, (non-ski) Les Fripouilles (☎ 450 79 84 84), Les P'tits Montagnys (☎ 450 75 80 03). Morzine: (ski/non-ski) Le Club des Piou-Piou (☎ 450 79 13 13), (non-ski) L'Outa (☎ 450 79 26 00)

**FOOD AND DRINK**
Coffee €2–2.50, bottle of house wine €12, small beer €3–4, soft drink €3, dish of the day €10–15

# La Plagne

ALTITUDE 1,250–2,050m (4,100–6,735ft)                    map: see pages 176–177

❋ **huge integrated skiing area** ❋ **spectacular views of Mont Blanc**
❋ **skiing convenience**

---

**Best for:** intermediates, high-mileage
cruisers, beginners, families, off-piste
skiers
**Not recommended for:** night-owls,
those looking for Alpine charm (in the
high-altitude villages)

---

La Plagne has now joined forces with
neighbouring **Les Arcs** to form **Paradiski**, a
ski area of mammoth proportions. Some
425km of groomed runs served by 141 lifts
make it one of the most extensive circuits in
the world. The double-decker Vanoise
Express cable-car now spans the Ponturin
gorge between the two resorts. However,
many would argue that La Plagne's own
225km of piste, together with some of the
most challenging off-piste powder-skiing in
the whole of the Tarentaise valley, was
already enough. Indeed, the owners of the
lift system (who also run Les Arcs) believe
that in the long term only 30 per cent of
skiers in either resort will actually make use
of the link. This poses the question of why
they have spent £11 million building it.

La Plagne consists of ten separate
'villages', of which six are purpose-built for
ski-in, ski-out convenience in the main,
high-altitude bowl up above the tree-line.
The other four are outlying villages in the
surrounding valleys, accessed by different
roads and linked by lifts into the main
skiing area. Overall, the resort has all the
ingredients of the perfect ski destination:
high-altitude snow surety, long runs and
piste-side accommodation. But its
undeniable reputation as a 'ski factory' for
intermediates can leave some visitors
dissatisfied.

Plagne Centre was the original resort
and sets standards of ugliness otherwise
achieved only in such monuments to 1960s'
architectural vandalism as Les Menuires
and Tignes. Aime-la-Plagne is styled as a
giant battleship and appears magnificent to
some, as it does monstrous to others, while

Belle Plagne, with its attractive village
centre and integrated arcs of apartment
buildings, is more appealing to most. Plagne
Bellecôte's semi-circle of reddish high-rise
blocks is more of an acquired architectural
taste, while Plagne Villages, Plagne Soleil
and Plagne 1800, the lowest of the bowl
resorts, nod to Savoyard tradition with their
low-rise, wood-clad complexes.

Of the outlying villages, the most rustic
is **Montchavin** where cats slink around
cobbled alleys and cowsheds. There is a
gondola link to neighbouring **Les Coches**.
Being close to the new Vanoise Express
cable-car to Les Arcs, these villages benefit
from extensive artificial snowmaking, which
is needed to keep the link open throughout
the season. More snow-cannon have been
introduced above the other valley villages of
**Montalbert** and **Champagny-en-Vanoise**.

## On-piste
top 3,250m (10,660ft) bottom 1,250m (4,100ft)

La Plagne is the consummate intermediate
skiers' resort, with red and blue runs
leading in all directions from the ski-in, ski-
out villages. Les Blanchets and Carella
chairs link Bellecôte to the summit of Roche
de Mio, which gives access to the some of
the resort's most challenging terrain, and
also to the Glacier de Bellecôte, whose
3,250-m summit is the resort's highest
point. Summer skiing is possible here.

With much of the resort above tree-level,
there is an abundance of wide-open,
motorway pistes throughout the main bowl.
For forest runs, there are beautiful routes
winding down to Montchavin, Les Coches,
Champagny and Montalbert. Skiers should
keep an eye out for poor weather, when the
links between these and the main bowl can
close, causing congestion and stranding
skiers. Generally, however, queues are
minimal – with the significant exception of
the bottleneck Arpette chair linking Plagne
Bellecôte to Les Coches.

For beginners, there are nursery slopes
at all the high-altitude centres, with easy

progressions on to blue runs, though a virtual absence of long greens can make things difficult for the more cautious. Montchavin, Les Coches and Montalbert also have nursery slopes and gentle blues. Champagny is the only resort area for beginners to avoid.

La Plagne has a general lack of black runs. There are a few steep, compelling pistes such as Les Etroits and Morbleu from Le Biolley ridge above Aime-la-Plagne, and the Emile Allais descent to the bottom of the outlying Charmettes chair.

For snowboarders there is a permanent half-pipe and terrain park at Plagne Bellecôte, a terrain park at Montchavin/Les Coches and a terrain park and boardercross course at Champagny.

## Off-piste
La Plagne holds some of the most exhilarating and varied powder-skiing in the Tarentaise valley. Highlights include a long, sweeping descent from the Bellecôte glacier down to Les Bauches, as well as the demanding Cul du Nant run from the back of the glacier into the Champagny-le-Haut valley. The western slopes of Le Biolley can be superb in spring snow.

## Tuition and guiding
The French Ski School (ESF) has branches in all the resort villages, offering group ski and snowboard classes, and individual lessons. A few small schools provide competition. In Plagne Centre there is Oxygène: 'our instructor worked hard with us and was extremely patient'. Groups are restricted to a maximum of eight at El Pro in Belle Plagne and at Evolution 2 in Montchavin and Les Coches. Plagne Centre also has a specialist school, Antenne Handicap, which can assess and provide lessons for most levels of physical or mental disability.

## Mountain restaurants
The standard of mountain restaurants in the La Plagne area continues to increase steadily. Au Bon Vieux Temps, below Aime-la-Plagne, remains popular for its sunny terrace and efficient service. The piste-side Le Forperet, on the way down to Montalbert, is another good bet for sun and spectacular views in fine weather. Down in the Ponturin valley near the Vanoise Express, the Auberge de Montagne chez Pat

du Sauget is well positioned for a stop to or from Les Arcs. Other recommended restaurants include Le Loup Garou and Le Petit Chaperon Rouge above 1800, and, for especially good value, La Rossa at the top of the Champagny gondola. Les Borseliers in Champagny serves 'excellent crèpes, *galettes* and *tartiflette*'.

## Accommodation
The British make up about 37 per cent of visitors to La Plagne, with all the mainstream tour operators, and many smaller ones, between them offering the full gamut of accommodation options – hotels, club-hotels, chalets and self-catering apartments.

In Plagne Centre, the three-star Paladien Terra Nova (☎ 479 55 79 00) has 'a great location and good food, though a bit impersonal'. In Plagne Village, the four-star Residence Aspen (☎ 479 55 75 75) is warmly praised.

In Belle Plagne, the four-star Les Montagnettes apartments (☎ 479 55 12 00) and Les Balcons de Belle Plagne apartments (☎ 479 55 76 76) are favourites among reporters. The two-star Hotel Mercure Eldorador (☎ 479 09 12 09) is 'in serious need of refurbishment, but the food is good'.

In Aime-la-Plagne, MGM's Les Hauts Bois apartments (☎ 0870 750 6820 in UK) are among the most luxurious in the resort. Residents have use of a stylish swimming-pool, sauna and steam room. In Montchavin the two-star Hotel Bellecôte (☎ 479 07 83 30) is recommended.

## Eating in and out
The four outlying villages have the widest selection of restaurants. In Montchavin, for example, Skanapia is warmly praised: 'great food in great surroundings'. For fine dining in the high-altitude resorts, La Soupe au Schuss in Aime-la-Plagne is a favourite, as are Le Matafan in Belle Plagne and Métairie in Plagne Centre. Le Refuge in Plagne Centre is recommended by reporters: 'a lovely, three-course meal for about €20 each, including wine and coffee'. Le Loup Blanc in Plagne 1800 is also recommended.

## Après-ski
'Resort nightlife was a dead loss,' was how one reporter put it. Party-goers will find the most action in Plagne Centre and Plagne

Bellecôte, particularly at Jet 37 and Saloon discos respectively. No Blem Café in Plagne Centre was 'busy, and it screens the football'. Le Mine in Plagne 1800 is decorated with 'original gear from a local silver mine'. Aime-la-Plagne has Bleu Night disco, while the main nightspot in Montchavin is Oxygène, and in Champagny is Le Galaxy.

Just below Plagne 1800 is the 1.5-km Olympic bob-sleigh track, which can be put to the test by visitors. The latest of these is a self-guiding mono-bob, which hurtles down the icy corridor averaging up to an adrenaline-pumping 100kph – although, at €95 per descent, you might question whether a euro per second represents good value for money.

## Childcare

Oxygène in Plagne Centre has a good reputation for children's classes in English. It and Evolution 2 in Montchavin and Les Coches are both recommended for their children's ski classes, in which group sizes are generally considerably smaller than with the ESF.

Crèches operate throughout the high-altitude villages, taking toddlers from two years old out on the mountain for snowy activities. The Mercure Eldorador Hotel in Belle Plagne has a children's club for four- to twelve-year-olds, and offers supervised children's meals, and Les P'tits Bonnets crèche in Plagne Centre takes infants from ten months to three years. In Montchavin, Club Bébés caters for nine-month- to three-year-olds.

# La Plagne: At a glance

**Tel** 33 479 09 79 79
**Email** bienvenue@la-plagne.com
**Website** www.la-plagne.com

### GETTING THERE
**Airports** Chambéry 2hrs, Geneva 2½hrs, Lyon 2½hrs
**Rail** Eurostar from Waterloo and Ashford to Bourg-St-Maurice, 15km
**Road** autoroute to Albertville, climb from Aime to other villages

### THE SKIING
**Linked/nearby resorts** Les Arcs, Tignes, Trois Vallées, Val d'Isère, Peisey-Vallandry
**Total of trails/pistes** 225km in La Plagne (5% beginner, 56% easy, 27% intermediate, 12% difficult) 425km in Paradiski area
**Lifts in area** 141 in Paradiski: 1🚡 16🚠 66🚡 58🚡
**Lift opening dates** 4 December 2004 to 30 April 2005. Summer skiing on Glacier de Bellecôte, closed for 2 weeks in May and 2 weeks in Sept

### LIFT PASSES
**Area pass** La Plagne only €181, Paradiski (linked Les Arcs/La Plagne area and one day in each of Val d'Isère/Tignes, Pralognan–La-Vanoise, Les Saisies) €225, both for 6 days
**Pensioners** La Plagne only 60–71yrs €154, Paradiski 60–71yrs €191, both for 6 days

### TUITION
**Ski & board** in all 10: ESF (☎ 479 09 00 40). Belle Plagne: El Pro (☎ 479 09 11 62). Champagny: International Snowride (☎ 663 12 32 28). Les Coches: Evolution 2 (☎ 479 04 20 83). Montchavin: Evolution 2 (☎ 479 07 81 85). Plagne Centre: Antenne Handicap (☎ 479 09 13 80), Oxygène (☎ 479 09 03 99)
**Guiding** ESF, Evolution 2

### CHILDREN
**Lift pass** La Plagne only 6–13yrs €136, Paradiski 6–13yrs €169, both for 6 days
**Ski & board school** El Pro, ESF, Evolution 2, Oxygène
**Kindergarten** (ski) through ski schools. (non-ski): Aime-la-Plagne: Les Lutins (☎ 479 09 04 75). Belle Plagne: ESF (☎ 479 09 06 68). Champagny-en-Vanoise: Les Cabris (☎ 479 55 06 40). Les Coches: Club Pirouette (☎ 479 07 83 54). Montalbert: ESF (☎ 479 09 77 24). Montchavin: Chat Bleu (☎ 479 07 82 82), Club Bébés (☎ 479 07 82 82). Plagne 1800: ESF (☎ 479 09 09 64). Plagne Bellecôte: La Maison de Dorothée (☎ 479 09 01 33). Plagne Centre: Garderie Marie Christine (☎ 479 09 11 81), Les P'tits Bonnets (☎ 479 09 00 83). Plagne Soleil: ESF (☎ 479 55 18 73). Plagne Villages: ESF (☎ 479 09 25 40)

### FOOD AND DRINK
Coffee €2–3, bottle of house wine €12, small beer €2.50–3.50, soft drink €3.20, dish of the day €12–14

# Risoul 1850

ALTITUDE 1,850m (6,068ft)                    map: see page 185

❋ skiing convenience ❋ value for money ❋ lack of queues
❋ late-season skiing ❋ reliable snow cover

**Best for:** beginners and intermediates, snowboarders, families, tree-skiers
**Not recommended for:** advanced skiers, skiing gourmets, night-owls

Purpose-built in the 1970s, Risoul 1850 has extensive and convenient family skiing and a reputation for reliable late-season snow, yet it remains an underrated destination. One reason is the transfer from Grenoble or Marseille, which one reporter aptly described as 'a big negative – very long and very hairy, especially when there is snow about, on one of Europe's highest roads'. However another commented: 'a thoroughly relaxing place for a holiday, refreshingly different from the hustle and bustle of Méribel'. The ski area of 57 lifts and 180km of piste is shared with neighbouring **Vars 1850** and is known as the Domaine de la Forêt Blanche.

Risoul's location far from any city means that the area is largely free of weekend overcrowding, and its clientèle is both family- and budget-oriented. It has long been a favourite with the British, but Eastern European visitors now supplant those from the UK among the 30 per cent of skiers who are not French.

The resort offers attractive, wood-and-stone apartment complexes, but its small downtown section is blighted by illegally parked cars, a lack of proper pavements and a ghastly profusion of billboards. However, reporters were impressed by the resort's convenience. As one reporter summed it up: 'Risoul may not be the prettiest place in the Alps and the transfer is long and difficult, but the payback is easy access to the slopes, a good variety of beginner and intermediate runs, and no long queues'.

## On-piste
top 2,750m (9,020ft) bottom 1,650m (5,412ft)
Risoul was 'an excellent base for two experienced if nervous parents and three speedy and decidedly un-nervous teenagers,' said one reporter. Lifts fan out from the village base, but the lift system still has a predominance of drag-lifts ('a bit of a pain'). A chair-lift takes you from the village all the way up to Payrefolle at 2,457m. Risoul offers three slalom race-training areas and a mogul-training course.

The Plate de la Nonne quad-chair takes you over to Vars 1850, and it is possible to ski back on blue runs. The green runs, with children's park and snowmaking at the bottom of Risoul, are some of the most attractive in Europe. The French Ski School (ESF) beginner area has its own bucket-lift.

Reporters praised the 'wide variety of interesting intermediate slopes'. The most notable pistes include the ridge-line run from Risoul's high point, Crête de Chabrières, and the return to the village from the liaisons on Razis, which requires a hike back up from below the car park. Virtually unskied are the long, wide, mogul-free reds into Vars-Sainte-Marie.

There are only eight black runs, which reporters say are graded thus more for their lack of grooming than their gradient.

Snowboarders rate Risoul as one of the best resorts in France, with freeriders spoilt for choice with its powder bowls. The Surfland terrain park on L'Homme de Pierre is regularly used for boardercross competitions; it has several quarter-pipes, an excellent half-pipe and numerous obstacles. Close to Surfland is a nursery slope that is ideal for beginner riders.

## Off-piste
Risoul has neither glaciers nor couloirs, but it does provide a lot of gladed powder-skiing after fresh snow. In the back bowl by Valbelle is a natural half-pipe shared by skiers and boarders. It is possible to ski below the resort to the old village of Risoul. The area to the skier's left of the Clos Chardon chair also offers reasonable challenges.

## Tuition and guiding
The ESF claims an average of ten skiers per class, but reporters have spotted groups of fifteen. However, we also have some favourable comments: 'instructors both cheerful and helpful'. The rival International Ski School (ESI) guarantees no more than eight pupils per class.

## Mountain restaurants
These are cheap enough but seriously lacking in cuisine and character. Barjo at the bottom of the Mayt chair on the Vars 1850 side offers overnight accommodation and food. Vallon and Valbelle are small spaghetti-and-*steak-frites* joints, while Le Têtras provides rooms and food. Vars L'Horizon at the top of the Sainte-Marie chair-lift is 'typically French'.

## Accommodation
The two-star Le Chardon Bleu (☎ 492 46 07 27) is the only hotel in Risoul 1850. Chalet accommodation is available, but most visitors opt for self-catering apartments ('excellent ski in, ski out apartments and chalets'). Les Mélèzes (☎ 492 46 03 47) is functional, seriously lacking in space, but in an 'excellent situation'. Le Belvédère (☎ 492 46 03 47) is bigger and better. A new residence, The four-star Balcons de Sirius (☎ 492 46 03 47)

opens for the 2004–5 season. There is no shuttle bus in the resort.

## Eating in and out
Cheap and plentiful are the burgers and *frites* at Snack Attack and Chez Robert. La Dalle en Pente and Le Cesier Snowboard Café have low prices and frequent special offers, and at La Cherine under Les Mélèzes apartments 'you sit at long tables and muck in – very good value'. L'Assiette Gourmande offers 'an altogether more sophisticated menu'.

## Après-ski
The Grotte du Yetti is a happy-hour haunt after the lifts close, while La Dalle en Pente has live bands and is open until 2am. Reporters commented that in high season late-night noise in the resort is a serious problem and that families should choose accommodation away from the village centre.

An unusual sport available here is 'ruissiling' – hiking with crampons and ice axes on frozen rivers.

## Childcare
Les Pitchouns crèche is conveniently located above the ESF and takes children from six months to six years of age. Both the ESF and ESI have children's learning areas.

# Risoul 1850: At a glance

**Tel** 33 492 46 02 60
**Email** o.t.risoul@wanadoo.fr
**Website** www.risoul.com

### GETTING THERE
**Airports** Grenoble 2½hrs, Marseille 3½hrs
**Rail** Montdauphin–Guillestre 17km
**Road** exit Grenoble–Briançon road towards Saint-Crepin and Guillestre

### THE SKIING
**Linked/nearby resorts** Vars 1850, Vars-Sainte-Marie
**Total of trails/pistes** 180km (47% easy, 41% intermediate, 10% difficult, 2% very difficult)
**Lifts in area** 57: 1⬡ 13⬠ 43⬤
**Lift opening dates** 4 December 2004 to 24 April 2005

### LIFT PASSES
**Area pass** Forêt Blanche (covers Risoul and Vars) €134.50 for 6 days

**Pensioners** Forêt Blanche 65–74yrs €115 for 6 days

### TUITION
**Ski & board** ESF (☎ 492 46 19 22), ESI (☎ 492 46 20 83)
**Guiding** through ski schools

### CHILDREN
**Lift pass** Forêt Blanche 5–11yrs €115 for 6 days
**Ski & board school** as adults
**Kindergarten** (ski) ESF and ESI mini-clubs as adults, (non-ski) Les Pitchouns (☎ 492 46 02 60)

### FOOD AND DRINK
Coffee €2–3, bottle of house wine €10–15, small beer €2.30–3.50, soft drink €2.50–4, dish of the day €10–16

# Sainte-Foy

**ALTITUDE 1,550m (5,084ft)**

## ❋ excellent off-piste ❋ uncrowded slopes ❋ burgeoning ski village

> **Best for:** advanced skiers and riders, powderhounds, day-trippers from other Tarentaise resorts
>
> **Not recommended for:** beginners to lower intermediates, families, gourmets, night-owls

For dedicated powder enthusiasts, Sainte-Foy was the great discovery of the 1990s. It began as a bold attempt by the unremarkable old farming community of the same name, on the road up from Bourg-St-Maurice, to market its outstanding terrain. Each winter, villagers watched the nose-to-tail cars heading for **Val d'Isère** and **Tignes** and thought 'why not us?' They therefore established their own little *station de ski*. For the happy years that followed, those in the know have commuted from Val d'Isère and Tignes to enjoy crowd-free groomed runs as well as exceptionally good off-piste. But now the secret is out. A chalet-building boom, headed by giant resort developer MGM, has caused Sainte-Foy to double in size.

## On the snow
**top 2,620m (8,596ft) bottom 1,550m (5,084ft)**

Three chair-lifts take you up to the Col de l'Aiguille and the starting point for 600m vertical of challenging piste and some dramatic powder descents. More lifts are needed to serve the expanded village, but so far planning permission has been refused on environmental grounds. A new chair-lift is planned for 2005–6 from the blue La Chapelle piste, which should create several new easy runs as well as providing additional off-piste possibilities.

The skiing receives rave reviews: 'no queues, empty pistes and awesome off-piste – who needs to go anywhere else?' enthused a reporter. The resort is also an excellent location for freeriders looking for natural drops and walls. Another reporter remarked: 'the piste map is a complete

smokescreen: it gives no indication of the hugeness of the off-piste terrain'. A guide is essential for enjoying the full off-piste potential.

Sainte-Foy's proximity to the Italian frontier means it is easy to organise a day's heli-skiing above **La Thuile** and **La Rosière**. Two outstanding itineraries are the Face Nord de Fogliettaz and the Couloir Dudu; the latter is an 800-m chute renowned for its spring powder. Both these runs end at Le Miroir, with its rustic eatery Chez Merie ('beautiful and cosy').

Other simple but atmospheric mountain eating-places include Les Brevettes, at the top of the first chair, as well as Maison à Colonnes, Chez Alison and the Bec de l'An at resort level. The French Ski School (ESF) offers group and private tuition for adults and children and has a good reputation.

## In the resort

'Plenty of French charm without the pretentiousness of other larger resorts,' was how one reporter described Sainte-Foy. Hotel Le Monal (☎ 479 06 90 07) is in the old village, and the British-owned Auberge sur la Montagne (☎ 479 06 95 83), in the neighbouring hamlet of La Thuile (not to be confused with the Italian resort of the same name), continues to receive praise: 'it has an ancient manor-house feel to it, and the chef was first class'.

Children aged three to eight are cared for at Club Enfants les P'tits Trappeurs, while Auberge sur la Montagne can organise childcare for its guests: 'really first rate,' commented a reporter. Beginners and small children can use the rope-tow lift.

> ## Sainte-Foy: At a glance
>
> **Tel** 33 479 06 95 19
> **Email** stefoy@wanadoo.fr
> **Website** www.saintefoy.net
> **Lifts in resort** 3: 3⏏
> **Lift opening dates** 18 December 2004 to 24 April 2005

# Serre Chevalier

ALTITUDE 1,200–1,500m (3,936–4,920ft)  map: see page 186

❄ large linked ski area ❄ attractive tree-lined slopes
❄ value for money ❄ varied off-piste

> **Best for:** intermediate cruisers seeking high mileage, snowboarders, families
> **Not recommended for:** non-skiers, those looking for quiet slopes (Chantemerle/Villeneuve), night-owls

'Le Grand Serre Che', as it is affectionately known to its thousands of loyal visitors, is the fourth largest ski area in France. 'This is indeed a superb and underrated resort,' enthused a reporter. Serre Chevalier is, in fact, not a resort in its own right but the collective name for more than a dozen villages and hamlets that line the main valley road between the Col du Lautaret and the ancient garrison town of Briançon.

Chantemerle (Serre Chevalier 1350) is the closest village to Briançon. Villeneuve–Le Bez (Serre Chevalier 1400) is the most central and lively ('a quaint old town oozing with character') and Monêtier-Les-Bains (Serre Chevalier 1500) is a pretty spa village that attracts the fewest tourists and has the highest skiing in the area. The old walled town of Briançon is directly linked by gondola to the substantial ski area. Buses connect all the villages and are commended as 'frequent and on time'. However, they do not go to all the lift stations so there is 'some tiresome walking'.

## On-piste
top 2,800m (9,184ft) bottom 1,200m (3,936ft)

As one reporter put it: 'The skiing is unbeatable – for all levels it is plentiful and wide ranging', and adept intermediates will particularly enjoy the 250km of cruising. The well-linked, albeit rather old-fashioned, lift system is covered by an efficient, electronic, hands-free lift pass. The three main mountain access points are from Villeneuve, Chantemerle and Briançon, with most of the lifts and pistes concentrated in the area above Villeneuve and Chantemerle. The Monêtier section, although less accessible, is the most appealing and is the least crowded in the whole area.

The Grand Alpe section above Chantemerle includes a decent but sometimes busy beginners' area, and Briançon has its own nursery slopes. There are commendable starter slopes at Monêtier and Villeneuve, with beginner lifts at their bases.

Monêtier has some enjoyable red pistes through the woods, such as that from Bachas at 2,180m down to the valley at Monêtier. The Cucumelle that connects Monêtier and Villeneuve is another recommended red: 'a long fun run with good potential for off-piste either side'.

Overall, Monêtier is the prime area for advanced skiers, although the high and exposed link with Villeneuve can sometimes be closed. Isolée is an exciting black, which starts on the ridge from L'Eychauda at 2,659m and plunges down towards Echaillon. Tabuc is a long black run through the woods with a couple of steep and narrow pitches. The Casse du Boeuf, a sweeping ridge through the trees back to Villeneuve, is, according to one reporter, 'better than sex, but more tiring'.

Snowboarders consider this to be one of the best resorts in France. The original terrain park is at the bottom of the Yret chair-lift, and the one at Villeneuve contains jumps, half- and quarter-pipes.

**WHAT'S NEW**
Bietonnet triple-chair upgraded to 6-person chair-lift

## Off-piste
The Fréjus–Echaillon section above Villeneuve provides some fine runs, with short and unprepared trails beneath the mountain crest. The Yret chair gives easy access to off-piste, including the testing face under the lift: 'take the less-explored La Montagnole route and discover the massive off-piste possibilities through the woods, over bridges and next to streams down to

the village of Monêtier', recommended one reporter.

## Tuition and guiding

We have generally favourable reports of the ESF in all the villages ('all the instructors speak good English, and groups were not too big'). Buissonnière ESI in Villeneuve received praise: 'the instructors all spoke excellent English and were very friendly, and the standard of teaching was high'. In all, Serre Chevalier has nine ski schools, with three of them specialising in off-piste tours. First Tracks, which is run by the ESF, is a specialist snowboarding school in Villeneuve, and Génération Snow is in Chantemerle. EurekaSki, the British-owned ski school run by BASI instructors in Monêtier, was praised by reporters: 'both of us had lessons and would thoroughly recommend it'.

## Mountain restaurants

The Pi Maï is 'the perfect piste-side restaurant. Great atmosphere, attentive service and superb food'. Café Soleil above Chantemerle is well located and has 'very well-prepared food and a great atmosphere, the best *vin chaud* and clean toilets, too'. Le Briance is also recommended. L'Echaillon is 'pretty and off the beaten track, with friendly staff', but is also said to be the 'poorest value for money'. Le Grand Alpe serves 'big portions', while Père et Noëlle is 'good value and lively'. L'Aravet was praised: 'the views were breathtaking, the food was very nice and great value'. Peyra Juana in Monêtier is 'a fabulous hut with a sun-soaked terrace. It serves excellent food with a friendly service'. Le Bachas above Monêtier was said to be 'pretty traditional. The food was good and the portions were excellent value for money'. Le Bivouac de la Casse is at the top of the Casse du Boeuf chair-lift. Le Relais de Ratier, situated at the Chantemerle's mid station, has a panoramic sun terrace.

## Accommodation

Most of Serre Chevalier's lodging is in apartments, and all accommodation can be booked through Serre Chevalier Reservations (☎ 492 24 98 80). The Altea, Vauban and Parc hotels are Briançon's three-stars, while the Pension des Ramparts is a small and simple hotel with a loyal following. The Grand Hotel at Chantemerle

is 'a modest place despite its name, and right opposite the lift station'.

Monêtier's Hotel Bonnabel is the only four-star in the valley. It has 23 rooms, of which 15 are duplexes. Also in Monêtier, Hotel Le Rif Blanc was said to be 'small, run by Brits, and the closest I've come to being at home in a hotel. However the rooms were small and the pipe work noisy'. Two-star Les Colchiques was praised as 'very friendly, the food was excellent and rooms of a decent size'. L'Auberge du Choucas is known for its gourmet cuisine. Le Lièvre Blanc in Villeneuve is a recommended British-owned two-star. Le Mont Thabor is a new three-star opening for the 2004–5 season, while Hotel des Glaciers (☎ 492 24 42 21) opened last season on the Col de Lautaret with wonderful views, and is the first four-star in the area. Chalet-Hotel Pi Mai (☎ 492 24 83 63), up the mountain in the hamlet of Fréjus, is 'wood-beamed, very comfortable, with great food'. Just outside Briançon, in the hamlet of Belvoir, is the area's most luxurious chalet, Chez Bear (☎ 492 21 11 70), which is run by a British couple ('a lovely old wooden building full of character').

## Eating in and out

A car is useful for visiting the many restaurants along the valley. In Villeneuve, Le Petit Duc is a friendly crêperie, and La Pastarele is recommended, Le Refuge serves fondue and *pierrade*, while Le Petit Lard is 'rustic, French and fantastic value'. Eau Petit Pont has 'a good-value set menu'. Le Bidule in Le Bez has a friendly ambience and specialises in fresh fish and seafood while La Manouille serves mountain specialities. Los Serranos in Chantemerle serves Mexican food. At Le Caribou in Monêtier 'the food in quality and presentation was delightful', Pére Benzol in Hotel Bonnabel serves gourmet fare, while Le Passé Simple in Briançon offers dishes from the seventeenth century. At Vauban, chef André Petit Pierre uses fresh produce in his cuisine.

## Après-ski

'In short – if you don't ski don't come,' said one reporter. Bars include Loco Loco ('if you want a chilled night out check it out'), Le Per et Noelle ('a friendly bar with lots of atmosphere') and the Bam Bam in

Villeneuve. Le Yeti and the Underground are the best late-night drinking places in Chantemerle; both provide live bands and stay open until 2am. Le Frog ('a very British clientèle') and La Baita discos in Villeneuve come alive at weekends. Le Cavaillou in Le Bez is highly recommended. Le Lièvre Blanc in Villeneuve is a riders' hangout with weekly live music. Bar Alpin has a 'really friendly atmosphere', as has the Bar Le Que Tai. Monêtier's restaurants and bars have a good ambience.

In Villeneuve, the Lucky Luc Ski received praise ('the staff were unfailingly friendly and helpful'), as did the Dr Feelgood shop at the base of the Aravet lift. Briançon is a bus ride away and has a hypermarket, a large Intersport and several other sports shops. The swimming-pool and fitness centre in Villeneuve contains a dedicated children's pool, Chantemerle's Altiforme health centre offers massage and beauty treatments, while Les Bains at Monêtier is a thermal spa with naturally hot water, at 37°C.

## Childcare

Each village has its own crèche and children's ski school. In Chantemerle, Les Poussins takes children from eight months. In Villeneuve, Les Schtroumpfs caters for little ones from six months, and Kids de l'Aventure is for children from seven years with activities such as dog-sledding. In Monêtier, Les Eterlous takes children aged eighteen months to six years.

The ESF Jardin des Neiges in all three resorts takes youngsters from three years. Génération Snow offers lessons to children aged seven to eleven years.

# Serre Chevalier: At a glance

**Tel** 33 492 24 98 98
**Email** contact@ot-serrechevalier.fr
**Website** www.serre-chevalier.com

## GETTING THERE
**Airports** Turin 1½hrs, Grenoble 2hrs, Lyon 3hrs
**Rail** Briançon 6km, regular bus service to resort
**Road** 2-hr journey from Grenoble relieved by spectacular rock formations

## THE SKIING
**Linked/nearby resorts** Alpe d'Huez, Les Deux Alpes, La Grave, Montgenèvre, Puy-St-Vincent
**Total of trails/pistes** 250km in linked area (19% easy, 69% intermediate, 12% difficult)
**Lifts in area** 74: 9🚠 19🚡 46🎿
**Lift opening dates** 27 November 2004 to 23 April 2005

## LIFT PASSES
**Area pass** Grande Serre Che (covers all centres as well as 1 day in each of Alpe d'Huez, Les Deux Alpes, La Grave, Montgenèvre, Puy-St-Vincent) €158 for 6 days
**Pensioners** Grande Serre Che 65–75yrs €112 for 6 days

## TUITION
**Ski & board** Chantemerle: ESF (☎ 492 24 17 41), Evasion ESI (☎ 492 24 02 41), Génération Snow 1350 (☎ 492 24 21 51), Legendre David (☎ 492

24 19 19), Montagne Aventure (☎ 492 24 05 51). Monêtier: ESF 1500 (☎ 492 24 42 66), EurekaSki (☎ 689 31 66 56, 01326 375710 in UK), Montagne et Ski (☎ 492 24 46 81). Villeneuve–Le Bez: Axesse (☎ 492 24 27 11), Buissonnière ESI (☎ 492 24 78 66), ESF 1400 (☎ 492 24 71 99), ESF First Tracks (☎ 492 24 71 99), Evasion ESI (☎ 492 24 02 41), Montagne à la Carte (☎ 492 24 73 20)
**Guiding** Compagnie des Guides de L'Oisans (☎ 492 24 75 90), Montagne à la Carte, Montagne et Ski

## CHILDREN
**Lift pass** Grande Serre Che 6–12yrs €112 for 6 days
**Ski & board school** as adults
**Kindergarten** Chantemerle: (ski/non-ski) ESF Jardin des Neiges (☎ 492 24 17 41), Génération Snow 1350 (☎ 492 24 21 51), Les Poussins (☎ 492 24 40 03). Monêtier: (ski/non-ski) ESF Jardin des Neiges (☎ 492 24 42 66), Les Eterlous (☎ 492 24 45 75). Villeneuve–Le Bez: (ski/non-ski) ESF Jardin des Neiges (☎ 492 24 71 99), Kids de l'Aventure (☎ 492 24 93 10), Les Schtroumpfs (☎ 492 24 70 95)

## FOOD AND DRINK
Coffee €1.50–2.50, bottle of house wine €12–15, small beer €2.50–3.50, soft drink €2.50–3.50, dish of the day €12–20

# La Tania

ALTITUDE 1,350m (4,429ft)                                             map: see page 181

❅ **part of giant Trois Vallées ski area** ❅ **skiing convenience**
❅ **reasonable prices** ❅ **large choice of chalet accommodation**
❅ **attractive village**

> **Best for:** all standards of skier and snowboarder, budget skiers in an expensive ski area, families
> **Not recommended for:** night-owls, those wanting a sophisticated resort

La Tania is a purpose-built but pleasant village that offers an alternative base to its expensive neighbours **Courchevel** and **Méribel**. It is situated a couple of kilometres by road from Le Praz (Courchevel 1300) and is linked by lift and piste to Courchevel 1850 as well as to Méribel via the Col de la Loze. The resort is served by a jumbo gondola and has developed its own village atmosphere. An attractive residential sector called Le Forêt, which is a collection of Scandinavian-style chalets set in the woods above the village, has greatly added to its charm as a no-frills family resort in a tranquil setting.

## On the snow
top 3,300m (10,825ft) bottom 1,300m (4,264ft)

La Tania has its own dedicated learning area, while second-weekers can cover immense distances on green and blue runs to (time permitting) the farther corners of **The Trois Vallées**. During a heavy snowfall or in flat light, the tree-lined slopes above La Tania provide some of the most enjoyable skiing in the whole of the Trois Vallées, but its position off the beaten track means that the area is always under-used. Snow-cannon made it possible last season to ski down to the resort right up until the closing date in late April.

The resort has its own branch of the French Ski School (ESF) as well as three independent schools: Arthur MacLean, Magic in Motion and Snow Ball. Olivier Houillot arranges off-piste guiding.

Le Bouc Blanc, at the top of La Tania gondola, provides what were considered by one reporter to be 'the best omelettes anywhere in the Trois Vallées, and the service is second to none – at this price level'. Pub Le Ski Lodge down in La Tania offers 'the cheapest lunches in the whole region'.

## In the resort
Many of the pleasant chalets attractively arranged in the woods above La Tania are run by British tour operators. Hotel Montana (☎ 479 08 80 08) in the village centre is 'excellent, modern and clean with large rooms, a piano bar and a small swimming-pool'. The Mountain Centre (☎ 01273 897525 in UK) consists of two wooden chalets with pine-clad, two- to four-bedded rooms, many of which are en suite. You can arrive and depart on any day of the week and decide on the day whether you want to eat in or out in the evening.

La Tania contains four reasonably priced restaurants including Pub Le Ski Lodge and La Taiga, which are described as 'welcoming and serve tasty, (relatively) inexpensive food'. The restaurant in Hotel Montana serves local and international dishes. La Tania's nightlife has much improved in recent years: the resort boasts a handful of bars with a relaxed atmosphere, headed by Pub Le Ski Lodge, which has live music on Tuesday nights.

The Maison des Enfants and the Jardin des Neiges non-ski and ski-kindergarten take children from three to twelve years old.

> ## La Tania: At a glance
> **Tel** 33 479 08 40 40
> **Email** info@latania.com
> **Website** www.latania.com
> **Lifts in area** 189 in Trois Vallées: 40🚠 68🚡 81🎿
> **Lift opening dates** 17 December 2004 to 24 April 2005

# Tignes

ALTITUDE 2,100m (6,888ft)                                    map: see page 187

## ❄ large well-linked ski area ❄ excellent lift system ❄ long ski season ❄ reliable snow record ❄ skiing convenience

**Best for:** all standards of skier and rider, early- and late-season skiers

**Not recommended for:** those seeking a traditional resort with village atmosphere, people who like tree-level skiing, non-skiers

France's principal high-altitude resort in the Haute Tarentaise has faced enormous criticism over the years because of its original, high-rise architecture. This dates from the 1960s and is wholly alien to Tignes' glorious mountain setting at the foot of the twin peaks of the Grande Motte and the Grande Casse. However, the resort has spent £35 million in the past five years in an effort to improve its appearance. New buildings, constructed in a much more sympathetic style than the old ones, are slowly replacing some of the worst 40-year-old architectural excesses, and so Tignes is undergoing an impressive renaissance. Many of the older buildings have been re-clad and apartment owners have been given financial incentives to carry out renovations. Of the two main villages in Tignes, Le Lac has been entirely remodelled with a tunnel bypass, and new buildings in Val Claret are much more appealing.

The hamlets of Tignes-le-Lavachet and even the much lower community of Tignes-les-Boisses are also all changing their appearance, although the valley farming community of Tignes-les-Brévières will always remain the most visually attractive.

Tignes' ski area is directly linked by gondola and high-speed chair-lift to neighbouring **Val d'Isère**, and the two resorts are jointly marketed as **L'Espace Killy**, after its most revered son Jean-Claude Killy, who swept the board of gold medals at the 1968 Winter Olympics. A vertical drop of 1,900m coupled with 97 lifts, including two high-speed funiculars, four gondolas and four cable-cars, form a hard-core infrastructure for mountain access that few resorts can match. Lack of skier demand throughout much of the summer, coupled with the need to service machinery and protect snow cover for when the crowds begin to arrive in mid-November, means that the glacier in Tignes is no longer open for 365 days of the year.

The original village of Tignes disappeared beneath the waters of the Lac de Chevril when the valley was dammed in 1952 as part of a hydro-electric scheme. The decision to flood it causes bitter resentment among locals even after half a century. The lake, enclosed by a dam that depicts a giant figure of Hercules, forms a reserve source of power that ironically has never been used.

Val d'Isère can be reached from Tignes by ski lifts or buses, although the latter are neither frequent nor cheap. If you have your own car and want a change of scenery, day-trips are also possible to **Les Arcs**, **La Plagne**, **La Rosière** and **Sainte-Foy**.

## On-piste
top 3,456m (11,335ft) bottom 1,550m (5,084ft)

Tignes' core skiing is on the Grande Motte, served by a modern funicular, which ferries skiers from Val Claret at 2,100m to the Panoramic restaurant at 3,030m in just six minutes. A cable-car and a network of chair- and drag-lifts serve the extensive summer ski area. It is usually possible to ski 1,400m vertical from the end of October until the lifts close in early May.

A modern network of lifts takes you from Le Lac towards the dramatic rock formation of L'Aiguille Percée, in one direction, or towards Tovière and Val d'Isère's more demanding ski area in the other. For most of the season there is further skiing down to the lower-lying hamlets of Tignes-les-Boisses at 1,850m and Tignes-les-Brévières at 1,550m.

Tignes has a good choice of blue runs on the glacier, but the usually chilly temperature is not conducive to learning.

The long descent to Val Claret is a test for even the fittest of intermediates with strong thigh muscles when taken without stopping.

'There's not a great deal on-piste for the advanced skier,' commented one reporter, and 'there aren't many black runs'. However, Sache, a long black with fierce moguls, starts from the blue Corniche run below L'Aiguille Percée and tests the best as it meanders down to Tignes-les-Brévières, where it merges with the red Pavot.

The Val Claret terrain park at Tignes has a half-pipe, a boardercross course and assorted obstacles. A terrain park operates on the Grande Motte Glacier in summer. The summer ski area comprises 20km of piste and is accessible to pedestrians.

## Off-piste

L'Espace Killy has some of the best lift-served off-piste in the world. Once you commit yourself, you are on your own and it is easy to get lost – or worse. Some years ago a tragedy involving a group of British doctors showed that avalanche danger can be extreme after a fresh snowfall. It is imperative to have an experienced local guide who can read the snow conditions and knows which routes are safe.

Some of the inviting powder easily reached from the top of the Grande Motte is deceptively crevassed, and incredibly steep couloirs lead down off the shoulders.

The top of the Col du Palet is the starting point for a long and beautiful tour of neighbouring valleys, including La Plagne and Les Arcs.

## Tuition and guiding

To get the best out of the ski area you need some expert help: Tignes has seven ski and snowboard schools as well as half-a-dozen recognised and licensed individual instructors. The ESF at Le Lac was warmly praised: 'the best value I have ever known. The standard of teaching ranged between good and superb'. Evolution 2 received mixed reviews: 'expert tuition from an expert skier', enthused one reporter. 'A little disappointing', said another, 'they didn't try very hard to get people into groups of similar standard – just a couple of questions about how good you are without even a quick ski off'. Evolution 2 also offers a range of non-skiing activities, including ice-diving under the lake. We have no reports of the FSI (International Ski

School). Snow Fun has been operating here for 16 years ('small classes and a cheerful English-speaking instructor'). Snocool at Le Lac, Kébra and Surf Feeling at Val Claret, are the specialist board schools, while 333, based at Val Claret, teaches both disciplines. Henri Authier at Le Lac specialises in bump skiing technique.

## Mountain restaurants

Le Panoramic, at the top of the Grande Motte funicular, is under new management and offers a self-service and separate waiter-service restaurant ('surprisingly good, with courteous staff'). At lunch-time many snow-users return to the valley, where restaurants are as busy as they are by night.

Upstairs at L'Arbina in Le Lac is 'a serious but reasonably priced gastronomic experience with a bargain daily *formule skier* menu, but you must book, even at lunch-time'. The Brasserie downstairs is full of atmosphere and serves regional specialities. The restaurant at the Col du Palet is described as 'very welcoming', while La Taverne at Val Claret is 'better and cheaper than most restaurants in the region'. Le Chalet du Bollin is recommended for 'its delicious crêpes and homemade tarts'.

## Accommodation

Most of the accommodation is in self-catering apartments, which vary dramatically in quality in direct relation to their age. The MGM spa complex (☎ 020-7584 2841 in UK) at Val Claret heads the list for the combination of comfort and convenience. Four-star Le Ski d'Or (☎ 479 06 51 60) in Val Claret has 'bright, spacious rooms'. All the accommodation in Le Lac's lavish Village Montana (☎ 479 40 01 44) is in large suites, some of which are duplexes, and some have saunas. Slightly lower down the price scale, Alpaka Lodge (☎ 479 06 45 30) is said to be 'extremely comfortable'. Also recommended are Le Lévanna (☎ 479 06 32 94) and Les Campanules (☎ 479 06 34 36), both at Le Lac.

The clutch of two-stars includes the well-positioned Hotel L'Arbina (☎ 479 06 34 78) at Le Lac decorated in Savoyard style with a small health centre, and Hotel La Vanoise (☎ 479 06 31 90) at Val Claret ('comfortable, the food was of a high standard and staff very pleasant; it really is ski-in, ski-out').

## Eating in and out

Tignes has 60 restaurants divided between the three villages. In Le Lac, Upstairs at Hotel L'Arbina is considered by many to be the best gourmet restaurant in the whole region. La Côte de Boeuf is 'heaven for meat-lovers'. In Le Lavachet at La Ferme des Trois Capucines, which claims to be the highest working farm in Europe, you can watch the cows behind a glass wall as you eat. In Val Claret, Le Caveau is 'a lovely underground restaurant with friendly service and lots of atmosphere'. La Pignatta is recommended as 'an Italian restaurant with huge courses and a lovely atmosphere'. Daffy's Café is a lively Tex-Mex, and Le Ski d'Or is praised for its fresh fish. La Pizzéria 2000 'is much more than your standard pizzeria – it also has fondue and raclette'. The five supermarkets in Tignes sell a wide range of food and other goods at mountain prices.

## Après-ski

Harri's Bar in Le Lavachet describes itself as 'a British pub that got lost and ended up on a mountain', while TC's provides lively competition. In Le Lac, Le Café de la Poste has live music, as does the Red Lion ('good fun and full each night'). In Val Claret, Grizzly's Bar, decorated with carved and stuffed bears of various sizes, is warmly recommended: 'one of the few drinking joints with character'. The Fish Tank 'is too much like a Brit bar on the Costa del Sol', while the Crowded House was 'fun for all age groups'. The discos in Val Claret are Sub Zero, which has live music ('a scream') and Blue Girl ('features themed evenings – including topless ones').

## Childcare

Les Marmottons is for children from two years old ('our four-year-old enjoyed it and learnt a lot, although there was a lot of French spoken, which alienated the four or five English kids'). The ESF at Tignes Le Lac and Val Claret offers all-day ski lessons with lunch from four years of age, and the ESI from five. Evolution 2 at Val Claret takes children from three years of age and provides free helmets.

# Tignes: At a glance

**Tel** 33 479 40 04 40
**Email** information@tignes.net
**Website** www.tignes.net

### GETTING THERE
**Airports** Chambéry 2hrs, Lyon 2½hrs, Geneva 3hrs
**Rail** Bourg-St-Maurice 26km, regular buses
**Road** autoroute to Albertville, continue through Moûtiers and Bourg-St-Maurice, fork right to Tignes. Steep climb into resort

### THE SKIING
**Linked/nearby resorts** Les Arcs, La Plagne, La Rosière, Sainte-Foy, Val d'Isère
**Total of trails/pistes** 300km in L'Espace Killy (15% easy, 47% intermediate, 38% difficult)
**Lifts in area** 97 in L'Espace Killy: 2⬛ 8⬛ 46⬛ 41⬛
**Lift opening dates** 2 October 2004 to 8 May 2005. Summer skiing on Grande Motte Glacier in July and August

### LIFT PASSES
**Area pass** L'Espace Killy €187 for 6 days

**Pensioners** L'Espace Killy 60–74yrs €159 for 6 days

### TUITION
**Ski & board** 333 (☎ 479 06 20 88), ESF (☎ 479 06 30 28), ESI (☎ 479 06 36 15), Evolution 2 (☎ 479 06 43 78), Henri Authier (☎ 479 06 36 38), Kébra (☎ 479 06 43 37), Snocool (☎ 615 34 54 63), Snow Fun (☎ 479 06 46 10), Surf Feeling (☎ 479 06 53 63)
**Guiding** Bureau des Guides (☎ 479 06 42 76), Tetra (☎ 479 41 97 07) and through ski schools

### CHILDREN
**Lift pass** L'Espace Killy 5–12yrs €140.50 for 6 days
**Ski & board school** ESF, ESI, Evolution 2, Snow Fun
**Kindergarten** (ski/non-ski) Les Marmottons (☎ 479 06 51 67)

### FOOD AND DRINK
Coffee €3.70, bottle of house wine €12–16, small beer €3.60, soft drink €3.50, dish of the day €12–20

# Val d'Isère

ALTITUDE 1,850m (6,068ft)

map: see page 187

❉ **large well-linked ski area** ❉ **excellent lift system** ❉ **lively après-ski** ❉ **reliable snow cover** ❉ **wonderful off-piste opportunities**

> **Best for:** intermediate to advanced skiers and riders, night-owls, early- and late-season skiers
>
> **Not recommended for:** second-week skiers, non-skiers, gourmets

Val d'Isère, situated at the head of the Tarentaise Valley, induces a level of passionate partisan commitment among its devotees that is unequalled elsewhere. Together with neighbouring **Tignes**, it forms a rugged, boundary-free, snow-sure playground that is marketed as **L'Espace Killy**. This best suits a breed of dedicated enthusiast who knows his or her own DIN setting and seeks to escape the corral of tame, pristine, piste-only skiing that is imposed by the commercial machinations of other, understandably safety-conscious, major French resorts. Two reasons for Val's appeal are apparent: firstly, its altitude and micro-climate ensure that skiing is possible from the beginning of December until early May. Secondly, its off-piste terrain is some of the most enjoyable, demanding and easily lift-accessed of any in Europe.

The emphasis on chalets and hotels rather than self-catering apartments has given Val a much more elevated profile over the years than mass-market Tignes. The British form a mighty 32 per cent of the skiers. They are so prevalent that you might be forgiven for thinking - as in Méribel - that English is the resort's primary language. However, unlike Méribel, Val d'Isère also has a dedicated 45 per cent following among French skiers - who view it, along with Chamonix, as one of the two best resorts in France for serious skiers. The two nationalities co-exist with a harmonious respect for each other's commitment to the mountain that is rarely found in the Trois Vallées.

During the French school holidays in February the pistes are inevitably crowded, but otherwise queuing is not a problem. Air

Val d'Isère (96.1 FM) gives up-to-date news on piste grooming, as well as weather and snow reports.

Val d'Isère meanders for a couple of kilometres from the purpose-built hamlet of La Daille to the old houses of Le Fornet, but its commercial heart is sandwiched between two roundabouts in the middle, with Val Village, a cluster of 'old-style' stone buildings, housing smart boutiques, surrounding the eleventh-century church.

The resort's free bus service, known as the *train rouge*, plies every few minutes from one end to the other, linking the different bed bases. However, buses between Val d'Isère and Tignes are neither frequent nor cheap. If you have your own car and want a change of scenery, day-trips to **Les Arcs**, **La Plagne**, **La Rosière** and **Sainte-Foy** are also possible.

## On-piste
top 3,456m (11,335ft) bottom 1,550m (5,084ft)

The quality of the skiing in the area is so varied and demanding that it has raised a whole generation of international experts who never ski anywhere else. Val d'Isère alone has eight major points of mountain access, including a high-speed underground funicular. A giant gondola, with 30-person cabins, from the village to the top of Bellevarde provides the speediest way of reaching most of the skiing.

In the 2003–4 season the six-person Lessières Express lift replaced the ancient double-chair, up-and-over link between Solaise and L'Iseran. Another important innovation in recent seasons has been the upgrade of the Tommeuse and Fresse chairs to high-speed detachables. These provide the important all-weather links to Tignes. Together with other modern lifts, including the Glacier Express, it is now perfectly feasible to ski the entire length of the area, from Le Fornet to Tignes and back in a single morning.

You don't have to be an expert to ski here, but you do need to be prepared for an alternative standard of piste-marking. Green means blue elsewhere. A 'benign' red would be classified as a black throughout Italy or Austria. The resort has acceptable – and free – nursery slopes right in the centre of the village, but there is little for the improving beginner.

Val d'Isère's half of L'Espace Killy divides into three sectors: Col de l'Iseran/Glacier de Pissaillas, Solaise and Bellevarde. The first two sectors are linked by the Lessières Express, but Solaise and Bellevarde join only at valley level – across the nursery slopes in the village centre. Bellevarde links easily with Tignes via the Tovière ridge/Col de Fresse.

Piste-grooming in Val d'Isère is of an exceptionally high standard. A programme of grass-seeding and the removal of stones during the summer months means that runs that used to need 70cm of snow are now perfectly skiable with only a 20cm base. However, the severity of the terrain makes it very susceptible to avalanches. In high winds or after a major dump the whole area is liable to temporary closure. Those in the know take a day out on the protected pistes of Sainte-Foy.

Val offers some exceptional freeriding as well as lots of natural cliffs and gullies for snowboarders. The terrain park, situated above La Daille, and accessed by the Mont Blanc chair-lift, has a half-pipe and two boardercross courses.

## Off-piste

For the expert, the real joy lies in the unlimited off-piste opportunities to be found in this wild region. It is essential to hire a local guide who can read the snow conditions and knows which routes are safe. In fresh powder the Charvet area is a particular favourite ('there is no greater thrill than cutting first tracks on the Face du Charvet or the Couloir Mont Blanc before skiing the Bec d'Aigle'). The Signal de l'Iseran/Pissaillas glacier sector provides some of the most dramatic runs, including, when conditions permit, the long descent through the Gorges de Malpasset.

## Tuition and guiding

Val possesses no fewer than 12 ski and snowboard schools. The French Ski School (ESF) has a strong presence ('kids' classes overcrowded with some fairly grumpy instructors'), but Anglo-Saxons tend to favour the alternatives. Pat Zimmer's Top Ski was the first independent ski school in France when founded in 1976 ('all the instructors are simply in a different class to their rivals'). We have positive reports of Mountain Masters and Alpine Experience, who also run primarily off-piste operations. Evolution 2, Snow Fun and Oxygène concentrate on the British market, but with emphasis on ski group and private ski lessons. We have had mixed reports of Evolution 2. The Development Centre, a small British school, received rave reviews.

## Mountain restaurants

Eating out at altitude is not L'Espace Killy's strongest point. La Fruitière, at the top of the La Daille gondola, and Le Signal, at the top of the Le Fornet cable-car, both have gourmet pretensions. L'Edelweiss, near the bottom of Le Fornet, was new for the 2003–4 season: 'a great addition to Val's lunch opportunities'. A Mongolian Yurt at Le Signal has 'a roaring log fire where you can stop for a dozen oysters or snails – wonderful'.

Other good establishments include Trifollet, off the OK descent to La Daille, and Les Tufs, beside the Funival bottom station. Bananas, in the resort, is a favourite among reporters – for the ambience rather than the quality of the food.

## Accommodation

Les Barmes de l'Ours (☎ 479 41 37 00) is Val's first four-star hotel of true international standard ('a serious spa and pool, as well as an abundance of bleached wood, black slate floors and painstakingly distressed furniture'). The Christiania (☎ 479 06 08 25) is another comfortable four-star and the Blizzard (☎ 479 06 02 07) is popular, while the three-stars Savoyarde (☎ 479 06 01 55) and Tsanteleina (☎ 479 06 12 13) enjoy a strong British following. Hotel Les Sorbiers (☎ 479 06 23 77) is in a renovated, wood-and-stone chalet style. The piste-side Hotel Brussel's (☎ 479 06 05 39) is praised, despite being 'stuck in a 1970s time warp'.

For self-caterers, Alpina Lodge Résidence (☎ 479 41 60 00) is recommended for 'location, prices, reasonable accommodation and very helpful staff', and Aspen Lodge (☎ 020-8875 1957 in UK) contains apartments that are 'extremely comfortable and in the best possible position on the high street'. Mountain Rooms (☎ 0700 2000 456 in UK) have a wide range of accommodation to rent.

## Eating in and out

La Grande Ourse ('a gastronomic outpost in the desert') is Val's premier shot at gourmet dining, and Chalet du Crêt has 'definitely the best food in town and great Savoyard ambience'. The Blizzard is 'exceptionally good', while Le Canyon is warmly praised for 'excellent food at not unreasonable prices, but service is unreasonably slow'. The Perdrix Blanche is renowned for its fresh fish and seafood. Casa Scara is praised too. Les Clochetons, just out of town in the Manchet Valley, provides a free minibus service as well as 'a great meal at a reasonable price in a lovely setting'. Val d'Isère has four supermarkets ('the Casino supermarket is much nicer than my local Tesco – and better stocked').

## Après-ski

Dick's Tea Bar remains the most celebrated disco in the Alps and is the only nightclub in the resort. It is hoped that its new owners Mark Warner will give it the makeover it

has been waiting for these past two decades. It closes at 4am. Earlier après-ski centres around Café Face, Le Petit Danois, Victors, the Pacific Bar, Le Pub and the Saloon Bar beneath Hotel Brussel's. British teenagers gather downstairs at Bananas.

## Childcare

ESF, Snow Fun, Oxygène and Evolution 2 all cater for beginners from three or four years old. Oxygène is highly praised ('our seven-year-old daughter was taught by a sympathetic young Brit who made the whole week enormous fun'). Billabong snowboard school is for riders aged seven and over. Top Ski runs 'Discover the Mountain' classes for experienced children aged twelve to seventeen.

The Village d'Enfants caters for three- to thirteen-year-olds from 8.30am to 6.30pm daily, with ski lessons for the older ones. Petit Poucet kindergarten collects and delivers children aged three and over from your chalet or hotel. The Jardin de Neige accepts youngsters from four to five years.

# Val d'Isère: At a glance

**Tel** 33 479 06 06 60
**Email** info@valdisere.com
**Website** www.valdisere.com

### GETTING THERE
**Airports** Chambéry 2hrs, Lyon 2½hrs, Geneva 3hrs
**Rail** Bourg-St-Maurice 30km, regular buses
**Road** autoroute to Albertville, continue through Moûtiers and Bourg-St-Maurice. Steep climb into resort

### THE SKIING
**Linked/nearby resorts** Les Arcs, La Plagne, La Rosière, Sainte-Foy, Tignes
**Total of trails/pistes** 300km in L'Espace Killy (15% easy, 47% intermediate, 38% difficult)
**Lifts in area** 97 in L'Espace Killy: 2🚠 8🚡 46🚡 41🎿
**Lift opening dates** 27 November 2004 to 8 May 2005. Summer skiing in July on Glacier de Pissaillas

### LIFT PASSES
**Area pass** L'Espace Killy €187 for 6 days
**Pensioners** L'Espace Killy 60–74yrs €159 for 6 days

### TUITION
**Ski & board** Alpine Experience (☎ 479 06 28 81),

Billabong (☎ 479 06 09 54), The Development Centre (☎ 615 55 31 56), ESF (☎ 479 06 02 34), Evolution 2 (☎ 479 41 16 72), Misty Fly (☎ 479 40 08 74), Mountain Masters (☎ 479 06 05 14), Oxygène (☎ 479 41 99 58), Ski Concept (☎ 688 67 25 63), Snow Fun (☎ 479 06 19 79), Tetra Horspiste (☎ 479 41 97 07), Top Ski (☎ 479 06 14 80), Val Gliss (☎ 479 06 00 72)
**Guiding** Bureau des Guides (☎ 479 06 94 03) and through ski schools

### CHILDREN
**Lift pass** L'Espace Killy 5–12yrs €140.50 for 6 days
**Ski & board school** Billabong, ESF, Evolution 2, Oxygène, Snow Fun, Top Ski, Val Gliss
**Kindergarten** (ski/non-ski) Evolution 2 Yéti Courses (☎ 479 41 16 72), Jardin de Neige (☎ 479 06 02 34), Petit Poucet (☎ 479 06 13 97), Snow Fun Club Nounours (☎ 479 06 16 79), Village d'Enfants (☎ 479 40 09 81)

### FOOD AND DRINK
Coffee €3.60, bottle of house wine €12–20, small beer €3.50–4, soft drink €3.50–4, dish of the day €12–20

# Val Thorens and the Belleville Valley

ALTITUDE Les Menuires 1,850m (6,068ft), St-Martin-de-Belleville
1,450m (4,757ft), Val Thorens 2,300m (7,544ft)                    map: see page 188

❋ adjoining resorts in the giant Trois Vallées ❋ skiing convenience
❋ extensive skiing for all standards ❋ snow-sure resort (Val Thorens)
❋ attractive old village (St-Martin)
❋ budget accommodation (Les Menuires)

---

**Best for:** all standards of skier and snowboarder, off-piste skiers, early- and late-season skiers (Val Thorens), anyone wanting village atmosphere (St-Martin)

**Not recommended for:** non-skiers, night-owls (St-Martin)

---

Val Thorens lays claim to being the highest ski village in western Europe and is the highest of the four principal resorts of the giant **Trois Vallées**. With its 189 lifts and 600km of prepared pistes, the Trois Vallées is the largest truly linked ski area in the world.

In fact, the Trois Vallées is no longer confined to three valleys but stretches over the back of Val Thorens into the Maurienne Valley and the Pointe de Bouchet ski area. It can be also accessed from Orelle, which is only a two-hour drive from Turin via the Fréjus tunnel. Consequently the number of Italians on the pistes has greatly increased.

At 2,300m, Val Thorens has the advantage of being the most snow-sure ski destination in France, with virtually guaranteed conditions from late November until early May. Its glacier usually opens for limited summer skiing during the French *Grandes Vacances* in July, but following damage to the permafrost during the August heat wave of 2003 it has remained closed.

On a blue-sky morning Val Thorens can be a place of magic, surrounded by pristine pistes that take you into the heart of the village, and a backdrop of glittering peaks dominated by the 3,562-m Aiguille de Péclet. But on a winter's afternoon when the weather closes in, few places in the Alps offer such an inhospitable environment. In flat light, the tree-less pistes lack any points of reference.

**Les Menuires** lies 450m vertical down the mountain road. This purpose-built resort was once known as the ugliest resort in the Alps, an image offset by low prices that allowed budget visitors a reasonable base from which to explore this otherwise wickedly expensive ski area. However, times are changing. The modern satellites of Reberty, Les Bruyères and Preyerand are positively attractive. This leaves only the central 1960s-built La Croisette as an architectural eyesore, but that too is slowly being transformed. In April 2004, the original *résidence* at the entrance to the resort was demolished and replaced by a smart new complex of MGM chalets. One inevitable consequence of this urban transformation is that prices are no longer significantly lower here than elsewhere in the Trois Vallées.

In complete contrast, **St-Martin-de-Belleville**, further still down the road to Moûtiers, is an old stone farming village. Many of the original barns have been turned into restaurants or chalets, but you can still buy fresh milk and local cheese.

## On-piste
3,300m (10,827ft) bottom 1,400m (4,593ft)

A high-tech series of constantly upgraded cable-cars, gondolas and chair-lifts serve the open slopes above and below Val Thorens, and a cable-car ferries advanced skiers and riders to the 3,230-m summit of the Cime de Caron. This is the starting point for the Combe de Caron, which is one of the most demanding black pistes in the region.

A Funitel gondola and a chair-lift take you up to the highest point of the ski area at 3,300m, while half-a-dozen other lifts transport skiers from Val Thorens and Les

Menuires to the ridge that divides the Belleville Valley from **Méribel**.

Enjoyable red and blue runs take you back down across undulating south-facing pastures to Les Menuires. A modern Funitel cluster-gondola provides an all-weather link between Val Thorens and the rest of the Trois Vallées. Another gondola from St-Martin connects with a fast quad-chair up to the Tougnette ridge and has much improved mountain access to Méribel. The Pointe de La Masse, on the other side of Les Menuires, and reached by gondola, offers delightful skiing for both intermediates and advanced snow-users.

## WHAT'S NEW

Grand Lac drag replaced by Granges 6-person chair-lift

All three Belleville Valley resorts have dedicated learning areas. The terrain park at Les Menuires is described as 'wild, with lots of jumps 'n' stuff'. In Val Thorens the park is situated on the Deux Lacs pistes and has a 110-m half-pipe as well as tables, hips, a hand-rail and a boardercross course.

Val Thorens also has a high-speed 6-km toboggan run with a drop of 700m vertical. It is operational only during skiing hours and is situated in the Tête Ronde sector, reached by the Péclet gondola.

## Off-piste

After a fresh dump, the Méribel ridge is the jumping-off point for the best powder in the region, with seemingly endless variations on the long route down towards St-Martin and Les Menuires. Long itineraries lead down from La Masse towards St-Martin. The powder runs from the summit of Cime de Caron include the scenic Itinéraire du Lou.

## Tuition and guiding

Val Thorens has four ski and snowboard schools. The ESI received one critical report: 'in spite of repeated requests for instruction, our private instructor seemed to think we wanted a guided tour of the blue runs in the area'. The other schools are the ESF, Ski Cool and Pros-Neige. The ESF also operates in Les Menuires and St-Martin.

## Mountain restaurants

L'Oxalys at Val Thorens is a 'welcome gastronomic lunch place'. Etape 3200 at the top of the Cime de Caron 'has the best view in the Trois Vallées, but be careful how you open your can of coke'. Le Galoubet is also recommended.

In Les Menuires, Chalet 2000 in the Reberty *quartier* is 'an undiscovered treat' with a shaded terrace. Chalet des Neiges has 'good food and a sunny terrace', and Quatres Vents at Les Bruyères 'maintains a consistent standard'. In St-Martin, Le Corbeley has 'a sunny terrace and good food', while L'Etoile de Neige is a lunchtime favourite with ski guides.

## Accommodation

Most visitors to Val Thorens stay in apartments or chalets. The standard of these has improved enormously in recent years. L'Oxalys four-star chalet complex is the smartest (☎ 479 00 20 51), while the four-star Fitz-Roy (☎ 479 00 04 78) is the pick of a cluster of hotels. The Val Thorens (☎ 479 00 04 33), Le Val Chavière (☎ 479 00 00 33) and Le Portillo (☎ 479 00 00 88) are recommended three-stars. Le Bel Horizon (☎ 479 00 06 08) and Le Sherpa (☎ 479 00 00 70) are cheaper options.

Les Menuires is mainly apartment territory and the standard has vastly improved in recent years, with luxury developments that include Les Alpage de Reberty, MGM's Hameau des Marmottes and Les Montagnettes. All can be booked through the reservations office (☎ 479 00 79 79). The three-star Hotel Maeva Latitudes (☎ 479 00 75 10) in Les Bruyères offers some of the best-value accommodation. The three-star L'Ours Blanc (☎ 479 00 61 66) at Reberty is also praised. In St-Martin, recommended hotels include the three-stars St-Martin (☎ 479 00 88 00), Alp'Hôtel (☎ 479 08 92 82) and Hotel Edelweiss (☎ 479 08 96 67) ('pleasant with a good restaurant').

## Eating in and out

L'Oxalys, run by celebrity chef Jean-Michel Bouvier, is 'worth coming on holiday just to eat here'. Chalet des Glaciers is its nearby rival. La Joyeuse Fondue, Le Vieux Chalet and Bloopers are all praised. Chamois d'Or serves 'excellent smoked salmon and avocado salad', and Le Blanchot is 'quite fantastic, with a great wine list'. La Paillotte is recommended for crêpes and fresh trout, while La Ferme de Rosalie specialises in casseroles ('home cooking at its best').

In Les Menuires, recommended eateries include La Marmite du Géant, La Ferme de Reberty and The Trattoria. Les Sonnailles has 'wonderful fondues, raclette and a delicious *tartiflette*'. In St-Martin, L'Eterlou boasts 'a sunny terrace and friendly staff', while La Montagnarde is 'strong on cheese and potatoes in hayloft-like surroundings'. La Voutte has 'good food and drink at fair prices'. Chef René Meilleur's La Bouitte, at nearby St-Marcel, has a Michelin star and is considered to be one of the finest restaurants in the region.

## Après-ski

The popular watering-holes at Val Thorens are Le Tango, the Ski Rock Café, the Viking Pub, and the Frog and Roast Beef. The renovated sports centre contains a health club as well as tennis and squash courts.

Après-ski in Les Menuires involves a wide range of sporting alternatives including skating, tubing and swimming, as well as concerts in the village hall for the less active. Among the lively bars are the Tilbury, L'Oisans and the Jungle Bungle. St-Martin has 'a couple of good bars, but is pretty quiet by night'.

## Childcare

In Val Thorens, skiing- and non-skiing children are cared for by the ESF at Village Montana and Village Roc. They provide all-day care for children from three months, with lessons for three-year-olds and over.

In Les Menuires, non-skiing children from three months are looked after at the Village des Schtroumpfs in La Croisette, and those from two-and-a-half years at the Village des Piou Piou in Bruyères. The ESF gives lessons from three years. In St-Martin, the Piou Piou takes skiing and non-skiing children from two-and-a-half ('a very clean nursery – but with little English spoken our kids found it rather daunting and they didn't learn much').

# Val Thorens and the Belleville Valley: At a glance

**Tel** Les Menuires 33 479 00 73 00 / St-Martin 33 479 00 20 00 / Val Thorens 33 479 00 08 08
**Email** Les Menuires and St-Martin: lesmenuires@lesmenuires.com / Val Thorens: valtho@valthorens.com
**Websites** www.lesmenuires.com / www.st-martin-de-belleville.com / www.valthorens.com

## GETTING THERE
**Airports** Chambéry 2hrs, Lyon 2½hrs, Geneva 3hrs
**Rail** Eurostar from Waterloo or Ashford to Moûtiers, 33km away
**Road** autoroute to Albertville, steep climb from Moûtiers

## THE SKIING
**Linked/nearby resorts** Courchevel, Les Menuires, Méribel, St-Martin-de-Belleville, La Tania
**Total of trails/pistes** 300km in the Belleville Valley (40% easy, 50% intermediate, 10% difficult), 600km in Trois Vallées
**Lifts in area** 189 in Trois Vallées: 40⬡ 68⬡ 81⬡
**Lift opening dates** Val Thorens: 1 November 2004 to 8 May 2005. Les Menuires: 11 December 2004 to end April 2005

## LIFT PASSES
**Area pass** Trois Vallées €204 for 6 days

**Pensioners** Trois Vallées 60–72yrs €164 for 6 days

## TUITION
**Ski & board** Les Menuires: ESF (☎ 479 00 61 43). St-Martin: ESF (☎ 479 00 61 43). Val Thorens: ESF (☎ 479 00 02 86), ESI (☎ 479 00 01 96), Pros-Neige (☎ 479 01 07 00), Ski Cool (☎ 479 00 04 92)
**Guiding** Bureau des Guides (☎ 479 00 08 08), Ski Safari Pepi Prager (☎ 479 00 01 23), Ski The 12 Valleys (☎ 479 00 00 95)

## CHILDREN
**Lift pass** Trois Vallées 5–13yrs €153.50 for 6 days
**Ski & board school** as adults
**Kindergarten** Les Menuires: (ski) ESF, (ski/non-ski) Village des Piou Piou (☎ 479 00 69 50), Village des Schtroumpfs (☎ 479 00 63 79). St-Martin: (ski/non-ski) Piou Piou (☎ 479 08 91 15). Val Thorens: (ski/non-ski) ESF Village Montana and Village Roc (☎ 479 00 02 86)

## FOOD AND DRINK
Coffee €3–3.50, bottle of house wine €14–20, small beer €3.50–5, soft drink €3.50–4, dish of the day €12–20

# Valmorel

**ALTITUDE 1,400m (4,592ft)**

## ❄ attractive resort architecture ❄ excellent children's facilities ❄ exceptional nursery slopes

**Best for:** beginners and intermediates, families, skiers on a budget

**Not recommended for:** advanced skiers, non-skiers, gourmets, night-owls

Valmorel is an unsophisticated family resort in the Tarentaise Valley, reached by road from Moûtiers. The village is architecturally pleasing and fits so snugly into its mountain environment that it is hard to believe that it was constructed only in 1976. Central Valmorel is often referred to as Bourg-Morel to distinguish it from the satellite residential areas, called *hameaux*.

## On the snow
**top 2,550m (8,364ft) bottom 1,250m (4,100ft)**

Valmorel shares a network of lifts and pistes with the popular destinations of St-François and Longchamp in the Maurienne Valley and the beginner resort of Doucy Combelouvière. The excellent nursery slopes are closed off to passing skiers and snowboarders, and children have a moving walkway at Les Piou Piou kindergarten as well as a totally enclosed area for three- to twelve-year-olds up the mountain.

It is important to note that the colour-coding on the local lift map is completely different from the rest of Europe: green is listed as easy, blue as intermediate, red as difficult, and black as very difficult.

With its family image, the resort does not normally attract many advanced skiers and riders, but good powder-skiing can be found down the ridge between Mottet and Gollet. Snowboarders have a boardercross course and half-pipe in the terrain park.

At the French Ski School (ESF), lessons are held in English in the afternoons and in French in the mornings, although one reporter complained that 'my wife and I found ourselves in a mainly French-speaking group during the afternoon'. However, 'the ski school was superb', commented another. Classics include telemark, cross-country, and off-piste.

The mountain restaurants are mostly self-service and offer value rather than *haute cuisine*. The Alpage cafeteria is recommended. Altipiano is smarter, while the Banquoise 2000 refuge has rustic tables and a log fire. Les 2 Mazots serves the best *croûte au fromage*, and Le Grenier is popular.

## In the resort
Auberge Planchamp (☎ 479 09 97 00) is a good-value three-star decorated in rustic Savoyard style with stripped pine walls and ceilings. Two-star Hotel du Bourg (☎ 479 09 86 66) is situated in the village centre, and three-star Hotel la Fontaine (☎ 479 09 87 77) has bigger, better rooms.

La Grange offers the ubiquitous range of Savoie foods, and you can also eat local specialities at La Ferme du Soleil and Le Champ de Lune. Planchamp is 'cosy with a great atmosphere' and L'Aigle Blanche, just outside the village, is worth trying. Jumbo Lolo serves Tex-Mex, Chez Albert has 'the best pizzas', while Le Petit Prince and Le Petit Savoyard have 'great menus'.

Les Nuits Blanches is the only disco. Top-20-type music is played in the Perce Neige, Café de la Gare and at La Cordée. Le Casbah is 'the most intimate and atmospheric bar'. The resort also has a cinema and an Internet café.

The resort's childminding service, Les Piou Piou, is run by the ski school and accepts children from eighteen months to six years and offers indoor and outdoor activities.

### Valmorel: At a glance

**Tel** 33 479 09 85 55
**Email** info@valmorel.com
**Website** www.valmorel.com
**Lifts in area** 52: 2 14 36
**Lift opening dates** 18 December 2004 to 24 April 2005

# Vaujany

ALTITUDE 1,050m (3,444ft)

---

✳ first-rate resort for families and for skiers in search of a challenge
✳ unspoilt village atmosphere ✳ lack of lift queues ✳ value for money

**Best for:** children of all ages, all standards of skier
**Not recommended for:** older night-owls, those looking for a large and lively resort

Vaujany is a sleepy farming community that would have slowly crumbled into agronomic oblivion but for a quirk of fate. Its fortunes took a turn for the better when compensation in the 1980s for a valley hydro-electric scheme made the village rich beyond its residents' wildest dreams. This explains why it boasts a state-of-the-art 160-person cable-car that links it directly into the 85-lift ski circuit of **Alpe d'Huez**. A separate gondola provides slower access to the main mountain.

## On the snow
top 3,330m (10,922ft) bottom 1,250m (4,101ft)

Vaujany's ski area starts at Montfrais, where two drag-lifts give access to green and blue runs. Alternative access is by the cable-car. From the top of the DMC gondola above Alpe d'Huez you can ski the long red Les Rousses into the Vaujany sector. A largely under-used piste takes you all the way down to the hamlet of L'Enversin d'Oz, linked to Vaujany by a cluster gondola. From the summit of Pic Blanc this represents a mighty vertical drop of 2,330m, which is claimed to be the longest fully lift-served run in the Alps.

The French Ski School (ESF) and Le Massif schools both provide ski lessons, and snowboarding lessons are now also offered in the resort.

Les Airelles is a simple restaurant built into the rock at the top of the Montfrais nursery lift. A host of other excellent mountain restaurants can be accessed on skis. These include Chez Passoud on the Oz piste below the top of the Alpette gondola, and Chalet du Lac Besson on the cross-country track.

## In the resort
Although considerable development has recently taken place, Vaujany still retains its rural atmosphere. There are four simple hotels in the village centre, including the Rissiou (☎ 476 80 71 00), which offers a good standard of accommodation. Its restaurant serves first-rate cuisine and wines. Les Cimes (☎ 476 79 86 50) has more basic accommodation. The upper village boasts some extremely comfortable and well-equipped apartments. There are several pleasant chalets in Vaujany and also in the neighbouring hamlet of La Villette, 1km away.

The nightlife in Vaujany centres around the bars of L'Etendard and the Rissiou, while the Swallow Bar is an animated meeting-place that attracts teenagers to early-20s, and comes complete with a pool table and giant video screen.

Vaujany has what reporters consider to be one of the best-equipped crèches in the French Alps for ages six months to five years and, if you have small children, this is a reason in itself for choosing the resort. Skiing children are divided into classes at the two ski schools. The ESF's Ski Adventure classes are for more intrepid youngsters. The Snow Garden is for children from four years of age, who are taught the basics by ESF instructors.

The resort also boasts an ice-skating rink, an impressive indoor swimming-pool and gym complex, and two small shopping malls – the lower of which has a car park connected to the cable-car station by escalator.

## Vaujany: At a glance

**Tel** 33 476 80 72 37
**Email** info@vaujany.com
**Website** www.vaujany.com
**Lifts in area** 85: 16🚠 24🚡 45🎿
**Lift opening dates** 4 December 2004 to 30 April 2005

# ITALY

# Arabba

**ALTITUDE 1,600m (5,248ft)**                                   map: see page 189

❄ **attractive small village** ❄ **demanding terrain** ❄ **high-quality hotels**

> **Best for:** advanced and intermediates skiers and snowboarders
>
> **Not recommended for:** beginner skiers, night-owls, non-skiers, cross-country skiers

This small, unspoilt village with only 2,500 beds and 30 lifts is surrounded by some of the most challenging skiing in the **Sella Ronda**. Indeed it has some of the best skiing in the whole 1,220km of piste included in the Dolomiti Superski lift pass, which covers some 460 – not necessarily linked – lifts in this beautiful corner of Italy.

Signposting is good and in recent years the local lift map has improved beyond all recognition. The principal language here is Italian, although Arabba is only a couple of kilometres south of the Sud Tirol border.

## WHAT'S NEW

Marmolada cable-car replaced for 2004–5
2 drag-lifts (no.10 and no.24) replaced with 2-seater chairs for 2004–5
Chair-lift no.13 becomes a 4-seater chair in 2004–5

## On the snow
**top 2,950m (9,676ft) bottom 1,600m (5,248ft)**

From the edge of the village a cable-car and a modern gondola rise to Porta Vescovo at 2,478m for the link into the Sella Ronda. A chair-lift from the first stage of the gondola takes you in the direction of the 3,342-m Marmolada, the highest point in the region, where the old cable-car is being completely replaced. On the other side of the village a chair-lift leads to Burz, at 1,943m, from where you can work your way towards **Corvara**.

We have received positive reports of the ski school: 'expert, informative tuition delivered in good English'. However, the nursery slope suffers from through-traffic, and the resort is not recommended for complete beginners.

## In the resort
The Grifone (☎ 0436 780034) is a modern five-star hotel with a first-rate reputation, although it is isolated outside the village. The four-star Sporthotel Arabba (☎ 0436 79321) has a strong following: 'we return year after year'. The three-star Portavescovo (☎ 0436 79139), which boasts a pool and fitness centre, is livelier and houses the Stübe Bar, which is a resort rendezvous. Other three-star hotels include the Evaldo (☎ 0436 79109), Olympia (☎ 0436 79135), the Royal (☎ 0436 79293), the Alpenrose (☎ 0436 750076) and Garni Laura (☎ 0436 780055). A further three-star, the Mesdi (☎ 0436 79119) opens for the 2004–5 season.

Al Table has 'very tasty pizzas and a pleasant atmosphere', and Pizzeria Sett Sass is also recommended. Arabba's nightlife is centred around Peter's Bar, the Sporthotel Bar and La Treina (which opened during 2003–4). However, reporters advise: 'This is not a place for those expecting boisterous après-ski activity'. The Ru de Mont is a recommended restaurant in the satellite village of Renaz. Arabba's public transport is limited to two daily buses to Corvara, and a car is strongly recommended for visiting nearby resorts.

The crèche and ski kindergarten look after children from two years on weekdays.

## Arabba: At a glance

**Tel** 39 0436 79130
**Email** arabba@infodolomiti.it
**Website** www.infodolomiti.it
**Lifts in resort** 30: 7☁ 15☁ 8☁. 460 in Dolomiti Superski area
**Lift opening dates** 27 November 2004 to early April 2005

# Cervinia

ALTITUDE 2,050m (6,726ft)                          map: see page 190

❄ **reliable snow** ❄ **long cruising runs** ❄ **lively atmosphere**
❄ **value for money** ❄ **beautiful scenery**

> **Best for:** beginners to intermediates, ski
> gourmets, late-season holidaymakers,
> families
>
> **Not recommended for:** advanced skiers
> and snowboarders, non-skiers, people
> wanting a quiet village and slopes

Cervinia remains by far the most popular
destination in Italy for British skiers, who
flock to this outwardly uninspiring resort
above the Aosta Valley on the Italian side of
Il Cervino, which is better known as the
Matterhorn. The reason for its popularity is
two-fold. At 2,050m, with slopes rising to
3,883m, it is one of Europe's most snow-
sure resorts, a place where long runs right
down to village level are virtually
guaranteed from the beginning of December
until early May. The terrain is also ideally
suited to both beginners and intermediates
– in short, 90 per cent of all skiers – in
search of long and undemanding cruising
runs against a beautiful backdrop.

The substantial ski area is linked with
**Zermatt**, and their joint ski area comprises
52 lifts. This is of considerable advantage to
the more accomplished skiers and
snowboarders in a mixed group, who will
enjoy the far more challenging pistes on the
Swiss side ('half of us spent the day happily
pottering around on easy blues in Italy,
while the rest of the party spent their
mornings in Switzerland'). You don't have
to buy the more expensive joint lift pass –
beginners should confine themselves to the
28 lifts on the Italian side – but, if you plan
to visit Switzerland more than once in a
week's holiday, it is financially worthwhile.
Alternatively you can pay a daily
supplement. The link is subject to rupture
in storms or high winds. Cervinia's skiing is
also connected to the nearby village of
Valtournenche (1,524m).

Mussolini, who was instrumental in the
resort's construction in the 1930s, decreed
the name should change from Breuil to the
more Italian-sounding Cervinia. A nucleus of
original buildings reflects the austere imperial
style of the time. Post-war edifices, thrown up
without regard for the extraordinarily
beautiful mountain environment, are stark,
but more recent additions have façades of
wood and natural stone.

Weekends see an influx from Milan and
Turin and parking is chaotic, despite six
parking areas (five free and one fee-paying).
There is no free ski bus, but a municipal bus
makes circuits to Cieloalto every 20 minutes
until 8pm.

Reporters praised Cervinia as 'very
reasonably priced'. The resort may not be as
chic as Cortina d'Ampezzo or even
Courmayeur, but it does have a vibrant
atmosphere.

## On-piste
top 3,883m (12,740ft) bottom 2,050m (6,726ft)

Italy's highest resort is often unfairly
dismissed by experienced skiers as a
playground for beginners and lower
intermediates – no match for its swanky
Swiss neighbour. Certainly it is true that,
despite warnings of *solo per esperti* (only
for experts), most of the handful of black
runs would be graded red on the Swiss side
of the mountain.

But the majority of visitors will be
perfectly content with the skiing Cervinia
has to offer ('slopes are the widest I have
come across'). The length and quantity of
its flattering red and blue runs provide
hours of effortless cruising, although
reporters criticised the lack of variety.

'Get on the lifts by 9.40am as they get
quite busy,' warned a reporter. This is
particularly true at high-season weekends
when long queues can form. Mountain
access is most direct from the gondola and
cable-car, but these are an irritating hike
uphill from the village. Access is also
possible from drag-lifts in the nursery area
to the left of the village, or from the satellite
areas of Cieloalto and by a modern 12-
person gondola from Valtournenche. Plan

Maison is the mid-mountain station from which the main lifts fan out, with a gondola and cable-car to Plateau Rosa and the Swiss border. If you are on a day visit from Zermatt do not underestimate the time it takes to work your way through the lift system back into Switzerland. Italian lifts close 30 minutes earlier than the Swiss ones; after that the journey between the two resorts is a costly six-hour taxi ride.

'Perfect to learn in', said one reporter. Cervinia's excellent snow record means that novices have good conditions on the conveniently accessed learning area at the village edge, on which they tend to spend no more than two days, before moving up to the network of green and blue pistes at Plan Maison. This is one of the few resorts where beginners can graduate quickly to high-altitude intermediate runs and explore almost the whole mountain in the course of their first fortnight on skis or board.

The 8-km Ventina (no.7 on the resort's piste map) from Plateau Rosa down to the resort is a classic Alpine cruise, which can be tackled by second-week skiers. The descent from the Klein Matterhorn to Valtournenche measures a mighty 22km and is long enough to reduce even the toughest skier's knees to noodles. Skiers who have been intimidated by steep slopes in Chamonix or Val d'Isère will find the gradual pitch of Cervinia's pistes both ego-boosting and useful for advancing technical skills.

However, the benign gradients can be frustrating for the more experienced. 'Not even a hint of challenge', commented one reporter. Zermatt's skiing is considerably more difficult, but the distances are too great to enable the Cervinia-based skier to do little more than scratch the surface on the Swiss side of the mountain ('time dictated that we had to confine ourselves to the Trockener Steg–Klein Matterhorn area, even though we really wanted to ride the Gornergrat railway. As it was, we nearly missed the connection home').

There is a terrain park at the Fornet chair-lift, which has a half-pipe, rails, boardercross course and music played over loudspeakers to complete the atmosphere.

## Off-piste

On powder days, especially when the wind closes upper lifts, the skiing among the trees on the shoulder above Cieloalto is a good off-piste option. More ambitious routes require guides and mountaineering gear. Heli-skiing and heli-boarding are available on the Italian side of the mountain and, in addition to ski-touring, provide access to a wealth of glacier runs.

## Tuition and guiding

We have mixed reports on the main Cervino School, while the Matterhorn Cervinia is new. One reporter commented that 'the Cervino seems prone to the follow-my-leader school of instruction', but another said that his private lesson with Cervino was 'money well spent'. Valtournenche has its own ski school. We have no reports of the other ski schools. Mountain guides from the local bureau in Cervinia charge considerably less than their Swiss counterparts, but have equal expertise on the border peaks.

## Mountain restaurants

Cervinia's mountain meals are not cheap by Italian standards but are still much better value than on the other side of the Matterhorn. Chalet Etoile, near the Rocce Nere chair-lift, is one of the finest mountain restaurants in the Alps, renowned for its pasta and polenta ('lobster spaghetti was just the best thing I've ever eaten'). Bar Ventina on the eponymous run down from Plateau Rosa, and Bar Bontadini on the Bontadini slope, also received favourable reviews. Bar Le Pousset, just below Laghi Cime Bianche, is recommended, as is Baita Cretaz on the nursery slopes. The Igloo – run by Pauline, an English exile – at the top of the Bardoney chair is praised for its tasty food and large portions. La Motta da Felice at the top of the Motta drag-lift is also not to be missed.

## Accommodation

Cervinia has virtually no chalet or self-catering accommodation, but boasts some 40 hotels. The Hermitage (☎ 01661 948998) is a four-star hotel with the highest standards of service, cuisine and price. Another four-star, the Punta Maquignaz (☎ 01661 949145), is an attractive wood-clad hotel close to the drag-lifts, and the four-star Sertorelli Sporthotel (☎ 01661 949797) is praised: 'fantastic – nothing but five-star service'. Two-star Hotel Grivola (☎ 01669 48287) was said to have 'tired accommodation, but the après-ski bar downstairs was one of the best in the resort', while another reporter added:

'watch out for the huge portions in the restaurant'. The Jumeaux (☎ 01661 949044) is 'pleasant, quiet and well run', although one reporter described the showers as 'the smallest in the world' and complained of poor sound-proofing. Da Compagnoni (☎ 01661 949068) on the main street is 'simple, convenient and welcoming'. Hotel Breuil (☎ 01661 949537) was rated 'clean, spacious and very acceptable'. Other recommended hotels include the four-star Petit Palais (☎ 01669 49371) ('staff and food were great') and the three-star Hotel-Residence Cielo Alto (☎ 01669 42774) 'hotel a little dated but the staff were great and the food wonderful'.

## Eating in and out
The resort has a reasonable range of restaurants, which are mostly good value. The Hermitage has 'truly outstanding cuisine', and Le Bistrot de l'Abbé is a close contender. La Nicchia is similarly rich for pocket and paunch, while La Tana is recommended for wild boar, venison and everything with *porcini* mushrooms. The Copa Pan received mixed reviews: 'we cannot recommend it highly enough,' said

one reporter, but 'very over-rated and rather over-priced,' complained another. La Maison de Saussure is the place to try typical Valdostana specialities, and it is hard to beat the pizzas at Al Solito Posto and the Matterhorn Pizzeria.

## Après-ski
Lino's Bar beside the ice-rink is busy when the lifts close. Skating is a passionate pastime here, but reporters complained that the nightlife lacks lustre. 'Like the skiing', said one reporter, 'it is all intermediate'. Ymeletrob cocktail bar is the liveliest venue ('great – with substantial bar snacks'), and the Copa Pan Irish bar is also busy, and serves Murphy's beer. The Dragon bar remains as well frequented as ever.

## Childcare
Biancaneve is the new non-ski kindergarten, and accepts children from two to eight years old, while small skiers can join the children's classes at the adults' ski schools. Kid Zone up at Plan Maison is a play area where children must be accompanied by a parent. The tourist office has a list of officially sanctioned babysitters but admits that few speak English.

# Cervinia: At a glance

**Tel** 39 01669 49136
**Email** breuil-cervinia@montecervino.it
**Website** www.montecervino.it

### GETTING THERE
**Airports** Geneva 2hrs, Turin 2hrs
**Rail** Châtillon 27km, regular buses to resort
**Road** take the Châtillon exit from the A5 Turin–Aosta autostrada. Cervinia is 28km

### THE SKIING
**Linked/nearby resorts** Valtournenche, Zermatt
**Total of trails/pistes** 200km in Cervinia (30% easy, 60% intermediate, 10% difficult), 350km with Zermatt
**Lifts in area** 62 with Zermatt: 2🚡 19🚠 20🚡 21🎿
**Lift opening dates** 23 October 2004 to 1 May 2005. Summer skiing on Plateau Rosa

### LIFT PASSES
**Area pass** (covers Cervinia, Valtournenche, Zermatt) €159–198 for 6 days, (covers Cervinia and Valtournence) €131–163, 1-day Zermatt supplement €26

**Pensioners** 65yrs and over: (covers Cervinia, Valtournenche, Zermatt) €120–149, (covers Cervinia and Valtournanche) €99–123

### TUITION
**Ski & board** Breuil (☎ 01661 940960), Cervino (☎ 01661 949034), Matterhorn Cervinia (☎ 01661 948451) Valtournanche (☎ 0166 92515)
**Guiding** Guide del Cervino (☎ 01661 948169), Heliski Cervinia (☎ 01661 949267)

### CHILDREN
**Lift pass** 8–13yrs: (covers Cervinia, Valtournenche, Zermatt) €120–149, (covers Cervinia and Valtournanche) €99–123. Free for under 6yrs with parent
**Ski & board school** as adults, Kid Zone (☎ 339 1599155)
**Kindergarten** (non-ski) Biancaneve (☎ 01669 40201)

### FOOD AND DRINK
Coffee €3, bottle of house wine €10, small beer €2–3, soft drink €3, dish of the day €15

# Champoluc–Gressoney–Alagna

ALTITUDE 1,568m (5,144ft)

❋ **excellent off-piste skiing** ❋ **villages with rustic charm**
❋ **high-quality local cuisine** ❋ **lack of lift queues**
❋ **uncrowded pistes** ❋ **value for money**

> **Best for:** intermediates, adventurous skiers and snowboarders, those on a budget, powderhounds (Alagna)
>
> **Not recommended for:** beginners, non-skiers, night-owls, families with young children

Champoluc is the best known of four linked resorts – Champoluc, Alagna, Gressoney-La-Trinité and Stafal – above the north-western corner of the Aosta Valley, which together form a 180km circuit connected by 30 lifts collectively known as Monterosa Ski. Although the resorts are close as the crow flies and connected by the lift system, it takes two hours to drive between any two of them. The Monterosa region is remote, supremely beautiful and remarkably uncommercialised.

Much of the skiing in the Champoluc and Gressoney valleys is given over to well-groomed pistes that are best suited to families and intermediates in search of high daily mileage and the feeling of going somewhere different each day. However, the Alagna end of the circuit is an altogether more serious proposition ('a resort for committed skiers and snowboarders looking for the kind of steep terrain that can frighten the daylights out of the faint-hearted').

Champoluc is reached by a long, winding road from the Turin–Aosta autostrada and is set around a church and a fast-running mountain river. The old quarter was built in the fifteenth century, but the village has expanded in recent years.

Gressoney is on a similar scale ('a one-horse town'), with a network of cobbled streets and wooden chalets surrounded by contemporary buildings. Gressoney-St-Jean, 5km down the valley, is larger and more attractive, while the outpost of Stafal is a modern hamlet above Gressoney-La-Trinité.

Alagna has unique wooden houses with built-in hay frames, and a charm all of its own. However it has recently been transformed by new lifts and a new piste. Its two-stage cable-car takes you up to Passa del Salati at 2,979m. The hopeless regional piste map was rated 'the worst I've seen' by one reporter, but signposts are plentiful and accurate.

The local buses serve the valley town of Verrès, but a car is essential if you want to explore the other ski resorts of the Aosta Valley, which include **Cervinia, Courmayeur, Pila** and **La Thuile** and **La Rosière**.

## On-piste
top 3,370m (11,056ft) bottom 1,200m (3,936ft)

The collection of slow chairs and ancient cable-cars have recently been updated, and a new lift from Alagna has been designed to run in high winds. All pistes in the central valley eventually lead to Stafal, which is the central link in the chain of lifts. Head up in the cable-car and chair-lift to the west and you reach the Colle Bettaforca, the departure point for the descents to Champoluc. Take the two-stage gondola to the east and you come to the Passo del Salati, the start of the new piste and many unpisted routes to Alagna. With slopes on both sides of the valley, Gressoney has the lion's share of the pisted skiing in the area.

### WHAT'S NEW

Alagna–Salati Peak drag-lift links Gressoney Valley and Valsesia
Funifor cable-car links Pianalunga with Salati Peak at Gressoney

There are two points of departure from Champoluc, one on the outskirts of the village and the other up the hill in Frachey, which provides quicker access to the main area. Three small satellite areas – Antagnod, Brusson and Gressoney-St-Jean – are not connected to the central system.

'Don't bother coming to Monterosa unless you have two to three weeks' experience', said one reporter. The best place for novices to learn is on the sunny nursery slope at Crest, at the top of the first stage of the Champoluc gondola. In Gressoney, beginners congregate around the Punta Jolanda lift, then progress to the wide plateau above Stafal on the Bettaforca side.

Both Gressoney and Champoluc offer plenty of intermediate cruising, although Stadio dello Slalom above Champoluc is a challenging red. One reporter described the run to Champoluc as 'one of the best-maintained runs I have ever seen'.

The best black piste in the area is the 7-km descent from the top of the Punta Indren towards Alagna, but even this would not be so severely rated in other resorts. The same could be said of the only mogul field, which is at Sarezza in Champoluc. Diretta Stafal is an exhilarating black run in the Gressoney valley.

The region has no terrain parks, although the absence of drag-lifts is a bonus. Indeed the whole of the Alagna sector has been described by the snowboarding hard core as a 'freeride paradise'.

## Off-piste
In the right conditions, Champoluc, Gressoney and Alagna present challenges that are made all the more testing by bumpy terrain and narrow defiles between rock walls. The Mos and the Bettolina in Gressoney should not be attempted without a guide. The same is true of most of the skiing in Alagna, where the cable-car provides access to huge snowfields that are prone to avalanche. The north-facing slopes in the Alta Valsesia National Park give a sense of extreme adventure, especially when accessed by the couloir at the top of the Malfatta. Alternatively, there is extensive heli-skiing, with glacier drops at over 4,000m in the Monterosa range. Ski-touring can also be arranged.

## Tuition and guiding
In Gressoney by no means all the ski instructors speak English, so you should request an English speaker when booking lessons. Champoluc, Gressoney and Alagna all have mountain guiding associations, and qualified Alpine guides are available through the respective tourist offices.

## Mountain restaurants
The mountain restaurants are numerous and of a very good standard,' said one

reporter, although another complained that 'some of the larger places were very functional and the service very slow indeed'.

Bedemie, on the route down to Gressoney from Gabiet, has 'a beautiful terrace and nourishing soup', while Albergho del Ponte above Gabiet is praised for its cheap and superlative spaghetti carbonara. Rifugio Guglielmina, reached by a short off-piste route from Passo del Salati, is recommended for its food and the view, and Bettaforca has 'the biggest and best mixed grill in the business'. La Baita Refuge offers superb mushroom pasta, friendly service, and is a convenient stop-off en route to Alagna. The Edelweiss at the top of the gondola at Crest, contains a café and a small waiter-service restaurant. The Belvedere (at the top of lift 12) is 'a small place with excellent views'. The Ostafa, at the top of chairs 8 and 9, served 'the best spaghetti carbonara I have ever eaten'.

## Accommodation
In Champoluc, the four-star Hotel Breithorn (☎ 0125 308734) looks like a farm building, but inside it is smart-rustic with wood-panelled walls, two restaurants and a spa. The three-star Hotel Castor (☎ 0125 307117) is described by one reporter as 'an absolute gem, Italian-owned but managed by an Englishman who has married into the family'. The three-star Hotel California (☎ 0125 307977) is one of the most unusual hotels in the Alps, decorated with a 1960s' music theme. Every bedroom is named after a rock star or band and is wired for sound – for example, the Bob Dylan Room or the Doors Room. The four-star Ayas (☎ 0125 308128) and three-star Hotel de Champoluc (☎ 0125 308088) are also recommended. Three-star Le Rocher (☎ 0347 2103073) opened in December 2003, and is a ten-minute walk to the lifts (there is a minibus). The owners are 'very friendly and helpful, the food was good, but our room suffered from a slight shortage of storage space'. The two-star Favre (☎ 0125 307131) is small and friendly.

The Hotel Mirella (☎ 0163 922965) in Alagna, a B&B with rooms over a cake shop, is 'a must'. Alternatives are the Genzianella (☎ 0163 923921) or the Monterosa (☎ 0163 923209). Self-catering is also available in some of the traditional Walser houses (☎ 08701 622 273 in UK).

Above Gressoney, at Stafal, the four-star Monboso (☎ 0125 366302) is 'of an excellent standard', while, in Gressoney itself, the three-star Hotel Lo Scoiàttolo (☎ 0125 366313) is equally comfortable but with a better ambience. The three-star Hotel Residence (☎ 0125 366148) was recently refurbished but 'the rooms were decidedly spartan, although the food and service were both good'.

## Eating in and out

Le Sapin in Champoluc looks unpromising but serves 'acceptable food at reasonable prices'. The Favre remains consistently good, with a bias towards gargantuan feasts of local game. Cuisine at the Villa Anna Maria was described as 'variable, but the restaurant has an honest wine list', while Le Petit Coq and La Grange at Frachey are recommended too. Capanna Carla in Gressoney provides typical local cuisine at reasonable prices. In Alagna, Fum Diss offers 'superb game and polenta', and Ristorante Unione Alagnese is 'not to be missed'. An Baker Wi offers a good selection of local and national wines.

## Après-ski

This is the kind of area where the nightlife is described by tour operators as 'informal and relaxed' – often a euphemism for dead in the winter. What there is takes place in the bars of family hotels, where locals and tourists drink and play cards. The Champoluc disco scene centres on the Gram Parsons in Frachey, while the relaxed nightlife in Gressoney consists of cafés such as the Hirsch Stube and the Petit Bar. Gamblers with their own transport can visit the casino in St-Vincent (25km from Champoluc, 70km from Gressoney). Alagna has added some new bars and restaurants.

## Childcare

Daycare in the area is extremely limited, with no crèche or kindergarten facilities in Champoluc apart from the Hotel Castor. The ski school takes children from five years old. Hotel Monboso, at Stafal, offers a mini-club for residents' children aged four to eight years. In Gressoney, the Residenza del Sole hotel looks after residents' children aged three to eleven. Skiers over six must join the adult classes. The resort also has a Baby Snowpark. Alagna's ski school accepts children from three years.

# Champoluc–Gressoney–Alagna: At a glance

**Tel** 39 0125 303111 / Alagna only: 0870 162 2273 in UK
**Email** kikesly@monterosa-ski.com / more@alagna.co.uk
**Website** www.monterosa-ski.com

## GETTING THERE
**Airports** Turin 1½hrs, Milan 2½hrs
**Rail** Verrès, then 26km by bus
**Road** Turin–Aosta autostrada to Verrès exit, then SR45

## THE SKIING
**Linked/nearby resorts** Cervinia, Chamonix, Courmayeur, Pila, La Thuile/La Rosière, Zermatt
**Total of trails/pistes** 180km (18% easy, 73% intermediate, 9% difficult)
**Lifts in area** 30 : 7🚠 17🚡 6🎿
**Lift opening dates** 4 December 2004 to 10 April 2005

## LIFT PASSES
**Area pass** (includes 1–3 days in other Aosta Valley resorts) €168 for 6 days

**Pensioners** 65yrs and over 25% reduction

## TUITION
**Ski & board** Alagna (☎ 0163 922961), Antagnod (☎ 0125 306641), Brusson (☎ 0340 5410632), Champoluc (☎ 0125 307194), Gressoney (☎ 0125 366015)
**Guiding** Alagna (☎ 0163 91310), Champoluc (☎ 0348 5186479) and Gressoney (☎ 0125 366 139) mountain guiding associations

## CHILDREN
**Lift pass** 25% reduction for 8–12yrs. 75% reduction in high season for under 8yrs, free in low season
**Ski & board school** as adults
**Kindergarten** Champoluc: (non-ski) Hotel Castor. Gressoney: (non-ski) Hotel Monboso, Residenza del Sole (☎ 0125 357 400)

## FOOD AND DRINK
Coffee €1, bottle of house wine €7, small beer €3, soft drink €2, dish of the day €8

# Cortina d'Ampezzo

**ALTITUDE 1,224m (4,015ft)**                                  **map: see page 191**

❅ **extensive nursery slopes** ❅ **spectacular scenery** ❅ **atmospheric town**
❅ **long runs** ❅ **excellent restaurants** ❅ **lively nightlife**

**Best for:** all standards of skier, gourmet
skiers, non-skiers, night-owls, families,
cross-country skiers
**Not recommended for:** budget skiers,
those wanting skiing convenience

If we had to single out one ski resort in the
world for the sheer beauty of its setting,
combined with an attractive town and a truly
all-round winter-sports resort, it would be
Cortina d'Ampezzo. Cortina sits in the
Ampezzo Valley in the Dolomite mountains,
less than two hours' journey by road from
Venice. Unlike its neighbours in the German-
speaking Sud Tirol, Cortina is Italian to its
voluptuous core and largely devoid of
German and Austrian tourists. Some 70 per
cent of its winter visitors are Italian.

The large, attractive town is centred
around the main shopping street of Corso
Italia and the Piazza Venezia with its green-
and-white bell-tower. The large, frescoed
buildings have an air of faded grandeur, and
the views of the pink rock-faces of Monte
Cristallo are sensational. More recent
architectural additions display a
sympathetic Italian Alpine style in keeping
with the town's dramatic surroundings. The
centre is mercifully traffic-free.

Such a smart resort, with a pedigree that
includes hosting the 1956 winter Olympics,
is markedly more expensive than other
Italian destinations. However, a failure over
the years to properly reinvest in the
mountain makes its membership of The Best
of the Alps, an exclusive club of a dozen top
resorts that includes St Anton, St Moritz
and Chamonix, somewhat questionable.

## On-piste
top 3,243m (10,640ft) bottom 1,224m (4,015ft)

The skiing is divided between the main
Tofana-Socrepes area to the west of town,
which is reached via the Freccia nel Cielo
cable-car, and Staunies-Faloria on the other
side of town, which consists of two sectors

separated by a minor road. A scattering of
smaller ski areas along the Passo Falzarego
road still belong to individual farmers. One
of these, Cinque Torri–Averau, reached by a
new four-seater chair, is uncrowded, with
breathtaking scenery.

Passo Falzarego, further down the road
and a 20-minute bus ride from the town
centre, links in one direction only into the
**Sella Ronda** circuit. At Passo Falzarego the
dramatic cable-car soars 640m vertical up a
cliff-face to Lagazuoi, followed by a
beautiful 11-km red run past a shimmering
turquoise ice-fall and several welcoming
huts before reaching Armentarola and **San
Cassiano** beyond. To return to Cortina from
Armentarola you take either a bus to
Falzarego or one of the waiting taxis to
Lagazuoi.

## WHAT'S NEW
4-seater chair-lift at Cinque Torri–Averau

The buses linking the town with the
various fragmented ski areas are infrequent
and hopelessly oversubscribed at peak
hours. To enjoy the skiing to its full, you
therefore need your own car.

Both Tofana and Faloria can be reached
on foot from most of the accommodation if
you are prepared for a hearty hike in ski
boots. Morning queues for the Tofana
cable-car are not a problem owing to the
late rising-time of the average Cortina
visitor – the morning rush-hour never starts
before 10.30am.

A long serpentine blue piste takes you
down from Tofana's mid-station to link
with Socrepes, one of the best nursery
slopes in Europe. The more isolated Miétres
is an equally gentle sector.

The majority of Cortina's skiing is of
intermediate standard ('great resort for
beginners to intermediates, but quite a few
button lifts'), with long runs in both the
main ski areas. Between the resort and Col
Drusciè, the Tofana cable-car travels over

gentle, tree-lined terrain and open fields with wide and easy trails, which cross rough roads without much warning to either skiers or drivers. Poor snow conditions often make these runs testing, which gives them their red and black gradings. However, snowmaking now covers up to 95 per cent of the terrain. The second stage of the cable-car climbs the sheer, rocky mountain-side to Ra Valles, in the middle of a pleasant bowl.

A day-trip into the Sella Ronda ski area should not be missed for anyone of intermediate standard and upwards. The good-value Dolomiti Superski lift pass covers Cortina and the Sella Ronda.

Higher up at Tofana, the Ra Valles sector at 2,700m offers the best snow in the resort. Near the bottom of the Tofana bowl, a gap in the rock gives access to an exhilarating black trail, which has a fairly steep, south-facing stretch in the middle. The run ends up at the Pié–Tofana–Duca d'Aosta chair-lifts, an area that itself offers some excellent runs including a couple of good blacks: the spectacular Canalone, and the Olympia downhill racecourse.

The most dramatic skiing is found between Cristallo and Cresta Bianche, two soaring cathedrals of granite that dominate the landscape. From the foot of Monte Cristallo, a four-stage chair climbs to Forcella Staunies, which starts with a steep black mogul field so sandwiched between the rock walls that it creates an illusion of narrowness. Halfway down, the bumps flatten out into a wide red race track.

Cortina has a small terrain park at Faloria and an additional new terrain park at Tofana. Cross-country is a popular sport, with six trails in the valley north and east of the resort giving a total 75km of loipe.

## Off-piste

After a fresh snowfall, Forcella Staunies becomes an appealing off-piste area, as do the higher reaches of Tofana. Guide Alpine arranges day ski-tours.

## Tuition and guiding

The main Scuola Sci Cortina has meeting-places at Socrepes, Pocol, Rio Gere and Miétres. Standards appear to be mixed, depending mainly on the level of English spoken by the instructor. Azzurra and Cristallo-Cortina are smaller alternatives. Snowboarding lessons are available through the Scuola Sci Cortina, Cristallo-Cortina and Dolomiti-Cortina.

## Mountain restaurants

Eating is a memorable experience in Cortina, and the choice of restaurants is extensive in the main ski areas, as well as being good value for money. Rifugio Duca d'Aosta is recommended, with its wood-panelled walls and heart-warming local dishes. Simple mountain fare can be eaten at Rifugio Son Forca, which is reached by a modern chair-lift from Rio Gere on the road separating the Cristallo and Faloria ski areas. Rifugio Pomedes is a summer climbing hut with hand-carved furniture and a varied menu. Reporters praised El Faral at the foot of Socrepes, and, in the same area, Col Taron, which serves delicious pasta.

The next stage down the mountain from the Duca d'Aosta is Baita Piè Tofana, a relaxed eating-place with a sun terrace and attractive interior. Rifugio Averau at Cinque Torri, reached by a rope-tow, has stunning views and some of the best mountain food in the resort. Homemade pasta is the speciality, and you can request three different types served on a single plate. Rifugio Lagazuoi is situated a steep but worthwhile walk from the top of the Falzarego cable-car. Le Sorei in the Lacadel ski area was new in 2003–4 and is 'a worth addition to the lunchtime choice'. Other highly rated eating-places are the Tondi restaurant, and Rifugio Scotoni on the long run down to Armentarola.

## Accommodation

Hotels range from the large international variety to simple, family-run establishments. A large number of private apartments and chalets are also available. The five-star Hotel Cristallo (☎ 0436 4281) with its new spa heads the list of luxury establishments. The five-star Miramonti Majestic Grand Hotel (☎ 0436 4201), situated 2km out of town, has improved under new ownership. The four-stars include the attractive Hotel de la Poste (☎ 0436 4271), an old coaching inn run for generations by the Manaigo family, which is 'comfortable, with huge bathrooms. Its position on the high street is convenient if rather noisy'. Also well located is the Hotel Ancora (☎ 0436 3261 on the Corso Italia, run by the indomitable Flavia Sartor, who uses the hotel to house her enormous collection of antiques and paintings. The Parc Victoria (☎ 0436 3246 is advantageously placed and comfortably furnished by the Angeli family, who own the hotel. The three-star, family-run Aquila (☎ 0436 2618) is highly recommended. The Italia (☎ 0436 5646) is a popular two-star, with wholesome food and a loyal following. Two-star Hotel Montana (☎ 0436 860498) is said to be 'centrally located, cosy, comfortable and friendly'. The Olimpia (☎ 0436 3256) is one of the cheapest and most central B&Bs.

## Eating in and out

Michelin-starred Tivoli on the edge of town has a warm ambience with delicious and often unusual cooking ('try the warm guineafowl salad with nuts and smoked bacon'). El Toulà is a converted barn with a rustic atmosphere and first-rate food. Tiny Leone e Anna has been serving Sardinian cuisine in Cortina for 30 years, while El Zoco has grilled meats. La Tavernetta, on the road to the ice rink, was new in 2003–4 and is warmly recommended. The Croda Café, Il Ponte, Vienna, La Perla and the Cinque Torri are all good for pizzas. Lago Ghedina, a 15-minute drive away from town, has 'outstanding food in an intimate lake-side setting'.

## Après-ski

In one week you can only scratch the surface of Cortina's après-ski', commented one reporter. At about 5pm the pedestrianised Corso Italia comes alive with promenading, fur-clad Italians: 'like a fashion show with mobile phones'.

Cortina's shopping is absorbing and varied and includes antique and jewellery shops, sportswear and designer boutiques, interesting delicatessens and the six-storey Cooperativa department store, an Aladdin's Cave that seems to sell everything, with reasonable prices to match. As one reporter remarked: 'it's the only town we know where the Co-op has marble floors and sells designer clothes'.

Before dinner the action starts at the Enoteca wine bar, a serious drinking spot with a magnificent cellar, which closes at 9pm. Jerry's Wine Bar is another popular meeting-place, and LP 26 is curious mix of *prosciutteria* and cocktail bar (with ham snacks). The late-night crowd head for the Blu Room, Bilbo's and the Area.

## Childcare

Cortina has some of the most extensive nursery slopes in Europe, but the extent of childcare varies from season to season as kindergartens come and go. Gulliver Park, which opened for 2003–4, cares for children from three months to twelve years. The ski schools offer lessons for children from five years.

# Cortina d'Ampezzo: At a glance

**Tel** 39 0436 3231
**Email** cortina@infodolomiti.it
**Website** www.infodolomiti.it

### GETTING THERE
**Airport** Venice 2hrs
**Rail** Calalzo–Pieve di Cadore 35km
**Road** A27 autostrada from Venice to Belluno, then route 51

### THE SKIING
**Linked/nearby resorts** Armentarola, Kronplatz, San Cassiano, San Vito di Cadore
**Total of trails/pistes** 140km in Cortina area (44% easy, 49% intermediate, 7% difficult), 1,220km in Dolomiti Superski region
**Lifts in area** 49 in Cortina area: 12🚡 24🚠 13🎿. 460 in Dolomiti Superski area
**Lift opening dates** mid-November 2004 to end April 2005

### LIFT PASSES
**Area pass** Dolomiti Superski €160–182 for 6 days
**Pensioners** Dolomiti Superski 60yrs and over €136–155 for 6 days

### TUITION
**Ski & board** Azzurra (☎ 0436 2694), Cristallo-Cortina (☎ 0436 870073), Dolomiti-Cortina (☎ 0436 862264), Scuola Fondo Ski Cortina (☎ 0436 4903), Scuola Sci Cortina (☎ 0436 2911)
**Guiding** Guide Alpine (☎ 0436 868505)

### CHILDREN
**Lift pass** Dolomiti Superski 7–15yrs €112–127 for 6 days
**Ski & board school** as adults
**Kindergarten** Gulliver Park (☎ 340 0558399)

### FOOD AND DRINK
Coffee €3, bottle of house wine €10–15, small beer €2–3.50, soft drink €2–3.50, dish of the day €11–15

# Courmayeur

ALTITUDE 1,224m (4,016ft)

## ❄ beautiful scenery ❄ lovely old town centre ❄ easy airport access ❄ superb restaurants

> **Best for:** intermediates, off-piste skiers and boarders, cross-country skiers, night-owls, gourmet skiers
>
> **Not recommended for:** people who want skiing convenience, those seeking challenging pistes

Courmayeur established its reputation as a climbing base for the forbidding granite peaks of Mont Blanc, and then as a popular nineteenth-century spa. Its role as an internationally acclaimed ski resort came only with the opening of the Mont Blanc tunnel in 1965, which linked the village with **Chamonix** and made Geneva airport a 90-minute drive away.

The heart of the old village is a charming maze of cobbled alleys. It is largely traffic free and lined with fashion boutiques, delicatessens and antique shops. There are numerous bars, cafés and restaurants, with a lively crowd. For anyone interested in observing the prolonged après-ski *passeggiata* along Via Roma, it is important to find accommodation within easy walking distance of the pedestrian precinct. Courmayeur is the favourite resort of the Milanese, a clientèle for whom lunch is frequently a greater priority than skiing, and it proudly boasts some of the finest mountain restaurants in the Alps.

## WHAT'S NEW

Boardercross slope at Plan de la Grabba

## On-piste
top 2,624m (8,609ft) bottom 1,709m (5,607ft)

'Don't expect long runs or a varied ski area,' said a reporter, 'but in good conditions the skiing is excellent'. The main mountain access is by cable-car across the river gorge. This takes you up to Plan Chécrouit, a sunny plateau 75m from the foot of the lifts. At the end of the day you can take the cable-car back down, with skis and boots left in lockers at Plan Chécrouit. The alternative is to ski down to Dolonne and take a ski bus back across the river to Courmayeur. The mountain can also be reached by cable-car from the hamlet of Va Veny.

Extensive investment in snow-cannon has done much to improve skiing on the lower slopes down to Plan Chécrouit, Dolonne and to Val Veny. However, the skiing is not satisfactory for everyone: the pisted runs are mainly short and lack challenge. Advanced skiers will be more interested in the separate off-piste area, reached by the three-stage Mont Blanc cable-car at La Palud, near the village of Entrèves on the tunnel side of Courmayeur. This also provides access to the Vallée Blanche on the Chamonix side of Mont Blanc.

The easiest slopes are somewhat hazardous, with those at Plan Chécrouit cramped by buildings and crowds of skiers descending from the main pistes. The main nursery slope is situated at the top of the Maison Vieille chair-lift. The baby slopes at the top of Val Veny and Dolonne are quieter.

The east-facing Chécrouit Bowl has many short intermediate runs served by a variety of lifts including a six-seater gondola. There are some surprisingly steep and narrow passages, even on some of the blue runs. The wooded, north-facing Val Veny side of the mountain is linked in a couple of places with the Chécrouit Bowl; the Val Veny side has longer and more varied pistes with two red runs and a black trail following the fall-line through the trees.

The pistes served by the Gabba quad-chair at the top of the ski area and to the west of Lago Chécrouit keep their snow well. The off-piste run underneath them is testing. The Youla cable-car above Lago Chécrouit provides access into a deep and sheltered bowl, which serves a single, uncomplicated red run with plenty of space for short off-piste excursions when snow conditions are good. Courmayeur has neither terrain park nor half-pipe, but the off-piste at Cresta d'Arp makes for some excellent freeriding.

Queuing for the Plan Chécrouit and Mont Blanc areas is much worse at weekends, when the crowds arrive from Turin and Milan. Quad-chairs at La Gabba, Aretu and Zerotta have eased some of the other bottlenecks on the mountain, but the Youla cable-car can still be a problem. Plan de la Grabba has a new 500-m boardercross slope offering parabolic curves and jumps.

Opportunities for cross-country skiing are enormous here, with a major Nordic centre at Val Ferret, a 15-minute drive away at the foot of the Grandes Jorasses. The centre offers four loipes totalling 30km, which wind through spectacular scenery.

Courmayeur is a good base from which to explore the substantial amount of skiing available in the Aosta Valley. A joint lift pass extends to **La Thuile** and **La Rosière** in one direction, and to **Champoluc– Gressoney–Alanga** in the other.

## Off-piste

The top of the two-stage cable-car at Cresta d'Arp is the starting point at 2,755m for some serious powder runs. Avalanche safety has been improved, but the service of a guide is still advised. One route takes you down 1,500m vertical to the satellite village of Dolonne or to the river bank near Pré-St-Didier; the other brings you through the beautiful Vallon de Youla to La Balme, a few kilometres from La Thuile.

From the nearby hamlet of La Palud, the Mont Blanc cable-car rises to 3,462m at Punta Helbronner, giving easy access to the Vallée Blanche by avoiding the dreaded ice steps. Alternatively, you can cruise the 10km back down the Toula Glacier to La Palud; it is steep at the top and involves a clamber along a fixed rope and the hair-raising negotiation of an exposed and awkward staircase. Heli-skiing on the Ruitor Glacier and from the ridge at the head of Val Veny is spectacular.

## Tuition and guiding

The standard of spoken English has improved greatly at the Scuola di Sci Monte Bianco in recent years, and the general verdict is that private instructors and guides are first rate, but that group instructors are often jaded. However, the strong presence of Interski, a British tour operator that has been allowed to establish its own ski school with British instructors for its mixed clientèle of adults and schoolchildren, has served to raise standards. Snowboard & Ski School Courmayeur is new, but as yet we have no reports.

## Mountain restaurants

Food in Courmayeur is taken just as seriously as skiing. There is probably nowhere you can eat better for less money in a greater variety of mountain restaurants. Prices are actually lower than in the resort itself. One reporter commented: 'it is hard to ski when you could be eating. The atmosphere in the huts scattered around the mountain is an integral part of our annual visit here'.

Rifugio Maison Vieille at Col Chécrouit has a large wood-burning stove and a great atmosphere ('it's worth coming to Courmayeur just to have lunch here'). The Christiania at Plan Chécrouit is also singled out for special praise: 'good meeting-point for families, great pizzas' and 'the freshest seafood I have ever tasted'. The Chiecco, situated just above Plan Chécrouit, serves full meals and 'heavenly desserts'. La Grolla at Peindeint on the Val Veny side merits a visit ('expensive, but worth it and difficult to find – thank goodness'). On the Mont Blanc side there are bars at each lift stage. The Rifugio Pavillon at the top of the first stage of the cable-car is reportedly superb and has a sun terrace. Rifugio Torino, at the next stage, is also said to be good.

## Accommodation

The resort has six four-star hotels including the Gallia Gran Baita (☎ 0165 844040), which is described as 'worthy of its rating, but too far out of town unless you have a car'. Few of the hotels, apartments and chalets are well situated for the main cable-car. However, the comfortable and expensive Hotel Pavillon (☎ 0165 846120) ('the service was impressive') is well placed 150m from the cable-car and boasts a swimming-pool and sauna. Three-star Hotel Courmayeur (☎ 0165 846732) is 'friendly, with a roaring log fire in the sitting area'. The family-run Bouton d'Or (☎ 0165 846729) is 'conveniently located, quiet, comfortable and has its own parking'. Three-star Hotel Meublé Laurent (☎ 0165 846687) was rated 'a good find. The recently renovated rooms were cosy and traditional, while the bathrooms were modern and clean'. Auberge de la Maison (☎ 0165 869811) in the quiet little hamlet of Entrèves ('an outstandingly stylish three-star') has friendly owners and comfortable rooms. I Maquis (☎ 0165 897649), also in Entrèves, is said to have an 'outstanding restaurant – incredibly contemporary and chic'. However, the hotel's nightclub 'stays open until 3am at weekends, which makes sleep impossible'.

## Eating in and out

Restaurants are varied, plentiful and lively. Pierre Alexis rates as one of the best in town ('an extraordinary wine list to complement great food'). Courmayeur also has plenty of pizzerias, including Mont Frèty ('wonderful for families'). Cadran Solaire is praised for both cuisine and ambience. La Maison de Filippo at Entrèves is an exercise in unparalleled gluttony; it offers a fixed-price menu of more than 30 courses. Ancien Casino is a new pizzeria.

## Après-ski

The evening begins with cocktails in the American Bar. The Bar Roma, with its comfortable sofas and armchairs, fills up early. Ziggi's is a cyber-café, the Red Lion is frequented by snowboarders and Cadran Solaire is where the sophisticated Milanese go. Bar Posta and Bar delle Guide both have a lively atmosphere, and there are also two discos.

For something completely different, you can now play golf on snow from the first stage of the Mont Blanc cable-car, where there is a panoramic driving range and an instructor to hand.

## Childcare

Kinderheim up at Plan Chécrouit looks after children from six months old. Staff pick up from the bottom of the cable-car in the village and return at the end of the day. Baby Club at the sports centre also cares for kids from six months old and is particularly useful for parents wanting to ski on the Mont Blanc side. The Scuola di Sci Monte Bianco and the Snowboard & Ski School Courmayeur both accept children from four years of age. The resort has four magic carpets.

# Courmayeur: At a glance

**Tel** 39 0165 842060
**Email** aiat.montebianco@psw.it
**Website** www.comune.courmayeur.ao.it

## GETTING THERE
**Airports** Geneva 1½hrs (through Mont Blanc tunnel), Turin 2hrs
**Rail** Pré-St-Didier 5km, regular buses from station
**Road** Autoroute Blanche from Geneva and continue through Mont Blanc tunnel

## THE SKIING
**Linked/nearby resorts** Alagna, Chamonix, Champoluc, Gressoney-La-Trinité, Pila, La Rosière, La Thuile
**Total of trails/pistes** 100km (20% easy, 70% intermediate, 10% difficult)
**Lifts in area** 19: 8⬆ 8⬆ 3⬆
**Lift opening dates** early December 2004 to late April 2005

## LIFT PASSES
**Area pass** Aosta Valley Skipass €161 for 6 days

**Pensioners** no reductions

## TUITION
**Ski & board** Interski (☎ 01623 456333 in UK), Scuola di Sci Monte Bianco (☎ 0165 842477), Snowboard & Ski School Courmayeur (☎ 0165 848254)
**Guiding** Air Vallée (☎ 0165 869814), Società delle Guide Alpine di Courmayeur (☎ 0165 842064)

## CHILDREN
**Lift pass** Aosta Valley Skipass 9–12yrs €121 for 6 days
**Ski & board school** Scuola di Sci Monte Bianco, Snowboard & Ski School Courmayeur
**Kindergarten** (ski/non-ski) Kinderheim at Plan Chécrouit (☎ 0165 842477), (non-ski) Baby Club at Forum Sports Centre (☎ 348 7623811)

## FOOD AND DRINK
Coffee €1–2, bottle of house wine €10, small beer €2.50–3.50, soft drink €2.50–3, dish of the day €8.50–20

# Kronplatz

ALTITUDE 900m (2,953ft)

## ❉ Europe's most sophisticated lift system ❉ value for money
## ❉ beautiful scenery

**Best for:** beginners, intermediates, high-speed cruisers, families

**Not recommended for:** powderhounds, anyone seeking skiing convenience, night-owls, sophistocates

Kronplatz is situated in the Sud Tirol, that rugged corner of the Alps that was once part of Austria but which has belonged to Italy since the end of World War I. This mainstream Alpine ski area is one of the best-kept secrets of European skiing – at least from a British point of view ('during a two-day visit I never once heard English spoken').

The dome-shaped mountain lies close to the Austrian border – **Innsbruck** is only 115km by road to the north. **Cortina d'Ampezzo** is an hour's drive away.

## On the snow
top 2,275m (7,464ft) bottom 900m (2,953ft)

Kronplatz, also known by its Italian name of Plan de Corones, is a ski area rather than a resort, and has enjoyed huge investment in recent years. Most of the 90km of runs are fairly undemanding reds and blues, but with a vertical drop of up to 1,320m they provide enormous enjoyment for intermediate and expert alike.

The principal means of access directly to the flat summit is by a gondola from near the village of Olang, or from Reischach near Bruneck. A third network of gondolas rises from Italian-speaking St Vigilio di Marebbe.

Advanced skiers and riders can concentrate on the black Sylvester run and the new and even more demanding Herrneg, a 1,320-m rollercoaster through the woods designed by Bernhard Russi, the former Swiss racer responsible for the last five Olympic downhill courses.

The resort has a half-pipe served by a six-person chair-lift. Six ski schools in the area provide tuition – Skischool Kronplatz, San Vigilio, Sporting Al Plan, Olang-Rasen, Cima,

and Gsieser Tal. The two specialist cross-country schools are Ski School Nordic in Brunek and Ski & Biathlon School Antholz. The good-value Dolomiti Superski lift pass gives access to 460 lifts in the region.

Reporters recommend the Cai restaurant ('good value for money'), which is close to the summit.

## In the resort
The nearby town of Bruneck (or Brunico), and 13 little villages scattered around the foot of the mountain, act as individual bed bases, connected to the lift stations by a regular free bus service.

The four-star Hotel Mirabell in Olang (☎ 0474 496191) has 'a great spa and is extremely convenient'. Alpenhotel Hubertus (☎ 0474 592104) and the Hotel Post (☎ 0474 496127) are recommended. In St Vigilio, Almhof-Hotel Call (☎ 0474 501043) and Parc Hotel Posta (☎ 0474 501010) are both praised, and in Bruneck Royal Hotel Hinterhuber (☎ 0474 541000) and the Petrus (☎ 0474 548263) head a long list of hotels for all price brackets.

Nightlife in the outlying villages consists of bars and the occasional disco busy at weekends only during the high season. St Vigilio boasts Le Morin Club disco and bar, and Bruneck offers some small measure of sophistication throughout the winter.

Croniworld on the summit of the mountain cares for skiing and non-skiing children aged three to eight years. Olang and St Vigilio both have kindergartens at resort level.

## Kronplatz: At a glance

**Tel** 39 0474 555447
**Email** info@kronplatz.com
**Website** www.kronplatz.com
**Lifts in resort** 30: 14⬤ 8⬛ 8⬛. 460 in Dolomiti Superski area
**Lift opening dates** 27 November 2004 to 10 April 2005

# Livigno

**ALTITUDE 1,820m (5,970ft)**                    map: see page 193

## ❄ duty-free prices ❄ skiing convenience ❄ reliable snow cover

---

**Best for:** beginners, ski-to-lunchers, ski-and-shoppers, budget skiers, telemarkers, night-owls

**Not recommended for:** advanced skiers and riders, non-skiers, people wanting a quiet village atmosphere

---

Livigno – the cheapest of Alpine resorts – is a duty-free village reached after a long transfer from Bergamo, Milan or Zurich airports. Its high location has earned it the nickname 'Piccolo Tibet' (Little Tibet). The resort's *raison d'être* is shopping, with stores dedicated to cheap alcohol, clothing and consumer durables.

The resort is divided into the four spread-out hamlets of Santa Maria, San Antonio, San Rocco and Trepalle. These are linked by a free but 'entirely inadequate' bus service. San Antonio provides the focal point, with hotels, restaurants and noisy bars.

---

### WHAT'S NEW
6-seater chair replaces drag-lift at Federia

---

### On the snow
top 2,797m (9,177ft) bottom 1,820m (5,970ft)

The core of the skiing is on the ski-in, ski-out, south-east-facing Carosello, and a two-stage gondola provides rapid access from the town to the highest point. The skiing is generally steeper on the west-facing side of the valley. A new six-seater chair replaces the drag-lift at Federia for the 2003–4 season.

The resort-level nursery area is close to the main thoroughfare, and the best slopes for progressive novices are from Monte della Neve and Mottolino to Trepalle.

Wide pistes mean that Livigno is a good place for novice snowboarders, but it presents few challenges for the experienced. Reporters rated the resort 'great for apprehensive skiers and mixed-ability families'.

In recent years, Inverno/Estate has become the major player amongst the five ski and snowboard schools. The main self-service restaurants at the top of the Mottolino and Carosello gondolas offer competitive prices, while La Costaccia is known for its outdoor barbecue. Also recommended are Tea Borch, below Carosello, and the Tea del Plan, below Costaccia.

### In the resort
Livigno boasts seven four-stars: the Golf Hotel Pare (☎ 0342 970263) and the Intermonti (☎ 0342 972100) are on the hill-side overlooking the town; the others are the Concordia (☎ 0342 990100), the Flora (☎ 0342 996034), the Amerikan (☎ 0342 996521), the Spöl (☎ 0342 996105) and the Posta (☎ 0342 996076). Convenient for both the nursery slopes and the après-ski are the Alpina (☎ 0342 996007), the Helvetia (☎ 0342 970066) and the Victoria (☎ 0342 970490).

Good restaurants include the Pesce d'Oro ('by far the best') and Camana Veglia, while the Bellavista wins many friends with its pizzas as does Mario's for 'classy pizza and pasta'.

Reporters rated the Kuhstall the best bar ('a great atmosphere'). Noisy alternatives include Tea del Vidal and Galli's. The Kokodi nightclub attracts British visitors.

Children's tuition is available at all the ski schools, while Mini Club Mottalino and Spazio Gioco Peribimbi are for small non-skiers. Ali Baba acts as both ski- and non-ski kindergarten. M'eating Point (sic) is for children from three years old.

---

### Livigno: At a glance

**Tel** 39 0342 996379
**Email** info@aptlivigno.it
**Website** www.aptlivigno.it
**Lifts in resort** 32: 3🚡 15🚠 14🎿
**Lift opening dates** 27 November 2004 to 1 May 2005. Summer skiing on the Stelvio Pass

# Madonna di Campiglio

ALTITUDE 1,550m (5,085ft)

## ❄ excellent nursery slopes ❄ first-rate piste-grooming ❄ beautiful scenery ❄ chic resort atmosphere

> **Best for:** beginners, intermediates, snowboarders, cross-country skiers
>
> **Not recommended for:** expert skiers, ski-to-lunchers, budget skiers

Madonna di Campiglio is one of Italy's smartest resorts. The atmosphere is congenial, with a predominantly modern architectural style and high standard of accommodation.

The ski area is officially rated as Italy's premier for piste-grooming, and the resort regularly hosts international winter sports events.

## On the snow
### top 2,505m (8,219ft) bottom 1,520m (4,987ft)

Madonna's three ski areas are cunningly interlinked at valley level by a snow-cannon-maintained piste that winds beneath a series of road bridges. An ancient cable-car climbs slowly up to the first area, 5-Laghi, from the centre of town. The second area is reached by a jumbo gondola to Pradalago at 2,100m, which is linked to the resorts of Marilleva and Folgarida. The four-seater Genziana chair-lift in the Pradalago area was new for 2003–4. The third area, Monte Spinale/Grostè, is dramatically positioned beneath the towering granite cliff faces of Pietra Grande and is accessed by high-speed gondola.

### WHAT'S NEW
6-seater chair-lift replaces 2 chairs in Grostè area for 2004–5

The resort has nine ski and snowboard schools. Novices taking tuition should not buy a lift pass, as they will be taken by bus to the private Campo Carlo Magno nursery area. Bambi, a second beginner area, is in the centre of Madonna. Blue runs make up more than half the slopes in the main Madonna area, which provides lots of long cruises on attractive tree-lined trails.

Madonna is also rated as one of the best snowboarding resorts in Italy. The Grostè

terrain park and boardercross course is at 2,500m. Another terrain park is on the 2,100-m Doss del Sabion, above the nearby resort of Pinzolo. Recommended mountain restaurants include Cascina Zeledria and Malga Boch.

## In the resort

'The resort has a very exclusive feel,' commented a reporter, 'I have never seen so many fur coats in my life'. Relais Club des Alpes (☎ 0465 440000) heads a list of 20 four-star hotels. Chalet Hermitage (☎ 0465 441558) is a 'bio-hotel' in an immense private park. 'The accommodation, food and quality of service were second to none, and the leisure facilities were equally impressive,' said one reporter. The Savoia Palace (☎ 0465 441004) is well positioned. Arnica (☎ 0465 440377) is a conveniently central, modern B&B, while Villa Principe (☎ 0465 440011) has some of the cheapest rooms in town. There are also chalet-apartments and self-catering establishments.

Notable mountain restaurants include Malga Montagnoli, Cascina Zeledria and Malga Boch. In town, Antico Focolare is the 'in' place to eat, along with Pappagallo and Cliffhanger. Le Roi serves the best pizzas.

Bar Suisse, the Franz-Josef Stube and Café Campiglio are the principal après-ski haunts. Bacchus is a lively new wine bar. Zangola, 3km out of town, and Cliffhanger are the discos.

Hotel Spinale runs a children's club, and Campilandia is the non-ski kindergarten. The resort has a magic carpet lift.

## Madonna di Campiglio: At a glance

**Tel** 39 0465 442000
**Email** info@campiglio.net
**Website** www.campiglio.to
**Lifts in resort** 22: 4🚠 12🚡 6🎿
**Lift opening dates** early December 2004 to late April 2005

# Sauze d'Oulx

**ALTITUDE 1,509m (4,951ft)**                                   map: see page 194

## ❄ giant intermediate ski area ❄ wild nightlife ❄ value for money

> **Best for:** intermediates, high-mileage cruisers, budget skiers, 20-something party-goers, off-piste skiers
>
> **Not recommended for:** early-nighters, sophisticates, gourmets, snowboarders

Sauze d'Oulx, situated close to the French border and just an hour's drive from Turin, has long held a reputation as a place where 'on the piste' is a 24-hour state of mind and body that has little or nothing to do with skiing. Despite strenuous efforts to shift its profile to that of a more sober family resort, good-natured pub culture still rules.

Sauze is a key component of the **Milky Way**, or Via Lattea, a complex web of 92 lifts linking five principal Italian resorts with the French border town of **Montgenèvre**. At its best, this is one of the great ski circuits of Europe, with 400km of groomed pistes that provide mainly intermediate terrain, but the region is by no means snow-sure. It is hoped that cover will be ample during the February 2006 Winter Olympics. Neighbouring **Sestriere** is the main host, but the freestyle events will take place in Sauze. As in other resorts in the Milky Way, Sauze d'Oulx hoteliers are concerned that fears of widespread piste closures during the Games will act as a deterrent to those who might otherwise visit during February 2006. However, such fears proved groundless at both the Salt Lake City and Nagano Olympics.

The old part of the town dates from the fifteenth century and has cobbled streets, but the main part, adjacent to the slopes, is a largely uninspiring collection of modern edifices constructed with budget rather than beauty in mind. Annoyingly, the resort bus service is not included in the lift pass.

## On-piste
top 2,507 m (8,225ft) bottom 1,360m (4,462ft)

Most of the improvements to the area brought about by the impending Olympics benefit Sestriere and **Cesana–Sansicario**.

But Sauze is to have a new chair-lift to Clotes, a new piste for the freestyle events, and improved snowmaking. The Sauze d'Oulx slopes face west and north, and the majority of them are below the tree-line. A quad-chair takes you up to the centre of the skiing at Sportinia, a sunny woodland clearing with a variety of restaurants. A network of lifts lead on up into the main ski area. Both the local lift map and trail-marking have improved substantially in recent years, although lift queues remain a problem.

The main nursery slope is at Sportinia; it is light and open, but often very crowded. Nursery slopes can also be found at Belvédère on the Genevris side, as well as in the village when there is snow. The Genevris/Moncrons/Bourget sector on the edge of the Milky Way circuit has some of the best slopes and is the ideal retreat on Saturdays and Sundays ('I had the area to myself') when the Italians arrive in force.

Sauze quite wrongly has a novice label attached to it, due to the predominance of beginner and early-intermediate skiers. In fact, some of the reds here could easily be graded black, and a few of the blacks (notably No. 33 and No. 21) are seriously challenging in difficult snow conditions.

Below Sportinia are wide runs back through the woods, graded red and black. Links to the rest of the circuit are via the 2,424-m Col Basset and 2,701-m Monte Fraiteve. From here you can ski down to Sestriere, or Sansicario and on to **Claviere** and Montgenèvre. Sauze has no special facilities for snowboarding.

## Off-piste
Monte Fraiteve, an exposed crest, is the start of the famous Rio Nero off-piste run, which is a long descent that follows a river gully down to the Oulx–Cesana road, 1,600m below. An infrequent bus service takes you back to the lifts at **Cesana–Sansicario**.

## Tuition and guiding
The Sauze d'Oulx Ski School has much improved in recent year, and has two rivals:

Sauze Project and Sauze Sportinia. The latter achieves a high standard of teaching, though one reporter complained that his instructor had only a few English phrases.

## Mountain restaurants

The five busy restaurants at Sportinia maintain a high standard. Chalet Genevris, in the area of the same name, is renowned for its fixed-price, lunchtime barbecue. Ciao Pais and the Highest Pizzeria in Italy are both praised. One reporter warned of a €3-per-person seating charge in some mountain restaurants 'even if you are just having a coffee'.

## Accommodation

The 39 hotels range from four four-stars to five one-stars and include six apartment complexes. Among the four-stars, Il Capricorno (☎ 0122 850273) is 'comfortable and quiet – a long way from the noisy nightlife', La Torre (☎ 0122 858301) is recommended, and Hotel Relais des Alpes (☎ 0122 859747) is said to be 'a great hotel'. The three-star Sauze (☎ 0122 850285) is 'clean and spacious', while Gran Baita (☎ 0122 850183) is praised as 'excellent – very clean, the staff are pleasant'. The two-star Hermitage (☎ 0122 850385) is recommended, along with the 'clean and comfortable' two-star Biancaneve (☎ 0122 850021). One reporter recommended staying in the one-star Hotel orso Bianco (☎ 0122 850226) at Sportinia.

## Eating in and out

Del Falco is praised ('atmosphere, food and wine all excellent') along with Old Inn, La Vecchia Pietra and Bruscetta. Del Borgo exudes 'a pleasant buzz'.

## Après-ski

The New Scotch Bar catches the early evening crowd and is awash with pints of Tartan long before dark. The Moncrons is equally popular. Later on, the action moves to the Cotton Club, Hotel Derby Bar ('mellow, with comfy sofas and chill-out music') and Osteria dei Vagabondi. The Village Café and Gran Trun both host live music six nights a week, while the Bandito, Schuss and Rimini Nord discos 'keep you dancing as long as you want'.

## Childcare

La Cinciarella accepts children from 13 months ('absolutely superb – I couldn't have wished for better childcare'). The ski schools offer kids' lessons from four years.

# Sauze d'Oulx: At a glance

**Tel** 39 0122 850700
**Email** sauze@montagnedoc.it
**Website** www.montagnedoc.it

### GETTING THERE
**Airport** Turin 1hr
**Rail** Oulx 5km, regular buses to resort
**Road** take the Oulx-Est exit off the A32 Turin–Bardonecchia autostrada

### THE SKIING
**Linked/nearby resorts** Clavière, Montgenèvre, Sansicario, Sestriere
**Total of trails/pistes** 120km in Sauze d'Oulx (27% easy, 61% intermediate, 12% difficult), 400km in the Milky Way
**Lifts in area** 92 in the Milky Way: 3⬆ 35⬆ 54⬆
**Lift opening dates** early December 2004 to mid-April 2005

### LIFT PASSES
**Area pass** Milky Way €138–155 for 6 days

**Pensioners** Milky Way 60–75yrs €127–143 for 6 days

### TUITION
**Ski & board** Sauze d'Oulx Ski School (☎ 0122 858084), Sauze Project (☎ 0122 858942), Sauze Sportinia (☎ 0122 850218)
**Guiding** Elisusa Heli-skiing (☎ 0122 623162), Guide Alpine Valsusa (☎ 0335 398984) and through ski schools

### CHILDREN
**Lift pass** Milky Way 8–12yrs €127–143 for 6 days
**Ski & board school** as adults
**Kindergarten** (ski) through ski schools, (non-ski) La Cinciarella (☎ 328 6445146)

### FOOD AND DRINK
Coffee €0.80–2, bottle of house wine €10, small beer €2.50–3, soft drink €2.50, dish of the day €12–15

# Selva Gardena

ALTITUDE 1,564–1,800m (5,130–5,904ft)                    map: see page 189

## ❋ most important resort in giant Sella Ronda ski area
## ❋ beautiful scenery ❋ good children's facilities

> **Best for:** all standards of skier and snowboarder, long-distance cruisers, families, foodies, cross-country enthusiasts
>
> **Not recommended for:** people who hate lift queues, early- and late-season skiers

Selva Gardena is the most popular resort in the **Sella Ronda**, a celebrated circuit of four valleys in the Dolomites that involves 90 minutes of lifts, 120 minutes of downhill skiing and an always undetermined joker factor of queuing time. In turn, the Sella Ronda is itself only part of the area covered by the Dolomiti Superski – the world's largest ski pass – which encompasses 1,220km of piste served by 460 lifts.

Whether the Sella Ronda is the world's largest ski area is open to debate, but it is certainly the most beautiful – the backdrop of craggy peaks and dramatic cliff faces, which take on a distinctive and glorious shade of rose-pink in the light of the setting sun, is without parallel.

Selva Gardena, or Wolkenstein as it is also known, is an unassuming village that sprawls in suburban style up the Val Gardena. The village maintains a quiet, unsophisticated charm, which makes it popular with families.

From Selva Gardena, the Sella Ronda can be skied in both directions, but clockwise involves less poling and skating. Signposting is good, but miss the crucial lift home and you are in for an expensive taxi ride.

## On-piste
top 2,950m (9,676ft) bottom 1,225m (4,018ft)

With its mainly blue and unproblematic red runs, the Sella Ronda is better for seeing some wonderful scenery than for really challenging skiing or snowboarding. Snow cover in recent seasons has been erratic, but this climatic handicap has been partially offset by heavy investment in modern snowmaking techniques.

Despite continuing innovations to the lift system, queues in the Sella Ronda can still become chronic at high-season weekends and during the Italian school holidays. You cannot hope to ski the whole Sella Ronda area in a week, or even in a season, but as one reporter put it, 'it's a lot of fun trying'.

The whole of the Sella Ronda is ideally suited to cruisers who really want to put some mileage beneath their skis each day in this outstanding setting. For Langlauf enthusiasts, the Dolomiti Superski area claims 1,033km of prepared loipe scattered throughout the region.

## Off-piste
For the best powder slopes, head for the Passo Pordoi cable-car. The long run down the Val de Mezdi is one of the most taxing in the Dolomites and should not be attempted without the services of a guide.

## Tuition and guiding
Tuition at the Selva Gardena ski school appears to be of a high standard: 'good teaching and no silly end-of-week races'. The standard of English spoken by instructors throughout the Sella Ronda appears to have improved dramatically in recent years. The other ski schools in Val Gardena are Santa Cristina and Ortisei. Dolomiti Ski Eagles specialises in off-piste and helping advanced skiers to improve.

## Mountain restaurants
The Dolomites abound with mountain eateries, with much the best to be found in the Italian- rather than the German-speaking sectors. Rifugio Lagazuoi is singled out as having 'spectacular value with amazing views', and Rifugio Pralongia is praised for 'well-prepared meals', while Villa Frainela at Dantercëpies serves 'homemade *Strudel* and traditional cakes that are to die for'. Panorama (on the Selva

Gardena side of the Dantercëpies piste) is 'a real sun-trap and has good food'.

## Accommodation

Sporthotel Gran Baita (☎ 0471 795210) is the pick of a dozen four-stars, together with the Aaritz (☎ 0471 795011) and the Alpenroyal (☎ 0471 795178). The centrally situated Hotel Antares (☎ 0471 795400) is also praised. The three-star Hotel Laurin (☎ 0471 795105) is a favourite among visitors and renowned for its food. We have good reports, too, of the Hotel Solaia (☎ 0471 795104). The Rodella (☎ 0471 794553) is 'family-run and beautifully clean with a lovely atmosphere', while the Stella (☎ 0471 795162) is 'simple, inexpensive and thoroughly recommended'. The more spacious Savoy (☎ 0471 795343) is praised for its restaurant. Hotel Continental (☎ 0471 795411) is well located for skiers beneath the Dantercëpies gondola, but 'non-skiers should note that the ten-minute walk into town can be steep and icy'.

## Eating in and out

The Laurinkeller remains famed for its steaks and spare-ribs, and Pizzerias Miravalle and Rino are popular. Other eateries include Armin's Grillstube, Scoiàttolo, Frëina and the restaurant in the Sporthotel Gran Baita. In nearby Santa Cristina, Plaza and Iman are recommended, along with Uridl for authentic local dishes. L'Medel ('try the venison with polenta and *porcini* mushrooms') is a wooden chalet set on the piste.

## Après-ski

'If you want nightlife, then you would be better off staying across the border in Austria', said one reporter. The Luislkeller is the most popular haunt, along with Goalie's Pub, the Laurinkeller and La Bula. Bar La Stua has twice-weekly folk-music evenings, and the Speckkeller can be lively, as can Bar 200 and Crazy Pub in Santa Cristina. Principal discos are the Dali and the Heustadl in Selva Gardena.

## Childcare

The Selva Gardena nursery slopes are based below the Dantercëpies gondola. In the kindergarten at the bottom of the Biancaneve drag-lift, toddlers and small children are taught by patient ski instructors.

# Selva Gardena: At a glance

**Tel** 39 0471 795122
**Email** selva@valgardena.com
**Website** www.valgardena.com

### GETTING THERE
**Airports** Innsbruck 1½hrs, Verona 2–3hrs, Milan and Munich 3–4hrs
**Rail** Chiusa 27km, Bressanone 35km, Bolzano 40km, regular buses
**Road** from the Brenner Pass take Chiusa/Val Gardena autostrada exit

### THE SKIING
**Linked/nearby resorts** Arabba, Armentarola, Campitello, Canazei, Colfosco, Cortina d'Ampezzo, Corvara, Ortisei, Pedraces, San Cassiano, Santa Cristina, La Villa
**Total of trails/pistes** 175km in Val Gardena, 1,220km in Dolomiti Superski area (30% easy, 60% intermediate, 10% difficult)
**Lifts in area** 83 in Val Gardena: 10🚠 36🚡 37🎿.
460 in Dolomiti Superski area
**Lift opening dates** 27 November 2004 to 3 April 2005

### LIFT PASSES
**Area pass** Dolomiti Superski €160–182 for 6 days
**Pensioners** Dolomiti Superski 60yrs and over €136–155 for 6 days

### TUITION
**Ski & board** Dolomiti Ski Eagles (Ski Academy) (☎ 0471 773182), Ortisei (☎ 0471 796153), Santa Cristina (☎ 0471 792045), Selva Gardena Ski School (☎ 0471 795156)
**Guiding** Catores Alpine School (☎ 0471 798223), Val Gardena Guides (☎ 0471 794133)

### CHILDREN
**Lift pass** Dolomiti Superski 7–15yrs €112–127 for 6 days
**Ski & board school** as adults
**Kindergarten** (ski/non-ski) Ortisei (☎ 0471 796153), Santa Cristina (☎ 0471 792045), Selva Gardena (☎ 0471 795156)

### FOOD AND DRINK
Coffee €2, bottle of house wine €10, small beer €2.50, soft drink €2.50, dish of the day €7–20

# Sestriere

**ALTITUDE 2,035m (6,675ft)**

map: see page 194

## ❄ varied off-piste opportunities ❄ lively nightlife
## ❄ extensive skiing terrain

> **Best for:** intermediates in search of high-mileage skiing, snowboarders, those requiring easy airport access
>
> **Not recommended for:** non-skiers, people wanting a traditional Alpine village atmosphere

Sestriere was controversially chosen, at the eleventh hour, over Crans Montana in Switzerland as the venue for the 2006 Winter Olympics – and it is now working hard on improvements to convince the world that the decision was the right one.

This is the smartest resort with the most challenging skiing in the whole of the **Milky Way**, or Via Lattea, which straddles the border between France and Italy and is reached more easily from Turin than Grenoble. In all, some 92 lifts serve 400km of mainly intermediate skiing that stretches beyond Sestriere to **Sauze d'Oulx**, Sansicario, **Clavière**, Cesana–Sansicario and the French border town of **Montgenèvre**.

What was once considered to be one of the most fashionable winter resorts in Europe was purpose-built in 1930 by Giovanni Agnelli, the founder of Fiat, who was frustrated that members of his family spent so much of their winter skiing abroad. Sestriere's location on a high, cold and barren pass is not enchanting, but the snow here is usually the best in the region. However, snowfall in recent seasons has been by no means reliable and this corner of the Alps, which includes the nearby French resort of **Serre Chevalier**, attracts a different weather system from mainstream destinations farther north.

The village is compact but, despite being essentially Italian, appears to lack soul. Its skyline is dominated by the twin towers of the Torre and the Duchi d'Aosta hotels that now both form a Club Med complex, and by the two copycat towers of the Villagio degli Atleti, built to house competitors in the highly successful 1997 Alpine Skiing World Championships. The staging of this event went a long way towards convincing members of the International Olympic Committee that Sestriere had the resources and flair to organise a Winter Games. Buses run to and from the satellites of Borgata and Grangesises.

## On-piste
### top 2,823m (9,262ft) bottom 1,839m (6,033ft)

In the run up to February 2006, the Sestriere end of the Milky Way is understandably benefiting from most of the new lifts. The old, slow triple Trebials chair between Borgata and Sestriere has been upgraded to a detachable quad. The old Garnel drag-lift has been replaced by a chair-lift from the new Olympic Village up to Alpette, with a tunnel to allow skiers to pass beneath the Sises piste, venue for the Olympic giant slalom.

Snow-cannon are being installed on a further 7km of nearby pistes that will be used as Olympic training runs. A new cable-car between Sestriere and Fraiteve will be completed in time for the games.

> **WHAT'S NEW**
>
> Trebials chair upgraded to detachable quad
> Garnel drag-lift replaced by chair
> Improved snowmaking on Olympic pistes

Sestriere's own considerable ski area divides into the two sectors of Monte Motta and Monte Sises. Both are accessed by quad chair-lifts and offer a variety of mainly red and black runs. The steep Motta drag- and chair-lifts serve the toughest slopes and climb to the top point of the Milky Way. Here the mogulled slopes beside the drag can have gradients of up to 30 degrees. Monte Sises has some more benign terrain, as well as a steep black run from the summit.

The resort has good beginner slopes close to the village, and a terrain park with boardercross, obstacles and a half-pipe.

## Off-piste

The most celebrated powder run in the region is the Rio Nero, which follows a river gully down to the Oulx–Cesana road from Monte Fraiteve. Both Monte Sises and Monte Motta offer outstanding alternatives after a fresh dump, but you do need a guide. Heli-skiing can be arranged through Guide Alpine Valsusa or Elisusa Heli-skiing.

## Tuition and guiding

Reports of the Sestriere Ski School are positive: 'our instructor spoke excellent English and tuition was friendly and competent'. Sestriere Extreme ski school offers night-skiing, freeriding and ski testing among its group and private lessons.

## Mountain restaurants

Bar Conchinetto is a traditional wood-and-stone restaurant noted for its polenta, while atmospheric La Gargote is more expensive, and Alpette is praised for its pasta.

## Accommodation

Sestriere's accommodation is in hotels, modern apartments and at Club Med (☎ 020-7348 3333 in UK). The restored four-star Grand Hotel Principi di Piemonte (☎ 0122 7941) is situated a kilometre out of town but has its own access lift to the Sises ski area. The four-star Hotel Cristallo (☎ 0122 77091) has 'a magnificent new swimming-pool'. Il Fraitevino (☎ 0122 77091), in the centre of town, and Banchetta (☎ 0122 70307), in the satellite of Borgata, are also recommended. The Biancaneve (☎ 0122 755176) is situated just outside the town.

## Eating in and out

Ristorante du Grandpère, in Champlas Janvier, is praised for its wild boar stew and polenta. Antica Spelonca offers 'a wonderful atmosphere'.

## Après-ski

Sestriere's nightlife is fairly lively and stylish when the Italians are in residence at weekends and in holiday periods, although at other times it is quiet. The Black Sun and Tabata discos are buzzing. Brahms Pub is Irish. Anno Zero, Pinky Bar, Kovo and People Pub are all popular, while Osteria Barabba and Kandahar attract a more mature clientèle.

## Childcare

Asilo Neve provides daycare from two years old. Club Med looks after its smallest members from four years.

# Sestriere: At a glance

**Tel** 39 0122 353099
**Email** sestriere@montagnedoc.it
**Website** www.sestriere.it

## GETTING THERE
**Airport** Turin 1½hrs
**Rail** Oulx 22km, buses to resort
**Road** take the Oulx-Est exit off the A32 Turin–Bardonecchia autostrada

## THE SKIING
**Linked/nearby resorts** Bardonecchia, Borgata, Cesana Torinese, Clavière, Grangesises, Montgenèvre, Sansicario, Sauze d'Oulx
**Total of trails/pistes** 120km in Sestriere (39% easy, 42% intermediate, 19% difficult), 400km in the Milky Way
**Lifts in area** 92 in the Milky Way: 3⬡ 35⬡ 54⬡
**Lift opening dates** early December 2004 to late April 2005

## LIFT PASSES
**Area pass** Milky Way €138–155 for 6 days

**Pensioners** Milky Way 60–75yrs €127–143 for 6 days

## TUITION
**Ski & board** Borgata Sestriere (☎ 0122 77497), Olimpionica (☎ 0122 76116), Sestriere Extreme (☎ 0122 76214), Sestriere Ski School (☎ 0122 77060)
**Guiding** Elisusa Heli-skiing (☎ 0122 623162), Guide Alpine Valsusa (☎ 0335 398984) and through ski schools

## CHILDREN
**Lift pass** Milky Way 8–12yrs €127–143 for 6 days
**Ski & board school** as adults
**Kindergarten** (non-ski) Asilo Neve (☎ 0122 755444)

## FOOD AND DRINK
Coffee €2, bottle of house wine €10, small beer €2–3, soft drink €2, dish of the day €15

# La Thuile

ALTITUDE 1,441m (4,728ft)

map: see page 195

❉ **modest resort in the Aosta Valley** ❉ **good snow record**
❉ **uncrowded slopes**

> **Best for:** all standards of skier and
> boarder, powderhounds, those who like
> uncrowded slopes
> **Not recommended for:** people wanting
> resort charm, families with small
> children, night-owls, ski-to-lunchers

The former mining town of La Thuile has
some overriding advantages over other
Italian resorts of comparable size:
inaccessibility, exceptionally favourable
snow record, and a lift link to **La Rosière** in
France. The Petit-St-Bernard Pass between
the two countries is closed in winter, so the
French and other foreigners can reach the
resort only by the Mont Blanc tunnel, while
remote road access in the Aosta Valley
keeps the Italians in Courmayeur. The result
is a ski area that even at its busiest remains
delightfully uncrowded.

## On the snow
### top 2,641m (8,665ft) bottom 1,176m (3,858ft)

The linked area's 150km of undulating blue
and red pistes provides plenty of scope for
the average motorway cruiser, while good
nursery slopes make it a sensible choice for
complete novices. The most testing black
runs are in the Touriasse sector from
Belvédère or Chaz Dura to the Petit-St-
Bernard Pass, between the San Bernardo
and Fourclaz chair-lifts. First-time visitors
to the resort will be surprised by the variety
and quality of La Thuile's off-piste. Better
still is the heli-skiing, which begins at the
top of the Ruitor Glacier (3,486m) on the
Italian side and progresses through the
glacial terrain before ending in the village of
Miroir (1,220m) over the border in France.
The descent to La Thuile itself is a real
adventure, complete with a short rope
section across an ice gully and a long walk
at the bottom.

The resort boasts a terrain park and a
good half-pipe. We have conflicting reports

of La Thuile's ski school: 'we made good
progress due to the small group size' but
'the instructor's English was very basic'.

La Thuile is the exception to the rule
that skiers invariably eat well on Italian
mountain tops. However, Roxi has 'the best
hot chocolate – more like hot mousse with
cream – and new superloos', while Riondet
is 'very friendly and cosy with an open fire'.

## In the resort

The resort has 13 hotels, almost all of
which are family-owned. The four-star
Planibel Hotel (☎ 0165 884541) or the
Planibel apartments (☎ 0165 884541) are
the most convenient and luxurious place to
stay: 'great value, quality and location',
remarked one reporter, and 'fab food' said
another. Three-star Les Granges (☎ 0165
883048) is warmly praised, as is Hotel du
Glacier (☎ 0165 884137). Chalet Alpina
(☎ 0165 884187) and Entrèves (☎ 0165
884134) head the list of two-stars.

Recommended restaurants include Le
Rascard, La Bricole and La Fordze. La Lisse
was said to be 'excellent'. Tables at Maison
de Laurent are available by reservation only.
Planibel's La Cage aux Folles, formerly the
Rendez-vous Bar, has a new owner. Bar La
Buvette near the gondola station attracts the
late-afternoon crowds. Night-owls go to the
Fantasia disco.

Il Grande Albero is the crèche for
children up to three years old, and Miniclub
La Thuile is a free, non-skiing kindergarten
for children from four years of age.

## La Thuile: At a glance

**Tel** 39 0165 884179
**Email** info@lathuile.it
**Website** www.lathuile.it
**Lifts in area** 37: 1⛷ 17⛷ 19⛷
**Lift opening dates** 28 November 2004 to 25 April
2005

# NEW ZEALAND
# Mt Ruapehu

ALTITUDE 1,625m (5,331ft)

❄ **dramatic volcanic scenery** ❄ **New Zealand's largest ski area**
❄ **longest vertical drop in Australasia**
❄ **challenging skiing and snowboarding**

> **Best for:** beginners and intermediates, tough and adventurous skiers, vulcanologists
> **Not recommended for:** fair-weather skiers, people worried about skiing on a live volcano

Mt Ruapehu, in the middle of North Island's Tongariro National Park, is New Zealand's largest and busiest ski area. It comprises **Whakapapa** on the north-western side of the volcano, and **Turoa**, on the south-western slopes.

Mt Ruapehu is famed for its unpredictable and rapidly-changing weather. On a clear day, the skiing can be excellent. During a wet, windy white-out, visibility can be so poor that the resort is barely skiable – particularly the more interesting terrain on the snow-encrusted Pinnacles area.

## On the snow
top 2,322m (7,616ft) bottom 1,605m (5,266ft)

Ruapehu has a mix of deep gullies, which provide natural half-pipes, narrow chutes and wide-open flanks. The Pinnacles on Whakapapa is a steep and challenging area that gives the resort its special cachet and is best skied in fresh or spring snow. Those in search of less challenging off-piste can try the Black Magic area.

The extremely easy beginners' area, Happy Valley, is also New Zealand's largest dedicated novice area. It is tucked away from the main slopes at Whakapapa, and normally opens in mid-June, in advance of the rest of the area. It has its own cafeteria, ski-hire building and free chair-lift access. Whakapapa has six on-mountain cafés.

Turoa shares the same lift pass and has Australasia's biggest vertical drop: 720m.

There is no easy way to get from one resort to the other on snow. Turoa is always the last resort in the country to close in early November, and offers fabulous spring skiing. The area has three on-mountain cafés.

## In the resort
Tourists generally stay in Whakapapa village, 6km down the road from the mountain. The elegant and expensive Grand Château (☎ 07 892 3809) is the focal point, while the cheaper Skotel (☎ 07 892 3719) is nearby. National Park Village is 22km away, but more convenient for access to both ski fields. Here, the Adventure Lodge & Motel (☎ 07 892 2991) offers a hearty breakfast and a spa. Howard's Lodge (☎ 07 892 2827) suits most budgets. The Mountain Heights Lodge and Motel (☎ 07 892 2833) is traditional.

The best restaurant in Whakapapa is the Ruapehu Room at the Grand Château, while Fergusons Café is a cheap alternative. National Park Village has the Basekamp Gourmet Burger Bar and a couple of cafés.

Ohakune is the après-ski capital of the North Island, offering a wide selection of accommodation, restaurants and a vibrant nightlife less than 40 minutes' drive from the skiing. The Powderhorn Chateau (☎ 07 385 8888) offers the most comfortable accommodation, while the Turoa Lodge (☎ 07 385 8274) has a choice of apartments or backpacker dorms.

## Mt Ruapehu: At a glance

**Tel** 64 7 892 3738
**Email** info@mtruapehu.com
**Website** www.mtruapehu.com
**Lifts in resort** Turoa 9: 4🚠 5🎿. Whakapapa 14: 7🚠 7🎿
**Lift opening dates** 18 June 2005 to early November

# NORWAY

# Hemsedal

ALTITUDE 650m (2,133ft)

❄ **fast modern lift system** ❄ **highest lift-served slopes in Scandinavia** ❄ **good off-piste**

**Best for:** families, intermediate cruisers, snowboarders, those seeking lively nightlife

**Not recommended for:** people wanting skiing convenience, families on a tight budget, early-season skiers, wine-lovers (very expensive)

Norway's mountains tend to lack vertical descent and challenge – but Hemsedal, situated between Oslo and Bergen, goes a considerable way towards remedying both shortcomings.

## WHAT'S NEW

Hollvinheisen 8-seater chair-lift replaces old 3-seater
Beginners' terrain park

## On the snow
top 1,497m (4,911ft) bottom 625m (2,050ft)

Hemsedal's craggy terrain provides the highest lift-served slopes in Scandinavia. Fast quad-chairs are gradually replacing the old drag-lifts to create a lift system, serving 42km of groomed runs. The new Hollvinheisen eight-seater serves some genuinely steep slopes, including a gladed run called Hjallerløypa, which merits a double-black classification. Even more extreme is Reidarskaret, a challenging off-piste adventure that starts with a steep, exhilarating couloir. A guide is recommended, and transport is required at the bottom.

Hemsedal Ski School offers instruction in good English. Kruse Toppur and Norske Opplevelser are the specialist ski guiding companies. The resort now has two terrain parks, one with a boardercross course.

The Hemsedal lift pass includes the smaller area of Solheisen, a few miles further along the valley, which has three drag-lifts and its own ski school. Hemsedal offers free ski passes for children under seven, along with free helmet rental.

There is one unexceptional mountain restaurant mid-mountain. At the base areas are two self-services, and a table-service restaurant called Skistua. Hemsedal Mountain Village, below the ski area, offers everything in one place including accommodation, the ski school and the Experten Sportsbar activity centre.

## In the resort
Hemsedal village is almost 3km from the slopes. Plans exist to bridge the gap by building a slope and a lift. The spacious and modern Skarsnuten Hotel is on the edge of the piste. Hemsedal has several small hotels including the popular Norlandia Skogstad, which is the focus for busy nightlife. For accommodation contact Hemsedal Booking (☎ 32 055060). The Garasjen overflows with skiers and snowboarders and the Skogstad Piano Bar and Hemsedal Café are equally popular. The restaurant at the Skarsnuten hotel is warmly recommended. Others include Anden Etage in the Norlandia Skogstad hotel.

The Troll Park area is ideal for children aged three and four. The Trollia crèche provides excellent slope-side babysitting for little ones from three months.

## Hemsedal: At a glance

**Tel** 47 32 055030
**Email** hemsedal@hemsedal.net
**Website** www.hemsedal.com
**Lifts in resort** 17: 6🚡 11🎿
**Lift opening dates** 13 November 2004 to 1 May 2005

# ROMANIA

# Poiana Brasov

**ALTITUDE 1,021m (3,350ft)**

✳ **attractive old town** ✳ **value for money** ✳ **vibrant nightlife**

**Best for:** beginners, young singles, families, those on a budget, anyone wanting to combine skiing with culture
**Not recommended for:** advanced skiers and riders, off-piste enthusiasts, teetotallers

'Simply Surprising' is Romania's advertising slogan – and so it is. The former Eastern Bloc country, whose economy, culture and architectural heritage suffered so appallingly at the hands of the Ceausescu dynasty, has risen from the ashes of the difficult post-Communist era to create a thriving ski tourism industry.

Poiana Brasov is the country's best-known resort, located in the attractive Carpathian Mountains, a three-hour drive north of Bucharest. The ski base is reached by a 15-minute drive up a mountain road from the medieval town of Brasov, which offers good shopping, restaurants and plenty of evening entertainment.

## On the snow
**top 1,775m (5,823ft) bottom 1,021m (3,350ft)**

The 14-km ski area may be small in comparison to the average Alpine resort but it offers ample challenge to beginners and wobbly intermediates wanting to practise their technique in pleasant, budget-priced surroundings. The summit of Mount Postavaru is reached by a choice of two ancient cable-cars and a gondola. They serve a handful of easy green and blue runs, as well as some more demanding terrain that is marked red or black according to its width rather than the gradient.

The main nursery slopes are at the bottom of the mountain, close to the Sport cable-car and the main hotels but, when there is little snow, beginners are taken to a gentle slope at the top of the gondola.

The six ski schools are Ana Hotels, Club Montana Schi, Euro Inter Ski, Impera International, Poiana SA and Valona Tour. The tuition is 'exceptionally good value. There is no shortage of ski school instructors who speak fluent English'.

Two mountain restaurants serve simple food ('beer 80p a pint, a bottle of house wine £2.50 and pizza £1.50').

## In the resort
Accommodation in Poiana exceeded the expectations of all reporters. Two new four-stars, the Piatra Mare (☎ 268 262029) and Hotel Tirol (☎ 268 262460), bring the total to four. The others are the Hotel Sport (☎ 268 407330) ('convenient for the skiing and comparable in quality to anywhere in the Alps') and Capra Neagrā (☎ 268 262122). Hotel Alpin (☎ 268 262111) is the only three-star. Of the six two-stars, Hotel Bradul and Hotel Poiana (☎ 268 407330 for both) are popular with British visitors.

Most resort restaurants are in hotels and serve typical Romanian dishes. Dinner at the Outlaws Hut is lively, starting with musicians playing around a log fire.

All the main hotels have discos or floor shows in high season. Vicky's Bar is recommended, along with Festival 39.

The adult ski schools all offer children's classes.

## Poiana Brasov: At a glance

**Tel** 40 268 550443 / 020-7224 3692 in UK
**Email** romaniatravel@btconnect.com
**Website** www.skiresorts.ro
**Lifts in resort** 10: 3🚡 1🚠 6🚟
**Lift opening dates** 15 December 2004 to 31 March 2005

# SPAIN

# Baqueira–Beret

ALTITUDE 1,500m (4,920ft)

## ❋ Spain's chic ski resort ❋ beautiful Pyrenean scenery ❋ relaxed atmosphere

> **Best for:** all standards of skiers and riders, off-piste enthusiasts, night-owls, adventurous diners, non-skiers
>
> **Not recommended for:** those wanting traditional village atmosphere, early-nighters and early-risers

Baqueira–Beret is Spain's answer to Megève – a smart and fashionable resort where not all the designer ski suits you see parading down the main street make it on to the snow. It lies at the head of the beautiful Val d'Aran, near Viella on the northern side of the Pyrenees; access from France is easy, and the drive from Toulouse airport takes two hours. The resort's proximity to the border means that French is widely understood, if not spoken. In keeping with its chic status, prices are higher than you might otherwise expect in Spain.

Baqueira is purpose-built in an aesthetically adequate style. The village lies beside the road that leads up to the very high Bonaigua Pass, which is often closed in winter. King Juan Carlos has made the resort 'by Royal Appointment' by setting up a home here. Beret is the second base area rather than a separate resort, and consists of little more than a car park and a cafeteria.

## On the snow
### top 2,510m (8,235ft) bottom 1,500m (4,920ft)

A bizarre quad-chair, which you ride without skis (you slot them into the back of the chair in front), takes you up to the mid-mountain station at 1,800m. The skiing takes place on four wide, well-linked mountains with a vertical drop of about 1,000m over varied, often exciting terrain. Most of it is suited to intermediates, but Where Goats Tumble poses a real challenge.

The development of the Bonaigua area has added some considerably more challenging pistes for good skiers and boarders. There is a half-pipe at Beret. Reporters widely praised the standard of piste-grooming and the amount of snowmaking. The resort claims a modest 93km of groomed piste. However, opportunities for easy and safe off-piste excursions abound – and effectively double the amount of terrain. At the Baqueira Ski School few of the instructors speak English.

## In the resort
The hotels are led by the five-star Melia Royal Tanau (☎ 973 64 44 46). Less well-heeled visitors can stay in the ageing but still acceptable four-star Hotel Montarto (☎ 973 63 90 01), the three-star Tuc Blanc (☎ 973 64 43 50) or the Hotel Val de Ruda (☎ 973 64 52 58) ('a pleasant three-star in a good position'). Chalet-hotel Salana (☎ 01457 821200 in UK) is warmly praised. Rafael Hotel La Pleta (☎ 973 64 55 50) is being refurbished.

Borda Lobato in Baqueira specialises in roast suckling pig and whole baby lamb 'carved at the table with garden shears', while Tamarro's has tapas. Other recommended restaurants include Era Mariqueria and Casa Irene in the hamlet of Arties. Cap del Port, a gothic folly, offers a gastronomic lunch. Tiffany's is the busiest nightclub.

The kindergarten accepts children from three months.

## Baqueira–Beret: At a glance

**Tel** 34 973 63 90 10
**Email** baqueira@baqueira.es
**Website** www.baqueira.es
**Lifts in resort** 30: 19🚡 11🎿
**Lift opening dates** end of December 2004 to end of April 2005

# SWEDEN

# Åre

ALTITUDE 384m (1,259ft)

## ❋ attractive village ❋ well-linked lift system ❋ highly rated ski school ❋ good choice of restaurants

**Best for:** all standards of skier and boarder, families

**Not recommended for:** people on a budget, after-lunch skiers in November and December (lack of daylight)

Åre is the most serious destination in Scandinavia for recreational skiers and snowboarders of all standards. It has a vertical drop of 1,040m, and its lifts, spread across four villages (linked on-mountain or by ski bus), serve 93km of piste. The transfer time is about 90 minutes from Östersund airport.

Those who come here find a charming village of pastel-painted houses and hotels on the shore of an enormous frozen lake. The outlying hamlets of Björnen, Duved and Tegefjäll are part of a Trois Vallées-style linked ski area with a sophisticated lift system that has been regularly upgraded in recent years, with a high-speed quad and a six-seater chair-lift taking skiers from the valley to the top station in under four minutes.

If you decide to visit early in the season, remember that at this northerly latitude the skiing day in Åre is short, with the sunset in January at 2.30 pm.

## On the snow
**top 1,420m (4,659ft) bottom 380m (1,312ft)**

The 1,420-m summit of Åreskutan, reached by a tow behind a snowcat, provides the launching point for one of Europe's most unusual and rewarding off-piste descents. The gradient is such that the lake far below fills your horizon for much of the run. The skiing is certainly comparable to a medium-sized Alpine resort, with challenging pistes including the Salombacken and the World Cup runs.

Beginners are well served by the Åre ski school, which enjoys a sound reputation and is staffed entirely by fluent English-speakers. Cross-country is popular here, with 56km of trails, of which 13km are floodlit. Children are well catered for, with a free lift pass.

## In the resort

The four-star Åregarden is 'much the best and most centrally located place to stay', while the Arefjällby Apartments 'vary quite enormously in standard'. The Diplomat Ski Lodge is warmly praised. What used to be the Sunwing Hotel is now, refurbished, the Åre Tott Hotel & Spa. The Backpackers' Inn ('cheerful') is the budget option. All accommodation can be booked at a central office (☎ 647 17700).

Restaurants include Grill Hörnan and Liten Krog, which 'has the best pizzas you could wish for'. Alcohol was said to be 'way cheaper than in Norway, and really not that expensive any more'. The Skier's Bar at the Diplomat Ski Lodge is the 'in' place after skiing. Later on, the Bygget at Arefjällby puts on the best live music.

There is a crèche for three- to five-year-olds, and a ski kindergarten, which takes up to five children per group. Apart from skiing, you can join a husky or snowmobile safari, try ice-climbing, fish for trout through a hole cut into the ice, and even sample 'snowfering' (windsurfing on snow).

### Åre: At a glance

**Tel** 46 647 17700
**Email** booking@areresort.se
**Website** www.skistar.com
**Lifts in resort** 40: 1🚡 2🚠 6🪑 31🎿
**Lift opening dates** early November 2004 to 1 May 2005

# SWITZERLAND

# Andermatt

**ALTITUDE 1,445m (4,740ft)**

❊ **huge off-piste potential** ❊ **excellent ski-touring**
❊ **traditional village centre**

> **Best for:** powderhounds, adventurous skiers and snowboarders, those wanting a quiet resort
>
> **Not recommended for:** intermediate cruising skiers, non-skiers, families with young children, night-owls

Andermatt is a retreat for a dedicated skiing minority. It boasts enormous off-piste opportunities and a reputation for generous dumps of snow, but is in fact one of Switzerland's lesser-known gems. Situated at a major Alpine crossroads on the route to the St Gotthard Pass into Italy, it was once one of the busiest of Swiss resorts. Now the high Urseren Valley, of which Andermatt is the main village, is underpassed by the Gotthard road and rail tunnels, making it a virtual dead-end in winter.

> **WHAT'S NEW**
>
> Monster half-pipe at Gurschen

## On the snow
**top 2,965m (9,725ft) bottom 1,445m (4,740ft)**

Four ski areas run along the sides of the Urseren Valley, between the Furka and Oberalp passes. The two main areas lie at either end of Andermatt, with the Gemsstock reached by two cable-cars ('can get very crowded') and the Gütsch by two chair-lifts. Two smaller and less popular areas are a train journey or drive to the south-west, above the villages of Hospental and Realp. Descents down the shaded face of the Gemsstock, which has 800m of severe vertical and treacherous off-piste skiing in the bowl, should not be tackled without a guide; nor should some of the long off-piste alternatives in other directions from the top-station. Beginners tend to ski

in the Nätschen area. Andermatt links with the villages of Disentis and Sedrun.

Mountain restaurants include Bergrestaurant Gurschen ('wholesome fare at reasonable prices'). Andermatt has a Swiss Snowsports School (SSS) for adults and children from four and a half years old. Off-piste guiding is with Alpine Sport-school, Bergschool Uri and Montanara.

## In the resort
Andermatt village has cobbled streets and a traditional character. However, it is one of Switzerland's major centres for the training of Alpine troops, and severe barrack buildings are a feature of the architecture. The heart of the old village receives little sun as it is hemmed in by mountains. Ski buses link Andermatt with the ski areas of Gemsstock and Winterhorn.

Accommodation is in a mixture of hotels and appealing old chalets. The five three-stars are Drei Könige & Post (☎ 41 887 0001), Monopol-Metropol (☎ 41 887 1575), Activ Kronen (☎ 41 887 0088), Hotel Aurora (☎ 41 887 1661) and Hotel Sonne (☎ 41 887 1226). Hotel Schweizerhof (☎ 41 887 1189) is 'a bit old but quite central'. Pension Guesthouse Sternen (☎ 41 887 1130) is reported to have a cosy atmosphere.

The limited après-ski includes Barokko Music Bar, Dancing Gotthard and Bar La Curva. There is no childcare available in the resort.

> ## Andermatt: At a glance
>
> **Tel** 41 41 887 1454
> **Email** info@andermatt.ch
> **Website** www.andermatt.ch
> **Lifts in area** 35 in Gotthard–Oberalp: 1🚠 3🚡 10🚏 21🎿
> **Lift opening dates** 1 November 2004 to 1 May 2005

# Crans-Montana

ALTITUDE 1,500m (4,920ft)

## ❊ easy airport access ❊ superb scenery ❊ lack of queues ❊ high standard of hotels

> **Best for:** intermediates, snowboarders, children, non-skiers
>
> **Not recommended for:** people wanting a quiet Alpine village, those who like easy mountain access, advanced skiers

In the 1890s the town of Crans-Montana was a centre for tuberculosis clinics, and the emphasis on health remains today. The resort of Crans-Montana has a host of hotels that contain wellness centres, enabling their elite, older patrons to enjoy a combination of skiing, health treatments and shopping at the resort's chic boutiques. This well-heeled, health-seeking clientèle mixes incongruously with a huge snowboarding crowd, which comes here for some of the best facilities in the Alps.

Crans-Montana sits on a sunny plateau, dotted with larches and lakes, and the view across the Rhône Valley is the most spectacular of all Alpine panoramas. However, it is sometimes hard to believe that this town owes its existence to the once-pure mountain air. The urban conglomeration sprawls untidily for more than 2km along a busy main road.

A funicular takes only 12 minutes to carry snow-users up to Crans-Montana from the valley town of Sierre. Swiss runs a weekly direct service on winter Saturdays between Heathrow and Sion, which is only 30 minutes from the resort.

## On-piste
top 3,000m (9,840ft) bottom 1,500m (4,920ft)

From Les Violettes a 30-person Funitel gondola gives direct access to the top of the ski area at Plaine-Morte. Alternative mountain access is by two gondolas from the Crans end of town, a gondola from the Montana district, and another from the neighbouring resort of Aminona.

Crans-Montana is an intermediate's resort with good beginner terrain. 'Long, open cruising runs in the sunshine leading down into the tree-line – I could wish for nothing better,' said one reporter. Starting at the top, beginners have three short but easy runs on the Plaine-Morte Glacier, where good snow is guaranteed. The nursery slopes down by the golf course in Crans are even easier, but susceptible to sun.

The largest conflux of intermediate pistes is in the Violettes sector, with winding trails through the woods. The Toula chair- and drag-lifts lead to steeper reds. Most exciting are the Nationale World Cup piste and the Chetseron. The only officially graded black run in the entire resort is a bumpy fall-line pitch on the ridge under the Toula chair-lift ('no more than a red really').

Crans-Montana is a very active snowboarding centre with first-rate tuition. The 25,000-square-metre terrain park is in Aminona and there is a half-pipe at Cry d'Err. Its 50km of Langlauf tracks include a 10-km loipe, set unusually at an altitude of 3,000m on the Plaine-Morte Glacier.

## Off-piste
With a guide, a number of itineraries are possible from the Plaine-Morte Glacier. These include a descent to the lake at Zeuzier, where by walking though tunnels and skiing a summer roadway you reach the ski lifts of the neighbouring resort of Anzère.

## Tuition and guiding
There are two branches of the Swiss Snowsports School (ESS) in Crans-Montana, while Ski & Sky organises group and private lessons. Surf Evasion and the Swiss Snowboard School, both affiliated with the Crans and Montana branches of the ESS, and Stoked are the specialist snowboard schools.

## Mountain restaurants
The resort has 13 mountain eateries, including the characterful Café de la Cure alongside the blue run down to Aminona, but the best inns are Merbé ('great food but

a little expensive') and Plumachit ('good atmosphere and food at an OK price'). The Cabane des Violettes is an authentic touring hut offering simple meals.

## Accommodation

Crans-Montana sports an impressive number of five-star hotels. Hostellerie Pas de l'Ours (☎ 27 485 9334), together with the Hotel Royal (☎ 27 481 3931) and Grand Hotel du Golf (☎ 27 481 4242), all in the district of Crans, head the luxury list, along with the five-star Crans-Ambassador (☎ 27 481 4811) in the Montana district.

The three-star Mont-Blanc (☎ 27 481 3143), on a hill above Crans, has 'the biggest terrace and best views'. In Montana, Hotel St George (☎ 27 481 2414) is 'conveniently placed with good food and service. However, the rooms are shamefully poky for a four-star'. Hotel de la Prairie (☎ 27 481 4421) in Montana is said to be 'the best three-star in town'.

## Eating in and out

At the Crans end of town, the most celebrated non-hotel gourmet dining is at the Nouvelle Rôtisserie and the Bergerie du Cervin, which specialises in Valais-style raclette and fondue. The Hostellerie Pas de l'Ours has splendid cuisine in an attractive dining-room. In the Montana sector, the modestly priced Auberge de la Diligence is renowned for its Middle Eastern cuisine, and Le Gréni is 'expensive but excellent – Roger Moore/aka James Bond's third home'.

## Après-ski

The most popular bars are Amadeus ('cheap beer and wine and good music') and the Constellation and the Cuban Punch Bar. The Indiana Café and New Pub both attract a young crowd. Teenagers flock to Montana's Number Two's for late drinking. The Absolut Disco is the most popular late-night haunt.

## Childcare

Fleurs des Champs kindergarten, next to Hotel Eldorado in Montana, cares for infants from three months ('excellent facilities although not all the staff speak English'). Garderie Zig-Zag, also in Montana, takes children between two and six years of age. We have good reports about ESS Montana's Jardin des Neiges up on the Grand Signal mid-station. ESS Crans also has a kindergarten next to the tubing slope.

# Crans Montana: At a glance

**Tel** 41 27 485 0404
**Email** information@crans-montana.ch
**Website** www.crans-montana.ch

### GETTING THERE
**Airports** Sion 30 mins, Geneva 1½hrs
**Rail** Sierre 15km, bus to resort
**Road** motorway E62 from Geneva to Sierre, short climb to resort

### THE SKIING
**Linked/nearby resorts** Aminona, Anzère, Bluche
**Total of trails/pistes** 140km (38% easy, 50% intermediate, 12% difficult)
**Lifts in area** 27: 1🚡 6🚠 6🚟 14🎿
**Lift opening dates** 27 November 2004 to 10 April 2005. Summer skiing on Plaine-Morte Glacier

### LIFT PASSES
**Area pass** SF268 for 6 days
**Pensioners** women 63yrs and over, men 65yrs and over, SF228 for 6 days

### TUITION
**Ski & board** ESS Crans (☎ 27 485 9370), ESS Montana (☎ 27 481 1480), Ski & Sky (☎ 27 485 4250), Stoked (☎ 27 480 2421), Surf Evasion (ESS Montana), Swiss Snowboard School (ESS Crans)
**Guiding** Air Glacier (☎ 27 329 1415), ESS Crans, ESS Montana, Helicopter Services (☎ 27 327 3060)

### CHILDREN
**Lift pass** 6–15yrs SF161, 16–19yrs SF228, both for 6 days
**Ski & board school** as adults
**Kindergarten** (ski/non-ski) ESS Crans, Fleurs des Champs (☎ 27 481 2367), Garderie Zig-Zag (☎ 27 481 2205), Jardin des Neiges (☎ 27 481 1480)

### FOOD AND DRINK
Coffee SF3.50–4, bottle of house wine SF20, small beer SF5, soft drink SF4, dish of the day SF19–20

# Davos

ALTITUDE 1,560m (5,117ft)                    map: see pages 196–197

## ✳ large linked ski area ✳ wide choice of mountain restaurants ✳ well-groomed slopes

**Best for:** intermediate cruisers, experienced skiers, snowboarders, off-piste enthusiasts, ski-tourers

**Not recommended for:** those looking for quiet village atmosphere, people wanting skiing convenience

Davos, at the foot of the Parsenn ski area, is the European birthplace of downhill skiing. The first pair of skis arrived here from Norway in the early 1880s and quickly became a success with both the locals and the large foreign community who came to visit the well-established sanatorium that had made this Switzerland's leading health resort.

In 1894 Arthur Conan Doyle of Sherlock Holmes fame wrote about his experiences in crossing the Maienfeld Furka Pass to **Arosa** and created worldwide publicity for this new winter sport. He captured the imagination of a generation of British, and what followed was nothing short of a snow rush. However, the first funicular railway did not open until 1931 and what was arguably the world's first drag-lift was constructed here in 1934.

Today Davos has grown into a modest but not particularly appealing town that is as well known for its international conference facilities (it is home to the annual meeting of the World Economic Forum) as for its skiing. The town, which claims to be the highest in Europe, straggles inconveniently for 6km from the railway station of Davos Dorf to Davos Platz. It consists largely of giant hotels, built in practical style, interspersed with expensive boutiques and a good range of other shops. Buses run regularly in a loop around the one-way system. Nevertheless, where to stay deserves serious consideration.

Davos Dorf is quiet and stately with handsome old hotels, while Davos Platz is the bustling commercial heart. Dorf gives the most direct access to the main ski area, but Platz has the lion's share of the nightlife. Enthusiasts will enjoy the Wintersport Museum at Platz, which traces the development of equipment and clothing through the years.

## On-piste
### top 2,844m (9,328ft) bottom 813m (2,667ft)

Much has changed since the Davos English Ski Club built its first mountain refuge in 1906, only to have it destroyed almost immediately in a fatal avalanche. Where there were once no lifts at all, there are now 50 spread over the Parsenn and a clutch of separate ski areas. The Parsenn, which Davos shares with **Klosters**, is the largest.

This is accessed most directly by the Parsennbahn funicular from Davos Dorf, which carries 200 passengers to the mid-station in just four-and-a-half minutes. From here the second stage of the old funicular or a six-person chair-lift takes you on up to the Weissfluhjoch, 180m below the 2,844-m Weissfluhgipfel, the highest point on the piste map.

The Weissfluhjoch is the starting point for a web of wide, sweeping runs that flatter your skiing technique. In mid-season snow conditions it is possible to ski 12km through a full 2,000m vertical drop down to Küblis and Serneus. Six of the lift companies that manage the skiing in the region have amalgamated, with the result that the slopes are well looked after, and access is enhanced by a hands-free electronic lift pass system. The Rega lift pass still does not cover the Schatzalp/Strela area.

This heartland of beautifully groomed pistes is ideally suited to intermediates. Nearly all the marked runs are blue or red, most are invitingly wide, and several are more than 10km long. The ones from the Weissfluhgipfel to the valley villages of Küblis, Saas and Serneus start high above the tree-line, then track down through the woods to the railway line, providing a degree of excitement that is definitely not attainable in more crowded places.

The Parsenn is supplemented by the five further ski areas, four of them on the other side of the Davos Valley and the fifth beyond Klosters. In the Davos catchment area, the peaks are Pischa, Jakobshorn and Rinerhorn. They are accessed by bus from Dorf, directly from Platz, or by bus or train from Glaris, which is the next stop on the line down to Chur ('buses and trains on time and comfortable'). All the ski areas offer plenty of easy terrain, so there is no excuse for not ranging far and wide.

Like many large, first-generation resorts, Davos is not the place to learn to ski from scratch. But if you must, the wide Bolgen nursery slope at the bottom of the Jakobshorn, a short walk from Platz, is the best starting point. In Dorf the equivalent is Bünda, which has a longer but steeper pitch. Since the mountains in the area become steeper near the bottom, the black runs are mostly confined to the lower sections, which means that they can be icy in all but the most favourable snow conditions. The advantage is that they are generally among trees, and therefore the visibility is always good. Gruelling bump runs on the Standard Ersatz and the Unterer Standard immediately above Davos Dorf offer considerable challenge. The most highly recommended black run starts on the Meierhofer Tälli at the top of the Parsenn and goes down to the hamlet of Wolfgang.

Throwing tradition out of the window, the area has embraced snowboarding with enthusiasm and admirable commercial acumen. The Jakobshorn area is ideal for riders, with lots of trees, a boardercross circuit, two half-pipes and night-riding.

Davos offers 75km of prepared cross-country trails on the valley floor and in the Sertigtal and Dischmatal areas. Evening expeditions can be made on the 2.5-km floodlit section, and dogs are allowed on some of the trails. The highlights of the cross-country year are the Davos Nordic World Cup and the 20-km Volks Langlauf.

## Off-piste

Excursions include skiing to Arosa in the tracks of Conan Doyle. This is an enjoyable but serious business, with a three- to four-hour climb to the Maienfeld Furka Pass above Frauenkirch, followed by a gentle descent through woods to the bottom of the valley and then a 40-minute plod up

through the town to the railway station for the three-hour return to Davos.

## Tuition and guiding

The Swiss Snowsports School (SSS) offers ski and snowboard classes for adults and teenagers. Half-day safety classes for off-piste beginners (with a maximum of six per group) are available, covering the use of ABS-rucksacks and avalanche transceivers. Daily or weekly guided ski-tours can be arranged between January and Easter. Top Secret Snowboarding School in Davos Platz is highly recommended for first-timers.

## Mountain restaurants

Intelligent use of the piste map makes it possible to locate the many small establishments in the woods on the way down to the outlying villages. The restaurant at the Teufi on the off-piste descent from the Jakobshorn is recommended, as is the Hotel Kulm in Wolfgang ('an excellent choice'). The Gallo Rosso at the Weissfluhjoch and Bruhin's Weissfluhgipfel are both praised.

## Accommodation

Davos has two five-star hotels: the Steigenberger Belvédère (☎ 81 415 6000), up on the hillside above Platz, and the Flüela (☎ 81 410 1717), opposite the railway station in Dorf. Both offer old-fashioned comfort in the stolid Swiss manner, a style emulated by many of their competitors in the four- and three-star brackets. The four-star Victoria Turmhotel (☎ 81 417 5300) at Dorf is warmly recommended: 'excellent health and fitness centre, and splendid food'. In Platz, the Waldhotel Bellevue (☎ 81 415 3747) is rich in tradition.

The Sunstar Park (☎ 81 413 1414) receives rave reports: 'quality, spacious hotel with high proportion of English guests,' said one reporter, and 'recommended highly for helpfulness and attention to the little details that make you feel pampered after a hard day on the slopes,' commented another. A third noted: 'a casual glance at the guest book revealed people who have been back eight times – and not without good reason. The six-course gala dinner on Sunday night was one of the best meals we have ever enjoyed on a skiing holiday'.

Kinderhotel Muchetta (☎ 81 404 14 24) is a specialist family hotel. The restaurant offers a children's buffet, the crèche cares for little ones from newborn, and the ski kindergarten is for beginners from four years old.

## Eating in and out

In Davos, as elsewhere in Switzerland, those who stray outside half-board deals must pay highly for the privilege. Money is well spent in Hubli's Landhaus, the Magic Mountain restaurant in the Waldhotel Bellevue, and the Stübli in the Flüela hotel. Try the Zauberberg restaurant in the Hotel Europe or the Goldener Drachen in the Hotel Bahnhof Terminus for Far Eastern cuisine. Local dining, at correspondingly lower prices, can be found in the outlying villages of Frauenkirch, Wolfgang and Laret.

## Après-ski

As one reporter put it: 'we were not unduly perturbed by the city feel of Davos and, whilst it is not chocolate-box scenery, it does have all the facilities of a city and therefore offers considerable non-skiing activities'. In the pre-dinner hours, major league ice-hockey matches take place in the handsome Sports Centre; other activities include skating on the largest natural ice-rink in Europe.

In the late afternoons, the high-lifers at Davos congregate in the Café Schneider in Platz and the Café Weber in Dorf, both specialists in temptation cakes. The most favoured bar is the rustic Chämi, which is full to bursting until closing time with revellers of all ages.

The area's pulsating nightlife can be found in Davos Platz, and especially in the Ex-Bar ('shoulder-to-shoulder drinking to rock and pop background from Status Quo to *When The Saints Go Marching In*'). The laser show at the Cabanna Club disco in Hotel Europe attracts a young crowd ('the best disco in town'), while the Carigiet bar in Hotel Steigenberger Belvédère and the Piano Bar Tonic in the Hotel Europe cater for an older clientèle. The Cava Grischa has techno and disco. Casino Davos houses 70 slot machines, and the Scala restaurant in the same building stays open until 1.30am. Riders hang out in the Bolgenschanze bar and disco.

## Childcare

The Swiss Snowsports School (SSS) offers children's classes for three-year-olds and upwards on Bünda or Bolgen ('great with all ages'), with supervised lunch and lifts included in the price, and a Bobo Wonderland playground, complete with cartoon characters, in each area. Pischa Kinderland cares for children from three years and also provides ski lessons. New Trend accepts children from four years.

# Davos: At a glance

**Tel** 41 81 415 2121
**Email** info@davos.ch
**Website** www.davos.ch

### GETTING THERE
**Airport** Zurich 2½hrs
**Rail** Davos Dorf and Davos Platz stations in resort
**Road** motorway Zurich–Landquart, further 79 km

### THE SKIING
**Linked/nearby resorts** Arosa, Gargellen, Glaris, Klosters, Küblis, Saas, Serneus, St Moritz, Wolfgang
**Total of trails/pistes** 370km in Davos/Klosters area (30% easy, 40% intermediate, 30% difficult)
**Lifts in area** 50: 2🚡 12🚠 9🚡 27🎿
**Lift opening dates** Parsenn ski area: 27 November 2004 to 17 April 2005

### LIFT PASSES
**Area pass** Rega Pass (covers all Davos and Klosters lifts, except Schatzalp/Strela) SF279 for 6 days

**Pensioners** Rega Pass 10% reduction for women 63yrs and over, and men 65yrs and over

### TUITION
**Ski & board** New Trend (☎ 81 413 2040), SSS (☎ 81 416 2454), Top Secret (☎ 81 413 7374)
**Guiding** through ski schools

### CHILDREN
**Lift pass** Rega Pass 6–12yrs SF103, 13–17yrs SF187, both for 6 days
**Ski & board school** as adults
**Kindergarten** (ski/non-ski) Bobo Wonderland (SSS), New Trend, Pischa Kinderland (☎ 81 417 6767)

### FOOD AND DRINK
Coffee SF4.50, bottle of house wine SF20–30, small beer SF5, soft drink SF5, dish of the day SF20–25

# Engelberg

ALTITUDE 1,020m (3,346ft)

## ❊ beautiful scenery ❊ reliable snow cover ❊ demanding off-piste ❊ short airport transfer

**Best for:** all standards of skier and snowboarder, night-owls, early- and late-season skiers, weekend skiers

**Not recommended for:** those wanting skiing convenience, luxury accommodation seekers

Engelberg's easy accessibility from Lucerne and Zurich marked its original spot as a spa on the fashionable Victorian European tour. Both before and after World War II it epitomised the high living associated with a Swiss ski resort. Engelberg faded from view during the ski boom years of the 1970s, but now the development of a modern lift system, combined with nostalgia for small, traditional resorts, has redefined its position on the world ski map. But it is better known in India than in Britain, because of its regular use in summer as a location for Bollywood films.

## On the snow
### top 3,028m (9,934ft) bottom 1,020m (3,346ft)

Access to the main Titlis ski area, with its craggy cliffs reminiscent of the Dolomites, is by modern gondola or a parallel, high-season combination of funicular and cable-car. It takes a full 40 minutes to reach Klein Titlis, the last section in the Rotair revolving cable-car. The high altitude guarantees a long season and the area is suited to all levels including experts.

The sunny pastures of Brunni, on the other side of the town, form an ideal beginner and intermediate ski area. There is a terrain park at Engstlen–Jochpass, and the resort has a 20-km cross-country course.

These high mountains lend themselves to ski-touring, but the Titlis Glacier is heavily crevassed and a local guide is essential. Dramatic and demanding off-piste runs include the Laub, a powder bowl with an enormous 1,120m vertical drop.

The Swiss Snowsports School (SSS) has the monopoly here, but it also has a reputation for excellence.

The Titlis-Stübli provides haute cuisine on the summit of Klein Titlis. Food is traditional Swiss, with an emphasis on fish. The Ritz at Gerschnialp offers simple mountain fare at reasonable prices. Untertrübsee has more atmosphere. The simple Brunnihütte has the best Käseschnitte and a good sun terrace.

## In the resort

The two four-stars are Hotel Ramada-Treff Regina (☎ 41 639 5858), which has the least atmosphere but provides good rooms and the best location, and Hotel Waldegg (☎ 41 637 1822), which is a long, steep walk above the town. The other hotels are all three-stars and include the comfortable Hotel Best Western Terrace (☎ 41 639 6666), reached by funicular. Hotel Europe (☎ 41 639 7575) is a magnificent Belle Epoque building in need of modernisation, and the family-run Hotel Spannort (☎ 41 637 2626) is a friendly place.

Axels is a new French restaurant with Swiss overtones that offers the best fine dining in the resort. The Spannort serves traditional Swiss food, while the Alpenclub has an eclectic menu that ranges from fondue and pizza to fusion.

The Spindle nightclub has been eclipsed in recent years by the Yukatan, but you can dance at both until dawn. Hotel Eden's Bistro on Dorfstrasse is sophisticated.

The ski school's Snowli Village takes children from three years for lessons and childcare with lunch included. There is no non-ski kindergarten, but babysitters can be booked through the tourist office.

## Engelberg: At a glance

**Tel** 41 41 639 7777
**Email** welcome@engelberg.ch
**Website** www.engelberg.ch
**Lifts in resort** 25: 1 🚠 9 🚡 8 🚟 7 🎿
**Lift opening dates** late November 2004 to late April 2005. Summer skiing on Titlis Glacier

# Flims and the Alpenarena

ALTITUDE 1,100m (3,609ft)

## ❄ large ski area ❄ choice of interesting hotels ❄ few British skiers

> **Best for:** beginners to intermediates, families, snowboarders, cross-country skiers
>
> **Not recommended for:** non-skiers, night-owls, those wanting skiing convenience (Flims Waldhaus)

The Alpenarena is the joint marketing name of Flims, **Laax** and Falera. It comprises 220km of linked piste in the heart of the Graubunden on the route of the famous Glacier Express train. The area is one of the largest and most popular in Switzerland, but still largely unknown to British skiers.

Flims is divided into the two hamlets of Flims Dorf, which is the livelier and more convenient place to stay, and Flims Waldhaus, which houses the best accommodation but is not within easy walking distance of the lifts. However, the larger hotels run a courtesy minibus service to the base-station. A free shuttle bus also connects Flims, Laax and Falera.

## On-piste
top 3,018m (9,902ft) bottom 1,100m (3,609ft)

The ski area spans the slopes beneath the peaks of the Vorab, La Siala and Cassons, divided in places by bands of rock and steep wooded gullies. Mountain access from Flims Dorf is by gondola or quad-chair. From the base-station of Laax–Murschetg, a cable-car links directly with the main mid-mountain station of Crap Sogn Gion, which can also be reached by chair-lift from Falera. Crap Sogn Gion is the gateway to a network of lifts leading up to the Vorab Glacier, at 3,018m. This is the starting point for the 4-km Weisse Schuss and the annual prom downhill that ends in Flims Dorf.

Novices make their first turns on nursery slopes at Flims Waldhaus or at each of the base-stations. Alpenarena is ideal for gaining confidence, with huge tracts of easy skiing terrain on La Siala and the Vorab.

Intermediates have the run of the whole area, with the exception of the unpisted top section of Cassons. Reporters particularly rate the red Masegn West run, served by the Alp Ruschein chair on the edge of the ski area below Crap Masegn.

The longest black run is the FIS downhill course from Crap Sogn Gion down to Laax–Murschetg, but it owes its colouring more to its racecourse status than to its degree of difficulty. More challenging descents are Sattel from Vorab and the unpisted Platt'Alva itinerary from Nagens. There are cross-country trails along the valley floor from Flims, and around the neighbouring villages of Trin and Sagogn, as well as in the high Bargis Valley above Flims.

In recent years Laax has become a popular snowboarding base. The Crap Sogn Gion and the Vorab Glacier areas each boast two well-maintained half-pipes and a terrain park.

## Off-piste
The off-piste potential is surprisingly high, with tree-level runs above Laax.

## Tuition and guiding
Snowboard Fahrschule and the Swiss Snowsports School (SSS) offer lessons in Flims, Laax and Falera. Ten other schools offer a wide variety of courses including off-piste and ski mountaineering.

## Mountain restaurants
Startgels, Naraus, Segnes and Cassons mountain eateries are praised by reporters. Capalari at Crap Sogn Gion serves 'new-wave Swiss fare at reasonable prices'. Two gourmet restaurants – the Elephant at Crap Masegn and the Tegia Larnags – are recommended.

## Accommodation
The five-star Park Hotels Waldhaus (☎ 81 928 4848) heads the list of accommodation at Flims Waldhaus. It comprises five buildings with opulent rooms connected by underground passages and covered walkways. Four-star Hotel Sunstar-Surselva (☎ 81 928 1800), also in Waldhaus, is said to be 'excellent and central', with a swimming-pool and health centre. In Flims Dorf, the four-star Hotel Adula (☎ 81 928 2828) is praised for

its children's facilities and also has a wellness centre. Four-star Alpenhotel Flims (☎ 81 927 9800) is praised along with the three-star Albana Sporthotel (☎ 81 927 2333).

The old village of Laax ('not a compact resort, and lacks character') is 5km to the west of Flims, with a modern satellite base-station at Laax–Murschetg and low-cost, on-mountain accommodation called Crap Sogn Gion Mountain Hostel (☎ 81 927 7373). Top choices in Laax are the three-star Posta Veglia (☎ 81 921 4466) and DesignHotel Riders Palace (☎ 81 927 9700). The latter describes itself as 'the first high-tech hotel in the Alps', and one reporter described it as 'a bizarre mixture of designer hotel and backpacker hostel'.

The farming hamlet of Falera offers a rustic alternative. The well-run three-star Hotel La Siala (☎ 81 927 2222) is warmly recommended.

## Eating in and out

Recommended restaurants include La Clav, in Hotel Adula, and Claveau Vegl in Flims Dorf for regional specialities. Pomodoro and Pizzeria Porta Sut in Flims Dorf were also favourites with reporters. In Laax, Romana specialises in Balkan cuisine and Riva has 'great cheesy cuisine'. Cas Seeli in Falera is recommended.

## Après-ski

The action focuses on the Iglu Music Bar and Club Angel, both in Flims Dorf. Alternatives are the quieter Livingroom in Dorf and Bellavista Bistro Bar in Waldhaus. In Laax, the options include the Crap Bar and the Casa Veglia at the base-station and Red Cat in the DesignHotel Riders Palace.

## Childcare

The SSS cares for children from two years old with lessons from four years, and we have positive reports. Park Hotels Waldhaus and Hotel Adula have crèches. Annina Hägler cares for non-skiers in Flims Dorf.

# Flims and the Alpenarena: At a glance

**Tel** 41 81 920 9200
**Email** tourismus@alpenarena.ch
**Website** www.alpenarena.ch

## GETTING THERE
**Airport** Zurich 2hrs
**Rail** Zurich via Chur, 3hrs
**Road** motorway Zurich–Chur, 18km by mountain road

## THE SKIING
**Linked/nearby resorts** Lenzerheide
**Total of trails/pistes** 220km (48% easy, 37% intermediate, 15% difficult)
**Lifts in area** 29: 11🚠 7🚡 11🎿
**Lift opening dates** 23 October 2004 to 17 April 2005

## LIFT PASSES
**Area pass** SF250–301 for 6 days
**Pensioners** women 63yrs and over, and men 65yrs and over, SF200–240 for 6 days

## TUITION
**Ski & board** Falera: SSS (☎ 81 921 3030). Flims Dorf: Alpine Action Unlimited (☎ 81 936 7474),

EuroBoard (☎ 81 925 2755), EuroSki (☎ 79 683 5642), Rock and Snow (☎ 78 679 7153), Roland Tuchschmid (☎ 79 742 6677), SSS (☎ 81 927 7181), Touchdown (☎ 78 830 5960), Yetis (☎ 79 635 3767). Flims Waldhaus: Mountain Fantasy (☎ 81 936 7077), Snowboard Fahrschule (☎ 81 927 7155), SSS (☎ 81 927 7171), Swissraft (☎ 81 911 5250). Laax: Inspiraziun Grischun (☎ 76 391 6894). Laax–Murschetg: SSS (☎ 81 927 7171)
**Guiding** through ski schools

## CHILDREN
**Lift pass** 6–12yrs SF85, 13–17yrs SF150.50, both for 6 days
**Ski & board school** as adults
**Kindergarten** Flims Dorf: (ski) SSS (☎ 81 927 7171), (non-ski) Annina Hägler (☎ 79 791 5221), Hotel Adula (☎ 81 928 2828). Flims Waldhaus: (ski) SSS, (non-ski) Park Hotels Waldhaus (☎ 81 928 4848)

## FOOD AND DRINK
Coffee SF3.80–4.40, bottle of house wine SF20–30, small beer SF5, soft drink SF4.20–4.50, dish of the day SF18–25

# Grindelwald

ALTITUDE 1,034m (3,393ft)                                                    map: see page 198

## ❋ old and cosmopolitan resort ❋ busy town with smart hotels
## ❋ large ski area ❋ beautiful scenery

**Best for:** intermediates, powderhounds,
ski-tourers, non-skiers

**Not recommended for:** families with
young ski-age children, those who want
doorstep skiing, early/late-season skiers

Grindelwald is the oldest of the three
principal ski villages in the Jungfrau region
of the Bernese Oberland – the other two
being **Wengen** and **Mürren**. This large and
busy, year-round resort spreads along the
valley floor between the soaring peaks of
the Wetterhorn and the Eiger on the one
side, and the gentler wooded slopes of the
First ski area on the other. There are few
more cosmopolitan resorts to be found in
the world, with myriad nationalities listed
among the guests here – not least the
Japanese, who arrive in large numbers to
visit the Jungfraujoch, which at 3,454m has
the highest railway station in Europe.

Railways have played an essential role in
the history of Grindelwald, Wengen and
Mürren. Trains provided the first means of
uphill transport when the first mountain
railways were built here in the 1880s, and
they are still pivotal to the lift system. The
three resorts share a lift pass that covers a
network of not only trains but also
gondolas, chairs and drag-lifts. While the
trains run to an exact and reliable Swiss
timetable, reporters complained that they
are a slow means of getting up the
mountain ('we seemed to waste half the day
waiting around and lost a lot of skiing
time').

## In-piste
top 2,501m (8,206ft) bottom 1,034m (3,393ft)

Grindelwald shares the Kleine Scheidegg
ski area, beneath the imposing north face of
the Eiger, with neighbouring Wengen. A
mountain railway takes you up to Brandegg,
Alpiglen and Kleine Scheidegg itself. From
here, the train continues up to the
Eigergletscher, the high point of the joint
ski area. Non-skiers can continue the
journey through a remarkable tunnel in the
Eiger and on up to the Jungfraujoch. A
network of chair-lifts and drag-lifts serves
mainly blue and red runs either back down
to Grindelwald or down to Wengen.

Alternative mountain access is provided by
a gondola from the satellite hamlet of Grund
to the 2,230-m Männlichen, which separates
the Grindelwald and Wengen valleys. From
here you can work your way through the lift
system up to Kleine Scheidegg.

Grindelwald has its own separate ski
area, First, reached by a gondola on the far
side of the village. From the top, three drag-
lifts and a couple of chair-lifts give access to
further blue and red runs. The nursery
slopes are situated right by the village, and
others are served by the Hohwald and
Bargelegg lifts, although beginners will
want to return to base via the First gondola.

First has a challenging black piste under
the gondola, but advanced snow-users will
be mainly interested in the top part of the
Kleine Scheidegg area. The train up to
Eigergletscher leads to the black runs of
Blackrock and Oh God.

Grindelwald has a large terrain park at
Oberjoch, with a boardercross course.

## Off-piste
The resort has superb powder possibilities,
with runs such as the White Hare beneath
the north face of the Eiger. Local mountain
guides are essential, and the
Bergsteigerzentrum is one of the most
famous guiding establishments in the world.

## Tuition and guiding
The Swiss Snowsports School (SSS) gives
mornings-only group lessons from Sunday to
Friday. Most, but by no means all, instructors
speak more than adequate English.

## Mountain restaurants
The Brandegg restaurant is famed for its
apple fritters ('remember to ask for the
sauce'). The Jägerstübli is a farmhouse

below Männlichen, with a 'cosy ambience', while the Aspen above Grund 'is sunny and welcoming'. The restaurant at Bort is 'pleasant and reasonably priced, but the food is not exceptional'. Hotel Wetterhorn on the way down to Grindelwald offers a 'convivial atmosphere and delicious food'.

## Accommodation

The five-star Grand Hotel Regina (☎ 33 854 8601) is partly decorated with eighteenth-century antiques and is famous for the ice sculpture in its grounds. A host of recommended four-star hotels include Hotel Spinne (☎ 33 854 8888) and Hotel Sunstar (☎ 33 854 7777). Four-star Hotel Kreuz & Post (☎ 33 854 5492) serves 'the best food we have ever experienced in a package-deal hotel'.

Of the three-stars, Hotel Alpenhof (☎ 33 853 5270) and Hotel Derby (☎ 33 854 5461) are also praised, as is Hotel Hirschen (☎ 33 854 8484). Three-star Hotel Bodmi (☎ 33 853 1220) on the nursery slopes is convenient for families.

## Eating in and out

The Derby-Bahnhof restaurant is one of the best places to dine. Reporters also speak warmly of the Schmitte in Hotel Schweizerhof. Kreuz & Post's Challi-Stübli is 'great for a special night out', as is the Adlerstube in the Hotel Sunstar. Erlebnisrestaurant Barry's serves innovative cuisine in a reconstructed mountain hut. Dinner at Restaurant Français is eaten to a background of live piano music.

## Après-ski

The Espresso bar draws a young crowd straight after skiing, while the Gepsi attracts a slightly older clientèle. Later on the Chälli bar in the Kreuz & Post, the Cava in the Derby and Herby's in Grand Hotel Regina are the most popular. The Plaza Club and the Mescalero rock on into the small hours.

## Childcare

The decision by the SSS to run group lessons only in the mornings seriously detracts from the Jungfrau's erstwhile reputation as an ideal area for families with young children. Kinderclub Bodmi caters for pre-ski children from three years in its play area by the nursery slopes. Kinderhort Sunshine takes children from one month old at Männlichen, while Kinderhort Murmeli at First accepts children from six months.

# Grindelwald: At a glance

**Tel** 41 33 854 1212
**Email** touristcenter@grindelwald.ch
**Website** www.grindelwald.ch

### GETTING THERE
**Airports** Zurich 2hrs, Geneva 3hrs
**Rail** station in resort
**Road** motorway Bern–Interlaken, short climb to Grindelwald

### THE SKIING
**Linked/nearby resorts** Lauterbrunnen, Mürren, Wengen
**Total of trails/pistes** 213km in Jungfrau Top Ski Region (28% easy, 57% intermediate, 15% difficult)
**Lifts in area** 41: 5🚡 7🚠 15🚟 14🎿
**Lift opening dates** 4 December 2004 to 17 April 2005. Summer skiing at Jungfraujoch

### LIFT PASSES
**Area pass** Jungfrau (covers Grindelwald, Mürren, Wengen) SF288 for 6 days

**Pensioners** Jungfrau from 62yrs SF259 for 6 days

### TUITION
**Ski & board** SSS (☎ 33 853 5200)
**Guiding** Bergsteigerzentrum (☎ 33 853 1200)

### CHILDREN
**Lift pass** Jungfrau under 6yrs SF25 (or free if with parent), 6–15yrs SF144, 16–19yrs SF230, all for 6 days
**Ski & board school** as adults
**Kindergarten** (ski/non-ski) Kinderclub Bodmi (☎ 33 853 5200), (non-ski) Kinderhort Murmeli (☎ 79 592 0209), Kinderhort Sunshine (☎ 79 632 8178)

### FOOD AND DRINK
Coffee SF4, bottle of house wine SF25–30, small beer SF4.50–5, soft drink SF4.50, dish of the day SF18–25

# Klosters

ALTITUDE 1,192m (3,911ft)                    map: see pages 196–197

❄ **large ski area with long runs** ❄ **traditional village**
❄ **well-groomed slopes**

**Best for:** gourmet skiers, off-piste enthusiasts, ski-tourers
**Not recommended for:** budget skiers, those wanting skiing convenience, families with beginner children

Klosters is a small, rural farming community with its own small ski area as well as the large Parsenn slopes, which it shares with **Davos** – its more urban neighbour. It welcomed its first wintersports enthusiasts in 1904, and has prospered from its connection with the British royal family, in particular Prince Charles. Despite its high 'by Royal Appointment' profile, it remains essentially a small Swiss village.

Klosters Platz is the main community and is centred on the railway station and the Gotschna cable-car, which gives access to the Parsenn. Klosters Dorf is a sleepy outpost at the bottom of the Madrisa lift system. The two parts of the resort are connected by a regular bus service. A new bypass road tunnel (not due to be finished until 2005) will enable Klosters to be pedestrianised and should solve the valley's unsightly traffic problem. Trains between Klosters and Davos are once again included in the lift pass.

## On-piste
top 2,844m (9,328ft) bottom 813m (2,667ft)

Most skiers and riders head from Platz for the Parsenn, and as a result the two-stage Gotschna cable-car is prone to queues. Once up the mountain, however, the crowds thin out and the Parsenn provides a pleasing combination of intermediate and steeper terrain.

The Parsenn is dominated by the 2,844-m Weissfluhgipfel above Davos. The Weissfluhjoch, 180m beneath the summit, is where the network of gently undulating pistes begins. However, the steeper slopes

at the Klosters end of the circuit are sufficiently long and demanding to deter all but truly accomplished skiers. In good snow conditions you can ski a 12-km run down to the villages of Küblis and Serneus. Those who profit most from the Klosters/Davos area are intermediates with the energy to ski all the hours the lift company allows.

The focus of the Madrisa, Klosters' own ski area, is a delightful beginner and family area on top of the mountain, although it is inconvenient for parents who want to spend time on the Parsenn. While snow cover is usually guaranteed on these sunny, user-friendly slopes, novices must buy a full lift pass and return by gondola at the end of the day. Complete beginners can use the Heidi lift, which is situated in the village.

Snowboarders congregate at the Jakobshorn terrain park, with its two half-pipes, boardercross circuit and night-riding.

## Off-piste
The longest, but by no means the most exciting, runs are the 18-km descents to Fideris and Jenaz, each with short climbing sections along the way. The Madrisa is the starting point for the trans-border loop to the Austrian hamlet of **Gargellen** at the head of the **Montafon** Valley.

## Tuition and guiding
The Saas Ski and Snowboard School (Saas S&S-S) is 'highly professional, with mainly young switched-on instructors with immaculate English'. Boardriding Klosters, the Swiss Snowsports School (SSS) and Bananas ('expert tuition for my son from a lass with lots of body-piercing') offer snowboard lessons.

## Mountain restaurants
Chesetta is renowned for its Rösti and other local specialities, as is the Serneuser Schwendi. The Gotschna at Serneus serves delicious cheese dishes. Berghaus Schifer is praised for its staff, who were unfailingly friendly, and for the reasonably priced food.

Another winner is the pizzeria at the end of the Schlappin run in Klosters Dorf. Madrisa has the Bergrestaurant Saaseralp.

## Accommodation

The four-star hotels are headed by Hotel Walserhof (☎ 81 410 2929), which has a top reputation and royal patronage. However, the Vereina (☎ 81 410 2727) is more comfortable, more conveniently situated and has a first-rate spa in its basement. The Chesa Grischuna (☎ 81 422 2222) is rustic and has a popular bar, while the modern Hotel Alpina (☎ 81 410 2424) has a small indoor swimming-pool and four new, feng shui-designed bedrooms. The 30-room Wynegg (☎ 81 422 1340) is a resort institution, run much like a large chalet for its mainly British guests. The overspill can find a quieter refuge in the Bundnerhof (☎ 81 422 1450) next door. Four-star Hotel Pardenn (☎ 81 423 2020) has been partly rebuilt. The Silvretta Parkhotel (☎ 81 423 3435) has good-sized rooms and a wellness area. One reporter warmly recommends Hotel Hirschen (☎ 81 330 5555) as 'hard to beat on value'.

Heading the list of luxury properties in Klosters is Eugenia (☎ 020-7384 3854 through Descent International in UK), a beautiful chalet with oak panelling, marble and stripped wooden floors, and pillared fireplaces.

## Eating in and out

The smartest restaurant in town is the Michelin-rated restaurant in the Hotel Walserhof, presided over by Switzerland's celebrity chef Beat Bolliger. Together with the Chesa Grischuna, the Walserhof must be booked days in advance in high season. The Wynegg serves meals that are more rustic than gastronomic. Fellini is a favourite place for tea and cakes after skiing, as well as for pizzas later on.

## Après-ski

The Steinbock Bar attracts locals as well as tourists. Alternative watering-holes include the Chesa Grischuna, and the Piano Bar in the Silvretta Parkhotel. For late-night dancing try the Casa Antica, the Kir Royal, the Rössli Bar and the Mountain Pub in Klosters Dorf.

## Childcare

Kids Land at Madrisa is for non-skiers from two years of age, while the Snow Garden is for skiers over four years and is situated at the Sports Centre at Klosters Platz.

# Klosters: At a glance

**Tel** 41 81 410 2020
**Email** info@klosters.ch
**Website** www.klosters.ch

### GETTING THERE
**Airport** Zurich 2½hrs
**Rail** Klosters Dorf and Klosters Platz stations in resort
**Road** motorway Zurich–Landquart, further 69km

### THE SKIING
**Linked/nearby resorts** Arosa, Davos, Gargellen, Glaris, Küblis, Saas, Serneus, St Moritz, Wolfgang
**Total of trails/pistes** 370km in Davos/Klosters area (30% easy, 40% intermediate, 30% difficult)
**Lifts in area** 50: 2🚠 12🚡 9🚢 27🚲
**Lift opening dates** Parsenn ski area: 27 November 2004 to 17 April 2005

### LIFT PASSES
**Area pass** Rega Pass (covers all Davos and Klosters lifts, except Schatzalp/Strela) SF279 for 6 days

**Pensioners** Rega Pass 10% reduction for women 63yrs and over, and men 65yrs and over

### TUITION
**Ski & board** Bananas (☎ 81 422 6660), Boardriding Klosters (☎ 81 420 2662), Saas S&S-S (☎ 81 420 2233), SSS (☎ 81 410 2828)
**Guiding** Adventure Skiing (☎ 81 422 4825), Berger Jürg (☎ 81 422 3636) and through ski schools

### CHILDREN
**Lift pass** Rega Pass 6–12yrs SF103, 13–17yrs SF187, both for 6 days
**Ski & board school** as adults
**Kindergarten** (ski) Snow Garden (☎ 81 410 2828), (ski/non-ski) Kids Land (☎ 81 410 2170)

### FOOD AND DRINK
Coffee SF4, bottle of house wine SF20–30, small beer SF5, soft drink SF5, dish of the day SF20–25

# Mürren

❄ **idyllic car-free mountain village** ❄ **intimate atmosphere**
❄ **steep skiing**

**Best for:** strong intermediates and advanced skiers, powderhounds

**Not recommended for:** beginners, those wanting a big ski area

raffic-free Mürren is the perfect example of classic Swiss mountain village that sits in ural splendour on a sunny ledge 550m above ae Lauterbrunnen Valley. It shares a lift pass, ut not a joint ski area, with **Wengen** and ₃rindelwald. All three resorts are reached by ain from the railway halt at **Lauterbrunnen**, ⁰hich acts an alternative budget base from hich to explore this corner of the Bernese ⁰berland. Distances are large and the lift ⁄stem slow. One reporter complained it took ₁ore than two hours to travel home to ⁄engen after skiing at Winteregg.

The mountain railway came here in ictorian times and is still the backbone of ₁e lift system. Henry Lunn, a non-skiing ₁ethodist minister and one-time lawn tennis ₃uipment salesman, is credited with ₁troducing the first-ever ski package holidays ₁ the region in the winter of 1910–11. To ₁courage the class-conscious British to come ₁ his tours, he founded the Public Schools ₁lpine Sports Club. His more distinguished ₁n, Sir Arnold, went on to found the ₁andahar Ski Club in Mürren, where slalom ₁cing was first introduced in 1922.

Mürren, as one reporter elegantly ₃scribed it, 'is like a coveted biscuit jar ₁dden above the kitchen cabinet. It is high ₃, difficult to reach, but full of delights ₁ce within your grasp'. Old chalets and ₁tels line the paths between the railway ₁ation at one end and the cable-car at the ₁her. The same British families, many of ₁em members of the Kandahar Club, have ₁en returning here for generations and ₁ve forged firm links with the local ₁llagers.

The village is reached by a steep rack-₁d-pinion railway from Lauterbrunnen, ₁llowed by a further stretch of track that winds from Grütschalp through Winteregg to the resort. Alternatively, you can take a cable-car up from Stechelberg in the valley.

## On-piste
### top 2,971m (9,748ft) bottom 796m (2,612ft)

Mürren's skiing is spread across three parallel ridges – the Schiltgrat, the Allmendhubel and the Maulerhubel – which run roughly north and south above the village.

Main mountain access is by cable-car to Birg at 2,676m and on to the summit of the Schilthorn at 2,971m. This is the starting point for the annual pro-am Inferno downhill race, which, when conditions permit, takes racers all the way down to Lauterbrunnen. The slopes on the top section of the mountain are steep, and although carefully groomed every morning they can become heavily mogulled later in the day. Two chair-lifts, Muttlern and Kandahar, allow skiing on the middle section of the mountain below Obere Hubel without having to return all the way down to the bottom of the cable-car. More benign terrain can be accessed from the village by the Schildgrat chair-lift or by a swift funicular that takes you up to meadows surrounding Allmendhubel.

Mürren is not an ideal resort for beginners. The small nursery slope is on the upper road behind Hotel Jungfrau. Another novice area lies at the top of the Allmendhubel lift and is served by a small drag-lift. The resort has a half-pipe.

## Off-piste
Off-piste skiing is extensive, if you know where to look. The Blumental is famous for its powder, and Hidden Valley from the summit of the Maulerhubel to Grutsch is a delight. Tschingelchrachen off the Schilthornbahn is often closed and should be treated with care as it is very steep.

## Tuition and guiding
We have favourable reports of the Swiss Snowsports School (SSS): 'sensible tips

from a local with lots of fascinating stories'. However, group lessons are only from Sunday to Friday mornings.

## Mountain restaurants
The Schilthorn Tavern has 'copious portions and reasonable prices'. Pension Sonnenburg is praised for its Rösti. Restaurant Birg is 'worth a visit, if only for the view from the terrace'. Gimmeln has 'tasty raclette and *Apfelküchen*'. The revolving Piz Gloria on the summit of the Schilthorn is praised: 'I had an imaginative salad – it took a full revolution to demolish it'. The Schilthornhütte, on the descent from here, is a mountain refuge serving simple dishes (a 'fun atmosphere').

## Accommodation
The four-star Hotel Eiger (☎ 33 856 5454), across the road from the railway station, boasts some luxurious suites as well as standard hotel rooms and apartments. The four-star Anfi Palace (☎ 33 856 9999) dates back to the Edwardian days of Henry Lunn, when it housed the first holidaymakers.

Of the three-stars, Hotel Jungfrau (☎ 33 855 4545) is 'the friendliest Swiss hotel we have ever stayed in. We couldn't believe the quality of the food we were served night after night'. The Alpenruh (☎ 33 856 8800)

at the Schilthornbahn end of the village has 'an excellent restaurant', the popular Edelweiss (☎ 33 856 5600) is 'convenient, clean and friendly' and the Blumental (☎ 33 855 1826) is also recommended.

## Eating in and out
Hotel Eiger's Stübli has a 'superb, if somewhat expensive, menu'. The Alpenruh comes well recommended, and the Belmont offers 'excellent value'. The Edelweiss and Stägerstübli are both praised, as is the Kandahar Snack ('cakes to die for').

## Après-ski
For such a small village, Mürren is surprisingly lively, although only during high season. The Ballon bar in the Anfi Palace, together with the Grübi in the Jungfrau and the Pub in the Belmont, are al popular. The Tächi bar in the Hotel Eiger is one of the main meeting-places. The Bliemlichäller disco in the Blumental and the Inferno disco in the Anfi Palace buzz in high season. Skating and curling are popular activities at the sports centre.

## Childcare
Non-skiing children from one month to five years are cared for in the Snowgarten.

# Mürren: At a glance

**Tel** 41 33 856 8686
**Email** info@muerren.ch
**Website** www.wengen-muerren.ch

**GETTING THERE**
**Airports** Zurich 3hrs, Geneva 4hrs
**Rail** station in resort
**Road** motorway Bern–Interlaken, road to Lauterbrunnen, railway or cable-car to resort

**THE SKIING**
**Linked/nearby resorts** Grindelwald, Lauterbrunnen, Wengen
**Total of trails/pistes** 213km in Jungfrau Top Ski region (28% easy, 57% intermediate, 15% difficult)
**Lifts in area** 41: 5🚟 7🚡 15🚠 14🎿
**Lift opening dates** 4 December 2004 to 17 April 2005

**LIFT PASSES**
**Area pass** Jungfrau (covers Grindelwald, Mürren, Wengen) SF288 for 6 days

**Pensioners** Jungfrau from 62yrs SF259 for 6 days

**TUITION**
**Ski & board** SSS (☎ 33 855 1247)
**Guiding** through ski school

**CHILDREN**
**Lift pass** Jungfrau under 6yrs SF25 (or free if with parent), 6–15yrs SF144, 16–19yrs SF230, all for 6 days
**Ski & board school** as adults
**Kindergarten** (non-ski) Snowgarten (☎ 33 856 8686)

**FOOD AND DRINK**
Coffee SF4, bottle of house wine SF25–30, small beer SF4.50–5, soft drink SF4.50 , dish of the day SF18–25

# Map section

## CONTENTS

## KEY TO MAPS

| | | PISTES | EUROPE | NORTH AMERICA |
|---|---|---|---|---|
| 🚠 | Cable-car | | Beginner | Easy |
| 🚡 | Gondola | | Easy | Intermediate |
| 🚡 | Chair-lift (inset figure denotes number of seats) | | Intermediate | |
| | | | Difficult | Difficult |
| 🚋 | Drag-lift | ♦ | | Very difficult |
| 🚞 | Funicular | ♦♦ | | |
| 🚃 | Mountain railway | ............ | Unpisted itinerary | Unpisted itinerary |

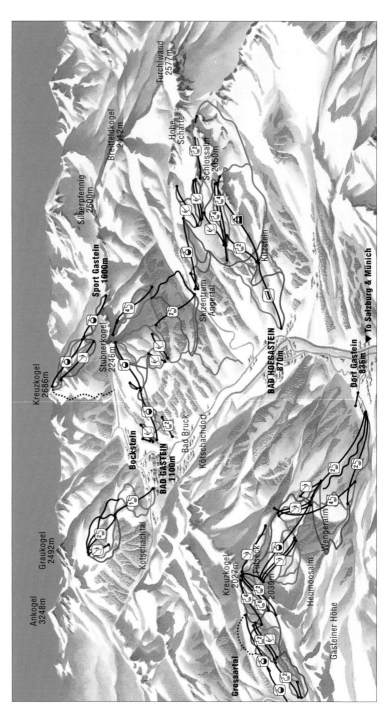

AUSTRIA   The Gasteinertal

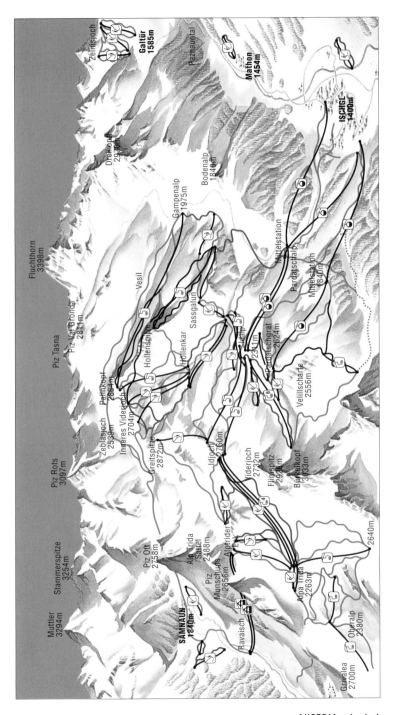

AUSTRIA   Ischgl

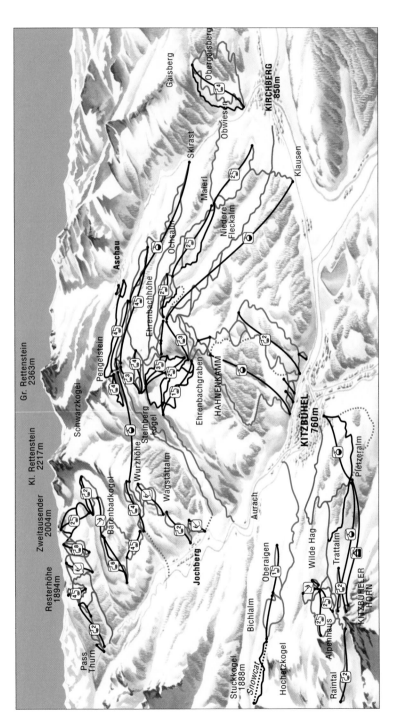

AUSTRIA Kitzbühel

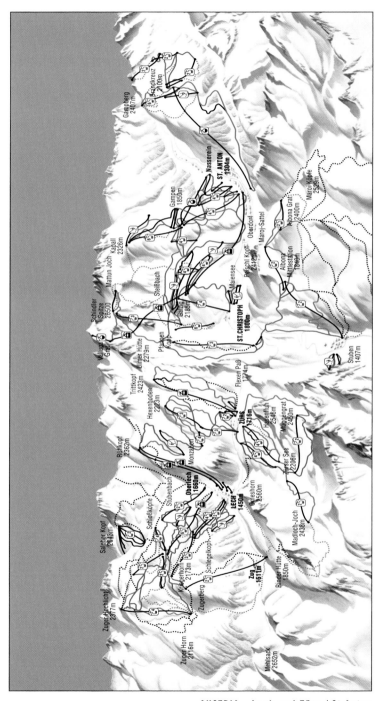

**AUSTRIA** Lech and Zürs / St Anton

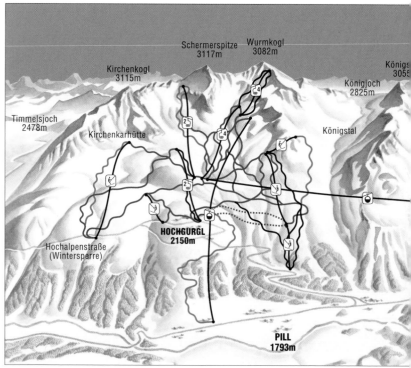

AUSTRIA   Obergurgl–Hochgurgl

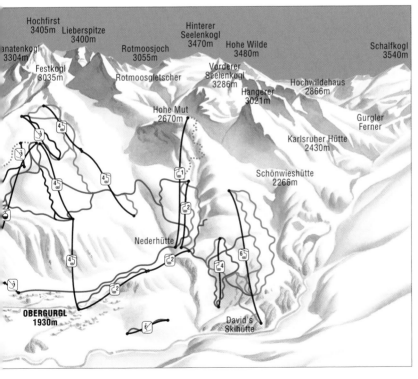

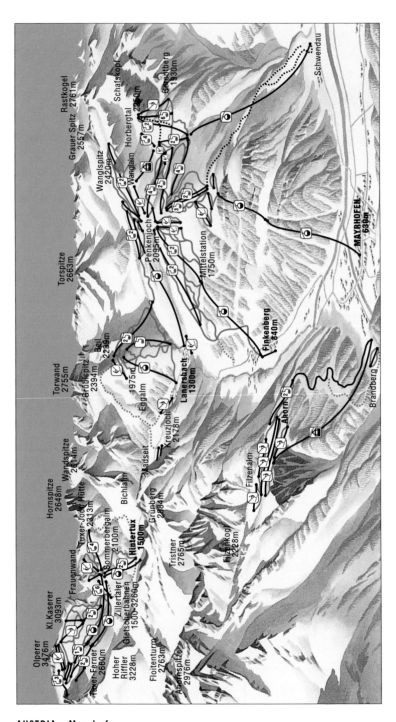

**AUSTRIA    Mayrhofen**

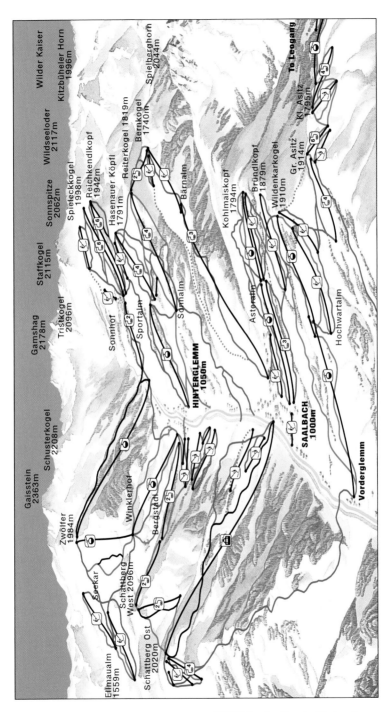

AUSTRIA   Saalbach–Hinterglemm

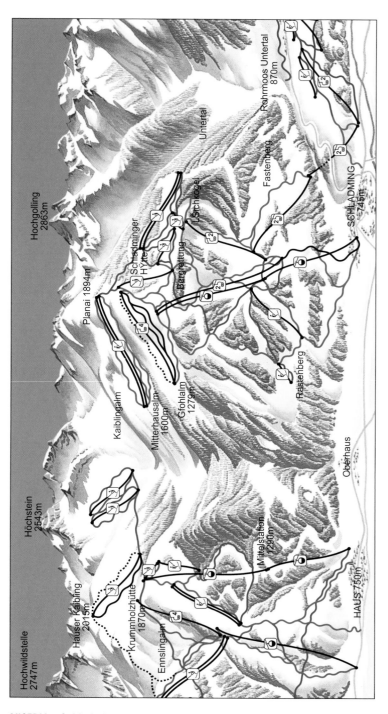

**AUSTRIA   Schladming**

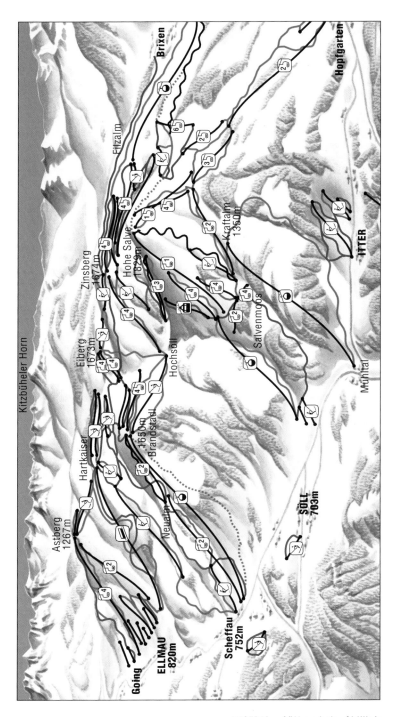

AUSTRIA   Söll and the SkiWelt

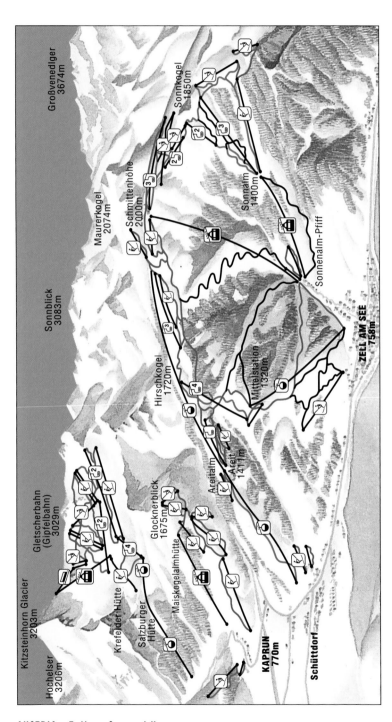

AUSTRIA    Zell am See and Kaprun

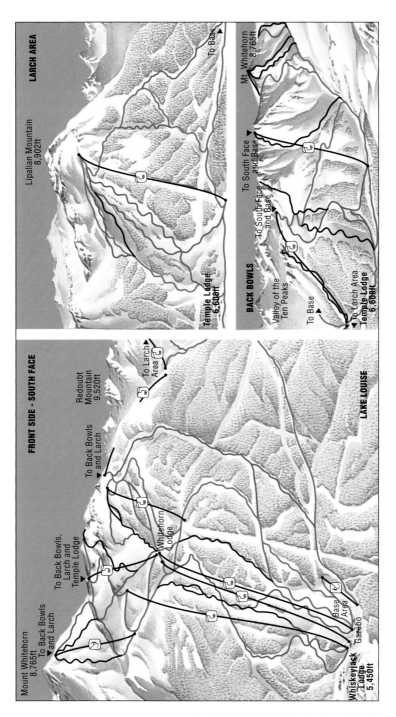

**LARCH AREA**

Lipalian Mountain
8,902ft

To Base

Temple Lodge
6,608ft

Mt. Whitehorn
8,765ft

To South Face
and Base

To South Face
and Base

**BACK BOWLS**

Valley of the
Ten Peaks

To Base

To Larch Area

Temple Lodge
6,608ft

**FRONT SIDE - SOUTH FACE**

Redoubt
Mountain
9,520ft

To Larch
Area

To Back Bowls
and Larch

Whitehorn
Lodge

Mount Whitehorn
8,765ft

To Back Bowls
and Larch

To Back Bowls,
Larch and
Temple Lodge

Base
Area

Gazebo

Whiskeyjack
Lodge
5,450ft

**LAKE LOUISE**

CANADA   Banff–Lake Louise, Alberta

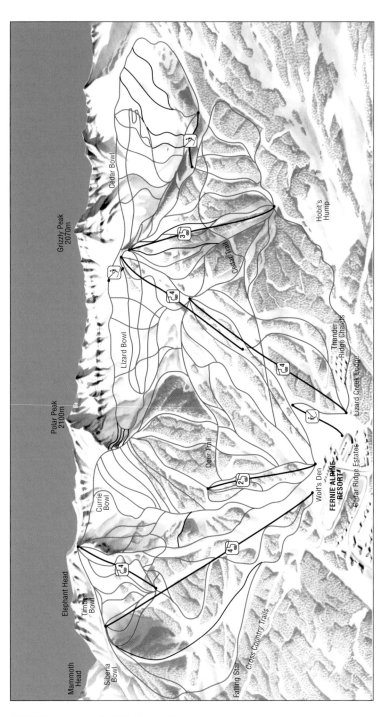

**CANADA   Fernie, British Columbia**

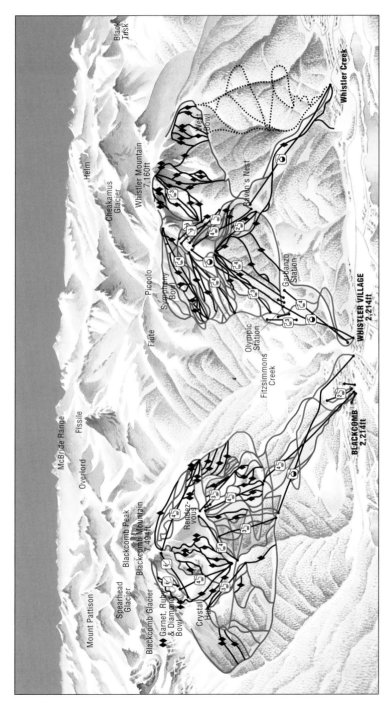

CANADA   Whistler, British Columbia

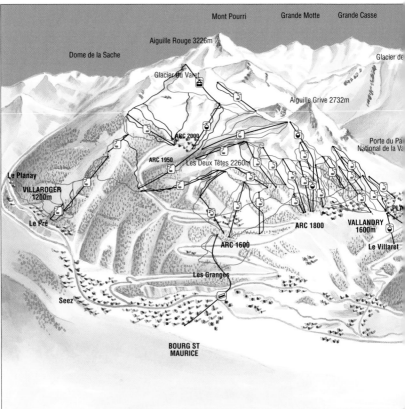

FRANCE   Les Arcs / La Plagne (Paradiski)

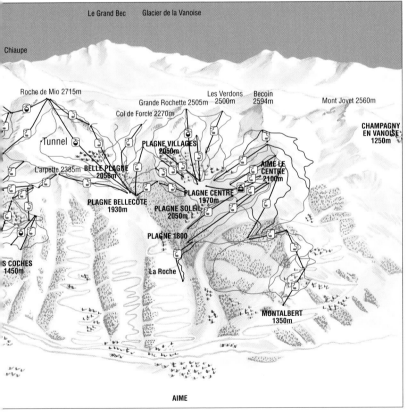

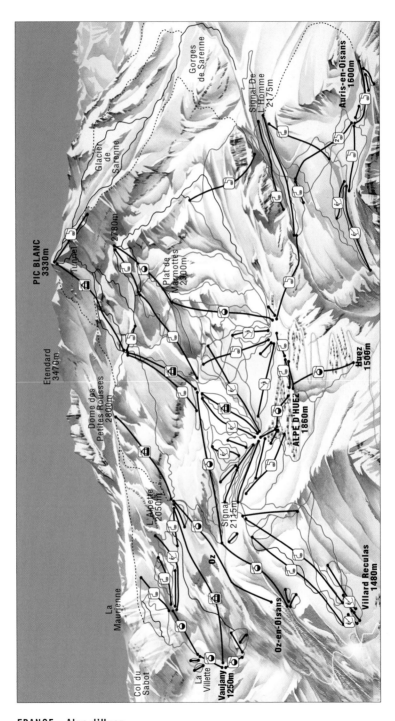

FRANCE Alpe d'Huez

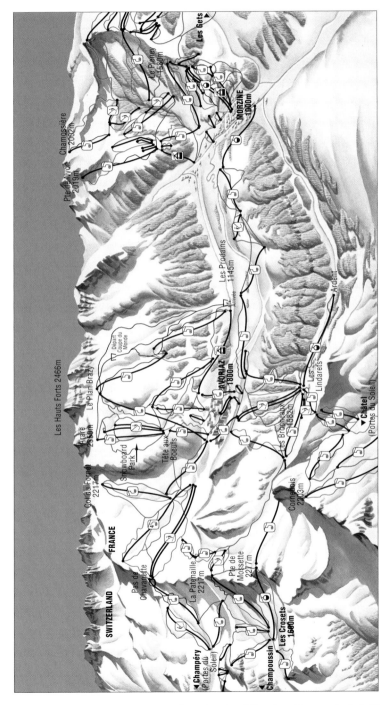

FRANCE   Avoriaz / Morzine (Portes du Soleil)

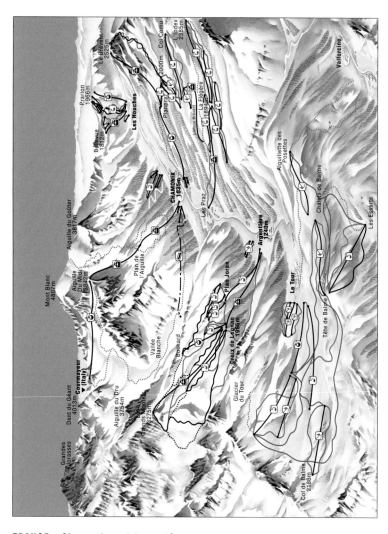

FRANCE   Chamonix and Argentière

## KEY TO MAPS

| | | PISTES | EUROPE | NORTH AMERICA |
|---|---|---|---|---|
| | Cable-car | ——— | Beginner | Easy |
| | Gondola | ——— | Easy | Intermediate |
| | Chair-lift (inset figure denotes number of seats) | ——— | Intermediate | |
| | | ——— | Difficult | |
| | Drag-lift | | | |
| | Funicular | ◆ | | Difficult |
| | | ◆◆ | | Very difficult |
| | Mountain railway | ·············· | Unpisted itinerary | Unpisted itinerary |

FRANCE   Courchevel / Méribel / La Tania (The Trois Vallées)

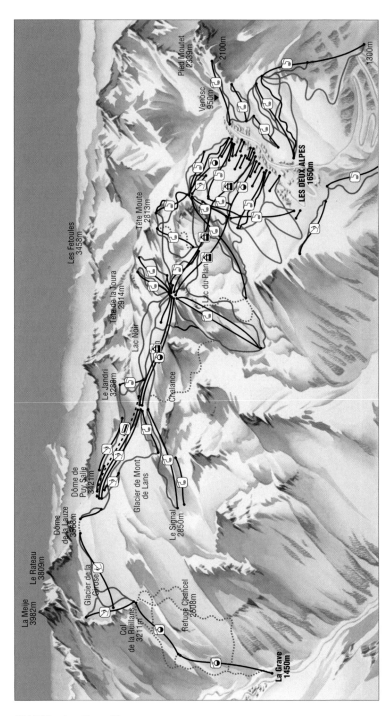

**FRANCE** Les Deux Alpes

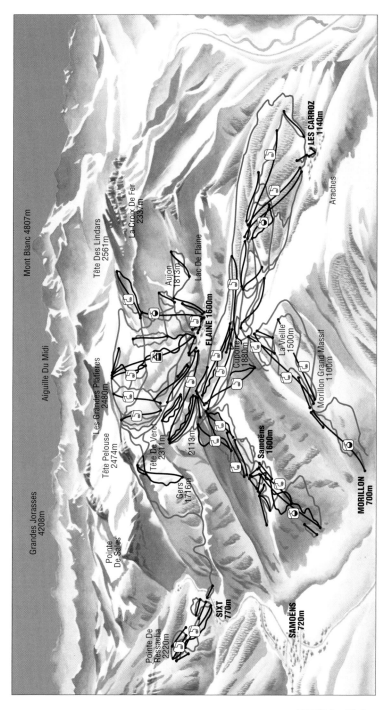

FRANCE   Flaine

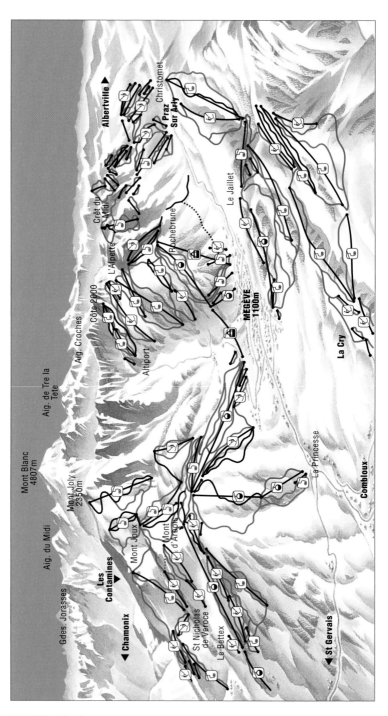

FRANCE  Megève

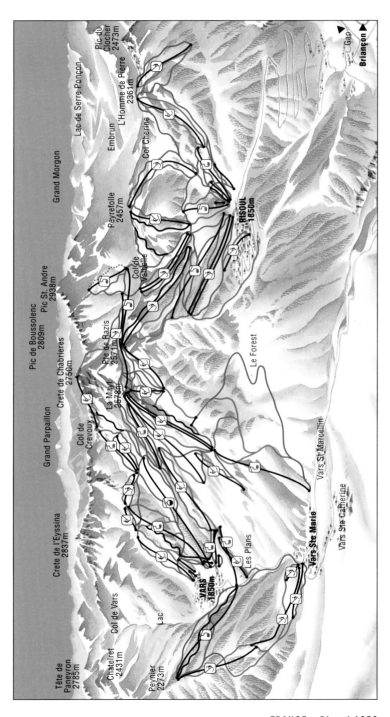

FRANCE   Risoul 1850

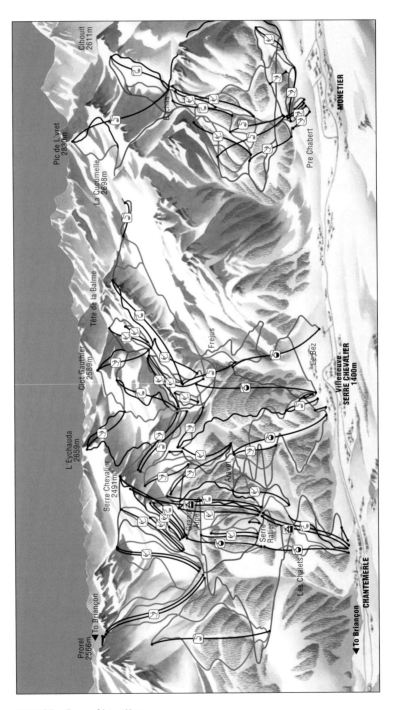

FRANCE   Serre Chevalier

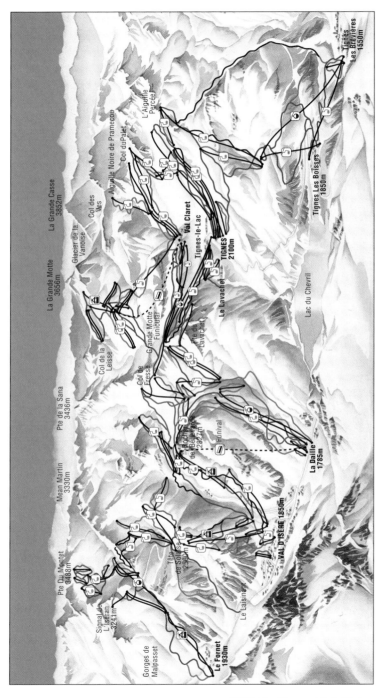

FRANCE   Tignes / Val d'Isère

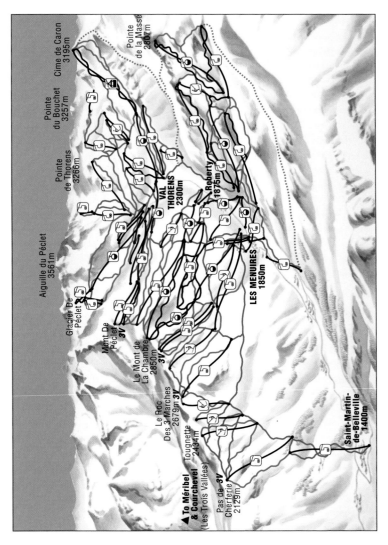

**FRANCE** Val Thorens and the Belleville Valley (The Trois Vallées)

## KEY TO MAPS

| | | | |
|---|---|---|---|
| 🚠 | Cable-car | **PISTES** | **EUROPE** | **NORTH AMERICA** |
| 🚡 | Gondola | | Beginner | Easy |
| 🚟 | Chair-lift<br>(inset figure denotes<br>number of seats) | | Easy | Intermediate |
| | | | Intermediate | |
| 🎿 | Drag-lift | | Difficult | |
| 🚞 | Funicular | ♦ | | Difficult |
| 🚃 | Mountain railway | ♦♦ | | Very difficult |
| | | ············· | Unpisted itinerary | Unpisted itinerary |

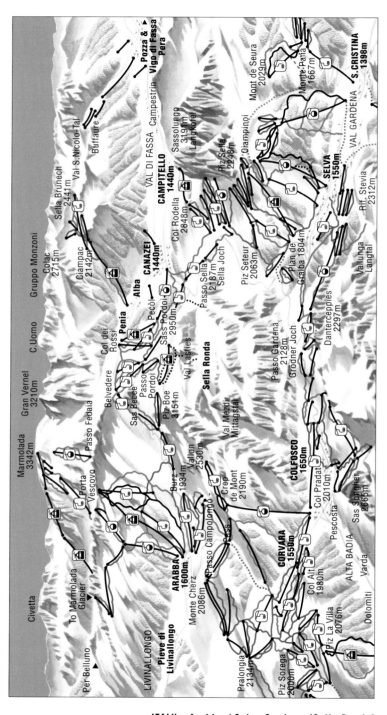

**ITALY   Arabba / Selva Gardena (Sella Ronda)**

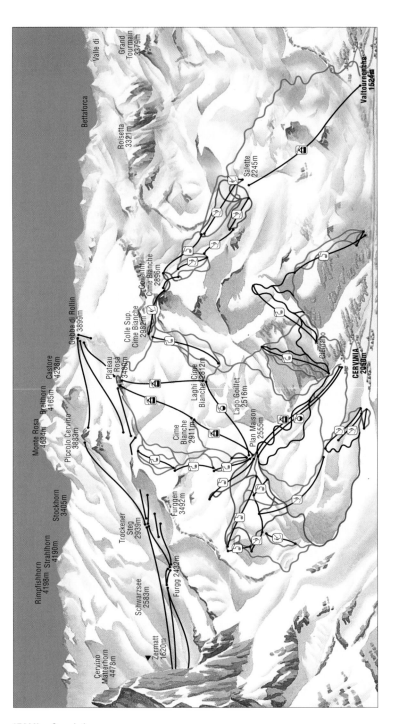

**ITALY** Cervinia

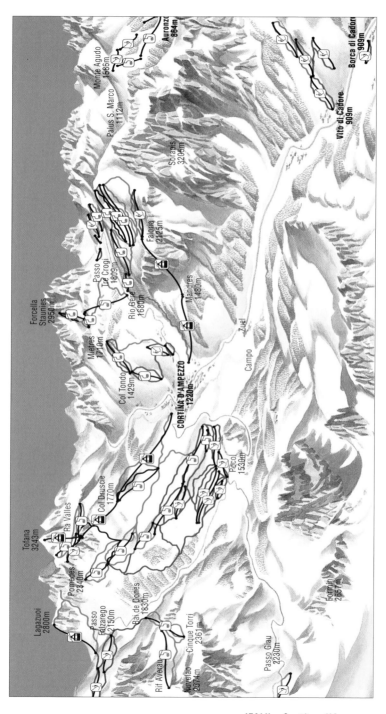

ITALY   Cortina d'Ampezzo

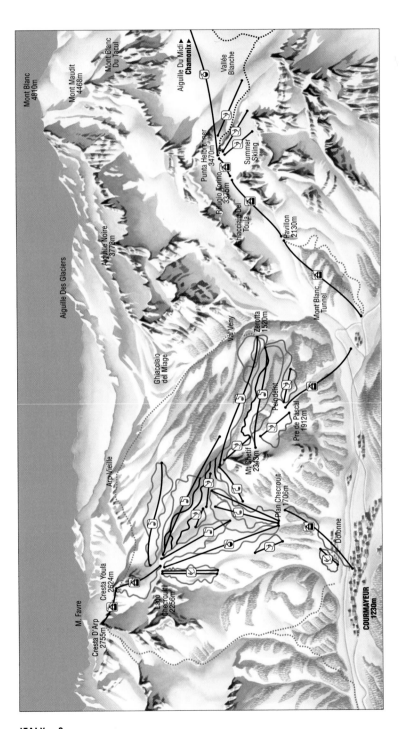

ITALY    Courmayeur

**ITALY   Livigno**

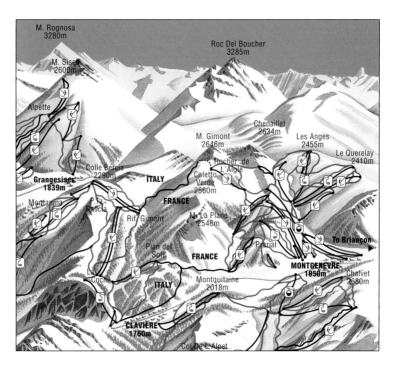

**ITALY   Sauze d'Oulx / Sestriere (The Milky Way)**

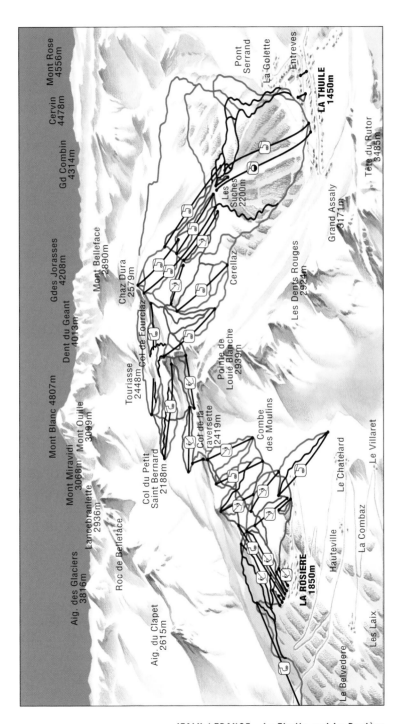

**ITALY / FRANCE    La Thuile and La Rosière**

Mont Rose 4556m
Cervin 4478m
Gd Combin 4314m
Gdes Jorasses 4208m
Dent du Geant 4013m
Mont Blanc 4807m
Mont Miravidi 3068m
Mont Ouille 3099m
Lancebranlette 2936m
Aig. des Glaciers 3816m
Roc de Belleface
Col du Petit Saint Bernard 2188m
Aig. du Clapet 2615m

Pont Serrand
La Golette
Entreves
LA THUILE 1450m
Tête du Rutor 3485m
Les Suches 2200m
Grand Assaly 317 Lm
Mont Belleface 2890m
Chaz Dura 2579m
Cerellaz
Les Dents Rouges 2924m
Col de Fourclaz
Pointe de Louié Blanche 2939m
Touriasse 2448m
Col de la Traversette 2419m
Combe des Moulins
Le Chatelard
Le Villaret
LA ROSIÈRE 1850m
Hauteville
La Combaz
Le Belvedere
Les Laix

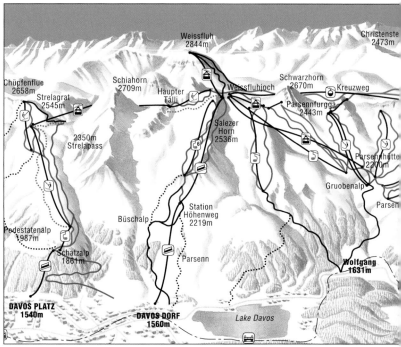

SWITZERLAND   Davos / Klosters

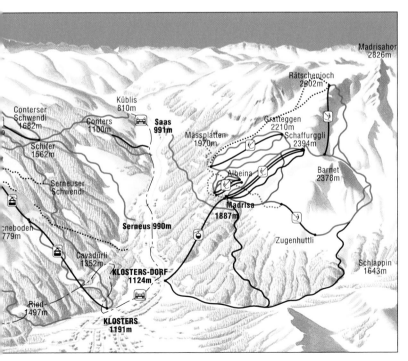

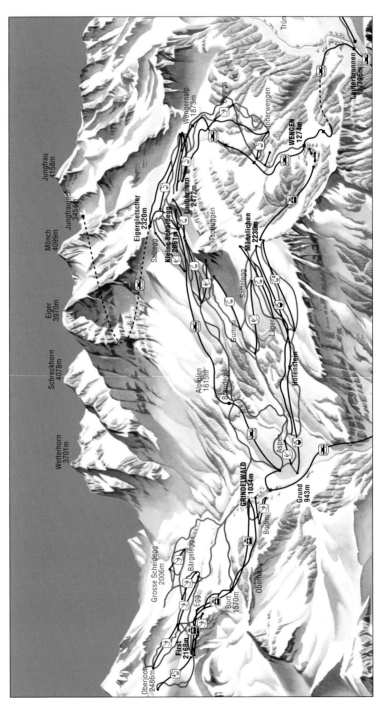

SWITZERLAND Grindelwald / Wengen (Jungfrau)

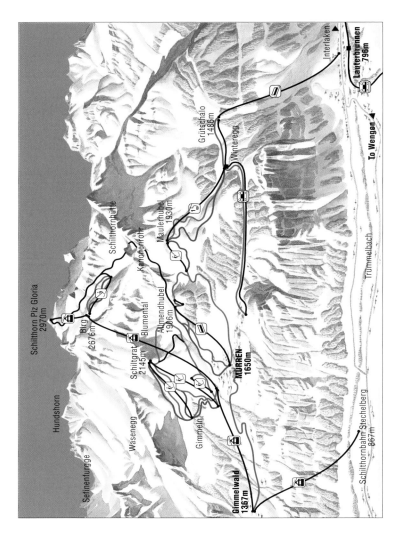

SWITZERLAND   Mürren (Jungfrau)

## KEY TO MAPS

| | | PISTES | EUROPE | NORTH AMERICA |
|---|---|---|---|---|
| | Cable-car | | | |
| | | | Beginner | Easy |
| | Gondola | | | |
| | | | Easy | Intermediate |
| | Chair-lift | | | |
| | (inset figure denotes number of seats) | | Intermediate | |
| | | | Difficult | |
| | Drag-lift | | | |
| | | ◆ | | Difficult |
| | Funicular | | | |
| | | ◆◆ | | Very difficult |
| | Mountain railway | | | |
| | | ············ | Unpisted itinerary | Unpisted itinerary |

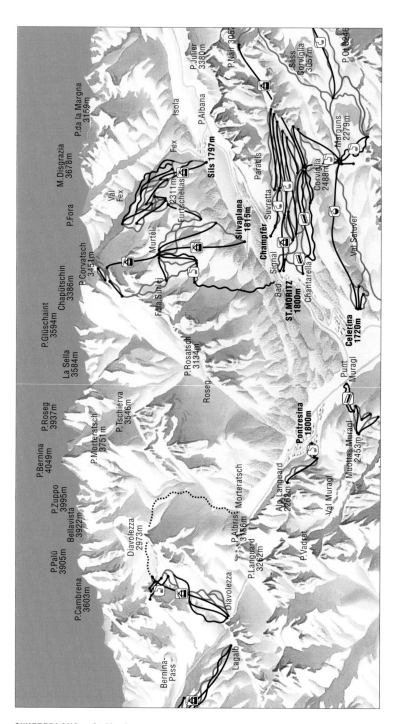

**SWITZERLAND** St Moritz

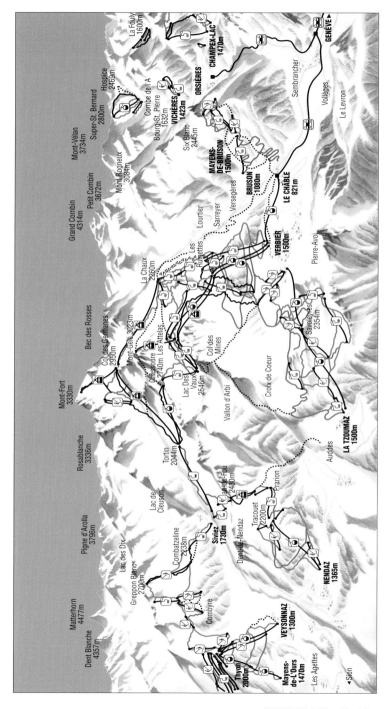

SWITZERLAND Verbier

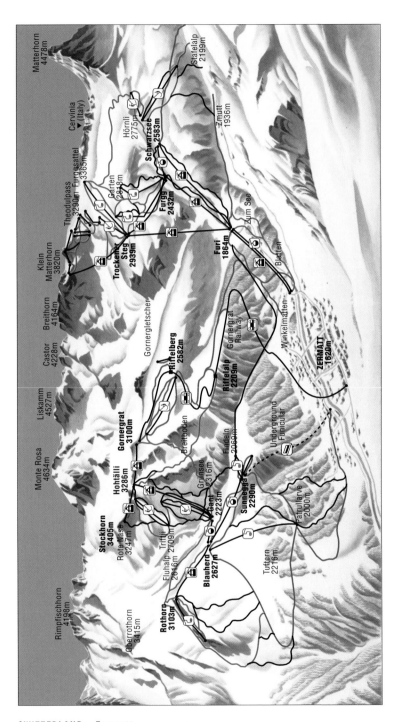

SWITZERLAND   Zermatt

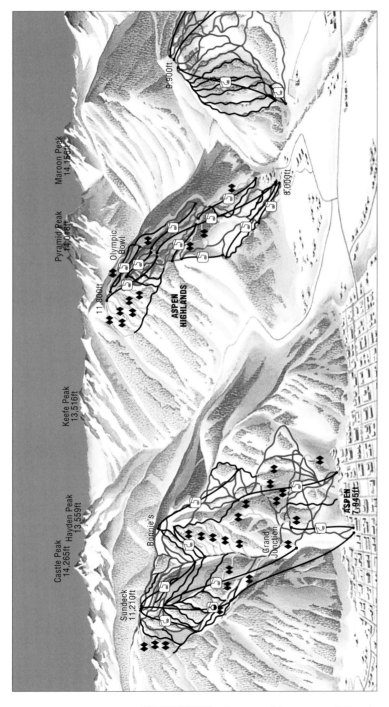

UNITED STATES    Aspen and Snowmass, Colorado

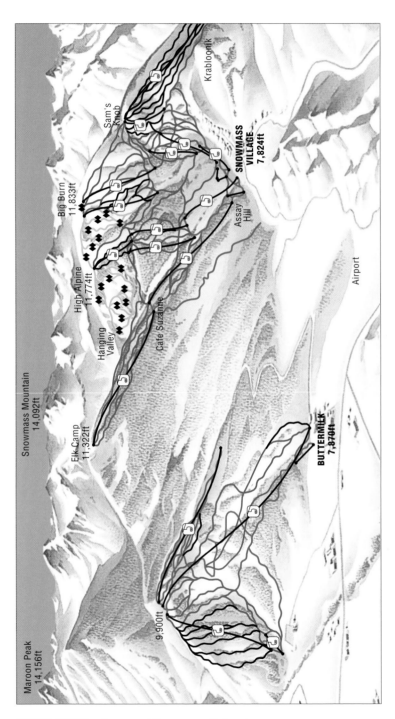

UNITED STATES    Aspen and Snowmass, Colorado

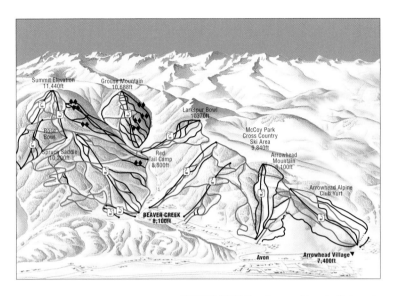

UNITED STATES    Beaver Creek, Colorado

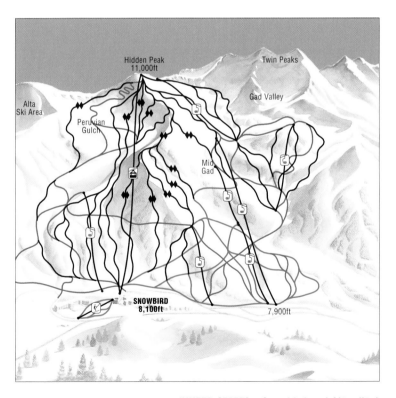

UNITED STATES    Snowbird and Alta, Utah

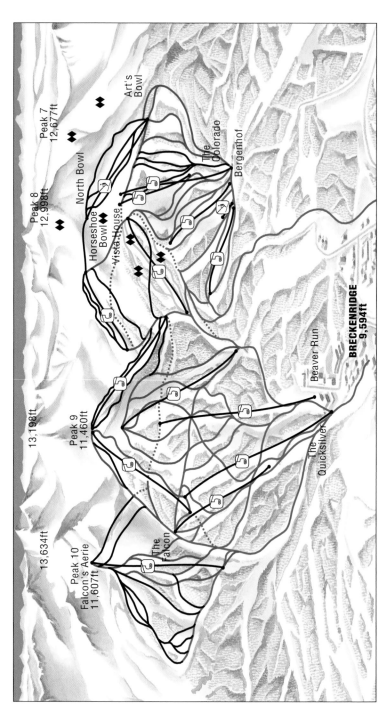

UNITED STATES    Breckenridge, Colorado

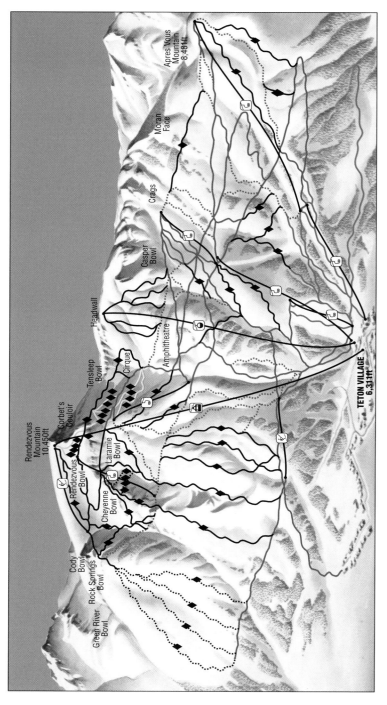

Apres Vous
Mountain 8,481ft

Moran
Face

Crags

Casper
Bowl

Headwall

Amphitheatre

Tensleep
Bowl

Cirquel

Corbet's
Couloir

Rendezvous
Mountain
10,450ft

Laramie
Bowl

Rendezvous
Bowl

Cheyenne
Bowl

Cody
Bowl

Rock Springs
Bowl

Green River
Bowl

TETON VILLAGE
6,311ft

**UNITED STATES** Jackson Hole, Wyoming

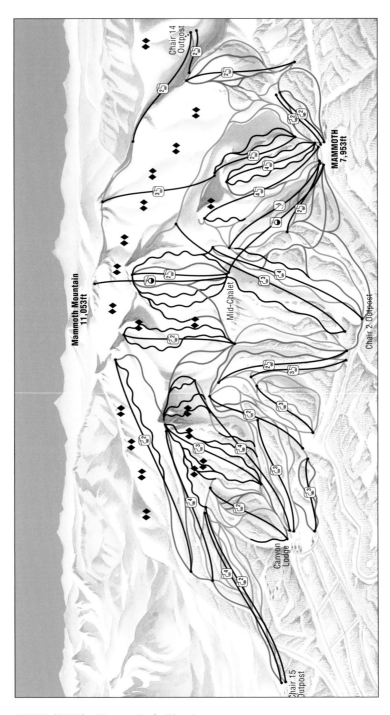

UNITED STATES    Mammoth, California

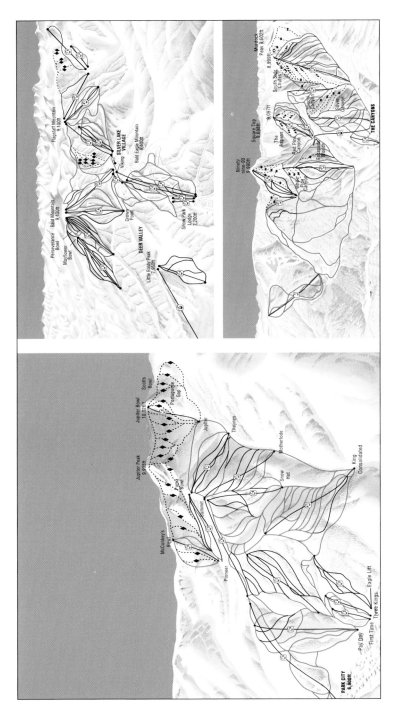

UNITED STATES   Park City Resorts, Utah

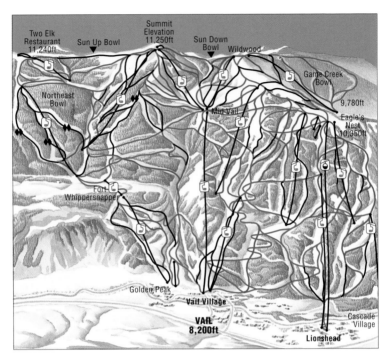

UNITED STATES    Vail, Colorado

## KEY TO MAPS

| | | PISTES | EUROPE | NORTH AMERICA |
|---|---|---|---|---|
| 🚠 | Cable-car | | | |
| 🚡 | Gondola | ——— | Beginner | Easy |
| 🚡 | Chair-lift (inset figure denotes number of seats) | ——— | Easy | Intermediate |
| | | ——— | Intermediate | |
| | | ——— | Difficult | |
| 🎿 | Drag-lift | | | |
| | | ◆ | | Difficult |
| 🚟 | Funicular | ◆◆ | | Very difficult |
| 🚃 | Mountain railway | •••••••••••• | Unpisted itinerary | Unpisted itinerary |

# Saas-Fee

ALTITUDE 1,800m (5,904ft)

## ✳ snow-sure resort ✳ attractive village ✳ glacier skiing

> **Best for:** beginners to intermediates, night-owls, snowboarders, ski-tourers, early- and late-season skiers
> **Not recommended for:** those looking for ski-in ski-out accommodation, adventurous intermediates

Saas-Fee is a delightfully unspoilt resort set against one of the most dramatic glacial backdrops in the Alps. Its narrow streets are lined with some 60 hotels interspersed with ancient barns and chalets of blackened wood. Designer ski shops rub shoulders with working farmhouses.

## On the snow

top 3,600m (11,811ft) bottom 1,800m (5,904ft)

At this altitude, snow cover is virtually guaranteed, and the long vertical drop of 1,800m provides a total of 100km of runs. Main mountain access is by the Alpin Express cable-car and the world's highest underground funicular system, the Metro Alpin, which rises to Mittelallalin. A network of lifts ('too many T-bars and not enough chairs') serves mainly intermediate terrain that is severely limited in scope by the surrounding glaciers. The risk of falling down crevasses is significant for anyone foolish enough to stray without a local guide. The great advantage of the area is its high altitude with pistes up to 3,600m and skiing on the glacier, which provides year-round skiing and snowboarding.

The Swiss Snowsports School (SSS) in Saas-Fee suffers from poor organisation and overcrowding, especially during peak holiday periods. Inconveniently, it offers group ski lessons only in the mornings from Monday to Friday. Reporters criticise the SSS: 'Our only real gripe was the ski school, of which our group's experiences were poor'. Snowboarding is big business here, and the SSS faces fierce competition from the Eskimos Snowboard School, which runs all-day courses for adults and children. The two terrain parks include one beneath Mittelallalin, the highest point of the ski area, which has a boardercross course, half-pipe and various obstacles.

'Some great mountain restaurants,' commended reporters. Recommended lunchtime restaurants include the Plattjen and the Gletschergrotte. The world's highest revolving restaurant at Mittelallalin received criticism: 'the worst food at the highest prices'.

## In the resort

Saas-Fee is traffic-free and you must leave vehicles at the large car park on the outskirts. Ski buses and electric taxis are not always available, making the position of your hotel of paramount importance.

Recommended hotels include the five-star Ferienart Resort & Spa (☎ 27 958 1900) as well as the four-stars Metropol (☎ 27 957 1001), Schweizerhof (☎ 27 958 7575) and Allalin Relais du Silence (☎ 27 957 1815). The three-star Fletschhorn Waldhotel (☎ 27 957 2131), set in the woods above Saas-Fee, houses a private art gallery and the Cäsar Ritz gourmet restaurant. Centrally-situated Unique Hotel Dom (☎ 27 957 5101) is said to be 'very impressive'.

Village eateries include the Hofsaal in the Schweizerhof and the Cheminée. The Fletschhorn Waldhotel has 'a delightful atmosphere and good food'. Saas-Fee offers 'plenty to do in the evenings'. The Crazy Night is the hippest techno venue, with a Chevy on the dance floor. Rowdy drinking is frequent at Nesti's Ski Bar. Popcorn in the Hotel Dom is the town's hot-spot ('lively, with good service and a comfortable mix of ages').

The Bears Club in the Hotel Berghof offers all-day care for children from four to six years old, while the Marmot Club is for little ones from one month of age.

## Saas-Fee: At a glance

**Tel** 41 27 958 1858
**Email** to@saas-fee.ch
**Website** www.saas-fee.ch
**Lifts in resort** 22: 1🚠 7🚡 1🚏 13🎿
**Lift opening dates** 4 December 2004 to 24 April 2005. Summer skiing on glacier from 3 July 2004

# St Moritz

**ALTITUDE 1,800m (5,904ft)**                    map: see page 200

## ❋ fine dining ❋ good snow record ❋ wealth of luxury hotels ❋ beautiful scenery ❋ wide range of other snowsports

> **Best for:** intermediate skiers and snowboarders, non-skiers, ski-gourmets, cross-country skiers, tobogganers, bob-sledders
>
> **Not recommended for:** beginners, budget skiers and boarders, those wanting skiing convenience, people looking for Alpine charm

St Moritz is an all-round winter sports resort located on two levels, above and along the shores of a fir-lined lake in the scenic Engadine Valley, three to four hours by road from Zurich. Dorf is the name used for St Moritz centre, and Bad is on the lake below.

Winter Alpine holidays were invented here in 1864 by the British, and, while other resorts have long since emulated its seasonal formula of snow fun, few have eclipsed its hedonistic allure. However, the urban architecture is bland: the beauty of St Moritz lies not in the views of the resort itself but in the views from it.

### WHAT'S NEW
Improved terrain park at Corviglia

The resort sets a world standard for luxury and indulgence. Skating, curling, golf, cricket, polo and a number of exotic horse-racing events take place throughout the winter on the frozen lake. The Cresta, the origin of the new Olympic sport of skeleton tobogganing, has been the ultimate demonstration of machismo for more than 100 years. Even in these emancipated times when political correctness normally rules, it still maintains a sexist men-only stance. Male novices aged over 18, with an introduction to the private St Moritz Tobogganing Club, can try their luck four mornings a week from Christmas to the end of February. Speeds of up to 100kph can be achieved by riders sledging down head-first on the ice.

But for the latest craze in a town hooked on adrenaline you should head for the bob-sleigh. The world's only natural ice bob-sleigh run snakes in a series of hideous hairpin bends down towards the satellite resort of **Celerina** and is regularly used for international competitions.

The new sport of bob-run skating is just what it says it is. You don ice-hockey skates and launch yourself down the track. Once you have started on the twisting ribbon of ice, there is no way of stopping. The run takes approximately 90 seconds and the most accomplished skaters make full use of the nine serpentine corners, skimming the top of the banking to reach speeds of up to 100kph.

St Moritz has twice been the venue for the Winter Olympics, and in 2003 the resort successfully hosted the Alpine Ski World Championships for the fourth time in its history.

The Upper Engadine regional ski pass covers 56 lifts and 350km of pistes from one end of the valley to the other. Celerina, **Pontresina**, Silvaplana and Sils Maria are outlying villages with ski lifts.

### On-piste
top 3,303m (10,834ft) bottom 1,720m (5,642ft)

The region divides into the sectors of Corviglia, Corvatsch and Diavolezza–Lagalb. The home mountain of St Moritz is Corviglia. The ski area can be reached by funicular from Dorf, by cable-car from Bad, by chair-lift from Suvretta or by gondola from Celerina.

The ski area continues up to 3,057m at Piz Nair, which is reached by a 100-person cable-car. The area has a funicular and gondola with leather seats. Corvatsch, on the other side of the valley, has more advanced terrain and is accessed from Sils Maria, Silvaplana and Surlej. Diavolezza and Lagalb, both at nearly 3,000m, are reached by train or bus.

Although much of the terrain is suitable for riders, the resort's high prices for accommodation and nightlife may be off-putting. The Diavolezza area is particularly recommended for freeriding. The new terrain park at Corviglia, reached by the Munt da San Murezzan chair-lift, contains a half-pipe and obstacle course.

The frozen lakes of the Engadine and the forest trails make St Moritz one of the most interesting and beautiful cross-country areas in the Alps, with loipe of every standard. A new cross-country ski centre opened in Bad in winter 2003–4. The 42-km Engadine Marathon is held each season in St Moritz and attracts thousands of entrants.

There are nursery slopes at Corviglia, and guests at the Suvretta House hotel even have their own beginner slope. However, because of the spread-out nature of St Moritz, this is not the ideal resort in which to learn to ski. A long, gentle blue run goes down from the Marmite restaurant on Corviglia, through the woods back into St Moritz, or all the way across to the cable-car at Bad. Every sector has some blue runs. The Furtschellas drag-lifts go up to blue runs at 2,800m above Sils Maria, but beginners will have to ride the cable-car down.

The highest skiing is found at Corvatsch, which links with red runs on Furtschellas. South-facing Corviglia has a number of flattering reds, and the run under the Piz Grisch chair holds its snow well. The least busy skiing, however, is out of St Moritz in the Lagalb sector. The base areas at Corviglia and Corvatsch both suffer from crowds during peak-season weeks.

The black Hahnensee run from the top of Corvatsch winds over open snowfields and on into the woods at the edge of Bad, providing around 8km of non-stop skiing for 1,600m vertical. At Diavolezza, the Schwarzer Hang black piste drops through bands of rock for some first-rate steep skiing down the Bernina black run all the way to the bottom.

## Off-piste
The steep face of Piz Nair provides incredible thrills when enough powder snow covers the sheer rock. The long glacier itinerary from the top of Diavolezza, around and over crevasses to Morteratsch, is one of the classic off-piste routes in the Alps. Heli Bernina and Heliswiss offer heli-skiing.

## Tuition and guiding
In 1929 the St Moritz and Suvretta were Switzerland's first ski schools, and today

they are both branches of the Swiss Snowsports School (SSS), as are Snowboard School St Moritz and the Wave Snowboard School. Altogether they employ 300 instructors. A high percentage of the resort's wealthy clients book private guides, which has resulted in four companies offering private guiding, along with two heli-ski operations.

## Mountain restaurants
Renowned among snow-users and gourmets alike, the Marmite, on Corviglia, is an essential lunch spot. Reservations are always necessary. The owner, Reto Mathis, whose father, Hartly, was the first man to bring *haute cuisine* to the high mountains, weighs caviar and truffles by the kilo. Also on Corviglia, the renovated Skihütte Alpina is great for pasta and rustic charm.

Piz Nair, higher up the mountain, has a new restaurant with Swiss–Italian cuisine and an extensive wine list, while Salastrains, beside the ski school meeting-place, has a big sun deck and specialises in Mediterranean dishes. The Suvretta owns three mountain eateries – the intimate Chassellas, the Chamanna, which is frequented by snowboarders, and Trutz Lodge, which boasts self-service and à la carte.

## Accommodation
In a town where more than half the hotels have four or five stars, your choice of accommodation says much about your bank balance and social prestige. The five-star Grand Hotel des Bains Kempinski (☎ 81 838 3838), next to the cross-country track in Bad, is the best new address. It has a spa offering everything from cosmetic surgery to massage with hot oils. It also houses what is already the smartest wine bar in town, and a casino.

Badrutt's Palace Hotel (☎ 81 837 1000), with its grotesque tower, is the most famous of the five-stars and has its own private ski school. The pastel blocks of the Kulm (☎ 81 836 8000) are preferred by Cresta members. The Suvretta House (☎ 81 836 3636) is a mini-resort within a resort, with its own spa, skating-rink, nursery slope and ski lift. The Carlton (☎ 81 836 7000) has a country-house atmosphere. The four-star Schweizerhof (☎ 81 837 0707) and Steffani (☎ 81 832 2101) hotels, both with active nightlife, are downtown and good value. Three-star Hotel Waldhaus am See (☎ 81 833 7676) is pleasant, albeit a brisk walk from the town centre. Hotel Arte (☎ 81 837 5858) is a new three-star place to stay in Dorf.

## Eating in and out

Hanselmann's in the town centre has been around for more than 100 years and serves coffee, pastries and delectable ice-cream. Lunch at the Chesa Veglia, an architectural museum-piece owned by the Palace Hotel, is not expensive compared with dinner. The Grischuna at the Hotel Monopol is 'expensive but delicious'. Jöhri's Talvo specialises in local venison and game from the valley, while the Suvretta's Trutz Lodge, reached by a chair-lift that runs at night, is open for evening fondue parties.

## Après-ski

Dance the night away on a table at the Moroccan-themed King's Club, if you can afford it ('to reserve a table means a minimum drinks bill of £165'). Vivai charges a more modest SF10 a drink, but you have to pay a SF25 entrance fee. Prince is 'fun, and marginally cheaper'. Wealthy

blue-bloods hide away in the shadows of the infamous members-only Dracula Club, founded by Brigitte Bardot's ex-husband and Sixties' playboy Gunther Sachs.

The Stübli at the Schweizerhof has late-night dancing on tables, and after 10pm is 'so crowded that you could not possibly fall off'. The Muli Bar hosts Country and Western music, Bobby's Bar is for the under-20s, and the Prince disco is opposite the Kulm hotel. The Cascade Bar and the Cava Bar in the Steffani hotel are both praised. The Devil's Place bar at Hotel Waldhaus am See claims the world's biggest range of malt whisky.

## Childcare

The kindergarten in the Schweizerhof accepts children over three years old on a daily basis, with lunch included. Suvretta House's Teddy Bear Club has a kindergarten for children from 12 months old, and a dedicated children's restaurant; both are for residents. Kempi Kids Club in the Grand Hotel des Bains Kempinski officially takes children from three years, although it will care for guests' babies as well. All the ski schools accept children over four years old.

# St Moritz: At a glance

**Tel** 41 81 837 3333
**Email** information@stmoritz.ch
**Website** www.stmoritz.ch

## GETTING THERE
**Airport** Zurich 3–4hrs
**Rail** station in resort
**Road** motorway Zurich–Chur, then over Julier Pass

## THE SKIING
**Linked/nearby resorts** Celerina, Champfèr, Livigno, Pontresina, Samedan, Sils Maria, Silvaplana, Surlej, Zuoz
**Total of trails/pistes** 350km in linked area (35% easy, 25% intermediate, 40% difficult)
**Lifts in area** 56: 3🄢 8🄖 18🄛 27🄥
**Lift opening dates** late November 2004 to early May 2005

## LIFT PASSES
**Area pass** Upper Engadine (covers Celerina, Pontresina, Sils Maria, Silvaplana, St Moritz and 1 day in Livigno) SF274–347 for 6 days
**Pensioners** no reductions

## TUITION
**Ski & board** SSS (☎ 81 830 0101)
**Guiding** AAA (☎ 81 832 2233), Bergsteigerschule Pontresina (☎ 81 838 8333), Heli Bernina (☎ 81 852 4677), Heliswiss (☎ 81 852 3535), SSS, The St Moritz Experience (☎ 81 833 7714)

## CHILDREN
**Lift pass** Upper Engadine 6–15yrs SF137–312, 16–19yrs SF247–312, both for 6 days
**Ski & board school** as adults
**Kindergarten** (ski) SSS (non-ski) Kempi Kids Club (☎ 81 838 3838), Schweizerhof (☎ 81 837 0707), Teddy Bear Club at Suvretta House (☎ 81 836 3636)

## FOOD AND DRINK
Coffee SF4–5, bottle of house wine SF30–40, small beer SF5–7, soft drink SF5–6, dish of the day SF20–25

# Verbier

LTITUDE 1,500m (4,920ft)                                    map: see page 201

❄ **challenging pistes and off-piste** ❄ **large ski area**
❄ **good sunshine record**

**Best for:** experienced skiers and riders,
affluent party-goers
**Not recommended for:** beginners,
families, nervous skiers, people on a
budget

A resort that has the right balance of
everything – a big thumbs up,' was how one
eporter described it. Not only does Verbier
ave an enormous range and variety of
hallenging pistes, but it also offers some of
Europe's most exciting lift-served, off-piste
kiing. Nowhere is there a more extensive
nenu of glaciers, couloirs and deep powder
owls for advanced skiers and riders. The
Savolèyres and Lac des Vaux sectors provide
more limited playground for intermediates.

During the boom years of the 1960s and
970s, Verbier became one of Europe's
nost famous ski resorts. Then lack of
nvestment in mountain facilities, coupled
vith an abysmal sterling rate of exchange in
he late 1980s, saw it plunge in popularity.
A revamped lift system and a high pound
ave done much to redress the balance in
ecent years. However, a surfeit of old lifts
emains and one can't help feel that once
gain the resort is ill-advisedly resting on
ts laurels.

Verbier comprises a mixture of
partment blocks and chalet-style wooden
uildings. Only 1,500 of the 15,000 beds
re in hotels, and none of these has
oorstep skiing. A church with a 20-m
pire, built in 1962, dominates the
traggling village.

The resort forms part of the so-called
our Valleys, the ski area it shares with its
eighbours – Thyon, **Veysonnaz**, and
Nendaz – comprises 410km of piste served
y 94 lifts with a hands-free, computerised
ft ticket. But in practice, few skiers
enture beyond the limits of the main
Verbier lifts. Also included in the lift pass is
he separate area of **Bruson**, which is being
onsidered by international resort builder

Intrawest for a repeat of its successful
development at Les Arcs.

## On-piste
top 3,330m (10,925ft) bottom 1,500m (4,920ft)

Verbier's best skiing is not visible from the
resort and is almost impossible to decipher
from the cramped piste map, which receives
universal criticism from reporters. The main
mountain access is by the two gondolas
from the Medran base area. Day visitors are
actively encouraged to leave their cars down
in Le Châble. From Les Ruinettes mid-
station, the Funispace gondola zips up to
Attelas at 2,740m. From here skiers can
ride a cable-car up to Mont Gelé (3,023m),
ski down into the intermediate Lac des
Vaux sector for chair-lift access to Tortin
and further cable-cars to Mont-Fort
(3,330m), or ski over to the south-facing
intermediate runs of La Chaux, where the
150-person Jumbo cable-car rises to the
glacial slopes of Gentianes and Mont-Fort.

'Not a resort for the faint-hearted,'
commented one reporter. 'Nowhere on
earth can such steep slopes be reached
directly from lifts,' said another. There is a
short nursery slope mid-town on the
Moulins golf course and another crowded
area on Esserts. Those certain of their
snowploughing technique can ski blue runs
higher up the mountain on the usually
excellent snow at Lac des Vaux.

The separate intermediate mountain of
Savolèyres has been extended with a
detachable six-person chair-lift. It benefits
from sunny south-facing slopes towards
Verbier and longer, better runs down its
back side to La Tzoumaz. However, it is
impossible to ski all the way down to Les
Savolèyres base-station on piste, which is a
cause of much complaint as skiers are
diverted sideways across the mountain to a
dead-end bus stop.

Except for the one run down Mont-Fort,
all of Verbier's black pistes are classified as
'ski itineraries'. Most notorious is Tortin, a
steep, wide slope that is often dangerous to

access because of exposed rocks at the top ('lack of new snow meant that the entry involved a roller-coaster ride of increasingly dangerous bumps before turning on to a near sheer pitch that promises jeopardy rather than joy').

Gentianes offers a huge scope for bumps. Col des Mines and Vallon d'Arbi are both accessed by a traverse beginning in Lac des Vaux. Marked itineraries down to Le Châble (800m) from Verbier are seldom skiable due to poor snow cover.

Snowboarders are welcomed in Verbier, with its awesome freeriding from Mont Gelé. The 120,000 square-metre terrain park at Les Chaux offers four different runs, separate boardercross and freestyle areas, and music and a bar at the base. Both Mont-Fort and Les Ruinettes have terrain parks with half-pipes and obstacles, and there is a park at Savolèyres.

## Off-piste

'The skiing is extraordinary', enthused reporters, 'more bumps, off-piste action and full-on powder skiing than you could wish for'. Just over a decade ago Creblet, the front face of Mont Gelé, and the back of Mont-Fort down to Cleuson were considered radical descents. These days, like other high-altitude runs such as Stairway to Heaven and Hidden Valley, they are skied out within an hour of a fresh snowfall. Reporters remarked on the good tree skiing at Bruson. Bec des Rosses (3,220m) is the venue for extreme snowboarding contests, and skiing off the back down into Fionnay wins jealous admiration. The 'North Face' of Mont-Fort, with its B52 and Poubelle variants, is routinely skied, despite its lethal start. The Grand Banana and Paradise are examples of off-piste sectors that are not so much difficult to ski as dangerous to access. The services of a qualified mountain guide are essential if you plan to ski or ride off-piste.

## Tuition and guiding

Verbier has five competing ski schools, which all have good reputations. British-run European Snowsport was the new kid on the block in 2003–4. It offers a series of courses limited to only six skiers. These include an introduction to off-piste, advanced off-piste, and women-only one-day clinics. We have mixed reports of the Swiss Snowsports School (ESS), which has expanded in recent years. La Fantastique, Adrénaline and No Limits make up the rest

of the competition. Bureau des Guides is the official mountain-guiding operation. Off-piste skiers should beware of local ski bums in Pub Mont-Fort offering illegal and uninsured guiding.

## Mountain restaurants

Chez Danny is a resort institution tucked away in the woods below the Ruinettes chair-lift. Other options include Cabane du Mont Fort, a mountain refuge off the La Chaux piste, and the upstairs waiter-service restaurant at Les Ruinettes. Au Vieux Verbier, back in town beside the Médran gondolas, is 'much the best for traditional Swiss mountain fare served with a smile'. Les Ruinettes, Tortin and Gentianes self-services are all described as 'uninspired and busy'. On Savolèyres, Buvette de la Marlenaz is far off-piste. Chez Simon is recommended by reporters: 'firmly non-smoking, and absolutely brilliant'.

## Accommodation

Le Chalet d'Adrien (☎ 27 771 6200) is Verbier's only five-star hotel. It has a pleasant bar, two restaurants and a small spa, but is not particularly central. The modest Hotel de Verbier (☎ 27 771 6688) in the village square is friendly, as is Serge Tacchini's Le Mazot (☎ 27 775 3550). Both are three-stars. Around the corner, four-star Hotel Vanessa (☎ 27 775 2800) is 'wonderfully convenient with good food'. The Montpelier (☎ 27 771 6131), also four star, received praise. Three-star Hotel Bristol (☎ 27 771 6577) is said to be extremely convenient. However, 'the hotel houses a disco on the first floor, which can provide some noise late into the night'. Other three-stars include Le Chamois (☎ 27 771 6402) and Le Phenix (☎ 27 771 6844), which is 'very comfortable, central and welcoming'. The simple Les Touristes (☎ 27 771 2147) is reported to be good value for money.

Some 90 per cent of British visitors stay in tour-operator-run chalets or in the wealth of self-catering apartments. The cheaper dormitory accommodation at the Bunker (☎ 27 771 6602), next to the snowboard centre, attracts an increasing number of young snowboarders.

## Eating in and out

Roland Pierroz, at the Hotel Rosalp, is presided over by the chef/owner of the same name. It still has the finest international cuisine in Verbier. The hotel's brasserie La Pinte du Rosalp is 'less formal and less expensive.' Le Caveau has 'truly amazing fondues'. Le Bouchon Gourmand has an intimate atmosphere and cuisine from south-western France. Hotel Montpelier's restaurant offers outstanding cuisine. Appartement in Chalet d'Adrien concocts 'French-international cuisine in small portions with unique flavours'. Chez Martin, Al Capone and Pizza Taxi all serve pizzas. A-team is for take-away pizzas.

## Après-ski

Friday and Saturday are the big nights in a resort that sees a huge influx of regular weekenders from Geneva and London. Hotel Farinet on the Place Centrale is under new ownership and has quickly established itself as the most popular spot in town. As the lifts close, what seems like half the population of Verbier crushes into the glass-sided terrace bar, which has live music. The hotel's inadequate restaurant has been replaced by a second bar – a comfortable lounge bar with deep leather sofas for those who prefer to talk as well as drink.

Offshore ('breakfasts and après-ski drinks take some beating') and Le Fer à Cheval are both busy by mid-afternoon. Chalet girls and ski bums flock to the Pub Mont-Fort ('lively, with cheap drinks'). Later on, Crok No Name acts as a sophisticated warm-up bar for the nightclubs, of which The Farm Club still dominates. Spirits or champagne prices hover around the £100 mark, but this does not deter the long line-up of affluent customers.The Moroccan-themed Casbah beneath the Hotel Farinet has replaced Marshal's. VIP guests have their own private room adjoining the dance floor. Taratata, known universally as Tara's, attracts a younger crowd. Entrance to most clubs is free, although some charge £5–10 in the final hours before their 4am closure.

## Childcare

The Kids Club skiing programme for children over three years is run by La Maison du Sport and based at the Moulins nursery site, which has its own lift and restaurant. Les Schtroumpfs has an excellent reputation for day-long indoor childminding (ages five months to seven years) and has now moved to the Moulins nursery site too.

# Verbier: At a glance

**Tel** 41 27 775 3888
**Email** info@verbier.ch
**Website** www.verbier.ch

## GETTING THERE
**Airport** Geneva 2hrs
**Rail** Le Châble 15mins
**Road** motorway Geneva–Martigny, then mountain road to resort

## THE SKIING
**Linked/nearby resorts** Bruson, Champex-Lac, Nendaz, Siviez, Thyon, La Tzoumaz, Veysonnaz
**Total of trails/pistes** 150km in Verbier, 410km in Four Valleys area (33% easy, 42% intermediate, 6% difficult, 19% very difficult)
**Lifts in area** 94: 17🚠 32🚡 45🎿
**Lift opening dates** mid-November 2004 to 24 April 2005

## LIFT PASSES
**Area pass** Four Valleys SF306 for 6 days. Family Pass (covers whole area) SF306 for 1st adult, 30%

reduction for 2nd, 30% reduction for 16–20yrs, 15% reduction for 17–20yrs
**Pensioners** Four Valleys 65yrs and over SF214 for 6 days

## TUITION
**Ski & board** Adrénaline (☎ 27 771 7459), ESS (☎ 27 775 3363), European Snowsport (☎ 27 771 6222), La Fantastique (☎ 27 771 4141), No Limits (☎ 27 771 5556)
**Guiding** Air Glaciers (heli-ski) (☎ 27 329 1415), Bureau des Guides (☎ 27 775 3363), No Limits (☎ 27 771 7250)

## CHILDREN
**Lift pass** Four Valleys 7–15yrs SF214 (part of Family Pass) for 6 days
**Ski & board school** as adults
**Kindergarten** (ski) Kids Club (☎ 27 775 3663), (non-ski) Les Schtroumpfs (☎ 27 771 6585)

## FOOD AND DRINK
Coffee SF3.50–4, bottle of house wine SF30, small beer SF5, soft drink SF5, dish of the day SF20

# Villars

**ALTITUDE 1,300m (4,265ft)**

## ❉ underrated intermediate ski area ❉ easy airport access
## ❉ popular resort for Britons

**Best for:** beginners, intermediates, families, snowboarders, weekenders

**Not recommended for:** advanced piste skiers and riders, off-piste enthusiasts

Villars sits above the Rhône Valley in the beautiful Vaudois Mountains, a 90-minute drive from Geneva.

Snow cover at this low altitude is often uncertain. However, Villars shares its ski area and a new electronic lift pass with the neighbouring resort of **Les Diablerets**, which has a 3,000m glacier. The downside of this promise of certain snow is that first you have to go to Les Diablerets then take a bus to the base-station of the glacier cable-car at Reusch.

### On the snow
**top 2,113m (6,932ft) bottom 1,300m (4,265ft)**

From the centre of Villars, a cog mountain railway transports skiers to the mid-mountain station of Bretaye at 1,800m. A gondola from the edge of town up to Roc d'Orsay just above Bretaye provides a speedy alternative means of access. A second gondola from the nearby village of Barboleusaz also feeds into the system.

### WHAT'S NEW

Hands-free electronic lift pass
Ski lift from Restaurant du Lac des Chavonnes to bottom of Petit Chamossaire chair

From Bretaye, the recently upgraded lift has speeded up journey times to the long blue and red cruising runs at Les Chaux and the pistes leading down through the woods to Les Diablerets.

The area is essentially suited to intermediates, although a couple of runs, including the black Bouquetin from Roc d'Orsay down to Villars, provide reasonable challenge. The terrain parks are at Bretaye and Les Chaux.

Both the traditional Swiss Snowsports School (ESS) and its rival, Villars Ski School, use the graduated-length method of teaching. Riderschool is the snowboarding specialist and specialises in freeride.

Le Mazot at Meilleret is said to be 'by far the best mountain restaurant'. Café Bretaye is praised by another reporter. Restaurant du Lac des Chevonnes is in a delightful lake-side setting at Bretaye and there is a new lift from here to the bottom of the Petit Chamossaire chair. Restaurant des Chaux was warmly praised by reporters.

### In the resort

Recommended hotels include the five-star Grand Hotel du Parc and the four-star Eurotel Victoria. La Renardière (☎ 24 495 2592) is described as 'a friendy three-star with a cosy atmosphere'. The four-star Hotel du Golf, three-stars Alpe Fleurie and Ecureuil are all said to be child-friendly. All hotels can be booked through a central reservations office (☎ 24 495 3232).

Recommended restaurants include Ecovets, Le Vieux Villars, Chez Sylvie and La Crémaillère. Pasta Basta in Chesières, Le Sporting in Villars and L'Escale at Gryon below Les Chaux are informal and less expensive alternatives.

Night action includes jazz at L'Alchemiste, live rock and pool at Café Central and drinking at Charlie's Bar. All ages dance the night away at El Gringo.

Snowli (the ESS kindergarten) and Villars Ski School both accept children from three years of age at Bretaye. La Trottinette in Villars centre looks after non-skiing children aged two months to six years.

### Villars: at a glance

**Tel** 41 24 495 3232
**Email** information@villars.ch
**Website** www.villars.ch
**Lifts in region** 38: 1⬛ 4⬛ 15⬛ 18⬛
**Lift opening dates** mid-December 2004 to mid-April 2005. Summer skiing on Les Diablerets Glacier

# Wengen

**ALTITUDE 1,274m (4,180ft)**                                    map: see page 198

❄ **car-free traditional mountain-side resort** ❄ **exceptional views**
❄ **large intermediate ski area**

---

**Best for:** beginners, intermediates, off-
piste skiers, mountain lunchers, railway
enthusiasts, non-skiers
**Not recommended for:** young ski-aged
children, advanced piste skiers

---

Wengen, together with neighbouring
**Grindelwald** and **Mürren** in this beautiful
corner of the Bernese Oberland, is the
birthplace of package ski tourism, in which
trains played – and continue to play – a crucial
role. The mountain railway came to the region
as early as the 1880s, bringing at first summer
and later winter tourists. The Downhill Only
Club, one of Britain's oldest surviving and still
active ski organisations, was formed in
Wengen in February 1925 to race against their
Kandahar Club rivals in Mürren.

Although recently expanded, Wengen is
basically a single pedestrian street of shops
and a cluster of hotels and chalets around
the railway station, which brings skiers up
from **Lauterbrunnen** and on to Kleine
Scheidegg. Trains stop at way-side halts
throughout the area, and run as accurately
as a Swiss watch to a timetable printed on
the back of the piste map.

---

## WHAT'S NEW
4-person chair-lift at Läger

---

The three resorts of Wengen, Mürren
and Grindelwald share a ski pass that
covers 41 lifts against the awesome
backdrop of the Eiger, Mönch and Jungfrau
mountains. Despite some recent
modification, the lift system is still in
serious need of an overall upgrade ('stay
above the Männlichen mid-station to avoid
the poor linking of the lower runs').

Snowfall in the region is extremely
variable, and natural cover cannot be relied
on either early or late in the season.
However, a network of snow-cannon can
usually make up for any shortfall.

## On-piste
top 2,320m (7,612ft) bottom 1,034m (3,393ft)

Mountain access from the village is by the
Männlichen cable-car to the ridge
separating the Wengen and Grindelwald
valleys. Alternatively, skiers can take the
train up to Kleine Scheidegg or the
Eigergletscher beyond. From here, a
network of chairs and drag-lifts serves runs
leading back to Wengen or down to
Grindelwald. Non-skiers can also take the
dramatic train ride from the Eigergletscher
through the Eiger and on up to the
Jungfraujoch, at 3,454m.

Wengen has an excellent nursery area in
the middle of the village. Blue and red runs
predominate throughout the ski area that it
shares with Grindelwald, but advanced
skiers will find that most of the handful of
blacks lack real challenge. However, the
World Cup racecourse which, at 4.5km is
the longest in the world, is testing.

Wengen has a terrain park with a variety
of jumps and obstacles, served by the Wixi
lift.

## Off-piste
The Wengen area has a great deal of easily
accessible off-piste skiing. The White Hare,
which starts from the foot of the
Eigerwand, is dramatic and exciting.

## Tuition and guiding
The Swiss Snowsports School (SSS) gives
mornings-only group lessons as well as
private lessons in the morning and
afternoon. The one-to-one Privat Ski and
Snowboard School 'has young English-
speaking teachers, who give friendly,
encouraging tuition'.

## Mountain restaurants
The Hotel Jungfrau at Wengernalp has
beautiful views, a friendly atmosphere and
the best Rösti ('avoid the gorgonzola. It will
blow your socks off'). The Kleine Scheidegg
station buffet 'has got to be the best station
buffet in the world'.

## Accommodation

The four-star Park Hotel Beausite (☎ 33 856 5161) is 'very friendly, great service, good food'. The four-star Hotel Sunstar (☎ 33 856 5111) provides family duplexes and a swimming-pool, and is one of the most conveniently placed hotels in town.

Of the three-stars, Bernerhof (☎ 33 855 2721) is 'friendly and comfortable', while Hotel Eiger (☎ 33 855 1131) is central and has long been a favourite among the British. The ski-in, ski-out Hotel Brunner (☎ 33 855 2494) is described as 'one of those Alpine secrets that visitors – many of them with children – like to keep to themselves'. Falken (☎ 33 856 5121) is 'delightfully old-fashioned' and 'very comfortable', and Hotel Alpenruhe (☎ 33 856 2400) is warmly recommended.

## Eating in and out

Most restaurants in Wengen are in hotels, but Sina's Italian is 'good value for money in a warm and friendly ambience'. Mary's Café offers cheese fondue accompanied by Alphorn-blowing contests on Tuesdays. Restaurant Hirschenstübli in the Hotel Hirschen specialises in fondue *chinoise*. The Berghaus is known for its fresh fish and the Bernerhof for fondue and raclette. On sunny days, Hotel Eiger and the Silberhorn have outdoor tables.

## Après-ski

The last ski trains of the day are full of families with toboggans going up to Wengernalp for the 4-km descent back to the village. The Tipi Après Ski Bar at Kleine Scheidegg is busier during the skiing day than in late afternoons. Crowds gather in Mary's Café, and the ice-bar outside Hotel Brunner is lively. For tea-and-cakes go to Café Grübi, which is full of atmosphere. The Tanne, Sina's Pub, Hot Chilli, Rocks Bar and Pickel Bar are popular watering-holes, while Tiffany's disco is in the Silberhorn. Wengen has a magnificent skating-rink.

## Childcare

Wengen's biggest single failing is its lack of childcare outside ski school. The Swiss Snowsports School (SSS) runs morning-only group lessons, which 'makes life almost impossible for families with small ski-age children. Parents effectively end their skiing day at lunch-time'. Alternatively you can book private lessons with Privat Ski and Snowboard School at any time of day. The non-ski Sylvie's Playhouse accepts children from 18 months to seven years and has a sound reputation.

# Wengen: At a glance

**Tel** 41 33 855 1414
**Email** info@wengen.ch
**Website** www.wengen-muerren.ch

### GETTING THERE
**Airports** Zurich 3hrs, Geneva 4hrs
**Rail** station in resort
**Road** motorway Bern–Interlaken, road to Lauterbrunnen, funicular to resort

### THE SKIING
**Linked/nearby resorts** Grindelwald, Lauterbrunnen, Mürren
**Total of trails/pistes** 213km in Jungfrau Top Ski region (28% easy, 57% intermediate, 15% difficult)
**Lifts in area** 41: 5🚡 7🚠 15🚋 14🎢
**Lift opening dates** 4 December 2004 to 17 April 2005. Summer skiing at Jungfraujoch

### LIFT PASSES
**Area pass** Jungfrau (covers Grindelwald, Mürren, Wengen) SF288 for 6 days
**Pensioners** Jungfrau from 62yrs SF259 for 6 days

### TUITION
**Ski & board** Privat Ski and Snowboard School (☎ 33 855 5005), SSS (☎ 33 856 2022)
**Guiding** through ski schools

### CHILDREN
**Lift pass** Jungfrau under 6yrs SF25 (or free if with parent), 6–15yrs SF144, 16–19yrs SF230, all for 6 days
**Ski & board school** as adults
**Kindergarten** (non-ski) Sylvie's Playhouse (☎ 33 855 3681)

### FOOD AND DRINK
Coffee SF4, bottle of house wine SF25–30, small beer SF4.50–5, soft drink SF4.50 , dish of the day SF18–25

# Zermatt

**ALTITUDE 1,620m (5,314ft)**                                          **map: see page 202**

## ❊ superb scenery ❊ Alpine charm ❊ luxury accommodation ❊ excellent ski school

**Best for:** gourmet skiers, powderhounds, non-skiers, beginners, advanced skiers and riders

**Not recommended for:** budget skiers, second-weekers

After decades of resting on the laurels of its outstandingly beautiful scenery dominated by the Matterhorn, Zermatt has finally seen it to upgrade its lift system and bring its ski area up to the demanding standards of one of the world's top five resorts. This has come about as a result of a merger between the three separate lift companies, and improvements continue to take place on an annual basis. 'If you were to visit only one resort in the world, this should be it,' enthused one reporter. Arriving by train from the hamlet of Täsch is a breathtaking experience – backpackers and fur-clad socialites alike are awestruck by the majesty of the high Alpine setting.

Zermatt was a settlement from the early Middle Ages and in its narrow lanes sheep are still shorn outside centuries-old wooden *mazots* (barns on stilts) beside gleaming modern hotels. The conflux of electric taxis and horse-drawn carriages on the main thoroughfare provides a fresh interpretation of 'car free'. Complimentary but inadequate ski buses link the separate ski areas.

Zermatt is linked across the back of the Klein Matterhorn with **Cervinia**. It is possible to buy a daily extension for Italy, but if you plan on more than one visit in a week it is worth buying the joint lift pass. The summer skiing area at Klein Matterhorn is open all year round.

## On-piste

top 3,899m (12,788ft) bottom 1,620m (5,314ft)

The three once-separate ski areas are linked, albeit tenuously, and the cable-car from Gant to Hohtälli effectively links the Sunnegga and Gornergrat areas and dispenses with the necessity of taking the

long, slow, but beautiful train journey up the Gornergrat.

The Matterhorn Express gondola takes skiers from the Klein Matterhorn base to Furi and on to Schwarzsee, providing an alternative route to Trockener Steg and doing away with the formerly heavy rush-hour congestion. The long, cold T-bar from Trockener Steg to Furggsattel is now a six-person covered chair that begins in Switzerland and ends in Italy. Reporters say that it is a major improvement but during its first winter of operation it was often closed due to high winds.

An underground funicular runs up to the Sunnegga sector, with sunny slopes continuing up to Blauherd and Rothorn, which are connected by an efficient cable-car. Most of the skiing suits competent intermediates, but more challenging slopes can be found in each sector.

Triftji is one of the most famous black runs in the Alps. Unfortunately, this and the other difficult trails under the Hohtälli–Rote Nase sector do not receive sufficient snow early on, so they are often closed until mid-January.

Zermatt is a serious destination for snowboarders, with stupendous possibilities for freeriding. Blauherd's terrain park has a special area for beginners. The Trockener Steg park contains slides and tubes. Klein Matterhorn has a year-round half-pipe.

## Off-piste

Zermatt has superb powder possibilities but a guide is essential, particularly for the Klein Matterhorn sector, which is heavily crevassed. A day's heli-skiing excursion to the Monte Rosa or the Alphubeljoch above Zermatt is a popular way to escape the pistes.

## Tuition and guiding

Since the establishment of Stoked The Ski School, Zermatt is no longer a 'closed' resort for complete novices. Indeed, this school is at the forefront of modern teaching techniques at all levels and is a compelling reason for choosing the resort. Its young, international team (all the full-time instructors are aged between 18 and 31) provides the competition that the old and staid Swiss Snowsports School (SSS) sorely lacked, although the SSS has slowly risen to the challenge and improved its standards. Stoked also runs a separate snowboarding school.

## Mountain restaurants

This is no place to pack a picnic – not when old wooden barns such as Chez Vrony in Findeln provide crystal glasses, starched napkins, sofas on the terrace and intimate nooks and crannies for serious dining. Also in Findeln, the Findlerhof and Paradies are warmly recommended. The centuries-old hamlet of Zum See houses a restaurant of the same name, which is run by Max and Greti and has an established reputation as one of Zermatt's best. Higher up in the Furi sector, Simi is the Rösti headquarters but also serves delicious salads at reasonable prices. Alphittä at Riffelalp has delectable pasta. Fluhalp, on the way to Gant, offers some of the finest food and certainly the best panorama of the Matterhorn. Stafelalp has unusual views of the Matterhorn and specialises in Rösti and sweet omelettes. Wherever you go, even in low season, it is essential to book in advance.

### WHAT'S NEW

6-person covered chair-lift from Riffelberg to Gifthittli
Gandegg and Theodulpass drag-lifts replaced by a single drag-lift

## Accommodation

Most accommodation is in hotels, of which there are 116 including three five-stars and 35 four-stars, but a handful of tour operators have catered chalets and it is also possible to rent surprisingly cheap apartments through the tourist office. The venerable Zermatterhof (☎ 27 966 6600) and the rival Mont Cervin (☎ 27 966 8888) are the five-star establishments in town, while up the mountain in the Gornergrat sector the Riffelalp (☎ 27 966 0505) is a luxurious mini-resort in its own right.

The four-star Monte Rosa (☎ 27 966 0333), a favourite of Sir Winston Churchill and the base from which Edward Whymper,

the Victorian mountaineer, set off to conquer the Matterhorn, exudes understated opulence. The four-star Alex (☎ 27 966 7070), an Alpine–Byzantine mélange, boasts a nightclub and swimming-pool, while its sister hotel, the Schlosshotel Tenne (☎ 27 967 4400) – tucked down an alleyway near the railway station – is just as bizarre. The modern Hotel Albana Real (☎ 27 966 6161) is warmly recommended, and Hotel Nicoletta (☎ 27 966 0777) and Hotel La Ginabelle (☎ 27 966 5000) are both commended for families.

Acclaimed three-stars include Hotel Holiday (☎ 27 967 1203), a family-run establishment with good food, close to the Sunnegga Express, and nearby Hotel Parnass (☎ 27 967 1179). Hotel Biner (☎ 27 966 5666), near the railway station, is a three-star with five-star facilities including a spa with huge swimming-pool. The hotel's modern interior includes a mixture of loft bedrooms and white-painted bedrooms containing works of art. Hotel Bijou (☎ 27 966 5151), two minutes' walk from the Klein Matterhorn lift, is praised by several reporters for its rooms and cuisine. Hotel City (☎ 27 966 3940) is said to be good value for money. The Excelsior (☎ 27 966 3500) is 'central, next to a bus stop, and caters for vegetarians'. We also have good reports of the Darioli B&B (☎ 27 967 2748).

A number of high-quality private chalets are available to rent, including four-star Haus Turquino (☎ 27 967 4503), Chalet Sunnu Biela (☎ 62 822 0555), Chalet Graziella (☎ 27 967 2041), Chalet Huwi (☎ 27 968 1130), and Chalet Nachtigall (☎ 27 967 1685).

## Eating in and out

Le Gitan in Hotel Darioli is highly praised. Lamb from the owner's own flock is succulent at the Schäferstübli in Hotel Julen. Le Mazot, an old favourite among reporters, also specialises in lamb. Hotel Albana Real houses Rua Thai, where exotic dishes are created by two chefs from the five-star Shangri-la Hotel in Bangkok. Casa Rustica is as pastoral as its name, and serves good food. Mood's is cutting edge, with a glass floor and ultra-modern designer furniture. Tony's Grotta has 'excellent, but expensive Italian food'. Cuisine at the Gourmetstübli in Hotel Schönegg (☎ 27 966 3434) has an Asian influence.

# Après-ski

Elsie's Bar, by the church, is irresistible for champagne and oysters or snails (despite the crowds and expense). The Post Hotel complex continues to cater for almost everybody, the Pink Elephant hosts live jazz, Le Village is for house music, and Le Broken is a traditional disco where dancing on huge beer barrels is encouraged until 3am. The former owners of the Post have moved to Mood's, taking their considerable cocktail-bar clientèle with them.

Hotel Alex's nightclub is sedate but is the only place where the 30-plus age group can dance to music that allows conversation. Grampi's Pub ('good service and a friendly atmosphere') is a glass-fronted haunt. Z'Alt Hischi is a small, atmospheric, 'rusty little nook' in the old part of town, with an extensive collection of Rolling Stones CDs. The North Wall, the Brown Cow, and the T-Bar in Hotel Pollux are where you find the resort workers. Vernissage is brimming with atmosphere and is unusually decorated with furniture and light fittings constructed from recycled eclectica such as old bicycle parts and bath plugs. Reporters rated the Papperla one of the coolest après-ski spots in town.

# Childcare

Stoked The Ski School has moved its children's ski school and Stoked Snowflakes Kids Club to a sunny location at the top of the Matterhorn Express at Schwarzee. It accepts children aged three to eight on a flexible basis. The SSS Snowli Snow Club ('where kids can jump around on the snow with a huge cuddly penguin') offers weekday ski courses for ages six to twelve and cares for four- to six-year-olds all day at its kindergarten at Riffelberg. Children meet outside the tourist information office then travel up (and down) by special train. The SSS also accepts children from six to twelve years with supervised lunch at Blauherd or Riffelberg. The resort has three magic carpets.

The kindergarten in Hotel Nicoletta takes kids from two to eight years on weekdays, with lunch included. Childminding for children from two-and-a-half is available at Hotel La Ginabelle's Kinderclub Pumuckel six days a week. Kinderparadies Zermatt has an indoor playground and accepts little ones from three months old, daily, and also runs a babysitting service until 10pm.

# Zermatt: At a glance

**Tel** 41 27 966 8100
**Email** zermatt@wallis.ch
**Website** www.zermatt.ch

## GETTING THERE
**Airports** Sion 1½hrs, Geneva 4hrs
**Rail** Geneva–Zermatt via Visp
**Road** park car in Täsch and complete journey by rail

## THE SKIING
**Linked/nearby resorts** Cervinia, Crans Montana, Grächen, Riederalp, Saas-Fee
**Total of trails/pistes** 200km in Zermatt (10% easy, 54% intermediate, 36% difficult), 400km with Cervinia
**Lifts in area** 62 with Cervinia: 2🚠 19🚡 20🎿 21🪑
**Lift opening dates** 27 November 2004 to 1 May 2005. Summer skiing on Klein Matterhorn Glacier

## LIFT PASSES
**Area pass** Zermatt only SF326, Zermatt–Cervinia SF368, both for 6 days

**Pensioners** Zermatt only 65yrs and over SF277, Zermatt–Cervinia 65yrs and over SF313, both for 6 days

## TUITION
**Ski & board** SSS (☎ 27 966 2466), Stoked The Ski & Snowboarding School (☎ 27 967 7020)
**Guiding** Air Zermatt (☎ 27 966 8686), Alpin Center (☎ 27 966 2460)

## CHILDREN
**Lift pass** Zermatt only 9–16yrs SF163, Zermatt–Cervinia 9–16yrs SF184, both for 6 days
**Ski & board school** as adults
**Kindergarten** (ski) Stoked Snowflakes Kids Club (☎ 27 967 4340), (ski/non-ski) SSS Snowli Snow Club (☎ 27 966 2466), (non-ski) Club Nico at Hotel Nicoletta (☎ 27 966 0777), Kinderclub Pumuckel at Hotel La Ginabelle (☎ 27 966 5000), Kinderparadies Zermatt (☎ 27 967 7252)

## FOOD AND DRINK
Coffee SF4–5, bottle of house wine SF30–40, small beer SF5–7 soft drink SF5–6, dish of the day SF20–28

# UNITED STATES

## Aspen and Snowmass

ALTITUDE 7,945ft (2,422m)                    map: see pages 203 & 20

❋ **skiing and snowboarding for all standards**
❋ **atmospheric Victorian town (Aspen)** ❋ **wide choice of restaurants**

---

**Best for:** families, off-piste skiers and snowboarders, ski gourmets, shoppers, night-owls, non-skiers, star-spotters
**Not recommended for:** people on a budget

---

The town of Aspen lies at the foot of Aspen Mountain (also known as Ajax), and its first claim to fame was as a silver-mining centre. Today it boasts about 200 shops and a wonderful variety of restaurants. Planners have managed to conserve the low-rise appeal of the original nineteenth-century mining town, with older buildings authentically refurbished and recent additions built in sympathetic style.

Aspen continues to attract big names in show business and sport, some of whom, such as Jack Nicholson, Michael Douglas, Melanie Griffiths and Antonio Banderas, have made their homes here. What these celebrities have in common is that they are all fanatical skiers. Indeed Aspen and Snowmass offer some of the best skiing in North America for all standards.

### WHAT'S NEW

High-speed quad-chair at Buttermilk West
High-speed chair-lift at Aspen Mountain

'The skiing and the resort is world class with some fabulous eating and drinking venues,' enthused reporters. Although considerably larger than most US ski resorts, Aspen's centre is relatively compact, and outlying hotels and the ski areas are served by a highly efficient bus service. Day-to-day living is more expensive than in any of Aspen's Colorado counterparts – apart from Vail. However, with a little care in your choice of

restaurants and nightlife, it is possible to have a moderately priced holiday.

Snowmass, which is nine miles out of town, is an alternative and cheaper accommodation base, and Aspen Highlands village, situated three miles from Aspen, is another slope-side option for serious skiers.

Aspen has its own airport, three miles from town. It is also an easy 70-mile drive from Eagle County/Vail airport.

### On-piste
top 12,518ft (3,815m) bottom 7,870ft (2,399m)

Aspen/Snowmass covers four separate mountains: Aspen Mountain, Aspen Highlands, Snowmass and Buttermilk. Aspen Mountain is strictly the reserve of good skiers and snowboarders – it has no beginner slopes. It suffers from having a rather antiquated gondola but it is well worth the uphill journey. Highlands offers the toughest, most radical terrain and greatly adds to Aspen's appeal for advanced skiers. Snowmass provides the best all-round skiing, while Buttermilk is ideal novices' terrain, with no hidden surprises.

The area below Buttermilk's West Summit is packed with green runs, and more advanced beginners will thrive on a large network of long blues. A new quad-lif at Buttermilk West has a mid-station stop t access the beginner skiing area. The nurser area at Snowmass hugs the lower slopes an is accessed by the Fanny Hill high-speed quad. At Aspen Highlands, the main nursery slopes are mid-mountain.

Of the four mountains, Snowmass has th largest intermediate appeal, with almost every run mid-mountain and below providin good cruising. The mountain is famous for it Big Burn area, where a clutch of blue trails provides almost unlimited scope for cruising Aspen Highlands has a range of green and blue trails for the less demanding. Plenty of strong intermediate skiing with top-to-bottom cruising is found on Aspen Mountain. The best area for middling skiers at Highlands is near the top of the mountain, where the Cloud Nine lift accesses runs such as Scarlett's, Grand Prix and Gunbarrel.

Aspen Mountain is riddled with short, sharp and quite steep double-black-diamond chutes, including the famous 'dump runs' such as Bear Paw, Short Snort and Zaugg Dump, which were created by miners' spoil. Walsh's is considered to be the most challenging trail. The area has a new high-speed chair-lift. At Highlands, the large and challenging gladed area to the left of the Exhibition quad-chair includes Bob's Glade, Upper Stein and Golden Horn Woods, which are all double-black-diamonds. With the addition of G-Trees, the whole bowl is now open for skiing and riding. Snowmass has the most double-black-diamond terrain of the four mountains, and real challenges can be found in the largely gladed chutes in the Hanging Valley Wall and Hanging Valley Glades. The Cirque has even steeper terrain mainly above the tree-line.

Buttermilk has ideal rolling terrain for riders as well as one of the largest terrain parks in the world, Crazy T'rain. Snowmass boasts a competition-sized half-pipe, a beginners' half-pipe and a terrain park, while superlative riding and skiing can be accessed by snowcat off the back of Aspen Mountain.

## Off-piste

Aspen Highlands offers some of the most exhilarating off-piste terrain in the valley, much of it accessed by the Loge Peak quad-chair at the top of the ski area. The chair follows a ridge with steep terrain on both sides. As you ride up, a dramatic area known as Steeplechase opens up on your left; this comprises about half-a-dozen steep chutes. On your right is even steeper terrain in Olympic Bowl, although the gradient is not always fully appreciable until you have progressed some way down the slopes. New steep areas in Highlands Bowl have been opened, offering some of the most radical terrain of any resort in the USA.

Snowmass has some new extreme terrain featuring spectacular cliff jumps that are not for the faint-hearted.

## Tuition and guiding

As well as traditional lessons, the Ski and Snowboard School of Aspen offers courses

including biathlon, powder clinics, race-training, skiing for the disabled, and seniors' and women's ski seminars. Too Cool For School provides teen skiing classes.

## Mountain restaurants

Cloud Nine Café at Highlands is a former ski patrol that has been transformed into a small gourmet restaurant (the nearest you will find to a European mountain restaurant in the US). On Aspen Mountain, Bonnie's is praised ('good food without silly prices') along with the Ajax Tavern.

At Snowmass, recommended restaurants include Gordon's High Alpine, Up 4 Pizza and Ullrhof. Sam's Knob is a welcoming little restaurant with white linen tablecloths and serves northern Italian fare, while Café Suzanne, at the bottom of the Elk Camp lift, specialises in French food.

Buttermilk has two mountain restaurants: Bumps at the base, which includes a rôtisserie and grill; and the Cliffhouse, at the top of the Summit Express.

## Accommodation

In Aspen, skiers who can afford to live like celebrities should try Hotel Jerome (☎ 970 920 1000), the Little Nell (☎ 970 920 4600) and the St Regis Aspen (☎ 970 920 3300). The St Regis' refurbishment will be complete for the 2004–5 season and includes 20 new rooms and suites, some with loft sleeping areas for families, as well as a new spa and restaurant. More modestly priced alternatives include Limelite Lodge (☎ 970 925 3025), Hotel Durant (☎ 970 925 8500) and the Innsbruck Inn (☎ 970 925 2980). The Aspen Mountain Lodge (☎ 970 925 7650) is a little more expensive but is also praised. St Moritz Lodge (☎ 970 925 3220) is a low-cost alternative base. Besides its regular hotel bedrooms, it has three-bedded dorm-style rooms.

Top-of-the-range accommodation at Snowmass includes the Silvertree Hotel (☎ 970 923 3520), the Snowmass Club (☎ 970 923 5600), the Chamonix (☎ 970 923 3232) and Crestwood (☎ 970 923 2450). More reasonably priced are the Snowmass Mountain Chalet (☎ 970 923 3900) and the Stonebridge Inn (☎ 970 923 2420). For those counting their cents, the Pokolodi Lodge (☎ 970 923 4310) and the Snowmass Inn (☎ 970 923 4302) are both close to the slopes, as are the Aspenwood (☎ 970 923 2711) and Laurelwood (☎ 970 923 3110) condominiums. The

Virtual Hostel, accessed on www.aspensnowmass.com, offers last-minute accommodation deals.

## Eating in and out

The St Regis Aspen houses Olives Aspen, which serves Mediterranean-inspired American food. Chart House on East Durant is well known for steaks and seafood, L'Hostaria is an authentic Italian restaurant, and Pacifica offers a fine selection of seafood and a caviar menu. Popular Mezzaluna serves pizzas and Italian specialities. Aspen features three gourmet Japanese restaurants – Kenichi, Takah Sushi and Matsuhisa – while Sage, in the Snowmass Club, is a bistro serving contemporary Colorado cuisine. Asie offers pan-Asian cuisine in hip surroundings, and the Colony features dining from the former British colonies. La Cocina, Little Annie's, the Steak Pit, Jimmy's, the Mother Lode and Ute City Bar are lower-priced. One reporter suggested: 'by night, eat at some of the best restaurants – but at the bar, not at a table. The same food in slightly smaller portions costs a fraction of the price'. Two new restaurants are Wild Fig, which opened to rave reviews in January 2004, and Umbria, which will open at the start of 2004–5.

## Après-ski

The Jerome Bar (better known as the J-Bar), where miners once congregated, offers Happy Hour beer at $1 a pint. The sundeck at the Ajax Tavern attracts the crowds when the lifts close, and Shooters is a Country and Western saloon with live bands. Mezzaluna serves inexpensive beers and pizzas. Aspen Billiards is casually elegant and smoke-free. Club Chelsea attracts a sophisticated clientèle, whereas the glitterati congregate at the Caribou Club. The health-conscious can try the Aspen Club and Spa or the new St Regis spa.

## Childcare

Aspen has an in-town nursery service (Kids Room) and a kindergarten at each mountain base. At Snowmass, Snow Cubs caters for children aged from eight weeks. Older children can join the Big Burn Bears or the Grizzlies. A new interactive Family Zone has been created at Snowmass. Powder Pandas at Buttermilk is for three- to six-year olds.

# Aspen and Snowmass: At a glance

**Tel** 1 970 925 1220
**Email** info@aspensnowmass.com
**Website** www.aspensnowmass.com

### GETTING THERE
**Airports** Aspen 10 mins, Eagle County/Vail 1½hrs, Denver 3½hrs
**Road** 3½hr drive from Denver on I-70 to Glenwood Springs, then Highway 82

### THE SKIING
**Linked/nearby resorts** none
**Total of trails/pistes** 4,893 acres on 4 mountains (16% easy, 40% intermediate, 24% difficult, 20% very difficult)
**Lifts in area** 37: 1🚠 32🚡 4🎿
**Lift opening dates** 25 November 2004 to 3 April 2005 (Buttermilk/Aspen Highlands) or 10 April 2005 (Aspen Mountain/Snowmass)

### LIFT PASSES
**Area pass** (covers all 4 mountains) $346–384 for 6 days, $307 for advance bookings
**Pensioners** 65–69yrs $294–372 for 6 days. Silver

Pass (unlimited skiing all season) for 69yrs and over $129

### TUITION
**Ski & board** Ski and Snowboard School of Aspen (☎ 970 925 1227)
**Guiding** Aspen Adventures (☎ 970 925 7625), Aspen Mountain Powder Tours (☎ 970 920 0720) and through ski school

### CHILDREN
**Lift pass** 7–17yrs $228–239 for 6 days
**Ski and board school** as adults, Too Cool For School (☎ 970 923 1227)
**Kindergarten** (ski) through ski school, one at each base area (☎ 970 925 1227), (non-ski) Aspen: Kids Room (☎ 701 456 7888), Buttermilk: Powder Pandas (☎ 970 923 1227). Snowmass: Big Burn Bears (☎ 970 923 0570 ), Grizzlies (☎ 970 923 0580), Snow Cubs (☎ 970 923 0563)

### FOOD AND DRINK
Coffee $2.50 (free at mountain bases), bottle of house wine $20–22, small beer $4.50, soft drink $2.50, dish of the day $10–20

# Beaver Creek

**ALTITUDE 8,100ft (2,470m)**  map: see page 205

❄ **good snow record** ❄ **long cruising runs** ❄ **excellent ski school**
❄ **top-rate children's facilities** ❄ **up-market resort**

---

**Best for:** beginners, intermediates, families, those wanting an introduction to off-piste

**Not recommended for:** budget skiers, ski-to-lunchers

---

Beaver Creek is an elegant family resort situated at the end of a private road, a 20-minute drive from its sister resort of **Vail**. The two are under the same giant corporate ownership and run a joint ski school and unlinked lift system, but there the similarity ends. While Vail is big and brash, Beaver Creek is more compact, with an intimate atmosphere and plenty of slope-side accommodation.

The resort exudes an air of sophistication and wealth that is reflected in its luxurious hotels, magnificent condos, designer boutiques and plethora of art galleries. Excellent childcare facilities and a scenic network of easy runs that are as immaculately groomed as its visitors consistently win it awards as one of America's top family resorts.

The Colorado Ticket lift pass entitles skiers to use the lift systems in Vail, **Breckenridge** and **Keystone** as well as the small but challenging ski area of **Arapahoe Basin**. Shuttle buses operate between Beaver Creek, Vail, Breckenridge and Keystone at a nominal charge.

## On-piste
top 11,440ft (3,488m) bottom 8,100ft (2,470m)

This substantial ski area includes the linked villages of Bachelor Gulch and Arrowhead. Main mountain access from Beaver Creek is by the Centennial Express chair, which takes you up to Spruce Saddle, the mid-mountain station. From here the Birds of Prey Express chair continues on to the summit of the ski area. You can also take the Bachelor Gulch Express from Bachelor Gulch or the Arrow Bahn Express from Arrowhead, and work your way along the adjoining mountains.

The beginner areas are at the base of the Haymeadow, at the top of the Birds of Prey Express lift and at Arrowhead. Long, cruising intermediate trails are the hallmark of Beaver Creek's skiing. The cross-mountain journeys to Bachelor Gulch and Arrowhead enable you to feel you are going somewhere, as opposed to the more usual American experience of skiing variations of the same terrain over and over again.

The Birds of Prey downhill course is one of the most testing in the business. When you stand on the aptly named Brink, the mountain falls away at a stomach-churning 45 degrees. Screech Owl and Osprey are usually heavily mogulled, while Royal Elk Glades is a steep double-black-diamond run from the top of the mountain. The Rose Bowl lift also serves a choice of black-diamond trails.

The resort has three terrain parks that attract as many twin-tipped skiers as they do snowboarders. Park 101, situated on Upper Sheephorn, is designed for park novices. Zoom is for accomplished riders, and has a half-pipe as well as the full range of rails, hips and spines.

## Off-piste
Early in the morning on new snow days in high season, the local powderhounds ignore Vail's inevitably crowded back bowls and head for Grouse Mountain. This provides some truly spectacular trails between the trees and along the edge of the ski area boundary.

## Tuition and guiding
The Vail/Beaver Creek Ski and Snowboard School is consistently praised for the teaching quality and the friendliness of its instructors. The resort offers a large disabled skiing programme.

## Mountain restaurants
Owing to the well-heeled nature of its clientèle, Beaver Creek takes lunch more seriously than many American resorts – but

unfortunately the public are unable to share the best part of it. At lunch-time Beano's Cabin remains a private club. The same applies to Zach's Cabin and Allie's Mountain Steakhouse. 'The few accessible outlets are heavily subscribed', said one reporter, 'and the best option is to return to the resort for lunch'. Beaver Creek Tavern offers gourmet burgers, and the Broken Arrow Café in Arrowhead has 'homemade soup and enormous club sandwiches'.

## Accommodation

The Park Hyatt Beaver Creek Resort and Spa (☎ 970 949 1234) and the Charter at Beaver Creek (☎ 970 949 6660) head the five-star list, along with Ritz-Carlton (☎ 970 748 6200) at Bachelor Gulch ('a truly hedonistic establishment with a magnificent spa'). The four-star Inn at Beaver Creek (☎ 970 845 5990) is adjacent to the Strawberry Park Express lift ('great comfort and a wonderful outdoor pool') and Trapper's Cabin (☎ 970 496 4040) is an exclusive hideaway in the woods, reached only on skis or by snowmobile. The ski-in, ski-out Townsend Place Condominiums (☎ 970 479 2868) are 'of an excellent standard and well located'.

## Eating in and out

Splendido at the Chateau is 'the ultimate in

fine dining American-style, at a cost you would expect', while SaddleRidge houses an extraordinary museum of Western memorabilia ('lovely atmosphere and setting'). Allie's, Beano's and Zach's are open by night to all. Beano's, reached by a motorised sleigh, has 'some of the best fine dining in the resort – a truly memorable evening'.The Mirabelle lies at the entrance to the resort ('best elk I have ever tasted'). Tramoniti serves 'superb lobster ravioli', and Toscani is Italian and 'an altogether less formal and more tasty option in relaxed surroundings'. The Blue Moose is a budget pizzeria.

## Après-ski

The Coyote Café, Beaver Creek Chophouse and Dusty Boot Saloon capture the main crowd, along with the Beaver Creek Tavern and McCoy's for live music. The Black Family Ice Rink is open until 10pm. The resort has three spas.

## Childcare

Beaver Creek ranks as one of the top US resorts for families ('one of the best resorts we've ever been to with our children'). The Small World Play School is the non-skiing kindergarten. It provides all-day care for children from three years of age.

# Beaver Creek: At a glance

**Tel** 1 970 845 9090
**Email** bcinfo@vailresorts.com
**Website** www.beavercreek.com

**GETTING THERE**
**Airports** Eagle County/Vail 45mins, Denver 2½hrs
**Road** 2½hr drive up I-70 through Eisenhower tunnel to Avon

**THE SKIING**
**Linked/nearby resorts** Arapahoe Basin, Arrowhead, Bachelor Gulch, Breckenridge, Copper Mountain, Keystone, Vail
**Total of trails/pistes** 1,625 acres (34% easy, 39% intermediate, 27% difficult)
**Lifts in area** 14: 13🚠 1🚡
**Lift opening dates** late November 2004 to late April 2005

**LIFT PASSES**
**Area pass** Colorado Ticket (covers Arapahoe Basin,

Beaver Creek, Breckenridge, Keystone, Vail) $234–426 for 6 days
**Pensioners** Colorado Ticket 65–69yrs $199–362 for 6 days, 70yrs and over $299 for season

**TUITION**
**Ski & board** Vail/Beaver Creek Ski and Snowboard School (☎ 970 845 5300)
**Guiding** through ski school

**CHILDREN**
**Lift pass** Colorado Ticket 5–12yrs $210–224 for 6 days
**Ski & board school** as adults
**Kindergarten** (ski) as ski school, (non-ski) Small World Play School (☎ 970 845 5325)

**FOOD AND DRINK**
Coffee $2.50, bottle of house wine $20, small beer $3.50–4, soft drink $2.50, dish of the day $10–16

# Breckenridge

**ALTITUDE 9,600ft (2,927m)**                    map: see page 206

❄ **lively town** ❄ **wide spectrum of bars and restaurants**
❄ **extensive and well-linked ski area** ❄ **reliable snow cover**

**Best for:** freeriders, skiers and snowboarders of all standards, under-30s night-owls, people on a budget, families, snowboarders

**Not recommended for:** anyone prone to altitude sickness or insomnia, ski-gourmets

Breckenridge's origins as a mid-nineteenth-century gold-mining town dominate Main Street, a commercial thoroughfare comprising rows of refurbished clapboard houses interspersed with neo-Victorian outlets wherever space permits. As a means of bridging the gap between old and new, garlands of fairy lights remain in place throughout the season, providing a sense of festivity. Modern Breckenridge is an encircling band of late-twentieth-century buildings that widens into a high-rise complex of hotels and condos at the base of the principal lifts. Here the tone is functional, with few concessions to architectural frivolity.

With a 90-minute transfer from Denver International Airport, Breckenridge is among the most accessible of the Colorado resorts. However, it is very high, making it difficult for some visitors arriving from sea-level to acclimatise quickly. The extremely low humidity combined with altitudes in excess of 12,000ft may cause dehydration and headaches – made worse by exercise – which can be avoided by resting, drinking plenty of water and abstaining from alcohol. We were constantly out of breath even though two of us are regular gym users and pretty fit,' was one comment. One reporter's tip is to spend the night in Denver on arrival in order to acclimatise before going on to the resort. The predominantly north- and east-facing slopes are vulnerable to high wind-chill factors. The upside of this is abundant snow that is frequently feather-light and invariably long-lasting.

In the 1980s, British skiers spearheaded the European invasion of Breckenridge, and it has remained in the top three in the international North American popularity league ever since – with first-timers particularly impressed by the easy welcome in the informal bars. As an added attraction, Vail Resorts, the owner of Breckenridge, offers a two-tier joint lift pass that includes its other resorts of **Keystone**, **Vail** and **Beaver Creek**, as well as local hill **Arapahoe Basin**. The more expensive version of the pass can be bought in Vail and Beaver Creek and allows you full use of the lift system in all resorts. The cheaper version, bought in Breckenridge or Keystone, permits you to ski in Vail and Beaver Creek for half the duration of the pass. A free bus service connects Breckenridge with Arapahoe Basin and Keystone, while a subsidised service takes skiers and snowboarders further afield to Vail and Beaver Creek. Vail Resorts also owns Heavenly in California.

## On-piste
### top 12,998ft (3,962m) bottom 9,600ft (2,927m)

It is hard to imagine anyone who loves mountains naming a row of peaks by rote, but that's what happened with Ten Mile Range near Breckenridge. As seen from the town, the lift system stretches from left to right across Peaks 10, 9, 8 and 7. The remainder diminish into the distance in their virgin state.

The existing system is easily accessed by the Quicksilver Super 6 next to the modern complex at the base of Peak 9. At the top, easy runs fan out to the Falcon SuperChair on Peak 10, the starting point for a network of predominantly advanced runs with some testing mogul fields. It is also possible to ski to the Mercury and Beaver Run SuperChairs on Peak 9, which has the most inviting cruising in the resort, plus Gold King, a terrain park designed for learner freeriders. Peak 7 is built for cruising, with huge rollers on all seven trails.

The SuperConnect lift is the easiest way to reach Peak 8, and the Vista Haus mid-station is the focal point for the chair-lifts that serve the network of blue and black trails on the lower slopes of Peak 8.

Easily accessed bowls and chutes make Breckenridge hugely popular with boarders, and away from groomed trails boarders outnumber skiers, especially on powder days. Experienced freeriders (as well as skiers) will enjoy the Freeway Terrain Park and the Breckenridge Super-Pipe, recently rated the best in Colorado by *Snowboarder* magazine. The Independence SuperChair has extended Breckenridge's boundaries into a glade area cut from the forest on the lower slopes of Peak 7.

## Off-piste

Breckenridge's expert terrain, created as a result of local demand for more 'European-style off-piste', covers the wide open upper slopes on Peaks 7, 8 and 9. The T-Bar takes snow-users into Peak 8's double-black-diamond zone, comprising Horseshoe, Contest, North and Cucumber Bowls, all of them ungroomed. Beyond that, you're on your own, hiking over 12,000ft to the radical Peak-top runs. Whale's Tail and Peak 7 Bowl are 1,500ft vertical above the T-Bar, but the sterner test is Peak 8's Imperial Bowl, a 2,700-ft vertical rise from the same starting point. This also provides access to the Lake Chutes, which have slopes of up to 50 degrees.

## Tuition and guiding

The 600-strong Breckenridge Ski & Ride School prides itself on having something for everyone, with a range of programmes that includes telemarking, terrain park sessions, women's seminars and 50+ Silver Skiing seminars ('taught by oldies for oldies'), in addition to regular group classes. It encourages everyone over the age of seven to enrol in its 'fast track' Burton Learn to Ride courses. Snowboarding is big here – indeed Breckenridge was one of the first resorts in Colorado to embrace the sport 20 years ago.

## Mountain restaurants

As yet, Breckenridge has no on-mountain gourmet lunching, but there are several convenient fast-food options designed for the American market. Ten Mile Station, at the top of the Quicksilver Chair between Peaks 9 and 10, has a heated outdoor deck, plus a fair-weather BBQ. The alternatives are Border Burritos at the Bergenhof ('salads by the pound'), Spencer's, which

does 'as much as you can eat' specials, at the bottom of Peak 9, as well as Sub Fusion (where you 'build your own sandwiches') and the food court at the Vista Haus on Peak 8.

## Accommodation

The resort has a choice of spacious rather than deluxe hotels, two large condominium resorts, an assortment of smaller apartment buildings and several restored Victorian inns. With the exception of the Lodge & Spa at Breckenridge (☎ 970 453 9300), located outside town with a shuttle bus to take guests to the slopes, all the main properties are within a five-minute walk of a lift. The main ski-in, ski-out options are the Village at Breckenridge (☎ 970 453 2000), on the Plaza near the ice-rink, and the massive Beaver Run Resort (☎ 970 453 6000) – a 500-room slope-side condo complex. The Great Divide Lodge (☎ 970 453 4500) is the only full-service hotel, while the smaller Breckenridge Mountain Lodge (☎ 970 453 2333) ('budget accommodation in a picturesque log cabin exterior') is particularly well placed for the Main Street nightlife. The Mountain Thunder Lodge (☎ 888 547 8092) offers comfortable accommodation and is a short walk from the town centre.

## Eating in and out

'Without doubt the main night entertainment is eating out, with bigger queues for the restaurants than on the slopes,' commented one reporter. Breckenridge has more than 100 restaurants offering international cuisine. The Hearthstone, converted from a Victorian brothel, scores highly for romantic atmosphere and creativity: the menu features granola-crusted elk chops. On the same street, the South Ridge Seafood Grill's inventive menu includes oysters flown in from Chesapeake Bay. The Blue River Bistro, Café Alpine and the Breckenridge Cattle and Fish Co. are also recommended for fine dining. The Steak and Rib on Maine Street was said to have 'huge helpings of bison, steaks and ribs at £40–45 for two with wine').

Bubba Gump Shrimp Co. serves Cajun specials and the Blue Moose is renowned for its pancakes. Mi Casa Mexican Cantina is popular ('good atmosphere – full works with a bottle of wine £60 for two'), as is the Columbine Café, which is said to serve the best breakfasts in town. The Red Orchid and the Bamboo Garden specialise in Mandarin and Szechwan dishes, while Mountain Flying

Fish is a new sushi restaurant. The range of Italian places includes St Bernard, the Main Street Bistro, Fatty's Pizzeria, Giampetro's Pasta and Michael's Pizzeria. Pierre's Riverwalk Café offers French cuisine.

In Breckenridge, eating in your condo is easy: Gourmet Cabby (☎ 970 543 7788) will deliver burgers, pizza, steak, sandwiches, Mexican and Chinese from 30 Breckenridge restaurants, plus beer, wine and spirits.

## Après-ski

As soon as the lifts close, Breckenridge comes into its own, with hard-core skiers and boarders transforming into dedicated party animals with the first taste of Mi Casa's legendary après-ski Margaritas. Follow this up in the Breckenridge Brewery ('enormous cheap meals and good beer – it was the liveliest bar on most nights, and rocked on disco night'), which sells draught beers brewed on the premises. Salt Creek Saloon is true Old West, with stuffed animal heads and pool tables. Eric's diverts the kids with pinball and pizza, while their parents drink jugs of beer and watch TV. Local pool players take on visitors at Ullr's Sports Grille, while the frontier-style Gold Pan, built circa 1879, kicks off with a three-hour Happy Hour (starting at 4pm) and goes on from there. Gracy O'Malley's is an Irish pub. The Julius Caesar Lounge, known as JC, is an English-style pub. Late-night action focuses on Sherpa & Yeti's and Cecilia's ('lacked atmosphere'); both have DJs or live bands at weekends and during the week in high season. The Back Stage Theater is 'strictly amateur but entertaining'.

Sadly the once-famous factory outlet stores at Silverthorne, a 20-minute drive away, are in serious decline ('prices for designer goods used to be a bargain, but half the stores seem to have closed and it's no longer worth the journey').

## Childcare

Breckenridge Children's Center offers slope-side crèches for children from two months and has two slope-side children's facilities at Peak 8 and Peak 9. Both have pagers for parents to hire, provide lunches and offer a non-skiing, outdoor snow-play programme. Advance reservations are essential during the busiest weeks.

Breckenridge Ski & Ride School accepts children from three years and is praised by reporters: 'I would definitely recommend Breckenridge to families with children who require warm coaxing into having lessons'. The resort has five magic carpet lifts and teenagers are catered for by the ski school's teens-only programme.

# Breckenridge: At a glance

**Tel** 1 970 453 5000
**Email** breckguest@vailresorts.com
**Website** www.breckenridge.com

## GETTING THERE
**Airports** Eagle County/Vail 1hr, Denver 1½hrs
**Road** follow I-70 from Denver to exit 203, then Highway 9

## THE SKIING
**Linked/nearby resorts** Arapahoe Basin, Beaver Creek, Copper Mountain, Keystone, Vail
**Total of trails/pistes** 2,208 acres (13% easy, 32% intermediate, 55% difficult)
**Lifts in area** 20: 15⬚ 5⬚
**Lift opening dates** late November 2004 to late April 2005

## LIFT PASSES
**Area pass** Colorado Ticket (covers Arapahoe Basin, Breckenridge, Keystone, as well as optional three days in Beaver Creek and Vail) $234–354 for 6 days
**Pensioners** Colorado Ticket 65–69yrs $199–300 for 6 days, 70yrs and over $299 for season

## TUITION
**Ski & board** Breckenridge Ski & Ride School (3 centres) (☎ 970 453 3272)
**Guiding** none

## CHILDREN
**Lift pass** Colorado Ticket 5–12yrs $150–170 for 6 days
**Ski & board school** as adults
**Kindergarten** (ski/non-ski) Breckenridge Children's Center (☎ 970 453 3258)

## FOOD AND DRINK
Coffee $2.50, bottle of house wine $20, small beer $3.50–4, soft drink $2.50, dish of the day $10–16

# Crested Butte

ALTITUDE 9,100ft (2,774m)

## ❋ attractive old town ❋ excellent off-piste ❋ highly regarded ski school

**Best for:** advanced skiers and snowboarders, those who enjoy the steep and deep

**Not recommended for:** high-mileage skiers, people requiring easy resort access

This small, historic mining town dates back to the nineteenth century. Today it is one of the most attractive ski resorts in Colorado and is situated three miles from the ski area, which also provides some good lodging at its base. Skiers fly into Gunnison airport, after changing planes at Denver.

## On the snow
top 12,162ft (3,707m) bottom 9,100ft (2,774m)

Crested Butte is renowned for its steep skiing ('the steepest lift-served terrain in North America'), and hosts ski-extreme championships. The Extreme Limits area offers over 400 acres of truly challenging terrain. At the opposite end of the scale, it also possesses some of Colorado's easiest lower intermediate skiing.

The resort came under new ownership in March 2004 and substantial improvements are planned. First in line is the new Prospect lift for 2004–5, carrying skiers from the Prospect housing development to the top of the Goldlink and Painter Boy lifts. The expansion will add five trails and 15 acres to the present 1,073-acre ski area. The North Face single-person platter lift is replaced by a T-bar. Future plans include rebuild of the mountain village and the addition of 400 acres of terrain on nearby Snodgrass Mountain.

Crested Butte Ski and Snowboard School offers workshops on turning skills, all-terrain and ski-racing. A new terrain park, on Lower Canaan beneath the Paradise chair, opened in 2003–4 featuring eight jumps and a host of rails. A super-pipe is being added for 2004–5. Kids' Park at the top of the Painter Boy lift is very popular.

On the mountain, the Ice Bar and Restaurant offers fine dining as well as a bar on the outside deck. Andiamo, in the

Paradise Warming Hut, is Italian and features a table-service lunch.

## In the resort
In the old town's Main Street, 40 of the original buildings, have been converted into shops and restaurants, giving the place a Wild West atmosphere. The town is overlooked by the Butte (pronounced as in 'beaut-iful' and meaning a mountain that stands alone). The Nordic Inn (☎ 970 349 5542) is a family-run ski lodge that is firmly recommended. The former Sheraton Resort has undergone a $5-million facelift and is now the Grand Lodge Crested Butte (☎ 970 349 8000). The alternative is Club Med (☎ 020-7348 3333 in UK) at the base area, which is linked to the old town by regular shuttle bus.

### WHAT'S NEW
Prospect lift adds five new trails to the ski area
Super-pipe in Lower Canaan terrain park

Recommended restaurants include the Buffalo Grille and Saloon, the Black Whale and Slogar. The Secret Stash is a 100-year-old miners' cabin serving BBQ foods and gourmet pizzas.

Crested Butte's nightlife has a cowboy atmosphere, and the Idle Spur has live music. Other hot-spots include Talk of the Town, the slope-side Hall of Fame, Kochevar's and the Eldo.

Children under two years old ski free, while those under 16 years pay their age in dollars per day for use of the ski lifts. The Baby Bears kindergarten takes potty-trained toddlers, while Cuddly Bears is for ages 13 months and over.

### Crested Butte: At a glance
**Tel** 1 970 349 2303 (0800 894085 in UK)
**Email** info@cbmr.com
**Website** www.skicb.com
**Lifts in resort** 13: 10🚠 3🎿
**Lift opening dates** 20 November 2004 to 10 April 2005

# Heavenly

ALTITUDE 6,500ft (1,982m)

## ☀ spectacular lake and desert scenery ☀ large ski area
## ☀ excellent tree-skiing

> **Best for:** beginners, intermediate cruisers, families, gamblers, night-owls
>
> **Not recommended for:** people who want doorstep skiing

Heavenly is the largest of 15 alpine resorts on the shores of beautiful **Lake Tahoe**. Its position, straddling the frontier between two states, gives it an intriguing split personality. From the top of the mountain you can choose to ski in Nevada, with views of the arid vastness of the Nevada Desert, or to head for the Californian side overlooking the lush beauty of Lake Tahoe. Down below you can stay on the Nevada side of the stateline in South Lake Tahoe – where garish, huge neon signs and monstrous casino complexes contrast with the more peaceful waterfront and its simple, single-storey homes – or you can choose Heavenly Village at the foot of the ski area. Reporters comment that the new village has given Heavenly the real identity as a ski resort that it previously lacked. Owners Vail Resorts have invested $25 million over three years on upgrading the resort – with the promise of a further $15 million to come.

## On-piste
### top 10,067ft (3,068m) bottom 6,200ft (1,890m)

Heavenly is one of America's larger ski areas, and almost all of its terrain is below the tree-line. The resort also features one of America's most extensive snowmaking programmes. Main mountain access is by a high-speed eight-person gondola from South Lake Tahoe. The alternative is to start from either Stagecoach or Boulder base on the Nevada side, or from California Lodge.

The resort offers several beginner areas: the Enchanted Forest at the California base, at Boulder base-lodge midway up the mountain on the California side ('wide open pistes, very uncrowded by European standards', and a new 15-acre beginners' area at the top of the gondola.

Most of the trails are ideally suited to intermediates – long cruisers bordered by banks of pine trees and enhanced by the stunning view of the lake. You can take the Sky Express chair and try Liz's or Betty's, then head to Nevada for the Big Dipper, Sand Dunes, Perimeter and Galaxy runs – the Nevada face consists mainly of blue runs.

The upper Californian side is generally fast, blue, cruising terrain with more difficult runs higher up. The linking of the ski area received criticism: 'it's a drag getting from the California side to the Nevada one for skiers. For snowboarders it's a real pain, too much flat stuff'.

> ### WHAT'S NEW
> 6-person chair-lift to replace old Waterfall and Powderbowl chairs on the Californian side

Milky Way Bowl provides challenging skiing, but the most advanced is in Mott Canyon and Killebrew Canyon. Steep chutes are cut through the trees, with runs such as Snake Pit and Widowmaker.

The resort features a superpipe with 17-ft walls, and three terrain parks with hits for all levels.

## Off-piste
Heavenly is reputed to have some of the best tree skiing in the Tahoe area on a powder day. The Milky Way, Mott Canyon and Killebrew Canyon are large expanses of mountain-side that remain ungroomed. But you need to arrive early after a big dump, as they are quickly skied out.

## Tuition and guiding
The Heavenly Ski & Snowboard School offers a full range of programmes including Learn to Ski – Easy as 1-2-3.

## Mountain restaurants
Lakeview Lodge and The Cabin are tucked away among the giant granite boulders at the top of Gunbarrel, overlooking Lake Tahoe on the Californian side. Sky

Meadows, also on the California side, has a daily barbecue. Boulder Lodge offers a bar, cafeteria and sundeck, while Stagecoach Lodge has a cafeteria. The Slice of Heaven Pizza Pub at the Stagecoach base-lodge is warmly recommended, while Stagecoach Lodge was said to be 'well worth a visit for the meatball sandwich'.

## Accommodation

The Tahoe Seasons Resort hotel complex (☎ 530 541 6700) is close to the lifts at the California base. Harrah's Lake Tahoe (☎ 702 588 6611) and the Lake Tahoe Horizon Casino Resort (☎ 775 588 6211) in South Lake Tahoe are two of the bigger casino-hotels; others include Caesar's Tahoe (☎ 702 588 3515) and Harveys Resort Hotel (☎ 775 588 2411) – all have good spas. The Marriott Timber Lodge (☎ 530 542 6600) is 'fabulous and right by the gondola'. The Station House Inn (☎ 530 542 1101) and the Timber Cove Lodge (☎ 530 541 6722) are acceptable motels that have been singled out by reporters. Much of the accommodation is in condominiums.

## Eating in and out

In South Lake Tahoe, the Summit in Harrah's is rated one of America's top 100 restaurants. Sammy Hafar's Cabo Wabo inside Harvey's is the 'best Mexican in town'. Fire & Ice Improvisational Grill offers fresh food cooked to order. Red Hut, Ernie's and Heidi's all remain popular for breakfast. The Naked Fish has 'outstanding sushi and a great atmosphere at a reasonable price'. The Chart House is more expensive but affords great views. The Blue Water Bistro on the Timber Cove Pier is highly praised by reporters.

## Après-ski

Heavenly is developing its own nightlife in the new village, but the lure of gambling and Vegas-style celebrity shows takes most visitors across the stateline into Nevada. Some excellent cabaret acts and pop concerts are staged here and often feature top artists. Fire & Ice, at the base of the gondola, is a popular resort meeting place.

## Childcare

The ski school accepts children from three years for a half- or full-day programme with skiing and games. Daycare is available for non-skiing children as young as six weeks, but reservations are essential.

# Heavenly: At a glance

**Tel** 1 775 586 7000
**Email** heavenlyinternational@vailresorts.com
**Website** www.skiheavenly.com

## GETTING THERE
**Airports** Reno 1½hrs, Sacramento 2hrs, San Francisco 4hrs
**Road** I-80 from San Francisco to Sacramento, I-50, then Highway 89

## THE SKIING
**Linked/nearby resorts** Alpine Meadows, Boreal, Diamond Peak, Donner Ski Ranch, Granlibakken, Kirkwood, Mount Rose, Northstar-at-Tahoe, Sierra-at-Tahoe, Ski Homewood, Soda Springs, Squaw Valley, Sugar Bowl, Tahoe Donner
**Total of trails/pistes** 4,800 acres (20% easy, 45% intermediate, 35% difficult)
**Lifts in resort** 27: 2⑤ 19⑤ 6⑨
**Lift opening dates** late November 2004 to late April 2005

## LIFT PASSES
**Area pass** $258–312 for 6 days. Regional pass (only available through tour operators and covers Alpine Meadows, Kirkwood, Northstar-at-Tahoe, Sierra-at-Tahoe, Squaw Valley) $270 for 5 out of 6 days
**Pensioners** 65yrs and over $138–174 for 6 days

## TUITION
**Ski & board** Heavenly Ski & Snowboard School (☎ 775 586 7000 ext 96218)
**Guiding** through ski school

## CHILDREN
**Lift pass** 5–12yrs $108–144 for 6 days
**Ski & board school** as adults
**Kindergarten** Day Care Center (☎ 775 586 7000 ext 96912)

## FOOD AND DRINK
Coffee $1.50–2, bottle of house wine $10–25, small beer $3.50, soft drink $2.50, dish of the day $10–15

# Jackson Hole

**ALTITUDE 6,311ft (1,924m)**

map: see page 207

### ❄ challenging terrain ❄ wide choice of moderate-to-luxury accommodation ❄ Wild West ambience

---

**Best for:** advanced skiers and riders, off-piste enthusiasts, beginners, families, non-skiers, foodies

**Not recommended for:** budget skiers, nervous intermediates, party-going teenagers

---

Some 100,000 skiers and 8,000 elk can't be wrong. Both spend each winter – or at least part of it – in Jackson Hole, a remote rural corner of Wyoming hailed by experienced skiers and boarders as the greatest winter sports destination on Earth. The resort offers a winning combination of spectacular scenery, yester-year cowboy values and facilities designed for Hollywood refugees following in the footsteps of long-term resident Harrison Ford.

The main square in Jackson Town establishes the Western tone, with picturesque boardwalks and arches made from antlers shed by the elks. In the evenings, the locals ride the lifts on the floodlit town hill at **Snow King**, but the best slopes are on Rendezvous Mountain, 12 miles away on the other side of the Snake River at Teton Village. During the day, this ski area is linked to Jackson town by a regular bus service.

### WHAT'S NEW
Crags expert terrain

In summer, Jackson plays host to three million visitors, who arrive by campervan en route to Yellowstone Park and Old Faithful, the world's largest geyser. In the winter, the resort returns to its cattle-town origins, helped not a little by the ski industry. Working ranches still surround the town, and horses are the secondary means of transport after the four-wheel-drive. Late-night revellers returning homewards should not be surprised to happen upon the occasional elk roaming the streets. Reporters praise Jackson as being 'large enough to be interesting, but small enough to get around easily'.

## On-piste
**top 10,135ft (3,135m) bottom 6,311ft (1,924m)**

The skiing above Teton Village is neatly arranged on two mountains, Rendezvous and Apres Vous. Apres Vous is prime beginners' territory, with a beginner network of runs at the bottom served by the Teewinot quad, and slightly more demanding intermediate terrain at the top, served by the Apres Vous quad. This natural progression offers a peaceful learning curve on slopes that are generally ignored by the macho individualists who make up Jackson's core clientèle. The adjacent freestyle terrain park and half-pipe is low-key, but popular with young skiers and boarders.

The Bridger gondola provides access to the intermediate area between the two mountains, a limited selection of predominantly blue runs served by the slow Casper Bowl triple-chair and criss-crossed by traverses linking the main areas. Advanced snow-users head for the rugged slopes, steep chutes and rock jumps on Rendezvous. Although the gondola accesses many of these, the hard core prefer to queue throughout the day for the venerable Aerial Tram, an ancient cable-car that offloads at the top of the windswept peak, the start of the longest vertical drop in the United States served by a single lift. The journey is accompanied by warnings of potential dangers, but in all but the most difficult snow conditions confident intermediates will have no trouble in picking out manageable descents – provided they remember that, in Jackson, expert-only double-black-diamond trails take no prisoners.

Riders are catered for by a groomed super-pipe and terrain park on Apres Vous Mountain, and a natural half-pipe on Dick's Ditch. Nearby **Grand Targhee** also provides a natural half-pipe for freestylers, but it is the freeriders who will really appreciate the area for its untracked snow.

## Off-piste

With grooming kept to a minimum on the steeper slopes, the challenging mixture of bowls and trees provides exceptional powder opportunities within the resort boundaries. The Rendezvous Trail connects the upper slopes to the Hobacks, an enormous south-facing area that is best tackled early in the day. Whichever route you choose through expansive snowfields divided by hidden gullies, you end up at the Union Pass Traverse, leading to the quad that takes you back to base. Fresh powder may last longer in the Moran Woods and Saratoga Bowl at the less fashionable end of the ski area, while the 20-minute hike up the Headwall opens up Casper Bowl. A further short walk takes you out of the resort area to Granite Bowl, a magnificent mile-long powder field followed by a wilderness traverse back to base, but it is avalanche-prone and so should not be attempted without a guide, transceivers and shovels. The same applies to Cody and Rock Springs Bowls off Rendezvous Mountain. The Crags area will open for the 2004–5 season, allowing adventurous skiers and snowboarders to hike to it for an additional 1,000ft vertical of steep chutes and tree-skiing.

However, the ultimate test of nerve is Corbet's Couloir, a leap into space off a cornice followed by a landing on a 50-degree slope. The size and configuration of the jump varies from year to year, providing the wannabes who peer anxiously over the edge with much pause for thought. Although the moment of derring-do often results in a spectacular 'yard sale', the adrenaline high lasts much longer than the time it takes to reassemble your equipment and ego.

## Tuition and guiding

The Jackson Hole Mountain Sports School runs comprehensive courses for all levels, starting with Learn to Turn and Learn to Ride and progressing to Turn it Up, Mountain Masters and Race Clinics through the timed Nastar gates. The demanding Steep and Deep Camp is extremely popular, while the Jackson Hole Alpine and Backcountry Guide Service is available for groups of one to five (pre-booking essential). Keen teenagers can join one of Jackson Hole's Team Extreme courses, run by the ski school. The

demanding four-day clinic for skiers and snowboarders aged between 12 and 17 is aimed at those who have outgrown regular ski school classes.

## Mountain restaurants

No one goes to Jackson Hole for its on-mountain lunches. The greatest plus at the self-service cafeteria at the bottom of the Casper Bowl lift is the roaring log fire, but this is more than offset by the crowds and indifferent food. The other options are Corbet's Cabin, a soup-and-sandwich facility at the top of the Tram, and a gloomy pizzeria at the top of the gondola. In Teton Village, the best bets are the Mangy Moose and upstairs at the Alpenhof ('delicious salads and burgers in a pleasant atmosphere').

## Accommodation

On arrival, most people head for Teton Village at the foot of Jackson Hole Ski Resort, 35 minutes away from the airport by 4WD. The alternative is the town of Jackson, which has the advantage of the lion's share of nightlife but is a 20-minute daily commute by bus to the mountain. Teton Village has ski-in, ski-out convenience, and now the sleek allure of five-star Snake River Lodge & Spa (☎ 307 732 6000) and the brand new Four Seasons Resort hotel (☎ 307 734 5040) weight the balance in its favour. The former, recently renovated and owned by Vail Resorts, has an indoor–outdoor swimming-pool built among the rocks with a quasi stage-set surrounding of whirlpools and waterfalls. Its spa specialises in Native American treatments. The plush Four Seasons Resort is the hotel of choice for those with fat wallets. It contains substantial bedrooms and family-sized suites all with connecting marble bathrooms, a kids' club and games room, state-of-the-art spa and fitness centre.

The Teton Club (☎ 307 734 9777), a deluxe condo development with maid service and a health club, is the most central place to stay in Teton Village, while Teton Mountain Lodge (☎ 307 734 7111) is more family-oriented. The old order includes the neo-Tyrolean Alpenhof Lodge (☎ 307 733 3242) and the cheaper Best Western Inn at Jackson Hole (☎ 307 733 2311). Alternatively, you can stay a (free) bus ride away from the slopes in one of the spacious Teton Village Condos: bookings through Jackson Hole Resort Lodging (☎ 307 733 3990).

The hedonistic Amangani (☎ 307 734 7333) is a minimalist marble palace set on a bluff halfway between Teton Village and Jackson town. Self-indulgent traditionalists may prefer neighbouring Spring Creek Ranch (☎ 307 735 8833).

In Jackson town, location is everything. The Wort Hotel (☎ 307 733 2190), a comfortable stagecoach inn a minute's walk from the main square, is the top choice, while the welcoming Parkway Inn (☎ 307 733 3143) appeals to more cost-conscious visitors.

## Eating in and out

In Teton Village, the Westbank Grill in the Four Seasons has an international menu and cosy atmosphere.The Mangy Moose is a resort institution and a particular favourite among families. Its busy restaurant serves Western cuisine in a vast barn building. GameFish in the Snake River Lodge and Spa concentrates on fish and smoked game, and Masa Sushi serves authentic Japanese fare. Calico is a modestly-priced Italian restaurant and bar on Teton Village Road. In Jackson, try Nikai Sushi ('mouth-wateringly fresh delicacies') and Old Yellowstone Garage, which is top-of-the-range Italian.

## Après-ski

The Mangy Moose has live music and a convivial atmosphere. The slope-side Peak in the Four Seasons Resort attracts skiers at the end of the day, but Teton Village has little life after dark, with lights out almost everywhere by 11pm. Those in search of serious drinking, shooting pool and dancing the Western Swing should head for the Million Dollar Cowboy Bar, on Jackson's Town Square. This huge saloon has stools made from Western saddles, live music and pool tables, all of them dominated by an unnervingly poised stuffed grizzly bear. The Snake River Brewing Company sells its own and other beers in neo-industrial surroundings. The Stagecoach in the nearby village of Wilson is a 'must go' on Sunday evenings, when locals and visitors crowd in for the live music. A word of warning: Jackson is strict about licensing laws, which forbid anyone under 21 to go to bars; over-21s must carry ID to show when asked.

## Childcare

The slope-side Kids' Ranch, based in Cody House, has its own dedicated corral complete with magic carpet lift and the Fort Wyoming playground. It offers childcare from six months to two years, and ski programmes for three- to twelve-year-olds. The resort has two rope-tows and a magic carpet. Annie's Nannies and Babysitting by the Tetons are the childcare options for small non-skiers.

---

# Jackson Hole: At a glance

**Tel** 1 307 733 2292
**Email** info@jacksonhole.com
**Website** www.jacksonhole.com

## GETTING THERE
**Airport** Jackson Hole airport 15 mins to Jackson,35 mins to Teton Village

## THE SKIING
**Linked/nearby resorts** Grand Targhee, Snow King
**Total of trails/pistes** 2,500 acres (10% easy, 40% intermediate, 50% difficult)
**Lifts in area** 10: 2☑ 8☑
**Lift opening dates** 4 December 2004 to 3 April 2005

## LIFT PASSES
**Area pass** $348 for 6 days
**Pensioners** 65yrs and over $286 for 6 days

## TUITION
**Ski & board** Jackson Hole Mountain Sports School (☎ 307 733 2553)
**Guiding** High Mountain Heli-skiing (☎ 307 733 3274), Jackson Hole Alpine and Backcountry Guide Service (☎ 307 739 2663)

## CHILDREN
**Lift pass** 14yrs and under $174 for 6 days
**Ski & board school** as adults
**Kindergarten** (ski/non-ski) Kids' Ranch (☎ 307 733 2553), (non-ski) Annie's Nannies (☎ 307 733 8086), Babysitting by the Tetons (☎ 307 730 0754)

## FOOD AND DRINK
Coffee $2.50–3, bottle of house wine $24, small beer $3.50, soft drink $2.50, dish of the day $10–15

# Mammoth

ALTITUDE 7,953ft (2,424m)　　　　　　　　　　　　　map: see page 208

❋ skiing and snowboarding for all standards ❋ large ski area
❋ long skiing season ❋ good sunshine and snow records

> **Best for:** snowboarders, early- and late-season holidaymakers, ski-and-shoppers
> **Not recommended for:** those who dislike remote locations, night-owls, ski-to-lunchers

To Europeans, California and snow may seem the strangest of associates. But the coastline of the Sunshine State is backed by the largest snowmaking machine in the world, otherwise known as the Pacific Ocean. Inland from the better-known beaches lie the high Sierra Nevada mountains, which attract a mighty 400 inches of snow each winter. When it is not snowing, the sun is shining – for an average 300 days each year.

Mammoth is the chief beneficiary of the snow, and with a formidable 27 lifts set in 3,500 acres it remains the largest single-mountain ski-and-snowboard destination in North America. The season officially runs from November to June and sometimes even extends to Independence Day in July.

Since a change of ownership in 1998, the resort has been undergoing a $830-million makeover. Improvements include the development of the Village on Minaret Road, the approach route to the existing resort. Work is approaching completion on what is conceived as a European-style ski community, linked to the main ski area by gondola and eventually a return ski trail.

The resort is situated 168 miles from Reno, and 307 miles from Los Angeles. But despite its remote location, skiers from Nevada and southern California think nothing of driving up for the weekend – or even the day.

A frequent, free shuttle bus runs to and from the ski-area bases at Main Lodge, Canyon Lodge and Juniper Springs, while an airport bus operates regularly between Reno and the town of Mammoth Lakes. The town's small airstrip is being rebuilt as a major regional airport, planned to be ready for the 2005–6 season.

Mammoth's sister resort of June Mountain, situated 20 miles away, acts as a useful refuge at weekends when Mammoth is prone to crowds. June offers benign and spectacularly beautiful runs and shares Mammoth's lift pass. There is, however, no free bus service between the two resorts.

## On-piste
top 11,053ft (3,369m) bottom 7,953ft (2,424m)

The main course is Mammoth Mountain, a superb peak for all standards of skier and rider. Four separate bases provide mountain access, but the two-stage, eight-person Panorama gondola from Main Lodge is the fastest way to the summit. Chairs 12, 13 and 14 give access to plenty of cruising terrain with runs such as Surprise, Secret Spot and Bristlecone. The majority of seriously challenging, double-black-diamond trails are reached from the top of the Panorama gondola and Chair 23. The upper half of the ski area offers open bowls, gullies and tree skiing.

Mammoth boasts three terrain parks. The original is reached by Thunder Bound Express from Main Lodge and includes a super-pipe, a 'super-duper' pipe, table-tops and other jumps. The two other terrain parks are at Canyon Lodge and below the Roller Coaster chair. JM2 at June Mountain has spines, pipes and rails.

## Off-piste
Skiing and riding are permitted everywhere within the boundary. There are even some out-of-bounds routes, such as Hole in the Wall, down which, with permission from the ski patrol, instructors are allowed to take clients. Almost all the expert terrain is left ungroomed.

## Tuition and guiding
The two ski schools offer a full range of courses that includes teen skiing and skiing for the disabled. Women's seminars are popular and you can fine-tune your slalom skills at A J Kitt's Ski & Race Camp.

## Mountain restaurants
The Parallax at McCoy Station features

Pacific Rim and Mediterranean food and is warmly recommended. Self-service cafeterias are located in Main and Canyon Lodges and at the mid-station of the gondola. The Mill Café at the bottom of Stump Alley is a cosier and more relaxing alternative. The Mountainside Grill in the Mammoth Mountain Inn and the Yodler Bar & Pub – a Swiss chalet shipped piecemeal from the Alps – are the other culinary options. Hennessey's is new, providing good food and great views from the summit of Mammoth Crest. It's open from breakfast until late into the evening.

## Accommodation
Enthusiasts wanting a head start in the mornings should stay at Mammoth Mountain Inn (☎ 760 934 2581), at the Main Lodge base or at the Austria Hof Lodge (☎ 760 934 2764) ('good value with good rooms') at Canyon Lodge. Juniper Springs & Sunstone Lodges (☎ 760 924 1102) offer slope-side self-catering. The Alpenhof Lodge (☎ 760 934 8558), located in the Village, is within easy access of the skiing and the town. In Mammoth Lakes, the Shilo Inn (☎ 760 934 4500) is warmly recommended. Double Eagle Resort & Spa (☎ 760 648 7004) at June Mountain has a swimming-pool and health club.

## Eating in and out
Skadi and Nevados are 'both excellent for a special night out', while Ocean Harvest specialises in seafood. Shogun is the best Japanese restaurant, and Matsu's offers an eclectic Far Eastern menu, including Thai and Chinese specialities. The Charthouse and the Mogul are recommended for steaks. Alpenrose provides cheese fondue.

## Après-ski
Skiers and riders gather at the Yodler when the lifts close. Canyon Lodge regularly has a live band. Later in the evening, the Clocktower pub at the Alpenhof is a popular resort rendezvous along with nearby Whiskey Creek. In town, Grumpy's Sports Bar attracts a young crowd. Shogun has a separate bar serving sushi and Japanese snacks. Dublin's is a new, traditional-style Irish pub. At Fever, the new nightspot inside Dublin's, you can dance the night away. At Lakanuki visitors can stop by in their ski boots for hula dancing and tropical drinks.

## Childcare
Canyon Kids and the Woollywood Sports School offer morning and afternoon lessons for children from four years, as well as daycare for small non-skiers.

# Mammoth: At a glance

**Tel** 1 760 934 0745
**Email** info@mammoth-mtn.com
**Website** www.mammothmountain.com

### GETTING THERE
**Airports** Reno 3hrs, Los Angeles 5hrs
**Road** I-395 from Los Angeles or Reno, then Highway 203

### THE SKIING
**Linked/nearby resorts** June Mountain
**Total of trails/pistes** 3,500 acres (25% easy, 40% intermediate, 35% difficult)
**Lifts in area** 27: 3 22 2
**Lift opening dates** 11 November 2004 to early June 2005

### LIFT PASSES
**Area pass** (covers Mammoth and June Mountain) $360 for 6 out of 8 days

**Pensioners** 65yrs and over $180 for 6 days

### TUITION
**Ski & board** Canyon Lodge Sports School (☎ 760 934 0708), Main Lodge Sports School (☎ 760 934 0708), A J Kitt's Ski & Race Camp (☎ 760 934 2571)
**Guiding** Mammoth Mountaineering School (☎ 760 924 9100)

### CHILDREN
**Lift pass** 7–12yrs $180 for 6 out of 8 days
**Ski & board school** Canyon Kids (☎ 760 934 0787), Woollywood Sports School (☎ 760 934 0685)
**Kindergarten** (ski/non-ski) as ski & board schools

### FOOD AND DRINK
Coffee $2.50, bottle of house wine $20–25, small beer $4, soft drink $2.50, dish of the day $12–20

# Park City Resorts

ALTITUDE The Canyons 6,800ft (2,073m), Deer Valley Resort 7,200ft (2,195m),
Park City Mountain Resort 6,900ft (2,104m)                    map: see page 209

## ❋ wide choice of adjacent resorts ❋ short airport transfer
## ❋ good skiing for all standards ❋ excellent snow record

> **Best for:** intermediate to advanced skiers, non-skiers, families (Deer Valley), gourmets (Park City), off-piste enthusiasts (The Canyons and Park City)
>
> **Not recommended for:** those wanting a compact resort and families with small children (Park City), people on a budget (Deer Valley)

A group of distinctively different resorts makes up the Park City Resorts ski area. A clutch of three – **The Canyons**, **Deer Valley Resort** and **Park City Mountain Resort** – are situated side by side, a 40-minute drive from Salt Lake City in Utah – the state that boasts the finest, driest powder snow in the world.

At present the three are under separate ownership. However, they do share a lift pass: the Ski Utah Passport covers **Alta**, **Brighton**, The Canyons, Deer Valley Resort, Park City Mountain Resort, **Snowbird**, **Solitude** and **Sundance**. It can be purchased only through a UK tour operator or Ski Utah (www.skiutah.com/international/passport). There is no Ski Utah Passport for children, who require separate resort passes.

Park City is the town for all three resorts. The heart is attractive Main Street, home to the Wasatch Brewery, the Egyptian Theater and a host of art galleries, boutiques, bars, coffee shops and restaurants. On the edge of town is Park City Mountain Resort, which is a moderately well-designed complex on three levels, with shops and cafés set around a skating-rink.

Unashamedly luxurious, Deer Valley lies one mile to the south-east, up a winding mountain road lined with multi-million-dollar homes. This is a resort where snowboarding is still banned and grooming counts, both on the meticulously pisted slopes ('like going skiing at Harrods') and with the clientèle.

The Canyons has developed from a small, local ski area into what is now the fifth largest ski resort in the United States, with the facilities to attract international skiers and snowboarders. The Utah Olympic Park, adjoining The Canyons, has a bob-sleigh and luge track. It is also one of the few places in the world where beginners can try their hand at ski-jumping.

## On-piste
The Canyons top 9,990ft (3,045m) bottom 6,800ft (2,073m)

Deer Valley top 9,570ft (2,917m) bottom 6,570ft (2,003m)

Park City Mountain Resort top 10,000ft (3,049m) bottom 6,900ft (2,104m)

The mountain above Park City was once one of the most important silver-mining areas in the world, and the first skiers were taken up through the mountain on a mine train before being raised to the surface on a mine hoist lift. Mountain access is now by two detachable six-person chair-lifts, which take 12 minutes to reach the Summit House Restaurant. The highest point is Jupiter Bowl. Snow-users of all standards will find suitable runs from the summit to the bottom of the Silverlode six-person chair. Reporters praised the trails as 'beautifully groomed and policed'.

Neighbouring Deer Valley is so exclusive that the staff, who unload the skis from your car and carry them to the snow, won't even accept tips. The resort's designer tag unfairly detracts from the skiing. In fact, its four mountains offer some of the greatest challenges in the region.

Not much of The Canyons ski area can be seen from the base, but a short walk takes guests to the Flight of The Canyons gondola and so to the Red Pine Lodge mid-station, and from here this resort's full magnificence is revealed. Again, the skiing suits all standards on the resort's eight peaks.

Riders and skiers at The Canyons are served by a terrain park on the front face of the resort, which is rated among the top ten in the USA. The half-pipe off Payday trail at Park City is illuminated at night.

No single one of the Park City resorts alone is worth the long journey from the UK but, taken together, and better still in conjunction with Snowbird, Alta and others nearby, this corner of Utah provides some of the world's finest skiing. A complimentary shuttle bus operates between the three resorts, but a hire car is a bonus for visiting other resorts in the surrounding area.

## Off-piste
Nearly all of the skiing at The Canyons is below the tree-line, and consequently the resort has some fabulous tree skiing. The backcountry skiing can be accessed from the top of the Crowning Glory and Ninety Nine 90 Express chairs. Empire Canyon at Deer Valley is the starting point for lots of powder runs including the Daley Chutes and Lady Morgan Bowl.

Park City's skiing is more demanding than the lift map suggests, with plenty of ungroomed options from the top of the Jupiter chair-lift. A guided programme called Ski Utah Interconnect Tour is a full-day off-piste adventure that takes you from Park City to Brighton, Solitude and Alta. Park City Powder Cats arranges guided snowcat-skiing or -boarding.

## Tuition and guiding
We have enthusiastic reports of the Park City Ski & Snowboard School: 'the best we have found anywhere'. Its Mountain Experience programme takes good intermediate to advanced snow-users on to Jupiter Peak. The Deer Valley Ski School offers group and private lessons. Perfect Turn at The Canyons offers learn-to-ski packages using graduated ski lengths to build up confidence.

## Mountain restaurants
At The Canyons, Lookout Cabin has a sophisticated menu and table service. The Silver Lake Lodge, on the slopes at Deer Valley, is home to three restaurants as well as a sunny outdoor barbecue. On a fine day, the rows of smart deckchairs contain more designer-suited sunbathers than you will see in any other US ski resort. The Mid-Mountain Lodge at Park City, a modified version of an old miners' dwelling, offers high-quality fast food ('heaven on a sunny day').

## Accommodation
At the Canyons (☎ 800 472 6309 for all accommodation), the Grand Summit Resort Hotel is an impressive slope-side complex, with a spa and outdoor swimming-pool. The Sundial Lodge provides accommodation on a rather less grandiose scale.

Slope-slide accommodation at Deer Valley is in large, luxurious condominiums and smart hotels, including the Lodges at Deer Valley (☎ 435 615 2600), Goldener Hirsch Inn (☎ 435 649 7770), Stein Eriksen Lodge (☎ 435 649 3700) and Chateaux at Silver Lake (☎ 435 649 4040).

In Park City, recommended hotels include the Silver King (☎ 435 649 5500), Radisson Inn (☎ 435 649 5000) and Yarrow Hotel (☎ 435 649 7000). The Marriott Summit Watch (☎ 435 647 4100) on Main Street is central. At the unusual Angel House Inn (☎ 435 647 0338) each of the nine rooms is modelled on a different angel. Best Western Landmark Inn (☎ 435 649 7300) at Kimball Junction is six miles out of town, but good value.

## Eating in and out
The Cabin, in the Grand Summit Resort Hotel at The Canyons, is one of the smartest eateries in the region. Alternatively the hotel's Cabin Lounge provides more informal dining. Smokie's SmokeHouse is family-friendly, with a Cajun menu and a barbecue.

Deer Valley has nine restaurants, including the Seafood Buffet at the Snow Park Lodge, which is warmly recommended. The Mariposa at Silver Lake Lodge offers fine dining.

Park City is a strong contender for the 'best dining' accolade in a US ski resort. The Claimjumper Steakhouse is an all-American establishment serving 'surf-and-turf'. Chimayo serves Mexican and South-western cuisine. Mikado boasts a wide selection of sushi. 'Excellent crab and enormous Pacific mussels' can be found at 350 Main. Grappa is classic Tuscan. The Riverhorse Café is American and trendy, and Banditos is new. Zoom, owned by Robert Redford, is the clear winner with its Californian cuisine with oriental overtones. For those counting their cents, Ruby Tuesday, at Kimball Junction, is a good-value diner.

## Après-ski
Late-night bars must conform to the strictures of a private club licence in Utah, but temporary membership is easily obtained.

Doc's at the Gondola is the watering-hole of choice for resort staff at The Canyons, but there is a shortage of options by night. The Après Ski Lounge at the Snow Park Lodge in Deer Valley is popular after skiing, but the best of the nightlife is in Park City. There, the No Name Saloon displays the local Park City Rugby Club memorabilia on its walls, alongside stuffed moose and elk heads. Legends in Legacy Lodge at the Park City ski base is a licensed club with live music.

The Factory Stores at Kimball Junction, a four-mile drive from Park City, is a large shopping centre selling end-of-the-line designer clothing at cut prices.

## Childcare

Perfect Kids, conveniently based in the Grand Summit Resort Hotel in The Canyons, offers daycare from eighteen months to nine years of age, and group ski and snowboard clinics. Their Skiers in Diapers programme offers private instruction for children from eighteen months.

Children from two months to twelve years in Deer Valley are looked after by the Children's Center, in the base-lodge at Snow Lodge, which underwent a $4.5 million renovation in 2003–4. The Deer Valley Ski School takes children from three-and-a-half to twelve years of age, and provides Teen Equipe lessons for 13- to 17-year-olds.

Although babysitting is available in town through a choice of three companies, Park City Mountain Resort does not have a ski kindergarten. Families with small children who want to ski would be better off in Deer Valley. The Park City Ski & Snowboard School provides tuition for children from three years.

# Park City Resorts: At a glance

**Tel** The Canyons 1 435 649 5400 / Deer Valley Resort 1 435 649 1000 / Park City Mountain Resort 1 435 649 8111
**Email** info@thecanyons.com / marketing@deervalley.com / pcinfo@pcski.com
**Websites** www.thecanyons.com / www.deervalley.com / www.parkcitymountain.com

## GETTING THERE
**Airport** Salt Lake City 40mins
**Road** follow I-80 from Salt Lake City to Kimball Junction, then Highway 224

## THE SKIING
**Linked/nearby resorts** Alta, Brighton, Snowbird, Sundance, Solitude
**Total of trails/pistes** The Canyons: 3,500 acres (14% beginner, 44% intermediate, 42% difficult). Deer Valley: 1,750 acres (15% easy, 50% intermediate, 25% difficult, 10% very difficult). Park City: 3,300 acres (18% easy, 44% intermediate, 38% difficult)
**Lifts in resorts** 15 at The Canyons: 1🚠 12🚡 2🪑. 19 at Deer Valley: 1🚠 18🚡. 14 at Park City: 14🚡
**Lift opening dates** The Canyons/Deer Valley/Park City 4 December 2004 to 10 April 2005

## LIFT PASSES
**Area pass** Ski Utah Passport (covers Alta, Brighton, The Canyons, Deer Valley, Park City Mountain Resort, Snowbird, Solitude, Sundance) $345–360 for 6 out of 10 days

**Pensioners** The Canyons 65yrs and over $192, Deer Valley 65yrs and over $246, Park City 65–69yrs $228, all for 6 days. Ski Utah Passport no discounts

## TUITION
**Ski & board** Deer Valley Ski School (☎ 435 645 6648), Park City Ski & Snowboard School (☎ 435 649 5496), Perfect Turn at The Canyons (☎ 435 615 3449)
**Guiding** Park City Powder Cats (☎ 435 649 6596), Ski Utah Interconnect Tour (☎ 801 534 1907), Wasatch Powderbird Guides Heli-skiing (☎ 801 742 2800)

## CHILDREN
**Lift pass** The Canyons 7–12yrs $192, Deer Valley 4–12yrs $180, Park City 7–12yrs $192, all for 6 days
**Ski & board school** as adults
**Kindergarten** The Canyons: (ski) Perfect Kids (☎ 435 615 3449), (non-ski) Daycare (☎ 435 615 8036). Deer Valley: (ski/non-ski) Children's Center (☎ 435 649 1000). Park City: (non-ski) Annie's Nannies (☎ 435 615 1935), Creative Beginnings (☎ 435 645 7315), Guardian Angel (☎ 435 783 2662)

## FOOD AND DRINK
Coffee $2.50–3, bottle of house wine $25, small beer $5, soft drink $2.70, dish of the day $12–20

# Smugglers' Notch

ALTITUDE 1,030ft (314m)

❄ **superb children's facilities** ❄ **outstanding ski school**
❄ **lack of queues**

> **Best for:** families, beginners, people seeking skiing convenience
>
> **Not recommended for:** those in search of long cruising runs, off-piste enthusiasts, night-owls, people who hate the cold, adults without children

Smugglers' Notch in Vermont takes its name from the nearby mountain pass that was used for contraband from Canada after the American War of Independence. Sensibly, because of the nature of its mainly gentle, pine-clad slopes, the resort has not tried to compete with its bigger sisters in Colorado and Utah, but has carved a niche in the family market. It regularly wins awards for its child-friendly facilities.

This is not a resort that attracts couples or singles; in fact you would not choose to come to 'Smuggs' if you did not have small children. The key is convenience, with the lifts and accommodation within a 1,000-ft radius, and apartments designed with families in mind. Smuggs is a small, unadorned village consisting mainly of condominiums. Sports shops in the village and in the Upper Mountain Lodge provide the necessary balaclavas and neoprene face masks, and one small supermarket sells provisions for self-caterers.

Stowe, Smuggs' more famous neighbour, used to be reached on skis from Smugglers' Notch via a tenuous connection, but sadly the resorts no longer have an agreement on a joint lift pass and the link is now closed.

## On-piste
top 3,640ft (1,109m) bottom 1,030ft (314m)

Morse is the beginners' mountain, conveniently situated in the village centre of Smugglers' Notch. Another novice area, Morse Highlands, is set halfway up the mountain and is serviced by five trails. From the top of Morse Mountain, at 2,250ft, you can ski along a green trail to the base of Madonna Mountain and back again.

More adept snow-users quickly move on from Morse to the other two mountains, which are reached by bus or on skis. Madonna Mountain offers some pleasant trails, and Sterling has long intermediate runs. The resort also features several sharp double-black-diamond trails, as well as the Black Hole, which is billed as 'the only triple-black-diamond in the east'. The trail directly below the Madonna Summit chair-lift is intimidating.

The old, fixed, double chair-lifts are in serious need of upgrading. The Madonna Summit lift has had a recent $500,000 facelift, but this was no substitute for the building of a detachable quad. However, the chairs' low capacity means that in high season the crowds are at the lift stations and not on the slopes.

Madonna boasts Prohibition Park with a 450-ft super-pipe, which is considered the best half-pipe in Vermont.

> ## WHAT'S NEW
> 40 acres of trails on Madonna Mountain

## Off-piste
There is some unpatrolled skiing through the trees, and locals rate skiing the back bowls from Smuggs after a new snowfall as some of the most challenging easily accessible back-country skiing on the East Coast.

## Tuition and guiding
Snow Sport University is the well-regarded ski and snowboard school. Special courses include 'Dad & Me' and 'Mom & Me'.

## Mountain restaurants
The former warming hut has been replaced with a 'post-and-beam' construction serving snacks and drinks. During the day, snow-

244 THE GOOD SKIING & SNOWBOARDING GUIDE 2005

users currently return to the two bases, where at Morse there is a choice of the Village Lodge, which houses the Green Mountain Café & Bakery, and Rigabello's Pizzeria. At Madonna base you can lunch at the Green Peppers Pub on soups and sandwiches. The Black Bear Lounge is a simple cafeteria.

## Accommodation

The Village at Smugglers' Notch offers a variety of self-catering apartments. The resort's condominiums are highly recommended for families. Reservations for all apartments can be made through the tourist information centre (☎ 0800 169 8219 in UK).

## Eating in and out

All the restaurants in and around Smugglers' Notch are child-friendly. At the Mountain Grille, children under 12 years old are charged half their age in dollars for all they can eat for breakfast. The Hearth & Candle restaurant is the only eatery that has a separate upstairs section – for adults without children. Three Mountain Lodge recreates an authentic Vermont atmosphere.

## Après-ski

Nightlife is geared to family entertainment and fun for children of all ages. The atmosphere is more Butlins-on-snow than Beaver Creek. After skiing, hot chocolate awaits you as you gather around a camp fire at the foot of Morse Mountain. Floodlit snowboarding and tubing down Sir Henry's Sliding Hill provide the later evening entertainment. Snowshoeing on Sterling Pond is another popular après-ski adventure. SmuggsCentral comprises a family-friendly swimming-pool, hot-tub and FunZone.

The Family Snowmaking Center is an educational experience you can ski to on your way home on the Meadowlark green trail. A self-drive snowmobile tour of the mountain is available by night.

## Childcare

Children are what Smuggs is all about. The only disadvantage is the numbingly low temperatures. Little ones from six weeks of age spend their days at Treasures Child Care Center, which features under-floor heating and giant fish tanks. The ski school ('outstanding and puts anything in Europe that we had experienced to shame') takes children to and from the slopes in a tractor-drawn trailer, and in the cold weather classes frequently return to base for hot chocolate, videos and snacks. The timed carving course provides endless on-slope entertainment for more proficient children. An all-day ski camp is open for children aged three to fourteen years and snowboarding for four to fourteen years old. The ski school runs daily programmes for older teenagers.

---

# Smugglers' Notch: At a glance

**Tel** 0800 169 8219 in UK
**Email** smuggs@smuggs.com
**Website** www.smuggs.com

## GETTING THERE
**Airports** Burlington 30 minutes, Boston 3½hrs
**Road** I-89 from Boston

## THE SKIING
**Linked/nearby resorts** Stowe
**Total of trails/pistes** 1,000 acres (22% easy, 53% intermediate, 25% difficult)
**Lifts in area** 8: 6⬚ 2⬚
**Lift opening dates** 26 November 2004 to mid-April 2005

## LIFT PASSES
**Area pass** $264–288 for 6 days

**Pensioners** 65–69yrs $188–200 for 6 days, 70yrs and over free

## TUITION
**Ski & board** Snow Sport University (☎ 0800 169 8219 in UK)
**Guiding** through Snow Sport University

## CHILDREN
**Lift pass** 7–18 yrs $188–200 for 6 days
**Ski & board school** as adults
**Kindergarten** Treasures Child Care Center (☎ 0800 169 8219 in UK)

## FOOD AND DRINK
Coffee $1.50, bottle of house wine $14–20, small beer $4–5, soft drink $1.50, dish of the day $10–14

# Snowbird and Alta

ALTITUDE Snowbird 7,740ft (2,359m), Alta 10,550ft (3,216m)          map: see page 205

❄ **impressive scenery** ❄ **snow-sure resorts** ❄ **short airport transfer**
❄ **retro resort (Alta)** ❄ **purpose-built village (Snowbird)**

> **Best for:** strong intermediate to advanced skiers, off-piste skiing, those who want skiing convenience and families (Snowbird)
>
> **Not recommended for:** beginners, snowboarders (Alta), night-owls, people seeking traditional village atmosphere (Snowbird), budget skiers

The best skiing in Utah is to be found up Little Cottonwood Canyon, at Snowbird and at the 1960s retro-resort of Alta, two contrasting destinations that share a lift link and a lift pass. Their alliance after decades of friendly but serious rivalry has created the most challenging European-style ski circuit for advanced skiers and riders in the whole of North America.

The canyon is rightly considered to be the home of 'champagne powder', a dream-like substance of talcum-type flakes. These have been freeze-dried in their journey over the desert from the distant ocean before being deposited in copious quantities on the steep slopes of the valley.

When Dick Bass, a Texan oilman, built Snowbird in the 1970s, he had apparently fallen under the spell of the latest concrete additions in the French Alps. Officially, the heart of the resort is Snowbird Center, the departure point for the cable-car. The Center comprises the Plaza Deck – an open space surrounded by limited shops on three levels. However, the mirrored walls of the Cliff Lodge, with its 11-storey atrium, dominate the long, narrow swathe of contemporary buildings and car parks.

The neighbouring resort of Alta exists in a time warp. While other ski resorts around the world vie with each other to build four-, six- and even eight-person chair-lifts to provide increasingly swifter access to their slopes, Alta has made a fortune out of standing still. The resort was built some 30 years before Snowbird and is immensely proud of the fact. Sadly, even Alta cannot

forever ignore simple refinements on the invention of the wheel. The 2004–5 season sees the replacement of the old Collins and Germania chairs with a bottom-to-top detachable quad serving Collins Gulch. But otherwise the atmosphere remains reminiscent of Austria in the 1960s, with cranky lifts leading to uncrowded slopes. Only leather lace-up boots, wooden skis and tea-dancing are missing from the tableau.

Alta is revered by powder skiers and generations of well-to-do families, who return here year after year to stay in expensive and comfortable, but far from luxurious, wooden lodges. Its cheap daily lift ticket makes it extremely popular with local skiers. It has rather more beginner and lower-intermediate terrain than Snowbird, and also phenomenal chutes and secret powder caches reached only by hiking.

Devotees refuse to accept that Snowbird is in the same class; realists are thankful that two outstanding powder resorts have joined forces. The mountain merger was made possible because of Snowbird's expansion into Mineral Basin – 500 acres of spectacular alpine terrain that adjoins Alta's boundary.

Visitors exploring different Utah resorts should be aware of the Ski Utah Passport, which covers all lifts in Alta, Park City Resorts (The Canyons, Deer Valley, Park City Mountain Resort), Snowbird, **Sundance** and **Solitude**. It can be purchased only through a UK tour operator or from Ski Utah (www.skiutah.com). There is no Ski Utah Passport for children and families must buy children's day tickets at each resort.

## On-piste
### top 11,000ft (3,352m) bottom 7,760ft (2,365m)

Snowbird boasts one of America's few cable-cars, known as aerial trams, which carries 125 skiers almost 3,000ft to the top of Hidden Peak in seven minutes. There is only one relatively easy run down: Chips, a three-mile trail back to the base area. Elsewhere, the higher skiing is dominated by bowls, chutes and gullies – an exciting arena for advanced skiers who enjoy powering through steep slopes on ungroomed snow.

Snowbird's Baby Thunder lift opens up a network of green runs as well as the slightly more demanding blue trail, Thunder Alley, all of which end up below the village. Complete beginners can ski off the Chickadee lift down by the Cliff Lodge. Otherwise, the Mid Gad and Wilbere lifts serve some of Snowbird's least intimidating terrain, as does the Baldy Express.

The biggest surprise in Alta is that a resort with such a macho reputation for deep powder should have so much easy, groomed skiing. Its network of blue trails criss-crosses the mountain. Both the Sugarloaf and Supreme lifts provide access to cruising runs such as Rock 'n' Roll and Devil's Elbow.

The ski area at Snowbird offers a number of well-groomed runs best suited to confident parallel skiers. Bassackwards, Election, Bananas and Lunch Run are all straightforward cruising trails. However, the ski area is littered with black-diamond slopes and intimidating double-black-diamond runs; considerable care should be taken to avoid embarking on a slope that may be too testing.

## WHAT'S NEW

Replacement of the old chair-lifts with detachable quad at Collins Gulch (Alta)
Super-pipe at Snowbird

Strong skiers in Snowbird are spoilt for choice, with everything from fairly easy, open-bowl skiing to very difficult bump chutes. With the exception of Chips, all the trails off Hidden Peak are classified as black-diamond or double-black-diamond. Challenging black runs through spruce and lodge-pole pine, such as Gadzooks and Tiger Tail, are reached from the Gad 2 lift. The Road To Provo traverse from Hidden Peak (also reached by the Little Cloud lift) leads to other demanding runs such as Black Forest and Organ Grinder.

In Alta, serious skiers head for the Supreme lift and runs such as Catherine's Area, So Long and Sidewinder. Devil's Castle and East Devil's Castle also provide spectacular skiing in powder conditions.

Snowboarders, who account for up to 20 per cent of lift tickets sold in other resorts, are banned from Alta on the grounds that their behaviour both on and off the mountain might inconvenience the regular visitors. How long this ban can be enforced,

given the shared lift pass with Snowbird, remains to be seen. Meanwhile snowboarders at Snowbird enjoy a superb choice of terrain that varies from gentle bowls to extreme chutes from Hidden Peak. There is also a new super-pipe for 2004–5.

## Off-piste

Snowbird's off-piste terrain is superb, and the key to it is the Cirque Traverse from Hidden Peak. From this narrow ridge skiers can drop off both sides into a large selection of chutes and gullies. Some are sandwiched between pines, which have been twisted and stunted by blizzards; others are guarded by imposing outcrops of granite. Plunges into Silver Fox, Great Scott and Upper Cirque on one side and Wilbere Chute, Wilbere Bowl, Barry Barry Steep and Gad Chutes on the other can be exhilarating in fresh snow but quite frightening in difficult conditions. There is also some awesome back-country skiing below Twin Peaks in Gad Valley.

Likewise, Alta becomes one huge powder playground after a fresh fall. It is vital to take local advice on where to find the best and safest runs.

## Tuition and guiding

Snowbird's Mountain School operates a variety of workshops including 'bumps-and-diamonds' and racing, as well as providing normal lessons. The Alf Engen Ski School at Alta was named after its founder, who taught skiing here in 1948.

## Mountain restaurants

The only restaurant on the mountain at Snowbird is at Mid Gad. Serious lunchers must return to the base area.

Alf's Restaurant and the Collins Grill, which are both on the slopes at Alta, are warmly recommended, as is the Albion Grill at Albion base area. Alta Lodge is 'great for a quiet lunch'.

## Accommodation

At Snowbird most people stay at Cliff Lodge and Spa ('much the smartest and most comfortable address here') or at one of the three other condominium lodges nearby: Lodge at Snowbird, The Inn and Iron Blosam Lodge (☎ 801 742 2222 for all reservations)

Alta's oldest and most charming lodge is Alta Lodge (☎ 801 742 3500), which has been attracting visitors since 1939 and was renovated in 1990. Other accommodation includes Alta Peruvian Lodge (☎ 801 742

000) and Rustler Lodge (☎ 801 742 2200),
oth of which have heated outdoor pools.

## ating in and out

nowbird boasts 12 restaurants, including
he Aerie at the top of Cliff Lodge, which is
nclosed by glass and provides continental
uisine. Anyone visiting the Sushi Bar must
e aged 21 or older. Keyhole Junction
pecialises in South-western cooking, while
he Wildflower Ristorante at Iron Blosam
odge features Italian food.

Alta's best food is found at Alta Lodge,
/here Chef Paul Raddon has presided over
he kitchens for more than 30 years. Here in
he heart of the world's first retro-resort,
eservations are chalked on a blackboard
nd wealthy guests from Boston and New
'ork dine at communal tables. Albion Grill,
lta Java and Goldminer's Daughter are
ocated at Alta's mountain bases.

## près ski

nowbird's bars are few in number and
ormal enough to deter all but the most
nthusiastic nightlifers. Immediately after
he lifts close, most people gravitate
owards Wildflower Lodge, Lodge Bistro
Lounge and Keyhole Cantina. The Tram
Club at Snowbird Center puts on live music
and dancing. Later on, the Aerie has live
jazz on Wednesdays and Saturdays. Cliff
Lodge houses a comprehensive spa with a
rooftop swimming-pool.

In Alta, après-ski entertainment is limited
to the slope-side hot-tub or the screening of
black-and-white ski films, followed by
drinks around a roaring log fire. Guests at
Alta Lodge swap tales in the Sitzmark Club.

## Childcare

Daycare for children of six weeks to twelve
years old is available at Camp Snowbird at
Cliff Lodge. The Mountain School at Camp
Snowbird also organises tuition for three- to
twelve-year-olds. One reporter described
Snowbird as 'the most child-friendly resort
I have ever been to'.

Alta's Alf Engen Ski School offers
children's lessons. Alta Lodge Kids'
Program is aimed at four- to ten-year-old
hotel residents and provides transport to
and from ski school, as well as après-ski
activities. Alta Children's Center provides
daycare for non-skiing children from
8.30am to 5pm daily.

# Snowbird and Alta: At a glance

**Tel** Alta 1 801 359 1078 / Snowbird 1 801 742 2222
**Email** info@altaskiarea.com / cres@snowbird.com
**Website** www.altaskiarea.com / www.snowbird.com

## GETTING THERE
**Airport** Salt Lake City 45mins
**Road** I-80 east to exit 6 of I-215 South, then
Highway 210

## THE SKIING
**Linked/nearby resorts** Brighton, The Canyons,
Deer Valley, Park City Mountain Resort, Solitude,
Sundance
**Total of trails/pistes** 4,700 acres (27% beginner,
38% intermediate, 35% advanced)
**Lifts in area** 26: 1🚡 18🚠 7🚋
**Lift opening dates** 15 November 2004 to 15 May
2005

## LIFT PASSES
**Area pass** (covers Alta and Snowbird) $312 for 6
days. Ski Utah Passport (covers Alta, Brighton, The
Canyons, Deer Valley, Park City Mountain Resort,
Snowbird, Solitude, Sundance) $345–360 for 6 out
of 10 days

**Pensioners** Alta 65yrs and over $53, Snowbird
65yrs and over $45, both per day. Joint lift pass and
Ski Utah Passport no discounts

## TUITION
**Ski & board** Alta: Alf Engen Ski School (☎ 801
359 1078). Snowbird: Mountain School (☎ 801
933 2170)
**Guiding** Ski Utah Interconnect Tour (☎ 801 534
1907), Wasatch Powderbird Guides Heli-skiing
(☎ 801 742 2800)

## CHILDREN
**Lift pass** Alta: $33 per day. Snowbird: 12 years and
under ski free with a paying adult.
**Ski & board school** as adults
**Kindergarten** Alta: (ski) Alf Engen Ski School, (non-
ski) Alta Children's Center (☎ 801 742 3042), Alta
Lodge Kids' Program (☎ 801 742 3500), Snowbird:
(ski) Mountain School, (non-ski) Camp Snowbird
(☎ 801 933 2256),

## FOOD AND DRINK
Coffee $1.50, bottle of house wine $25–30, small
beer $3, soft drink $1.50, dish of the day $8–12

# Squaw Valley

ALTITUDE 6,200ft (1,890m)

## ❊ scenic Lake Tahoe resort ❊ good intermediate terrain ❊ steep skiing and snowboarding

**Best for:** intermediates, accomplished skiers and riders, cross-country skiers, families

**Not recommended for:** non-skiers, those wanting a large linked ski area

Squaw Valley, on the north shore of beautiful Lake Tahoe, provides steep and demanding terrain coupled with a brand-new village and beautiful scenery in a corner of the Sierra Nevada that has a long skiing tradition. As far back as 1856, John 'Snowshoe' Thompson, a Norwegian immigrant, used to carry the mail on skis between the mining camps in these mountains. Until the railway was built in 1872, skiing was the miners' only winter link with the outside world. In 1960 Squaw Valley successfully hosted the Winter Olympics, despite a virtual absence of lifts at the time, and has since managed to maintain an international image. Phases one and two of a major building programme, undertaken by the giant Canadian resort developer Intrawest, are now complete, providing additional restaurants, shopping and entertainment.

### WHAT'S NEW
Double-chair-lift added to Far East beginners' area

Tahoe City, a ten-minute drive from Squaw Valley on the north shore of the lake, is a small town that exudes considerable atmosphere and boasts several appealing restaurants on the lake-side. The lake is surrounded by no less than 15 alpine ski resorts and another eight cross-country centres. Together they offer more than 100 lifts, giving access to 17,520 acres of skiing and riding. Squaw shares an interchangeable lift pass with five of them – Alpine Meadows, **Heavenly**, Kirkwood, Northstar-at-Tahoe and Sierra-at-Tahoe. A car is useful for exploring the enormous amount of skiing

on offer, although public transport is efficient and frequent.

## On-piste
top 9,050ft (2,758m) bottom 6,200ft (1,890m)

The skiing at Squaw Valley takes place on six peaks: Granite Chief, Snow King, KT-22, Squaw Peak, Emigrant and Broken Arrow. The area is divided into three sectors, but the 32 lifts, rather than the runs, are colour graded. All the main lifts on KT-22, Squaw Peak and Granite Chief are black-diamond, while those on Snow King and Emigrant are blue. Intermediates will find a huge amount of skiing – the highlight being a three-mile trail from the High Camp area down to the mountain base. The main mountain access is via the Gold Coast Funitel.

The main beginner area is located adjacent to the High Camp Bath and Tennis Club at the top of the mountain and is accessed by cable-car. Three areas are of particular appeal to intermediates: the pistes off the Squaw Creek and Red Dog lifts, the area off the Gold Coast Express chair-lift, and the tree runs off the Shirley Lake Express chair-lift. A new double-chair-lift has been added to the Far East beginners' area, improving access for novice skiers and snowboarders.

The Mainline terrain park comes complete with a host of treats for riders. KT-22 is a particularly good area for freeriders in search of challenge and excitement. The old Riviera terrain park and half-pipe under the chair-lift of the same name is open until 9pm.

## Off-piste
Squaw was the birthplace of the American extreme skiing movement and boasts some seriously steep couloirs as well as open bowl skiing. The most radical terrain is to be found off the KT-22, Headwall, Cornice II and Granite Chief chair-lifts.

## Tuition and guiding
The Squaw Valley Ski & Snowboard School runs a wide variety of programmes.

## Mountain restaurants

The resort has over 40 eateries and bars, both on the mountain and in the base village. These include the Gold Coast, at the top of the Funitel, which features a barbecue, restaurants and bars on three levels. High Camp boasts five.

## Accommodation

Condominiums in the new village (☎ 530 584 1000) are said to be 'elegant and comfortable', and the Resort at Squaw Creek (☎ 530 583 6300) is a large ski-in, ski-out complex near the base. The Squaw Valley Lodge (☎ 530 583 5500) is close to the base lifts, while the Squaw Valley Inn (☎ 530 583 1576) offers some of the most stylish accommodation. PlumpJack (☎ 800 323 7666) is a modern minimalist hotel with a renowned restaurant. Other accommodation is at The Olympic Village Inn (☎ 530 583 1576).

## Eating in and out

Squaw Valley now has 29 restaurants and bars, including the eateries in the new village such as Mamasake Sushi, High Sierra Grill and Tantara Bakery Bistro & Beyond. Glissandi is a high-priced Italian, and Graham's (in the valley) is cosy. Resort at Squaw Creek and PlumpJack are warmly praised. The Bridgetender ('delicious and affordable burgers'), Wolfdales ('Japanese-inspired cuisine') and Sunnyside in nearby Tahoe City are recommended, along with Za's and upmarket Christy Hill's overlooking the lake. The Cottonwood, Moody's Bistro and Pianettas, a ten-minute drive away in Truckee, are also praised.

## Après-ski

At Squaw there is music at Bar One in the base village. Other post-slope options include Salsa, the Balboa Café, Le Chamois, the PlumpJack and the Red Dog Saloon, where the locals drink. The High Camp Bath and Tennis Club is open until 9pm with tubing and ice-skating in winter, and swimming during the spring. Night-skiing and boarding are included in the daily lift ticket.

## Childcare

The Children's Centre at the base of the mountain is for three- to twelve-year-olds, and is convenient for families. Parents can deliver their offspring and buy their tickets at the same time. At Squaw Kids Ski & Snowboard School instructors teach children aged four to twelve years. As part of Squaw's upgrade, the Papoose Learning Area has been improved and boasts two new drag lifts.

# Squaw Valley: At a glance

**Tel** 1 530 583 6985
**Email** squaw@squaw.com
**Website** www.squaw.com

### GETTING THERE
**Airports** Reno 1hr, San Francisco 4hrs
**Road** I-80 from Reno or San Francisco, then Highway 89

### THE SKIING
**Linked/nearby resorts** Alpine Meadows, Heavenly, Kirkwood, Northstar-at-Tahoe, Sierra-at-Tahoe
**Total of trails/pistes** 4,000 acres (25% easy, 45% intermediate, 30% difficult)
**Lifts in area** 32: 3🚡 25🚠 4🎿
**Lift opening dates** 15 November 2004 to 31 May 2005

### LIFT PASSES
**Area pass** (resort only) $290 for 6 out of 8 days.
Regional pass (only available through tour operators and covers Alpine Meadows, Heavenly, Kirkwood, Northstar-at-Tahoe, Sierra-at-Tahoe) $270 for 5 out of 6 days
**Pensioners** 65–75yrs $174 for 6 days

### TUITION
**Ski & board** Squaw Valley Ski & Snowboard School (☎ 530 581 7263)
**Guiding** through ski school

### CHILDREN
**Lift pass** 12yrs and under $30 per day
**Ski & board school** Squaw Valley Kids Ski & Snowboard School (☎ 530 581 7166)
**Kindergarten** (ski/non-ski) Children's Centre at Squaw Valley Kids Ski & Snowboard school (☎ 530 581 7225)

### FOOD AND DRINK
Coffee $2, bottle of house wine $25–35, small beer $3.50, soft drink $2.50, dish of the day $10–12

# Steamboat

ALTITUDE 6,900ft (2,103m)

## ❄ modern lift system ❄ good snow cover ❄ wide range of restaurants ❄ Wild West town

> **Best for:** beginners, snowboarders, families
>
> **Not recommended for:** expert piste skiers

Steamboat lies at the foot of Rabbit Ears Pass in Routt County, north-west Colorado, a three-and-a-half hour drive from Denver. It is a genuine cowboy town. Each January it hosts The Cowboy Downhill, a unique slalom with roping and saddling elements contested by more than 100 professional rodeo riders in full costume.

### On the snow
top 10,568ft (3,221m) bottom 6,900ft (2,103m)

The skiing at Steamboat covers 2,939 acres on six mountains: Mount Werner, Sunshine Peak, Storm Peak, Thunderhead Peak, Christie Peak and Pioneer Ridge. The area's modern lift system is backed up by extensive snowmaking.

> ### WHAT'S NEW
> Quad-chair in Sunshine Bowl

The Steamboat gondola takes snow-users up to the Thunderhead mid-station, and four high-speed quads allow them to fan out rapidly over the upper slopes. The Morningside Park Bowl off the back of Storm Peak provides gentle terrain and better access to Mount Werner. The Pioneer Ridge sector opens up 12 trails, mainly for advanced skiers. A new quad-chair in Sunshine Bowl gives good access to popular runs such as Tomahawk, Quickdraw and Flintlock. The Mavericks super-pipe, at 660ft, is claimed to be the longest in North America. The base of the gondola is an ideal novice area and is served by six beginner lifts.

Steamboat Ski School has a good reputation for teaching children and beginners. Steamboat Powder Cats runs day snowcat-skiing trips to Buffalo Pass, a few miles out of town.

The most sophisticated lunch option is Hazie's at the Thunderhead mid-station. The alternative sit-down choice, Ragnar's at Rendezvous Saddle, specialises in Scandinavian dishes.

## In the resort

Visitors stay at the purpose-built Steamboat base area, or four miles away in the town of Steamboat Springs. The Steamboat Grand Resort & Conference Center (☎ 970 871 5500) and the Sheraton Steamboat (☎ 970 879 2220) are praised. In the Old Town area of Steamboat Springs, the Harbor Hotel (☎ 970 879 1522), Alpiner Lodge (☎ 970 879 1430), Hampton Inn & Suites (☎ 970 871 8900), Fairfield Inn (☎ 970 870 9000), Comfort Inn (☎ 970 879 6669) and Holiday Inn (☎ 970 879 2250) are all popular.

When the lifts close, beer lovers gather at Slopeside and the Tugboat in Ski Time Square, as well as at the Steamboat Brewery and Tavern on Lincoln Avenue in Steamboat Springs. Other watering-holes include Chaps, the Bear River Bar & Grill, Dos Amigos, Levelz and the Tap House.

Smart restaurants include Sevens at the Sheraton and The Cabin at the Steamboat Grand. Fine dining can be found at L'Apogee, Antares, Tobianos, Hazie's, Giovanni's, Ragnar's, Café Diva and the Steamboat Yacht Club. There is Chinese food at the Panda Garden and the Canton, sushi at Yama Chan's and Mexican at La Montana. The Cottonwood Grille is recommended for Pacific Rim cuisine.

The Kids Vacation Center accepts two- to six-year-olds, and babies and non-skiing children are looked after at Kiddie Corrall Child Care.

> ## Steamboat: At a glance
>
> **Tel** 1 970 879 6111
> **Email** info@steamboat.com
> **Website** www.steamboat.com
> **Lifts in resort** 20: 1🚡 17🚠 2🎿
> **Lift opening dates** 24 November 2004 to 10 April 2005

# Stowe

ALTITUDE 1,300ft (396m)

❄ **classic New England village** ❄ **dramatic mountain scenery**
❄ **varied terrain** ❄ **well-groomed trails**

**Best for:** skiers and snowboarders of all standards, ski-gourmets

**Not recommended for:** people who want ski-in ski-out convenience, night-owls

The eighteenth-century town of Stowe attracts wealthy Bostonians and New Yorkers as well as ten per cent of its skiers from Britain – several hotels have UK freephone numbers for booking direct.

Stowe is a typical Vermont town of red-and-white, weatherboarded houses set around a steepled, white church on attractive Main Street, where most of the shops and some of the hotels are located. Much of the accommodation is strung out along the highway that winds for five miles up to the ski base. However, construction is underway on Stowe's $300-million, ten-year plan of improvements that will give the resort new base-lodges, lifts, trails and accommodation.

## WHAT'S NEW

Double-chair on Spruce Peak replaced by high-speed detachable quad

## In the snow

Top 3,640ft (1,109m) bottom 1,280ft (390m)

The skiing takes place outside the village centre with 49 trails on two mountains on either side of the valley road. The ten-year plan envisages a lift link; for now, a free bus shuttles continuously between the two – only a five-minute ride, but an irritation, especially for groups of mixed ability divided between the two mountains.

Spruce Peak has a broad, protected nursery area, where most of the beginner ski school classes take place; higher up are a variety of mainly blue, wooded runs. Across the valley road on Mount Mansfield, the highest peak in Vermont, two fast lifts serve nearly all the trails. An eight-person gondola

up to the Cliff House Restaurant offers a choice of mainly blue runs down, while the Cliff Trail links over to the main part of Mansfield. On this sector a high-speed quad carries skiers to the self-service Octagon Web Café, with superb views. On the upper part of the mountain are some thrillingly steep double-black-diamonds. The 'Front Four'– Starr, Liftline, National and Goat – are rightly considered some of the toughest slopes in the Eastern States, especially in icy conditions.

Stowe Ski & Snowboard School offers group and private lessons.

## In the resort

The Inn at the Mountain (☎ 802 253 3656) is the only slope-side accommodation. In the village, the Green Mountain Inn (☎ 802 253 7301) is based around a private house dating to 1833, with a year-round heated outdoor pool and health club.

Options along the mountain road include the friendly, family-run Golden Eagle Resort (☎ 0800 328 7865 in UK). The Partridge Inn opposite is top choice for seafood; next door Pie in the Sky serves good-value pizzas. Stoweflake (☎ 0500 892 522 in UK) looks like a classic family-run New England inn, but is actually a major hotel with a huge spa comprising 29 treatment rooms and an indoor waterfall. Across the road is the lively Shed microbrewery. Four miles out of town is the opulent, Austrian-style Trapp Family Lodge (☎ 802 253 8511).

Cubs Daycare Center opens at 8am daily and accepts children from six weeks of age. The resort has a magic carpet lift.

### Stowe: At a glance

**Tel** 1 802 253 3000
**Email** info@stowe.com
**Website** www.stowe.com
**Lifts in resort** 11: 1🚠 8🚡 2🎿
**Lift opening dates** mid-November 2004 to mid-April 2005

# Taos

ALTITUDE 9,207ft (2,807m)

※ **steep-and-deep skiing** ※ **exotic desert surroundings**
※ **historic town of Taos** ※ **recommended ski school**

**Best for:** advanced skiers, non-skiers wanting a cultural experience
**Not recommended for:** snowboarders

Taos likes to describe itself as 'the last bastion of pure skiing – a lot of sun, snow, mountains . . . and no snowboarders'. Provided you prefer two planks to one, the Taos Ski Valley possesses a charm that is all its own. Although it is at the same latitude as Rome, the snow in this north-facing bowl in the Carson National Forest is surprisingly good. A few miles down the road, the cacti and sagebrushes that characterise the New Mexican desert stretch as far as the eye can see. The town of Taos, an art-led, cosmopolitan melting pot with a dominant Native American culture, is 20 miles away.

The Taos Ski Valley was created by the legendary Ernie Blake, a German-born Swiss who discovered what he recognised as perfect skiing terrain while flying over the Rockies in the early 1950s. In 1956 Blake was joined by the French racer Jean Mayer in an enterprise that still combines Teutonic efficiency with Gallic flair. Mayer also had a gastronomic interest, which he indulged at Hotel St Bernard. Blake was a firm believer in ski classes, and he created the best ski school in the country. Its founder died in 1989, but Taos continues in the same distinguished tradition.

## On the snow
top 11,819ft (3,603m) bottom 9,207ft (2,807m)

Taos has 105 trails and the mountain is imposing, especially from the village perspective. Al's Run, the tough mogul field under the lift line, makes such an impression that a notice reassures visitors of easier skiing further up the mountain.

While this is true, there is also even more difficult skiing, especially off the high traverse, where trails such as Oster, Tresckow and Stauffenberg (German officers who plotted against Hitler) testify to the

founder's anti-Nazi stance during World War II. Sir Arnold Lunn, the father of modern European skiing, is also commemorated on the trail map. The key run in the beginners' area is Honeysuckle, while intermediates should head for Porcupine and Powderhorn, both ego-boosting cruisers.

Taos Ski Valley is the ski school for adults and children, and still has an excellent reputation. Specialist courses include a race camp, a mogul camp, Ski-the-Steeps and telemarking. Children have a maximum class size of nine pupils. Non-skiers aged six weeks to three years are cared for at the Children's Center.

## In the resort
Taos Ski Valley is extremely compact, and hotel accommodation is limited. Hotel St Bernard (☎ 505 776 2251) is usually booked out for the next season by early August. Thunderbird Lodge (☎ 505 776 2280) is comfortable and hosts live jazz, while The Inn at Snake Dance (☎ 505 776 2277) has the most modern rooms. The Sagebrush Inn (☎ 505 758 2254) was built in 1929 and is in Taos town. The other hotels are Rio Hondo Condos (☎ 505 776 2347) and the Kandahar (☎ 505 776 2226). A new complex of deluxe condos, a spa and restaurant opens in December 2004. Four miles down the valley, the adobe Quail Inn Ridge Resort (☎ 505 776 2211) features a desert ambience, tennis courts and an outdoor swimming-pool.

Kids' nights with entertainment and teen party nights are regularly organised in the resort.

## Taos: At a glance

**Tel** 1 505 776 2291
**Email** tsv@skitaos.org
**Website** www.skitaos.org
**Lifts in resort** 12: 10⑤ 2⑤
**Lift opening dates** 22 November 2004 to 3 April 2005

# Telluride

**ALTITUDE 8,725ft (2,660m)**

## ❄ atmospheric old town ❄ good skiing for all standards ❄ wide choice of restaurants

**Best for:** advanced piste skiers, non-skiers, snowboarders
**Not recommended for:** people who prefer not to go to remote destinations

An old mining town in a beautiful box-canyon in the San Juan Mountains of Colorado, Telluride has a colourful history. At the height of the gold rush, 5,000 prospectors crowded into the town, the name of which derives either from tellurium, a non-metallic element in gold and silver ore, or less probably from 'to hell you ride' – a sobriquet that could apply to Butch Cassidy, who robbed his first bank on Main Street in 1889 before escaping on horseback.

The wide street, dominated by the New Sheridan Hotel – which was new in the Victorian times – and the original court house, is architecturally little changed today. Four miles away by road lies the modern piste-side Mountain Village Resort, which is connected to the town by gondola. The development of condominiums, shops and a golf course there triggered a property boom and attracted a number of Hollywood investors.

Both town and Mountain Village are equally convenient for the skiing, although the delightful town is itself one of the prime reasons for visiting this remote corner of Colorado. Montrose Regional Airport is 65 miles from the resort and accessible via Chicago, Dallas/Fort Worth, Houston and Newark. Alternatively you can fly direct to Telluride Regional Airport, just six miles from Telluride, via Denver or Phoenix.

## In the snow
**Top 12,247ft (3,734m) bottom 8,725ft (2,660m)**

The backbone of the area is See Forever, a long, rolling blue run from the top of the skiing to the Mountain Village.

The Galloping Goose area, isolated to one side of the Mountain Village, is perfect for beginners. Aggressive skiers and riders head for the double-black-diamond Spiral

Stairs or Gold Hill for short but steep off-piste glades. Expansion into Prospect Bowl has almost doubled Telluride's lift-served terrain, to 1,700 acres, in recent years. The giant terrain park with a half-pipe is the largest in Colorado.

Telluride's Ski & Snowboard School offers adult group and private lessons as well as tuition for children from three to twelve.

On-mountain dining takes place at Alfred's, Giuseppe's, Big Billie's, Gorrono Ranch and That Pizza Place.

## In the resort
The New Sheridan Hotel (☎ 800 200 1891) is central and traditional, with a handsome mahogany bar, while the restaurant serves fashionable dishes of elk, venison and ostrich. The Ice House (☎ 800 544 3436) is modern, central, smart and convenient for the Oak Street base-station, while the best-placed hotel in town is Camel's Garden (☎ 888 772 2635), right next to the gondola station. Up at Mountain Village, the sprawling Peaks Resort (☎ 800 789 2220) at Mountain Village is 'the ultimate in luxury spa hotels', and Hotel Telluride is a new boutique hotel.

Restaurants in Telluride offer everything from sushi to gourmet French fare. Options include Limeleaf, which serves 'new Asian' cuisine, and Rustico, which is Italian, while Allred's has innovative cuisine.

The Children's Nursery is for kids aged two months to three years, and the Afternoon Kids Club offers free après-ski entertainment for those attending ski school classes. Mountain Village Nursery and Annie's Nannies are for babysitting.

---

### Telluride: At a glance
**Tel** 1 866 287 5015
**Email** info@telluride.com
**Website** www.tellurideskiresort.com
**Lifts in resort** 18: 3 🚡 13 🚠 2 🎿
**Lift opening dates** 24 November 2004 to 3 April 2005

# Vail

ALTITUDE 8,120ft (2,475m)                                    map: see page 21

❄ **reliable snow record** ❄ **smart hotels and restaurants**
❄ **large ski area** ❄ **excellent ski school** ❄ **big mogul fields**
❄ **substantial off-piste terrain**

---

**Best for:** children, those seeking creature comforts, skiers and riders of all levels of experience, off-piste novices

**Not recommended for:** those on a budget, mountain-lunchers, late-night clubbers

---

Through a relentless programme of annual improvement, Vail maintains its position as the showcase of American skiing. It continues to woo domestic and international skiers by offering the largest single mountain ski area in the United States, served by 34 mainly high-speed lifts.

Over the past eight years the resort's owners, Vail Resorts, have injected some $110 million into mountain facilities and they have now turned their attention to the resort itself. In a bold initiative, Vail is to raze ugly buildings which date from the 1970s to create what will be an entirely new village out of the existing suburb of Lionshead, at an initial estimated cost of $380 million.

For some visitors, the primping and pampering of an otherwise mediocre stretch of mountain-side signals the danger of homogenising the skiing and snowboarding experience to the level of a Disney-style theme park. The Yellow Jackets ski patrol operates speed traps in designated slow-skiing zones, and offenders are liable to lose their lift passes without warning. However, for others, Vail personifies the perfect winter playground, a place where fine hotels and gourmet restaurants are matched by seamless corduroy slopes and dedicated lift attendants.

Anyone expecting a classic Rocky Mountain settlement at their journey's end is in for a disappointment. The pedestrianised village centre is built in neo-Tyrolean style with outlying communities that sprawl for several miles along the busy I-70 freeway. Vail shares a two-tier lift pass – the Colorado Ticket – with its sister resort **Beaver Creek**, ten miles to the west as well as **Breckenridge** and **Keystone**. There is a regular subsidised shuttle service between them. The small but challenging ski area of **Arapahoe Basin** is also included in the lift pass although it is not owned by Vail Resorts. The more expensive version of the Colorado Ticket can be bought in Vail and Beaver Creek and allows you full use of the lift system in all resorts. The cheaper version, bought in Keystone and Breckenridge, allows you to ski in Vail and Breckenridge for half the duration of the pass.

## On-piste
top 11,570 ft (3,526m) bottom 8,120ft (2,475m)

Vail stretches along Highway I-70 from Golden Peak to Cascade Village with six main means of mountain access. Queues tend to form only at peak times for the main Vista Bahn Express and Eagle Bahn Gondola, and at the Mid-Vail station. All these lifts are served by an efficient ski-bus system.

The two beginner areas are at Golden Peak and Eagle's Nest. The former, at the east end of the mountain, includes a number of easy runs and short lifts at the base area. Fort Whippersnapper, at the mid station of the Riva Bahn lifts, is an extensive ski-in, ski-out playground for children. At Eagle's Nest, reached directly by the gondola from Lionshead, are several easy runs and an activity centre that includes tubing, skating and snowmobiling.

The front face of Vail is essentially an intermediate's mountain spiced with some vicious bump runs ('Highline, Roger's Run and Blue Ox are mogul heaven'). Most skiers head to the top of the mountain via the Vista Bahn to mid-Vail ('worst queues of anywhere in the region'), where two high-speed quads let you explore the central est side of the mountain. Gandy Dancer is a lovely roller-coaster'. Skipper, off the Windows Road catwalk, is little skied and an provide considerable challenge, while Ouzo, Ouzo Glade and Ouzo Woods, off Taro, all offer first-rate tree skiing. Look Ma and Challenge, under the Wildwood xpress chair, really test technique in good now. Kangaroo Cornice, under the Wildwood Express chair, and North Rim, nder the Northwoods Express, are also well worth trying. Intermediates favour the ong, cruising runs from the Northwoods xpress, or the easier trails off Game Creek xpress lift. For fast and smooth cruising ou can take the runs off Eagle's Nest idge, such as Lodgepole, Berries and edges, down to the Avanti chair or all the way to the base.

The Golden Peak terrain park features a uper-pipe with 18-ft walls. There is also a maller park on Bwana, which has jumps nd rails.

## ff-piste

he Back Bowls, accessed from the top of e mountain, provide Vail's off-piste skiing nd snowboarding. The area is ideally uited to beginner and inexperienced deep-now skiers, who get a chance to find their et in a controlled and lift-served nvironment that is mainly gentle in pitch. ndeed one reporter commented: 'it is hard work out how they managed to come up ith so many names for similar side-by-side uns on the same stretch of mountain'. evertheless, it is rewarding for anyone to ake fresh tracks here, with plenty of utes, drop-offs and tree skiing to be und once you know where to look.

Blue Sky Basin, Vail's most recent 645-cre addition off-piste, is where to find the xperts. 'Stupendous skiing that gives Vail ue status among powderhounds,' enthused ne reporter. 'Blue Sky is the business, but ke care at the top of Lover's Leap, or you nd yourself on top of a 15-ft rock, with owhere to go,' commented another.

The Minturn Mile takes you down rough some scenic and challenging terrain the small town of Minturn; Margaritas or tchers of beer at the Saloon here make a easant end to the outing.

## ition and guiding

ail/Beaver Creek Ski and Snowboard chool has the monopoly and prices are consequently iniquitously high. However, the standard of teaching is exceptional ('a single lesson here was worth a week of classes in France'). Ex-British Olympic racer Martin Bell works for Vail as an ambassador-at-large and you can book a private lesson with him. The school meets at six separate locations: at the base of Golden Peak and Lionshead, and in Vail Village, as well as at Two Elk, Mid-Vail and Eagle's Nest. Reporters continue to comment on the high quality of instruction and the friendly attitude of the teachers: 'the ski school is excellent – my group varied from two to five people and the instructor was happy to tailor the content to what we wanted to do'. The school employs 150 snowboard teachers, with dedicated teenage classes in high season. Extreme skiing is also on offer, as well as skiing for the disabled, telemark, women's clinics and terrrain park instruction.

## Mountain restaurants

Two Elk Lodge, on the ridge separating the Front Face from the Back Bowls, is a cavernous self-service. One reporter noted that 'the restaurant has now augmented the standard hamburger and hot dog fare with Oriental dishes such as sushi and stir-fry with noodles or rice'. The Lodge at Vail's Cucina Rustica offers a 'good-value Italian lunchtime buffet'. The Wildwood Smokehouse is renowned for its chicken and wild rice soup, and Buffalo's at Chair 4 has 'great buffalo burgers'. Larkspur at the base of Golden Peak, Garfinkels, and Bart & Yeti's at Lionshead are recommended, as are Pepi's and Los Amigos in Vail Village.

## Accommodation

The Lodge at Vail (☎ 970 476 5011) is owned by the resort and remains one of the most luxurious hotels, together with the Sonnenalp Resort (☎ 970 476 5656). The Evergreen Lodge (☎ 970 476 7810) heads the second rank. The Marriott Mountain Resort (☎ 970 476 4444) is rated among the best in Vail. Cheaper is Roost Lodge (☎ 970 476 5451) in West Vail. Antlers at Vail (☎ 970 476 2471) has had a recent makeover, and the renovated Vail Mountain Lodge and Spa (☎ 970 476 0700) is highly recommended. Landmark Townhouses in Lionshead (☎ 970 479 2868) are 'convenient and extremely well-appointed'.

## Eating in and out

The Vail Valley features an enormous choice of restaurants, serving food of every nationality from Mexican to Thai and Japanese. Terra Bistro is 'an upmarket brasserie with an Oriental–Italian focus'. Montauk Seafood Grill in Lionshead 'specialises in oysters and wonderful Rocky Mountain trout'. Russell's 'offers the world from *Wienerschnitzel* to Alaskan crab legs'. Bully Ranch at the Sonnenalp Resort is renowned for its Western-style beef and barbecue menu. The Wildflower in the Lodge, La Tour and the Left Bank are also strongly recommended for a special night out, as are the Tyrolean and the Lancelot Inn. Montauk in Lionshead features superlative seafood: 'quite outstanding, some of the best food in the resort'. Mezzaluna and Billy's Island Grill in Lionshead are both favourites with locals. Up the Creek is praised for its 'excellent duck', and May Palace in the West Vail Mall is a recommended Chinese restaurant.

The resort continues to receive criticism for its high prices: 'no family-priced restaurants to be found; everywhere is upscale', said one reporter. For cheaper food, try Pazzo's Pizzeria. Reporters advised taking the car to Minturn and eating in the Saloon ('noisy, friendly, cheap, with plentiful Mexican food').

## Après-ski

Chill out at the Blue Moon bar at Eagle's Nest ('much the best curry in Vail') after tubing, ski-biking, orienteering, and a choice of other after activities at Adventure Ridge, at the top of the Eagle Bahn gondola. Down in the resort, Mickey's Piano Bar at the Lodge is where to spot celebrities. The Red Lion in Bridge Street is the most popular après-ski bar with live music. The Tap Room & Sanctuary has dining and dancing. Numerically named 8150 is a fashionable nightclub. The Ore House offers happy-hour prices. Bully Ranch at the Sonnenalp and Hypnotik were both warmly praised by reporters.

## Childcare

Vail is recommended for children: 'my young kids were able to glide down a well-marked catwalk in complete safety from the top of every lift', said one reporter. The Small World Play School at Golden Peak and at Lionshead is a non-ski kindergarten. The Children's Ski and Snowboard School at both locations is for kids from seven to fourteen years of age. After-skiing children's and family programmes include Kids' Night Out, for children aged five to thirteen, with dinner and activities.

# Vail: At a glance

**Tel** 1 970 476 9090
**Email** vailinfo@vailresorts.com
**Website** www.vail.com

### GETTING THERE
**Airports** Eagle County 40 mins, Denver 2½hrs
**Road** take I-70 east from Denver and follow through Eisenhower tunnel to Vail

### THE SKIING
**Linked/nearby resorts** Arapahoe Basin, Beaver Creek, Breckenridge, Keystone
**Total of trails/pistes** 5,289 acres (28% easy, 32% intermediate, 40% difficult)
**Lifts in area** 34: 1⑤ 24⑤ 9⑤
**Lift opening dates** late November 2004 to late April 2005

### LIFT PASSES
**Area pass** Colorado Ticket (covers Arapahoe Basin, Beaver Creek, Breckenridge, Keystone, Vail) $234–426 for 6 days

**Pensioners** Colorado Ticket 65–69yrs $199–362 for 6 days, 70yrs and over $299 for season

### TUITION
**Ski & board** Vail/Beaver Creek Ski and Snowboard School (☎ 970 476 3239)
**Guiding** through ski school

### CHILDREN
**Lift pass** Colorado Ticket 5–12yrs $210–224 for 6 days
**Ski & board school** as adults
**Kindergarten** (ski) Children's Ski and Snowboard School (☎ 970 476 3239), (non-ski) Small World Play School (☎ 970 479 3285)

### FOOD AND DRINK
Coffee $2.50, bottle of house wine $20, small beer $3.50–4, soft drink $2.50, dish of the day $10–16

# Winter Park

**ALTITUDE 9,000ft (2,743m)**

## ✳ easy airport access ✳ excellent piste-grooming ✳ efficient lift system

**Best for:** intermediate cruisers, budget skiers, early- and late-season skiers

**Not recommended for:** snowboarders, partygoers

Winter Park is the closest major ski resort to Denver, which is only 67 miles away, and a high number of skiers and snowboarders commute here at weekends by a special Ski Train, which conveniently deposits them at the foot of the lifts. An Amtrak rail service stops at nearby Fraser on a daily basis. What has always been a good Colorado resort is now set to get even better. The municipally-owned Denver ski area is now being run on a 50-year lease by giant Canadian resort developer Intrawest, which has announced plans to invest $100 million in Winter Park over the next decade. Sadly, only $10 million of this sum has been set aside for new lifts.

The original village of Winter Park is an inconvenient two miles from the ski area and plans to build a gondola from the old village to mid-mountain have yet to materialise. A regular ski bus service links it to the ski base area, which also has accommodation and has undergone considerable development in recent years.

## On the snow
**top 12,057ft (3,676m) bottom 9,000ft (2,743m)**

The skiing in Winter Park is highly rewarding, with long, wide trails, challenging mogul fields, few mid-week queues, efficient lifts, perfectly manicured slopes and usually reliable snow conditions.

The area is divided into two main sections: Winter Park/Vasquez Ridge, which has mostly intermediate trails, and Mary Jane, which features hard-bump skiing as well as tree-level runs and long blues from the Parsenn Bowl. Winter Park has two terrain parks and a super-pipe.

Winter Park Ski & Snowboard School offers tuition ('private lessons were cheap and the boarding lessons were of a very high quality'). Special courses include bump clinics, a mogul camp and a ride festival, as well as women-only and men-only programmes. The daily free mountain-guiding service is warmly recommended by reporters as the best way to learn your way around the ski area of 2,770 acres.

Mountain restaurants include the Dining Room at the Lodge at Sunspot, which is on the summit of Winter Park Mountain. Snoasis is a mid-mountain meeting place with a daily Happy Hour from 2pm. The Club Car, at the base of Mary Jane, and Derailer Bar, at the base of Winter Park, both offer waiter-service menus.

Neighbouring Berthoud Pass now no longer operates as a ski area.

## In the resort
The choice is between the base-area village and the town. The village is built around the ski-in, ski-out Zephyr Mountain Lodge, with a restaurant, pub and ski shop as well as over 200 condominiums. Additional lodging near the slopes is at Winter Park Mountain Lodge ('adequate, but nothing special'), the Vintage Hotel and Iron Horse Resort. Options in downtown Winter Park include the Super 8 Lodge, the Olympia Lodge and Sundowner Motel (☎ 970 726 5587 for all reservations).

Après-ski choices include the Club Car, the Derailer Bar and the Crooked Creek Saloon.

Winter Park Resort Adventure Junction Children's Center runs ski and snowboard programmes, while the Children's Center Daycare looks after children from two months to five years. The resort has four magic carpet lifts.

### Winter Park: At a glance

**Tel** 1 970 726 5514
**Email** wpinfo@skiwinterpark.com
**Website** www.skiwinterpark.com
**Lifts in resort** 20: 18⬠ 2⬡
**Lift opening dates** 17 November 2004 to 17 April 2005

# World resort index

## Abondance, France

This tiny historic village lies 7km from **La Chapelle d'Abondance** and is not connected by lifts into the main **Portes du Soleil** system. However, an hourly bus service links the village into the main Portes du Soleil circuit. Abondance has its own small ski area with a dedicated children's area on the slopes beneath the Col de l'Ecuelle, served by a gondola and a series of six drag-lifts. The resort has a micro-park for snowboarding children. Recommended hotels include the two-star La Rocaille (☎ 45 07 301 74), Hotel Les Touristes (☎ 450 73 02 15) and Le Ferraillon (☎ 450 73 07 75).

**Tel** 33 450 73 02 90
**Email** ot@valdabondance.com
**Website** www.valdabondance.com
**Ski area** top 1,800m (5,906ft) bottom 930m (3,050ft)
**Lifts in area** 207 in Portes du Soleil: 14⊙ 82⊙ 111⊙
**Tour operators** none

## Adelboden and Lenk, Switzerland

Adelboden is an unspoilt village of wooden chalets located on a sunny terrace at the foot of the Wildstrubel massif. Nearby Lenk is a traditional spa village. The two resorts share a 170-km ski area, which a reporter described as 'good and varied skiing mainly for intermediates and above, but somewhat spread out'. A six-seater gondola enhances the lift links between the resorts. A new six-person chair-lift connects Metschmaad to Metschstand for 2004–5. The Timeless Private Ski and Snowboarding School is, according to one reporter, 'highly recommended and infinitely superior to the alternative SSS'. Lift passes for more than four days give you one day's free skiing in **Gstaad**.

Kindergartens in both resorts care for children from three years. Recommended hotels in Adelboden include the four-star Beau Site (☎ 33 673 2222), Parkhotel Bellevue (☎ 33 673 8000) and the Arena Hotel Steinmattli (☎ 33 673 3939). The three-stars Adler Sporthotel (☎ 33 673 4141), Hotel Bären (☎ 33 673 2151) and Hotel Waldhaus und Huldi (☎ 33 673 1531) were all praised by reporters. In Lenk, Hotel Krone (☎ 33 736 3344) has a kindergarten. Restaurant Alpenblick 'is worthy of its reputation for having the best food in town'. Arte Bar is 'a relaxing modern hideaway for discerning skiers'.

**Tel** Adelboden 41 33 673 8080 / Lenk 41 33 733 3131
**Email** info@adelboden.ch / info@lenk.ch
**Websites** www.adelboden.ch / www.lenk.ch
**Ski area** top 2,357m (7,733ft) bottom 1,068m (3,503ft)
**Lifts in area** 39: 8⊙ 8⊙ 23⊙
**Tour operators** Interhome, Kuoni, Made to Measure, Swiss Travel Service

## Alagna, Italy

See *Champoluc–Gressoney–Alagna*, page 122

**Tour operators** Original Travel, Momentum, Ski Freshtracks, Ski Weekend

## Alpbach, Austria

See page 18

**Tour operators** Crystal, Inghams, Interhome, Made to Measure, Neilson School Groups

## Alpe d'Huez, France

See page 67

**Tour operators** Airtours, Alpine Elements, Chalet World, Club Med, Crystal, Erna Low, First Choice, French Freedom, French Life, Inghams, Interhome, Lagrange, Leisure Direction, Made to Measure, Mark Warner, Neilson, On The Piste, Panorama, Ski Activity, Ski Expectations, Ski France, Ski Freshtracks, Ski Independence, Skibound, Ski Miquel, Ski Supreme, Skitopia, Skiworld, Thomson, Tops Travel, Wasteland

## Alpendorf, Austria

See *Salzburger Sportwelt Amadé*, page 303

## Alta, Utah, US

See *Snowbird and Alta*, page 245
**Tour operator** Ski the American Dream

## Altenmarkt, Austria

See *Salzburger Sportwelt Amadé*, page 303
**Tour operators** Interhome, Made to Measure, Sloping Off

## Alyeska, Alaska, US

Alaska's steep-sided, deeply furrowed peaks with outstanding helicopter- and snowcat-skiing have for some years been the cult destination for extreme skiers and snowboarders. Alyeska is a small, family-oriented resort frequented mostly by locals from Anchorage, 40 miles away. It has a 60-person cable-car that departs from inside the Alyeska Prince Hotel. The base-station is barely above sea level, yet Alyeska enjoys phenomenal snow and astonishing scenery. Unfortunately, its northerly latitude and maritime climate mean that blue-sky days are limited and weather conditions can be extreme.

Most resort trails in the 1,000-acre ski area are unthreatening to intermediates. However, the North Face couloirs offer considerable challenge. The ski school, Alyeska Mountain Resort Learning Center, has a sound reputation. Babysitting can be arranged through guest services.

The 307-room Alyeska Prince Hotel (☎ 907 754 1111) accommodates most visitors. Hotel staff will awaken guests who so request when the famed Northern Lights make an appearance.

**Tel** 1 907 754 1111
**Email** info@alyeskaresort.com
**Website** www.alyeskaresort.com
**Ski area** top 3,939ft (1,200m) bottom 250ft (76m)
**Lifts in area** 9: 1🚡 6🚠 2🎿
**Tour operators** Frontier Ski, Inghams, Ski All America

## Andermatt, Switzerland

See page 146
**Tour operators** Made to Measure, Ski Freshtracks

## Aonach Mor, Scotland

See *Nevis Range*, page 295

## Apex, BC, Canada

Apex is a small resort in the Okanagan Valley with a big reputation for uncrowded, quality skiing amid beautiful scenery. It is situated a 30-minute drive up a private road from the valley town of Penticton, an hour's drive from Kelowna Airport with connectons to Vancouver and Calgary.

A quad and a triple chair-lift give access to a surprisingly varied selection of runs on Beaconsfield Mountain. The front face is largely given over to blue and fairly easy single-black-diamonds leading back down to the village and the bottom of the triple chair. From the top of the quad-chair, the long green Grandfather's trail that winds around the shoulder – and eventually back to the village – gives access to a series of short, sharp double-black-diamonds that will test the best.

The Snow Sport and Adventure Centre houses the Ski and Snowboard School and the Rippin Rascals Kids' Club, and is the central point for all resort activities. The Billy Goat Hut is a cosy log cabin perched at the top of the Quickdraw Quad. The other lunchtime alternatives are the Hog on the Hill at the area base, Salty's on the Mountain, and the Longshot Cafeteria in Apex Village. The Coast Inn Apex (☎ 250 979 3939) provides the smartest slope-side accommodation. Saddleback Lodge (☎ 250 292 8118) is 'a welcoming and luxurious B&B' and Sheeprock Lodge (☎ 250 292 855) offers 'the best *pierrade* outside France'). Double Diamond Hostel (☎ 250 292 8256) is the cost-saving alternative, located in the heart of the village. Salty's serves good Thai cuisine, and the Gunbarrel Saloon is a popular après-ski bar with food, which is also open for lunch.

**Tel** 250 292 8222
**Email** info@apexresort.com
**Website** www.apexresort.com
**Ski area** top 7,197ft (2,180m) bottom 5,197ft (1,575m)
**Lifts in area** 4: 2🚠 2🎿
**Tour operator** Ski Safari

## Arabba, Italy

See page 118

**Tour operators** Inghams, Momentum, Neilson, Original Travel, Ski Expectations

## Arapahoe Basin, Colorado, US

Arapahoe Basin – or 'A-Basin' – is a small area that can be skied either on its own local pass or on the two-tier **Vail**, **Beaver Creek**, **Breckenridge** and **Keystone** lift pass purchased in one of these four resorts. The pass is cheaper (but with restricted access to Vail and Beaver Creek) if bought in either Breckenridge or Keystone. The high altitude of A-Basin means that snow cover is assured until May. Almost every run down the middle is intermediate or beginner terrain, but, at the top of the ski area, Palavicinni is one of the longest and steepest bump runs in North America, and the Alleys and East Wall provide some exciting off-piste.

A-Basin has a ski and snowboarding school, but no accommodation. The nearest is six miles away at Keystone. The Legends Café and the 6th Alley Bar are the two most popular après-ski venues. Kids' Room accepts children from four months to seven years with optional one-to-one lessons for older children, while Children's Center Nursery caters for children from one to three years old.

**Tel** 1 970 496 7077
**Email** abasin@a-basin.net
**Website** www.arapahoebasin.com
**Ski area** top 13,050ft (3,967m) bottom 10,780ft (3,283m)
**Lifts in area** 5: 5🚡
**Tour operators** see Keystone

## Arcalis, Andorra

Arcalis is a ski area without a village, situated at the end of a remote and beautiful valley in the middle of the principality, a 20-minute drive from the villages of Ordino and La Massana. 'Some of the most challenging and certainly the most unknown skiing in Andorra', was how one reporter described the resort. Hotel Rutllan (☎ 83 50 00) in La Massana is described as 'the perfect jumping-off point', both for Arcalis and for **Pal–Arinsal**.

The kindergarten cares for little ones from twelve months old, while Snowgarden looks after children aged four to nine years. Visitors to the resort are almost exclusively Spanish.

**Tel** 376 73 70 80
**Email** skiandorra@skiandorra.ad
**Website** www.skiandorra.ad

**Ski area** top 2,624m (8,609ft) bottom 1,940m (6,363ft)
**Lifts in area** 13: 5🚡 8🚡
**Tour operators** none

## Les Arcs, France

See page 69

**Tour operators** Airtours, Alpine Elements, Chalet World, Club Med, Crystal, Equity, Erna Low, Esprit, Finlays, First Choice, French Freedom, French Life, Inghams, Interhome, Lagrange, Leisure Direction, Made to Measure, Neilson, On The Piste, PGL, Ski Activity, Ski Amis, Ski Adventures, Ski Beat, Ski Freshtracks, Ski Independence, Ski Olympic, Ski Supreme, Skitopia, Skiworld, Thomson, Total Ski, Wasteland

## Åre, Sweden

See page 145

**Tour operators** Neilson, Neilson School Groups, Norvista

## Argentière, France

See *Chamonix and Argentière*, page 75

**Tour operators** AWWT, Collineige, Erna Low, French Life, Interhome, Lagrange, McNab, Peak Retreats, Ski Freshtracks, Ski Hillwood, Ski Weekend, Skiworld, White Roc

## Arinsal, Andorra

See *Pal–Arinsal*, page 296

## Arosa, Switzerland

Arosa is suitable for anyone in search of the complete winter-sports experience rather than just skiing, and is best suited to beginners and unadventurous intermediates. The top of the Hörnli is the starting point for a variety of ski-tours to neighbouring resorts. The resort has a dramatic half-pipe and is keen to promote snowboarding. The choice of tuition lies between the SSS, ABC Wintersport Instruction and the Private Berufs ski and snowboard schools.

Arosa Kulm (☎ 81 378 8888) and the Tschuggen Grand Hotel (☎ 81 378 9999) are the two five-stars, while Waldhotel National (☎ 81 378 5555) is 'convenient, comfortable, but lacking in style'. Each bedroom at Hotel Eden (☎ 81 377 0261) is individually decorated with a theatrical theme. Hotel Cristallo (☎ 81 378 6868) was described by reporters as 'a good place with very smart bathrooms and four-posters'. Hotel Alpensonne (☎ 81 377 1547) is also praised.

Carmennahütte is the best of half-a-dozen mountain eateries, all of which are reachable on foot. Resort restaurants include Aahen Thai in the Arosa Kulm, Hotel Obersee, Hotel Quellenhof, Bajazzo, the Grischuna, Les Cigales and the Grottino Pizzeria (open until midnight). The Kitchen (in Hotel Eden), Crazy, Halligalli and Nuts are the nightclubs.

**Tel** 41 81 378 7020
**Email** arosa@arosa.ch
**Website** www.arosa.ch
**Ski area** top 2,653m (8,702ft) bottom 1,800m (5,904ft)
**Lifts in area** 13: 3🚠 6🚡 4🎿
**Tour operators** Interhome, Kuoni, Made to Measure, Momentum, Powder Byrne, Swiss Travel Centre, Swiss Travel Service, White Roc

## Aspen and Snowmass, Colorado, US

See page 224

**Tour operators** AWWT, Carrier, Crystal, Erna Low, Lotus Supertravel, Made to Measure, Momentum, Rocky Mountain Adventures, Seasons in Style, Ski Activity, Ski All America, Ski the American Dream, Ski Independence, Ski Safari, Ski Solutions, Skiworld, Trailfinders, United Vacations

## Auffach, Austria

See *Wildschönau*, page 44

## Auris-en-Oisans, France

Auris consists mainly of apartment blocks and, though somewhat isolated from the bulk of the skiing in the **Alpe d'Huez** ski area, is well positioned for outings to **Les Deux Alpes**, **Briançon / Serre Chevalier** and **La Grave**. The Hotel Beau Site (☎ 476 80 06 39) attracts predominantly French guests. Down the hillside in the old village is the more traditional Auberge de Forêt de Maronne (☎ 476 80 00 06) with its fine cuisine, as well as a variety of chalets and gîtes to rent.

**Tel** 33 476 80 13 52
**Email** auris-en-oisans@wanadoo.fr

**Website** www.auris-en-oisans.com
**Ski area** top 3,330m (10,922ft) bottom 1,600m (5,249ft)
**Lifts in area** 85: 16🚠 24🚡 45🎿
**Tour operators** none

## Aviemore, Scotland

See *Cairngorm Mountain (Aviemore)*, page 266

## Avoriaz, France

See page 72

**Tour operators** Airtours, Alpine Elements, Chalet Snowboard, Club Med, Crystal, Erna Low, First Choice, French Freedom, French Life, Lagrange, Leisure Direction, Made to Measure, Neilson, On The Piste, Original Travel, Ski Independence, Ski Supreme, Skiworld, Thomson, Trail Alpine, White Roc

## Axamer Lizum, Austria

This somewhat characterless ski station offers the best range of skiing and boarding within immediate reach of **Innsbruck**. Axamer is one of the top snowboarding resorts in Austria, with riders sometimes outnumbering the skiers. The resort has a renowned world-class terrain park and a half-pipe.

The pick of the skiing is accessed by a fast quad-chair from the car park or by a funicular that climbs the ridge to the top of the area. From here the Olympic women's downhill course provides a demanding descent. Across the narrow valley, a long chair-lift serves either a black run to Axamer Lizum village or gives access to a sunny, easy piste that takes you back down the valley to Götzens.

The Gipfelhaus, at the top of the mountain railway at Hoadl, boasts home cooking and panoramic views. The four-stars Lizumerhof (☎ 5234 68244) and Hotel Kögele (☎ 5234 68803) are recommended. Alpinhotel Lizumer Bergheim (☎ 5234 65796) ('excellent simple food and the staff are like family' is situated 30 metres from the lifts). Off Limits is the main bar.

**Tel** 43 5125 9850
**Email** info@innsbruck.tvb.co.at
**Website** www.innsbrucktourist.info
**Ski area** top 2,343m (7,687ft) bottom 874m (2,867ft)
**Lifts in area** 10: 1�carriage 5🚡 4🎿
**Tour operators** Crystal, Neilson School Groups, PGL, Thomson

## Bad Gastein and Bad Hofgastein, Austria

See *The Gasteinertal*, page 19

## Bad Kleinkirchheim and St Oswald, Austria

Bad Kleinkirchheim – or BKK as it is usually known – is the home resort of Austrian super-hero Franz Klammer. The ski area is linked to the neighbouring village of St Oswald, and together they provide 90km of mainly intermediate pistes. However, the World Cup downhill course (designed by Klammer) offers considerable variety and challenge. BKK has a floodlit terrain park.

The wide choice of hotels includes the stylish five-star Thermenhotel Ronacher (☎ 4240 282) and Hotel Pulverer-Thermenwelt (☎ 4240 744). Four-star Hotel Almrausch (☎ 4240 8484) is 'quite superb, with good food'. Three- to six-year-olds can join the ski kindergarten.

**Tel** 43 4240 8212
**Email** info@bkk.at
**Website** www.badkleinkirchheim.at
**Ski area** top 2,000m (6,560ft) bottom 1,080m (3,543ft)
**Lifts in area** 26: 4⃞ 4⃞ 18⃞
**Tour operators** Alpine Tours, Crystal, PGL, Sloping Off, Slovenija Pursuits

## Banff–Lake Louise, Alberta, Canada

See page 47

**Tour operators** Airtours, AWWT, Crystal, First Choice, Frontier Ski, Inghams, Lotus Supertravel, Made to Measure, Neilson, Neilson School Groups, Nonstopski, Rocky Mountain Adventures, Seasons in Style, Ski Activity, Ski All America, Ski the American Dream, Ski Freshtracks, Ski Independence, Ski Safari, Skiworld, Solo's, Thomson, Trailfinders, United Vacations, Virgin Snow, Wentworth Travel

## Bansko, Bulgaria

This lovely old town is situated 150km south of Sofia and about an hour's drive beyond **Borovets**. It lies in the shadow of the 2,915-m peak of Vihren, the highest mountain in the beautiful Pirin range, close to the borders with Macedonia and Greece.

The main focus of the skiing is located out of town at Shiligarnika, the largest of three small ski areas and best suited to novices and low intermediates. A €30 million investment project has provided a range of new lifts, including an eight-person gondola and three detachable chairs.

Children are cared for at the Ulen Junior Ski Club, which is part of the Ulen Ski and Snowboard School.

Hotel Bansko (☎ 7 443 4221) and the Pirin (☎ 7 443 8051) are praised, along with the Strajite (☎ 7 443 2367). All have four stars. The Dedo Pene, a converted eighteenth-century town house, and the equally atmospheric Mexana Rumen Baryakov are highly recommended restaurants. The Torino cabaret bar is unexpectedly up-market and popular with prosperous-looking Sofians.

**Tel** 359 7443 8060
**Email** alliance@bansko.bg
**Website** www.banskoski.com
**Ski area** top 2,000m (6,560ft) bottom 936m (3,079ft)
**Lifts in area** 12: 1⃞ 5⃞ 6⃞
**Tour operators** Balkan Holidays, Neilson, Neilson School Groups

## Baqueira–Beret, Spain

See page 144

**Tour operator** Ski Miquel

## Bardonecchia, Italy

This large and traditional market town near the Italian end of the Fréjus tunnel lies close to **Montgenèvre** and **Sestriere**, but is not part of **The Milky Way** circuit. The resort is popular with Italians, who flood in from Turin at weekends. The surprisingly large and challenging ski area, spread over three sectors, is praised for its lack of crowds 'even during half-term week'. We have favourable reports of Ski School Bardonecchia: 'excellent, even though it was busy'. Childcare for small children is non-existent.

El Gaucho and Il Caminetto are recommended restaurants. The nightlife is limited to a dozen rather dull bars. Hotels are quite spread out and include the three-star Des Geneys Splendid (☎ 0122 99001), Asplenia (☎ 0122 999870), La Nigritella (☎ 0122 980477) and Park Hotel Rosa (☎ 0122 902087).

Tel 39 0122 99032
Email bardonecchia@montagnedoc.it
Website www.montagnedoc.com
Ski area top 2,750m (9,022ft) bottom 1,290m (4,232ft)
Lifts in area 24: 9⬜ 15⬜
Tour operators Crystal, First Choice, Neilson, Neilson
School Groups, Ski High Days, Skitopia, Thomson

## Barèges and La Mongie, France

Barèges and La Mongie form the largest ski area in the Pyrenees, sharing 100km of wide, mainly easy-to-intermediate pistes on both sides of the Col du Tourmalet. The area is prone to overcrowding at weekends. Of the two, La Mongie is the better base for complete beginners, with easy slopes immediately around the resort. However, the one-street spa village of Barèges has considerably more atmosphere. La Mongie boasts a boardercross course and three other dedicated snowboard spots at different points around the ski area.

The French Ski School (ESF) and Ecoloski in Barèges both have a ski kindergarten for children from four years. The two non-ski kindergartens accept youngsters from two to six years, and Hélios is an activity centre for three- to 12-year-olds. La Mongie has a ski and non-ski kindergarten.

Chez Louisette is a popular mountain restaurant and Le Bastan is 'cheerful and cheap'. Le Yeti in La Mongie is also rated. Recommended hotels in Barèges include the two-stars Hotel Igloo (☎ 562 92 68 10) and Hotel Europe (☎ 562 92 68 04). La Mongie has one three-star hotel, Le Pourteilh (☎ 562 91 93 33), plus a handful of two-stars and apartment blocks, including the smart Résidence Le Montana (☎ 562 91 99 99).

Nightlife in Barèges centres on Le Jonathan disco. Le Pitchounet serves a good brasserade and La Rozell crêperie is warmly praised. Le Nem is Chinese. In La Mongie, Auberges des Neiges has 'great meals at reasonable prices'. Bar de la Plage and Le Mazot are popular après-ski venues.

Tel Barèges 33 562 92 16 00 / La Mongie 33 562 91 94 15
Email ot@bareges.com / info@bagneresdebigorre-lamongie.com
Websites www.bareges.com / www.bagneresdebigorre-lamongie.com
Ski area top 2,350m (7,708ft) bottom 1,250m (4,100ft)
Lifts in area 43: 3⬜ 12⬜ 28⬜
Tour operators Borderline, Lagrange, Pyrenean Mountain Tours, Tangney Tours

## Bariloche, Argentina

See Gran Catedral (Bariloche), page 278

## Beaver Creek, Colorado, US

See page 227

Tour operators AWWT, Carrier, Crystal, Elegant Resorts, Momentum, Seasons in Style, Ski Activity, Ski All America, Ski the American Dream, Ski Independence, Ski Safari, Skiworld, United Vacations, Virgin Snow

## Big White, BC, Canada

See page 50

Tour operators AWWT, Crystal, Frontier Ski, Ski Activity, Ski All America, Ski the American Dream, Ski Independence, Ski Safari, Skiworld

## Bled, Slovenia

The attractive old spa town of Bled looks on to a seventeenth-century church on an island in the middle of a lake. Its main ski area is 8km away at Zatrnik, where four lifts serve 15km of easy wooded slopes in a bowl; these are ideal for beginners in good snow conditions but provide little challenge for intermediates. Another even smaller area is Straza, which has two lifts on a nursery slope; both areas have artificial snowmaking. One reader commented that thin ice on the lake can be a hazard ('I know, because I fell through and tested the emergency services and hospital for treatment for hypothermia – very good').

Grand Hotel Toplice (☎ 4 579 10 00) is the resort's five-star hotel, and the four-star hotels are the quiet Golf Hotel Bled (☎ 4 579 20 00), set slightly away from the main centre; Vila Bled (☎ 4 579 15 00), an elegant residence set in its own grounds on the shore of Lake Bled; the Park Hotel (☎ 4 579 30 00) ('excellent top-floor swimming-pool') and Kompas Hotel Bled (☎ 4 578 21 00). The resort has nineteen restaurants, three pubs and a casino. Cross-country skiing and ski-touring are also available. Recommended après-ski venues include Pub Bled and the bar in Hotel Kompas. The Rock Bar has live music.

Tel 386 4 578 05 00
Email info@dzt.bled.si

**Website** www.bled.si
**Ski area** top 1,800m (5,940ft) bottom 503m (1,650ft)
**Lifts in area** 6: 2⑤ 4⑨
**Tour operators** Crystal, Thomson

## Borgata, Italy

This is a small resort five minutes by road from **Sestriere**, with an infrequent bus service between the two. Hotel Hermitage (☎ 0122 70346) is recommended ('nice rooms, but the food was not up to much'). Reporters who stayed in the Nube d'Argenta self-catering apartments (☎ 0122 70263) all praised them as 'clean, modern and convenient for the lifts'.

We have had complaints about the ski school ('very poor, with limited spoken English, but the teachers were pleasant enough'). Shopping is almost non-existent and the nightlife is quiet ('a couple of sleepy bars'). As one reporter put it: 'when the sun goes down, it is time to eat then go to bed'.

**Tel** 39 0122 755449
**Email** borgata@montagnedoc.it
**Website** www.montagnedoc.it
**Ski area** top 2,823m (9,262ft) bottom 1,840m (6,035ft)
**Lifts in area** 92 in Milky Way: (3⑥ 35⑤ 54⑨
**Tour operators** see Sestriere

## Bormio, Italy

Bormio offers limited high-speed cruising, but a high top-lift altitude normally allows the season to last well into April. Its slopes, a few minutes' walk from the town centre, will be the venue in 2005 for the Alpine Skiing World Championships. The resort shares a lift pass, but not a link, with the neighbouring village of **Santa Caterina**, while the nearby Stelvio Glacier offers summer skiing. The lift pass is also valid for **Livigno**, which is an hour's drive away, as well as nearby San Colombano.

Of the seven ski schools, the Bormio Valtellina is highly recommended for its friendly, English-speaking instructors. The ski schools take children from four years, while the crèche at the Contea di Bormio Ski School accepts little ones from three years. The favoured lunch spot is La Rocca, an old-fashioned hut on the main trail down to Bormio 2000.

Recommended four-star hotels include the Posta (☎ 0342 904753), Rezia (☎ 0342 904721) the Palace (☎ 0342 903131) and Baita dei Pinia (☎ 0342 9043460) ('excellent hotel, 400m from the gondola'), while the Derby (☎ 0342 904433), Nevada (☎ 0342 910888) and Funivia (☎ 0342 903242) are good three-stars.

The best places to eat regional dishes are the Rasiga ('a beautifully converted saw mill'), the Vecchia Combo, Al Filo and Osteria dei Magri. The Braulio houses a micro-brewery and a wine bar. The Lord Byron attracts teens and 20-somethings. Gordy's and Sotto-Sotto are popular alternatives. The late-night focus is on the King's Club disco ('a relic from the 1970s').

**Tel** 39 0342 903300
**Email** apt.bormio@provincia.so.it
**Website** www.valtellinaonline.com
**Ski area** top 3,012m (9,879ft) bottom 1,225m (4,018ft)
**Lifts in area** 17: 3⑥ 7⑤ 7⑨
**Tour operators** Equity, Interhome, PGL, Skitopia, Sloping Off

## Borovets, Bulgaria

Borovets is 73km from Sofia and set in a pine forest at the foot of Mount Moussala, the highest peak in the Balkans. But like much of Eastern Europe the resort has squandered the natural beauty of its setting by erecting buildings of dubious architectural merit.

The extent – 40km – of the skiing surpasses anything found elsewhere in the country, but the ancient lift system consists only of an ageing gondola, a quad-chair, an antique single-chair and 13 assorted drag-lifts. The inevitable queues and lack of adequate piste-grooming are a constant source of irritation: 'as a group of beginners we were expected to continue our classes on a mixture of ice, rock and grass that turned into wet slurry in the afternoons'. The skiing is divided into two separate sectors, linked by a long walk on an ice-rutted road.

Principal access to the main area is by an outmoded six-person gondola. The Markoudjik sector above it offers the best of the resort's skiing, which is mainly above the tree-line with a highest ski point of 2,540m. The separate Martinovi Baraki area comprises the quad chair-lift and four drag-lifts, but the top section can be reached only by the single-chair-lift, which is prone to enormous queues. All the nursery slopes are located at the base of this area.

Both main ski schools are well regarded, and English is widely spoken. The Peter Popanguelov School for Expert Skiing has ten instructors and offers its services 'for those who want to hone their skiing skills to world champion class'. The Rila Hotel kindergarten takes non-skiers from two years old and skiers aged four years. Ski school classes do not have lift priority.

Accommodation is almost exclusively hotel-based, with the conveniently located Samokov standing out as by far the best example. It offers a range of modern facilities including a swimming-pool and bowling alley, and it also has a nightclub and 'American' bar. The giant Rila Hotel is more basic but of reasonable standard. Hotels Breza and Mura are both popular. It is advisable to book hotels through one of the many tour operators to the resort.

Mamacita's serves steaks, White Magic is good value, and the Hungry Horse offers 'English food'. Off-slope activities are plentiful and entertainment cheap. Club Slide is a new nightspot in Hotel Mura, the Buzz Bar and Happy Duck are for après-ski drinks, and Franco's has karaoke.

**Tel** 359 2 987 97 78
**Email** none
**Website** www.bulgariaski.com
**Ski area** top 2,540m (8,333ft) bottom 1,323m (4,339ft)
**Lifts in area** 9: 1🚠 2🚡 6🚟
**Tour operators** Airtours, Balkan Holidays, Balkan Tours, Crystal, First Choice, Inghams, Neilson, Neilson School Groups, Thomson

## Breckenridge, Colorado, US

See page 229

**Tour operators** AWWT, Crystal, Erna Low, Inghams, Neilson, Rocky Mountain Adventures, Ski Activity, Ski All America, Ski the American Dream, Ski Independence

## Briançon, France

See *Serre Chevalier*, page 103

**Tour operators** see page 307

## Brides-les-Bains, France

This resort is a budget base for people wishing to ski the giant **Trois Vallées** ski area and is linked by a gondola to **Méribel**.

The old spa town has 21 hotels including four three-stars: Grand Hotel des Thermes (☎ 479 55 38 38), Hotel le Versea (☎ 479 55 27 44), Hotel Amélie (☎ 479 55 30 15) and Hotel le Golf (☎ 479 55 28 12). Brides has eight restaurants, a few shops and a spa.

**Tel** 33 479 55 20 64
**Email** tourism@brides-les-bains.com
**Website** www.brides-les-bains.com
**Ski area** top 2,952m (9,685ft) bottom 1,400m (4,593ft)
**Lifts in area** 198 in Trois Vallées: 39🚠 69🚡 90🚟
**Tour operators** Airtours, AWWT, Erna Low, First Choice, French Life, Lagrange, Leisure Direction, Made to Measure, On The Piste, Peak Retreats, Ramblers, Ski Independence, Ski Weekends & Board Breaks, Snowcoach

## Brienz, Switzerland

See *Meiringen–Hasliberg*, page 291

## Brighton, Utah, US

Utah's oldest ski area, at the top of Big Cottonwood Canyon and 45 minutes' drive from Salt Lake City, opened in 1936. It remains a small, scenic resort with 850 acres of terrain, 80 per cent of which is rated intermediate to advanced. There is some radical skiing off the back of Millicent in the Wolverine Cirque. The Brighton Ski School teaches all standards, and the Kinderski and Young Riders cater for children from four to seven years.

The Alpine Rose is a simple, slope-side cafeteria. A limited choice of accommodation is headed by the slope-side Brighton Lodge (☎ 801 532 4731).

**Tel** 1 801 532 4731
**Email** info@skibrighton.com
**Website** www.skibrighton.com
**Ski area** top 10,750ft (3,277m) bottom 8,755ft (2,668m)
**Lifts in area** 8: 7🚡 1🚟
**Tour operator** Equity, Ski the American Dream

## Brixen-im-Thale, Austria

At the far end of the **SkiWelt** is the last fully connected resort of the area. A six-person gondola and covered high-speed chair lead up to Hohe Salve. Rudi's Bar, Brixener Stadl and Cheers Pub are the main après-ski hang-outs. Brixen's two ski and board schools are Skischule Brixen and Skischule Aktiv.

**Tel** 43 5334 8433
**Email** brixen@skiwelt.at
**Website** www.brixenimthale.at
**Ski area** top 1,829m (6,001ft) bottom 800m (2,624ft)
**Lifts in area** 93 in SkiWelt: 11◐ 34◑ 48◒
**Tour operators** none

## Bruson, Switzerland

There are plans for a direct gondola from the valley train station in Le Châble to the top of Bruson and a new Les Arcs-style village, but for the moment Bruson remains uncrowded and boasts some of the best steep powder skiing available on the Four Valleys ski pass.

The four lifts serve just 30km of groomed pistes. With some hiking, however, long excursions down to Sembrancher and Orsières over snow-filled pastures, then a free train-ride back to Le Châble, are possible. Access is by free bus from Le Châble, itself connected to **Verbier** by gondola or another free bus. Bruson has two hotels, apartments midway up the mountain, and one restaurant.

**Tel** 41 27 776 1682
**Email** bagnestourisme@verbier.ch
**Website** www.verbier.ch
**Ski area** top 2,445m (8,022ft) bottom 1,100m (3,543ft)
**Number of lifts** 4: 2◑ 2◒
**Tour operators** none

## Cairngorm Mountain (Aviemore), Scotland

Aviemore is located about 120 miles north of Edinburgh and Glasgow on the A9 and is the nearest town to the Cairngorm Mountain ski area, which lies ten miles to the east. The Cairngorm Mountain funicular provides the main mountain access to a surprisingly challenging ski area that also has plenty of novice terrain. Like all Scottish resorts, Cairngorm suffers from the vagaries of the weather, but when the snow is good it rivals Alpine resorts of comparable size. Planning a holiday in advance will always be a gamble that is unacceptable to many southerners with the option of a shorter journey to Geneva.

When conditions allow, the area usually boasts at least one terrain park. The Ski School and Zippy Boarding School offer tuition at all levels, with lessons for children

on demand. A crèche is available at the nearby Hilton Coylumbridge Hotel (☎ 01479 810661). The Uphill Ski Club runs classes for disabled skiers in the resort.

The town of Aviemore is in the process of a major redevelopment, providing a range of leisure facilities as well as new shops and restaurants based in the Aviemore Highland Resort. Recommended places to stay include the three-star Cairngorm Hotel (☎ 01479 810233) and the Hilton Coylumbridge Hotel. The Cairngorm Hotel and The Old Bridge Inn are traditional meeting places. The Winking Owl, Mackenzies, and the Basement Bar are the most lively après-ski haunts, along with Café Mambo and a new late-night venue called The Vault. RD's has replaced Littlejohn's as one of the best restaurants in town, and PH22 is a new pizza house ('just what was needed after a long, cold day-out'). The Gallery at Inverdruie, a mile outside Aviemore, is also praised. Non-ski activities include clay pigeon shooting, dog-sledding and off-road driving courses.

**Tel** (01479) 810363
**Email** info@cairngormmountain.com
**Websites** www.cairngormmountain.com / www.ski.visitscotland.com
**Ski area** top 1,100m (3,608ft) bottom 550m (1,804ft)
**Lifts in area** 17: 1◐ 2◑ 14◒
**Tour operator** Ski Norwest

## Campitello, Italy

See *Canazei and the Val di Fassa*, below

## Canazei and the Val di Fassa, Italy

Canazei is a large and attractive village in the Val di Fassa. It is a principal player in the **Sella Ronda** ski circuit, popular with British skiers, and the best place in the area to stay for non-skiing activities and a lively nightlife. The village is a tangle of narrow streets, with a mixture of old farm buildings, new hotels and some delightful shops. A gondola provides direct access into the Sella Ronda lift system.

The Kinderland crèche and kindergarten, run by the Canazei Marmolada ski school, caters for children and offers a mixture of daycare and lessons for the older ones.

The four-stars Astoria (☎ 0462 601302) and La Perla (☎ 0462 602453) are the most

luxurious hotels in town. The Croce Bianca
(☎ 0462 601111) is also warmly
recommended. The Dolomiti (☎ 0462
601106) is built in grand hotel style, while
Hotel Bellevue (☎ 0462 601104) is well
placed for the skiing. The three-star Hotel
Faloria (☎ 0462 601118) has 'reasonable
prices and is only 250m from the lift station'.

Popular après-ski spots include the Rose
Garden, the Esso Bar ('cool, intimate, and
with a mix of locals and Brits'), the Husky,
La Teneta, Frog's Pub and El Binocol.

The other main resort in the Val di Fassa
is **Campitello**, which together with a
scattering of outlying villages provides an
alternative bed base. The resort is set back
from the main road and is ideal for
complete beginners, with some of the area's
best nursery slopes right on the doorstep. A
cable-car gives access to the Sella Ronda.
Hotels include the four-stars Diamant Park
(☎ 0462 750440) and Gran Chalet
Soreghes (☎ 0462 750060).

The villages of Alba, Vigo di Fassa,
**Moena**, Pozza di Fassa, Soraga and Mazzin
are all connected by a free ski bus. Each of
these little communities has its own tiny ski
area. Altogether the Val di Fassa offers
about 200km of pistes, with a half-pipe in
Alba. Park Bimbo Neve in Pozza di Fassa,
Mini Club Tananai in Vigo di Fassa and
Babylandia in Moena all offer care for
skiing and non-skiing children.

**Tel** Campitello 39 0462 750500 / Canazei 39 0462 602466
**Email** info@fassa.com
**Website** www.fassa.com
**Ski area** top 2,949m (9,676ft) bottom 1,320m (4,330ft)
**Lifts in area** 52: 9⃞ 26⃞ 17⃞
**Tour operators** Crystal, Equity, First Choice, Inghams,
Interhome, Thomson

## The Canyons, Utah, US

See *Park City Resorts*, page 240

**Tour operators** Ski Independence, Ski the American
Dream, United Vacations

## Cardrona, New Zealand

See *Wanaka (Cardrona and Treble Cone)*,
page 320

## Les Carroz, France

This is an increasingly important resort in
the Grand Massif, France's fourth largest ski
area, which is centred on **Flaine**. The resort
is more attractive than its big sister and is
popular with families and weekend visitors.
The gondola and chair-lift are a steep walk
from the village centre, but within easy
reach of some attractive old hotels including
Les Airelles (☎ 450 90 01 02), Les Belles
Pistes (☎ 450 90 00 17) and Croix de
Savoie (☎ 450 90 00 26). There have been
recent additions of sympathetic apartment
blocks including MGM (☎ 020-7584 2841
in UK), and the old part of the village has
been renovated. Bars L'Hacienda and La
Baraka offer après-ski entertainment. La
Souris Verte cares for non-skiers from three
months to five years old, and Le Club des
Loupiots accepts skiing and non-skiing
children from four to twelve years.

**Tel** 33 450 90 00 04
**Email** carroz@lescarroz.com
**Website** www.lescarroz.com
**Ski area** top 2,480m (8,134ft) bottom 1,140m (3,740ft)
**Lifts in area** 72: 6⃞ 28⃞ 38⃞
**Tour operators** AWWT, Erna Low, French Life, Lagrange,
Leisure Direction, Peak Retreats, Ski Independence

## Cauterets, France

This attractive thermal spa is situated only
40km from Lourdes airport. The skiing is
best suited to novices and intermediates,
taking place in the exposed Cirque du Lys
bowl and accessed by a two-stage cable-car,
which also brings skiers back to the resort
at the end of the day. The terrain park has a
boardercross course as well as a variety of
obstacles. Nearby **Pont d'Espagne** is a
separate ski area with four lifts, which is
renowned for its 37km of cross-country
trails. The two ski schools at Cauterets are
the ESF and Snow Fun. Garderie Les
Marmottes accepts children from two
months and the Mini-Club cares for three-
to seven-year-olds.

Recommended three-star hotels include
Hotel Bordeaux (☎ 562 92 52 50) and
Hotel-Résidence Aladin (☎ 562 92 60 00).
Restaurants La Flambée pizzeria, La
Raclette and the Aladin are all praised by
reporters. Après-ski centres on a handful of
bars including Le St-Trop, as well as a
casino, a couple of discos and ice-skating.

**Tel** 33 562 92 50 50
**Email** acceuil@cauterets.com
**Website** www.cauterets.com
**Ski area** top 2,350m (7,710ft) bottom 1,000m (3,280ft)
**Lifts in area** 15: 1⬡ 5🔺 9⬆
**Tour operator** Lagrange

## Cavalese, Italy

Cavalese is the best-known resort of the **Val di Fiemme**, the collective name given to the 11 small towns and villages in the Trentino region. Its own ski area of Alpe Cermis is reached by cable-car from the town. The other significant ski areas in the valley are Latemar, above the villages of Pampeago and Predazzo, and Bellamonte-Alpe Lusia, above the village of Bellamonte. Passo Rolle and Passo Lavazè are two other small resorts further along the valley. A sixth small area, Ziano di Fiemme, has night-skiing. The Fiemme-Obereggen area lift pass gives access to more than 100km of groomed pistes, and all the areas are linked by free shuttle bus. Val di Fiemme is the headquarters of Italian cross-country skiing and boasts 150km of trails.

Hotels in Cavalese include Park Hotel Azalea (☎ 0462 340109) and the Bellavista (☎ 0462 340205). Kindergartens Cermislandia, Pampeago and Gardone all accept children from three years.

**Tel** 39 0462 241111
**Email** info@valfiemme.net
**Website** www.valdifiemme.info
**Ski area** top 2,230m (7,316ft) bottom 980m (3,215ft)
**Lifts in area** 49: 7⬡ 27🔺 15⬆
**Tour operators** Alpine Tours, Thomson

## Celerina, Switzerland

A village atmosphere, old stone houses painted with the local graffito designs and ski access to the Corviglia ski area make Celerina an attractive and quiet alternative bed base to **St Moritz**. The village has its own ski and snowboard school, Engadin Snow and Fun. Zwergliclub in the four-star Hotel Cresta Palace (☎ 81 836 5656) offers daycare for children from three years. Cresta Kulm (☎ 81 836 8080) is the other four-star, while Hotel Misani (☎ 81 833 3314) is 'a bizarre mixture of Alpine and modern'.

**Tel** 41 81 830 0011
**Email** info@celerina.ch

**Website** www.celerina.ch
**Ski area** top 3,057m (10,030ft) bottom 1,720m (5,643ft)
**Lifts in area** 56: 3⬛ 8⬡ 18🔺 27⬆
**Tour operator** Made to Measure

## Cervinia, Italy

See page 119

**Tour operators** Alpine Answers, Club Med, Crystal, Elegant Resorts, Erna Low, First Choice, Inghams, Interhome, Momentum, Ski Freshtracks, Ski Solutions, Ski Supreme, Ski Weekend, Skiworld, Thomson

## Cesana-Sansicario, Italy

The attractively shabby old village of Cesana-Torinese dates from the twelfth century and is set on a busy road junction at the foot of the Italian approach to the Montgenèvre Pass. It is rather confined and shaded, and accommodation is mainly in apartments and a few hotels. The chair-lifts up to the skiing above **Clavière** and the purpose-built village of Sansicario are a long walk from the centre, and the place can be safely recommended only to those with a car. The Chaberton (☎ 0122 89147) is a three-star hotel, and there are half-a-dozen small one-stars. Restaurant La Selvaggia specialises in regional dishes, while the smart Fraiteve is renowned for its truffles. Nightspots include the Cremeria Rinaldo e Luciana bar.

Halfway up the west-facing mountain-side, Sansicario consists mainly of apartment buildings and a neat shopping precinct connected by covered walkways. Facilities for beginners, especially children, are good. A ski- and non-ski kindergarten provides daycare for three- to eleven-year-olds, and the resort has its own ski school. The choice of après-ski facilities is limited to a couple of bars and the Black Sun disco. Accommodation is mostly in apartments of a generally high standard, but with a few comfortable hotels. The most attractive is the Rio Envers (☎ 0122 811333), a short walk from the centre.

**Tel** 39 0122 89202
**Email** cesana@montagnadoc.it
**Website** www.montagnadoc.it
**Ski area** top 2,823m (9,262ft) bottom 1,350m (4,428ft)
**Lifts in area** 92 in Milky Way: 3⬡ 35🔺 54⬆
**Tour operator** Momentum

# Chamonix, France

See *Chamonix and Argentière*, page 75

**Tour operators** Airtours, Alpine Answers, Alpine Elements, Alpine Weekends, A.P.T. Holidays, Bigfoot, Classic Ski, Club Med, Club Pavilion, Collineige, Corporate Ski Company, Crystal, Erna Low, Esprit, First Choice, Flexiski, French Freedom, French Life, Huski, Inghams, Interhome, Lagrange, Leisure Direction, Momentum, Mountain Leap, Neilson, On The Piste, Original Travel, Peak Retreats, Ski Expectations, Ski France, Ski Independence, Ski Solutions, Ski Supreme, Ski Weekend, Skiworld, Thomson, White Roc

# Champagny-en-Vanoise, France

See *La Plagne*, page 97

**Tour operators** Erna Low, Lagrange, Made to Measure

# Champéry, Switzerland

This traditional Swiss village is linked into the **Portes du Soleil** ski area. The one-way main street is lined with attractive wooden chalets, hotels, shops and restaurants. A 125-person cable-car takes you up to the mid-mountain station at Planachaux. The Swiss Ski School (ESS) and the Freeride Company organise ski and snowboard lessons. Champéry has a gentle nursery slope in the middle of the village, with a rope-tow. The ESS accepts children from three years.

Recommended hotels include Hotel Suisse (☎ 24 479 0707), Hotel National (☎ 24 479 1130) and Hotel Beau-Séjour (☎ 24 479 5858) – all are comfortable and welcoming. Auberge du Grand-Paradis (☎ 24 479 1167) is highly rated by reporters, while Hotel la Rose des Alpes (☎ 24 479 1218) offers value for money.

Restaurants include the Grand-Paradis du Nord, Les Pervenches and Le Centre. Mitchell's, the Bar des Guides, Le Levant, Le Pub, La Crevasse, Les Mines d'Or and le Farinet provide evening entertainment. The comprehensive sports centre boasts indoor and outdoor ice-rinks, swimming-pools and a fitness centre.

**Tel** 41 24 479 2020
**Email** info@champery.ch
**Website** www.champery.ch
**Ski area** top 2,350m (7,708ft) bottom 1,053m (3,455ft)
**Lifts in area** 207 in Portes du Soleil: 14🚠 82🚡 111🎿
**Tour operators** Made to Measure, Piste Artiste, White Roc

# Champex-Lac, Switzerland

Unfortunately for **Verbier**-based skiers, this charming little neighbour has opted out of the Four Valleys lift pass, so you must buy a separate pass to enjoy the limited but nearly always crowd-free 25km of pistes. Powder on the north face remains good for weeks, and the resort's clientèle rarely ventures into the untracked snow among the trees. Champex houses a small branch of the Swiss Snowsports School (SSS).

Hotel Belvédère (☎ 27 783 1114) is said to be 'outstandingly characterful'. One piste is floodlit at night, and other activities include a 7-km toboggan run from La Breya, a natural half-pipe and an ice-climbing pyramid.

**Tel** 41 27 783 2828
**Email** info@champex.ch
**Website** www.champex.ch
**Ski area** top 2,188m (7,178ft) bottom 1,470m (4,823ft)
**Lifts in area** 4: 2🚡 2🎿
**Tour operators** none

# Champoluc, Italy

See *Champoluc–Gressoney–Alagna*, page 122

**Tour operators** Alpine Tracks, Crystal, Esprit, Momentum

# Champoussin, Switzerland

Champoussin is a mini-resort of modern, rustic-style buildings that are almost all apartments ('highly recommended'), and a main hotel, the Résidence Royal Alpage Club (☎ 244 768300). The hotel boasts a sauna, swimming-pool, games room and disco, and runs its own kindergarten and mini-club. Après-ski is limited to the hotel and two restaurants: Le Poussin bar/restaurant and Chez Gaby, which runs a snowcat service from the village in the evening. Floodlit skiing takes place on Wednesday evenings, and the thermal baths 10km away at Val d'Iliez are worth a visit.

The small ski school does not elicit impressive reports, and we have received mixed views on the resort from reporters: 'great for family holidays, but singles, extreme skiers and snowboarders should look elsewhere'.

**Tel** 41 244 7683 00

**Email** hotel.royal.alpage@portesdusoleil.com
**Website** www.portesdusoleil.com /
www.royalalpageclub.com
**Ski area** top 2,350m (7,708ft) bottom 1,680m (5,512ft)
**Lifts in area** 207 in Portes du Soleil: 14⊙ 82⊙ 111⊙
**Tour operators** none

## Chamrousse, France

Situated only a 30-minute drive from
Grenoble, Chamrousse is the closest ski
area to the city. It comprises an
unattractive, albeit reasonably convenient,
collection of buildings on two levels – 1650
and 1750 – and the ski area covers 73km of
piste. There is a boardercross slope and
half-pipe. The French Ski School (ESF) and
the International Ski School both offer the
full range of lessons. Les Marmots ski
kindergarten accepts children from three to
twelve years and also caters for non-skiers
from three months.

Hotel Bellevue (☎ 476 89 97 73) is
situated at the bottom of the piste. Also
recommended are Hotel L'Hermitage (☎
476 89 93 21) and the simpler Virage (☎
476 89 90 63) and La Datcha (☎ 476 89
91 40). Chamrousse's other facilities
include 25 restaurants and bars, an ice-rink
and an indoor swimming-pool.

**Tel** 33 476 89 92 65
**Email** info@chamrousse.com
**Website** www.chamrousse.com
**Ski area** top 2,255m (7,398ft) bottom 1,700m (5,577ft)
**Lifts in area** 26: 1⊙ 9⊙ 16⊙
**Tour operator** Lagrange

## La Chapelle d'Abondance, France

This old farming community, 6km down the
valley from **Châtel**, straddles both sides of
the road without any defined centre. On
one side, two long chair-lifts take you up to
Crêt Bèni at 1,650m, from where a series of
drags serves a choice of mainly easy runs
through the pine forest. On the other side of
the road a gondola and a chair-lift link into
**Torgon** and Châtel. Two-star hotels Les
Cornettes (☎ 450 73 50 24) and Alti 1000
(☎ 450 73 51 90) have swimming-pools
and fitness centres. Les Cornettes also
houses one of the best restaurants in the
region.

**Tel** 33 450 73 51 41
**Email** ot-chapelle@portesdusoleil.com

**Website** www.portesdusoleil.com
**Lifts in area** 207 in Portes du Soleil: 14⊙ 82⊙ 111⊙
**Ski area** top 1,700m (5,577ft) bottom 1,010m (3,313ft)
**Tour operators** none

## Chateau d'Oex, Switzerland

See *Gstaad*, page 279

**Tour operator** Alpine Tours

## Châtel, France

Châtel is a pleasant farming village in the
giant **Portes du Soleil** ski area. Unfortunately,
precious little planning has gone into the
development of the village, which consists of
random buildings up towards the Morgins
Pass and Switzerland, and down the hillside
and along the valley towards the Linga lift
and the connection with **Avoriaz**.

The French Ski School (ESF) has a solid
reputation, although some reporters
experienced classes of up to 20 pupils. Ski
Surf Ecole Internationale is warmly praised
('tuition is excellent'). Ecole de Ski Francis
Sports is an alternative ski school, while
Bureau des Moniteurs Virages, Snowride
and Henri Gonon are the other ski and
board schools. Les Mouflets caters for non-
skiing children from ten months to six
years. Le Village des Marmottons is for
youngsters from two to eight years old,
with a mixture of games and skiing for the
older ones.

Location of accommodation is important
and it is well worth checking out the
distance from a main lift before booking.
Hotel Fleur de Neige (☎ 450 73 20 10) is
praised for the quality of its food: 'more like
a restaurant with rooms than a hotel'. Hotel
Castellan (☎ 450 73 20 86) is 'simple, but
with excellent food', while Hotel Les
Rhododendrons (☎ 450 73 24 04) is
'perfectly located and typically French'.

Restaurants include Le Monchu on the
Swiss border ('absolutely the best food and
atmosphere in town'), La Bonne Ménagère,
which is popular, and the Vieux Four ('slow
service but food is good, basic French').
Evening entertainment is limited to a
handful of bars including the Tunnel, L'Isba
and L'Avalanche.

**Tel** 33 450 73 22 44
**Email** touristoffice@chatel.com
**Website** www.chatel.com

**Ski area** top 2,350m (7,708ft) bottom 1,200m (3,936ft)
**Lifts in area** 207 in Portes du Soleil: 14🚡 82🚠 111🎿
**Tour operators** AWWT, First Choice, Freedom Holidays, Interhome, Lagrange, Leisure Direction, Peak Retreats, Ski Independence, Ski Rosie, Ski Supreme, Skitopia, Skiworld, Tops Travel

## Clavière, Italy

Clavière is a small village on the Franco–Italian border and is linked into the **Milky Way** ski area. The village consists of little more than nine hotels and a row of shops. Reporters commented that it has a pleasant, relaxed atmosphere; it is tightly enclosed by wooded slopes, and the nursery area is small and steep ('definitely not the place for beginners. My partner has taken a lot of convincing to go skiing again'). Lifts give access to the skiing above **Montgenèvre** and **Cesana–Sansicario**, with easy runs back from both. There is a 15-km cross-country circuit trail up to Montgenèvre as well as a floodlit skating-rink.

Hotels include the Grand Albergo Clavière (☎ 0122 878787), Passero Pellegrino (☎ 0122 878914), Pian del Sole (☎ 0122 878085) and Savoia (☎ 0122 878803). Recommended restaurants are L'Gran Bouc, Gallo Cedrone, Pizzeria Kilt and La Montanina. Nightlife is limited to a few bars.

**Tel** 39 0122 878856
**Email** claviere@montagnedoc.it
**Website** www.montagnedoc.it
**Ski area** top 2,293m (7,523ft) bottom 1,760m (5,773ft)
**Lifts in area** 92 in Milky Way: 3🚡 35🚠 54🎿
**Tour operators** Crystal, Equity, First Choice, Momentum, Ski High Days, Skibound

## La Clusaz, France

This large, spread-out resort, a one-hour drive from Geneva airport, has managed to retain much of its charm as a working mountain village centred around an old church and a fast-flowing stream. New buidings have been constructed in chalet style and blend into the picturesque Alpine setting. Snow cover can be a problem here, since the village lies at 1,100m and the skiing goes up to only 2,600m. The 40 lifts of nearby Le Grand-Bornand are included in the regional Aravis lift pass.

The five ski areas are spread around the sides of a number of neighbouring valleys. Mountain access to Beauregard and L'Aiguille is by lifts from the resort centre, including a new cable-car. The other three areas (Balme, L'Etale and Croix-Fry/Merdassier) are reached from various points along the valleys via a satisfactory ski-bus network. The skiing is best suited to intermediates, but there is a substantial amount of more demanding terrain – particularly in the La Balme sector.

La Clusaz has three ski schools: the ESF ('the instruction was excellent and very hard work'), Sno Académie and Aravis Challenge ('both first rate'). There is a terrain park on Aiguille ('world class'). Club des Mouflets is the non-ski kindergarten, while Club des Champions provides daycare with optional ski lessons.

Recommended hotels include the three-stars Beauregard (☎ 450 32 68 00), Les Chalets de la Serraz (☎ 450 02 48 29), L'Alpage de Tante Pauline (☎ 450 02 63 28), Le Vieux Chalet (☎ 450 02 41 53) and Hotel Alpen'roc (☎ 450 02 58 96).

Restaurants Le Chalet du Lac in the Confins Valley and the gastronomic Symphonie in the Hotel Beauregard are warmly praised, along with L'Arbé, La Scierie, and L'Alpage de Tante Pauline. Après-ski centres around a few bars including La Braise, while Le Pressoir is the 'in' place for snowboarders. Resort workers meet in the Grenier. L'Ecluse has a glass dance-floor over the river, while Le Club 18 offers live bands and attracts the locals and an older clientèle.

**Tel** 33 450 32 65 00
**Email** infos@laclusaz.com
**Website** www.laclusaz.com
**Ski area** top 2,600m (8,528ft) bottom 1,100m (3,608ft)
**Lifts in area** 54: 5🚡 14🚠 35🎿
**Tour operators** Classic Ski, Crystal, Interhome, Lagrange, Leisure Direction, Made to Measure, Ski Weekend, Skiworld

## Les Coches, France

See *La Plagne*, page 97

**Tour operators** Erna Low, Family Ski Company, Leisure Direction, Ski Independence

## Colfosco, Italy

Colfosco has easy access to both **Selva Gardena** and **Corvara**'s skiing, although the village also has a small ski area of its own with good nursery slopes. Recommended hotels are the Capella (☎ 0471 836183), Alta Badia (☎ 0471 836616) and Kolfuschgerhof (☎ 0471 636188). Speckstube Peter, Mesoles, La Stria, Matthiaskeller and Tabladel are the most popular eating-places.

**Tel** 39 0471 792277
**Email** info@valgardena.com
**Website** www.valgardena.com
**Ski area** top 2,950m (9,676ft) bottom 1,650m (5,412ft)
**Lifts in area** 83 in Val Gardena: 10🚠 36🚡 37🚪
**Tour operator** Momentum

## El Colorado, Chile

See *Valle Nevado*, page 317

**Tour operators** Momentum, Scott Dunn Latin America, Ski All America, Ski Safari

## Les Contamines-Montjoie, France

This unspoilt resort is just over the hill from **Megève**. It has a keen following despite the fact that the whole set-up is awkward. The long village is on one side of the river, the ski area on the other, and Le Lay base-station is a 1-km uphill walk from the centre. However, a regular shuttle bus runs between the village and the lifts.

The east-facing bowl, which makes up the ski area, holds its snow well and offers a good alternative when neighbouring resorts have none. Off-piste enthusiasts can find virtually untouched powder all over the area after a fresh snowfall. Two efficient gondolas take snow-users up to a plateau at 1,470m, where a further gondola leads to Le Signal and the start of the skiing. Almost half of the 44 runs are intermediate, with the higher runs towards Mont Joly steeper and more testing.

Garderie Croc'Noisettes offers daycare and lessons for children from one to seven years, and the Jardin des Neiges is open only in the mornings during the French school holidays.

The six mountain restaurants include 'a lovely little restaurant at the top of the Ruelle lift on the Belleville side' and 'a fairly large, pleasant restaurant at Etape'. La Chemenaz (☎ 450 47 02 44) is the only three-star hotel. Nightlife is limited to a skating-rink, two discos and a cinema.

**Tel** 33 450 47 01 58
**Email** info@lescontamines.com
**Website** www.lescontamines.com
**Ski area** top 2,500m (8,202ft) bottom 1,164m (3,818ft)
**Lifts in area** 24: 3🚠 6🚡 15🚪
**Tour operators** Classic Ski, Club Europe, Interhome, Lagrange, Total Ski

## Copper Mountain, Colorado, US

This resort, situated on the Denver side of the Vail Pass, has recently been the subject of a $400-million makeover. The smart base is markedly more attractive than the original construction, with the car-free village set around four new lodges and plazas with shops and restaurants. Reporters feel that Copper Mountain is well worth a visit.

There is a natural tendency for the tree-lined trails to become more difficult as you move east (left on the piste map). Therefore, advanced skiers and boarders tend to stick to the main face of Copper Peak, and beginners will find little beyond their capabilities on the west side of the resort. In between, the terrain is mainly intermediate. Copper Bowl and Spaulding Bowl provide some of the best off-piste skiing in Colorado, with the latter full of natural jumps and lips for riders. Copper Mountain possesses a total of 125 groomed trails, and the mountain summit is reached in eight minutes by the Super Bee chair-lift.

Belly Button Babies kindergarten accepts little ones from two months old, and its stablemate, the Belly Button Bakery, caters for children over two years and skiers over three years of age.

Most of the accommodation is in apartments. Restaurants include Endo's Adrenaline Café, Salsa Mountain Cantina and the Imperial Palace – a Chinese that 'does a first-class take-away'. Creekside has 'the greatest pizzas', and the Rocky Mountain Chocolate Factory is recommended too. The Indian Motorcycle Café and Lounge features contemporary cuisine in a relaxed atmosphere.

The Copper Mountain Racquet and Athletic Club boasts excellent facilities, including a swimming-pool, indoor tennis and racket-ball.

**Tel** 1 970 968 2882
**Email** cmr-res@ski-copper.com
**Website** www.coppercolorado.com
**Ski area** top 12,313ft (3,767m) bottom 9,712ft (2,926m)
**Lifts in area** 19: 15🚠 4🚡
**Tour operators** AWWT, Crystal, Equity, Erna Low, Neilson, Neilson School Groups, Ski Activity, Ski All America, Ski the American Dream, Ski Independence, Skiworld, Thomson, United Vacations

## Le Corbier, France

Le Corbier is part of one of the largest ski areas in the Maurienne Valley, sharing 225km of terrain with the neighbouring resorts of Les Bottières, **St Jean d'Arves**, **St-Sorlin d'Arves** and La Toussuire. Set against the magnificent backdrop of Les Aiguilles d'Arves, the Massif de Belladonne and La Meije, the skiing is ideal for beginners and low intermediates, with 40 per cent of the 75km of pistes graded as easy. There are two terrain parks, and the area boasts four mountain restaurants. A new swimming-pool and fitness centre have been added for 2004–5.

Families are well catered for, with a snowpark for children from three years, and the Famille Nombreuse lift pass means that, in families with five or more members, one child skis free.

Most of the accommodation in Le Corbier is in self-catering apartments, including Maeva Résidence des Pistes (☎ 479 56 32 99). The resort also has a couple of two-star hotels: Hotel Mont Corbier (☎ 479 56 70 27) in the centre and Le Grillon (☎ 479 56 72 59), 3km away towards Villarembert. The choice for eating out lies between the hotels, three pizzerias and Le St Moritz restaurant, which serves cuisine described as 'gastronomic savoyarde'. Nightlife centres around a couple of bars and at Le Sweet Disco Club.

**Tel** 33 479 83 04 04
**Email** info@le-corbier.com
**Website** www.le-corbier.com
**Ski area** top 2,600m (8,530ft) bottom 1,550m (5,085ft)
**Lifts in area** 76: 26🚠 50🚡
**Tour operators** Equity, Erna Low, Lagrange, On The Piste, Ski Independence

## Coronet Peak, New Zealand

See *Queenstown (Coronet Peak and The Remarkables)*, page 301

## Cortina d'Ampezzo, Italy

See page 125

**Tour operators** Alpine Answers, Crystal, Elegant Resorts, Inghams, Momentum, Original Travel, Ski Freshtracks, Ski Equipe, Ski Expectations, Ski Solutions, White Roc

## Corvara, Italy

This pleasant **Sella Ronda** resort is strategically placed for some of the best skiing in the region. Planac Parkhotel (☎ 0471 836210) is a smart four-star, while Hotel Posta Zirm (☎ 0471 836175), the old post house at the bottom of the Col Alto chair-lift, keeps alive the tradition of the tea-dance ('fantastic fun'). The ski school includes a kindergarten for children from three years old, but English is not widely spoken. One reporter warmly recommended the Raetia Café for its wide selection of teas. La Stüa de Michil in Romantik Hotel La Perla (☎ 0471 831000) is an eighteenth-century Tyrolean Stube.

**Tel** 39 0471 792277
**Email** info@valgardena.com
**Website** www.valgardena.com
**Ski area** top 2,950m (9,676ft) bottom 1,550m (5,085ft)
**Lifts in area** 83 in Val Gardena: 10🚡 36🚠 37🚡
**Tour operators** Momentum, Pyrenean Mountain Tours

## Courchevel, France

See page 78

**Tour operators** Airtours, Alpine Answers, Alpine Weekends, Altitude Holidays, Chalet World, Corporate Ski Company, Crystal, Elegant Resorts, Erna Low, Esprit, Finlays, First Choice, Flexiski, French Life, Inghams, Lagrange, Leisure Direction, Le Ski, Lotus Supertravel, Mark Warner, Momentum, Mountain Leap, Neilson, On The Piste, Oxford Ski Company, PGL, Powder Byrne, Scott Dunn Ski, Seasons in Style, Silver Ski, Simply Ski, Ski Activity, Ski Amis, Ski Expectations, Ski France, Ski Freshtracks, Ski Independence, Ski Olympic, Ski Solutions, Ski Supreme, Ski Val, Ski Weekend, Skiworld, Thomson, Total Ski, White Roc

## Courmayeur, Italy

See page 128

**Tour operators** Alpine Answers, Alpine Weekends, Crystal, First Choice, Inghams, Interhome, Interski, Mark Warner, Momentum, Ski Expectations, Ski Freshtracks, Ski Solutions, Ski Weekend, Skiworld, Thomson, White Roc

## Crans Montana, Switzerland

See page 147

**Tour operators** Corporate Ski Company, Crystal, Inghams, Interhome, Kuoni, Momentum, Oxford Ski Company, PGL, Powder Byrne, Skiworld, Swiss Travel Centre, Swiss Travel Service

## Crested Butte, Colorado, US

See page 232

**Tour operators** AWWT, Ski the American Dream, Ski Independence, Skiworld, United Vacations

## Les Crosets, Switzerland

Les Crosets is a tiny ski station in the heart of the open slopes on the Swiss side of the **Portes du Soleil**. It is popular with riders and has its own snowboard school as well as a terrain park. The hamlet is fairly functional and, apart from a visit to the Sundance Saloon disco, has no obvious appeal to anyone but serious snow-users who want an early night. However, four of the slopes are floodlit for skiing and riding until 11pm each Wednesday and Saturday.

Hotel Télécabine (☎ 24 479 0300) is simple, British-run and serves excellent food. Half a dozen eateries on the piste are also open in the evening. The Swiss Snowsports School (ESS) has a branch here, and there is also a mini-club.

**Tel** 41 24 477 2077
**Email** info@lescrosets.com
**Website** www.lescrosets.com
**Ski area** top 2,350m (7,708ft) bottom 1,660m (5,445ft)
**Lifts in area** 207 in Portes du Soleil: 14🚡 82🚠 111🎿
**Tour operators** none

## Dachstein Glacier, Austria

See *Salzburger Sportwelt Amadé*, page 303

## Davos, Switzerland

See page 149

**Tour operators** Alpine Answers, Corporate Ski Company, Flexiski, Inghams, Interhome, Kuoni, Momentum, PGL, Ski Expectations, Ski Freshtracks, Ski Gower, Ski Weekend, Skiworld, Swiss Travel Centre, Swiss Travel Service, White Roc

## Deer Valley, Utah, US

See *Park City Resorts*, page 240

**Tour operators** AWWT, Ski the American Dream, Ski Independence, United Vacations

## Les Deux Alpes, France

See page 81

**Tour operators** Airtours, Chalet World, Club Med, Crystal, Equity, Erna Low, First Choice, French Freedom, French Life, Inghams, Interhome, Lagrange, Leisure Direction, Mark Warner, Neilson, On The Piste, Panorama, Peak Retreats, Ski Activity, Ski Independence, Ski Supreme, Skiworld, Thomson, Tops Travel

## Les Diablerets, Switzerland

Les Diablerets is a sprawling village with mainly chalet accommodation. It is situated near **Gstaad**, and its glacier provides snow-sure skiing throughout most of the year. Les Diablerets' intermediate ski area is linked on mountain to neighbouring **Villars**. The Eurotel Victoria (☎ 24 492 3721), Hotel des Diablerets (☎ 24 492 0909) and Mon Abri (☎ 24 492 3481) are recommended. Hotel Le Chamois (☎ 24 492 2653) has an in-house kindergarten. Auberge de la Poste and Le Café des Diablerets are singled out for culinary praise. The nightlife is quiet and centres on a few bars and discos, including the Pote Saloon and B'Bar. Les Vioz is 'a cosy venue for a *vin chaud* after the last run down'.

**Tel** 41 24 492 3358
**Email** info@diablerets.ch
**Website** www.diablerets.ch
**Ski area** top 2,113m (6,932ft), bottom 1,300m (4,265ft)
**Lifts in area** 47: 1🚡 6🚠 11🎿 29🎿
**Tour operators** Crystal, Interhome, Momentum, PGL, Ski Gower, Sloping Off, Solo's, Swiss Travel Service, Thomson

## Durango, Colorado, US

This purpose-built, alpine-style resort, 25 miles from Durango airport, received enthusiastic praise from reporters: 'it has an old-town feel in an unspoilt forest area of the Rockies'. The ski area boasts 85 trails covering 1,200 acres.

Snowboarders and freestyle skiers are well catered for with the new Paradise Freestyle Arena with hits, rails, and a half-pipe, as well as the Pitchfork Terrain Park. The Adaptive Sports Association provides lessons for disabled skiers and is ranked as one of the best ski schools of its type in the USA. The kindergarten accepts non-skiing children from two months old, and from three years for skiing.

Powderhouse and Dante's ('downstairs self-service, upstairs sit-down service') are the only two on-mountain restaurants. Purgy's in the village centre serves pizzas to live music. Powdermonkey Grill is a ten-minute, free shuttle-bus ride from the centre and received favourable reports.

Hotels include the Purgatory Village Hotel (☎ 970 385 2100), The Inn at Durango Mountain (☎ 970 247 9669), and Sheraton Tamarron Resort (☎ 970 259 2000). The Twilight View Condos are recommended. Durango village boasts nine B&Bs, many with fireplaces and hot-tubs. All accommodation bookings can be made through Durango Central Reservations (☎ 800 982 61030).

**Tel** 1 970 247 9000
**Email** lwright@durangomountain.com
**Website** www.durangomountainresort.com
**Ski area** top 10,822ft (3,299m) bottom 8,793ft (2,680m)
**Lifts in area** 10: 10C
**Tour operators** AWWT, Ski Independence

## Ellmau, Austria

Ellmau is the biggest resort in the **SkiWelt** circuit in the Austrian Tyrol, with easy access into the system and a choice of pleasant accommodation. Hotel Christoph (☎ 5358 3535), a five-minute walk from the main access lift, was described as excellent, with super large rooms'. Sporthotel Ellmau (☎ 5358 3755) and Hotel Hochfilzer (☎ 5358 2501) are both four-stars. The more luxurious Relais & Chateaux Der Bär (☎ 5358 2395) has a health club. Ellmau's nightlife rivals that of

Söll, with Pub Memory, Ellmauer Alm, Heldenbar and the Tenne all lively destinations. The après-ski venues include Disco Ötzi Bar, La Cantina (Mexican) and Pub 66. The Kaiserbad water chutes and adventure swimming-park are popular.

Both the Ellmau and Hartkaiser ski schools are praised by reporters. We have no reports of Top Schischule und Snowboard or Freaks on Snow Snowboardschule. Children aged six months to four years are cared for at Max & Moritz.

**Tel** 43 5358 2301
**Email** info@ellmau.at
**Website** www.ellmau.at
**Ski area** top 1,829m (6,001ft) bottom 820m (2,690ft)
**Lifts in area** 93 in SkiWelt: 11⑤ 34⑤ 48⑨
**Tour operators** Airtours, Crystal, Inghams, Interhome, Neilson, Ski Astons, Thomson

## Engelberg, Switzerland

See page 152

**Tour operators** Corporate Ski Company, Crystal, Inntravel, Interhome, Kuoni, Momentum, Oak Hall, Swiss Travel Service, Waymark, White Roc

## L'Espace Killy

See *Tignes*, page 107, and *Val d'Isere*, page 110

## Falls Creek and Mount Hotham, Australia

Falls Creek and Mount Hotham are Victoria's major resorts. They share a lift pass and are linked by a helicopter service. The six-minute flight is almost two-and-a-half hours quicker than by road. The area is served by its own Mount Hotham airport, 20km from the resort.

Falls Creek Alpine Resort is on the edge of the Bogong High Plains, four hours' drive from Melbourne. It is a European-style, ski-in ski-out village with accommodation among the gum trees. Parking is at the base of the village, and luggage is transported to your lodge by snowcat. You can ski directly to eight different lifts from every lodge, and altogether there are more than 92 trails spread across four distinct areas. The largest snowmaking system in Australia covers the principal runs, and the resort has an impressive terrain park. Nearby Mount McKay offers 38 hectares of back-country skiing.

Mount Hotham is the highest alpine resort in Victoria, with most of the slopes lying below the village. Runs such as Mary's Slide, the Chute and Gotcha are quite challenging, while intermediates tend to gather in the Heavenly Valley region. Dinner Plain, Mount Hotham's architect-designed sister village, provides reasonably priced accommodation and is situated 10km from the mountain, linked by an efficient free bus service. The Hotham Heights Chalets, adjacent to the Village Chair, are ski-in, ski-out.

**Tel** Falls Creek 61 3 5758 3224 / Mount Hotham 61 3 5759 4444
**Email** mhsc@hotham.com.au / frcm@fallscreek.com.au
**Websites** www.fallscreek.com.au / www.hotham.com.au
**Ski area** top 1,861m (6,105ft) bottom 1,450m (4,757ft)
**Lifts in area** 13 in each resort: 10⑤ 3⑨
**Tour operators** none

## Fernie, BC, Canada

See page 51

**Tour operators** AWWT, Crystal, Frontier Ski, Inghams, Nonstopski, Ski Activity, Ski All America, Ski Freshtracks, Ski Independence, Ski Safari, Ski the American Dream, Virgin Snow

## Fieberbrunn, Austria

Ten kilometres up the road from **St Johann in Tirol** lies the sprawling village of Fieberbrunn. 'A brilliant place – I can't recommend it too highly', enthused one reporter, and 'a great family resort', said another. Its small but attractive ski area is north-facing and is a snowpocket. The main skiing is at tree-level, with lifts giving access to a network of mainly long and easy runs totalling 35km. There are two ski schools – Rosenegg and Fieberbrunn – and we have favourable reports of both. The resort kindergarten takes children from 12 months. Austria Trend Sporthotel Fontana (☎ 5354 56453) and Hotel-Pension Lindauerhof (☎ 5354 56382) are the most convenient for the lifts, while Schlosshotel Rosenegg (☎ 5354 56201) is also recommended.

**Tel** 43 5354 563330
**Email** info@pillerseetal.at
**Website** www.pillerseetal.at

**Ski area** top 2,020m (6,627ft) bottom 800m (2,625ft)
**Lifts in area** 11: 3⑤ 3⑤ 5⑨
**Tour operators** Snowscape, Tyrolean Adventures

## Filzmoos, Austria

See *Salzburger Sportwelt Amadé*, page 303

**Tour operators** Inghams, Winetrails

## Finkenberg, Austria

See *Mayrhofen*, page 29

**Tour operator** Crystal

## Flachau, Austria

See *Salzburger Sportwelt Amadé*, page 303

**Tour operators** Club Europe, Interhome, PGL

## Flaine, France

See page 84

**Tour operators** Classic Ski, Club Med, Crystal, Erna Low, French Freedom, French Life, Inghams, Leisure Direction, Neilson, On The Piste, Ski Freshtracks, Ski Independence, Ski Supreme, Skiworld, Thomson

## Flims and the Alpenarena, Switzerland

See page 153

**Tour operators** Alpine Answers, Corporate Ski Company, Interhome, Kuoni, Powder Byrne, Momentum, Ski Freshtracks, Skiworld, Swiss Travel Centre, Swiss Travel Service, White Roc

## Font-Romeu, France

Situated 90km from Perpignan and 200km from Toulouse, Font-Romeu is set on a sunny plateau known for its mild climate, making it unreliable for snow at the beginning and end of the season. Half the total skiing terrain is covered by snow-cannon. A gondola links the purpose-built ski station with the village 4km away. The 52km of piste suit beginners to intermediates and families. Weekend queues are a problem as the resort is popular with both French and Spanish skiers.

The ESF and ESI are the two ski and snowboard schools. Children are cared for at a choice of Pyrénées 2000 and the Font Romeu crèches, while small skiers can join one of the two Jardins d'Enfants with their children-only T-bars. The resort has a terrain park. Cross-country skiing is prominent here, with 80km of loipe and two specialist schools.

There are two dozen hotels and pensions, including four three-stars: Hotel Carlit (☎ 468 30 80 30), Le Grand Tetras (☎ 468 30 01 20), La Montagne (☎ 468 30 36 44) and Sun Valley (☎ 468 30 21 21). The resort also boasts two children's holiday centres, where those as young as seven years old can stay during their school holidays. The resort's après-ski activities include a wide variety of shops and restaurants, a casino, cinemas, a choice of discos and bars, and an ice-hockey stadium. Font-Romeu is a training centre for dogs and dog-handlers in the sport of dog-sledding.

Tel 33 468 30 68 30
Email office@font-romeu.fr
Website www.font-romeu.fr
Ski area top 2,250m (7,382ft) bottom 1,700m (5,577ft)
Lifts in area 27: 1⟦⟧ 1⟦⟧ 7⟦⟧ 18⟦⟧
Tour operators Lagrange, Solo's

## La Foux d'Allos, France

See *Pra-Loup*, page 300
Tour operator Club Europe

## Fulpmes, Austria

See *Stubaital*, page 312

## Galtür, Austria

In comparison with neighbouring **Ischgl**, Galtür is normally an oasis of calm. However, the small ski area is prone to heavy crowds during the high-season February weeks. The resort is connected to Ischgl by free shuttle bus during the day.

Galtür's 40km of pistes are at Wirl, an outpost reached in five minutes by a free and frequent shuttle bus. The skiing is gentle and well suited to beginners and families; the kindergarten accepts little ones from three years. The area is also a notable centre for ski-touring, especially in spring.

The most popular bars are Tommy's Garage, off the main square, and s'Platzli in

the cellar of Hotel Rössle. Others include the Pyramidenbar in the village centre, along with Weiberhimmel and the Huber-Stadl at the ski area. The family-run Flüchthorn Hotel (☎ 5444 55550) offers a warm welcome in a central location. The Post (☎ 5444 5232) is also convenient.

Tel 43 5443 8521
Email galtuer@netway.at
Website www.galtuer.com
Ski area top 2,300m (7,546ft) bottom 1,585m (5,200ft)
Lifts in area 10: 3⟦⟧ 7⟦⟧
Tour operators First Choice, Inghams, Made to Measure

## Gargellen, Austria

Gargellen is a chalet-style village in the **Montafon**, close to the border with Switzerland. A variety of hotels include the four-star Madrisa (☎ 5557 6331), which was built at the beginning of the twentieth century. Hotel Heimspitze (☎ 5557 63190) is rated 'excellent'. The resort boasts a modern eight-person gondola. There are 36km of pistes, extensive off-piste and free ski buses that connect Gargellen to the neighbouring resorts of Gaschurn and St Gallenkirch. The village kindergarten accepts children from two years old.

Tel 43 5557 6303
Email tourismus@gargellen.to
Website www.gargellen.to
Ski area top 2,300m (7,546ft) bottom 1,430m (4,692ft)
Lifts in area 8: 1⟦⟧ 2⟦⟧ 5⟦⟧
Tour operator Made to Measure

## The Gasteinertal, Austria

See page 19

Tour operators Club Europe, Crystal, First Choice, Inghams, Interhome, Made to Measure, Neilson School Groups, Ski Miquel, Skibound

## Geilo, Norway

This traditional resort midway between Bergen and Oslo is only a 30-minute drive from Dagali airport. It is especially recommended for cross-country skiers as one of the centres on the famous Hardangevidda Plateau. The downhill skiing, which comprises 36 pistes, is relaxed and best suited to novices and intermediates. The two main ski areas are inconveniently situated on either side of a wide valley, with the resort in the middle. 'Difficult to ski both sides of the valley in one day, which makes it not ideal if you have kids in the ski school and want to make it a family lunch,' said one reporter, 'The ski bus (between areas) is limited'.

The main ski area, Geilohovda, has the widest selection of pistes, while the Vestlia area, on the other side of the valley, provides the easiest skiing. 2003–4 saw the opening of a third family area served by a quad-chair and a drag-lift at Kikut. This is linked to the Vestlia area by a six-person chair-lift and a blue run.

Geilo has three ski schools and the largest terrain park in Norway, situated at Fugleleiken. There is also a second, much smaller, one at Vestlia. 'The skiing is great for children,' enthused a reporter. The excellent Troll Club kindergarten ('warm and friendly') at Vestlia offers indoor and outdoor activities for children under three years.

At lunch-time sun-lovers congregate on the terrace of the stately Dr Holms Hotel. The Highland Hotel is recommended. The Vestlia Hotel is 'warm and comfortable, the food was excellent'. The Forest Cabins near the Vestlia lift were said to be 'first-rate value for money'. All accommodation can be booked through a central number (☎ 320 95940).

The Låven bar at the Vestlia Hotel is a popular après-ski venue, together with Skibaren in the Dr Holms. Highdance is the disco. The dog-sleigh rides on the frozen lake are recommended.

**Tel** 47 320 95900
**Email** turistinfo@geilo.no
**Website** www.geilo.no
**Ski area** top 1,178m (3,864ft) bottom 800m (2,624ft)
**Lifts in area** 19: 5🚠 14🎿
**Tour operators** Crystal, Headwater, Inntravel, Neilson, Neilson School Groups, Thomson

## Les Gets, France

See page 94

**Tour operators** AWWT, Descent International, Family Ski Company, Lagrange, Oxford Ski Company, Peak Retreats, Ski Activity, Ski Expectations, Ski Famille, Ski Hillwood, Ski Independence, Total Ski, Skiworld

## Glencoe, Scotland

Glencoe *closed down when its operators, the Glenshee Chairlift company, went into receivership in May 2004. We hope that a way will be found of reopening the resort in the future.*

**Tel** (01855) 851226
**Email** info@ski-glencoe.co.uk
**Website** www.ski-glencoe.co.uk

## Glenshee, Scotland

Glenshee *closed down when the Glenshee Chairlift company went into receivership in May 2004. We hope that a way will be found of reopening the resort in the future.*

**Tel** (01339) 741325
**Email** info@ski-glenshee.co.uk
**Website** www.ski-glenshee.co.uk

## Going, Austria

Fully linked into the **SkiWelt**, with the best views of the Wilder Kaiser and a large nursery slope, Going is beginning to be noticed by the British, not least because of the exceptional five-star Hotel Stanglwirt (☎ 5358 2000), which has indoor swimming, tennis and a Lipizzaner riding school. Going has its own ski and snowboard school called Schwaiger, and Krabblestube Max und Moritz is the kindergarten.

**Tel** 43 5358 2438
**Email** info@going.at
**Website** www.going.at
**Ski area** top 1,829m (6,001ft) bottom 800m (2,624ft)
**Lifts in area** 93 in SkiWelt: 11🚡 34🚠 48🎿
**Tour operator** Solo's

## Gran Catedral (Bariloche), Argentina

San Carlos de Bariloche, in Patagonia, is home to Gran Catedral – Argentina's oldest and most famous ski resort – better known simply as Bariloche. It is a large, attractive resort in the south-west, not far from the Chilean border. The scenery is impressive: the three-peaked Tronador (3,554m) dominates one horizon; Nahuel Huapi the other.

Some 20km from the bustling city and perched high above the spectacular lake of Nahuel Huapi, Gran Catedral – so called because of the cathedral-like rock formations high above the resort – is sophisticated, cosmopolitan and vibrant. Bariloche is South America's biggest single resort, with a modern lift system, 50 runs, a vertical drop of 1,000m and the biggest snowmaking system in South America. The area offers an expanse of wide-open, largely intermediate slopes with good, high-speed cruising and abundant off-piste.

Natural early-season cover can be sparse, although the lower slopes around the main chair-lift are covered by snow-cannon. Alternative nursery slopes are situated at the top of the mountain. The summit of Piedra del Condor is the site of a terrain park with a half-pipe. Lado Bueno (Alta Patagonia) and Robles Catedral are the ski schools. Hotels include the five-star Panamericano and the four-stars Hotel Nevada and Hotel Edelweiss. Bariloche's nightlife is effervescent.

**Tel** 54 2944 423776
**Email** none
**Website** www.bariloche.com
**Ski area** top 2,050m (6,725ft) bottom 1,050m (3,445ft)
**Lifts in area** 32: 1🚡 11🚠 20🎿
**Tour operator** Andes

## Gran Valira, Andorra

See *Pas de la Casa*, page 13, and *Soldeu–El Tarter–Canillo*, page 14

## Grand Targhee, Wyoming, US

This small resort just inside the Wyoming border and 47 miles from **Jackson Hole** is blessed with a first-rate snow record, which is why the main attraction here is snowcat skiing and boarding. This is only by previous arrangement, as the cat takes a maximum of ten passengers, plus the guide and a patrolman. If you can't get a booking, the resort's main 2,000-acre ski area offers reasonable challenge and more cultured powder opportunities. Grand Targhee has a ski and snowboard school, a kindergarten, a small shopping centre and limited restaurants. Prices are notably lower than those in Jackson Hole, and a new family package means that children under 14 stay

and ski free. The Trap offers 'friendly table service, ski videos and a good variety of local beers', and accommodation (☎ 800 827 4433 for booking office) includes the Teewinot Lodge, Targhee Lodge and Sioux Lodge Condominiums.

**Tel** 1 307 353 2300
**Email** info@grandtarghee.com
**Website** www.grandtarghee.com
**Ski area** top 10,230ft (3,118m) bottom 8,000ft (2,438m)
**Lifts in area** 8: 8🎿
**Tour operator** AWWT

## La Grave, France

See page 87

**Tour operators** Lagrange, Peak Retreats, Ski Freshtracks, Skiworld

## Gressoney, Italy

See *Champoluc–Gressoney–Alagna*, page 122

**Tour operators** Crystal, Momentum

## Grindelwald, Switzerland

See page 155

**Tour operators** Corporate Ski Company, Crystal, Elegant Resorts, Inghams, Interhome, Kuoni, Momentum, Powder Byrne, Ski Freshtracks, Ski Gower, Skiworld, Solo's, Swiss Travel Centre, Swiss Travel Service, Thomson, White Roc

## Gstaad, Switzerland

This village attracts a spectacularly wealthy clientèle. It stands at only 1,000m, with none of the local skiing above 2,200m, which means that snow cover can be unreliable. The redeeming factor is the proximity of **Les Diablerets** glacier, where the lifts go up to 2,979m. Regulars argue that the sheer extent of the intermediate skiing included in the Ski Gstaad lift pass – 250km of piste (nearly half of it rated as easy) and ten villages – makes up for the lack of challenge.

The local skiing is inconveniently divided into three separate areas. Regular ski buses to the surrounding villages of Rougemont, Saanenmöser and Schönried give access to slopes offering more scope. The other villages covered on the lift pass are St Stephan, Zweisimmen, Lauenen, Gsteig, Saanen and **Château d'Oex**. Gstaad has terrain parks at Hornberg above Saanenmöser, at Rinderberg above Zweisimmen and on the Eggli at Gstaad. There are 140km of cross-country loipe. Recommended mountain restaurants include Chemihütte ('by far the best') above St Stephan, and Cabane de la Sarouche at Château d'Oex.

The best-known hotel is the Palace (☎ 33 748 5000), which has fairytale turrets and sits on the hill like a feudal castle. The Grand Hotel Park (☎ 33 748 9800) is opulent. The four-star Bernerhof (☎ 33 748 8844) is close to the railway station and the Christiania (☎ 33 744 5121) has individually designed bedrooms. The four-star Olden (☎ 33 744 3444) is cosy.

Recommended restaurants include the Sonnenhof, La Cave in the Olden hotel and the sixteenth-century Chlösterli. Café du Cerf in Rougemont is a typical Swiss restaurant with live music at weekends. The Palace's Greengo nightclub is the main late-night venue for those who can afford it. The locals meet at Richi's. Other haunts include Pubbles in the Hotel Boo in Saanen and Club 95 at the Sporthotel Victoria.

**Tel** 41 33 748 8181
**Email** gst@gstaad.ch
**Website** www.gstaad.ch
**Ski area** top 2,979m (9,744ft) bottom 1,000m (3,280ft)
**Lifts in area** 63: 15🚠 17🚡 31🎿
**Tour operators** Corporate Ski Company, Headwater, Momentum, Seasons in Style, Ski Expectations, Skiworld, White Roc

## Guthega, Australia

See *Perisher–Blue*, page 299

## Hafjell, Norway

See *Lillehammer*, page 288

**Tour operators** Crystal, Ramblers

## Happo'one and Hakuba Valley, Japan

Happo'one is the biggest ski area in the Nagano Prefecture's resort-studded Hakuba Valley, and arguably the best single resort in Japan. The Tsugaike Ridge Mountains rise to almost 3,047m and the valley lies 200km from Tokyo. It is linked to the capital by the *shinkansen* (bullet train). As well as offering splendid mountain scenery, some challenging terrain and longer-than-average runs, Happo'one is one of the prettiest ski villages in the country. It has a good mix of terrain. Another plus point is the quick access to other ski areas in the valley, including Hakuba 47, Iwatake, Goryu-Toomi and Sunalpina Sanosaka. Accommodation includes the Omoshiro Hasshinchi hotel (☎ 81 261 72 6663) at the base of Happo'one. It has four restaurants and a nightclub, as well as indoor and outdoor swimming-pools. The Hotel Lady Diana & St George's (☎ 81 261 75 3525 is also recommended.

**Tel** 020-7734 6870 in UK
**Email** info@jnto.co.uk
**Website** www.snowjapan.com
**Ski area** top 1,830m (6,007ft) bottom 760m (2,493ft)
**Lifts in area** 33: 1🚠 32🎿
**Tour operators** none

## Hasliberg, Switzerland

See *Meiringen–Hasliberg*, page 291

**Tour operator** Kuoni

## Haus-im-Ennstal, Austria

Haus is a quiet village linked into the **Saalbach–Hinterglemm** area. Its farming origins are still in evidence, although it has a considerable amount of holiday accommodation in guesthouses and apartments. There are cafés and a couple of shops. Recommended four-stars include Hotel Hauser Kaibling (☎ 3686 23780), with a swimming-pool and good cuisine; Hotel Gasthof Herrschaftstaverne (☎ 3686 2392), which has a wellness centre with indoor pool, whirlpool and sauna; and traditional Dorfhotel Kirchenwirt (☎ 3686 2228) in the village centre. Gasthof Reiter (☎ 3686 2225) is a fine old chalet that is much cheaper than most of the accommodation, and the Panoramahotel Gürtl (☎ 3686 2383) is a quiet family-run hotel well situated for the cable-car.

A gentle nursery slope lies between the village and the gondola station, and snowboarders are catered for with a half-pipe. Skischule Brandner, WM-Ski und

Snowboardschule Dachstein-Tauern all
offer tuition.

**Tel** 43 3686 22340
**Email** info@haus.at
**Website** www.en.skiamade.com
**Ski area** top 2,015m (6,611ft) bottom 750m (2,460ft)
**Lifts in area** 64 in Planai Four Mountain Ski Connection:
🚠 19🚡 38🚋
**Tour operators** none

## Heavenly, California, US

See page 233

**Tour operators** AWWT, Equity, Neilson, Ski All America, Ski
the American Dream, Ski Independence, Ski Safari,
Skibound, Trailfinders, United Vacations

## Hemsedal, Norway

See page 142

**Tour operators** Crystal, Neilson, Neilson School Groups,
Norvista, Thomson

## Hintertux, Austria

See *Tux im Zillertal*, page 316

## Hinterglemm, Austria

See *Saalbach–Hinterglemm*, page 34
**Tour operators** see Saalbach, page 303

## Hochgurgl, Austria

See *Obergurgl–Hochgurgl*, page 31
**Tour operators** see Obergurgl, page 295

## Hopfgarten, Austria

Hopfgarten is a quiet, traditional Tyrolean
village in the **SkiWelt** circuit dominated by
the twin yellow towers of its impressive
church, yet despite its friendly, low-key
atmosphere few British are found here. Poor
mountain access has acted as a deterent and
Hopfgarten can expect a new lease of life
with the replacement of the old chair-lift by
a new gondola planned for 2004–5. The
village has a long-established Antipodean
following, and spirited nightlife and dancing
can be found at the 02 disco and the Cin-
Cin. Accommodation includes Aparthotel

Hopfgarten (☎ 5335 3920) and Sporthotel
Fuchs (☎ 5335 2420), which one reporter
described as 'comfortable, clean, but with a
small lounge area'.

**Tel** 43 5335 2322
**Email** info@hopfgarten.tirol.at
**Website** www.hopfgarten.com
**Ski area** top 1,829m (6,001ft) bottom 622m (2,040ft)
**Lifts in area** 93 in SkiWelt: 11🚠 34🚡 48🚋
**Tour operators** Contiki, First Choice, PGL, Seasons in Style

## Les Houches, France

This large village in the **Chamonix** valley
has its own reasonably sized ski area and
includes an FIS World Cup downhill course
considered by racers to be second only to
the Hahnenkamm in Kitzbühel in technical
difficulty. A choice of cable-car, gondola or
chair-lift provides mountain access to a
much-underrated area with magnificent
views of the Mont Blanc massif. The skiing
is suitable for all standards, although much
of the terrain is demanding. The French
national ski team regularly trains here, and
there is a permanent slalom and giant
slalom racecourse on the mountain, which
is used by the British Ski Academy, a skiing
school for young British hopefuls that is
based in Les Houches.

By rights the resort should be included
in the Chamonix lift pass, but the two
neighbours fell out over revenue-sharing a
decade ago. However, it is included in the
regional Evasion Mont Blanc pass. Les
Houches has the best tree-skiing in the
valley and, in flat light conditions, this is
where you will find the cognoscenti. It is
also one of the few places in the world
where novices can learn to ski jump.

Children aged three months to three
years are cared for in the village crèche. La
Garderie des Chavants, by the gondola
station, looks after children aged three to
ten. Recommended hotels include the three-
stars Beau-Site (☎ 450 55 51 16), Chris-Tal
(☎ 450 54 50 55) and Hotel du Bois (☎
450 54 50 35).

**Tel** 33 450 55 50 62
**Email** info@leshouches.com
**Website** www.leshouches.com
**Ski area** top 1,860m (6,102ft) bottom 1,000m (3,280ft)
**Lifts in area** 18: 2🚠 4🚡 12🚋
**Tour operators** AWWT, Erna Low, French Life, Interhome,
Lagrange, Leisure Direction, Peak Retreats, Ski
Expectations, Sloping Off

## Hungerburg, Austria

See *Innsbruck*, below

## Igls, Austria

Igls, 5km from **Innsbruck** towards the Europabrücke and the Italian border, is a fine example of a traditional Tyrolean village but with limited skiing – the Olympic downhill run presenting the biggest challenge. Considerable snowmaking allows skiing to continue throughout March. The two nursery slopes are covered by snow-cannon and are a five-minute walk from the village centre. Non-skiing children can attend Bobo's Children's Club from Monday to Friday.

The village is small and uncommercialised, with sedate hotels and coffee houses, excellent winter walks and the Olympic bob-run, which is open to the public. There are four mountain restaurants, with the one at the top of the cable-car receiving substantial praise.

The Sporthotel Igls (☎ 5123 77241) is singled out for its cuisine, while the five-star Schlosshotel (☎ 5123 77217) receives good reports. Hotel Batzenhäusl (☎ 5123 8618) is recommended for comfort and cuisine. Nightlife is not Igls' strongest point, but the bars at the Bon Alpina and the Astoria are the more exciting spots. The Sporthotel disco is open until late.

**Tel** 43 5125 9850
**Email** info@innsbruck.tvb.co.at
**Website** www.innsbrucktourist.info
**Ski area** top 2,247m (7,372ft) bottom 900m (2,953ft)
**Lifts in area** 6: 1🚡 2🚠 3🎿
**Tour operator** Inghams

## Innsbruck, Austria

The city of Innsbruck enjoys a reputation as a minor ski resort in its own right, but its true significance for the skier and snowboarder is as a jumping-off point for a host of big-name resorts in the Tyrol and even the Arlberg. These can be reached daily by bus, although a hire car adds convenience and flexibility.

Innsbruck has twice hosted the Winter Olympics and enjoys the advantage of its own international airport, which is enclosed by dramatic, towering mountain ranges on either side of the Inn Valley. Its 'own' small but steep ski area is to be found just outside the city above **Hungerburg** on the south-facing slopes of the Hafelekar. Five other ski areas are within easy reach.

The city's smartest hotel is the five-star Europa-Tyrol (☎ 5125 9310), which is attractively wood-panelled and boasts the well-respected Europastüberl restaurant. Four-stars include The Penz (☎ 5125 75657) ('smart designer hotel in city centre'), as well as the Hotel-Restaurant Goldener Adler (☎ 5125 71111) and Romantikhotel Schwarzer Adler (☎ 5125 87109), both of which have recommended restaurants. Hotel Maximilian (☎ 5125 9967) on the edge of the Old Town, is family-run, and Hotel Bierwirt (☎ 5123 42143) has been owned by the same family for 300 years. At the lower end of the price scale are many pensions, including Gasthof Koreth (☎ 5122 6262) ten-minutes from the city centre, and Weinhaus Happ (☎ 5125 82980) in the Old Town.

**Tel** 43 512 59850
**Email** office@innsbruck.info
**Website** www.innsbruck.info
**Ski area** top 2,334m (6,250ft) bottom 580m (1,903ft)
**Lifts in area** 60 in six ski areas: 1🚡 9🚟 21🚠 29🎿
**Tour operators** Made to Measure, Neilson School Groups, Ramblers

## Interlaken, Switzerland

This attractive town is set between two lakes at the foot of the dramatic Eiger, Munch and Jungfrau mountains. Interlaken makes a good base for people who would rather stay in a sophisticated town than in a ski resort. From the town centre it is a short train ride to Lauterbrunnen, where you can take the cable-car up to **Mürren**, or a train to **Wengen** and **Grindelwald**. The prime place to stay is the once very traditional Grand Hotel Victoria-Jungfrau (☎ 33 828 2828), which has recently been renovated, adding a strikingly minimalist spa wing complete with spa bedrooms for those who want to spend most of their time wallowing in the indoor/outdoor swimming-pool and generally relaxing.

**Tel** 41 33 826 5300
**Email** mail@interlakentourism.ch
**Website** www.interlakentourism.ch
**Ski area** (Mürren) top 2,971m (9,748ft) bottom 796m (2,612ft)

**Lifts in area** 41 in Jungfrau Top Ski Region: 5⬛ 7◉ 15◯ 14◯
**Tour operators** Erna Low, Swiss Travel Service

## Ischgl, Austria

See page 22

**Tour operators** First Choice, Inghams, Made to Measure, Original Travel, Seasons in Style, Ski Solutions, Sloping Off

## Isola 2000, France

Isola is the most southerly ski area in France and, in reasonable weather conditions, it is a 90-km drive north of Nice up a winding all-weather road with dramatic drop-offs. The purpose-built resort offers 120km of piste and boasts a respectable vertical drop of 810m. Created with families in mind, it has a convenient complex of shops, bars, economically designed apartments and hotels, and a large, sunny nursery area. An increasing number of tour operators feature the resort in their brochures, and British skiers make up a big slice of the winter business. Many own apartments in the resort.

The ski area is limited, but varied enough for beginners, families with small children, and intermediates. The non-ski Miniclub kindergarten accepts children from two to five years old, and the ski kindergarten, Le Caribou, caters for little ones from four years.

Isola's original building, the ugly and soulless Front de Neige Centre, is right on the slopes. The more attractive, wood-clad additions behind it improve the resort's aesthetic appeal. Hotel Le Chastillon (☎ 493 23 26 00) and Hotel Diva (☎ 493 23 17 71) are the only four-stars, and the three-stars Hotel Pas du Loup (☎ 493 23 27 00) and Hotel de France (☎ 493 02 17 04) are also recommended. Restaurants include La Starving in Le Hameau, La Dolce Vita, La Buissonnière, L'Edelweiss, La Raclette and Le Crocodile. Nightlife largely revolves around a dozen bars and the two discos, La Cuba Loca and La Tanière.

**Tel** 33 493 23 15 15
**Email** isola@nicematin.fr
**Website** www.isola-2000.com
**Ski area** top 2,610m (8,561ft) bottom 1,800m (5,904ft)
**Lifts in area** 22: 1◉ 10◯ 11◯

**Tour operators** Club Pavilion, Crystal, Erna Low, French Life, Lagrange, Made to Measure, On The Piste, PGL

## Itter, Austria

Itter has only 850 visitor beds, but a fast gondola nearby with no queues for the uphill journey, plus the longest run in the **SkiWelt** (8.5km), make it a quieter, cheaper alternative to **Söll**. The Schidisco in Gasthof Schusterhof (☎ 5335 2681) and the Dorfpub are perhaps not up to the decibel levels of Söll but sufficient for most. Salvista Stadl is a popular après-ski bar next to the gondola. Sporthotel Tirolerhof (☎ 5335 2690) has a bowling alley, and the resort also offers tubing and floodlit tobogganing. Leo Fuchs is the ski school for adults and children.

**Tel** 43 5335 2670
**Email** itter@skiwelt.at
**Website** www.skiwelt.at
**Ski area** top 1,829m (6,001ft) bottom 703m (2,306ft)
**Lifts in area** 93 in SkiWelt: 11◉ 34◯ 48◯
**Tour operators** none

## Jackson Hole, Wyoming, US

See page 235

**Tour operators** AWWT, Crystal, Inghams, Momentum, Seasons in Style, Ski Activity, Ski All America, Ski the American Dream, Ski Freshtracks, Ski Independence, Ski Safari, Trailfinders, United Vacations, Virgin Snow

## Jasper, Alberta, Canada

The most northerly and arguably the most beautiful of Canadian resorts is set among the glaciers, forests, frozen lakes and waterfalls of Jasper National Park. The ski area at **Marmot Basin**, a 20-minute drive from the town, is not large but the terrain is extremely varied, with open bowls, steep chutes and glades cut through the trees. The addition of Eagle Ridge, along with Sugar Bowl and Birthday Bowl, has greatly enhanced the advanced terrain, and the ski school offers its Outer Limits Mountain Experience Programme for those wanting to explore the new area.

A dozen hotels are headed by the Fairmont Jasper Park Lodge (☎ 780 852 3301), a huge hotel on the outskirts of town. The Chateau Jasper (☎ 780 852

5644), close to the downtown area, is 'extremely comfortable'. Whistlers Inn (☎ 780 852 3361), a budget hotel named after a local mountain, is small and central, with its own Italian restaurant, pub and wildlife museum. Little Rascals Nursery is for children from nineteen months to six years.

**Tel** 1 780 852 3816
**Email** info@skimarmot.com
**Website** www.skimarmot.com
**Ski area** top 8,534ft (2,601m) bottom 5,534ft (1,686m)
**Lifts in area** 8: 6⑤ 2⑨
**Tour operators** Crystal, Frontier Ski, Inghams, Neilson School Groups, Seasons in Style, Ski Activity, Ski All America, Ski Independence, Ski Safari, Ski the American Dream, Virgin Snow

## Kandersteg, Switzerland

This delightful village in the Bernese Oberland is particularly popular with cross-country skiers and has 75km of loipe. But it also has some commendable Alpine skiing for beginners. Mountain access is via a chair-lift to Oeschinen, where a couple of drag-lifts take you up to a small assortment of easy runs. A cable-car outside the village also gives access to a drag-lift that serves two blue runs as well as a long and more challenging descent to the valley. Hotels include the five-star Royal Park (☎ 33 675 8888), the four-star Waldhaus Doldenhorn (☎ 33 675 8181) and the Schweizerhof (☎ 33 675 8181). The three-star Victoria Ritter (☎ 33 675 8000) is also praised. The Berestübli, Alfa-Soleil and Au Vieux Chalet are all recommended restaurants. Evening entertainment takes place at the High Moon Pub and the hotel bars.

**Tel** 41 33 675 8080
**Email** info@kandersteg.ch
**Website** www.kandersteg.ch
**Ski area** top 1,920m (6,299ft) bottom 1,200m (3,937ft)
**Lifts in area** 8: 1⑥ 1⑤ 6⑨
**Tour operators** Headwater, HF Holidays, Inghams, Inntravel, Kuoni, Swiss Travel Service, Waymark

## Kaprun, Austria

See *Zell am See and Kaprun*, page 45

**Tour operators** Airtours, Crystal, Esprit, First Choice, Inghams, Interhome, Neilson, PGL, Ski Astons, Thomson

## Keystone, Colorado, US

Purpose-built Keystone is one of the nearest Colorado resorts to Denver and is popular with families. It was almost entirely rebuilt in the 1990s.

The resort boasts North America's largest night-skiing arena. On Keystone Mountain you can ski from summit to base on a choice of trails, all of which are open after dark. The 861 acres of Erickson and Bergman Bowls have now been opened for snowcat skiing.

Keystone is included in the cheaper version of the Colorado Ticket. This lift pass allows you to ski in nearby **Arapahoe Basin** as well as in **Vail** and **Beaver Creek** for half the duration of your stay.

The skiing is laid out on three interlinked mountains, one behind the other and each progressively more challenging. The huge Outback area, the size of both other mountains combined, is protected from the wind and provides an excellent introduction to advanced skiing. The resort also has one of the biggest and best-designed terrain parks in North America.

The nursery at Keystone Children's Center cares for babies from two months, and the Snowplay Programs are for children aged three years and above.

The Alpenglow Stube is without question the highest – at 11,444ft – *haute cuisine* in North America. The most characterful accommodation is at the Ski Tip Lodge, which used to be an old stagecoach inn. Keystone Ranch is a bus ride away from the skiing and is 'rather spread out'. All accommodation may be booked through central reservations (☎ 970 496 4386).

The restaurants at Ski Tip Lodge and the Keystone Ranch were both praised. Kickadoo Tavern, Great Northern Tavern and Inxpot provide après-ski entertainment while Snake River Saloon has live music and two pool tables. Grassy's Pub and Killian's Bar are also popular.

**Tel** 1 970 496 4386 (UK agent 01708 224773)
**Email** keystoneinfo@vailresorts.com
**Website** www.snow.com
**Ski area** top 12,200ft (3,719m) bottom 9,300ft (2,835m)
**Lifts in area** 22: 2⑥ 13⑤ 7⑨
**Tour operators** AWWT, Crystal, Erna Low, Neilson, Neilson School Groups, Ski Activity, Ski All America, Ski Independence, Ski Safari, Ski the American Dream, Skiworld, Trailfinders, United Vacations

## Kicking Horse, BC, Canada

See page 54

**Tour operators** AWWT, Crystal, Frontier Ski, Ski All America, Ski Independence, Ski Safari, Ski the American Dream, Skiworld

## Killington, Vermont, US

Killington normally attracts 250 inches of snow each winter, yet the snowmaking system is so sophisticated that the resort can manage perfectly well without a trace of the real thing. It is the first resort in the east to open, and the last to close – in May or even June.

Reporters' biggest complaint was that Killington lacks a heart, with most of the hotels, condominiums, restaurants and bars sprawled along the five-mile approach road from the main highway.

Seven peaks provide plenty of skiing and riding for all grades, but by European standards the emphasis is on mileage rather than variety. The beginner slopes encourage a gentle learning curve. The Perfect Turn Discovery Center, Killington's introduction to skiing and snowboarding, is praised ('I do not think you could go to a better place to learn to ski'), while another reporter commented: 'I would recommend it as the ideal place for a young child to learn'. The resort shares a lift pass with neighbouring Pico, and boasts three terrain parks, a super-pipe and a boardercross racecourse. The Friendly Penguin nursery cares for babies from six weeks.

Snowshed base is recommended by reporters as the best place to stay if you don't have a car. The Inn of the Six Mountains is close to the nightlife and runs its own courtesy bus to the lifts, and the Killington Grand Hotel is a slope-side condominium-hotel. The Killington Lodging and Travel Service (☎ 0800 893670 in UK) is the central booking office for accommodation.

Hemingway's restaurant near the skyship base is warmly recommended ('food excellent, but pricy'). Other eateries include Claude's, Casey's Caboose and Santa Fe. The Pickle Barrel is the centre of the evening action, with a season-long schedule of big-name bands playing every weekend. The Wobbly Barn attracts a noisy crowd and combines steakhouse dining with live rhythm-and-blues.

**Tel** 1 802 422 3333 / 0800 893670 in UK
**Email** info@killington.com
**Website** www.killington.com
**Ski area** top 4,241ft (1,293m) bottom 1,165ft (354m)
**Lifts in area** 31: 3⊙ 22⊡ 6⊗
**Tour operators** Crystal, Equity, Inghams, Neilson School Groups, Ski Activity, Ski All America, Ski Independence, Skibound, Ski the American Dream, Ski Safari, Solo's, Thomson, Trailfinders, United Vacations, Virgin Snow

## Kimberley, BC, Canada

Kimberley is located in the south-east corner of British Columbia at the foot of the Purcell Mountains and within easy reach of **Fernie**. The ski village is a five-minute drive from the Bavarian-style town of Kimberley and four-and-a-half hours from Calgary airport. The front face has gentle fall-line family runs, while the Backside area, reached by the Easter triple-chair, offers much more demanding terrain that includes more than a dozen black-diamond trails. The slopes are open at night from Tuesday to Saturday, and include the longest illuminated trail in the country. Daycare is available to children from 18 months.

The ski village, with its log-panelled-style Canadian mountain architecture, is rather spread out, and the best place to stay is in the lower village within easy reach of the Northstar Express quad. In the ski village the choice of accommodation includes the ski-in, ski-out Polaris (☎ 877 286 8828) and the Trickle Creek Residence Inn by Marriott (☎ 877 282 1200). Mingle's Grill serves western cuisine and Kelsey's in the Trickle Creek is for a casual lunch or dinner. Après-ski bars are Kelsey's and the Stemwinder Pub in Polaris Lodge.

**Tel** 1 250 427 4881
**Email** info@skikimberley.com
**Website** www.skikimberley.com
**Ski area** top 6,500ft (1,981m) bottom 4,035ft (1,230m)
**Lifts in area** 9: 5⊡ 4⊗
**Tour operators** Frontier Ski, Inghams, Ski Activity, Ski the American Dream, Ski Safari, Virgin Snow

## Kirchberg, Austria

Kirchberg used to be the no-frills dormitory village that gave you a back door into **Kitzbühel**'s skiing at knock-down prices, but without that resort's medieval charm. This once-poor relation, only 6km away around the shoulder of the Hahnenkamm, still gives alternative access to Kitzbühel's main ski area but circumstances have changed and it now has 8,000 tourist beds. The resort has its own small beginner and intermediate lifts on the Gaisberg, and offers access to the Hahnenkamm by a two-stage chair, the Klausen gondola and a second gondola that rises from a giant car park between Kirchberg and Aschau. It has a kindergarten, Kinderclub Total, and three ski schools: Skischool Total, Skischool Kirchberg and Aktiv.

Choose where you stay with care in relation to both price and where you want to ski. The Tiroler Adler (☎ 5357 2327) is neither particularly convenient nor cheap, but is one of the best hotels in town. Hotel Alexander (☎ 5357 2222) and Hotel Metzgerwirt (☎ 5357 2128) are recommended. Restaurant Rosengarten in the Hotel Taxacherhof (☎ 5357 2527) is run by one of Austria's celebrated young chefs ('not to be missed'). The nightlife is just as busy as in Kitzbühel but less sophisticated. Charley's Club and Le Moustache are among the main centres of activity. The 3.8-km toboggan run on the Gaisberg is floodlit in the evenings.

**Tel** 43 5357 2309
**Email** info@kirchberg.at
**Website** www.kirchberg.at
**Ski area** top 2,000m (6,562ft) bottom 850m (2,788ft)
**Lifts in area** 57: 6⊙ 29⊡ 22⊙
**Tour operators** Interhome, Neilson School Groups, Skiworld

## Kitzbühel, Austria

See page 24

**Tour operators** Airtours, Corporate Ski Company, Crystal, Elegant Resorts, First Choice, Inghams, Interhome, Momentum, Neilson, Original Travel, Panorama, PGL, Seasons in Style, Ski Astons, Ski Freshtracks, Ski Solutions, Skiworld, Snowscape, Thomson

## Klosters, Switzerland

See page 157

**Tour operators** Descent International, Elegant Resorts, Flexiski, Inghams, Kuoni, Momentum, Mountain Leap, Powder Byrne, Seasons in Style, Ski Expectations, Ski Freshtracks, Ski Solutions, Swiss Travel Centre, Swiss Travel Service, White Roc

## Kranjska Gora, Slovenia

Kranjska Gora is situated in a pretty flat-bottomed valley between craggy wooded mountains. It is close to the Italian and Austrian borders and is Austrian in ambience. Hotels are improving, although are still not comparable in standard to cosy Austrian Gasthofs. The four nursery runs are short, wide and gentle and set at the edge of the village; the transition to real pistes is rather abrupt, with the mountains rising steeply from the valley floor. The longest run, Vitranc, is reached by chair-lift to the top of the ski area and is graded red. The other lifts go only halfway up the small mountain, which means limited skiing and the risk of poor snow cover.

The Alpine Ski Club offers group and private lessons, although only private lessons are available for snowboarding and cross-country. The Zgornjesavska valley has 40km of Langlauf tracks. Children are catered for in the ski school but there is no kindergarten.

The Kompass, one of Kranjska Gora's best hotels, has a swimming-pool and disco. The modern Hotel Larix is recommended for its location and facilities, and Hotel Prisank has a friendly atmosphere. Other options are the HIT Casino and the Hotel Lek, as well as the Hotel Spik. The Razor apartments are situated 200m from the lifts. Accommodation can be booked through the tourist office or via a tour operator.

**Tel** 386 4588 1768
**Email** tic@kranjska-gora.si
**Website** www.kranjska-gora.si
**Ski area** top 1,630m (5,348ft) bottom 810m (2,667ft)
**Lifts in area** 20: 5⊡ 15⊙
**Tour operators** Balkan Holidays, Crystal, Slovenija Pursuits, Solo's, Thomson

## Kronplatz, Italy

See page 131
**Tour operators** Momentum, Sloping Off

## Lake Louise, Alberta, Canada

See *Banff–Lake Louise*, page 47
**Tour operators** see page 262

## Lake Tahoe, California, US

See *Heavenly*, page 233; *Squaw Valley*, page 248

**Tour operators** Crystal, Lotus Supertravel, Neilson School Groups, Ski Activity, Ski All America, Ski the American Dream, Skibound, Thomson, Virgin Snow

## Lauterbrunnen, Switzerland

Lauterbrunnen is the valley railway junction near **Interlaken** that gives access to the higher and better-known resorts of **Mürren**, **Wengen** and **Grindelwald**. Hotels here provide a convenient, much cheaper, but rather soulless, base from which to explore by rail the skiing in this corner of the Bernese Oberland. However, as one reporter put it: 'I was not prepared for the sheer beauty and scale of the region'. Mürren, reached by a steep rack-and-pinion railway, provides the closest skiing. It is possible to ski back down again to Lauterbrunnen, but lack of cover at this low altitude means that for most of the winter skiers have no option but to return by railway at the end of the day. The three-star hotels Schützen (☎ 33 855 2032) and Silberhorn (☎ 33 856 2210) are recommended. 'The après-ski could do with a boost,' said one reporter.

**Tel** 41 33 856 8568
**Email** info@lauterbrunnen-tourismus.ch
**Website** www.wengen-muerren.ch
**Ski area** (Mürren) top 2,971m (9,748ft) bottom 796m (2,612ft)
**Lifts in area** 41 in Jungfrau Top Ski Region: 5⬛ 7◉ 5⬙ 14⬙
**Tour operators** Oak Hall, Ski Miquel

## Lech, Austria

See *Lech and Zürs*, page 26

**Tour operators** Alpine Answers, Alpine Tracks, Corporate Ski Company, Crystal, Elegant Resorts, Erna Low, Flexiski, Inghams, Lotus Supertravel, Momentum, Original Travel, Powder Byrne, Seasons in Style, Scott Dunn Ski, Ski Expectations, Ski Solutions, Total Ski, White Roc

## The Lecht, Scotland

Scotland's smallest ski area has a network of short lifts on both sides of the A939 Cockbridge–Tomintoul road. It lies 56 miles west of Aberdeen and about 45 miles from **Glenshee** and **Cairngorm Mountain**. The area is best suited to beginners ('an amazingly good nursery area, which got the whole family going') and intermediates living within reasonable driving distance. The longest run is 900m. Extensive snowmaking is a precaution against the vagaries of Scottish weather, and the area has a tubing slope and a small terrain park. Parking is free and the single café is licensed. The nearest accommodation is the Allargue Arms (☎ 01975 651410), three miles away at Corgarff; a choice of hotels and B&B options six miles away at Tomintoul includes the Gordon Hotel (☎ 01807 580206).

**Tel** (01975) 651440
**Email** info@lecht.co.uk
**Website** www.lecht.co.uk
**Ski area** top 793m (2,600ft) bottom 643m (2,109ft)
**Lifts in area** 14: 1⬙ 13⬙
**Tour operators** none

## Las Leñas, Argentina

See page 16

**Tour operators** Andes, Scott Dunn Latin America

## Lenk, Switzerland

See *Adelboden and Lenk*, page 258

## Lenzerheide and Valbella, Switzerland

Lenzerheide used to attract a fair number of British families but in recent years has decreased in popularity. Yet the area has considerable charm and a number of lifts have been upgraded in recent years ('what a fantastic find – minimal queues even when the resort is full'). The villages of Lenzerheide and Valbella lie at either end of a lake in an inconveniently wide, wooded pass running from Churwalden to Parpan, Lantsch and Lenz, with high mountains on either side. The skiing is in two separate sectors, Rothorn and Danis-Stätzerhorn, on either side of the pass. None of these pistes is particularly difficult, although the Rothorn cable-car opens up some off-piste skiing.

The main street of Lenzerheide has some attractive old buildings, and hotels include the four-stars Sunstar (☎ 81 384 0121) and Romantik Guarda Val (☎ 81 385 8585). Valbella has less character, being no more than a large community of hotels and concrete holiday homes crammed on to a hillside. Posthotel Valbella (☎ 81 384 1212) and the Valbella Inn (☎ 81 384 3636) are its only four-stars. As alternative bases to Lenzerheide, Churwalden is the ideal gateway to the skiing, Parpan is a typical Grison village, while Lantsch and Lenz are the starting points for Langlauf.

**Tel** 41 81 385 1120
**Email** info@lenzerheide.ch
**Website** www.lenzerheide.ch
**Ski area** top 2,865m (9,397ft) bottom 1,500m (4,920ft)
**Lifts in area** 39: 3⛷ 11⛷ 25⛷
**Tour operators** Made to Measure, Skiworld

## Leogang, Austria

Leogang – an amalgamation of ten farming hamlets – claims the title of longest village in Europe. A smart, modern gondola takes skiers and snowboarders up to Berghaus Asitz at 1,758m, from where a quad-chair and a six-seater chair link you into the **Saalbach** circuit. Accommodation is in a mixture of hotels and chalets. The four-star Salzburgerhof (☎ 6583 7310) is 'definitely the most convenient place to stay'. Others nearby include Gasthof Rupertus (☎ 6583 8466), Asitz Stub'n (☎ 6583 8556) and Fortshofgut (☎ 6583 8545). The St Leonhard (☎ 6583 8542) is an eight-minute walk from the lift.

Five cross-country trails total more than 40km, and snow rafting is also available. The kindergarten in Hotel Krallerhof takes children from two years of age. Nightlife centres on the Outback Bar at the bottom of the gondola.

**Tel** 43 6583 8234
**Email** info@saalfelden-leogang.at
**Website** www.leogang-saalfelden.at
**Ski area** top 2,096m (6,877ft) bottom 800m (2,625ft)
**Lifts in area** 55: 11⛷ 14⛷ 30⛷
**Tour operator** Inntravel

## Levi, Finland

See page 66

**Tour operators** Inghams, Norvista

## Leysin, Switzerland

This resort above the town of Aigle is one of the top resorts in Switzerland for snowboarders ('virtually no drag-lifts, which makes it a complete delight'). The area boasts 60km of piste. Most of the skiing and riding is in the popular Mayen/Berneuse area, reached by a choice of two cable-cars. Snowboarders have a quarter-pipe and terrain park between Berneuse and Mayen. Central Résidence is the local kindergarten, and takes children from two years old.

The all-glass revolving restaurant of Kuklos at Berneuse is said to be 'worth a visit, if only for the views of 29 peaks'. The other mountain eateries are Les Fers and Buvette Mayen. Best-placed accommodation for the skiing is found in the four-star Hotel Classic-Terrasse (☎ 24 493 0606) ('large, comfortable rooms, which are a little overheated') and the simple Bel-Air (☎ 24 494 1339). The Hiking Sheep (☎ 24 494 35 35) is a renovated Art Deco building run as a hostel with better-than-usual dormitories and a log fire, TV/games room and cyber café. La Fromagerie is a cheese restaurant as well as a museum. The town has two sports centres and a handful of bars and nightclubs, including the Top Pub.

**Tel** 41 24 494 2244
**Email** info@leysin.ch
**Website** www.leysin.ch
**Ski area** top 2,800m (9,186ft) bottom 1,200m (3,937ft)
**Lifts in area** 15: 1⛷ 8⛷ 6⛷
**Tour operators** Interhome, Sloping Off, Solo's, Swiss Travel Centre

## Lillehammer, Norway

Lillehammer resembles an American frontier town, with its clapboard houses and single main street. The nearest skiing is based 15 minutes' drive north at **Hafjell**, which possesses 26km of prepared trails. The more challenging pistes are from Hafjelltoppen (1,050m) down either the Kringelas or Hafjell run. Kvitfjell, 50km from Lillehammer, was created as the downhill course for the Winter Olympics; its 4km of skiing is limited but provides a steeper challenge than anywhere else in the region.

The Radisson SAS Lillehammer (☎ 61 86000) is reported to be the best hotel in town. The Rica Victoria (☎ 612 50049) is also recommended.

The Troll Club is a ski kindergarten for children aged four to six years, and the non-ki kindergarten is for ages two to seven, with activities such as face painting and magic shows.

**Tel** 47 612 50299
**Email** info@hafjell@.no
**Websites** www.lillehammerturist.no / www.hafjell.com
**Ski area** top 1,050m (3,444ft) bottom 200m (656ft)
**Lifts in area** 10: 3🚡 7🚞
**Tour operators** Crystal, Inntravel, Norvista

## Livigno, Italy

See page 132

**Tour operators** Airtours, Equity, Inghams, Interhome, Neilson, Panorama

## Long-Zhu Erlongshan, China

This is Heilongjiang province's second resort and is much smaller than **Yabuli**. It is situated at Bin Xian, only 56km from Harbin. The ski area has four lifts serving eight different runs. Such is the growth of skiing in Heilongjiang that by 2005 the province expects to attract one million skiers annually.

**Tel** 86 451 791 3640
**Email** liulifeng68@yahoo.com.cn
**Website** none
**Ski area** top 1,371m (4,500ft) bottom 266m (872ft)
**Lifts in area** 4: 2🚡 2🚞
**Tour operators** none

## Loveland, Colorado, US

Loveland is a small, high ski area that traditionally vies with **Killington** and others to be the first resort in the US to open at the end of October or in early November. It is located on the Continental Divide 53 miles west of Denver and 12 miles east of Silverthorne. With its usually reliable snow cover, reasonable prices and more than 1,365 acres of varied terrain, Loveland has been a local favourite for decades. The most difficult skiing is at Loveland Basin with its bumps, glades and bowl skiing, while beginners head for the easier slopes at Loveland Valley.

Mountain eating is based around simple cafeteria-style restaurants featuring burgers and daily specials. There is also a

delicatessen, and an outdoor barbecue on warm weather days. The Wedge and Fireside bars both serve bar food. Loveland Ski and Snowboard School offers adult and child tuition, as well as telemark and women-only ski courses. The nearest accommodation to the ski area is at the Silver Mine Lodge (☎ 877 733 2656) in Silver Plume, 10 miles from Loveland; at Georgetown, 12 miles away, where the choice includes Georgetown Mountain Inn (☎ 569 3201); or at the Peck House (☎ 569 9870) in Empire, 14 miles to the east.

**Tel** 303 571 5580
**Email** loveland@skiloveland
**Website** www.skiloveland.com
**Ski area** top 13,010ft (3,965m) bottom 10,600ft (3,231m)
**Lifts in area** 11: 9🚡 2🚞
**Tour operators** none

## Macugnaga, Italy

This resort is made up of five villages: Borca, Isella, Pecetto, Pestarena and Staffa. Together they offer 38km of piste and lie at the foot of the spectacular east face of the Monterosa, close to the Swiss border and a two-hour drive from Turin. Macugnaga's proximity to the border has resulted in a style of buildings more in keeping with Switzerland than with Italy.

Staffa and Pecetto have their own small ski areas, which are linked by ski bus. One reporter summed up the area as 'a marvellous introduction to skiing'. Off-piste enthusiasts can hire a local mountain guide to ski over the back of Monte Moro to **Saas-Fee** in Switzerland.

The villages between them have 15 hotels, including Hotel Dufour (☎ 0324 65529) in Staffa's main square, which is said to be 'clean and friendly, with plentiful and delicious food'. Hotel Zumstein (☎ 0324 65490) is well positioned. Also recommended is Hotel Girasole (☎ 0324 65052) ('it makes up for its lack of luxury with its welcome and great food').

Restaurants include the Miramonti ('good lunchtime pizzas and great fondue nights') in Pecetto, the Glacier ('you must book at weekends') and Ghiacci del Rosa at the Mt Belvedere base. 'A family resort with hardly any nightlife, but if you want to ski and relax there is no better place,' said one reporter. The Big Ben disco 'appears to be in a 1960s time warp'.

**Tel** 39 0324 65119
**Email** sviva@libero.it
**Website** www.macugnaga-online.it
**Ski area** top 2,984m (9,790ft) bottom 1,327m (4,353ft)
**Lifts in area** 12: 2🚠 3🚡 7🎿
**Tour operators** Neilson, Neilson School Groups

## Madesimo, Italy

This small, attractive resort, centred around an old church, is situated a two-hour drive north of Bergamo. It is right on the Swiss border and close enough for a trip to **St Moritz**. The old village has narrow streets with a few shops and some old converted farmhouses, as well as some less pleasing concrete buildings.

The skiing in the Valle Spluga ski area is mostly intermediate and is concentrated on the usually uncrowded slopes of the 2,984-m Pizzo Groppera, with long runs leading down into the neighbouring Valle di Lei. The high altitude normally ensures reasonable snow conditions. The 50-km area contains mostly red pistes and some challenging black trails, including the famous Canelone run. There are two terrain parks and a half-pipe. The nursery slopes are pleasant and served by a quad chair-lift, and the Madesimo Ski School has a reputation for small classes ('excellent, with plenty of English-speaking instructors').

Hotels include the four-star Emet (☎ 0343 53395) and the family-run Andossi (☎ 0343 57000), which provides a fitness room and a lively bar. The Harlequin (☎ 0343 53005) has 'small rooms, but a brilliant location and delicious hot chocolate in the hotel bar'. Hotel Cascata e Crystal (☎ 0343 53108) offers first-rate facilities, including a swimming-pool, piano bar and a mini-club for children aged four and over. You can ski back to most of the accommodation.

**Tel** 39 0343 53015
**Email** splugadomani@madesimo.com
**Website** www.madesimo.com
**Ski area** top 2,984m (9,790ft) bottom 1,530m (5,018ft)
**Lifts in area** 17: 1🚠 14🚡 2🎿
**Tour operator** Inghams

## Madonna di Campiglio, Italy

See page 133

**Tour operators** Crystal, Equity, Erna Low, Inghams, Interhome, Momentum, Ski Expectations, Ski Freshtracks, Solo's

## Mammoth, California, US

See page 238

**Tour operators** AWWT, Crystal, Ski Activity, Ski All America, Ski Independence, Ski Safari, Ski the American Dream, Skiworld, United Vacations, Virgin Snow

## Marmot Basin, Alberta, Canada

See *Jasper*, page 283

## Le Massif, Québec, Canada

This unusual resort is a 45-minute drive from **Québec City**. It is possibly the only ski destination where you arrive by car at the top rather than the bottom of the mountain. It also has one of the most enchanting views of any resort in the world. So steep is the angle of descent down the principal run that you feel that at any moment you are liable to tumble off the mountain and on to the majestic ice flows of the St Lawrence river far below.

The resort has a high-speed quad-chair that takes you up to the top of the women's downhill course, which acts as a permanent training centre for the Canadian national team.

**Tel** 1 418 632 5876
**Email** info@lemassif.com
**Website** www.lemassif.com
**Ski area** top 2,644ft (806m) bottom 118ft (36m)
**Lifts in area** 5: 3🚡 2🎿
**Tour operators** Frontier Ski, Ski the American Dream

## Mayrhofen, Austria

See page 29

**Tour operators** Airtours, Crystal, Equity, First Choice, HF Holidays, Inghams, Neilson, Ski Astons, Snowcoach, Thomson

## Megève, France

See page 88

**Tour operators** Alpine Answers, AWWT, Classic Ski, Corporate Ski Company, Erna Low, French Life, Interhome, Lagrange, Momentum, Mountain Leap, Peak Retreats, Ski Barrett-Boyce, Ski Independence, Ski Solutions, Ski Supreme, Ski Weekend, Skiworld, Stanford Skiing, White Roc

## Meiringen–Hasliberg, Switzerland

Meiringen–Hasliberg is situated in the
Bernese Oberland, halfway between
Lucerne and Interlaken. The resorts have
joined forces with Brienz–Axalp to market
themselves as **Brienz**–Meiringen–Hasliberg.
Meiringen is best known for the
Reichenbach Falls, where Sir Arthur Conan
Doyle's character Sherlock Holmes fell to
his untimely death during his final struggle
with arch-villain Moriarty.

The area has 60km of slopes, 40 per cent
of which are rated intermediate. Mountain
access is by cable-car from Meiringen via
Hasliberg Reuti and on to the main ski area,
or by gondola from Hasliberg Wasserwendi
at 1,160m. The terrain here is ideal for
snowboarders, with a half-pipe and natural
obstacles that form Switzerland's first
'natural snowboard park'.

The resorts do not have a crèche, but the
Swiss Snowsports School (SSS) has a ski
kindergarten and is rated as 'excellent – I
find it hard to imagine better facilities for
teaching children'.

The five mountain restaurants in the ski
area include the Alpen Tower, with its
scenic lookout. Among the Meiringen hotels
are the Alpin Sherpa (☎ 33 972 5252),
Parkhotel du Sauvage (☎ 33 971 4141) and
three-star Sporthotel Sherlock Holmes (☎
33 972 9889). Hasliberg's 16 hotels include
the Bären (☎ 33 971 6022) and the
Bellevue (☎ 33 971 2341). Hotel Brienz
(☎ 33 951 3551) and Grandhotel
Giessbach (☎ 33 952 2525) are in Brienz.

**Tel** 41 33 972 5050
**Email** info@alpenregion.ch
**Website** www.alpenregion.ch
**Ski area** top 2,433m (7,982ft) bottom 1,061m (3,481ft)
**Lifts in area** 22: 4🚡 5🚠 13🎿
**Tour operators** Kuoni, PGL

## Les Menuires, France

See *Val Thorens and the Belleville Valley*,
page 113

**Tour operators** Club Med, Erna Low, Family Ski Company,
First Choice, French Freedom, French Life, Interhome,
Lagrange, Leisure Direction, Neilson, On The Piste, PGL, Ski
Independence, Ski Supreme, Skibound, Wasteland

## Méribel, France

See page 91

**Tour operators** Airtours, Alpine Action, Alpine Answers,
Alpine Elements, Belvedere Chalets, Bonne Neige, Chalet
World, Club Med, Club Pavilion, Cooltip, Corporate Ski
Company, Crystal, Descent International, Elegant Resorts,
Erna Low, First Choice, French Freedom, French Life,
Inghams, Interhome, Lagrange, Leisure Direction, Lotus
Supertravel, Mark Warner, Meriski, Momentum, Mountain
Leap, Neilson, On The Piste, Oxford Ski Company, PGL,
Purple Ski, Scott Dunn Ski, Seasons in Style, Silver Ski,
Simply Ski, Ski Activity, Ski Amis, Ski Beat, Ski Blanc, Ski
Cuisine, Ski Expectations, Ski France, Ski Freshtracks, Ski
Independence, Ski Olympic, Ski Solutions, Ski Supreme,
Skiworld, Snowline, Thomson, Total Ski, VIP, White Roc

## The Milky Way, Italy

See *Clavière*, page 271; *Montgenèvre*, page
292; *Sauze d'Oulx*, page 134; *Sestriere*,
page 138

## Moena, Italy

See *Canazei and the Val di Fassa*, page 266

## La Mongie, France

See *Barèges and La Mongie*, page 263
**Tour operators** Lagrange, Tangney Tours

## Mont-Sainte-Anne, Québec, Canada

With a vertical drop of more than 2,000ft,
56 trails covering 40 miles, and skiing on
three sides of the mountain, Mont-Sainte-
Anne is one of the most significant ski and
snowboarding areas in eastern Canada.
Rolling, well-groomed intermediate terrain
is interspersed with some surprisingly steep
double-black-diamond trails.

The resort enjoys magnificent views
across the drifting ice-pack of the St
Lawrence river and **Québec City**, 25 miles
away. Like all destinations in Quebec,
Mont-Sainte-Anne – nicknamed La Belle et
La Bête (Beauty and the Beast) – can be
very cold in the depths of winter. In spite of
this, 15 trails are open for night-skiing and
-snowboarding on what is claimed to be the
biggest illuminated vertical drop in Canada.
The Carte-Blanche multipass allows skiers

and boarders to visit the nearby resorts of **Stoneham, Le Massif** and Le Relais.

There are two terrain parks as well as two half-pipes. The Children Center welcomes children from six months to ten years, and Kinderski and Kindersnow programmes mix games with ski or snowboard lessons for children of four years and over.

For convenience, most people stay at the Chateau Mont-Sainte-Anne (☎ 418 827 5211), at the base area, or the Chalets Mont-Sainte-Anne (☎ 418 827 5776), a condominium complex close by.

**Tel** 1 418 827 4561
**Email** info@mont-sainte-anne.com
**Website** www.mont-sainte-anne.com
**Ski area** top 2,625ft (800m) bottom 575ft (175m)
**Lifts in area** 15: 1⑥ 8⑤ 6⑨
**Tour operators** Frontier Ski, Inghams, Ski the American Dream, Ski Independence, Skibound, Skiworld

## Montafon, Austria

See *Gargellen*, page 277

**Tour operator** Made to Measure

## Montalbert, France

See *La Plagne*, page 97

**Tour operators** none

## Montchavin, France

See *La Plagne*, page 97

**Tour operator** Made to Measure

## Montgenèvre, France

Montgenèvre is an old stone village perched on the col separating France from Italy between Briançon and Turin. It is France's only village included in **The Milky Way** ski circuit.

The village has been pleasantly developed for tourism and retains considerable charm. Montgenèvre has its own ski area, a good mix of mainly blue and red runs above the village reached by an assortment of lifts taking you up to the 2,680-m summit of Le Chalvet. But the main interest lies in the vast expanses of intermediate terrain afforded by the Milky Way. The awkward link to **Clavière** has

been improved in recent years by a quad chair-lift up to Colletto Verde. Montgenèvre has a terrain park with a half-pipe at 2,100m in the Gondrans area.

The French Ski School (ESF) received sound reports: 'first class – patient instructors all with good spoken English'. The Garderie cares for children aged six months to six years. Apeak ski and snowboard school runs a children's programme with free snowboard lessons on Sunday morning.

The accommodation is mostly in apartments. The pick of half-a-dozen, less-than-luxurious hotels are the three-star Napoléon (☎ 492 21 92 04) and the more attractive three-star Valérie (☎ 492 21 90 02), near the church. The new two-star Alpis Cottia (☎ 492 21 90 09) is said to be 'delightful and charming'.

Restaurants include La Ca del Sol, Les Chalmettes, L'Estable ('home-cooked cuisine'), Pizzeria Le Transalpin, Le Refuge and smart Le Jamy. La Ca del Sol and Le Graal are popular bars, and the Blue Night Club is the disco. Montgenèvre has a good skating-rink.

**Tel** 33 492 21 52 52
**Email** info@montgenevre.com
**Website** www.montgenevre.com
**Ski area** top 2,680m (8,793 ft) bottom 1,850m (6,070ft)
**Lifts in area** 92 in Milky Way: 3⑥ 35⑤ 54⑨
**Tour operators** Airtours, Club Europe, Crystal, Equity, French Life, Lagrange, Neilson, Ski France, Skibound, Skitopia

## Montriond, France

Montriond is little more than a suburb of **Morzine**, with no discernible centre and a number of simple, reasonably priced hotels. A bus links it to the resort's gondola, which provides direct access to the main lifts. The British Alpine Ski and Snowboarding School has a branch here. The Auberge la Chalande is the 'best restaurant we've found in the Portes du Soleil area', according to reporters.

**Tel** 33 450 79 12 81
**Email** ot.montriond@valleedaulps.com
**Website** www.portesdusoleil.com
**Ski area** top 2,350m (7,708ft) bottom 950m (3,116ft)
**Lifts in area** 207 in Portes du Soleil: 14⑥ 82⑤ 111⑨
**Tour operators** none

## Morgins, Switzerland

Morgins is a few kilometres from **Châtel** and is the border post with France. It is a relaxed, residential resort linked into the **Portes du Soleil** circuit. Most of the accommodation is in chalets and apartments ('good accommodation, not expensive'). The two-star Hotel La Reine des Alpes (☎ 24 477 1143) is said to be 'more than adequate'. Also recommended is the two-star Hotel Beau-Site (☎ 24 477 1138). The resort has a crèche, of which we have positive reports, but the large nursery slope in the centre of the village is prone to overcrowding. Early-evening après-ski is limited to a skating-rink, indoor tennis and a few bars. The SAF disco provides lively late-night entertainment.

**Tel** 41 24 477 2361
**Email** touristoffice@morgins.ch
**Website** www.morgins.ch
**Ski area** top 2,000m (7,710ft) bottom 1,350m (4,428ft)
**Lifts in area** 207 in Portes du Soleil: 14🚡 82🚠 111🎿
**Tour operators** Ski Morgins, Ski Rosie

## Morillon, France

The old village of Morillon has a sixteenth-century church and is linked by road or gondola to the purpose-built satellite of Morillon 1100. Together they have some 10,000 visitor beds and make a popular second-home resort for the French. Morillon has seven of its own lifts and is linked into the Grand Massif ski area, of which **Flaine** is the best-known resort. The children's village accepts little ones from six months up to ten years of age. Most of the accommodation is in chalets, apartments and gîtes. Le Morillon, a two-star hotel (☎ 450 90 10 32), has a recommended restaurant.

**Tel** 33 450 90 15 76
**Email** otmorill@ot-morillon.fr
**Website** www.ot-morillon.fr
**Ski area** top 2,480m (8,134ft) bottom 700m (2,296ft)
**Lifts in area** 72 in Grand Massif: 6🚡 28🚠 38🎿
**Tour operator** AWWT, Erna Low, French Life, Lagrange, Peak Retreats, PGL

## Morzine, France

See page 94

**Tour operators** Alpine Elements, Alpine Tracks, Alpine Weekends, Chalet Snowboard, Crystal, Esprit, First Choice, French Life, Inghams, Lagrange, PGL, Seasons in Style, Ski Activity, Ski Chamois, Ski Expectations, Ski Weekend, Skibound, Skiworld, Snowline, Thomson, Trail Alpine, White Roc

## Mount Buller, Australia

Mount Buller is the principal area for Melbourne-based skiers, situated a three-and-a-half-hour (250-km) drive north-east from the city, through Ned Kelly country. It has the largest lift capacity in Australia, with a comprehensive network serving 80km of trails – the longest of which is 2.5km. There are some long cruising runs, including Little Buller Spur and Wombats, and trails that run from the high-altitude snow gums through to the snowline. The Buller Chutes behind the Summit are genuine black-diamond runs. The scenery is some of the most impressive in the Victorian Alps, with extensive views across the gum forests. The Breathtaker Hotel (☎ 3 5777 6377) describes itself as Australia's first 'alpine spa retreat'. The Schuss Lodge (☎ 3 5777 6007) is a small hotel with 27 beds and some magnificent views.

**Tel** 61 3 5777 6077
**Email** info@mtbuller.com.au
**Website** www.mtbuller.com.au
**Ski area** top 1,804m (5,917ft) bottom 1,390m (4,559ft)
**Lifts in area** 22: 13🚠 9🎿
**Tour operators** none

## Mount Hotham, Australia

See *Falls Creek and Mount Hotham*, page 275

## Mount Hutt, New Zealand

This most famous of New Zealand's resorts is situated a 35-minute drive from Methven and 90 minutes' drive from Christchurch airport. It has magnificent views across the Canterbury Plains and is consistently the first resort in Australasia to open each winter. The skiing can be excellent, although unpredictable weather has given the resort the rather harsh sobriquet of 'Mount Shut'. Mount Hutt has one of the most extensive snowmaking systems in the southern hemisphere. The South Face runs, which end up below the base area, account for its advertised 672-m vertical drop. Local heli-skiing is available. The resort has two half-pipes and the ubiquitous (in New Zealand) bungee jump. The base area features a clock tower, café and restaurant, and the village of Methven has a wide range of accommodation.

**Email** david@mthutt.co.nz
**Website** www.mthutt.co.nz
**Ski area** top 2,075m (6,808ft) bottom 1,585m (5,200ft)
**Lifts in area** 9: 2⑤ 7⑨
**Tour operators** none

## Mt Ruapehu, New Zealand

See page 141

**Tour operators** none

## Mürren, Switzerland

See page 159

**Tour operators** Inghams, Kuoni, Momentum, Ski Freshtracks, Skiworld, Swiss Travel Centre, Swiss Travel Service

## Naeba, Japan

This bustling, all-night ski area in the Niigata Prefecture is one of the most frenetic resorts in the northern Japanese Alps. It is dominated by the Naeba Prince (☎ 81 25 789 2211), the largest ski hotel in the world, with a shopping arcade, Sega amusement area, health centre and more than 40 restaurants, including one that stays open all night. At weekends, when packed bullet trains and buses disgorge their human cargo, an almost absurd number of skiers floods the slopes – the record stands at 40,000 in one weekend. The resort has 28 trails and a terrain park.

**Tel** 020-7734 6870 in UK
**Email** info@jnto.co.uk
**Website** www.snowjapan.co.uk
**Ski area** top 1,800m (5,905ft) bottom 900m (2,953ft)
**Lifts in area** 28: 3⑥ 25⑤
**Tour operators** none

## Nassfeld, Austria

This growing Carinthian resort boasts 100km of piste, of which over 60 per cent is graded intermediate. One reporter commented: 'an excellent find for the good intermediate social skier who enjoys plenty of runs, beautiful scenery and good mountain restaurants, but does not want to pay top prices'. Nassfeld also claims to have the longest cable-car in the Alps – the Millennium-Express being 6,000m long and taking 17 minutes to climb from the valley in three stages. However, the resort's increasing popularity has resulted in peak-season overcrowding. The two terrain parks include a boardercross course, quarter-pipe, jumps and a twin-pipe. The resort is known for its exemplary childcare, with a choice of Bobo-Miniclub and the Daycare Kindergarten.

Nassfeld has 11 four-star hotels, including the Alpen Adria (☎ 4282 2666), with a swimming-pool; Berghotel Presslauer (☎ 4285 209) ('very welcoming with good food'); and Hotel Berghof (☎ 4285 8271), which features a nightclub with live music. The resort also has 23 three-stars and a handful of Gasthofs. Eating out is either in the hotels or at a choice of two Italian restaurants. The Stüberl in Hotel Wulfenia is a highly rated restaurant.

**Tel** 43 4285 8241
**Email** info@skiarena.at / info@hermagor.at
**Websites** www.skiarena.at / www.hermagor.com
**Ski area** top 1,500m (4,921ft) bottom 600m (1,969ft)
**Lifts in area** 40: 5⑥ 17⑤ 18⑨
**Tour operators** PGL, Sloping Off, Slovenija Pursuits

## Nendaz, Switzerland

Nendaz offers cheaper accommodation than **Verbier** but complicated and inefficient access to the best of the Four Valleys skiing, although a free bus does run from Nendaz to **Siviez**. However, one reporter rated it as 'ideal for beginners'. The ESS and Neige-Aventure ('highly recommended') are the ski schools, while Le P'tit Bec is a kindergarten for children aged eighteen months to seven years.

**Tel** 41 27 289 5589
**Email** info@nendaz.ch
**Website** www.nendaz.ch
**Ski area** top 3,330m (10,925ft) bottom 1,365m (4,478ft)
**Lifts in area** 94 in Four Valleys: 17⑥ 32⑤ 45⑨
**Tour operator** Interhome

## Neustift, Austria

See *Stubaital*, page 312

## Nevis Range, Scotland

Nevis Range is Scotland's nearest equivalent to an Alpine resort. It is located seven miles north of Fort William and close to Ben Nevis, Britain's highest mountain. Its own mountain, **Aonach Mor**, has 20km of piste. The ski area is reached from the car park by a modern, six-seater gondola. This takes you up to the Snowgoose Restaurant, from where a quad-chair and a series of drag-lifts fan out ('the views are stunning, with mouth-watering scenery in every direction'). The longest run is just over 2km. The Braveheart chair-lift gives easy access to the back bowls of the Coire Dubh, which provide excellent off-piste terrain after a fresh snowfall. Queues for the return gondola journey down the mountain can be huge when the weather is good in high season. Aonach Mor boasts a terrain park on the summit with rails, boxes, ramps and jumps. The kindergarten accepts children from three years. In addition to the restaurant at the top of the gondola, snack bars are located at the foot of the Goose and Rob Roy T-bars, and a small café located at the base station.

The delightful hamlet of Torlundy offers a choice of B&Bs, although most of the accommodation is in Fort William, an old loch-side town with a strong tourist appeal. Nearby hotels include the nineteenth-century Inverlochy Castle (☎ 01397 702177), which is set in 200 hectares of grounds and has sumptuous bedrooms. One reporter praised the Moorings Hotel (☎ 01397 772797): 'a friendly three-star'. The Milton Hotel (☎ 01397 702331) provides a health club, and the Crannog restaurant enjoys a good reputation for its seafood.

**Tel** (01397) 705825 for snow info / (01397) 703781 for tourist info
**Email** info@nevisrange.co.uk
**Websites** www.nevisrange.co.uk / www.ski.visitscotland.com
**Ski area** top 1,221m (4,006ft) bottom 655m (2,148ft)
**Lifts in area** 12: 1⬚ 3⬚ 8⬚
**Tour operator** Ski Norwest

## Niederau, Austria

See *Wildschönau*, page 44
**Tour operators** see page 321

## Nozawa Onsen, Japan

The neighbour to better-known **Shiga Kogen** is refreshingly old-world: a Japanese Mürren with an excellent ski museum. The busy, narrow streets of the picturesque little spa village are marred by traffic and imbued with the scent of sulphur from the 13 public hot-spring bath-houses. From downtown Nozawa, the slopes are reached in an arduous fashion by a steep walk up narrow streets, followed by two long escalators. The area is satisfyingly varied with some steep pitches, but, infuriatingly, two of the best runs are reserved for race training and competitions. Mountain restaurants are unusually plentiful but there is little Western food available. Accommodation is mainly in *ryokans* (inns) and small hotels. The central Kameya Ryokan (☎ 82 269 852124) is recommended.

**Tel** 020-7734 6870 in UK
**Email** info@jnto.co.uk
**Website** www.snowjapan.co.uk
**Ski area** top 1,650m (5,414ft) bottom 560m (1,837ft)
**Lifts in area** 29: 2⬚ 26⬚ 1⬚
**Tour operators** none

## Oberau, Austria

See *Wildschönau*, page 44
**Tour operator** Inghams

## Obergurgl, Austria

See *Obergurgl–Hochgurgl*, page 31
**Tour operators** Airtours, Crystal, First Choice, Inghams, Neilson, Ski Expectations, Ski Freshtracks, Ski Solutions, Thomson

## Obertauern, Austria

See page 33
**Tour operators** Club Europe, First Choice, Inghams, Thomson

## Oppdal, Norway

Oppdal lies 120km south of Trondheim and is one of Norway's largest most northerly downhill resorts. It offers 78km of pistes – the most challenging marked trails being Bjorndalsloypa, Hovdenloypa and Bjerkeloypa on the front face of Hovden, the central ski area.

The Vangslia area also features a mixture of terrain, while Stolen at the other end of the resort is made up entirely of beginner and intermediate pistes. The fourth area, Adalen, is set in a huge bowl behind Hovden and is dominated by long, mainly blue cruising runs. At 1pm, for a fee, snowcats will take up to 50 skiers at a time to the top of the mountain at Blaoret for sightseeing and an additional 240m vertical of off-piste skiing. Oppdal also boasts 60km of cross-country trails covering a variety of terrain; five of its tracks are floodlit.

The resort possesses six mountain restaurants: one at the bottom of each base area and two more at the top of the Hovden and Stolen lift complexes. Only the Vangslia lifts are without a mid-mountain restaurant of any description.

The 72-room Quality Hotel Oppdal (☎ 724 00700) is close to the quiet railway station ('cosy and quaint, despite its size'), while the Oppdal Motel (☎ 724 20600) is well equipped, with three- and six-bed rooms. Vangslia Fjelltun (☎ 724 00801) contains log-built apartments on the edge of the piste. Although Oppdal is a fair-sized town, nightlife is limited to a few bars and restaurants.

**Tel** 47 724 00470
**Email** heidi@oppdal.com
**Website** www.oppdal.com
**Ski area** top 1,300m (4,265ft) bottom 545m (1,788ft)
**Lifts in resort** 17: 2🚠 15🎿
**Tour operators** none

## Oz-en-Oisans, France

The small, purpose-built village of Oz Station lies above the old village of Oz-en-Oisans. It is reached by a fast all-weather road from the valley in only 20 minutes and thereby provides a back door into the lift system. Two gondolas branch upwards in different directions, one to L'Alpette above Oz-en-Oisans and the other in two stages to the mid-station of the DMC gondola above Alpe d'Huez. The shopping is limited and the nightlife consists of four restaurants and bars.

Hotel Le Hors Piste (☎ 476 79 40 25) is small with just 16 rooms, a small selection of bars and restaurants, an ice-skating rink and an indoor climbing wall. The village has an ESF ski and board school and a garderie that takes children from six months to six years old.

**Tel** 33 476 80 78 01
**Email** info@oz-en-oisans.com
**Website** www.oz-en-oisans.com
**Ski area** top 3,330m (10,922ft) bottom 1,350m (4,429ft)
**Lifts in area** 84: 15🚠 25🚡 44🎿
**Tour operator** Lagrange

## Pal–Arinsal, Andorra

The ski areas of Arinsal and Pal are now linked by a 50-person cable-car to create a single area of 63km of easy and intermediate groomed runs. The resort has a high percentage of riders among its clientèle. Arinsal's 40,000-square-metre FreeStyle Area contains a half-pipe, jumps and other obstacles, as well as a bumps area, slalom and carving area. The Nursery caters for children from twelve months, and the Snowgarden is for four- to eight-year olds.

The mountain restaurants serve 'ubiquitous burgers 'n' beer in surroundings that make up in price for what they lack in charm'. Other eateries include Igloo, offering Chinese cuisine, and Obelix, which is Mexican. Quo Vadis is a popular bar with videos. In Arinsal, The Poblado apartments (☎ 83 51 22) are recommended. Attitude and service at the Grand Hotel Font (☎ 83 52 94) came under fire from reporters. The modern Residència Daina (☎ 83 60 05) is a 15-minute walk from the centre, while Residència Janet (☎ 83 50 88) is a small family-run establishment on the outskirts. Recommended restaurants include El Rusc ('excellent food in amicable surroundings'). Pal has no accommodation, but La Barda restaurant offers 'authentic Catalan cuisine and a great night out'.

**Tel** 376 73 70 00
**Email** palarinsal@arinsal.com
**Website** www.palarinsal.com
**Ski area** top 2,573m (8,442ft) bottom 1,550m (5,084ft)
**Lifts in area** 28: 1🚠 11🚡 16🎿
**Tour operators** Airtours, Crystal, First Choice, Inghams, Neilson, Panorama, Thomson

## Pamporovo, Bulgaria

Pamporovo is a small resort 85km from the historic town of Plovdiv. The majority of its accommodation is in nine hotels strung out between the centre and the lift station, about a ten-minute journey by free ski bus. Most of the hotels face the area's only ski mountain, Snezhanka, the summit of which is crowned by the Bulgarian equivalent of the British Telecom Tower. Pamporovo claims an average of 272 sunny days each year. Unfortunately, it does not always snow on the other days.

There is one black run (optimistically called 'The Wall'), which is immediately beneath the summit, and a couple of good-quality red runs on either flank. One of these is the resort's longest, at 4km. Otherwise, the whole place is mostly geared to novices and lower intermediates. Lift queues are rare, except for a 15-minute spell in the morning when all the ski school classes set off simultaneously.

The locals claim that the Pamporovo Ski School is internationally renowned, although one reporter queried whether this might be for 'the grumpiness of its instructors'. Another, who chose the resort for a week's snowboarding course, reported that her instructor was 'charming, helpful, could board like a dream but, alas, wasn't all that gifted at passing on his undoubted talent'. The ski school kindergarten caters for children aged five to eight years.

Of the resort's hotels, the Pamporovo is rated as very comfortable and has a swimming-pool, and the Perelik was described as 'basic but comfortable – unless your room is above the disco that closes at 3am'. The hotel also houses Pamporovo's main shopping centre and a swimming-pool. The Finlandia also has a pool. Hotels are bookable through UK tour operators or Balkantourist (☎ 2 981 86 26).

The Chevermeto restaurant is recommended for its 'folk' nights, when whole sheep are roasted over open fires and dancers in traditional dress provide a colourful floor show.

**Tel** 359 2 987 97 78
**Email** webmaster@bulgariatravel.org
**Website** www.bulgariatravel.org
**Ski area** top 1,925m (6,316ft) bottom 1,450m (4,757ft)
**Lifts in area** 8: 5🄳 3🄵
**Tour operators** Balkan Holidays, Balkan Tours, Crystal, First Choice, Inghams, Thomson

## Panorama Mountain Village, BC, Canada

Panorama Mountain Village lies a two-hour drive to the south-west of **Banff–Lake Loiuse** and is on the edge of the Bugaboos mountain range, best known for its heli-skiing. More than half of the 2,847 acres of terrain is designated easy to intermediate, with long, sweeping runs making the most of the impressive 4,000-ft vertical drop. Two quad-chairs have replaced the old double-chair and T-bar that provided main mountain access and have greatly improved the appeal of the resort. The Outback region in Taynton Bowl, which was formerly heli-ski territory, offers access to nearly 1,000 acres of glade skiing, chutes and gullies in what the resort calls 'back-country within bounds'. RK Heli-skiing is based in the village, and flies directly from the resort. The resort is part of the Canadian Rockies Super Pass, enabling you to ski at eight other resorts, including Banff–Lake Louise, **Fernie**, Nakiska, **Kimberley** and Fortress Mountain.

The School of Skiing and Boarding is 'friendly and well-organised'. Daycare is available at Wee Wascals for children aged nineteen months to five years.

This attractive family resort has most of the accommodation in ski-in, ski-out condominiums. These include Panorama Springs/Ski Tip/Tamarack Lodge (the resort's most luxurious condominiums, adjacent to the Springs Waterpark), Horsethief Lodge, Toby Creek Lodge, Hearth Stone and Wolf Lake Townhomes. New are the Aurora Townhouses and 1000 Peaks Lodge, with its 'mountain boutique interior' and 35 suites. Bookings for all these are available through Panorama Mountain Village Reservations (☎ 250 342 6941).

The T-Bar & Grill is reasonably priced, and the Jackpine pub is 'great for a pint and darts'. The Starbird is for affordable family dining. After-skiing activities include relaxing at the Panorama Springs outdoor waterpark, or taking the shuttle bus to the valley town of Invermere to bathe in the radium hot springs.

**Tel** 1 250 342 6941
**Email** paninfo@intrawest.com
**Website** www.skipanorama.com
**Ski area** top 7,800ft (2,360m) bottom 3,800ft (1,158m)
**Lifts in area** 9: 6🄳 3🄵
**Tour operators** Frontier Ski, Inghams, Ski Activity, Ski the American Dream, Ski Independence, Ski Safari, Ski All America, Skiworld, Virgin Snow

## Park City Mountain Resort, Utah, US

See *Park City Resorts*, below

## Park City Resorts, Utah, US

See page 240

**Tour operators** AWWT, Crystal, Momentum, Ramblers, Ski Activity, Ski the American Dream, Ski Independence, Ski Safari, Ski All America, Skiworld, Thomson, United Vacations

## Paradiski, France

See *Les Arcs*, page 69; *Peisey–Vallandry*, right; *La Plagne*, page 97

## La Parva, Chile

See *Valle Nevado*, page 65

**Tour operator** Andes

## Pas de la Casa, Andorra

See page 13

**Tour operators** Airtours, Crystal, First Choice, Inghams, Lagrange, Neilson, Panorama, Thomson

## Passo Tonale, Italy

Passo Tonale is a resort with exceptional snow quality, beginner-to-easy intermediate terrain, and extensive ski-touring and off-piste. It is 100km from Bolzano and shares 70km of skiing with the charming village of **Ponte di Legno**. Hotels hug the single roadway, but fortunately there is little through-traffic by night. The only bus runs seven times daily to Ponte di Legno.

Mountain access is on either side of the main road, with most of the chair- and drag-lifts starting from the south-facing snowfields. The only cable-car is a 1-km walk west from the village. The resort has four ski and snowboard schools. Instructors at both Tonale–Presena and Ponte di Legno–Tonale are described as 'unspoilt, simple and sympathetic'. We have also received a favourable report for the Castellaccio ski school. G&G is the specialist snowboard school. The Miniclub

in the Hotel Miramonti cares for small non-skiers, while Fantaski is the ski kindergarten.

Negritella, up the mountain, is praised. Hotels include the Orchidea (☎ 0364 903935) ('family-owned and excellent'), Hotel Redivalle (☎ 0364 903814) and the historic Mirandola Hospice (☎ 0364 903933), where resident guests must rely on snowmobile transport, which is available until 2am. The two-star Biancaneve (☎ 0364 903997) features bright orange décor in a 12-storey, white tower block but serves good food. Sporthotel Vittoria (☎ 0364 91348) includes a pub with live music.

In town, intimate décor and delicious gorgonzola *Spätzle* are found at Il Focolare, while La Torretta is praised for its pizzas. Cady, Nico's and the UFO are popular bars, along with Pub Miramonti and Crazy Horse. El Bait is quiet and cosy, Antares features live music and Heaven is equally busy.

**Tel** 39 0364 903838
**Email** tonale@valdisole.net
**Website** www.valdisole.net
**Ski area** top 3,069m (10,069ft) bottom 1,883m (6,178ft)
**Lifts in area** 25: 1🚠 14🚡 10🎿
**Tour operators** Airtours, Alpine Tours, Club Europe, Crystal, Equity, Inghams, Neilson, Neilson School Groups, PGL, Skibound, Skitopia, Sloping Off, Thomson

## Peisey–Vallandry, France

This cluster of low-lying villages in the **Les Arcs** ski area – namely Peisey, Vallandry and Nancroix – used to be regarded as a tree-level bolt-hole in bad weather and a haven for French families wanting to avoid the commercial realities of the true *station de ski*. However, the higher area of Plan Peisey is now the site of the double-decker Vanoise Express cable-car linking Les Arcs to **La Plagne**. The two once-separate ski areas, with 144 lifts and 420km of piste, have been renamed **Paradiski**.

Nancroix is the starting point for 39km of cross-country trails. Vallandry is a village of mainly low-rise, chalet-style buildings with a few shops, and together with the small ski area of Plan Peisey it is linked by gondola to Peisey in the valley below.

**Tel** 33 479 07 94 28
**Email** info@peisey-vallandry.com
**Website** www.peisey-vallandry.com
**Ski area** top 3,226m (10,581ft) bottom 1,350m (4,428ft)
**Lifts in area** 141: 1🚟 16🚠 66🚡 58🎿
**Tour operators** Alpine Elements, Esprit, Ski Hiver

# Perisher–Blue, Australia

The linked resorts of Perisher and Smiggins, Blue Cow and **Guthega** in New South Wales form the largest ski area in Australia. The best way to reach the main complex is by train: the modern Ski Tube takes skiers through 10km of tunnels on a 20-minute journey to Perisher and Blue Cow from Bullocks Flat. However, you can also drive up the Kosciuszko Road.

Blue Cow prides itself on its testing terrain and the high proportion of black-diamond runs. Accelerator is the longest run in the Perisher–Blue area. However, 60 per cent of the terrain is graded intermediate. Guthega has some challenging short, sharp runs such as Parachute, Bloody Mary and Mother-in-Law. The area's half-pipe has been voted the best in Australia.

Improvements to mountain facilities, to the value of Aus$750,000, are being made. These include more pygmy-possum crossings beneath the piste to protect the little marsupials from skiers and riders on runs such as Zali's and Sidesaddle at Blue Cow. New to the slopes for the 2005 season is the southern hemisphere's first eight-seater detachable chair.

Transport from the Perisher terminal complex to all the lodges is on caterpillar vehicles. The best accommodation is in the Perisher Valley Hotel (☎ 2 6459 4455), which has 31 rooms and suites. The Perisher Manor (☎ 2 6457 5291) is a family-run, ski-in ski-out establishment, and the Lodge (☎ 2 6457 5341) at Smiggins is a no-smoking, Austrian-style hotel with a swimming-pool. Heidi's Chalet (☎ 2 9743 0911) is opposite the lifts at Smiggins.

**Tel** 61 2 6459 4419
**Email** dave.kirwan@perisher.com.au
**Website** www.perisherblue.com.au
**Ski area** top 2,034m (6,672ft) bottom 1,605m (5,264ft)
**Lifts in area** 49: 1⬛ 13☐ 35☐
**Tour operators** none

# Pila, Italy

Pila is linked to the regional capital, Aosta, by an 18-minute gondola ride. It is a compact but surprisingly challenging ski area with a full range of pistes for all levels and plenty of easily accessible off-piste. It offers 70km of mainly intermediate trails that are included in the Aosta Valley lift pass. The area has a terrain park with a half-pipe and obstacles. Five mountain restaurants are dotted around the slopes ('good-quality food at low prices'). Pila Ski and Snowboard School organises all-day tuition for adults and children, and the Ski School Mini Club cares for children from ten months.

Hotels include the ski-in, ski-out Etoile de Neige (☎ 0165 521541) ('very friendly, good food, but rather firm beds') and the Printemps (☎ 0165 521246), which has a disco. Pila boasts ten restaurants as well as shops and cafés.

The impressive gondola link to the valley makes it perfectly feasible to commute from Aosta to Pila, or to **Courmayeur** and the other resorts included in the lift pass. The valley is seriously blighted by commercial development, but the pedestrianised centre of the old Roman town of Aosta is delightful. Hotel Europe (☎ 0165 236363), in the centre, is 'quiet, traditional and a thoroughly comfortable base'.

**Tel** 39 0165 521148
**Email** info@pila.it
**Website** www.pila.it
**Ski area** top 2,750m (9,022ft) bottom 1,750m (5,741ft)
**Lifts in area** 12: 1⬛ 1☐ 9☐ 1☐
**Tour operators** Crystal, Interski, Momentum, Ski Supreme

# Pitztal, Austria

The Pitztal lies in the Wildspitze area to the south of Imst in the Austrian Tyrol. The region comprises four villages, with St Leonhard the main accommodation base close to the Pitztaler Glacier and Rifflsee skiing area. The skiing at Rifflsee is for all levels, with 70 per cent of the ski terrain classified as easy. The glacier skiing is accessed by fast underground funicular and the highest gondola in Austria. The area has a wide range of hotels, including the four-star ski-in, ski-out Alpinhotel (☎ 5413 86361) at the glacier base station.

**Tel** 43 5414 86999 / 5413 8288 (Pitztaler Glacier)
**Email** info@pitztal.com
**Website** www.tiscover.at/pitztal
**Ski area** top 3,440m (11,283ft) bottom 2,880m (9,446ft)
**Lifts in area** 11: 1⬛ 1☐ 2☐ 7☐
**Tour operators** none

## La Plagne, France

See page 97

**Tour operators** Airtours, Chalet World, Club Med, Crystal, Equity, Erna Low, Esprit, Finlays, First Choice, French Freedom, French Life, Inghams, Interhome, Lagrange, Leisure Direction, Mark Warner, Neilson, On The Piste, Silver Ski, Ski Activity, Ski Amis, Ski Beat, Ski Expectations, Ski France, Ski Freshtracks, Ski Independence, Ski Olympic, Ski Supreme, Skibound, Skitopia, Skiworld, Thomson

## Poiana Brasov, Romania

See page 143

**Tour operators** Airtours, Balkan Holidays, Balkan Tours, Inghams, Neilson, Neilson School Groups, Solo's

## Pont d'Espagne, France

See *Cauterets*, page 267

## Ponte di Legno, Italy

See *Passo Tonale*, page 298

## Pontresina, Switzerland

With no big lifts of its own, Pontresina is about midway between the outlying Diavolezza sector of **St Moritz** and the Corviglia sector. Grand Hotel Kronenhof (☎ 81 842 0111) is the only five-star in the resort. Kochendorfer's Albris (☎ 81 838 8040) is a relatively inexpensive three-star hotel. The Steinbock (☎ 81 842 6371) is comfortable and traditional. The four-star Saratz Hotel (☎ 81 839 4000) is highly praised – the style is traditional mixed with modern, and it has a renowned restaurant and a kindergarten for children from three years. Allegra Garni (☎ 81 838 9900) is the resort's newest hotel.

**Tel** 41 81 838 8300
**Email** info@pontresina.com
**Website** www.pontresina.com
**Ski area** top 2,978m (9,770ft) bottom 1,800m (5,904ft)
**Lifts in area** 56: 3🚡 8🚠 18🚡 27🎿
**Tour operators** Made to Measure

## The Portes du Soleil, France

See *Avoriaz*, page 72; *Champéry*, page 269; *Châtel*, page 270; *Morgins*, page 293; *Morzine*, page 94

## Portillo, Chile

See page 64

**Tour operators** Andes, Crystal, Exsus, Momentum, Scott Dunn Latin America, Ski All America, Ski Safari, Skiworld

## Pra-Loup, France

This popular resort in the Alpes de Haute Provence was named after the wolves that once frequented these pine forests. The 167km of piste is shared with neighbouring **La Foux d'Allos**. The skiing takes place on two main mountains, accessible by cable-car from the top of the village at 1600. Pra-Loup has an extensive range of beginner and intermediate trails, including open-bowl skiing and good tree-line runs with spectacular scenery. The off-piste is extensive (you will need a guide), but there are only five black runs. Weekend queues are said to be 'fearsome'. The ESF and ESI ski schools are rated as 'excellent'. Les P'tits Loups day nursery caters for children from six months to six years.

The resort is split into the two villages of 1500 and 1600, which are linked by a chair-lift and consist of a collection of hotels and apartments built in the 1960s, along with some older chalets. Hotel Club Les Bergers (☎ 492 84 14 54) is recommended ('the nicest of hotels'), while Hotel Le Prieuré (☎ 492 84 11 43) is 'very welcoming, warm and comfortable'. Le Loup Garou and Le Sham'rock are the hottest nightspots.

**Tel** 33 492 84 10 04
**Email** info@praloup.com
**Website** www.praloup.com
**Ski area** top 2,500m (8,202ft) bottom 1,600m (5,249ft)
**Lifts in area** 53 with La Foux d'Allos: 7🚠 12🚡 34🎿
**Tour operators** Equity, French Life, Lagrange

## Puy-St-Vincent, France

Puy-St-Vincent is an established resort 20km from **Briançon**, three hours' drive from Grenoble or Turin and on the edge of the Ecrins National Park. Its micro-climate usually ensures secure late-season snow cover along with 300 days of sunshine per year.

The 67km of piste in the small but challenging area has enough variety to suit all standards of skier, although most runs are classified as blue or red. From Puy-St-Vincent 1600 two chair-lifts give easy access to the main skiing, and queues are rare outside school holidays.

The ESF and the ESI offer group lessons and a range of courses, and the ESI runs classes for British children during the peak holiday weeks. The resort has a small terrain park that is floodlit at night, and a cross-country track. Other activities include night-skiing and weekly torchlight descents that children can take part in. Altitude Restaurant 2000 is a self-service with a good selection of dishes.

Puy-St-Vincent 1400 is an unspoilt mountain village. It is connected by a double chair-lift and a drag-lift to 1600, which is dominated by an aging central apartment block. Newer *résidences,* a few chalets and a handful of shops and restaurants have been built on the edge of the piste, and the higher village is the better bet if you want doorstep skiing. The newest and best of the apartments here are in the Mona Lisa building. At 1400 are a three-star hotel, the Saint Roche (☎ 492 23 32 79), and three two-stars.

Also in the lower village are two recommended restaurants – the St-Vincent and Cadran Solaire. Among the simple but friendly restaurants in the higher village are the rustic La Chaumière, Le Petit Chamois ('one of the best breakfasts'), and La Rozelle crêperie, all of which serve local dishes. There are several bars including one with karaoke.

Les P'tits Loups kindergarten at 1600 takes children from 18 months. Two UK tour operators – Snowbizz and Esprit – offer childcare programmes for little ones aged six months and over, and Snowbizz organises its own ski classes for children and adults. During holiday weeks it runs a race camp for older children under the expert tuition of an ex-racer, who also coaches budding French stars. Any 10- to 16-year-old who can ski parallel can join in and race against French children from the resort's Club de Sport in competitions every afternoon.

**Tel** 33 492 23 35 80
**Email** courrier@puystvincent.net

**Website** www.puystvincent.com
**Ski area** top 2,750m (9,022ft) bottom 1,400m (4,593ft)
**Lifts in area** 16: 5⑤ 11⑨
**Tour operators** Esprit, Interhome, Lagrange, Snowbizz Vacances

## Québec City, Canada

Romantic, beautifully preserved and reasonably priced, Québec acts as a convenient bed-base from which to explore several delightful little ski areas, each of which is worth a couple of days' attention. A regular winter shuttle bus service operates between the city, **Stoneham** (20-minute drive) and **Mont Saint Anne** (30 minutes away). **Le Massif** (also 30 minutes away) offers dramatic piste views of the frozen St Lawrence River. **Québec** city was built in 1608 and its cobbled streets added in the eighteenth-century. It is on two levels: an upper one that contains the fortress and a lower one, the Quartier Petit Champlain; the two are connected by a cable-railway. The city has a wide choice of bistros, shops, and art galleries on both levels, and is now home to a thriving club scene.

The Fairmont Chateau Frontenac (☎ 418 692 3861) is a striking hotel at the heart of the city and overlooks the St Lawrence River. Two less exalted alternatives are Le Clos Saint-Louis (☎ 418 694 1311) inside the old city walls, and Auberge Saint-Pierre (☎ 418 694 7981) in the old port.

**Tel** 1 418 649 2608
**Email** bit@cuq.qc.ca
**Website** www.quebecregion.com
**Ski area** (Stoneham) top 2,075ft (632m) bottom 695ft (211m) / (Mont-Saint-Anne) top 2,625ft (800m) bottom 575ft (175m)
**Lifts in area** (Stoneham) 8: 5⑤ 3⑨ / (Mont-Saint-Anne) 15: 1⑤ 8⑤ 6⑨
**Tour operator** Neilson School Groups

## Queenstown (Coronet Peak and The Remarkables), New Zealand

Six resorts come under the marketing umbrella of the Southern Lakelands, based around Queenstown and **Wanaka**. Queenstown is a lively and picturesque lakeside town situated in the south-west of the South Island. It is flanked by two separate resorts, which operate interchangeable lift passes. The traditional but modernised resort is **Coronet Peak**, with six lifts and a vertical drop of 420m, providing a wide variety of good all-round skiing. The nursery slope now claims the longest magic carpet lift (146m) in the world. **The Remarkables** was constructed more recently. The resort is visually exciting, but has fewer options than Coronet Peak. From Queenstown, The Remarkables range seems impossibly steep, with the peaks resembling a set of sharp, pearly-white teeth, dominating the shoreline of Lake Wakatipu. Fortunately, the ski area is on the other side, where gentle bowls belie the severity of the mountains. The award-winning Remarkables Lodge (☎ 3 442 2720) is the closest hotel to the resort.

**Tel** Coronet Peak 64 3 442 4634 /
The Remarkables 64 3 442 4617
**Email** andy@coronetpeak.co.nz /
hamish@theremarkables.co.nz
**Website** www.queenstown-nz.co.nz
**Ski area** top 1,957m (6,421ft) bottom 1,200m (3,937ft)
**Lifts in area** 10: 6⛷ 4⛷
**Tour operators** none

## Red Mountain, BC, Canada

See page 56

**Tour operators** AWWT, Frontier Ski, Nonstopski, Ski Safari

## The Remarkables

See *Queenstown (Coronet Peak and The Remarkables)*, page 301

## Riksgränsen, Sweden

Riksgränsen in Swedish Lapland is 300km into the Arctic Circle and 90 minutes from Stockholm. Being so far north, the sun doesn't set during midsummer (mid-May to mid-June), so you can ski, snowboard or heli-ski until 1am. Hotel Riksgränsen (☎ 980 400 800) has a spa and swimming-pool.

**Tel** 46 980 400 800
**Email** info@rikgransen.nu
**Website** www.riksgransen.nu
**Ski area** top 909m (2,982ft) bottom 500m (1,640ft)
**Lifts in area** 5: 2⛷ 3⛷
**Tour operators** Norvista, Original Travel

## Risoul 1850, France

See page 100

**Tour operators** Crystal, Erna Low, First Choice, French Life, Interhome, Lagrange, Neilson, Neilson School Groups, On The Piste, Ski Independence, Skitopia, Thomson, Tops Travel, Wasteland

## Rohrmoos, Austria

This diffuse satellite of **Schladming** has easy skiing to and from many of its hotel doorsteps. Among the choice of good-value hotels and guesthouses are the Austria (☎ 3687 61444) and the Waldfrieden (☎ 3687 61487). Both are well placed at the point where the lower, gentle slopes of Rohrmoos meet the steeper slopes of Hochwurzen. The smarter Schwaigerhof (☎ 3687 61422) boasts an excellent position on the edge of the pistes and is one of the few places with a swimming-pool. The Schütterhof (☎ 3687 61205) is also warmly recommended.

Après-ski is informal and centres on the hotel bars. The Tauernalm is the main meeting point. Café Perner is a tea-time favourite, and Knappenkeller in Rohrmoos is busy later on. Tritscher and the Hopl ski schools operate here, and Blue Tomato is the snowboard school. Max and Moritz Club is the non-skiing kindergarten for children aged two to five years. Hotel Seiterhof (☎ 3687 61194) is highly praised ('wonderful apartments that are much cheaper than any tour operator's if booked direct').

**Tel** 43 3687 61147
**Email** info@rohrmoos.at
**Website** www.rohrmoos.at
**Ski area** top 1,850m (6,070ft) bottom 870m (2,854ft)
**Lifts in area** 46: 7⛷ 19⛷ 20⛷
**Tour operators** none

## La Rosière, France

La Rosière is an attractive little resort tucked away in the Haute Tarentaise above Bourg-St-Maurice and linked across the Petit-St-Bernard Pass with **La Thuile** in Italy to form what is marketed as Espace San Bernardo. In winter, the road ends in a bank of snow outside the Relais du Petit-St-Bernard hotel. Just beyond the hotel lie the kennels of the St Bernard dogs, which have maintained a presence here as rescuers of snowbound travellers since the seventeenth century. The resort's lift system has been bought by new developers and we can expect to see much-needed improvements over the next decade. The first phase is the constructon of two six-person chair-lifts.

La Rosière has wide-open slopes well suited to beginners and intermediates. Several short nursery slopes are near the resort, with more at the altiport nearby. The 500-m-long terrain park is reached by the Poletta drag-lift.

The French Ski School (ESF) enjoys a sound reputation ('competitively priced, small classes; a good standard of tuition and English spoken'). The International Ski School (ESI) 'has friendly instructors' and we also have glowing reports of Evolution 2. Les Galopines nursery takes care of children from twelve months to three years, and Club L'Oisirs is for non-skiers aged three to twelve years.

Mountain restaurants include La Traversette, at the bottom of the Fort chair, and L'Ancolie, a pleasant inn with homemade food at the outlying hamlet of Les Eucherts. Also in Les Eucherts is Chalet Le Montana (☎ 479 06 82 66), which houses apartments that are 'spacious, well-equipped, well-maintained and exceptional value'. Hotel accommodation is limited in La Rosière, but the Relais du Petit-St-Bernard (☎ 479 06 80 48) is ideally situated at the foot of the pistes. The family-run Hotel Le Solaret (☎ 479 06 80 47) is recommended too.

The Relais du Petit-St-Bernardis has a restaurant, and others include L'Ancolie and Le Chalet ('the best food in the resort'). What limited nightlife there is starts at Le P'tit Relais when the lifts close. Le Pub extends a warm welcome, and Le Roc Noir is the favourite watering-hole for British seasonal workers. Arpin's Bar has karaoke, and La Terrasse du Yéti is another popular meeting-place.

**Tel** 33 479 06 80 51
**Email** info@larosiere.net
**Website** www.larosiere.net
**Ski area** top 2,641m (8,665ft) bottom 1,176m (3,858ft)
**Lifts in area** 37: 1⑤ 17⑤ 19⑤
**Tour operators** Crystal, Erna Low, Esprit, Ski Olympic, Thomson

## Saalbach, Austria

See *Saalbach–Hinterglemm*, page 34

**Tour operators** Airtours, Club Europe, Crystal, Equity, First Choice, Inghams, Interhome, Neilson, Panorama, PGL, Skiworld, Thomson, Wasteland

## Saas-Fee, Switzerland

See page 211

**Tour operators** Crystal, Erna Low, Inghams, Interhome, Kuoni, Momentum, Oak Hall, PGL, Ski Freshtracks, Ski Gower, Ski Independence, Skiworld, Sloping Off, Swiss Travel Centre, Swiss Travel Service, Thomson

## Sainte-Foy, France

See page 102

**Tour operators** Alpine Elements, Alpine Weekends, Skiworld

## Les Saisies, France

This small resort is halfway between the beautiful Beaufortain valley and Val d'Arly. It is primarily a cross-country resort with 80km of loipe, but it also boasts 34 alpine pistes, of which more than half are on easy tree-lined slopes. Other facilities include a boardercross course, terrain park and a slalom course. The hotels are headed by the four-star Calgary (☎ 479 38 98 38), which is in the village centre with a health club, swimming-pool and gourmet restaurant. The other hotels are the one-star Meteor (☎ 479 38 90 79) and two-star Cascade (☎ 479 38 70 00).

**Tel** 33 479 38 90 30
**Email** info@lessaisies.com
**Website** www.lessaisies.com
**Ski area** top 2,000m (6,562ft) bottom 1,650m (5,413ft)
**Lifts in area** 26: 11⑤ 15⑤
**Tour operators** AWWT, Classic Ski, Erna Low, French Life, Inntravel, Lagrange, Peak Retreats

## Salzburger Sportwelt Amadé, Austria

The four valleys of **Flachau, St Johann im Pongau, Wagrain** and **Zauchensee** lie only 45 minutes from Salzburg and provide an important linked playground for intermediates. The statistics for this ski arena are impressive: a dozen resorts with 350km of skiing, served by 130 lifts. Cross-country skiers are well served by 160km of trails along the valleys, and St Johann has a terrain park.

Wagrain and Flachau are the most convenient and attractive bases from which to explore the circuit. St Johann has its own small, separate ski area, and the link into the rest of the Sportwelt Amadé is via the hamlet of **Alpendorf**, a 3-km ski-bus ride away. The pistes offer plentiful eating-places, from small huts to larger self-services. The area is included in the 25-resort Skiverbund Amadé regional lift pass.

Each of the resorts has at least one ski school, and St Johann has four. Vitamin B and Board Unlimited are two specialist boarding schools in Alpendorf.

Accommodation in St Johann and Alpendorf includes the four-star Dorfhotel Tannenhof (☎ 6412 52310), the luxurious Sporthotel Alpenland (☎ 6412 70210), the three-star Hotel Brückenwirt-Tennerhof (☎ 6412 42590) and Gasthof-Pension Taxenbacher (☎ 6412 4288). The resort's nightlife is limited. The inconvenient bus journey to Alpendorf means that St Johann is not ideal for families.

In Wagrain, Hotel Grafenwirt (☎ 6413 7162) is discreetly up-market; Hotel Enzian (☎ 6413 8502) and the Wagrainerhof (☎ 6413 8204) are also both recommended. The ski kindergarten accepts children from three years.

Neighbouring Flachau continues to expand. The main accommodation is in large, chalet-style hotels, as well as apartment blocks. Beginners learn to ski on a gentle piste in the village. There is a non-ski kindergarten, and the Griessenkar Ski School takes children from three years. Flachau's recommended hotels include the four-star Vierjahreszeiten (☎ 6457 2981) and the luxurious Hotel Tauernhof (☎ 6457 23110).

The market town of **Altenmarkt** is a centre for the local sportswear and ski equipment industries. A modest ski area is linked to neighbouring Radstadt, but the main skiing is a bus ride away at Zauchensee or Flachau. The kindergarten cares for children from three years old. The pleasant village has 22 hotels, including six of a luxury standard.

**Filzmoos** is another small village, dating from the early twentieth century, when it was a popular holiday destination for the wealthy

Viennese. Today it has a ski area served by 17 lifts, shared with neighbouring Neuberg. The **Dachstein Glacier** is only 18km away, and the rest of the ski region is reached by bus via Flachau. The kindergarten takes children from three years old and has English-speaking staff. The choice of accommodation in 25 hotels and the selection of apartments is large in relation to the size of the village, which is famed as the hot-air ballooning capital of Austria.

**Tel** 43 6457 2929
**Email** info@salzburger-sportwelt.com
**Website** www.salzburger-sportwelt.com
**Ski area** top 2,188m (7,177ft) bottom 650m (2,132ft)
**Lifts in area** 97: 11⛷ 36⛷ 50⛷. 262 in Skiverbund Amadé.
**Tour operators** see *Flachau* page 310, *St Johann im Pongau* page 319, *Wagrain* page 322, *Zauchensee* page 322

## Samnaun, Switzerland

Lost in an inaccessible pocket in the mountains on the Austrian–Swiss border, Samnaun lives off its duty-free status and its well-established ski links with **Ischgl**. The resort has a strong following among Swiss families, but has not yet achieved major international status. Recommended on-mountain eateries are the Schmugglers Alms and the Samnaunerhof. Hotels include Chasa Montana (☎ 81 861 9000), Hotel Post (☎ 81 861 9200) and Hotel Silvretta (☎ 81 868 5400). The Gästekindergarten takes potty-trained children all day Monday to Friday.

**Tel** 41 81 868 5858
**Email** info@samnaun.ch
**Website** www.samnaun.ch
**Ski area** top 2,864m (9,394ft) bottom 1,840m (6,035ft)
**Lifts in area** 44: 2⛷ 3⛷ 21⛷ 18⛷
**Tour operators** none

## Samoëns, France

'One of the most beautiful and charming French ski villages I have ever seen' was how one reporter described Samoëns, which is linked into the Grand Massif ski area. Traditional-style bars and restaurants abound in what is a resort largely undiscovered by other nationalities. A lift from Samoëns village at 720m whisks skiers up to the ski area at 1,600m in eight minutes.

The ESF was described as 'fantastic – even over New Year we had small groups'. The resort also boasts eight mountain guides, a crèche for children from three months and a ski kindergarten for three- to six-year-olds. Cross-country skiers have 90km of loipe and a specialist ski school.

The three-star Neige et Roc (☎ 450 34 40 72) is recommended, together with Les Drugères (☎ 450 34 43 84). The resort's B&Bs include Chez Bobeau (☎ 450 34 98 95) and Les Gîtes de Plampraz (☎ 450 34 95 98). There are two dozen restaurants.

**Tel** 33 450 34 40 28
**Email** info@samoens.com
**Website** www.samoens.com
**Ski area** top 2,480m (8,134ft) bottom 700m (2,296ft)
**Lifts in area** 78 in Grand Massif: 6⊙ 25⊡ 47☒
**Tour operators** AWWT, French Life, Interhome, Lagrange, Peak Retreats

## San Cassiano, Italy

San Cassiano is a small road-side village that is linked into the **Sella Ronda**. It has some good skiing and snowboarding for beginners and early intermediates. Long, easy runs go down to the village from Pralongia and Piz Sorega. Reporters mentioned the lack of spoken English in the resort, which attracts mainly wealthy Italians. Hotel Rosa Alpina (☎ 0471 849500) is a large and comfortable hotel in the village centre and, with a live band, is also the focal point for nightlife. Its restaurant creates local dishes with a gourmet twist. The Ski Bar is recommended for tasty, cheap pizzas, and the Capanna Alpina, Saré and Tirol are all busy restaurants. La Siriola is an elegant restaurant with a 1,500-strong wine list and innovative dishes. Rosa Alpina, Fanes and the restaurant in Hotel Diamant are also expensive. Rifugio Scotoni (☎ 0471 847330) is a ski-touring hut serving delicious food, situated at 1,986m in the San Cassiano Valley.

**Tel** 39 0471 792277
**Email** info@valgardena.com
**Website** www.valgardena.com
**Ski area** top 2,950m (9,676ft) bottom 1,537m (5,041ft)
**Lifts in area** 83 in Val Gardena: 10⊙ 36⊡ 37☒
**Tour operator** Momentum

## San Martino di Castrozza, Italy

San Martino is on the eastern edge of the Trentino Dolomites, surrounded by wild forest with pink mountain peaks above. In 1700, the violin-maker Stradivari used to go into the same woods to select the spruce for his violins. Skiing started at San Martino di Castrozza in the early 1930s, and it has developed into three separate areas (two of which are linked) with 60km of piste.

The resort was praised as having 'no half-term queues, a complete lack of snowboarders, and the charm of a low-profile ski station', although 'the majority of lifts were old-fashioned and slow, and nightlife is non-existent'.

Nuova Scuola Nazionale di Sci accepts adults and children from five years. Gruppo Guide Alpine and Aquile de San Martino supply guides for the long off-piste descents of the Pale Highlands, and the Rosetta cable-car is open all winter for ski-touring and snowshoeing expeditions.

Accommodation includes four-star Hotel Savoia (☎ 0439 68094) and the three-star Hotel-Residence Colfosco (☎ 0439 68224). Kindergarten Tognola, on the slopes at Rifugio Tognola, accepts little ones from three years.

**Tel** 39 0439 768867
**Email** info@sanmartino.com
**Website** www.sanmartino.com
**Ski area** top 2,385m (7,825ft) bottom 1,450m (4,757ft)
**Lifts in area** 16: 3⊙ 9⊡ 4☒
**Tour operators** Momentum

## Santa Caterina, Italy

Santa Caterina is a quiet, attractive village with a 30-km ski area. Reporters rated it 'a great resort for family holidays or groups with beginners. It was English half-term week and I have never skied on less crowded slopes'. It is situated 30 minutes by bus from **Bormio** (with which it shares a lift pass), up a mountain road that is a dead-end in winter when the Gavia Pass is closed. Local skiing is on the north-east-facing slopes of the Sobretta ('the views and peace in the valley are second to none'). The higher slopes are fairly steep and graded black; some intermediate trails wind down between the trees.

The Santa Caterina Ski School received favourable reviews: 'the ski school was great'. The Bimbi Sulla Neve kindergarten cares for children six days a week. Cross-country is popular here, and there is also a natural ice-skating rink. The San Matteo Hotel (☎ 0342 925121) is recommended for comfort and food. Nightlife is limited, with one fairly large disco and a number of cosy bars that remain open until after midnight.

**Tel** 39 0342 935598
**Email** apt.santa.caterina@provincia.so.it
**Website** www.valtellinaonline.com
**Ski area** top 2,725m (8,940ft) bottom 1,738m (5,702ft)
**Lifts in area** 8: 1⑤ 7⑨
**Tour operators** Airtours, Momentum

## Sauze d'Oulx, Italy

See page 134

**Tour operators** Airtours, Crystal, Equity, First Choice, Inghams, Momentum, Neilson, Panorama, Ski High Days, Thomson

## Scheffau, Austria

Scheffau is a component of the **SkiWelt** ski area centred around better-known mass-market **Söll**. Hotel residents at Scheffau are given priority over the sometimes extensive lift queue for the eight-person gondola, which provides a direct link into the SkiWelt. The ski school, due to 'popular demand' operates only in the morning. Hotel Alpin Scheffau (☎ 5358 85560) has comfortable, en-suite bedrooms and a swimming-pool. The resort was recommended as 'a viable alternative to Söll, particularly if you are not a party animal'. CC-Pub, Conny's Corner and the Pub Royal are the only nightspots.

**Tel** 43 5358 7373
**Email** scheffau@skiwelt.at
**Website** www.scheffau.com
**Ski area** top 1,829m (6,001ft) bottom 752m (2,467ft)
**Lifts in area** 93 in SkiWelt: 11⑥ 34⑤ 48⑨
**Tour operators** Crystal, Esprit, Ski Astons, Thomson

## Schladming, Austria

See page 36

**Tour operators** Crystal, Equity, Interhome, Made to Measure, Oak Hall, PGL, Skibound, Sloping Off

## Seefeld, Austria

Seefeld, with its frescoed medieval architecture, is a small version of **Innsbruck**, **Kitzbühel** and the other beautiful towns of the Austrian Tyrol. The resort is stylish and sophisticated and has seven luxury hotels, a casino, an extensive health centre and horse-drawn sleighs. The village centre is pedestrianised.

The resort's main winter activity is cross-country skiing, with 270km of loipe. But it also has three small, alpine ski areas: Geigenbühel ('perfect for beginners'), Gschwandtkopf, a low peak next to the cross-country track used mainly by the ski school, and Rosshütte, the more extensive area with steeper runs and a long off-piste trail. All three areas are reached from the village centre by the free bus service.

The five-star hotels include the Klosterbräu (☎ 5212 26210), a former sixteenth-century monastery. Others recommended are the Creativhotel Viktoria (☎ 5212 4441), Aparthotel Schönruh (☎ 5212 2447) and the less pricy Hotel Bergland (☎ 5212 2293). The four-star Karwendelhof (☎ 5212 2655) is in the pedestrian precinct. The Kaltschmid (☎ 5212 2191) was highly rated: 'the free kindergarten, combined with excellent staff, ensured a relaxing stay for all the family'. The luxury Gartenhotel Tümmlerhof (☎ 5212 2571) is set in its own park and offers daycare and a children's playground. The resort kindergarten is in the Olympia Sport and Congress Centre.

Gourmets can try the Alte Stube in the Karwendelhof hotel. Café Nanni and Café Moccamühle are popular for après-ski. The Big Ben bar is as English as you would expect, and the Britannia Inn is another popular pub. Monroe's disco-bar attracts the late-night crowd, as do the Miramare and the popular Postbar in the Hotel Post. The Kanne in the Klosterbräu hotel, the centre of the village's social life, has live music.

**Tel** 43 5212 2313
**Email** info@seefeld.at
**Website** www.seefeld.at
**Ski area** top 2,100m (6,890ft) bottom 1,200m (3,937ft)
**Lifts in area** 30: 2⑥ 7⑤ 21⑨
**Tour operators** Crystal, Inghams, Interhome, Made to Measure, Skiworld, Thomson, Waymark

## Sella Ronda, Italy

See *Arabba*, page 118; *Canazei and the Val di Fassa*, page 266; *San Cassiano*, page 305; *Selva Gardena*, page 136

## Selva Gardena, Italy

See page 136

**Tour operators** Crystal, Esprit, First Choice, Inghams, Momentum, Thomson, Total Ski

## Serfaus, Austria

Exclusive Serfaus in the Tyrol attracts a mainly Austrian, German and Dutch clientèle to its beginner and intermediate slopes and its smart hotels. The village is car-free and has an unusual underground railway, which runs on air cushions rather like a hovercraft. This transports snow-users from the far end of the village to the ski lifts and contributes to the peaceful atmosphere in the resort.

Serfaus majors in 'wellness' and has five specialist hotels: the Löwe and Bär (☎ 43 5476 6058) are advertised as 'families-only' hotels, containing spas and impressive swimming-pools. The other five-star spa hotels are Wellnesshotel Schalber (☎ 5476 6770) and Wellnesshotel Cervosa (☎ 5476 62110), while Hotel Drei Sonnen (☎ 5476 5207) is a four-star with a spa.

The Serfaus ski area is linked to the villages of Fiss and Ladis, making a total of 160km of piste. The ski kindergarten is called Kinderschneealm; Baby-Kindergarten and Murmlinest are the non-ski kindergartens, and the resort has a designated Kinder-Restaurant, as well as a large number of magic carpet lifts. Other activities include cross-country on 111km of trails.

**Tel** 43 5476 62390
**Email** info@serfaus.com
**Website** www.serfaus.com
**Ski area** top 2,684m (8,806ft) bottom 1,427m (4,682ft)
**Lifts in area** 53: 1🚡 9🚠 10🚦 33🎿
**Tour operators** Alpine Tours, Made to Measure

## Serre Chevalier, France

See page 103

**Tour operators** Airtours, Alpine Elements, Club Med, Crystal, Equity, Erna Low, First Choice, French Life,

Hannibals, Inghams, Interhome, Lagrange, Leisure Direction, Neilson, Neilson School Groups, Panorama, PGL, Ski Expectations, Ski France, Ski Independence, Ski Miquel, Ski Supreme, Skibound, Skitopia, Sloping Off, Thomson, Tops Travel, Wasteland

## Sestriere, Italy

See page 138

**Tour operators** Club Med, Crystal, Equity, Inghams, Interhome, Momentum, Neilson, Thomson

## Shiga Kogen, Japan

This is Nagano's largest ski area. It is an extraordinary patchwork of 21 different ski bases, served by 71 lifts, dotted over six interlinked mountains. None of the sectors is big or particularly difficult; in Alpine terms the whole area would make up just three or four linked resorts of reasonable size. A competent skier or rider could cover all the terrain in a couple of days. The highest point – the 2,305-m summit of Mount Yoketeyama – is not infrequently obscured by freezing mist or blizzards. Accommodation includes Villa Alpen (☎ 81 269 34 2731), which has its own ski school and equipment rental shop in the Sun Valley resort, and Hotel La Neige Higashikan (☎ 81 261 72 7111) at Shiga Kogen.

**Tel** 020-7734 6870 in UK
**Email** info@jnto.co.uk
**Website** www.snowjapan.co.uk
**Ski area** top 2,305m (7,562ft) bottom 1,228m (4,028ft)
**Lifts in area** 71: 4🚡 66🚠 1🎿
**Tour operators** none

## Sierra Nevada, Spain

Sierra Nevada lies in Andalucia, 32km from the ancient Moorish city of Granada, and offers mainland Europe's most southerly skiing. The presence of a ski resort here seems at complete odds with the nearby resorts of Marbella and Malaga. The purpose-built village in which most skiers stay (at 2,100m) is known as Pradollano. The ski area is extremely vulnerable to bad weather, and the mountain range as a whole is exposed to high winds. Skiing is as likely to be interrupted by too much snow as too little. But when conditions are good, the skiing can be excellent and the views striking; on a clear day you can even see Morocco.

The village is short on alpine charm yet is 'certainly nowhere near as ugly as the Andorran resorts'. Because of its proximity to Granada and the Costa del Sol, it suffers from extreme crowding at weekends and on public holidays.

Accommodation is mainly in hotels. The Sol Melia Sol y Nieve (☎ 958 48 03 00) and the four-star Sol Melia Sierra Nevada (☎ 958 24 91 11) are convenient and pleasant. The former runs a mini-club for children between five and eleven years of age. The four-star Hotel Maribel (☎ 958 24 91 11) is warmly praised. A kindergarten cares for children aged three months to four years.

Restaurants include the Andalusi, Pizzeria La Bodega, the Monachil, and Genil. Early-evening entertainment focuses on the Crescendo bar. Other recommended venues include Sticky Fingers, Soho and Mango. A dozen clubs, such as Sala Muley in the Sol Melia Sierra Nevada, provide dancing.

**Tel** 34 958 24 91 00
**Email** sierranevada@cetursa.es
**Website** www.sierranevadaski.com
**Ski area** top 3,470m (11,385ft) bottom 2,100m (6,888ft)
**Lifts in area** 19: 2⑥ 10⑤ 7⑨
**Tour operator** Thomson

## Silver Star, BC, Canada

See page 57

**Tour operators** AWWT, Crystal, Frontier Ski, Ski Activity, Ski the American Dream, Ski Independence, Ski Safari, Ski All America, Skiworld

## Sinaia, Romania

Sinaia is a spa town where the Romanian royal family used to spend their summers. Its once-elegant hotels and casinos have an air of faded grandeur. The resort is as popular in summer as in winter, and visitors come here from all over Eastern Europe to take the waters.

The skiing is basic, but the setting is charming. A two-stage cable-car from the town, its top section duplicated by a chair-lift, serves long easy runs down the front of the mountain when snow conditions permit. These runs are poorly marked and are

consequently challenging in uncertain visibility. The main area is on exposed, treeless slopes behind the mountain and on subsidiary peaks beyond. It consists of short intermediate runs with some variety, and scope for off-piste. Four-star hotels include New Montana (☎ 40 24 431 2751), Hotel Anda, (☎ 40 24 430 6020) and the recently renovated Palace (☎ 94 024 431 2051). The three-star Sinaia (☎ 40 24 431 1551) is recommended by one reporter. Of the 16 restaurants in town, 11 are based in hotels. Nightlife is centred around a few bars including the German Pub. The Black Horse and Blue Angel discos provide late-night entertainment.

**Tel** 40 21 314 9957 or 020-7224 3692 UK
**Email** uktouroff@romania.freeserve.co.uk
**Website** www.romaniantourism.com
**Ski area** top 2,219m (7,280ft) bottom 855m (2,805ft)
**Lifts in area** 10: 2⑥ 2⑤ 6⑨
**Tour operators** none

## Siviez, Switzerland

Skiers desperate to save money and determined to be first up Mont-Fort in the **Verbier** ski area might consider Siviez. It is sunny and at the hub of the Four Valleys, with a high-speed chair link to the Gentianes–Mont-Fort cable-cars. Accommodation is limited to one hotel, a concrete apartment block and a youth hostel.The Ecole de ski Arc-en-Ciel offers adult lessons, as well as special courses for children aged two to six with their parents.

**Tel** 41 27 289 5589
**Email** info@nendaz.ch
**Website** www.nendaz.ch
**Ski area** top 3,330m (10,925ft) bottom 1,730m (5,676ft)
**Lifts in area** 94 in Four Valleys: 17⑥ 32⑤ 45⑨
**Tour operators** none

## SkiWelt, Austria

See *Ellmau*, page 275; *Going*, page 278; *Hopfgarten*, page 281; *Scheffau*, page 306; *Söll and the SkiWelt*, page 39

## Smugglers' Notch, Vermont, US

See page 243

**Tour operator** Ski Safari

## Snow King, Wyoming, US

This small ski area is in Jackson town and a free shuttle-bus ride from Teton Village and **Jackson Hole** ski resort. The ski area with its 300 acres of terrain is 'interesting enough for a day's skiing and very quiet'. The lower slopes are floodlit, and skating and tubing are also available. Reporters praised the area as 'a good place to learn to ski – the lower slopes are more gentle than at Jackson Hole'.

Accommodation is in the Snow King Resort Hotel and Condominiums (☎ 307 733 5200) at the base or elsewhere in Jackson.

**Tel** 1 307 733 5200
**Email** info@snowking.com
**Website** www.snowking.com
**Ski area** top 7,808ft (2,380m) bottom 6,237ft (1,901m)
**Lifts in area** 4: 3⬚ 1⬚
**Tour operators** Momentum, Ski All America, Ski Freshtracks, Ski Independence, Ski Safari, Ultimate Leisure

## Snowbird and Alta, Utah, US

See page 245

**Tour operators** (Snowbird only) Ski Independence, Skiworld, United Vacations; (both) Ski the American Dream

## Snowmass, Colorado, US

See *Aspen and Snowmass*, page 224

**Tour operators** see page 261

## Sölden, Austria

See page 38

**Tour operators** Made to Measure, Neilson, Neilson School Groups, Thomson

## Soldeu, Andorra

See *Soldeu–El Tarter–Canillo*, page 14

**Tour operators** Airtours, Club Pavilion, Crystal, First Choice, Inghams, Lagrange, Neilson, Panorama, Ski Freshtracks, Skiworld, Thomson

## Solitude Mountain Resort, Utah, US

Solitude is situated a 45-minute drive from Salt Lake City in the heart of Big Cottonwood Canyon in Utah's Wasatch National Forest. The underrated, ski-in ski-out resort is family-owned and full of charm. State-of-the-art machinery ensures that half the mountain is groomed on a rotating basis.

Seven lifts serve 1,200 acres of terrain. About 50 per cent of pistes are rated intermediate and the resort has a convenient hands-free lift pass. Beginners head for the Moonbeam II lift for easy runs such as Little Dollie and Pokey-Pine, while the mainly benign blues served by the Eagle Express quad provide plenty of cruising territory. The Moonbeam Ski and Snowboard Academy for Kids is part of Solitude Ski School and teaches four- to twelve-year-olds.

The Last Chance Mining Camp is a large and airy self-service on the piste, and the Creekside Restaurant is conveniently set at the base of the lifts and is open for lunch. In the evening, the seven restaurants include St Bernard's, which is the smartest venue; it also serves a first-rate breakfast. The only post-slope entertainment is found in the Thirsty Squirrel pub.

All accommodation (☎ 801 536 5707 for reservations) is of a high standard. There are comfortable ski-in, ski-out apartments in the Creekside Lodge and in the Powderhorn Lodge, as well as at the four-star Inn at Solitude, which contains the St Bernard's restaurant and a good spa. The Crossings townhouses are well equipped and each has its own hot-tub, fireplace, private deck and double garage. The Silver Fork Lodge (☎ 801 533 9977) in the Wasatch National Forest overlooks Solitude.

**Tel** 1 801 534 1400
**Email** info@skisolitude.com
**Website** www.skisolitude.com
**Ski area** top 10,035ft (3,059m) bottom 7,988ft (2,435m)
**Lifts in area** 8: 8⬚
**Tour operators** Ski the American Dream, Ski Independence

## Söll, Austria

See *Söll and the SkiWelt*, page 39

**Tour operators** Airtours, Crystal, First Choice, Inghams, Neilson, Neilson School Groups, Panorama, PGL, Ski Astons, Ski Hillwood, Thomson

## Squaw Valley, California, US

See page 248

**Tour operators** Made to Measure, Ski All America, Ski Independence, Ski the American Dream, United Vacations

## St Anton, Austria

See page 41

**Tour operators** Airtours, Alpine Answers, Alpine Tours, Crystal, Elegant Resorts, Erna Low, Esprit, First Choice, Flexiski, Inghams, Interhome, Lotus Supertravel, Mark Warner, Momentum, Neilson, Original Travel, Simply Ski, Ski Activity, Ski Equipe, Ski Expectations, Ski Solutions, Total Ski, Ski Val, Skiworld, Snowscape, Thomson, White Roc

## St Christoph, Austria

St Christoph is a small, attractive village directly linked into the **St Anton** ski area. It consists of little more than a cluster of restaurants and hotels, of which was the luxury Arlberg-Hospiz (☎ 5446 2611) is the most famous and comfortable. The hotel is on the site of the original hospice, built in 1386 as a refuge for pilgrims crossing the Arlberg Pass. St Christoph has five other hotels as well as the Bundes Ski Academy, where future ski and snowboard instructors go to train. The resort is a quiet alternative to bustling St Anton. Nightlife is limited but 'the wine list in the Hospiz – especially the vintage clarets – is world class'.

**Tel** 43 5446 22690
**Email** st.anton@netway.at
**Website** www.stantonamarlberg.com
**Ski area** top 2,811m (9,222ft) bottom 1,800m (5,90 6ft)
**Lifts in area** 83 on Arlberg Ski Pass: 7🚡 3🚡 36🚡 37🚡
**Tour operators** Elegant Resorts, Flexiski, Inghams, Made to Measure, Momentum, Powder Byrne, Scott Dunn Ski, Seasons in Style

## St-Gervais, France

As a spa resort, St-Gervais has attracted tourists since 1806 and today is popular with families wanting a cheaper alternative to **Megève**. Spa treatments are available in the hot springs. Nearby Le Bettex at 1,400m is a quieter village with a few comfortable hotels and some cross-country skiing.

The main ski area of St-Gervais has 79 lifts on the slopes of Mont d'Arbois, and is linked with that of Megève. It has a terrain park with a half-pipe and is accessed by a fast, 20-person gondola from the edge of the resort to Le Bettex. The second stage goes up to St-Gervais 1850. This is a popular and often-crowded entrance to Megève's pistes. Skiing on the Mont Blanc side of St-Gervais is served by the Tramway, a mountain railway that climbs slowly to the Col de Voza at 1,653m, where it links to the skiing above **Les Houches**. Hotel-Restaurant Igloo and the Terminus in Le Fayet area have good reputations for their cuisine.

St-Gervais has three nursery-slope lifts and two kindergartens. The ESF at St-Gervais and St Nicholas, and the ESI at Le Bettex, all offer standard lessons, as well as cross-country, slalom and telemark. The two local mountain-guiding companies are Compagnie des Guides de St-Gervais and Guides des Cimes, and both can organise heli-skiing.

Hotels include three-star Le Carlina (☎ 450 93 41 10), with an indoor pool, Chalet l'Igloo (☎ 450 93 05 84) and the quiet Arbois Bettex (☎ 450 93 12 22): all at the edge of the piste. A reporter recommended the Regina (☎ 450 47 78 10), with its reasonable prices and friendly staff. La Flèche d'Or (☎ 450 93 11 54) is recommended. St-Gervais has a moderate range of restaurants, with 4 Epices and L'Eterle both good value. Le Four and Le Robinson serve a variety of local specialities, while La Tanière and La Chalette are traditional. La Nuit des Temps is the only disco and the town has a casino.

**Tel** 33 450 47 76 08
**Email** welcome@st-gervais.net
**Website** www.st-gervais.net
**Ski area** top 2,350m (7,708ft) bottom 860m (2,821ft)
**Lifts in area** 79 in Evasion Mont Blanc: 1🚡 9🚡 28🚡 41🚡
**Tour operators** APT Holidays, French Life, Interhome, Lagrange, Peak Retreats, Snowcoach

## St-Jean d'Arves, France

See *Le Corbier*, page 273

**Tour operators** AWWT, Crystal, Peak Retreats, Ski France, Thomson

## St Johann im Pongau, Austria

See *Salzburger Sportwelt Amadé*, page 303

**Tour operator** PGL

## St Johann in Tirol, Austria

St Johann in Tirol is a bustling town with a ski area of 60km. Its expansion from a pretty Tyrolean village to a sprawling, light-industrial town has done little for its charm. However, the centre, with its ornately frescoed buildings and old coaching inns, remains largely unspoilt, and the heavy traffic is confined to the outskirts.

The resort is particularly geared towards beginners, with six nursery-slope lifts scattered between the town and the hamlet of Eichenhof, which is served by ski bus. The rolling lower pastures are ideal novice terrain, with a choice of blue runs higher up to which beginners can progress after a few days. A modern, eight-seater gondola up the Harschbichl from Penzing on the edge of Oberndorf has greatly improved mountain access and added some considerably more challenging skiing to the area.

All three ski schools offer tuition, with Ski School St Johann rated as 'very well organised'. The resort has a terrain park with a 60-m half-pipe. Non-ski Miniclub St Johann cares for children from two to four years and the ski schools take children from three years. Almost every piste has a welcoming mountain hut at the top, bottom or part-way down. The cross-country skiing is extensive and covers 70km of prepared tracks.

The central feature of St Johann is the three-star Gasthof-Hotel Post (☎ 5352 2230), which dates from 1225 and is beautifully frescoed. Hotel Park (☎ 5352 2226), near the gondola, is also recommended, and we have favourable reports of Hotel Fischer (☎ 5352 62332) ('good food, helpful staff and comfortable rooms'). Erlebnishotel Kizbühlerhorn (☎ 5352 6940) near the base of the new Penzing gondola makes an alternative, tranquil base.

Popular bars include Bunny's ('very lively'), Max's ('a great place'), Humungus ('intimate atmosphere') and Café Rainer. The restaurant in the Gasthof Post is recommended, Lange Mauer is a Chinese restaurant, and Masianco serves Italian and Mexican food.

**Tel** 43 5352 633350
**Email** info@st.johanntirol.at
**Website** www.st.johanntirol.at
**Ski area** top 1,700m (5,576ft) bottom 670m (2,198ft)
**Lifts in area** 17: 3🚠 4🚡 10🎿
**Tour operators** Crystal, Snowscape, Thomson

## St-Lary, France

This resort, 80km from Lourdes, is a typically Pyrenean village of stone-built houses and one main, rather narrow street. The 100km of pisted skiing is suitable for beginners to intermediates, and it takes four minutes to walk from the village centre to the cable-car to St-Lary Pla d'Adet (1,700m), a small but dull, modern ski station with some accommodation. This is linked by road and by lift to an alternative base at St-Lary La Cabane (1,600m). The fourth base area of St-Lary Espiaube (1,600m) is also reached by road, or on skis from Soum de Matte. The 100-km ski area is mainly treeless and lacks variety. Two chair-lifts give rapid access to St-Lary 2400, and the extension of the ski area into the neighbouring Auron Valley and up the snow-sure glacier on Mont Pichaleye has greatly add to the resort's appeal. St-Lary has two terrain parks: one that ranks in the top five in France, and a second designed for kids. Three crèches care for non-skiing children.

Hotel Mercure Coralia (☎ 562 99 50 00), Hotel La Terrasse Fleurie (☎ 562 40 76 00) and Les Arches (☎ 562 49 10 10) are all recommended, while the Christiania (☎ 562 98 40 62) is new. At Espiaube, Hotel La Sapinière (☎ 562 98 44 04) provides reasonable accommodation. The resort boasts more than 30 restaurants and a range of shops.

**Tel** 33 562 39 50 81
**Email** st-lary@wanadoo.fr
**Website** www.saintlary.com
**Ski area** top 2,515m (8,251ft) bottom 830m (2,723ft)
**Lifts in area** 32: 2🚠 11🚡 19🎿
**Tour operators** French Life, HF Holidays

## St-Martin-de-Belleville, France

See *Val Thorens and the Belleville Valley*, page 113

**Tour operator** Thomson

## St Moritz, Switzerland

See page 212

**Tour operators** Club Med, Corporate Ski Company, Elegant Resorts, Flexiski, Inghams, Interhome, Kuoni, Momentum, Oak Hall, Powder Byrne, Seasons in Style, Ski Freshtracks, Ski Gower, Ski Solutions, Skiworld, Swiss Travel Centre, Swiss Travel Service

## St-Sorlin d'Arves, France

See *Le Corbier*, page 273

**Tour operators** AWWT, Crystal, Lagrange, Peak Retreats, Ski France, Thomson

## St Wolfgang, Austria

This resort at the heart of Austria's lake district acts as a pleasant accommodation base for people wishing to ski the gentle Postalm plateau, a spectacular 35-minute drive away. An additional 77km of skiing is available at Gosau, an hour's drive. St Wolfgang has its own nursery slope just outside the village.

**Tel** 43 6138 8003
**Email** info@wolfgangsee.at
**Website** www.stwolfgang.at
**Ski area** top 1,600m (4,763ft) bottom 550m (1,800ft)
**Lifts in area** 8 at Postalm: 8⬛. 41 with Gosau: 2⬛ 5⬛ 34⬛
**Tour operators** Crystal, Inghams, Thomson

## Steamboat, Colorado, US

See page 250

**Tour operators** AWWT, Crystal, Lotus Supertravel, Ski Activity, Ski All America, Ski the American Dream, Ski Independence, Ski Safari, Skiworld, United Vacations

## Stoneham, Québec, Canada

Stoneham is notable for having the most extensive night-skiing in Canada. Being situated just 20 minutes from Québec City and having 17 illuminated trails that open daily from 3pm to 10pm, it is enormously popular with local skiers on weekday evenings. With 32 trails spread over four mountains, and a vertical drop of 1,380ft, Stoneham is one of the three largest ski areas in the province. It boasts three terrain parks, including a super-pipe with 17-ft walls, and a 1km-long boardercross course. Kidz Island is a kindergarten for infants and offers skiing tuition for children from three to twelve years.

Set in the floor of a horseshoe-shaped valley – and as a result sheltered from the often harsh East Coast winds – the base area is small but, because of the visiting city folk, après-ski is lively. There are five restaurants located at the mountain base, including Feu Follet, which has French cuisine. Stoneham Hotel (☎ 418 848 2411) is the only lodging at the base.

**Tel** 1 418 848 2415
**Email** info@ski-stoneham.com
**Website** www.ski-stoneham.com
**Ski area** top 2,075ft (632m) bottom 695ft (211m)
**Lifts in area** 8: 5⬛ 3⬛
**Tour operators** Equity, Frontier Ski, Inghams, Ski the American Dream, Skibound

## Stowe, Vermont, US

See page 251

**Tour operators** Crystal, Inghams, Neilson School Groups, Ski Activity, Ski All America, Ski the American Dream, Ski Independence, Ski Safari, Trailfinders, United Vacations, Virgin Snow

## Stubaital, Austria

**Neustift** is the main community of the broad and lush Stubai Valley, a 15-minute drive from **Innsbruck**. Despite recent expansion it remains traditionally Tyrolean at heart, and is centred on a magnificent and ornately decorated church. Slightly farther away is **Fulpmes**, with its own good skiing, branded as Schlick 2000.

Neustift has a gentle ski area on wooded north-facing slopes and is also the main base for the Stubai Glacier, a 20-minute drive away at the end of the valley. Schlick 2000's skiing is in a sheltered bowl on the 2,230-m Sennjoch.

When all of the lifts are open, the Stubai Glacier is one of the most extensive summer ski areas in Europe. Twin gondolas take you up to the network of lifts. When snow is scarce elsewhere, the slopes can become unbelievably crowded; German bank holidays should be avoided. The glacier is usually closed in January and for a month in the summer. The Stubai Superskipass also covers a small area at Milders and assorted lifts in the valley. There is a kindergarten for children aged three years and over, based at the Stubai middle station.

Recommended hotels in Neustift include the Jagdhof (☎ 5226 2666) ('wonderful five-star with great atmosphere'), the Tirolerhof (☎ 5226 3278) ('excellent food and a warm welcome') and the Sporthotel Neustift (☎ 5226 2510). Nightlife is lively n the Romanastuben. Keen skiers and riders tay in the comfortable Alpenhotel Mutterberg (☎ 5226 8116) at the base of he Stubai lifts. The Gamsgarten restaurant ias a good choice of reasonably priced food.

In Fulpmes, the Alpenhotel Tirolerhof ☎ 5225 62422), Hotel Alte Post (☎ 5225 >2175) and Haus Sonnegg (☎ 5225 64062) ire all recommended. Restaurants include he Leonardo Da Vinci ('popular and good value') and the Gasthaus Hofer, which erves 'simple, plain Austrian farmhouse are'. The Café Corso, the Ossi-Keller, Platzwirt and Dorfalm discos are popular at ight.

el 43 5225 62235
mail info@stubai.at
Iebsite www.stubai.at
ki area Fulpmes top 2,200m (7,218ft) bottom 937m 3,074ft), Neustift top 3,200m (10,499ft) bottom 1,000m 3,281ft)
ifts in area 25: 5⬡ 11⬠ 9⬦
our operators Alpine Tours, Esprit, Made to Measure

## Stuben, Austria

This village was named after the warm parlour – or *Stube* – of a solitary house on he Arlberg Pass where pilgrims used to helter in the eighteenth century. Only 32 iouses have been added since then, and tuben has a mere 104 residents and 650 uest beds. The Hotel Post (☎ 5582 7610), ow a four-star, was where mail-coach rivers changed horses for the steep journey p the pass. With its small collection of five iotels and restaurants, Stuben is an ideal ase for the Arlberg. Stuben Ski School has pedigree that goes back to the beginning f Alpine skiing. It also teaches children rom five years of age.

el 43 5582 399
mail info@stuben.at
Iebsite www.stuben.com
ki area top 2,811m (9,222ft) bottom 1,407m (4,616ft)
ifts in area 82 on Arlberg Ski Pass: 10⬡ 38⬠ 34⬦
our operators none

## Sun Peaks, BC, Canada

ee page 58

our operators AWWT, Crystal, Frontier Ski, Made to easure, Ski Activity, Ski All America, Ski the American ream, Ski Freshtracks, Ski Independence, Ski Safari

## Sun Valley, Idaho, US

Sun Valley is America's oldest ski resort, and home to the world's first chair-lift. It has been a magnet for the Hollywood élite since it opened in 1936 amid a fanfare of publicity. Previously, Americans in search of organised skiing had had to travel by sea to Europe. The resort's site, near the dilapidated mining town of Ketchum, Idaho, was chosen for its terrain and its sunshine records.

Throughout its history, Sun Valley has tried with moderate success to remain competitive with newer destinations. Millions of dollars have been spent on detachable quad-chairs as well as one of the world's largest, automated snowmaking systems.

The 2,054-acre ski area is divided between Dollar/Elkhorn, the site of some of the original lifts, and the much more demanding slopes of Bald Mountain, which has earned a reputation as one of the best single ski mountains in the United States with its 3,400-ft vertical drop.

Ernest Hemingway, who lived in Ketchum but never skied here, is commemorated with his own trail. In the golden era of Sun Valley, you might easily have found yourself sharing a chair-lift with Gary Cooper, Marilyn Monroe, Bing Crosby or Judy Garland. They have gone forever, but you still have a chance of finding yourself riding a lift with Clint Eastwood or Arnold Schwarzenegger. The ski school is said to be 'well organised, with good tuition and flexibility'. Sun Valley Playschool caters for children aged six months to six years.

Elkhorn Resort and Sun Valley Lodge are recommended: 'very comfortable suites and rooms'. Bookings should be made through Sun Valley Central Reservations (☎ 800 634 3347).

The upmarket clientèle has encouraged the establishment of some excellent restaurants, on and off the mountain. Day-lodges at Warm Springs, River Run and Seattle Ridge are 'luxurious and magnificent'. The restrooms are 'scrupulously clean with marble surfaces, infrared controls and – in one place – a grandfather clock'. The Soupçon and the Evergreen Bistro offer gourmet dining, while the Pioneer Steakhouse – Clint Eastwood's favourite – is cheerful and much cheaper. Bald Mountain Pizza is 'excellent, with a good range of wines'.

**Tel** 1 208 726 3423
**Email** ski@sunvalley.com
**Website** www.sunvalley.com
**Lifts in area** 18: 18⑤
**Ski area** top 9,150ft (2,789m) bottom 5,750ft (1,753m)
**Tour operators** AWWT, Ski Activity, Ski All America, Ski Independence, Skiworld

## Sundance, Utah, US

This traditional little Utah resort, created by Robert Redford, has old boardwalks and an atmosphere of a bygone age. It is a 55-minute drive from Salt Lake City, or a 40-minute scenic drive through the Heber Valley from **Park City Resorts**. Lift queues are a rarity here, yet Sundance offers a variety of terrain ranging from wide open trails to bowl skiing.

Sundance's skiing is recommended for families, and lift pass prices are reduced for children up to 12 years. At the Artisans Center, children can join arts and crafts clubs, and 24-hour babysitting can be arranged through the resort. Sundance Ski & Snowboard School offers tuition to adults and to children from four years.

The two restaurants, the Tree Room and the Foundry Grill, serve regional dishes and are open for lunch and dinner. The Tree Room is named after the tree growing through its centre and is decorated with Native American art along with Robert Redford's personal collection of Western memorabilia. The Owl Bar was once frequented by Butch Cassidy's Hole-In-The-Wall Gang in its original location in Wyoming, before being transported to Sundance. Resort accommodation is in the rustic yet elegant Sundance Cottages (☎ 801 225 4107), which are decorated with colourful Navajo rugs and handmade furniture.

**Tel** 1 801 225 4107
**Email** info@sundanceresort.com
**Website** www.sundanceresort.com
**Ski area** top 8,250ft (2,515m) bottom 6,100ft (1,859m)
**Lifts in area** 4: 3⑤ 1⑨
**Tour operators** , Ski the American Dream, Ski Independence, Ski Safari

## Sunday River, Maine, US

Sunday River, six miles north of Bethel in Maine, is one of the largest East Coast resorts. The picturesque state suffers at times from sparse natural snow, but given low temperatures this is of little consequence thanks to an arsenal of custom-built cannon that can cover up to 92 per cent of the total terrain.

The range and quality of the skiing compares favourably with that of a medium-sized resort in Italy or France. Fortunately, Sunday River is situated in a rural area sufficiently far from New York not to suffer from the overcrowding to which the Vermont resorts are prone.

Sunday River is flanked at one end by the Grand Summit Hotel (☎ 207 824 3500) and at the other by the Jordan Grand Resort (☎ 207 824 5000) ('large, clean room, excellent staff and very efficient service'). In between lies the main base area beneath a ridge of eight peaks offering a variety of terrain, ranging from beginner trails to Chutzpah, one of the ten most extreme trails in eastern US.

The Perfect Turn Ski and Snowboard School offers a wide range of instruction: 'excellent tuition and so well organised'. Tiny Turns Childcare intersperses play with private ski lessons until your child is ready for group ski school.

The resort is rider-friendly, with facilities including four terrain parks, a separate mini-pipe for beginners and a super-pipe. Floodlit tubing at the White Cap Fun Centre is a popular evening activity.

Restaurants include Legends in the Grand Summit Hotel ('at best mediocre, and certainly not cheap') and Rosetto's (average quality, fairly cheap'). The small town of Bethel is the quintessential Maine community, with better restaurants and a plethora of craft shops. Nightlife is muted.

**Tel** 1 207 824 3000
**Email** info@sundayriver.com
**Website** www.sundayriver.com
**Ski area** top 3,140ft (957m) bottom 800ft (244m)
**Lifts in area** 18: 15⑤ 3⑨
**Tour operators** Crystal, Equity Ski, Ski the American Dream, Ski Independence, Ski Safari, Skibound, Thomson, Virgin Snow

## Sunshine Village, Alberta, Canada

See *Banff–Lake Louise*, page 47

## La Tania, France

See page 106

**Tour operators** Airtours, Alpine Action, Chalet World, Club Pavilion, Crystal, Erna Low, First Choice, French Freedom, French Life, Lagrange, Leisure Direction, Le Ski, Neilson, Silver Ski, Ski Activity, Ski Amis, Ski Beat, Ski France, Ski Independence, Ski Supreme, Ski Weekends & Board Breaks, Snowline, Thomson, Wasteland

## Taos, New Mexico, US

See page 252

**Tour operators** AWWT, Ski the American Dream, Ski Independence, Skiworld

## Telluride, Colorado, US

See page 253

**Tour operators** AWWT, Crystal, Ski All America, Ski the American Dream, Ski Independence, United Vacations

## Termas de Chillán, Chile

This is South America's most exotically located resort, set against a backdrop of smoking volcanoes and bubbling sulphur springs 480km south of Santiago and 80km east of Chillán. The 28 groomed runs are spread across 10,118 hectares of unusually varied terrain. A vertical drop of 1,100m is possible for those prepared to hike above the lifts. The excellent off-piste includes the 14-km Shangri-La run, with its volcanic scenery, and Pirigallo – one of the resort's most celebrated itineraries, which comes complete with fumaroles belching sulphur fumes.

Termas de Chillán is popular with snowboarders, who are attracted by the long vertical drop. The resort also contains Chile's first terrain park and half-pipe. The Gran Hotel (☎ 233 1313) has expensive ski-in, ski-out accommodation and a magnificent indoor and outdoor hot-water pool fed by pipes directly from the volcano. The villages of Las Trancas and Los Lleunques, both within a 30-minute drive,

have more reasonably priced accommodation.

**Tel** 562 233 1313
**Email** msaez@termaschillan.cl
**Website** www.andesweb.com
**Ski area** top 2,500m (8,200ft) bottom 1,800m (5,900ft)
**Lifts in area** 9: 4⬚ 5⬚
**Tour operators** Andes, Exsus, Momentum, Scott Dunn Latin America, Ski Safari

## Thredbo, Australia

See page 17

**Tour operators** none

## La Thuile, Italy

See page 140

**Tour operators** Crystal, First Choice, Inghams, Interski, Momentum, Neilson, Thomson

## Tignes, France

See page 107

**Tour operators** Airtours, Alpine Elements, Chalet World, Club Med, Crystal, Erna Low, Esprit, First Choice, French Life, Inghams, Interhome, Lagrange, Leisure Direction, Mark Warner, Momentum, Neilson, On The Piste, Seasons in Style, Ski Activity, Ski Amis, Ski Expectations, Ski Freshtracks, Ski Olympic, Ski Solutions, Ski Supreme, Ski Val, Skitopia, Skiworld, Thomson, Total Ski, Wasteland

## Torgon, Switzerland

Torgon is perched above the Rhône close to Lac Lèman on the outer edge of the **Portes du Soleil**. Although it is in Switzerland, it is linked in one direction with **La Chapelle d'Abondance** and in the other with **Châtel**, both of which are in France. The distinctive and none-too-pleasing A-frame architecture contains comfortable apartments (☎ 24 481 2414). There is little else to do here but ski. The Jardin des Neiges kindergarten takes children from three years of age.

**Tel** 41 24 481 3131
**Email** tourisme@torgon.ch
**Website** www.torgon.ch
**Ski area** top 2,350m (7,708ft) bottom 1,100m (3,608ft)
**Number of lifts** 207 in Portes du Soleil: 14⬚ 82⬚ 111⬚
**Tour operator** Interhome

## Treble Cone, New Zealand

See *Wanaka (Cardona and Treble Cone)*, page 320

## Tremblant, Québec, Canada

See page 59

**Tour operators** Carrier, Crystal, Elegant Resorts, Equity, Erna Low, Frontier Ski, Inghams, Neilson, Neilson School Groups, Ski the American Dream, Ski Independence, Ski Safari, Ski All America, Skibound, Skiworld, Thomson, Trailfinders, United Vacations, Virgin Snow

## The Trois Vallées, France

See *Brides-les-Bains*, page 265; *Courchevel*, page 78; *Les Menuires*, page 291; *Méribel*, page 91; *St-Martin-de-Belleville*, page 311; *La Tania*, page 106; *Val Thorens and the Belleville Valley*, page 113

## Trysil, Norway

Norway's largest ski area is situated a two-and-a-half-hour drive from Oslo. Trysil is reputed to have the most reliable snow cover anywhere in Norway. Its 65km of piste are spread across the wooded slopes of Trysilfjellet, with a 685-m vertical drop. The resort features an impressive terrain park with a half-pipe, rails, jumps and boxes, as well as three separate children's ski areas. The 100km of cross-country trails (3km are floodlit for night-skiing) wind through the woods on the lower half of the mountain.

Accommodation is in hotels and 'brilliant cabins and apartments' for self-caterers, including the Trysilfjell Aparthotel (☎ 624 52350), which is right on the slopes. The old village of Trysil, 2km away from the slopes, is where the Norlandia Trysil Hotel (☎ 624 50833) and Trysil-Knut (☎ 624 48000) are based, both of which are highly recommended. The area has a dozen restaurants and a range of après-ski venues, including Stallen on the mountain at Knettsetra, and Skipub'n, Laaven, Heiskroken and Sindrestua at the Trysil Tourist Centre.

**Tel** 47 624 51000
**Email** info@trysil.com
**Website** www.trysil.com

**Ski area** top 1,132m (3,714ft) bottom 600m (1,969ft)
**Lifts in area** 25: 5⑤ 20⑨
**Tour operator** Neilson

## Turoa, New Zealand

See *Mt Ruapehu*, page 141

**Tour operators** none

## Tux im Zillertal, Austria

Tux im Zillertal is the marketing name for five villages in the Tuxer valley, the main one of which is **Hintertux**. It boasts the steepest glacier skiing in Austria and, snow permitting, is open 365 days a year (20km of the piste is open all summer). It also offers the most advanced skiing and snowboarding on the otherwise strictly low-altitude Zillertal Superskipass.

The glacier is prone to overcrowding in winter when conditions are poor elsewhere, but hotel residents receive priority in the lift queue. Mountain access is by a four-person gondola, and a double chair-lift takes you up to the foot of the glacier at Sommerbergalm. The two-stage Gletscherbus Funitel gondola carries skiers and snowboarders in sit-down comfort to the top of the glacier at 3,250m.

Nowhere on the glacier is the skiing overly challenging, with most runs groomed and free of bumps. However, the pistes are considered to be the best year-round downhill training ground in Europe, and national teams spend much of their summer here.

The Tuxer Valley winds steeply north-east for 17km to **Mayrhofen**, requiring a 45-minute (free) skiers' shuttle transfer to Mayrhofen from Hintertux. Buses run every 15 minutes during the morning peak hours and hourly until 2am.

The handful of modern, four-star hotels in Hintertux includes Hotel Bergfried (☎ 5287 87239), which has a swimming-pool.

**Tel** 43 5287 8506
**Email** info@tux.at
**Website** www.tux.at
**Ski area** top 3,250m (10,663ft) bottom 1,500m (4,920ft)
**Lifts in area** 21 on Hintertux Glacier: 5⑥ 10⑤ 6⑨
**Tour operators** none

# Vail, Colorado, US

See page 254

**Tour operators** AWWT, Carrier, Crystal, Elegant Resorts, Erna Low, Inghams, Lotus Supertravel, Made to Measure, Momentum, Neilson, Rocky Mountain Adventures, Ski Activity, Ski the American Dream, Ski Freshtracks, Ski Independence, Ski Safari, Ski Solutions, Ski All America, Skiworld, Thomson, Trailfinders, United Vacations, Virgin Snow

# Val Cenis, France

The old unspoilt villages of Lanslebourg and Lanslevillard in the Haute Maurienne join together to form the resort of Val Cenis. The villages have a selection of restaurants, bars and shops that offer a traditional community ambience. The skiing on 80km of piste is for all standards, particularly beginners to intermediates. The eight two-star hotels include La Vieille Poste (☎ 479 05 93 47) and Le Val Cenis (☎ 479 05 80 31).

**Tel** 33 479 05 23 66
**Email** info@valcenis.com
**Website** www.valcenis.com
**Ski area** top 2,800m (9,186ft) bottom 1,400m (4,593ft)
**Lifts in area** 22: 1⊙ 11⊡ 10⊗
**Tour operators** AWWT, Erna Low, Lagrange, Leisure Direction, MGS Ski, On The Piste, Peak Retreats, Snowcoach

# Val di Fassa, Italy

See *Canazei and the Val di Fassa*, page 266

# Val di Fiemme, Italy

See *Cavalese*, page 268
**Tour operators** Momentum, Ramblers

# Valfréjus, France

The modern resort of Valfréjus was built around the old wood-and-stone hamlet of Charmaix above the town of Modane. Valfréjus boasts a ski area of more than 52km of piste and 12 lifts, as well as a cross-country trail. Hotel Club MMV Le Valfréjus (☎ 492 12 62 12) is a Savoyard-style three-star in the heart of the village, while Le Grand Vallon (☎ 479 05 08 07) is a two-star with superb views of the resort.

**Tel** 33 479 05 33 83
**Email** info@valfréjus.com
**Website** www.valfrejus.com

**Ski area** top 2,737m (8,980ft) bottom 1,550m (5,085ft)
**Lifts in area** 12: 2⊙ 4⊡ 6⊗
**Tour operators** AWWT, French Life, Lagrange, On The Piste, Peak Retreats

# Val d'Isère, France

See page 110

**Tour operators** Airtours, Alpine Answers, Alpine Weekends, Chalet World, Club Med, Crystal, Descent International, Elegant Resorts, Erna Low, Finlays, First Choice, French Freedom, French Life, Inghams, Interhome, Lagrange, Le Ski, Leisure Direction, Lotus Supertravel, Mark Warner, Momentum, Mountain Leap, Neilson, On The Piste, Oxford Ski Company, Scott Dunn Ski, Seasons in Style, Silver Ski, Simply Ski, Ski Activity, Ski Amis, Ski Beat, Ski Expectations, Ski France, Ski Freshtracks, Ski Independence, Ski Solutions, Ski Supreme, Ski Val, Ski Weekend, Skibound, Skiworld, Snowline, Thomson, Total Ski, VIP, Wasteland, White Roc, YSE

# Val Thorens, France

See *Val Thorens and the Belleville Valley*, page 113

**Tour operators** Airtours, Chalet World, Club Med, Crystal, Erna Low, First Choice, French Freedom, French Life, Inghams, Interhome, Lagrange, Leisure Direction, Neilson, On The Piste, Panorama, Ski Activity, Ski Amis, Ski Expectations, Ski France, Ski Freshtracks, Ski Independence, Ski Supreme, Skiworld, Thomson, Total Ski, Ultimate Leisure, Wasteland

# Valle Nevado, Chile

See page 65

**Tour operators** Andes, Crystal, Exsus, Momentum, Scott Dunn Latin America, Ski All America, Ski Safari, Skiworld

# Valloire, France

Valloire is an attractive, reasonably large village set in an isolated bowl above the Maurienne Valley. It is still very much a traditional French farming community. The 150km of skiing is divided between three areas – La Sétaz, Le Crey du Quart and Valmeinier – on adjacent mountains reached by two gondolas that start a few minutes' walk from the centre of the village.The skiing is not difficult and the slopes are rated 'fantastic for beginners and intermediates alike'. Les Aiglons Garderie cares for non-skiing children aged six months to six years from 9am to 5pm, it is closed on Saturday.

Accommodation includes Le Sétaz
(☎ 479 59 01 03), Grand Hotel de Valloire
et du Galibier (☎ 479 59 00 95) and a
range of apartments and chalets. There are
20 restaurants, a dozen bars and an ice-rink.

**Tel** 33 479 59 03 96
**Email** info@valloire.net
**Website** www.valloire.net
**Ski area** top 2,600m (8,528ft) bottom 1,430m (4,690ft)
**Lifts in area** 32: 2⊙ 16⊙ 14⊙
**Tour operators** AWWT, Crystal, Erna Low, French Life,
Leisure Direction, Peak Retreats, Ski France, Ski
Independence, Skibound, Snowcoach, Thomson

## Valmorel, France

See page 116

**Tour operators** Airtours, Crystal, Erna Low, French Life,
Lagrange, Leisure Direction, Made to Measure, Neilson,
Neilson School Groups, Ski Independence, Ski Supreme,
Thomson

## Vars 1850, France

Vars 1850, with its 18,000 beds, is larger,
less attractive and also less welcoming to
the British than neighbouring **Risoul 1850**.
The old village is linked by drag-lift to the
modern station, but you have to hike across
town to access the Vars gondola and high-
speed chair to Risoul 1850. The skiing is
said to offer 'plenty of wide, open cruising
blues for timid intermediates'. The local
ESF was criticised as having 'few English-
speaking instructors'. The baby club takes
children from six months, and the ski
school accepts children from four years.
'There is very little in the way of après-ski',
said one reporter.

**Tel** 33 492 46 51 31
**Email** vars.ot@pacwan.fr
**Website** www.vars-ski.com
**Ski area** top 2,750m (9,020ft) bottom 1,850m (6,068ft)
**Lifts in area** 57 with Risoul: 1⊙ 13⊙ 43⊙
**Tour operators** Interhome, Lagrange, On The Piste,
Tops Travel

## Vaujany, France

See page 117

**Tour operators** AWWT, Erna Low, Lagrange, Leisure
Direction, On The Piste, Peak Retreats, Ski Independence,
Ski Peak

## Vent, Austria

Vent is a small resort with just 15km of piste
and a total of 900 beds. However, what it
does have is some good off-piste skiing. The
resort has one ski and snowboard school for
adults and children, called Serafin Kleon,
and a mountain guiding company. Small
non-skiers are cared for either at Kinderland
or in the kindergarten in the Familyhotel
Vent (☎ 5254 8102). The resort has seven
hotels and the same number of restaurants,
a bar and a disco. There is a magic carpet
lift. A free bus takes skiers to **Sölden** and
**Obergurgl–Hochgurgl**.

**Tel** 43 5254 8193
**Email** info@vent.at
**Website** www.vent.at
**Ski area** top 2,680m (8,793ft) bottom 1,900m (6,234ft)
**Lifts in resort** 4: 1⊙ 3⊙
**Tour operators** French Life, Neilson School Groups

## Verbier, Switzerland

See page 215

**Tour operators** Alpine Answers, Alpine Weekends,
Corporate Ski Company, Crystal, Descent International,
Erna Low, First Choice, Flexiski, Inghams, Interhome, Lotus
Supertravel, Momentum, Mountain Leap, Original Travel,
Oxford Ski Company, Peak Ski, Simply Ski, Ski Activity,
Ski Expectations, Ski Freshtracks, Ski Independence,
Ski Solutions,, Ski Verbier, Skiworld, Swiss Travel Service,
Thomson, Total Ski, White Roc

## Veysonnaz, Switzerland

This is a useful back door into the Four
Valleys, reached by a winding 13-km
mountain road from Sion. Old gondolas
take you up into the resort's own
considerable ski area of 400km of piste
from the little village and, more
conveniently, from a second base area 3km
away at Mayen-de-L'Ours. A bus service
connects the two. The red piste de L'Ours,
the main fall-line run, is a natural
racecourse that is regularly used by the
Swiss national team. Thyon, an unexpected
piste-side community situated at the top of
the Mayen-de-L'Ours gondola, is little more
than a collection of apartment blocks and a
hotel. From here a series of blue runs take
you down to the sunny hamlet of Les
Collons, or alternatively a red run connects

with **Siviez** and **Verbier**. Hotel Magrappé
(☎ 27 207 1817) is 'warm, comfortable
and friendly'.

**Tel** 41 27 207 1053
**Email** tourism@veysonnaz.ch
**Website** www.veysonnaz.ch
**Ski area** top 3,330m (10,925ft) bottom 1,400m (4,593ft)
**Lifts in area** 94 in Four Valleys: 17⌖ 32⌖ 45⌖
**Tour operators** none

## Villard-de-Lans, France

The capital of the Vercors is a small,
typically French town near Grenoble that
offers some good skiing for beginners and
intermediates. The 139km of piste starts
from a separate ski centre, Côte 2000, 2km
by bus from the main village. Together with
the resort of Corrençon, the area offers
62km of piste as well as a terrain park and
two permanent slalom courses. Villard-de-
Lans is also a major cross-country centre.
The village has a wide choice of hotels and
apartments, including three-star hotels Le
Christiania (☎ 476 95 12 51) and Le
Dauphin (☎ 476 95 95 25), and two-star
Les Bruyères (☎ 476 95 11 83). It also
boasts 30 restaurants and numerous bars.

**Tel** 33 476 95 10 38
**Email** info@ot-villard-de-lans.fr
**Website** www.ot-villard-de-lans.fr
**Ski area** top 2,170m (7,119ft) bottom 1,160m (3,806ft)
**Lifts in area** 29: 2⌖ 7⌖ 20⌖
**Tour operators** AWWT, Lagrange

## Villard-Reculas, France

This rustic old village is linked into the **Alpe
d'Huez** ski area by a quad chair-lift. Much
has been done in recent years to renovate the
village, and there are now a number of
apartments, the Beaux Monts hotel (☎ 476
80 43 14) and some converted cowsheds and
barns. Sustenance is provided by one small
supermarket and a couple of bars and
restaurants, including the popular Bergerie. A
blue piste from the bottom of the Petit Prince
lift runs to the village, offering an alternative
blue route to the steeper red Souveraine. The
ESF has a branch in the village, and the Club
des Loupiots crèche accepts children for two
hours a day. The road to Allemont on the
valley floor is wide and easily accessible in
winter, but the one-track road to Huez is
normally closed during the season.

**Tel** 33 476 80 45 69
**Email** info@villard-reculas.com
**Website** www.villard-reculas.com
**Ski area** top 3,330m (10,922ft) bottom 1,500m (4,921ft)
**Lifts in area** 84: 15⌖ 25⌖ 44⌖
**Tour operators** none

## Villars, Switzerland

See page 218

**Tour operators** Club Med, Corporate Ski Company, Crystal,
Erna Low, Inghams, Interhome, Kuoni, Momentum, Ski
Independence, Ski Weekend, Skiworld, Swiss Travel Centre,
Swiss Travel Service, Thomson, Wasteland

## Voss, Norway

Despite its low altitude, Voss provides a
reasonable ski area for beginners and lower
intermediates. The 40km of prepared pistes
include three black runs, two of which are
reasonably challenging, and some off-piste.
Enthusiasts of cross-country skiing will
certainly not be disappointed with 60km of
prepared loipe close to the centre, although
more is available in the valleys around the
area. The resort's historic hotel is the
Fleischer (☎ 565 20500), which is wood-
built in traditional style.

**Tel** 47 565 20800
**Email** info@visitvoss.no
**Website** www.visitvoss.no
**Ski area** top 945m (3,100ft) bottom 91m (300ft)
**Lifts in area** 9: 1⌖ 4⌖ 4⌖
**Tour operators** Crystal, Inghams, Neilson School Groups,
Norvista

## Wagrain, Austria

See *Salzburger Sportwelt Amadé*, page 303
**Tour operator** PGL

## Waidring, Austria

This unspoilt village is less than 20km from
**St Johann in Tirol** and is situated in the
same snowpocket as **Fieberbrunn**. The
quiet resort is known for its family skiing,
with convenient nursery slopes in the village
centre. It boasts 25km of piste, with the
main skiing at Steinplatte, 4km from the
village and well suited to beginners and
intermediates. The area is served by a new

six-person chair-lift. We have favourable reports of the Waidring Ski School ('excellent tuition for both skiers and snowboarders').

The Stallenalm is the recommended mountain restaurant. Hotel Waidringerhof (☎ 5353 5228) has a swimming-pool and a pleasant dining-room, and the central Hotel Tiroler Adler (☎ 5353 5311) is also recommended. Zardini's is the most popular après-ski venue. Nightlife is relaxed and informal, and the Schniedermann Bar and the Alte Schmiede are both popular.

**Tel** 43 5353 5242
**Email** waidring@netway.at
**Website** www.tiscover.com/waidring
**Ski area** top 1,860m (6,102ft) bottom 780m (2,558ft)
**Lifts in area** 8: 1🚡 7🚠
**Tour operators** Thomson, Tyrolean Adventures

## Wanaka (Cardrona and Treble Cone), New Zealand

Wanaka is a less-vibrant alternative bed base to **Queenstown** from which to explore the main South Island skiing. From here, the ski areas of Cardrona and Treble Cone, as well as the Waiorau Nordic Ski Area and the Wanaka Snow Park (New Zealand's first whole-mountain terrain park) are all within a 30-minute drive. The road between Queenstown and Wanaka is sealed, making the other Southern Lakelands resorts of Coronet Peak and The Remarkables even more accessible.

**Cardrona** has a 30-km ski area serviced by three chair-lifts, a drag-lift and three magic carpet lifts. The ski area is known for its dry snow and reliable season, which runs from late June until early October, and over half the area is classed as intermediate. Cardrona has the country's largest terrain park and four half-pipes.

Wanaka is also the gateway to **Treble Cone**, one of the country's top resorts, which houses New Zealand's first six-seater chair. Advanced skiers and freeriders can hike for 20 minutes to the 2,100-m summit to enjoy some of the best off-piste in the area, and there is good heli-skiing nearby in the Harris Mountains. Treble Cone has exceptional views across picturesque Lake Wanaka and the Matukituki Valley, as well as Mount Aspiring. There are two half-pipes and a recently enlarged terrain park. Treble

Cone is regularly voted the best snowboarding area in Australasia.

**Tel** Cardrona 643 443 8651 / Treble Cone 643 443 7443
**Email** nigel@cardrona.com / kim.manunui@treblecone.co.nz
**Websites** www.cardrona.com / www.lakewanaka.co.nz / www.treblecone.co.nz
**Ski area** Cardrona top 2,060m (6,759ft) bottom 1,670m (5,479ft), Treble Cone top 1,860m (6,102ft) bottom 1,200m (3,936ft)
**Lifts in area** 9 in Cardona and Treble Cone: 5🚡 4🚠
**Tour operators** none

## Wengen, Switzerland

See page 219

**Tour operators** Club Med, Crystal, Inghams, Interhome, Kuoni, Momentum, Ski Expectations, Ski Freshtracks, Ski Gower, Ski Solutions, Skiworld, Swiss Travel Centre, Swiss Travel Service, Thomson

## Westendorf, Austria

Westendorf is part of the **SkiWelt** ski circuit in the Tyrol but is linked only by bus and not by lift into the main complex. It is more snow-sure than elsewhere in the SkiWelt, and skiing on the 45km of pistes goes up to a higher altitude and can certainly be more challenging. However, flat roads between lifts are an irritating feature. The gondola, which provides main mountain access, is a 1-km walk or free bus ride from town. The alternative is to take a chair to the top of the nursery slopes and ski to the gondola. A regular bus plies between **Brixen-im-Thale** and the resort.

Westendorf is one of the most attractive of all the SkiWelt villages and has a genuine Tyrolean atmosphere coupled with a vigour lacking in some of the others. Its substantial accommodation base is almost equal to Söll's, making for lively entertainment as well as a family atmosphere. 'The après-ski atmosphere fantastic, although limited amount of bars for the young, free and single', commented a reporter. Gerry's Inn, the Post, Wunderbar and the Mosquito Bar are all recommended. Four-star Hotel Jakobwirt (☎ 5334 6245) is praised for its 'friendly staff, good food, good facilities and a central location'. The other four-stars are the Glockenstuhl (☎ 5334 6175) and the Schermer (☎ 5334 6268). Hotel Post (☎ 5334 6202) is recommended as a family hotel and described as 'well located, the staff were friendly'.

**Tel** 43 5334 6230
**Email** info@westendorf.com
**Website** www.westendorf.com
**Ski area** top 1,892m (6,207ft) bottom 789m (2,589ft)
**Lifts in area** 14: 2⬡ 7⬡ 5⬡
**Tour operators** Inghams, Interhome, Thomson

## Whakapapa, New Zealand

See *Mt Ruapehu*, page 141

**Tour operators** none

## Whistler, BC, Canada

See page 61

**Tour operators** AWWT, Carrier, Crystal, Elegant Resorts, Erna Low, First Choice, Frontier Ski, Inghams, Lotus Supertravel, Momentum, Neilson, Rocky Mountain Adventures, Seasons in Style, Ski Activity, Ski All America, Ski the American Dream, Ski Freshtracks, Ski Hillwood, Ski Independence, Ski Miquel, Ski Safari, Ski Solutions, Skiworld, Solo's, Thomson, Total Ski, Trailfinders, United Vacations, Virgin Snow

## Whitewater, BC, Canada

Whitewater is a delightful little ski area close to the attractive and laid-back Victorian town of Nelson. Its two lifts give direct access to an extraordinary large amount of challenging gladed trails as well as some spectacular – but avalanche-prone – off-piste that includes Powder Keg Bowl and Catch Basin. Some 20 per cent of the terrain is given over to easy runs, while the remainder is divided equally between intermediate and advanced skiing. Whitewater Snow School offers the full range of instruction ('really friendly people'). Whitewater Toddler cares for children aged eighteen months to six years. Mike's Pub at the base lodge is renowned for the quality of its food.

Reporters comment that Whitewater is not worth more than a couple of enjoyable days unless powder conditions exist, but the real attraction is Nelson. The lakeside town, close to the border with Montana, has become a haven for lotus-eaters who have tired of city life ('Haight-Ashbury of the twenty-first century, but without the hassle'). Inn the Garden (☎ 250 352 3226)

is a recommended B&B hotel in the centre of Nelson ('lots of character and friendly owners'). All Season's Café is one of the varied choice of eateries in town.

**Tel** 1 250 354 4944
**Email** info@skiwhitewater.com
**Websites** www.skiwhitewater.com / www.nelsonbc.ca
**Ski area** top 6,700ft (2,042m) bottom 5,400ft (1,646m)
**Lifts in area** 3: 2⬡ 1⬡
**Tour operator** Ski Safari

## Wildschönau, Austria

See page 44

**Tour operators** Airtours, First Choice, Interhome, Neilson, Neilson School Groups, Panorama, PGL, Thomson

## Winter Park, Colorado, US

See page 257

**Tour operators** AWWT, Crystal, Equity, Lotus Supertravel, Made to Measure, Neilson, Neilson School Groups, Ski the American Dream, Ski Independence, Ski Safari, Ski Activity, Ski All America, Skiworld, Thomson, United Vacations, Virgin Snow

## Yabuli, China

Yabuli is China's premier resort. Situated 194km north-west of the city of Harbin, the resort is open to skiers for 120 days a year and is trying double its present 45km of ski terrain. The longest run is a respectable 5km, with a vertical drop of 600m. Yabuli is also the location for a separate, private ski area used until now for competitions and by army skiers. The main hotel is the four-star Windmill Villa (☎ 451 345 5168), which has a swimming-pool and restaurant, and is within walking distance of the slopes.

**Tel** 86 451 345 5088
**Email** info@yabuliskiresort.com
**Website** www.yabuliskiresort.com
**Ski area** top 1,944m (6,378ft) bottom 1,374m (4,508ft)
**Lifts in area** 9: 9⬡
**Tour operators** none

## Zao, Japan

Zao, in the Yamagata Prefecture, retains its spa-town charm in spite of its size – being one of the biggest resorts in Japan, with 186 hectares of terrain on Mount Jizo. Zao is situated two-and-a-half hours from Tokyo by *shinkansen* (bullet train), and its slopes (accessed by a rather ancient cable-car) are famous throughout the country because of a huge forest of 'snow-ghosts' – fir trees that, during icy blasts of maritime winds, become encrusted with hoar frost and snow to form vast cohorts of weird monster shapes. To add to the surreal nature of the resort, 50 metres above the top of the cable-car is a gigantic statue of Zao Zizo, a *jizo-bosatsu* (guardian-deity), which is said to protect the peak. Some 90 per cent of this impressively large ski area is best suited to beginners and intermediates. Apart from one steep run that would merit a double-black-diamond rating in the United States, the resort holds little appeal for advanced skiers. However, reporters agreed that the volume of skiing and the nearby Zao Onsen hot springs made up for this.

Accommodation is mainly in traditional *ryokan* inns, which include the recommended Zao Onsen Eko (☎ 23 694 9533).

**Tel** 020-7734 6870 in UK
**Email** info@jnto.co.uk
**Websites** www.zao-spa.or.jp / www.snowjapan.com
**Ski area** top 1,736m (5,696ft) bottom 780m (2,599ft)
**Lifts in area** 42: 1⌷⍝ 36⌷⍝ 5⌷⍝
**Tour operators** none

## Zauchensee, Austria

See *Salzburger Sportwelt Amadé*, page 303
**Tour operators** Ski Hillwood, Sloping Off

## Zell am See, Austria

See *Zell am See and Kaprun*, page 45

**Tour operators** Airtours, Club Europe, Crystal, First Choice, Inghams, Interhome, Neilson, Neilson School Groups, PGL, Ski Astons, Skibound, Skiworld, Thomson

## Zell am Ziller, Austria

After Mayrhofen, Zell am Ziller is the second most substantial valley resort in the Zillertal area. The name should not be confused with Kaprun's twin resort near Salzburg, Zell am See. In fact, Zell am Ziller is the antithesis of a ski resort. Sitting in the Ziller river valley at 1,250m, it is a bustling, commercialised market town. Neither of Zell's own two areas, Kreuzjoch or Gerlosstein, is within walking distance of the town. Kreuzjoch's centrepiece is a swift, eight-person gondola, and Gerlosstein has twin cable-cars – testimony to the crowds that flock in from Germany each weekend. The four-star Sport und Wellnesshotel Theresa (☎ 5282 22860) and the three-star Hotel Englhof (☎ 5282 3134) are warmly praised.

**Tel** 43 5282 22810
**Email** info@zell.at
**Website** www.zell.at
**Ski area** top 2,505m (8,219ft), bottom 1,250m (4,101ft)
**Lifts in area** 55: 4⌷⍝ 28⌷⍝ 23⌷⍝
**Tour operators** PGL, Sloping Off

## Zermatt, Switzerland

See page 221

**Tour operators** Alpine Answers, Corporate Ski Company, Crystal, Elegant Resorts, Erna Low, Inghams, Interhome, Kuoni, Lotus Supertravel, Momentum, Oak Hall, Powder Byrne, Scott Dunn Ski, Seasons in Style, Simply Ski, Ski Expectations, Ski Freshtracks, Ski Independence, Skiworld, Swiss Travel Centre, Swiss Travel Service, Total Ski, Thomson, White Roc

## Zürs, Austria

See *Lech and Zürs*, page 26

**Tour operators** Corporate Ski Company, Crystal, Elegant Resorts, Inghams, Made to Measure, Momentum, Powder Byrne, Seasons in Style, Ski Solutions

# Safety on the slopes

Prevention of injury should always be a primary consideration when skiing or boarding, and it is crucial to be aware of your surroundings at all times. Mountain weather can change at a moment's notice and varies dramatically at different altitudes. Always dress with this in mind and be prepared for all conditions. Several layers of clothing are best, and it is always better to be too hot than too cold. More heat escapes through the head than any other part of the body, so you should never set off without a hat, nor without sunglasses or goggles.

## Frostbite and hypothermia

Exposure to bad weather can result in frostbite or hypothermia. Frostbite is the excessive cooling of small areas of the body – usually the fingers, toes, nose, cheeks or ears. The affected tissue turns white and numb. This is called first-degree frostbite and can be dealt with by immediate, gentle rewarming. Do not vigorously rub the affected areas, expose them to extreme heat or bathe them in hot water. In cold conditions, watch out for signs of frostbite in your companions.

Hypothermia results from a sharp drop in the body's temperature. It is difficult to diagnose, but some of the more obvious symptoms are physical or mental lethargy, sluggishness, slurring of speech, bouts of shivering and abnormal vision.

## Child safety

All children should wear safety helmets when skiing, preferably with chin guards. Helmets can be worn on their own, or over a thin balaclava or hat on extremely cold days. Unfortunately, except in a few Scandinavian resorts, helmets are not yet compulsory on the piste. A steadily increasing number of adults now wear helmets for recreational skiing and snowboarding, and we applaud this trend.

Never ski with a baby or small child in a backpack – anyone, however competent, can catch an edge and fall, and it is always possible that someone could crash into you.

## Rules of the slopes

The FIS (International Ski Federation) has established rules of conduct for skiers and snowboarders. The following is a summary.

- **Respect** Do not endanger others.
- **Control** Adapt the manner and speed of your skiing to your ability and to the general conditions on the mountain.
- **Choice of route** The skier or snowboarder in front of you has priority – leave enough space between you and him or her.
- **Overtaking** Leave plenty of space when overtaking a slower skier.
- **Entering and starting a run** Look up and down the mountain each time before starting on or entering a marked run.
- **Stopping** Only stop at the edge of a piste or where you can be seen easily by other skiers and snowboarders.
- **Climbing** When climbing up or down, always keep to the side of the piste.
- **Signs** Obey all signs and markers – they are there for your safety.
- **Assistance** In the case of an accident, provide help if you can and alert the rescue service.
- **Identification** All those involved in an accident, including witnesses, should exchange names and addresses.

All the above rules are legally binding and apply to skiers and snowboarders. You could be in serious trouble if you are to blame for an accident while in breach of these rules.

## Off-piste

Outside the marked pistes and itineraries are areas that are NOT protected from mountain dangers. Only venture off-piste with a fully qualified guide from the local Bureau des Guides or ski school. This rule applies particularly to glacial terrain, where the risk of crevasses is added to that of avalanches.

Listen to your guide; learn basic snowcraft and how to read a slope. It is important to remember, however, that guides can be fallible and that you alone must take responsibility for decisions concerning your safety.

## Avalanche danger

Signs and flags around the ski area should warn you when avalanche danger is present, but do not rely on these alone. Take local professional advice. Even when there is no warning of avalanches, there could be localised snow slides.

Both the unified European and the North American avalanche risk scales are numbered 1 to 5 and colour-coded, with 5 the most dangerous level.

In the event of an avalanche, try to ski to the side. If you fall, try to get rid of your skis, poles and backpack. The chances of survival after an avalanche deteriorate rapidly after the first five minutes beneath the surface of the snow. Make swimming motions with your arms and legs and fight to stay on the surface. Intensify your efforts as the avalanche slows and try to keep your nose and mouth free of snow.

## Accident procedure

Speed is essential when an accident has occurred. Stay calm and follow these guidelines.

- **Secure the accident area** Protect the casualty by planting crossed skis in the snow a little way above the accident. If necessary, post someone above the accident site to give warning to other skiers.
- **First aid** Assess the general condition of the casualty. Check for pulse.
- **Airway** Make sure nothing is obstructing the mouth or throat.
- **Breathing** If the casualty is not breathing, administer artificial respiration (mouth-to-mouth resuscitation). If the casualty is breathing but unconscious, turn him or her on to the side to minimise the risk of choking.
- **Limbs** Protect any fractured limb from movement. Do not remove the ski boot if there is injury to the lower leg as it will act as a splint.
- **Circulation** Bind any wound using a clean handkerchief or scarf and **keep the casualty warm**. Give nothing to eat or drink, especially not alcohol. If the casualty appears to be in shock, he or she should be encouraged to lie with the head lower than the feet.
- **Alert the rescue service** Contact the ski patroller, ski teacher or lift attendant. Give the place of accident (piste name and nearest piste-marker), the number of people injured and the types of injury.
- **Establish the facts of the accident** Take the names and addresses of the people involved and of witnesses. Note the place, time and circumstances of the accident, the terrain, snow conditions, visibility, markings and signs.
- **Report the accident to the police as soon as possible.**

# Winter sports insurance

Buying travel insurance is the boring part of planning any kind of holiday. Therefore it can be tempting to take the insurance offered as part of your ski holiday package. However, for both economy and peace of mind, you would be better off contacting a ski insurance specialist (see list on page 327). If you plan to ski more than once in a season or travel as a family or couple, an annual policy makes economic sense.

To avoid unpleasant and expensive surprises when you make a claim, you need to make sure that the limits imposed by the policy cover the activities you plan to indulge in and the value of your ski or snowboard equipment – whether your own or hired.

You should ensure that your policy covers:

- at least £1 million in medical expenses
- all mountain rescue expenses
- the cost of an air ambulance back to the UK
- at least £1 million (£2 million for a trip to North America) for your personal liability, in case you accidentally injure someone or damage property
- the reimbursement of costs involved in cancelling or cutting short your holiday
- the cost of pre-paid ski or snowboard lessons, lift passes and, if appropriate, hired equipment you are unable to use because of illness or injury
- the cost of travelling to another resort if lack of snow makes this necessary.

## Cover for you

It is not difficult to find a policy that will provide the essential levels of cover listed above, but it may take a little more time to find a policy that suits your personal circumstances. You need to be aware that insurers may refuse to pay out if you hurt yourself in any way other than while skiing recreationally on piste.

### Snowboarding

A handful of insurance companies do not provide cover for snowboarding. Several others demonstrate their ignorance of the subject by agreeing to cover boarders only if they do not venture away from marked runs.

### Racing

Ski-racing is normally excluded from standard policies, and many skiers will be surprised to learn that this exclusion is usually extended to children's end-of-week ski school competitions, as well as the permanent timed slalom courses that are common in resorts in Europe and North America.

### Off-piste

The off-piste question affects riders and skiers alike. Some insurers take the view that anyone wanting to go off-piste has a death wish, so will not pay out if you have an accident while skiing (or boarding) off-piste. Others cover off-piste only if you are accompanied by a mountain guide. This definition is so vague that it may or may not cover you if you go accompanied by a qualified ski instructor who does not have a separate mountain-guide qualification. Choose a policy that allows you to go off-piste without a guide – and check the insurer's definition of terms. However, no policy will cover you off-piste if the avalanche risk is above 3.

Heli-skiing may be covered as standard, but it is unlikely there will be automatic cover for ski-touring with skins (whether it involves climbing or not) unless you pay an extra premium.

## Other activities

Do not assume that it is only expert skiers and riders, taking greater risks, who need to worry about their insurance cover. The more cautious insurers will also refuse to pay a claim if you have an accident while taking part in popular après-ski activities such as tobogganing, ice-skating, parapente, dog-sledding or snowmobiling. Make sure that your policy covers you for any such extra-curricular activity you may want to try.

## Inactivity

Most insurers pay a fixed daily allowance of about £25 to £35 if lack of snow or severe weather conditions keep you off the slopes. However, what constitutes 'lack of snow' or 'piste closure' is very carefully defined. The insurer is unlikely to pay out if you can be transported to a neighbouring resort or if a token lift is kept open by a resort.

## Cover for equipment

Many people wrongly assume that if their skis are damaged or stolen, their insurer will pay to replace them as new. This will happen only if they are insured under your house contents policy, so, given the high cost of buying boots, skis and snowboards, we recommend this as essential. Most travel insurers take age and wear-and-tear into account when assessing a claim.

## Theft of equipment

Unless you are prepared to buy – and use – special ski locks, most insurers will not pay a claim if your skis are stolen while you are having lunch or stopping for a quick drink at a mountain restaurant – although they may be prepared to be more lenient if you can show that you took other precautions to prevent theft, such as leaving your skis in mixed pairs. It is best to look for one of the handful of insurers who will not penalise you for leaving your skis or board unlocked while on the slopes.

Leaving skis and boards unlocked and unattended *away* from the slopes is a different matter. You are very likely to have a claim refused if equipment is stolen because you failed to lock it away securely. This applies to leaving equipment locked to a car roof rack overnight.

## Replacement equipment

Although you are unlikely to recover the cost of buying new equipment if you are unfortunate enough to lose or damage it, most insurers *will* pay from £100 to £500 (depending on the insurer) towards the cost of hiring replacement kit. It is also likely that, within similar limits, your insurer will reimburse you for having to hire equipment if yours failed to arrive at the resort at the same time as you did.

## Insurance for rental equipment

Check what a policy will pay out if you lose or significantly damage hired skis or a board. If nothing else, it will help you to answer the vexed question of whether or not you should take the usually iniquitously expensive insurance that the hire shop will offer you.

# Ski insurance companies
The following organisations specialise in winter sports cover.

**American Express**
Tel (0800) 700737
Email insurance@AEXP.com
Website www.americanexpress.co.uk

**BIBA**
Tel 020-7623 9043
Email enquiries@biba.org.uk
Website www.biba.org.uk

**Columbus Direct**
Tel 020-7375 0011
Email administration@columbusdirect.com
Website www.columbusdirect.com

**Direct Travel Insurance**
Tel (01903) 812345
Email info@direct-travel.co.uk
Website www.direct-travel.co.uk

**Endsleigh Insurance Services**
Tel 020-7436 4451
Website www.endsleigh.co.uk

**Europ Assistance**
Tel (01444) 442211
Email customerservices@europ-assistance.co.uk
Website www.europ-assistance.co.uk

**Essential Travel Insurance**
Tel (0870) 343 0015
Email customerservices@essentialtravel.co.uk
Website www.essentialski.co.uk

**Fogg Travel Insurance**
Tel (01623) 631331
Email sales@fogginsure.co.uk
Website www.fogginsure.co.uk

**James Hampden**
Tel (0870) 243 0756
Email info@jameshampden.com
Website www.primary1.co.uk

**Kidski**
Tel (0870) 4106092
Email charles@kidski.co.uk
Website www.kidski.co.uk
*Nanny Goat Cover is a policy that pays for childcare or ski guides to look after children in the event of parent's accident or illness*

**Liverpool Victoria**
Tel (0800) 373905
Website www.liverpool-victoria.co.uk

**Medicover**
Tel (0870) 735 3600
Website www.medi-cover.co.uk

**Mondial Assistance**
Tel (0800) 777148
Email enquiries@mondial-assistance.co.uk
Website www.mondial-assistance.co.uk

**MPI**
Tel (01428) 664363
Email info@mpibrokers.com
Website www.mpibrokers.com

**MRL Insurance Direct**
Tel (0870) 876 7677
Email service@mrlgroup.co.uk
Website www.MRLinsurance.co.uk

**Options**
Tel (0870) 848 0870
Email options@inter-group.co.uk
Website www.optionsinsurance.co.uk

**Primary Direct**
Tel (0870) 444 3434
Email customersupport@primarydirect.co.uk
Website www.primarydirect.co.uk

**Ski Club of Great Britain**
Tel (0845) 458 0780
Email skiers@skiclub.co.uk
Website www.skiclub.co.uk

**Snowcard Insurance Services**
Tel (01327) 262805
Email enquiries@snowcard.co.uk
Website www.snowcard.co.uk

**Sportscover Direct**
Tel (0117) 922 6222
Email info@sportscover.co.uk
Website www.sportscover.co.uk

**Whiteley Insurance Consultants**
Tel (01422) 348411
Email support@kingfisher-insurance.com
Website www.kingfisherinsurance.com

**World Ski**
Tel (0870) 757 2288
Email info@worldski.co.uk
Website www.worldski.co.uk

**Worldwide Travel Insurance**
Tel (01892) 833338
Email sales@worldwideinsure.com
Website www.worldwideinsure.com

# Tour operators

B elow is a list of ski and snowboard operators that offer inclusive holiday packages or accommodation in ski resorts. Before booking, you should satisfy yourself that the company is protected by adequate bonding, trust funds or insurance. All packages involving air travel are required by law to be protected by an ATOL bond. Other recognised bonding schemes include ABTA and AITO (see contact details below). These schemes ensure that if the company goes bust before you travel you will get your money back, and if it goes bust while you are abroad you will be brought home. As an additional safeguard, if you pay at least part of the deposit by credit card you may be able to claim a refund from the credit-card company if the company collapses, provided the holiday itself is priced at more than £100. Make sure the payment slip is made out to the tour operator, not to a travel agent. Bookings are made entirely at your own risk.

**Bonding schemes contact details**

Air Travel Organisers' Licensing (ATOL) 020-7453 6430/6360, www.caa.co.uk

Association of British Travel Agents (ABTA) 020-7307 1907, www.abta.com

Association of Independent Tour Operators (AITO) 020-8744 9280, www.aito.co.uk

**Airtours Ski & Snowboard**
Holiday House, Sandbrook Park,
Sandbrook Way, Rochdale OL11 1SA
**Tel** (0870) 241 8964
**Websites** www.airtours.co.uk /
www.mytravel.com
*Mass-market UK subsidiary of Mytravel,
with hotel, chalet and apartment holidays in
Andorra, Austria, Bulgaria, Canada, France,
Italy and Romania*

**Alpine Action**
Marine Suite, The Old Town Hall,
Southwick BN42 4AX
**Tel** (01273) 597940
**Email** sales@alpineaction.co.uk
**Website** www.alpineaction.co.uk
*Small operator with en-suite chalets in
Méribel and La Tania*

**Alpine Answers Select**
The Business Village, 3–9 Broomhill Road,
London SW18 4JQ
**Tel** 020-8871 4656
**Email** select@alpineanswers.co.uk
**Website** www.alpineanswers.co.uk
*Tailor-made arm of specialist ski travel
agency*

**Alpine Elements**
Tulip House, 70 Borough High Street,
London Bridge SE1 1FX
**Tel** (08700) 111360
**Email** info@alpineelements.co.uk
**Website** www.alpineelements.co.uk
*Catered ski & snowboard holidays in
France. Also seasonal holidays for 1 to 6
months for working professional and gap-
year students*

**Alpine Tours**
South Granary, East Stour Farm,
Ashford Road, Chilham CT4 7DH
**Tel** (01227) 738388
**Email** sales@alpinetours.co.uk
*Long-established, family-run schools and
groups operator with particular expertise in
Austria, Italy, Switzerland and Spain*

**Alpine Tracks**
40 High Street, Menai Bridge, Anglesey
LL59 5EF
**Tel** (01248) 717440
**Email** info@alpinetracks.com
**Website** www.alpine-tracks.com
*Chalet and hotel holidays in Lech, Morzine
and Champoluc*

**Alpine Weekends**
95 Dora Road, London SW19 7JT
Tel 020-8944 9762
Email info@alpineweekends.com
Website www.alpineweekends.com
*Tailor-made operator to 5 resorts in France, as well as to Courmayeur and Verbier*

**Altitude Holidays**
Suite 787, 2 Old Brompton Road, London SW7 3DQ
Tel (0870) 870 7669
Email info@altitudeholidays.com
Website www.altitudeholidays.com
*Small catered chalet operator in Courchevel*

**Andes**
37A St Andrews Street, Castle Douglas DG7 1EN
Tel (01556) 503929
Email john@andes.org.uk
Website www.andes.org.uk
*South American skiing and climbing specialist offering holidays and ski tours to main Chilean and Argentinian resorts*

**A.P.T. Holidays**
PO Box 125, Rayleigh SS6 9SX
Tel (01268) 783878
Email info@ski-express.net
Website www.ski-express.net
*Ski weekends by coach to a hotel at Le Fayet near St-Gervais and Chamonix*

**AWWT**
1 Lonsdale Gardens, Tunbridge Wells TN1 1NU
Tel (01892) 511894
Email ian@awwt.co.uk
Website www.awwt.co.uk
*Tailor-made hotel and apartment holidays in a wide range of resorts in North America and France*

**Balkan Holidays**
Sofia House, 19 Conduit Street, London W1S 2BH
Tel (0845) 130 1114
Email sales@balkanholidays.co.uk
Website www.balkanholidays.co.uk
*Mass-market operator to Bulgaria, Slovenia and Romania*

**Balkan Tours**
61 Ann Street, Belfast BT1 4EE
Tel 028-9024 6795
Email mail@balkan.co.uk
Website www.balkan.co.uk
*Holiday specialist in its 30th year, operating to resorts in Bulgaria and Romania, with direct flights from Belfast and Dublin*

**Belvedere Chalets**
Peach House, Gangbridge Lane, St Mary Bourne SP11 6EW
Tel (01264) 738257
Email info@belvedereproperties.net
Website www.belvedereproperties.net
*Small specialist operator with top-of-the-market catered chalets in Méribel*

**Bigfoot Travel**
Griffins Court, 24–32 London Road, Newbury RG14 1JX
Tel (0870) 300 5874
Email enquiry@bigfoot-travel.co.uk
Website www.bigfoot-winters.com
*Hotels, chalets and apartments in the Chamonix Valley*

**Bonne Neige Ski Holidays**
PO Box 42, Crewe CW2 7FH
Tel (01270) 256966
Email ukoffice@bonne-neige-ski.com
Website www.bonne-neige-ski.com
*Small independent tour operator, now in its 10th year, with two luxury chalets and hotel accommodation in Méribel*

**Borderline**
Les Sorbiers, 65120 Barèges, France
Tel 00 33 562 92 68 95
Email info@borderlinehols.com
Website www.borderlinehols.com
*Holidays to company's own hotel in Barèges in the French Pyrenees*

**Canterbury Travel**
42 High Street, Northwood HA6 1BL
Tel (01923) 822388
Email reservations@laplandmagic.com
Website www.laplandmagic.com
*Lapland specialist with skiing, snowboarding and cross-country holidays to Luosto in Finland, 90 minutes south of the Arctic Circle*

**Carrier North America**
Church Street, Wilmslow SK9 1AX
Tel (01625) 547040
Email aspects@carrier.co.uk
Website www.carrier.co.uk
*4- and 5-star deluxe hotel holidays in Aspen, Vail, Beaver Creek, Whistler and Québec*

**Chalet Snowboard**
31 Aldworth Avenue, Wantage OX12 7EJ
Tel (0870) 800 4020
Email info@csbmountainholidays.com
Website www.csbmountainholidays.com
*Specialist snowboard holidays based in company's own chalets in Morzine and Avoriaz*

**Classic Ski**
Ober Road, Brockenhurst SO42 7ST
**Tel** (01590) 623400
**Email** info@classicski.co.uk
**Website** www.classicski.co.uk
*Small operator offering holidays in the French Alps with tuition for singles and couples over 50, weekday flights and flexible-length stays*

**Club Europe**
Fairway House, 53 Dartmouth Road,
London SE23 3HN
**Tel** (0800) 496 4996
**Email** ski@club-europe.co.uk
**Website** www.club-europe.co.uk
*Schools operator with ski programmes in Austria, France and Italy*

**Club Med**
115 Hammersmith Road, London
W14 0QH
**Tel** (0845) 367 6767
**Email** sarah.mason@clubmed.com
**Website** www.clubmed.co.uk
*Ski programme in France, Switzerland, Italy, Japan and the US. Flights, transfers, full-board accommodation, ski pass, tuition, après-ski entertainment and insurance all included in the price, as well as childcare in many resorts*

**Club Pavilion**
The Mezzanine, 56 Landsdowne Place,
Hove BN3 1FG
**Tel** (0870) 241 0427
**Email** info@conceptholidays.co.uk
**Website** www.conceptholidays.co.uk
*Specialists in affordable ski and weekend breaks*

**Collineige Ski**
30–32 High Street, Frimley GU16 7JD
**Tel** (01276) 24262
**Email** sales@collineige.com
**Website** www.collineige.com
*A large portfolio of catered and uncatered chalets in Chamonix and Argentière. Guiding/instruction and childcare available on request*

**Contiki**
Wells House, 15 Elmfield Road, Bromley
BR1 1LS
**Tel** 020-8290 6422
**Email** travel@contiki.com
**Website** www.contiki.com
*Holidays for 18–35s in Hopfgarten, Austria, by coach or air*

**Cooltip Mountain Holidays**
Ashcourt, Main Street, Long Riston,
Hull HU11 5JF
**Tel** (01964) 563563
**Email** info@cooltip.com
**Website** www.cooltip.com
*Small operator with catered chalet-apartments in Méribel*

**The Corporate Ski Company**
Spectrum House, Bromells Road,
London SW4 0BN
**Tel** 020-7627 5500
**Email** alexj@vantagepoint.co.uk
**Website**
www.thecorporateskicompany.co.uk
*Corporate ski trips to major resorts in the Alps*

**Crystal Holidays**
King's Place, 12–42 Wood Street,
Kingston-upon-Thames KT1 1SH
**Tel** (0870) 160 6040
**Email** skires@crystalholidays.co.uk
**Website** www.crystalski.co.uk
*Mass-market operator with wide range of holidays throughout Europe and both North and South America*

**Descent International**
Riverbank House, Putney Bridge Approach,
London SW6 3JD
**Tel** 020-7384 3854
**Email** sales@descent.co.uk
**Website** www.descent.co.uk
*One of the few operators catering for the extreme top end of the chalet market, with chalets in Méribel, Val d'Isère, Les Gets, Klosters, Verbier and Zermatt*

**Directski**
Unit 4B-5, Blanchardstown Corporate Park,
Dublin 15, Ireland
**Tel** (0800) 587 0945
**Email** sales@directski.com
**Website** www.directski.com
*Dublin-based online operator with holidays to France, Austria, Italy and Andorra*

**Elegant Resorts**
The Old Palace, Chester CH1 1RB
**Tel** (01244) 897333
**Email** enquiries@elegantresorts.co.uk
**Website** www.elegantresorts.co.uk
*Worldwide 4- and 5-star deluxe hotel and villa tour operator with an established reputation in skiing*

**Equity Ski / Rocket Ski**
Dukes Lane House, 47 Middle Street,
Brighton BN1 1AL
**Tel** (01273) 299299 / 262626
**Email** ski@equity.co.uk /
info@rocketski.com
**Websites** www.equity.co.uk /
www.rocketski.com
*Holidays to hotels and chalets in 36 resorts
in Austria, France, Italy and North America.
Associate company, Rocket Ski, is an online
booking service for ski holidays to Austria,
France, Italy and North America*

**Erna Low**
9 Reece Mews, London SW7 3HE
**Tel** (0870) 750 6820 / 020-7584 7820
(brochure line)
**Email** info@ernalow.co.uk
**Website** www.ernalow.co.uk
*The oldest independent ski tour operator,
with a wide selection of self-catering
apartments in France, Switzerland, Austria
and Italy, as well as hotels. New ski
programme to selected resorts in North
America featuring apartments and hotels.
Also spa holidays to a wide range of resorts
worldwide*

**Esprit Ski / Total Holidays**
185 Fleet Road, Fleet GU51 3BL
**Tel** (01252) 618300 / (0870) 163 3633
**Email** travel@esprit-holidays.co.uk
**Websites** www.esprit-holidays.co.uk /
www.skitotal.com
*Family specialist to 15 resorts in France,
Italy and Austria, with dedicated nurseries,
exclusive ski classes and activity clubs.
Associate company Total Holidays has a
large portfolio of catered chalets in Austria,
Canada, France, Italy and Switzerland*

**Exsus**
23 Heddon Street, London W1B 4BQ
**Tel** 020-7292 5050
**Email** travel@exsus.com
**Website** www.exsus.com
*Specialist tailor-made operator to South
America, with luxury accommodation*

**Family Ski Company**
Bank Chambers, Walwyn Road, Colwall,
Malvern WR13 6QG
**Tel** (01684) 540333
**Email** enquiries@familyski.co.uk
**Website** www.familyski.co.uk
*Family specialist providing childcare with a
growing number of chalets in the Portes du
Soleil as well as in Paradiski and Reberty /
Les Menuires*

**Finlays Skiing**
2 Abbotsford Court Business Centre,
Kelso TD5 7BQ
**Tel** (01573) 226611
**Email** info@finlayski.com
**Website** www.finlayski.com
*Long-established small chalet company with
a dedicated following in Courchevel, Val
d'Isère and Paradiski*

**First Choice Ski**
Olivier House, 18 Marine Parade,
Brighton BN2 1TL
**Tel** (0870) 754 3477
**Email** sales@fcski.co.uk
**Website** www.firstchoice.co.uk/ski
*Mainstream winter sports operator with a
collection of chalets, hotels and apartments
across Europe and North America*

**Flexiski**
Olivier House, 18 Marine Parade,
Brighton BN2 1TL
**Tel** (0870) 909 0754
**Email** reservations@flexiski.com
**Website** www.flexiski.co.uk
*Luxury arm of First Choice Ski (see above),
with holidays of variable length to chalets
and hotels in Austria, France and
Switzerland*

**Freedom Holidays**
PO Box 46, Petworth GU28 9ZX
**Tel** (01798) 861 881
**Email** freedomhols@hotmail.com
**Website** www.freedomholidays.co.uk
*Tailor-made weekends and weeks in
apartments, chalets and hotels in Châtel in
the Portes du Soleil*

**French Freedom Holidays**
44 Newdown Road, Southpark, Scunthorpe
DN17 2TX
**Tel** (01724) 290660
**Email** info@french-freedom.co.uk
**Website** www.skifrance4less.co.uk
*Self-drive holidays to the northern French
Alps, specialising in Chamonix and Val
d'Isère*

**French Life**
Kerry Street, Horsforth, Leeds LS18 4AW
**Tel** (0870) 4292180
**Email** ski@frenchlife.co.uk
**Website** www.frenchlifeski.co.uk
*Selection of budget ski holidays for the
independent traveller, mainly focused on
self-drive to the French Alps*

**Frontier Ski**
6 Sydenham Avenue, London SE26 6UH
**Tel** 020-8776 8709
**Email** info@frontier-travel.co.uk
**Website** www.frontier-ski.co.uk
*Small Canadian specialist with a dedicated following*

**Hannibals**
Farriers, Little Olantigh Road, Wye,
Ashford TN25 5DQ
**Tel** (01233) 813105
**Email** sales@hannibals.co.uk
**Website** www.hannibals.co.uk
*Specialist operator with hotels, chalets and self-catering apartments in Serre Chevalier*

**Headwater Holidays**
The Old School House, Chester Road,
Northwich CW8 1LE
**Tel** (01606) 720199
**Email** info@headwater.com
**Website** www.headwater.com
*Walking holidays specialist with cross-country ski programme for groups in Austria, Finland, France, Italy, Germany and Norway. Downhill ski holidays to Kandersteg in Switzerland*

**HF Holidays**
Imperial House, Edgware Road,
London NW9 5AL
**Tel** 020-8905 9558
**Email** info@hfholidays.co.uk
**Website** www.hfholidays.co.uk
*Group holidays that include instruction in cross-country skiing and snowshoeing in Austria, France, Italy, and Switzerland*

**Huski Chalet Holidays**
63A Kensington Church Street,
London W8 4BA
**Tel** 020-7938 4844
**Email** ski@huski.com
**Website** www.huski.com
*Long-established Chamonix chalet operator, also offering hotels, apartments and weekend skiing*

**Inghams**
10–18 Putney Hill, London SW15 6AX
**Tel** 020-8780 4433
**Email** travel@inghams.co.uk
**Website** www.inghams.co.uk
*Major tour operator with chalets and hotel holidays in 95 resorts in 12 countries. Aims for the top end of the mass market but also has its own separate luxury programme with scheduled flights*

**Inntravel**
Nr Castle Howard, York YO60 7JU
**Tel** (01653) 617906
**Email** winter@inntravel.co.uk
**Website** www.inntravel.co.uk
*Walking holidays specialist with a dedicated following. Offers cross-country, snowshoeing and Alpine programmes to resorts in Austria, Italy, France, Norway, Sweden and Switzerland*

**Interhome**
383 Richmond Road, Twickenham
TW1 2EF
**Tel** 020-8891 1294
**Email** info@interhome.co.uk
**Website** www.interhome.co.uk
*Swiss company (part of Hotelplan/Inghams group) with a large database of self-catering ski-drive chalets and apartments throughout the Alps*

**Interski**
Acorn Park, Commercial Gate,
Mansfield NG18 1EX
**Tel** (01623) 456333
**Email** email@interski.co.uk
**Website** www.interski.co.uk
*Long-established schools operator to the Italian Aosta Valley with an add-on adult and family programme, an air, coach and self-drive packages. The company has its own equipment rental and ski school with BASI instructors, based in Pila, Courmayeur and La Thuile*

**Kuoni Travel**
Kuoni House, Deepdene Avenue,
Dorking RH5 4AZ
**Tel** (01306) 747 000
**Email** switzerland.sales@kuoni.co.uk
**Website** www.kuoni.co.uk
*Long-established mainstream hotel operator to Switzerland*

**Lagrange**
168 Shepherds Bush Road, London W6 7PB
**Tel** 020-7371 6111
**Email** info@lagrange-holidays.co.uk
**Website** www.lagrange-holidays.co.uk
*British branch of a giant French operator that offers a wide range of self-catering accommodation in 100 ski resorts in the Alps, the Pyrenees and Andorra*

**Leisure Direction**
Image House, Station Road, London
N17 9LR
**Tel** 020-8324 4042
**Email** sales@leisuredirection.co.uk
**Website** www.leisuredirection.co.uk
*Established ski-drive operator with an expanded programme to 36 French resorts*

**Le Ski**
25 Holly Terrace, Huddersfield HD1 6JW
**Tel** (0870) 754 4444
**Email** mail@leski.com
**Website** www.leski.com
*Family-run chalet company with a long-established pedigree to Courchevel 1650, Val d'Isère and La Tania. Offers childcare and owns a complex of 6 chalets in Val d'Isère*

**Lotus Supertravel**
Sandpiper House, 39 Queen Elizabeth
Street, London SE1 2BT
**Tel** 020-7962 9933
**Email** ski@lotusgroup.co.uk
**Website** www.supertravel.co.uk
*Good quality chalets and tailormade holidays to Europe and North America*

**Made To Measure Holidays**
1 South Street, Chichester PO19 1EH
**Tel** (01243) 533333
**Email** sales@mtmhols.co.uk
**Website** www.mtmhols.co.uk
*Long-established operator specialising in tailor-made and flexible holidays to a wide range of resorts in Europe and North America*

**Mark Warner**
10 Old Court Place, London W8 4PL
**Tel** (0870) 770 4226
**Email** sales@markwarner.co.uk
**Website** www.markwarner.co.uk
*Family holiday specialist with 30 years' experience, offering chalet-hotel holidays with childcare or adult-only holidays in 8 major French ski resorts, as well as Courmayeur and St Anton*

**McNab Mountain Sports**
Harbour House, Crinen, Lochgilphead
PA31 8SW
**Tel** (01546) 830243 / 0033 450 54 22 84
**Email** info@mcnab.co.uk
**Websites** www.mcnab.co.uk /
www.kommunity.com
*Off-piste snowboarding courses and technical clinics based at a catered chalet in Argentière. Also summer freestyle/freeride snowboard camps in Les Deux Alpes*

**Meriski**
1st Floor, Carpenters Buildings, Carpenters
Lane, Cirencester GL7 1EE
**Tel** (01285) 648518
**Email** sales@meriski.co.uk
**Website** www.meriski.co.uk
*Luxury chalet accommodation in Méribel*

**MGS Ski**
109 Castle Street, Saffron Walden
CB10 1BQ
**Tel** (01799) 525984
**Email** skimajor@aol.com
**Website** www.mgsski.com
*Small, well-established family operator offering apartments in Val Cenis in France*

**Momentum Ski**
162 Munster Road, London SW6 6AT
**Tel** 020-7371 9111
**Email** sales@momentumski.com
**Website** www.momentumski.com
*Tailor-made operator specialising in weeks and weekends to the Alps and North America, together with a corporate programme. Italy and Switzerland a particular strength*

**Moswin's Germany**
Moswin House, 21 Church Street,
Oadby, Leicester LE2 5DB
**Tel** 0116-271 9922
**Email** germany@moswin.com
**Website** www.moswin.com
*Holidays in Garmisch Partenkirchen in Germany*

**Mountain Leap**
25 Eccleston Square, London SW1V 1NS
**Tel** 020-7931 0621
**Email** info@mountainleap.com
**Website** www.mountainleap.com
*Tailor-made holidays to Chamonix, Courchevel, Klosters, Megève, Méribel, Val d'Isère and Verbier. Also specialises in large groups and corporate hospitality events*

**Neilson / Neilson School Groups**
Locksview, Brighton Marina, Brighton
BN2 5HA
**Tel** (0870) 333 3347/3620
**Email** sales@neilson.com /
infoschools@neilson.com
**Websites** www.neilson.com /
www.neilsonschools.com
*Major tour operator with hotels, apartments and chalets in 10 countries. Separate school and adult groups operation to destinations in Austria, Bulgaria, France, Italy, Norway, Romania, Sweden and North America. The company is part of Thomas Cook*

**Nonstopski**
79 Leathwaite Road, London SW11 6RN
**Tel** (0870) 241 8070
**Email** info@nonstopski.com
**Website** www.nonstopski.com
*Fully-inclusive courses in Fernie, Red
Mountain and Banff*

**Norvista**
31–35 Kirby Street, London EC1N 8TE
**Tel** (0870) 744 7315
**Email** reservations@norvista.co.uk
**Website** www.norvista.co.uk
*Scandinavian specialist offering holidays to
Finland, Norway and Sweden*

**Oak Hall Skiing and Snowboarding**
Oak Hall, Otford TN15 6XF
**Tel** (01732) 763131
**Email** office@oakhall.co.uk
**Website** www.oakhall.co.uk
*Christian holidays to 10 resorts in Austria
and Switzerland*

**On The Piste**
28 Great King Street, Macclesfield
SK11 6PL
**Tel** (01625) 503111
**Email** sales@onthepiste.com
**Website** www.onthepiste.com
*French Alps specialist offering tailor-made
travel for school groups, students and adults
by coach or air*

**Original Travel Company**
Crombie Mews, 11A Abercrombie Street,
London SW11 2JB
**Tel** 020-7978 7333
**Email** info@originaltravel.co.uk
**Website** www.originaltravel.co.uk
*Up-market short-break specialist offering
exclusive holidays with a difference,
including heli-skiing, ski-touring and off-
piste to Austria, France, Italy, Sweden and
Switzerland*

**The Oxford Ski Company**
3 Barn Business Centre, Great Rissington,
Cheltenham GL54 2LH
**Tel** (01451) 810300
**Email** info@oxfordski.com
**Website** www.oxfordski.com
*Tailor-made luxury holidays in luxury
chalets, private lodges and hotels in France
and Switzerland. Also specialises in small
and large-scale hosted corporate events*

**Panorama Holidays**
Panorama House, Vale Road, Portslade
BN41 1HP
**Tel** (0870) 750 5060 / (0870) 241 5026
(24-hr brochure line)
**Email** panorama@phg.co.uk
**Website** www.panoramaholidays.co.uk
*Ski and snowboard holidays to Andorra,
Austria, France and Italy, with chalets,
hotels and apartments. The company is part
of the Mytravel group*

**Peak Retreats**
The Old Workshop, 34 Middle Street,
Southsea PO5 4BP
**Tel** (0870) 770 0408
**Email** reservations@peakretreats.co.uk
**Website** www.peakretreats.co.uk
*French Alps specialist for self-catering
chalets, apartments and family-run hotels in
off-beat resorts*

**Peak Ski**
White Lilacs House, Water Lane,
Bovingdon HP3 0NA
**Tel** (01442) 832629
**Email** peakski@which.net
**Website** www.peakski.co.uk
*Small catered chalet operator in Verbier
with 19 years' experience*

**PGL Ski**
Alton Court, Penyard Lane, Ross-on-Wye
HR9 5GL
**Tel** (0870) 162 6622
**Email** ski@pgl.co.uk
**Website** www.pgl.co.uk
*Major schools operator to Austria, France,
Italy, Switzerland and US*

**Piste Artiste**
128 Old Brompton Road, London SW7 3SS
**Tel** contact by email only
**Email** reserve@pisteartiste.com
**Website** www.pisteartiste.com
*Self-catered chalets in Champéry,
Switzerland*

**Powder Byrne**
250 Upper Richmond Road, London
SW15 6TG
**Tel** 020-8246 5300
**Email** enquiries@powderbyrne.co.uk
**Website** www.powderbyrne.com
*Luxury tailored ski holidays to Switzerland,
Austria and France, with children's clubs
and crèches*

**Purple Ski**
Hamilton Cottage, Chapel Hill, Speen
HP27 0SL
**Tel** (01494) 488633
**Email** michael@purpleski.com
**Website** www.purpleski.com
*Small luxury chalet operator in Méribel*

**Pyrenean Mountain Tours**
2 Rectory Cottages, Wolverton, Tadley
RG26 5RS
**Tel** (01635) 297209
**Email** pmtuk@aol.com
**Website** www.pyrenees.co.uk
*Small operator with ski, ski-touring and
snowshoeing holidays to hotels or self-
catering apartments in Barèges in the
French Pyrenees and Corvara in the
Dolomites*

**Ramblers Holidays**
PO Box 43, Welwyn Garden City
AL8 6PQ
**Tel** (01707) 331133
**Email** info@ramblersholidays.co.uk
**Website** www.ramblersholidays.co.uk
*Walking holidays specialist with group
cross-country holiday programme to
Achenkirch and Innsbruck in Austria, and
Dobbiaco and the Val di Fiemme in Italy*

**Rocky Mountain Adventures**
Charlotte House, 67–83 Norfolk Street,
Queens Dock, Liverpool L1 0BG
**Tel** (0870) 366 5442
**Email** info@rockymountain.co.uk
**Website** www.rockymountain.co.uk
*Specialises in full-season chalet holidays in
Aspen, Banff, Whistler, Breckenridge and
Vail*

**Scott Dunn Ski**
Fovant Mews, 12 Noyna Road, London
SW17 7PH
**Tel** 020-8682 5050 (SD Ski) /
020-8682 5030 (SD Latin America)
**Email** ski@scottdunn.com /
latin@scottdunn.com
**Website** www.scottdunn.com
*Up-market operator with ski programme
that includes a portfolio of catered chalets
in Zermatt, Courchevel 1850, Méribel and
Val d'Isère. Also runs childcare operation.
Scott Dunn Latin America offers holidays to
major resorts in Argentina and Chile*

**Seasons in Style**
Telegraph House, 246 Telegraph Road,
Heswall CH60 7SG
**Tel** 0151-342 0505
**Email** sales@seasonsinstyle.co.uk
**Website** www.seasonsinstyle.co.uk
*5-star deluxe worldwide hotel operator with
a growing ski programme to Austria, France,
Switzerland, Canada and US*

**Silver Ski**
Conifers House, Grove Green Lane,
Maidstone ME14 5JW
**Tel** (01622) 735544
**Email** karen@silverski.co.uk
**Website** www.silverski.co.uk
*Catered chalets in Paradiski, Trois Vallées
and Val d'Isère*

**Simply Ski**
Kings Place, 12–42 Wood Street,
Kingston upon Thames KT1 1SG
**Tel** 020-8541 2209
**Email** ski@simply-travel.co.uk
**Website** www.simplyski.co.uk
*Worldwide villa specialist with chalet
operation to Courchevel, Méribel, Val d'Isère,
Verbier, Zermatt, St Anton and many resorts
in US. The company is part of Thomson*

**Ski 2**
The Old Forge, High Street, Twyford
O21 1RF
**Tel** (01962) 713330
**Email** info@ski-2.com
**Website** www.ski-2.com
*Champoluc specialist, offering total
flexiblity of travel dates and length of stay.
Also has its own crèche and ski school*

**Ski Activity**
Lawmuir House, Methven PH1 3SZ
**Tel** (01738) 840888
**Email** sales@skiactivity.com
**Website** www.skiactivity.com
*Chalets, hotels and apartments in 11 resorts
in France, as well as in Verbier, St Anton,
and 25 resorts in North America*

**Ski Adventures**
14A Graham Road, Malvern, WR14 2HN
**Tel** (01684) 560707
**Email** enquiries@skiadventures.co.uk
**Website** www.skiadventures.co.uk
*Quality piste-side catered chalet
accommodation in Les Arcs 1600*

**Ski All America**
117 St Margarets Road, Twickenham
TW1 2LH
**Tel** (0870) 167 6676
**Email** sales@skiallamerica.com
**Website** www.skiallamerica.com
*Chalets, hotels and apartments in a large portfolio of resorts in North and South America*

**Ski the American Dream**
31 Beaufort Court, Admirals Way,
Waterside, South Quay, London E14 9XL
**Tel** (0870) 350 7547
**Email** holidays@skidream.com
**Website** www.skidream.com
*The original independent hotel and apartment operator to North America*

**Ski Amis**
122–126 High Road, London NW6 4HY
**Tel** 020-7692 0850
**Email** info@skiamis.com
**Website** www.skiamis.com
*Well-established company offering self-catering apartments and chalets in Courchevel, Méribel, Paradiski, La Tania, Tignes, Val d'Isère and Val Thorens*

**Ski Astons**
Clerkenleap, Broomhall, Worcester
WR5 3HR
**Tel** (01905) 829200
**Email** ski.astons@virgin.net
**Website** www.skiastons.co.uk
*Schools specialist with all-inclusive holidays to resorts in Austria and Switzerland*

**Ski Barrett-Boyce**
3 Mayfields, Brighton Road KT20 6QZ
**Tel** (01737) 831184
**Email** info@skibb.com
**Website** www.skibb.com
*Family-run company offering chalet holidays in Megève, with instruction and childcare*

**Ski Beat**
Metro House, Northgate, Chichester
PO19 1BE
**Tel** (01243) 780405
**Email** ski@skibeat.co.uk
**Website** www.skibeat.co.uk
*Chalets with childcare in Les Arcs, Mèribel, La Plagne, La Tania and Val d'Isère*

**Ski Blanc**
89 Palmerston Road, Buckhurst Hill
IG9 5NH
**Tel** 020-8502 9082
**Email** sales@skiblanc.co.uk
**Website** www.skiblanc.co.uk
*Small operator with a range of catered chalets in Les Allues village below Méribel*

**Ski Chamois**
18 Lawn Road, Doncaster DN1 2JF
**Tel** (01302) 369006
**Email** sales@skichamois.co.uk
**Website** www.skichamois.co.uk
*Small chalet-hotel operator in Morzine, with own childcare programme*

**Ski Cuisine**
49 Burgess Road, Southend-on-Sea
SS1 3AX
**Tel** (01702) 589543
**Email** skicuisine@dial.pipex.com
**Website** www.skicuisine.co.uk
*Small company with catered chalets in Méribel*

**Ski Equipe**
79 London Road, Alderley Edge SK9 7DY
**Tel** (0870) 444 5533
**Email** info@ski-equipe.co.uk
**Website** www.ski-equipe.co.uk
*Small operator with chalets in Cortina d'Ampezzo and St Anton*

**Ski Expectations**
Jasmine Cottage, Manor Lane,
Great Chesterford CB10 1PJ
**Tel** (01799) 531888
**Email** ski.expectations@virgin.net
**Website** www.skiexpectations.com
*Small tailor-made hotel and catered chalet operator to major resorts in Europe*

**Ski Famille**
Unit 2, Clare Hall, Parsons Green, St Ives
PE27 4WY
**Tel** (0845) 644 3764
**Email** info@skifamille.co.uk
**Website** www.skifamille.co.uk
*Specialist family-run chalet operator for families in Les Gets in the Portes du Soleil, with free childcare programme*

**Ski France**
PO Box 371, Bromley BR1 2ZJ
**Tel** (0870) 787 3402
**Email** ski@skifrance.co.uk
**Website** www.skifrance.co.uk
*Travel by rail, air or self-drive to France, with chalets, hotels and apartments*

**Ski Freshtracks**
The White House, 57–63 Church Road,
Wimbledon, London SW19 5SB
**Tel** (0845) 458 0784
**Email** holidays@skifreshtracks.co.uk
**Website** www.skifreshtracks.co.uk
*Ski Club of Great Britain's programme of
weeks, weekends and specialist courses for
skiers and riders of different standards, both
with and without instruction and guiding*

**Ski Gower**
2 High Street, Studley B80 7HJ
**Tel** (01527) 851411
**Email** pc@gowstrav.demon.co.uk
**Website** www.skigower.co.uk
*Tailor-made holidays in Switzerland for
schools and groups*

**Ski High Days**
Fire Clay House, Netham Road, Bristol
BS5 9PJ
**Tel** 0117-955 1814
**Email** sales@high-days.co.uk
**Website** www.skihighdays.com
*Group tour operator with an increasingly
large presence in Sauze d'Oulx, Claviere and
Bardonecchia in Italy*

**Ski Hillwood**
Lavender Lodge, Dunny Lane, Chipperfield
WD4 9DD
**Tel** (01923) 290700
**Email** sales@hillwood-holidays.co.uk
**Website** www.hillwood-holidays.co.uk
*Specialist family operator with childcare
programme to Söll and Zauchensee in
Austria and Les Gets and Argentière in
France. Also holidays in Whistler*

**Ski Hiver**
119A London Road, Waterlooville
PO7 7DZ
**Tel** (02392) 428586
**Email** skihiver@aol.com
**Website** www.skihiver.co.uk
*Catered chalets with childcare programme
to Peisey-Nancroix in Paradiski*

**Ski Independence**
Broughton Market, Edinburgh EH3 6NU
**Tel** (0870) 555 0555
**Email** ski@ski–i.com
**Website** www.ski–i.com
*Largest independent operator to US and
Canada, with hotels, chalets and
apartments in 41 North American resorts.
Extensive French and Swiss programme to
30 French and Swiss resorts, with option to
fly or drive for week or weekend stays*

**Ski Miquel**
73 High Street, Uppermill, Oldham
OL3 6AP
**Tel** (01457) 821200
**Email** ski@miquelhols.co.uk
**Website** www.miquelhols.co.uk
*Long-established chalet, hotel and
apartment operator to Alpe d'Huez, Bad
Gastein, Baqueira-Beret, Lauterbrunnen in
Switzerland, Serre Chevalier and Whistler*

**Ski Morgins**
The Barn House, 1 Bury Court Barns,
Wigmore HR6 9US
**Tel** (01568) 770681
**Email** info@skimorgins.com
**Website** www.skimorgins.com
*Small specialist operator to Morgins in
Switzerland*

**Ski Norwest**
8 Foxholes Cottages, Foxholes Road,
Horwich, Bolton BL6 6AL
**Tel** (01204) 668468
**Email** skinorwest@aol.com
**Website** www.skinorwest.com
*Self-drive and coach holidays to Scottish
resorts*

**Ski Olympic**
PO Box 396, Doncaster DN5 7YS
**Tel** (01302) 328820
**Email** info@skiolympic.com
**Website** www.skiolympic.com
*Chalets and hotels in 7 French resorts,
including own chalet-hotel at Vallandry in
Paradiski ski area*

**Ski Peak**
Barts End, Crossways Road, Grayshott
GU26 6HD
**Tel** (01428) 608070
**Email** info@skipeak.com
**Website** www.skipeak.com
*Small, dedicated operator that has built its
own chalets and apartments and manages
its own hotel in the cult resort of Vaujany in
the Alpe d'Huez ski area. The operator
provides a British nanny for the local crèche*

**Ski Rosie**
L'Alpage 8B, route du Petit Châtel,
74390 Châtel, France
**Tel** 00 33 450 81 31 00
**Email** rosie@skirosie.com
**Website** www.skirosie.com
*Small, long-established operator with one
catered chalet, apartments and hotels in
Morgins and Châtel in the Portes du Soleil*

**Ski Safari**
1 Hova Villas, Hove BN3 3DH
**Tel** (01273) 223680
**Email** info@skisafari.com
**Website** www.skisafari.com
*Specialist operator with hotels and apartments in North America. Self-drive adventures through Canada*

**Ski Solutions à la Carte**
84 Pembroke Road, London W8 6NX
**Tel** 020-7471 7777
**Email** alc@skisolutions.com
**Website** www.skisolutions.com
*Tailor-made arm of specialist ski travel agency, with hotels and apartments in all major resorts in the Alps and North America. You can expect staff to have knowledge of both the resorts and properties*

**Ski Supreme**
24 Howard Court, Neraton Estate, East Kilbride G74 4QZ
**Tel** (01355) 260547
**Email** info@skisupreme.co.uk
**Website** www.skisupreme.co.uk
*Self-drive and accommodation-only holidays in 19 resorts in France, and Cervinia and Pila in Italy*

**Ski Val**
The Ski Barn, Middlemoor, Tavistock PL19 9DY
**Tel** (0870) 746 3030
**Email** post@skival.co.uk
**Website** www.skival.co.uk
*Catered chalets and chalet-hotels in Courchevel, Tignes, Val d'Isère and St Anton*

**Ski Verbier**
25 The Coda Centre, 189 Munster Road, London SW6 6AW
**Tel** 020-7385 8050
**Email** info@skiverbier.com
**Website** www.skiverbier.com
*Established up-market operator in Verbier, with 10 catered chalets and one hotel*

**Ski Weekend**
Darts Farm Village, Topsham, Exeter EX3 0HQ
**Tel** (0870) 060 0615
**Email** info@skiweekend.com
**Website** www.skiweekend.com
*Weekends and short breaks combined with high-mountain guiding and specialist courses, mainly to Chamonix Valley but also to other destinations in Switzerland and Italy. A corporate programme is also available*

**Ski Weekends & Board Breaks**
67 Orsett Road, Grays RM17 5HJ
**Tel** (0870) 442 3400
**Email** sales@harris-travel.com
**Website** www.skiweekends.com
*Flexible-length holidays by coach and air to own hotel in Brides-les-Bains below Trois Vallées, and to chalets in La Tania*

**Skibound**
Olivier House, 18 Marine Parade, Brighton BN2 1TL
**Tel** (0870) 900 3200
**Email** sales@skibound.co.uk
**Website** www.skibound.co.uk
*Market leader for school trips to Austria, France, Italy and North America. Part of the First Choice group*

**Skitopia**
40 Lemon Street, Truro TR1 2NS
**Tel** (01872) 272767
**Email** ski@tjm.co.uk
**Websites** www.skitopia.com / www.skitopia.biz
*Specialists in hotel and chalet holidays to the French Alps and Italy, for schools and adults*

**Skiworld**
Skiworld House, 3 Vencourt Place, London W6 9NU
**Tel** (0870) 900 3200 (Europe) / (0870) 787 9720 (North America)
**Email** sales@skiworld.ltd.uk
**Website** www.skiworld.ltd.uk
*Largest independent ski tour operator, with major chalet programme in the Alps and North America*

**Sloping Off**
31 High Street, Handley, Salisbury SP5 5NR
**Tel** (01725) 552833 / (01202) 292197
**Email** hilary@slopingoff.fsnet.co.uk
**Website** www.sloping-off.co.uk
*Schools and groups operator to resorts in Austria, France, Italy and Switzerland*

**Slovenija Pursuits**
New Barn Farm, Tadlow Road, Royston SG8 0EP
**Tel** (0870) 220 0201
**Email** enquiries@slovenijapursuits.co.uk
**Website** www.slovenijapursuits.co.uk
*Established operator to Slovenian resorts and to Nassfeld and Bad Kleinkirchheim in Austria. Also organises heli-skiing and ski safaris in Slovenia*

**Snow Safari**
1351 route des Chavant, 74310
Les Houches, France
**Tel** 0033 450 54 56 63
**Email** elaine@chaletsavoy.com
**Website** www.chaletsavoy.com
*Small chalet specialist to Chamonix Valley
with mountain guiding*

**Snowbizz Vacances**
69 High Street, Maxey PE6 9EE
**Tel** (01778) 341455
**Email** info@snowbizz.co.uk
**Website** www.snowbizz.co.uk
*Small, long-established operator to Puy-St-
Vincent in France, with extensive childcare
and own ski-school programme with race-
training for children aged 10 to 16*

**Snowcoach**
146–148 London Road, St Albans
AL1 1PQ
**Tel** (01727) 866177
**Email** info@snowcoach.co.uk
**Website** www.snowcoach.co.uk
*Ski and snowboarding holidays to France
and Austria. Travel by air, coach or self-
drive for 1-week stays and short breaks*

**Snowline**
Collingbourne House,
140–142 Wandsworth High Street,
London SW18 4JJ
**Tel** 020-8870 4807
**Email** ski@snowline.co.uk
**Website** www.snowline.co.uk
*Well-established chalet operator with wide
range of catered properties in Morzine,
Méribel, La Tania and Val d'Isère.
Childcare service with private nannies in
Trois Vallées, plus crèche in Val d'Isère*

**Snowscape**
108 Wylds Lane, Worcester WR5 1DJ
**Tel** (01905) 357760
**Email** skiandboard@snowscape.co.uk
**Website** www.snowscape.co.uk
*Weekly and flexible holidays to Austria for
groups and individuals*

**Solo's Holidays**
54–58 High Street, Edgware HA8 7EJ
**Tel** (0870) 072 0700
**Email** travel@solosholidays.co.uk
**Website** www.solosholidays.co.uk
*Holidays for singles in 14 resorts in Austria,
Canada, France, Italy, Romania, Slovenia,
Switzerland and US*

**Stanford Skiing**
16 Sherlock Road, Cambridge CB3 0HR
**Tel** (01223) 477644
**Email** info@stanfordskiing.co.uk
**Website** www.stanfordskiing.co.uk
*Long-established specialist operator with
chalets and hotels in Megève*

**Swiss Travel Centre (Plus Travel)**
30 Bedford Street, London, WC2E 9ED
**Tel** 020-7734 0383
**Email** sales@stc.ch
**Website** www.switzerlandtravelcentre.co.uk
*Specialist hotel operator to 16 Swiss resorts*

**Swiss Travel Service**
Bridge House, 55–59 High Road,
Broxbourne EN10 7DT
**Tel** (0870) 191 7281
**Email** swiss@bridge-travel.co.uk
**Website** www.swisstravel.co.uk
*Major hotel operator to 19 resorts in
Switzerland. Travel by scheduled flights
with rail transfers, or by rail or car from UK*

**Tangney Tours**
3 Station Court, Borough Green TN15 8AF
**Tel** (01732) 886666
**Email** info@tangney-tours.com
**Website** www.tangney-tours.com
*Pilgrim charter operator to Lourdes, with a
small ski programme in nearby Barèges in
the French Pyrenees*

**Thomson Ski & Snowboarding**
King's Place, 12–42 Wood Street,
Kingston-upon-Thames KT1 1JY
**Tel** (0870) 606 1470
**Email** info@thomson-ski.com
**Website** www.thomson-ski.co.uk
*Major tour operator to over 80 resorts in 11
countries, with group discounts and
childcare facilities. Same parent company as
Crystal and Simply Ski*

**Tops Travel**
Lees House, 21 Dyke Road, Brighton
BN1 3GD
**Tel** (01273) 774666
**Email** sales@topstravel.co.uk
**Website** www.topstravel.co.uk
*Club hotels and chalets in 5 French resorts*

**Trail Alpine**
Cordelia House, James Park, Dyserth,
Rhyl LL18 6AG
**Tel** (0870) 750 6560
**Email** info@trailalpine.co.uk
**Website** www.trailalpine.co.uk
*Small operator with a chalet in Morzine*

**Trailfinders**
215 Kensington High Street, London W8 6BD
**Tel** (0845) 050 5900
**Website** www.trailfinders.com
*Largest independent travel company in UK, with new tailor-made programmes to resorts including Banff–Lake Louise, Breckenridge, Heavenly, Killington and Whistler*

**Tyrolean Adventures**
56 Poynder Road, Corsham SN13 9LZ
**Tel** (01249) 701627
**Email** fluck@pafluck.freeserve.co.uk
**Website** www.tyroleanadventures.com
*Small operator offering holidays by coach, inclusive of ski pass and ski hire, based at a hotel in Hochfilzen 15 miles from Kitzbühel*

**United Vacations**
PO Box 377, Bromley BR1 1LY
**Tel** (0870) 606 2222
**Email** uvuk@unitedvacations.com
**Website** www.unitedvacations.co.uk
*Tour operator arm of United Airlines, with tailor-made holidays to resorts across North America*

**Vertical Reality Verbier**
6 Osborne Road, Westcliff, SS0 7DW
**Tel** (077) 36 44 3156
**Email** info@verticalrealityverbier.com
**Website** www.verticalrealityverbier.com
*Small operator with 6 chalets in Verbier, which are let either fully catered or on a B&B basis*

**VIP**
Collingbourne House,
140–142 Wandsworth High Street,
London SW18 4JJ
**Tel** 020-8875 1957
**Email** ski@vip-chalets.com
**Website** www.vip-chalets.com
*Well-established luxury chalet operator with an expanding portfolio of properties in Val d'Isère and Méribel. Childcare service with private nannies in both resorts, plus crèche in Val d'Isère*

**Virgin Snow**
The Galleria, Station Road, Crawley
RH10 1WW
**Tel** (0870) 990 4212
**Email** reservations.services@virginholidays.co.uk
**Website** www.virgin.com/holidays
*The tour-operator arm of Virgin Atlantic. Offers hotel and fly-drive holidays to 20 destinations in North America and South Korea*

**Wasteland Ski Company**
9 Disraeli Road, London, SW15 2DR
**Tel** (0870) 844 4644
**Email** ru@wastelandski.com
**Website** www.wastelandski.com
*The largest student operator, which will also tailor-make family and group holidays and has a dedicated team for running large-scale events*

**Waymark Holidays**
44 Windsor Road, Slough, SL1 2EJ
**Tel** (01753) 516477
**Email** info@waymarkholidays.com
**Website** www.waymarkholidays.com
*Long-established cross-country ski operator to hotels in Austria, Finland, France, Italy, Norway and Switzerland*

**Wentworth Travel**
Wentworth House, Station Parade, Virginia Water GU25 4AE
**Tel** (01344) 844622
**Email** enquiries@wentworthtravel.com
**Website** www.wentworthtravel.com
*Spa and luxury hotel specialist with holidays to Banff–Lake Louise*

**White Roc Weekends**
69 Westbourne Grove, London, W2 4UJ
**Tel** 020-7792 1188
**Email** snow@whiteroc.co.uk
**Website** www.whiteroc.co.uk
*Weekend and longer tailor-made holidays for individual and corporate clients to Austria, France, Italy and Switzerland, with a choice of 22 resorts and an emphasis on characterful, good-quality hotels*

**YSE**
The Business Village, Broomhill Road, London SW18 4JQ
**Tel** 020-8871 5117
**Email** sales@yseski.co.uk
**Website** www.yseski.co.uk
*Large Val d'Isère specialist with a wide range of chalets, from comfortable to luxurious, with travel by charter flights.*

# Directory

## Contents

## National and state tourist offices

**Andorran Delegation**
020-8874 4806
www.andorra.ad

**Argentinian Consulate**
020-7318 1300

**Australian Tourist Commission**
(09068) 633235 (brochure line)
www.australia.com

**Austrian National Tourist Office**
020-7629 0461
www.austria-tourism.at

**Bulgaria, Embassy of the Republic of**
020-7584 9400
www.bulgariaski.com

**Canada, Visit**
(09068) 715000 (brochure line)
www.travelcanada.ca

**Chile, Consulate of**
020-7580 1023
www.visitchile.org

**Czech Tourist Authority**
(09063) 640641 (brochure line)
www.visitczechia.cz

**Finnish Tourist Board**
020-7365 2512
www.visitfinland.com

**French Government Tourist Office**
(09068) 244123 (brochure line)
www.franceguide.com / www.skifrance.fr

**Italian State Tourist Office**
020-7408 1254
www.enit.it

**Japanese National Tourist Organisation**
020-7734 9638
www.seejapan.co.uk

**New Zealand Tourism Board**
(09050) 606060
www.newzealand.com

**Norwegian Tourist Board**
(09063) 022003 (brochure line)
www.visitnorway.com

**Romanian National Tourist Office**
020-7224 3692
www.rotravel.com

**Scottish Tourist Board**
0131-332 2433
www.visitscotland.com

**Slovenian Tourist Office**
(0870) 225 5305
www.slovenia-tourism.si

**Spanish Tourist Office**
020-7486 8077
www.tourspain.es

**Swedish Travel & Tourism Council**
(00800) 308 03080 (international freephone)
www.visit-sweden.com

**Switzerland Travel Centre**
(00800) 100 20030 (international freephone)
www.myswitzerland.com

## US NATIONAL AND STATE TOURIST INFORMATION
**US Embassy**
Switchboard 020-7499 9000
Visa Information Line (09068) 200290 (24-hr)
www.unitedstatesvisas.gov

**California**
www.visitcalifornia.com

**Colorado**
www.visitcolorado.com

**Maine**
www.visitmaine.com

**Nevada**
(0870) 523 8832 (brochure line)
www.visitnevada.com

**New England**
www.skinewengland.com

**New Hampshire**
www.visitnh.gov

**Rocky Mountain International**
(09063) 640655
www.rmi-realamerica.com

**Utah**
www.utah.com

**Vermont**
www.travel-vermont.com

# Ski travel agents
**Alpine Answers**
020-8871 4656
www.alpineanswers.co.uk
*Also a tour operator*

**Avant-Ski**
0191-285 8141, www.avant-ski.com

**Chalet World**
(01743) 231199, www.chaletworld.co.uk
*Agency for tour operator chalets*

**Directski**
www.directski.com
*Dublin-based online ski travel agent*

**Erna Low**
(0870) 750 6820, www.ernalow.co.uk
*Agent for Paradiski, Intrawest Europe and MGM apartments. Also a tour operator*

**The First Resort**
www.thefirstresort.com
*Online holiday booking, cheap flights and information for snow-users*

**Ifyouski**
www.ifyouski.com
*Online holidays*

**Iglu**
www.iglu.com
*Online travel and accommodation*

**Independent Ski Links**
(01964) 533905, www.ski-links.com
*Agency offering holidays to the Alps and North America*

**Momentum Ski**
020-7371 9111
www.momentumski.com
*Also a tour operator*

**Mountain Beds**
020-7924 2650
www.mountainbeds.co.uk
*Apartment booking agency in Verbier*

**Packyourskis**
www.packyourskis.com
*Online agents for ski destinations and flights*

**Ski Deals**
www.skideals.com
*Online holiday agency*

**Ski McNeill**
(02890) 666699, www.skimcneill.com

**Ski Solutions**
020-7471 7700, www.skisolutions.com
*Also a tour operator*

**Ski & Surf**
020-8958 2418, www.skisurf.com

**Ski Travel Centre**
0141-649 9696
www.skitravelcentre.co.uk

**Skiers Travel**
(0870) 010 0032
www.skiers-travel.co.uk

**Snow Finders**
(01858) 466888, www.snowfinders.com

**Snow Line**
(0870) 333 0064, www.snow-line.co.uk

**World Ski & Travel**
(0114) 279 7300, www.worldski.co.uk

# Airlines

## NATIONAL

The major airlines listed below offer
international scheduled flights to airports
close to ski areas

**Air Canada**
(0870) 524 7226, www.aircanada.ca

**Air France**
(0845) 084 5111, www.airfrance.co.uk

**Alitalia**
(0870) 544 8259, www.alitalia.co.uk

**American Airlines**
020-736-50777, www.aa.com

**Austrian Airlines**
(0870) 124 2625, www.aua.com

**British Airways**
(0870) 850 9850
www.ba.com

**Continental Airlines**
(01293) 776464, www.continental.com

**Delta Airlines**
(0800) 414767, www.delta.com

**Lufthansa**
(0845) 773 7747, www.lufthansa.com

**Northwest Airlines**
(08705) 074074, www.nwa.com

**Swiss**
(0845) 601 0956, www.swiss.com

**United Airlines**
(0845) 844 4777
www.unitedairlines.co.uk

**Virgin Atlantic Airways**
(01293) 747747
www.virgin-atlantic.com

## CHARTER

Contact the following charter airlines for
seat-only fares from a large number of
UK airports

**Air 2000 / First Choice**
(0870) 366 1557, www.firstchoice.co.uk

**Britannia Airways**
(0800) 000747, www.britanniadirect.com

**Excel Airways**
(0870) 167 7747, www.excelairways.com

**JMC / Thomas Cook**
(0870) 566 6222, www.thomascook.com

**Monarch Airlines**
(01582) 400000, www.flymonarch.com

**Mytravel / Airtours**
(0870) 241 2567, www.uk.mytravel.com

## NO-FRILLS

Increasingly popular way of flying for
independent travellers. Pay as you go,
with no meals or drinks included

**bmibaby**
(0870) 264 2229, www.bmibaby.com

**easyJet**
(0870) 600 0000, www.easyjet.com

**Flybe**
(0871) 700 0535, www.flybe.com

**Jet 2**
(0870) 737 8282, www.jet2.com

**Ryanair**
(0871) 246 0000, www.ryanair.com

**Thomson Fly**
(0870) 190 0737, www.thomsonfly.com

## Breakdown insurance
**AA Five Star Services**
(0800) 444500, www.theaa.com

**Autohome**
(0800) 371280, www.autohome.co.uk

**Britannia Rescue**
(01484) 514848
www.britanniarescue.com

**Direct Line Rescue**
(0845) 246 8999, www.directline.com

**Europ Assistance**
(01444) 442211
www.europ-assistance.co.uk

**First Assist**
020-8763 1550, www.firstassist.co.uk

**Green Flag National Breakdown**
(0845) 767 0345, www.greenflag.com

**Key Connect**
(01924) 207000, www.keithlambert.com

**Leisurecare Insurance Services**
(01793) 750150

**Mondial Assistance**
020-8681 2525
www.mondial-assistance.co.uk

**RAC Travel Services**
(0800) 550055, www.rac.co.uk

## Channel crossings
**Brittany Ferries**
(0870) 536 0360
www.brittanyferries.com
*Portsmouth–Caen*

**Eurotunnel**
(0870) 535 3535, www.eurotunnel.com
*Folkestone–Calais*

**Hoverspeed**
(0870) 524 0241, www.hoverspeed.com
*Dover–Calais, Newhaven–Dieppe*

**Norfolkline**
(0870) 870 1020, www.norfolkline.com
*Dover–Dunekerque*

**P&O Ferries**
(0870) 242 4999
www.poportsmouth.com
*Portsmouth–Le Havre,
Portsmouth–Cherbourg,
Portsmouth–Caen*

(0870) 129 6002, www.ponsf.com
*Hull–Zeebrugge, Hull–Rotterdam*

(0870) 600 0600, www.posl.com
*Dover–Calais*

**Seafrance**
(0870) 571 1711, www.seafrance.com
*Dover–Calais*

**Stena Line**
(0870) 570 7070, www.stenaline.com
*Harwich–Hook of Holland*

## Ski roof-boxes
**Karrite Europe**
(01440) 760000, www.karrite.co.uk

**The Roof Box Company**
(01539) 621884, www.roofbox.co.uk

**Thule**
(01275) 340404, www.thule.co.uk

## Snow chains
**AA**
(0870) 550 0600, www.theaa.com

**Brindley Chains**
(01925) 825555
www.brindley-chains.co.uk

**RAC**
(0800) 550055, www.rac.co.uk

**RudChains**
(01227) 276611, www.rud.com

**Snowchains**
(01732) 884408, www.snowchains.co.uk

# Going by rail

The following 'snow trains' to the French Alps stop at Moûtiers, Aime and Bourg-St-Maurice

**Eurostar**
(0870) 518 6186, www.eurostar.com
*A weekly overnight service leaves London Waterloo on Friday evening, arriving in the Tarentaise valley the following morning. The return train departs on Saturday evening. An additional daytime service departs on Saturday morning, in each direction*

**Rail Europe**
(0870) 584 8848
www.raileurope.co.uk / www.sncf.com
*Agents for tour operators' chartered Snowtrain, which leaves Calais on Friday night, arriving in the French Alps on Saturday morning, and departs on Saturday evening, arriving in Calais Sunday morning*

*Also agents for SNCF couchette servicice, departing Paris Gare du Nord for the Alps on Friday evening, arriving Saturday morning, and leaving the Alps on Saturday evening, arriving Sunday morning. Services connect with Eurostar to London Waterloo but involve a change of train, though not of station*

*Also agents for SNCF daily and couchette Intercity services to the French Alps from Paris Gare du Lyon*

# Weather and snow

**www.skiclub.co.uk**
*Snow reports and 6-day weather forecasts on more than 250 resorts across Europe and North America*

**www.snow-forecast.com**
*Worldwide snow data*

## AVALANCHE WARNINGS
**www.avalanches.org**
*Collective site for Europe*

**Austria**
0043 5522 1588, www.lawine.at
Salzburgerland 0043 662 1588
www.lawine.salzburg.at

Tyrol 0043 512 1588, www.lawine.at.tirol
Voralberg 0043 5522 1588
www.vorarlberg.at/lawine

**Andorra**
0033 892 68 10 20 *99

**Canada**
001 250 837 2435, www.avalanche.ca

**France**
0033 892 68 10 20 www.meteo.fr

Hautes Pyrénées
0033 892 68 10 20 *65

Haute Savoie
0033 892 68 10 20 *73

Isère
0033 892 68 10 20 *38

Savoie
0033 892 68 10 20 *74

**Italy**
0039 0461 230030, www.aineva.it

**Scotland**
(01479) 861264, www.sais.gov.uk

**Spain**
0034 93 567 1500, www.icc.es

**Switzerland**
0041 81 417 0111, www.slf.ch

**US**
www.csac.org

# Ski-touring
**The Alpine Ski Club**
www.alpineskiclub.org.uk
*Britain's oldest ski-mountaineering organisation*

**The Eagle Ski Club**
020-8959 2214, www.eagleskiclub.org.uk
*Ski-touring & ski mountaineering club*

**Mountain Experience**
(01663) 750160
www.mountainexperience.co.uk
*Private guiding and courses. Off-piste and ski-touring in France, Italy and Switzerland*

**Ski Club of Great Britain**
(0845) 458 0780, www.skiclub.co.uk
*Ski-touring holidays*

# Heli-ski companies

The following are selected companies and (where available) their agents in the UK. Many of these agents offer tailor-made heli-skiing to destinations in addition to those listed

**Air Vallée** (*Aosta Valley*)
www.airvallee.it
Agent: Momentum 020-7371 9111

**Bella Coola Helisports** (*BC*)
www.bellacoolahelisports.com
Agents: Elemental Adventure (0870) 738 7838, James Orr Heliskiing (01799) 516964

**Canadian Mountain Holidays** (*BC*)
001 403 762 7100, www.cmhski.com
Agent: Powder Skiing in North America 020-7736 8191

**Chugach Powder Guides** (*Alaska*)
www.chugachpowderguides.com

**Crescent Spur** (*mid-BC*)
www.crescentspurheliski.com
Agent: James Orr

**Great Canadian Heliskiing** (*Selkirk & Purcell*)
www.greatcanadianheliski.com
Agents: Frontier Ski 020-8776 8709, James Orr

**H20 Heli Ski Guides** (*Alaska*)
www.h2oguides.com

**Himachal** (*India*)
www.himachal.com
Agents: Elemental Adventure, Ski Club of Great Britain 020-8410 2022

**Klondike Helisking** (*Yukon*)
www.atlinheliski.com
Agent: Ski Club of Great Britain

**Last Frontier Heliskiing** (*Northern BC*)
www.lastfrontierheli.com
Agents: Elemental Adventure, James Orr

**Mica Heli-guides** (*BC*)
www.micaheliguides.com
Agent: Elemental Adventure

**Mike Wiegele Helicopter Skiing** (*BC*)
www.wiegele.com

**Peace Reach Heli Ski** (*Northern BC*)
www.peacereachheliski.com
Agent: James Orr

**Robson Helimagic** (*Valemount*)
www.robsonhelimagic.com

**Selkirk Tangiers** (*BC*)
www.selkirk-tangiers.com
Agents: James Orr, Ski Club of Great Britain

**TLH Heliskiing** (*BC*)
www.tlhheliskiing.com
Agents: Elemental Adventure, James Orr, Momentum, Ski Club of Great Britain

**Valdez Heli-camps** (*Alaska*)
www.valdezhelicamps.com
Agent: Elemental Adventure

**Yak & Yéti** (*the Caucasus*)
www.yak-yeti.com
Agent: Elemental Adventure

# Ski courses

The organisations listed below specialise in ski-clinic holidays and race training. Note that several of the companies in *Tour operators* also offer ski courses

**Ali Ross**
020-7471 7777, www.skisolutions.com
*Organised through Ski Solutions*

**Berthon Ski**
0033 479 06 45 73
www.berthon-ski.com
*Bumps and freeride camps in France, Heli-skiing and snowcat-skiing in Canada*

**British Alpine Ski and Snowboarding School**
(01237) 451099 / (07092) 362591
*Ski courses in Avoriaz, Les Gets, Montriond, Morzine and Tignes*

**British Ski Academy**
020-8399 1181 / 0033 450 544059
www.britskiacad.org.uk
*Racing courses in Les Houches combined with academic study for 8- to 18-year olds*

**The Development Centre**
0033 615 55 31 56, www.tdcski.com
*British ski-coaching organisation in Val d'Isère, also offering BASI courses*

**EurekaSki**
(01326) 375 710 / 0033 679 46 24 84
(December to April)
www.eurekaski.com
*BASI instructors offering ski tuition in Serre Chevalier*

**Ice**
www.iceski.org
*The International Centre of Excellence for Snowsports Instructors offering courses in Val d'Isère*

**Improve Your Skiing**
(0870) 122 5549
www.improveyourskiing.com
*Bumps, off-piste, race training and adventure courses organised by Phil Smith in Canada, Chile and France*

**Inspired to Ski**
(0870) 128 8989
www.inspiredtoski.com
*Ski performance courses run by Sally Chapman in Tignes and Val d'Isère*

**The International Academy**
(02920) 672500
www.international-academy.com
*Professional ski and snowboard instructors' courses in USA, New Zealand, Canada, Switzerland and Chile*

**Lauralee Bowie Ski Adventures**
001 604 689 7444
www.skiadventures.net
*Personalised coaching in Lake Louise and Whistler*

**Mountain Tracks**
020-8877 5773
www.mountaintracks.co.uk
*Guided adventure skiing to Western Alps and Canada, plus exotic locations such as Morocco and Patagonia*

**Nonstopski**
020-8772 7852, www.nonstopski.com
*Intensive instruction in Fernie, Red Mountain and Banff, with the aim of qualifying as a Level 1 Canadian ski or board instructor*

**Optimum Ski Courses**
(01279) 641951, www.optimumski.com
*Ski clinics in Les Arcs and Tignes with BASI trainer*

**Piste to Powder Mountain Guided Adventures**
(01661) 824318 / 0043 6641 746 282
www.skimountaineering.com
*Ski courses with BASI instructors in St Anton*

**Roland Steiger**
0033 450 54 43 53
www.roland.stieger@libertysurf.fr
*Ski courses in Chamonix Valley*

**Rookie Academy**
www.rookieacademy.co.nz
*Ski-instructor training in New Zealand*

**Ski Club of Great Britain**
(0845) 458 0780, www.skiclub.co.uk
*Ski courses for all standards, both on- and off-piste*

**Ski Instructor Training**
www.skiinstructortraining.co.nz
*Ski-instructor training in New Zealand*

**Team Excel**
0191-584 7619
www.teamexcel.net
*Summer and winter race training for adults and children in Europe, New Zealand and North America*

**The Telemark Ski Company**
(01248) 810337
www.telemarkskico.com
*Specialists in telemark and cross-country instruction, and tours*

**Top Ski**
0033 479 06 14 80
www.topskival.com
*Ski clinics in Val d'Isère and Tignes*

## Ski recruitment agencies

**Free Radicals**
www.freeradicals.co.uk

**Jobs in the Alps**
www.jobs-in-the-alps.com

**Natives**
(08700) 463377, www.natives.co.uk

**Ski Connection**
www.skiconnection.co.uk

**Voovs Ltd**
(01707) 396511, www.voovs.com

## Gap-year skiing

These companies offer short, intensive ski instructor courses

**Nonstopski**
*See Ski courses*

**Peak Leaders**
(01337) 860079
www.peakleaders.co.uk

**Ski Le Gap**
(0800) 328 0345, www.skilegap.com
*Instructors' programme in Tremblant*

## Skiing organisations and clubs

**Association of British Tour Operators to France (ABTOF)**
(01989) 769140
www.holidayfrance.org.uk

**Association of British Travel Agents (ABTA)**
020-7637 2444, www.abta.com

**Association of Independent Tour Operators (AITO)**
020-8744 9280 / (0870) 751 8080
(brochure line)
www.aito.co.uk

**British Association of Ski Patrollers**
(01855) 811443, www.basp.org.uk
*Safety officers at Scottish resorts and UK artificial slopes*

**British Association of Snowsport Instructors (BASI)**
(01479) 861717, www.basi.org.uk

**British Bobskeleton Association**
(01225) 323696
www.british-bobsleigh.com

**British Bobsleigh Association**
(01225) 826802
www.british-bobsleigh.com

**British Mountain Guides**
(01834) 871694, www.bmg.org.uk
*Qualified British guides operating around the world*

**British Ski Club for the Disabled**
(01747) 828515, www.bscd.org.uk

**Freestyle Snowsports**
(07973) 561502
www.freestylesnowsports.co.uk
*Organisation for freestyle development in the UK, including courses at home and in the Alps*

**Ski Club of Great Britain**
(0845) 458 0780, www.skiclub.co.uk
*The leading club for British skiers*

**Snowsport England**
0121-501 2314
www.snowsportsengland.com
*Alpine racing club for children aged five and over*

**Snowsport Industries of Great Britain**
0131-557 3012, www.snowlife.org.uk
*Trade association for manufacturers and retailers of wintersports clothing and equipment*

**Snowsport GB**
0131-445 7676, www.snowsportgb.com

**Snowsport Scotland**
0131-445 4151, www.snsc.demon.co.uk
*The national body for snowsports in Scotland*

**Snowsport Wales**
029 2056 1904
www.website.lineone.net
*The national body for snowsports in Wales*

**The Uphill Ski Club of Great Britain**
(01479) 861272
www.ccksb.freeserve.co.uk
*Organisation for disabled skiers*

**World Ski & Snowboard Club**
(0870) 757 2288, www.worldski.co.uk
*Discounted equipment and travel for members*

## Artificial snow

**Snow Park**
(08700) 344437
www.thesnowpark.co.uk
*Outdoor snow slope in Stroud, Kent, with terrain park and tubing*

**The SnowDome, Tamworth, Staffordshire**
(08705) 000011, www.snowdome.co.uk

**Xscape Snowzone Castleford, West Yorkshire**
(0871) 222 5671, www.xscape.co.uk

**Xscape Snowzone, Milton Keynes**
(0871) 222 5670, www.xscape.co.uk

## Dry slopes

A full list of the 70 or so slopes in the UK is available from the Ski Club of Great Britain. Some of the largest include the following

**Bearsden Ski Club, Glasgow**
0141-943 1500, www.skibearsden.co.uk

**Gloucester Ski and Snowboard Centre**
(0870) 240 0375, www.gloucesterski.co.uk

**Hemel Ski Centre, Hemel Hempstead**
(01442) 241321, www.hemel-ski.co.uk

**Llandudno Ski and Snowboard Centre**
(01492) 874707, www.jnll.co.uk

**Midlothian Ski Centre, Edinburgh**
0131-445 4433

**Rossendale Ski Centre, Lancashire**
(01706) 226457
www.ski-rossendale.co.uk

**Sheffield Ski Village**
(0114) 276 9459
www.sheffieldskivillage.co.uk

**Wycombe Summit, High Wycombe**
(01494) 474711
www.wycombesummit.com

## Retail outlets

**47 Degrees**
020-7384 1747, www.47degrees.com
*Well-respected ski store with 4 branches in London*

**Blacks**
020-7361 0060, www.blacks.co.uk
*Outdoors and ski shop with branches throughout the UK, also online catalogue*

**Boardwise**
020-8994 6769, www.boardwise.com
*Specialist snowboarding outlet with 4 shops in the UK and online catalogue*

**Ellis Brigham**
020-7395 1010, www.ellis-brigham.com
*Ski and mountaineering store with 15 outlets in the UK and online catalogue*

**Kidski**
(01202) 631222, www.kidski.co.uk
*Affordable children's skiwear, with online catalogue*

**Snow + Rock**
(0845) 100 1000
www.snowandrock.com
*Specialist ski and mountaineering outlet with10 stores in the UK and online catalogue*

## Injury repair

**Bodyfactor**
020-7420 1440 / (01932) 564364,
www.bodyfactor.co.uk
*Assessment at Snow + Rock in London or Chertsey for program of specific exercises for skiing*

**Ski Inquiry**
www.ski-inquiry.com
*Comprehensive information on snowsports injury and prevention*

**Technology in Motion**
020-8944 9919
www.technologyinmotion.co.uk
*UK importer of The Edge and CT12 knee braces for ski injuries*

## Online resources

**www.0–21.co.uk**
*News and reviews for snowboarders*

**www.euroskidirect.co.uk**
*Location maps and resort trail maps*

**www.goski.com**
*Information and reader opinions, in particular on US resorts*

**www.ski.co.uk**
*Links to tour operators, clothing and equipment companies, and recruitment*

**www.skicentral.com**
*Mainly North American information*

**www.skijungle.com**
*A list of 2,400 ski and snowbound websites worldwide*

**www.snow.co.nz**
*All you need to know about skiing in New Zealand*

**www.snowboardbritain.com**
*Information for riders, including summer training camps, dry slopes, jobs and equipment*

**www.snowlife.org.uk**
*Full list of British ski and board shops*

# Reporting on the resorts

Your reports are an invaluable contribution to the book. The readers who send the best letters before 30 April 2005 will receive a free copy of *The Good Skiing & Snowboarding Guide 2006*.

Use the structure below and send your report to Dept CD, Consumers' Association, FREEPOST, 2 Marylebone Road, London NW1 4DF. No stamp is needed. Please use a separate sheet for each resort.

You can also email reports to *goodskiandsnowguide@which.net*.

## Resort report guidelines

### Basics
Your name and address
Your skiing experience
Resort name and country
Date of visit
Your operator
Hotel/chalet/apartment in which you stayed

### Verdicts
Give your reaction to our 'best for' and 'not recommended for' verdicts on the resort. Comment on the resort's suitability for skiers of different standards, snowboarders, families, après-skiers, and so on. Feel free to make nominations for the Golden Ski Awards.

### Lifts
Tell us news of new or upgraded lifts and lift queues.

### Runs
Give remarks on piste-grooming, the lift system and the accuracy of the piste map. Comment on any favourite runs and off-piste descents.

### Mountain restaurants
Give specific recommendations for restaurants and comment on the type and quality of food, as well as prices.

### Ski and board schools
Name the school on which you are commenting. Give remarks on tuition, language and group size.

### Children's facilities
Name the school, ski- and/or non-ski kindergarten on which you are commenting. Give remarks on staff attitude and approach to tuition.

### Transport within the resort
Comment on the reliability and cost of the transport, as well as on parking and the value of having a car.

### Shopping
Report on the range of shops.

### Eating out
Tell us about the range and type of restaurants; give specific recommendations, commenting on the type of food, prices and atmosphere.

### Après-ski
Give remarks on the range and style of bars and discos, with their prices.

### Accommodation
Name the apartment, chalet or hotel on which you are commenting. Give your advice on the choice of location within the resort.

### Prices
Give general observations on the cost of meals and drinks. Examples should include the price of a cup of coffee, a soft drink, a small beer, a bottle of local wine, and the dish of the day in a mountain restaurant.

### Summary
What did you particularly like about the resort? What aspect of the resort came as a surprise (pleasant or otherwise)? Would you go back there?

# Ski Club of Great Britain
# and *The Good Skiing & Snowboarding Guide*

The Ski Club of Great Britain has developed an unrivalled knowledge of the skiing and snowboarding world over the last hundred years, and is now looking forward to its next century. The Club continues to enjoy a strong association with *The Good Skiing & Snowboarding Guide.* Together they can offer you the best membership rate available to new members.

## EXCLUSIVE HALF-PRICE ONE-YEAR MEMBERSHIP OFFER
### INDIVIDUAL: £24.50    FAMILY: £35

This is your opportunity to join the UK's largest and most active snowsports organisation. As a member, you will receive hundreds of benefits that are unavailable elsewhere.

☆ Savings of between 5% and 15% off holidays booked with over 60 tour operators

☆ Comprehensive on- and off-piste insurance cover

☆ Skiing and boarding with Ski Club reps in over 40 premier resorts in Europe and North America

☆ Access to the Club's Information Department, an unbiased and invaluable resource to help you make the right decision on every aspect of snowsports

☆ Discounts and offers from outlets including Snow + Rock, Blacks, Ellis Brigham and hundreds of local independent snowsport retailers. Offers also from dry and real slopes in the UK, gyms, resort rental shops and ski schools, and on train fares and car hire

☆ Four issues of *Ski and Board,* the Club magazine

☆ A holiday programme tailored specifically to suit your skiing ability

This offer is subject to the production of the corner flash on page 1 and to signing a direct debit for your second and subsequent subscriptions. The offer expires on 30 April 2005 and may not be used in conjunction with any other offers. For further information, call the Ski Club's Membership Department on **0845 45 807 82** or visit its website at **www.skiclub.co.uk**.